Karl Löwith

From Hegel
to Nietzsche

the revolution in nineteenth-century thought

Translated from the German by David E. Green

COLUMBIA UNIVERSITY PRESS

New York

Columbia University Press Morningside Edition
Columbia University Press
New York   Chichester, West Sussex
Copyright © 1964 Holt, Rinehart and Winston, Inc.

Originally published in Germany under the title *Von Hegel zu Nietzsche: Der
revolutionäre Bruch im Denken des neunzehnten Jahrhunderts.* Copyright © Europa Verlag
AG. Zürich. Reprinted by permisison of Henry Holt and Company Inc.

Library of Congress Cataloging-in-Publication Data

Löwith, Karl, 1897–1973.
[Von Hegel zu Nietzsche. English]
From Hegel to Nietzsche : the revolution in nineteenth-century
thought / Karl Löwith ; translated from German by David E. Green.
p.   cm.
Translation of: Von Hegel zu Nietzsche.
Reprint. Originally published: New York : Holt,
Rinehart and Winston, 1964.
Includes bibliographical references and index.
(pbk.)
1. Philosophy, Modern—19th century.
2. Hegel, George Wilhelm Friedrich, 1770–1831.
3. Sociology.
4. Religious thought—19th century.
I. Title.
[B803.L613 1991]
190'.9'034—dc20
91-13225
CIP

p 10 9

190.9
LÖWITH

Contents

The Origin of the Spiritual Development of the Age in Hegel's Philosophy of the History of the Spirit

The Philosophy of History Becomes
the Desire for Eternity

Part Two
Studies in the History of the
Bourgeois-Christian World

Foreword to the Morningside Edition

Hans-Georg Gadamer

As a contemporary and old friend and colleague of Karl Löwith, I can only contribute from memory a prefatory word to this English-language reissue of his *From Hegel to Nietzsche*. We were bound by our work and our intellectual development in Marburg until 1935, then again after 1953 in Heidelberg. I can still see before me his serious, and in his youth, extremely introspective figure. In addition, we were joined by growing up together and especially by our heated discussion because of our different philosophical tendencies. And that was precisely what the students and young researchers in Marburg as well as in Heidelberg valued so much. Löwith began by writing on Nietzsche and ended his prolific career writing on Paul Valéry. Hegel was not, in fact, his subject, and especially not the metaphysics and the formative influence that emanated from it in antiquity, in the Middle Ages, and in the nascent modern era. In other words, what was at the core of my own research and study was remote to him. Thus we mutually complemented each other, and thus too our students could test themselves against us.

Löwith's approach was basically Schopenhauer's determined distancing, as well as his critique of the academic world and its concept of values. Thus the young Karl Löwith, returning after

World War I, was attracted by the revolutionary pathos of the young Heidegger. Later he saw in Nietzsche the unsurpassable radicalism whom no one else, not Husserl, nor Heidegger, nor we others who were young with him, could match. But Marxism, which Löwith tried to connect with Kierkegaard, could not win him over.

With a rare penetration and brilliant verbal artistry he knew instead how to uncover the evidence of humaneness underpinning the ideas of the great historical figures and the structure of their conceptual subtleties. It was not accidental that the sober skepticism and the virtually Egyptian fatalism of his view of life could not find a real model in any philosopher: not in Hegel but rather in Goethe; nor yet in Nietzsche but moreso in Jakob Burckhardt. For what Löwith sought was an inner independence, particularly in the face of the multiple perspectives of the contradictory systems of thought and their mutually incompatible effects on life and on society. As he handed us his first book, *The Individual in the Role of Societal Man*, he had added "The Individual Karl" to his own first name. He could also have titled the book *The Unique One and His Possession*, even if the extremism of the creator of that title, Eugen Dühring, remained foreign to him. Even in Nietzsche the *amor fati* alone was entirely to his taste. His plea for nature allowed him to share Goethe's dissatisfaction with history—and that concerned particularly the history of salvation, as his famous book, *Meaning in History*, makes clear. The whole of European philosophy must have seemed to him—particularly in view of his love of Italy and of the art of life of the Italians—an ultimate hypocrisy which never overcame its Christian remnants and denied itself total inherence in this world. He could release an astonishing amount of humanity and vital reality at the periphery of the barren heath of the conceptual practices of philosophy, turn it into fertile soil upon which a multiplicity of ideas and of the "spiritual animal kingdom" could feed. Thus his *From Hegel to Nietzsche* should not be read as a work of history, nor as a recounted story, but as a walk, with ever new perspectives on the occurrences and curiosities of the nineteenth century.

When he was driven out of his country because of his Jewish roots he was able, after much effort, to secure a prestigious position at the Imperial University of Sendai in Japan, where he could teach in German. Just before Japan's entry into the war, he was admitted into the United States. But the world of the Far

East retained its magic for him throughout his life, even after he returned to Germany.

The world of antiquity, which also lacked a concept of history, was for Löwith, who lacked a humanistic background, only attractive from afar. But he constantly ran into this world in Nietzsche. The classical philosophy which most easily found a response in him was, primarily, Stoicisim, and thus he particularly loved the essay "Of the World," which comes to us in the Aristotelian corpus. He did not like to hear, as I had to tell him, that this was not Aristotle but a much later work influenced by the Stoic circle.

That is how insistently, how unshakably he pursued his fight against all illusions of transcendence. The son of a painter, he saw the colorful reflection that life was, for Goethe as well as for him, passing by him with quiet grief and with stoical calm and dignity. And so *From Hegel to Nietzsche* will accompany many in their ramble through the nineteenth century and will reward them with splendid vistas.

—translated by Luna Carne-Ross and Edith Kurzeil

Preface to the First Edition

Hegel and Nietzsche are the two end points between which the historical course of the German spirit in the nineteenth century moves. But, because Hegel's work has usually been viewed as the brilliant culmination of the systems of idealism, and random portions have been excerpted from Nietzsche's works for opportunistic use, caution has been necessary in the case of each. Hegel seems to stand very far removed from us and Nietzsche very near, if we consider only the latter's influence and the former's works. In fact, though, Hegel's work, mediated through his pupils, had an effect upon intellectual and political life which it would be difficult to overestimate, while the numerous influences exerted by Nietzsche since 1890 have given birth to a German ideology only in our own time. The Nietzscheans of yesterday correspond to the Hegelians of the 1840's.

In contrast to the academic petrifaction of Hegel's system by scholars of Hegel and the popular warping of Nietzsche's writings by worshipers of Nietzsche, the following studies seek to bring accurately to life the epoch which starts with Hegel and ends with Nietzsche, "transcribing" the philosophical history of the nineteenth century within the horizon of the present. To transcribe history does not mean to counterfeit the irrevocable power of what has taken place once and for all, or to increase vitality at the expense of truth, but to do justice to the vital fact of history so that the tree may be known only by its fruits, the father by his son. The twentieth century has clarified and made explicable the actual events of the nineteenth. In the process, the deadly consistency of philosophical development since Hegel has made easier the pursuit of the consecutive stages which have led to such an extreme result.

Nevertheless, these studies in the history of the spirit are not a contribution to *Geistesgeschichte* in the usual sense of the word, the principles of which, having evolved from Hegel's metaphysics of the spirit, have been so attenuated that they are now trivial. The spirit, as subject and substance of history, is no longer a foundation, but, at best, a problem. Hegel's historical relativism has as its beginning and end "absolute knowledge," in relation to which every stage in the unfolding of the spirit is a mark of progress in consciousness of freedom; the knowledge of the "spirit" achieved by the historical sciences is not even relative, for there is no measuring stick by which to evaluate the temporal process. All that is left of the spirit is the "spirit of the age." But yet, even if only to be able to understand the age as an age, a point of view is necessary which will transcend the bare events of the age. But because the equation of philosophy with the "spirit of the age" gained its revolutionary power through Hegel's pupils, a study of the age from Hegel to Nietzsche ultimately will have to yield the question: Is the essence and "meaning" of history determined absolutely from within history itself; and, if not, then how?

The following studies in the history of the German spirit in the nineteenth century do not seek to give a complete history of nineteenth-century philosophy, especially since material completeness of historical comprehension is not only unattainable, but would be contrary to the meaning of causal historical relationship. In the real history of the world, as of the spirit, insignificant occurrences very quickly can become significant events; on the other hand, what seems eventful, very quickly can lose all meaning. It is nonsense, therefore, whether in advance or in conclusion, to fix the totality characteristic of an epoch in all its facets. The process of shift of meaning is never concluded, because, in history, it is never determined at the beginning what will result at the end. The purpose of these studies is solely to point out the decisive turning point between Hegel's consummation and Nietzsche's new beginning, in order, with the light of the present, to illuminate the epoch-making significance of an episode which has fallen into oblivion.

In the perspective of an age which thought itself superior, the nineteenth century seemed capable of being comprehended in a single catchword and already of being "overcome"; but even Nietzsche was still aware of being both a conqueror *and* an heir. In the perspective of history as a whole, an epoch is neither praiseworthy nor blameworthy; each is both debtor and creditor. Thus the past century, too, has its front runners and "fellow travelers," its prominent men and its average men, figures both lucid and opaque in its rank and file. The nineteenth century is Hegel and Goethe, Schelling and romanticism, Schopenhauer and Nietzsche, Marx and Kierkegaard—but also Feuerbach and Ruge, B. Bauer and Stirner, E. von Hartmann and Dühring. It is Heine and Börne, Hebbel and Büchner, Immermann and Keller, Stifter and Strindberg, Dostoevski and Tolstoi; it is Stendhal and Balzac, Dickens and Thackeray, Flaubert and Baudelaire, Melville and Hardy, Byron and Rimbaud, Leopardi and d'Annunzio, George and Rilke; it is Beethoven and Wagner, Renoir and Delacroix, Munch and Marées, van Gogh and Cézanne. It is the age of the great historical works of Ranke and Mommsen, Droysen and Treitschke, Taine and Burckhardt, and of fantastic growth in the natural sciences. Not least, it is Napoleon and Metternich, Mazzini and Cavour, Lassalle and Bismarck, Ludendorff and Clémenceau. It extends from the great French Revolution to 1830, and thence to the First World War. Blow upon blow, for good or ill, it forged technological civilization, and spread abroad over the whole earth inventions without which we can no longer even picture our daily lives.

Who could deny that our life is firmly based upon this century, thus understanding Renan's question—which is also the question of Burckhardt, Nietzsche, and Tolstoi—*De quoi vivra-t-on après nous?* Were there an answer to this question based solely upon the spirit of the age, the final, honest word of our generation, born before 1900 and come to maturity during the First World War, would be a resolute resignation, a resignation without profit; for renunciation is easy when it renounces most.

Sendai (Japan)

Spring, 1939

From Hegel to Nietzsche

Part One

Studies in the History of the German Spirit During the Nineteenth Century

Introduction:
Goethe and Hegel[1]

Goethe made German literature into world literature, and Hegel made German philosophy into world philosophy. Their productive power was of complete normality, because their goal was in complete harmony with their ability. What comes after them cannot be compared for breadth of vision and energy of accomplishment; it is exaggerated or exhausted, extreme or mediocre, and more promising than productive.

In 1806 Napoleon came through Jena and Weimar; in the same year, Hegel finished *Die Phänomenologie des Geistes* and Goethe the first part of *Faust*, two works in which the German language attained its broadest fullness and most extreme compactness. Yet the relationship between Hegel and Goethe is much less obvious than that between other German philosophers and men of letters, so that it gives rise to the appearance that they merely lived alongside each other, without working in common. While Schiller was influenced by Kant, and the romantics by Fichte and Schelling, Goethe's view of the world of nature and man was determined by none of the classical philosophers. His work needed no philosophical props, because its own thought was deep, and his scientific studies were produced by the same imaginative power that produced his poetry.

Thus "Hegel *and* Goethe" cannot mean that their life work is mutually dependent or interwoven, but the connection may indeed mean that between Goethe's intuition and Hegel's comprehension there exists an inner relationship which points to both a proximity and a separation. To see that each paid his due to the work and influence of the other is to recognize the distance they preserved in their association. While each did his own work, the mode of thought in which they worked was the same in its essentials. The difference which both separates and unites them becomes clear when we observe that Goethe's "primary phenomena" and Hegel's "absolute" encounter each other just as respectfully as did Goethe and Hegel in their personal lives.[2]

Their mutual relationship extends over three decades. A few diary entries and oral remarks by Goethe, together with the few letters they exchanged, are all that document their relationship. In his works Hegel makes a few passing references to Goethe, with more detail about the theory of color in both editions of the *Encyklopädie*.[3] Goethe reprinted a passage from one of Hegel's letters dealing with the same subject in the *4. Heft zur Naturwissenschaft*. And yet their relationship went beyond this outward co-operation.

On April 24, 1825, Hegel writes to Goethe describing the inner motives of his "dependence, or even devotion": "For when I look back over the course of my spiritual development I see you interwoven everywhere, and I could call myself one of your sons; from the nourishment you have given me, my inner self has obtained strength to resist abstraction, and has ordered its course aright by your system as by a beacon."[4] This corresponds to Goethe's statement to Varnhagen, after Hegel's death, that he experienced a deep sense of grief over the loss of this "highly talented, important leader," who had been such a "well-grounded man and friend, active in all fields. . . . The foundations of his theory lay outside my horizon, but wherever his actions touched on more, or even impinged upon my efforts, I always reaped a great spiritual benefit."[5] Even further from Goethe than the dogmatic foundations of Hegel's own theories lay the subsequent constructions of the members of the Hegelian school, although he also mentions with approval well-stated observations made by them. For example, even when he was seventy-eight years old he studied a book by Hinrichs on ancient tragedy, and used it as the point of departure for an important conversation.[6] Another of Hegel's pupils, L. von Henning, lectured at the University of Berlin on Goethe's theory of color—Goethe furnished him with the necessary material. The most independent of Hegel's pupils of that era was the legal philosopher E. Gans; he gives an account of a conversation Goethe once had with him: "He [Goethe] said, if philosophy would take it upon itself to give attention to the things and articles it treated, it would become all the more effective, also coming into more contact with the empiricists. But the question would always arise whether it was possible to be at the same time both a great scholar and observer and also an important generalizer and summarizer. . . . He acknowledged Hegel's many insights both in nature and in history; but he could not refrain from questioning whether his philosophical ideas would not have to undergo continual modification in order to conform to the new discoveries which would undoubtedly constantly be made, losing thereby their categorical nature. . . . Then he came to the *Jahrbücher*. He disliked a certain awkwardness and discursiveness in the individual articles; he criticized my recension of Savigny's *History of Roman Law in the Middle Ages* on the grounds that I was trying to make the author do something he did not intend. . . ."[7]

Here Goethe rejects the forceful importation of an alien system of thought; similarly, in a letter to Hegel, he emphasizes that in his scientific works he is concerned not with an "opinion to be put across" but with a "methodology to be demonstrated." Anyone might make use of it as he likes, as a tool.[8] But this reservation is followed immediately by a recognition of Hegel's efforts which shows how strongly Goethe, too, was opposed to all undisciplined caprice. "With great satisfaction I hear from many sources that your effort to educate young men to follow you is bearing fruit; it is necessary that somewhere in this amazing age a theory spread out from a central point, which can be of theoretical and practical benefit to one's life. Of course there is no preventing the hollow skulls from losing themselves in vague ideas and fine-sounding, empty words. This has a bad effect on the better minds; for, perceiving the erroneous methodologies in which the others have been entangled since youth, they withdraw into themselves, becoming abstruse or transcendental."[9] Quite apart from Hegel's "theory," the desire for a firm basis which could be passed on united Goethe with Hegel's spiritual "activity." This difference characterizes the whole relationship between Goethe and Hegel; it is expressed drastically in a conversation with Kanzler Müller: "I do not want to know any details of Hegelian philosophy, although I am somewhat attracted to Hegel himself."[10] Somewhat later, in a more conciliatory mood, Goethe writes to Hegel himself: "I keep my mind as open as possible to the gifts of the philosopher, and rejoice each time I can appropriate something which has been discovered by an ability nature was not willing to grant me."[11] Thus during the entire course of his life Goethe felt himself at once attracted to and repelled by Hegel's philosophy,[12] and yet basically he was sure that they agreed in spirit. This is beautifully expressed in his last letter to Zelter: "Fortunately, the nature of your talent is focused on the single note—that is, the moment. Now, since a sequence of consecutive moments itself is always a kind of eternity, it has been granted you always to remain constant in the midst of flux, thus fully satisfying both me and the spirit of Hegel, to the extent I understand him."[13]

1 Goethe's Idea of Primary Phenomena and Hegel's Comprehension of the Absolute

a The Unity of Principle

What appealed to Goethe about Hegel was nothing less than the principle of his spiritual activity: mediation between self-being (*Selbstsein*) and being other (*Anderssein*). In Goethe's idiom, Hegel placed himself in the middle, between subject and object, while Schelling emphasized the breadth of nature, and Fichte, the height of subjectivity.[14] "Where object and subject meet, there is life; when Hegel places himself between object and subject by means of his philosophy of identity and lays claim to this position, we must do him honor."[15] Similarly, Hegel had to see Goethe's subjectivity, the universal content of his self-being. Goethe's diagnosis of the "universal sickness of the age" corresponds exactly to his fierce criticism of the shallow subjectivity of the romantics: they are incapable of divesting themselves productively of their subjectivity and venturing into the world of objects.[16] To discover and establish the mid-point between subject and object, between being *pro se* and being *per se*, between the internal and the external, was the motivating force behind Hegel's entire philosophy of mediation, from his first systematic fragment to the *Logik* and *Encyklopädie*.

Through this philosophy, substance was to become subject, and the subject substantial. Similarly, Goethe's naïve philosophizing centers upon the problem of harmony between the self and the world.[17] The contradiction between them and its neutralization—under the terms subjective "idea" and objective "experience," what is "apprehended" by the senses and what is "conceived"—are discussed not only in the famous exchange of letters with Schiller,[18] but also in four special essays: *Der Versuch als Vermittler von Objekt und Subjekt* ("Experiment as Mediator between Object and Subject"), *Einwirkung der neueren Philosophie* ("The Influence of Recent Philosophy"), *Anschauende Urteilskraft* ("Intuitive Judgment"), and *Bedenken und Ergebung* ("Reflection and Resignation").

Goethe says that, in the process of viewing the universe, man cannot fail to venture ideas and construct concepts with the aid of which he attempts to understand the essence of God or of nature. "Here we come face to face with our real difficulty, . . . that between the idea and the experience there seems to be a certain gulf fixed; we exert all our strength to cross it, in vain. In spite of this, we strive constantly to overcome this gap by means of reason, understanding, imagination, faith, feeling, madness, and, if nothing else will serve, with absurdity. Finally, after constant strenuous effort, we discover that the philosopher might indeed be right who states that no idea is fully congruent with experience, but admits that idea and experience can, indeed must, be analogous."[19] The philosopher mentioned here is Kant, and the work in which he forges a unity out of conceptualizing reason and sense perception is the *Kritik der Urteilskraft*. Of the *Kritik der reinen Vernunft*, on the other hand, Goethe remarks that it lies completely outside his field. Only one thing in it seems to him worthy of attention, that it renews the "ancient primary question": "How much of our spiritual existence is derived from our own self, and how much from the external world?" He himself, he continues, had never separated the one from the other; whenever he philosophized in his own way, he had done so with unconscious naïveté, believing that his ideas really were "before his eyes."[20] Both as poet and as scientist, he, like nature, had always proceeded both analytically and synthetically. "The systole and diastole of the human spirit was to me like a second respiration, never apart, always pulsing." Yet for all of this he had no words, not to mention phrases. He had been kept from penetrating into the labyrinth of Kant's *Kritik der reinen Vernunft*, at times by his poetic gift, at times by his human understanding, although he believed he understood a few chapters and had gained much from them for his personal use.

This relationship to Kant underwent a change with the appearance of the *Kritik der Urteilskraft* (1790), which he had to thank for an "extremely light-hearted period." Quite in line with his own work and thought, it taught him to view as a unity the products both of nature and of the human spirit (i.e., art), so that aesthetic and theological judgment illuminated each other. "I rejoiced that the art of poetry and comparative natural science are related so closely to each other, both being subject to the same faculty of judgment."[21] But at the same time Goethe had a critical awareness that his use of Kant's study went beyond the limits drawn by Kant. His mind did not want to be restricted to a purely discursive power of judgment; he claimed for himself that intuitive understanding which was, for Kant, an *intellectus archetypus*, that is, an idea, which is not a property of human nature. "Indeed the author seems here to have in mind a divine understanding, but only when we bring ourselves to a higher level of morality through faith in God, virtue, and immortality, and approach the primal being (first principle). It might also happen the same way in the intellectual realm: through perception of nature, eternally creating, we might make ourselves worthy of spiritual participation in its products. Although at first, unconsciously and compelled by an inner drive, I pressed indefatigably toward that original, typical entity, even succeeding in constructing a representation in conformity with nature, nothing now could keep me from encountering courageously the 'adventure of reason,' as the old man of Königsberg himself calls it."[22] This was also the point at which Hegel began in his treatise on faith and knowledge (1802), only to draw from Kant's *Kritik der Urteilskraft* the conclusions which put an end to subjective idealism and brought "understanding" to "reason." Both interpret the power of judgment as the productive midpoint mediating between the concept of nature and that of freedom, bringing to light a "region of identity." Kant's reflections on "reason in its reality," as beauty standing objectively before the eyes (in art) and as organization (in nature), already defined formally the true concept of reason, although he was unaware that with his idea of intuitive understanding he was in the realm of speculation. In fact, with the notion of an archetypal understanding, he already had in his hands the key to unlock the riddle of the relationship between nature and freedom.

Hegel and Goethe—and Schelling too—took this latter idea from Kant and used it as a point of departure. Both attempted the "adventure of reason" by placing themselves—disregarding discursive understanding—in the middle between personal existence and the existence of the world. The difference between their ways of mediation resides in the fact that Goethe sees the unity from the point of view of nature as it is perceived, but Hegel from the point of view of the *historical spirit*. This corresponds to the fact that Hegel recognizes a "cunning of reason," and Goethe a cunning of nature. In each case, it lies in the fact that the affairs of men are subordinated to the service of a whole.

b The Difference in Exposition

However much their differing views of the absolute—as "nature" or as "spirit"—characterize the relationship between Hegel and Goethe, no contrast in principle is indicated, only a difference in the manner of its exposition. When Goethe speaks of nature, trusting that it also speaks through him, he means the reason behind everything that lives, just as the primary phenomena are themselves a kind of reason, more or less permeating all created things.[23] When Hegel speaks of spirit, confident that it also speaks through him, he understands thereby nature as the otherness of the idea, while the spirit is a "second nature." As a consequence of this difference and agreement, Goethe, with benevolent irony, could recommend his "primary phenomena" for friendly reception by the "Absolute" on an occasion of a gift-giving. Nevertheless, it did not seem to him proper to speak of the absolute "in the theoretical sense," precisely because he always kept it before his eyes, seeing it in its manifestations.[24]

After a visit from Hegel, Goethe wrote to Knebel that the conversation had aroused in him the desire to be together with Hegel at more length, "for what in the printed communications of such a man appears to us abstruse and unclear, because we cannot utilize it immediately for our own needs, immediately becomes our own in the course of live conversation, because we perceive that we are in agreement with him in basic thoughts and ideas, and mutual development and elucidation of them could probably lead to rapprochement and agreement." At the same time, Goethe was conscious of Hegel's approval: "Your gracious approval of the major trends of my thoughts confirms me all the more in the same; and I believe that I have made notable progress in many areas, if not in terms of the whole, then for me and my soul. May all that I am yet capable of achieving always be built upon what you have established and continue to develop."[25] This could just as easily have been written by Hegel to Goethe, for in fact the work of the one built upon that of the other. However great the difference in the type and range of their personalities, however rich and active Goethe's life was in comparison to Hegel's prosaic existence, they were at one in the basis of their work, through their recognition of "what exists." For this reason they denied the pretensions of individuality, which is only destructive, never philosophically constructive, because it has a conception of freedom which is only negative.[26]

However much Goethe's free flexibility within the fixed framework of pursuit of his goal differed from Hegel's constructive violence, the breadth of their mighty spirits exalted them both equally high above the everyday view of the world. They did not seek to know how things are in relation to us, but rather to perceive and to recognize what they are in and of themselves. When, in his essay on experiment, Goethe says that, like an indifferent and yet divine being, one must seek and study "what is" and not "what pleases," it is quite in line with what Hegel says about pure thought in the preface to his *Logik* and *Encyklopädie*. Both valued *theoria*, in the original sense of "pure vision," as the highest form of activity.

Observation of objects at the same time revealed to both their own nature, for which reason they rejected merely reflective self-knowledge as untrue and unfruitful. "I hereby confess that the great duty 'know thyself,' which sounds so important, has always seemed to me to be suspect, like a trick of priests in secret conspiracy who would like to confuse man through unfulfillable demands and lead him away from his proper activity in the external world to a false interior contemplation. A man knows himself insofar as he knows the world, which he perceives only within himself, and himself only within it. Every new object, properly examined, reveals a new organ within us."[27] On the same grounds Hegel, too, rejects "the complacent devotion of the individual to his own beloved individuality," that is, that which differentiates him as a particular individual being from the universal being of the spirit and the world.[28] Their conception of growth and existence is directed at an existence which emerges from itself, objectifies itself, within the world. This concern about questions of phenomena of an objective world, undistorted by machines, also characterizes Goethe's relationship with Hegel in matters pertaining to the theory of color. From the very beginning this was the actual concrete point of contact between them, although it was within this area, natural philosophy, that recognition and following were denied them. The way they reached an understanding of the problem of light and color shows most clearly the divergence in their method of procedure and in the manner in which they looked at their own work.[29]

In the foreground of their correspondence one is aware of a feeling of mutual assistance, approval, and corroboration, especially on the part of Goethe, who calls Hegel an "amazingly accurate and acute man" whose words on the theory of color are ingeniously clear and penetrating, although not equally accessible to everyone. Hegel, he states, has penetrated so deeply into his work on optical phenomena that he himself has only now understood it clearly.[30] The divergence in attitude which lurks in the background appears only in the form of a polite irony, by means of which each asserts the individuality of his own method before the other. Goethe expresses this ironic distance in a well-considered choice of words in his letter of October 7, 1820, in which he insists upon the obvious nature of his "idea," carefully differentiating his method of communication from an opinion which must prevail. We see it also in the previously mentioned dedication of the drinking glass, which conciliatorily preserves the distance between the "absolute" and the "primary phenomenon." He expresses his reservations more directly in a conversation on dialectics preserved by Eckermann: Goethe distrusts the dialectic method because it might be misused in order to turn falsehood into truth. One who is "dialectically sick," however, can be healed once more by honest study of nature; for nature is always and eternally true, and will not let such sickness prevail.[31]

Hegel expresses his irony in his stubborn designation of Goethe's primary phenomenon, based on observation, as a philosophical "abstraction," because it isolates from something which is empirically complex something pure and simple, and stresses it. "Your Excellency may call your procedure in the pursuit of natural phenomena a naïve method; I believe I may yield sufficiently to my faculty as to see and admire therein the abstraction by means of which you have held fast to the simple, basic truth, only inquiring after conditions, discovering them, and throwing them into relief."[32] Goethe has discovered thereby something which is primarily merely visible, a transitory certainty of the senses, a "simple observational relationship"; he has "elevated it to the level of thought," and made it "permanent." We read much the same material in Hegel's intricate letter of thanks for the drinking glass which has been sent him: Just as throughout the ages wine has been a mighty support of natural philosophy, by inspiring the drinker and thus proving "that there is spirit in nature," so this glass demonstrates the ingenious (*geistvoll*) phenomenon of light. He wishes thereby to retain his faith in the transubstantiation "of thought into phenomenon and phenomenon into thought." In a letter of February 24, 1821, Hegel writes that he has "understood nothing" of the many machinations of other color theorists, although in his case understanding comes before all else, and the "dry phenomenon" means nothing more to him than an awakened desire to understand it, that is, to comprehend it spiritually. This is just what Goethe has accomplished (more than he himself realized) through his "spiritual sense of nature," by breathing into nature an "intellectual breath"; this and this alone is worth talking about.[33] "The simple and abstract, which you most appropriately called the primary phenomenon, you set in first place, then show its concrete manifestations as arising through the addition of further modes of effect and conditions, and regulate the entire process in such a way that the sequence progresses from the simpler conditions to the more complex. When this arrangement has been made, that which is complex now appears in all its clarity through this decomposition. To trace the primary phenomenon, to distinguish it from other, accidental surroundings, to conceive it abstractly, as we say—this I consider a matter of great intellectual understanding of nature. Similarly, I consider this whole process to be the truly scientific portion of knowledge in this field."[34] Hegel interprets Goethe's primary phenomena under the aspect of "essence" (*Wesen*). The interest they might hold for the philosopher consists in the fact that such a "preparation," that is, something made prominent by the spirit, can actually be used for philosophical ends. "At the outset our absolute is something like an oyster, grey, or completely black—just as you like. If we have struggled with it in the direction of air and light to the point where it desires the same of itself, we need windows if we are to bring it out completely into the light of day; our schemata would vanish into mist if we sought merely to transfer them into the motley confusion of a resistant world. It is here, it seems to us, that Your Excellency's primary phenomena prove immensely useful; in this twilight, both worlds greet each other, our abstruse world and phenomenal existence—intellectually and conceptually through its simplicity, visibly or sensibly through its sensuousness."[35] For Hegel, then, Goethe's primary phenomena do not assume the status of an idea, but rather an entity intermediate between the intellectual and the sensual, mediating between pure essential concepts and the accidental appearances of the sensual world. Hegel is even clearer in the next sentences, where he no longer masks his disagreement with Goethe, but openly declares it: "Now when I discover that Your Excellency shifts the realm of the unsearchable and incomprehensible into the region where we dwell, . . . from which we seek to justify your view and primary phenomena, to understand them—one might say prove, deduce, construe them, etc.—I know at the same time that Your Excellency, even though you may not be grateful to us for this, even though in fact your own views might attack the taunt of 'natural philosophy,' will at least be so tolerant as to allow us to conduct ourselves with what is yours in our own innocent manner. In spite of everything, this is not the worst that has befallen you, and I can rely on the fact that Your Excellency understands the ways of human nature, how, whenever someone has done anything worthwhile, others come running, wanting to see something of their own accomplished in the process. In spite of all this, we philosophers have one enemy in common with Your Excellency, namely, metaphysics."

Thus finally the common element seems reduced to defense against a common foe, the negation of that "damned bad metaphysics" of the physical scientists (Newton), who do not push on to a concrete notion, but subordinate abstract rules to empirical facts. With all Goethe's receptiveness toward the "significant agreement" of such an "important man," the reservation in Hegel's recognition of his goals and accomplishments could not simply escape his notice. His reply merely hints at this through a reference to Hegel's "friendly attitude" toward the primary phenomena.

In two letters of earlier date their methodological difference seems to be an unbridgeable gulf. In 1807, Hegel writes to Schelling about Goethe's theory of color: "I have seen a portion of the same; out of hatred for the cogitation with which others have ruined the matter, he restricts himself completely to the empirical, rather than progressing beyond it to the other side, to the notion, which will succeed, at most, in becoming dimly visible."[36] What Hegel here calls a mere dim visibility of the notion means for Goethe a genuine self-revelation of the phenomena, in contrast to which Hegel's proofs of God seem to him "out of date,"[37] and his dialectical constructions an abuse. In 1812, referring to a passage in Hegel's preface to *Phänomenologie* in which Hegel describes the phases of plant development—from the bud to the flower and the fruit—as a kind of dialectic progress, he writes: "It is probably impossible to say anything more monstrous. To seek to destroy the eternal reality of nature through a bad sophistical joke seems to me completely unworthy of a rational man. If an empiricist, his mind chained to the earth, remains blind to ideas, one will pity him and allow him to go his way, will indeed derive much profit from his efforts. But when an outstanding thinker, who penetrates within an idea and knows quite well what it is worth, in and of itself, and what higher value it contains, in describing an immense process of nature, makes a joke of it, distorting it sophistically, denying and destroying it by means of words and phrases which artificially contradict each other, one simply does not know what to say."[38]

The illusion of perspective from Goethe's point of view, which affected his relationship with Hegel, rests in the fact that the "idea" as understood by Hegel was not intended to describe a process of nature but a process of the spirit. By it Hegel did not mean the reason of nature—which to him was powerless, while it was all-powerful to Goethe—but the reason of history; and Hegel viewed the spirit of Christianity as the absolute in the history of the spirit. The actual disagreement between Goethe and Hegel thus becomes comprehensible in their attitudes toward Christianity and toward history.[39]

2   Rose
and Cross

a   Goethe's Rejection of
Hegel's Association of Reason
With the Cross

In 1830, for his sixtieth birthday, Hegel received from his pupils a medal, displaying on the face his portrait, and on the reverse an allegorical representation: left, a male figure, seated, reads from a book; behind him is a pillar upon which an owl crouches; at the right stands the figure of a woman holding fast to a cross which towers above her; between the two, turned toward the seated figure, is a naked genius whose raised arm points to the cross on the other side. The attributes owl and cross allow no doubt concerning the intended meaning of the representation: the middle figure of the genius mediates between philosophy and theology. This medal is still in the possession of the Goethe collection; at Hegel's request, Zelter conveyed it to Goethe.[40] Of it Zelter said, "The head is good, and not unlike him; but I cannot be happy with the reverse. Who can demand that I love the cross if with that I am forced to share its burden?" When Goethe received the copy intended for him, after Hegel's death, he wrote on June 1, 1831 to Zelter, "The praise-worthy profile on the medal is very well designed by any standard. . . . I do not know what to say of the reverse. To me, it seems to open an abyss which I have always kept at a good distance during my progress toward eternal life." To this, Zelter replied, "I can easily believe that the Hegelian medal disturbs you, it was long enough in my possession; but you would really open your eyes in astonishment if you would inspect the contents of our new museum. Nothing but the hands of great artists, hands which have fallen into sin through the most tasteless representations!" Half a year later, Goethe returns once more to the subject of his thorough dislike: "It is impossible to tell what it is supposed to signify. That I have known how to honor and adorn the cross, as a man and as a poet, I have proved with my stanzas ["Die Geheimnisse"]; but that a philosopher should lead his pupils to this barren contignation[41] via a detour over the grounds and abysses of being and nonbeing—that I cannot accept. That can be had cheaper and stated better." Thus Goethe's annoyance is directed neither against the allegorical representation as such, nor against the Christian allegory; about the same time he himself devised an allegorical device for Zelter, and in "Die Geheimnisse" as well as in *Wilhelm Meister* and *Faust* he employed Christian symbolism "as a man and as a poet." What he objects to is that upon Hegel's medal the Christian symbol of the cross, in its philosophical sense, is applied and misapplied on the detour via reason, instead of theology being left at the distance from philosophy which befits them both. His letter continues: "I have a medal from the seventeenth century with the portrait of a high Roman cleric; upon the reverse, Theologia and Philosophia, two noble women, stand opposite each other, the relationship so beautifully and purely conceived, so perfectly satisfying and delightfully expressed, that I keep the medal secret, in order to give it into the possession of one who is worthy of it, should I find such a man." Further on, Goethe opposes the cross, towering above all else, on another basis:

in its harshness and crudity it stands opposed to the "human" and the "reasonable," which are indispensable.[42] A week after receiving the Hegel medal, and referring to his design for the Zelter medal, he writes: "An airy, decorative cross is always a cheerful object; the loathsome wood of the martyrs, the most repugnant object under the sun, no man in his right mind should be concerned to excavate and erect." Yet when one is eighty-two years old one must allow "the dear, accursed world to continue in its fool's life, as it has for millennia, in the name of God."[43] Goethe's interest at that time in the device for Zelter, together with the temporal proximity of this remark to his ill humor regarding the Hegel medal, render it probable that the Zelter medal, too, has some relationship to that cross which, contrary to everything rational, stands upon the Hegel medal, receiving through a genius its mediation with philosophy. Goethe rebelled against such an introduction of Christianity into philosophy. In a conversation with Eckermann on February 4, 1829, he says with regard to the philosopher Schubarth: "Just like Hegel, he, too, drags the Christian religion into philosophy, although it has no business there. The Christian religion is a mighty entity in itself, by means of which a sunken and miserable mankind from time to time has worked its way once more to the surface. When this effect is accorded it, it is exalted above all philosophy, and needs no support from it. Similarly, the philosopher does not need the approval of religion to demonstrate certain theories such as eternal existence." The same view is evidenced once more in a conversation with Kanzler Müller, occasioned by the confession of faith of a "rational believer."[44] But it is characteristic of Hegelian philosophy, which includes everything in its dualities, that it is a philosophy of the spirit based on the Christian logos, a philosophical theology. We have a metaphor for this amalgamation of the reason of philosophy with the theology of the cross in a famous passage from the preface to *Rechtsphilosophie*, where Hegel calls reason a "rose within the cross of the present."[45] Of course, this image is not connected with the allegorical representation upon Hegel's medal, which has a cross but not a rose; but it illustrates Hegel's conception of the unity of philosophical reason and the Christian cross.

Lasson has given an exhaustive interpretation of Hegel's statement, reducing the theological significance of the cross until it disappears in a universal "dichotomy" which is reconciled by reason. Nevertheless, he himself points out the connection between Hegel's metaphor and the sect of the Rosicrucians,[46] as well as with Luther's

coat of arms, with Hegel's own Lutheranism, and with the third
centenary of the Reformation (1817). But if the cross means only
dissociation between self-conscious spirit and presently existing
reality, why then—one must ask in disagreement with Lasson's interpretation—does Hegel, in such a conspicuous place, label this
estrangement with the basic Christian concept of the cross? Obviously because he understands both the estrangement and reconciliation to exist, from the very beginning, in the realm of the history of
the spirit, having in mind Christ's death upon the cross, though
understanding the "spirit" of Christianity philosophically. Reason is
a rose within the cross of the present, not because every estrangement strives by its very nature for reunion, but because the agony
of the estrangement and reconciliation have already taken place
within history in the suffering God.[47] But Goethe's objection to
Hegel's "contignation" is the more significant in that Goethe himself, in "Die Geheimnisse," used the metaphor of a cross garlanded
with roses as a symbol of his idea of the "purely human."

b Goethe's Association of
Humanity With the Cross

The content of the poem is briefly as follows: A young monk
loses his way in the mountains, finally arriving at a monastery above
whose door there is the symbol of a cross garlanded with roses.
Within the monastery twelve knightly monks are assembled, who
had formerly been scattered in secular life. Their spiritual leader is
a mysterious unknown man who bears the name "Humanus." In
contrast to this personification of pure and universal humanity, each
of the twelve others represents a particular nation or religion, with
his own way of thinking and seeing. Through their life together
under the leadership of Humanus, they have been granted the one,
inclusive spirit which is his. He now wishes to leave them. There is
no longer any need for his presence, after he has had his effect upon
them all.

Thus the religion of humanity is not a particular religion among
others, nor does it consist in the mere common beliefs of various
religions, as in Lessing's parable; it means "the eternal duration of
an elevated human condition." Despite this, Goethe's own statement
refers the cross with the roses to the Christian events of Holy Week.
To this faith of "half a world" Goethe gives "a completely new
significance" by mitigating the theological rigor of the Christian

cross and by exalting it to a symbol of pure humanity. The roses
lend softness to the "rude wood." The symbol is not surrounded by
any words of explanation; its meaning is, rather, to become visible
mysteriously, to remain, like Faust, a "riddle manifest." The human
mystery of the Christian cross is hinted at by the "hardly understood word" of self-liberation through self-conquest. To "die and
be born" makes up Goethe's humanistic Good Friday. To this extent, both Goethe and Hegel humanized (or spiritualized) Luther's
theology of the cross; in the metaphor of rose and cross, they interpreted the device of Luther and that of the Rosicrucians within
the secular realm.

There was nevertheless a divergence in their use of the same
symbol. For Goethe, it remains a symbol which cannot be comprehended in words; for Hegel, it merely serves to illustrate a relationship which can be comprehended by concepts. Goethe absorbs
Christianity into humanity, and "Die Geheimnisse" reveals the
nature of the "purely human." Hegel subsumes Christianity in
reason, which, as the Christian logos, is the "absolute." Goethe
allows the rose of humanity to wind freely about the cross, and
philosophy to remain separate from Christianity; Hegel removes the
rose of reason into the midst of the cross, and philosophical thought
incorporates the dogmatic concepts of theology. In Goethe's interpretation of his poem, the story is placed in Holy Week; but for him
the celebration of the crucifixion and resurrection of Christ means
only the "ratification" (*Besiegelung*) of an elevated human condition. Hegel's philosophy seeks to remove the seal from the historical event of Holy Week by turning it into a "speculative Good
Friday," making of Christian dogmatics a philosophy of religion,
which identifies Christian suffering with the idea of the highest freedom, and Christian theology with philosophy.[48] Goethe objected to
this association from the ground up. Precisely because he knows
how to honor the Christian cross "as a man and as a poet," he finds
the detour of the philosopher repugnant, doing honor neither to the
Christian faith nor to the reason of man.

c   The Lutheran Sense
of Rose and Cross

Measured against the original Lutheran sense of rose and cross,
the divergence between Hegel and Goethe in their attitude toward
Christianity pales into insignificance. Luther's device has a black

cross in the midst of a heart surrounded by white roses; its meaning can be read from the legend: *Des Christen Herz auf Rosen geht, wenn's mitten unterm Kreuze steht* ("The Christian's heart walks upon roses when it stands beneath the cross"). In a letter written in 1530 to Lazarus Spengler, Luther explains more precisely the meaning of the device: "Because you desire to know whether my seal is rightly conceived, as a mark of friendship I shall let you have my first thoughts, which I wanted to fix upon my seal as upon a stamp of my theology. First should be a cross: black, within the heart, which would have its natural color, that I may remind myself that faith in Him who was crucified makes us blest. For as one believes with his heart, one is justified. Now the fact that it is a black cross mortifies, and is intended to produce pain; yet, it allows the heart to retain its natural color, does not destroy nature, that is, does not kill but rather keeps alive—*Justus enim fide vivet, sed fide crucifixi*. But such a heart should stand in the midst of a white rose, to show that faith yields joy, comfort, and peace. . . . The rose is to be white, not red, for the color white is the color of the spirits and all angels. Such a rose stands in a field the color of heaven, for such joy in spirit and in faith is a beginning of the heavenly joy which is to be: now already comprehended within, held through hope, but not yet manifest." We can read a summary in antithetical form in a passage written in 1543, in juxtaposition with the device: "Because Adam lives (that is, sins), death swallows up life. But if Christ dies (that is, is justified), life swallows up death."

This Christian interpretation of the rose and cross stands in as great a contrast to Hegel's rational reinterpretation as to Goethe's humanistic reinterpretation. For, paradoxically, the heart of the Christian rests upon roses only when, following Christ, it assumes the cross of suffering, thus standing "beneath" the cross. The cross in the Christian sense is not mitigated through humanity, nor has it within itself a rose as a rational center. It is as nonhumanistic and nonrational as is the Christian in comparison to the natural man, that is, Adam. Therefore it is only in a very attenuated sense that one can speak of Hegel's and Goethe's Protestantism.

d Hegel's and Goethe's "Protestantism"

Hegel's Protestantism rests upon the fact that he understood the principle of the spirit, and thus the principle of freedom, as the conceptual development and consummation of Luther's principle of assurance of justification by faith.[49] He practically identifies the perceptions of reason with faith. "This perception has been called faith. It is not historical (externally objective) faith. As Lutherans—I am one and will remain so—we have only that original faith."[50] In this rational faith which knows that man's destiny of freedom rests on his immediate relationship with God, Hegel viewed himself as a Protestant. In this way he reconciled the absolute dichotomy between faith and reason which Luther himself so radically established. Ultimately, to Hegel, Protestantism is identical with the "universal insight and education" which it effected. "Our universities and our schools are our churches." Therein rests the essential contrast with Catholicism.

Like Hegel, Goethe esteemed the Reformation as liberation from the "shackles of intellectual narrow-mindedness," while for Luther it was the restoration of true Christianity. "Once more we have courage," we read in a conversation about the Reformation from the last year of Goethe's life, "to stand with our feet firmly planted upon God's earth, conscious of ourselves in our God-given human nature."[51] Neither Goethe nor Hegel had any qualms about how little a Christianity whose meaning resides in a man's ability "to feel, as a man, great and free" might have in common with its original meaning. Goethe said, "We shall all grow gradually from a Christianity of word and faith to a Christianity of disposition and deed." This statement marks the beginning of the road which led from Hegel to Feuerbach, and further into radical crises. The contrasting attempts of Nietzsche and Kierkegaard, once more to force the decision between paganism and Christianity, are determined reactions to that amorphous Christianity represented by Hegel and Goethe.

e   Goethe's Christian Paganism and Hegel's Philosophical Christianity

Goethe's statements regarding Christ and Christianity oscillate between a remarkable pro and con; this derives not from any vague vacillation, but from a defiant irony which shuns the either-or. "To me, Christ remains a highly significant but problematic entity"[52]—a remark which in the mouth of anyone else would be the symptom of a trivial education; coming from Goethe, it comprehends a world of contrasting lines of thought, which his extraordinary moderation held in balance.

Goethe once described himself as a "decided non-Christian," to whom the discovery of the earth's movement about the sun meant more than the entire Bible, and another time as perhaps the only true Christian, as Christ would have him be[53]—a contradiction—beside which stand the comments (in the same conversation): the pederasty of the Greek is as old as mankind, it is rooted in the nature of man even though contrary to nature; and, the sanctity of Christian marriage is of inestimable value, although marriage itself is unnatural!

The ambiguous tension of Goethe's statements about Christianity extends through sixty years. The *Prometheus* fragment of 1773 is already not only a rebellion against the gods, but—as Jacobi and Lessing at once understood[54]—an attack upon the Christian faith in God. It was followed in 1774 by *Der Ewige Jude*, an attack upon the Church and clergy. A year later Goethe sends a reply to Herder apropos the latter's *Erläuterungen zum Neuen Testament*, thanking him for a "stimulating heap of rubbish." If only the whole doctrine of Christ were not so illusory as to be an insult to his human intelligence, he would be immensely pleased by the subject itself, as well as Herder's treatment of it.

In 1781, upon receipt of Lavater's published letters, he writes: "I have never looked so gladly upon your Christ and admired him as much as I have done through these letters." It exalts the soul and furnishes occasion for the most wonderful meditations to see Lavater grasp with ardor this "crystal vessel," fill it to the very brim with his own bright red draught, and drink it down. "I grant you this pleasure gladly, for without it you must needs be miserable. With your wish and desire to derive everything possible from an individual, and with the impossibility that an individual can ever satisfy you, it is glorious that an image has been left to us from ancient times, into which you can pour your All, and, seeing yourself reflected in it, worship yourself. But I can only call it unjust, an act of robbery not befitting your good name, that you should pluck from the thousands of fowls of the air their priceless feathers as though they had been usurped in order to embellish your own bird of paradise with them, an action which must appear to us grievous and unendurable, we who devote ourselves to the study of all wisdom revealed through men and Man, as sons of God worshiping him within ourselves and within all his children. I quite understand that you can do nothing to change this, and that you are justified in your own eyes. But, since you repeatedly preach your own faith and doctrine, I also find it necessary repeatedly to show you our own, a brazen, unshakable rock of humanity, which you and all Christendom may occasionally dampen with the waves of your sea, but can neither innundate nor cause to tremble upon its foundations." More pointedly, he writes to Herder in 1788: "It remains true: the fairy tale of Christ is the reason that the world is able to go forward another ten meters without anyone coming to his senses; it takes as much strength of knowledge, understanding, and wisdom to defend it as to attack it. Now the generations are confused, the individual is a wretched thing no matter what party he declares himself for, the whole is never a whole, the human race tosses to and fro upon trivialities, none of which would be so important did it not exert great influence upon points which are so essential to man!" About six years later, after a renewed study of Homer, Goethe states in a conversation that he has just realized what indescribable mischief the "Jewish nonsense" brought upon us. "Had we never come to know the melancholy of the Orient, had Homer remained our Bible, how different a form would mankind have achieved!" Thirty years later, in a letter to Zelter on the occasion of the performance of some Passion music, we find similar sentiments: "Hopefully 'Jesus' Death' will bring you a joyous Easter this time, also. The clergy has learned so well how to reap a profit from this most wretched of all events; the painters, too, have profited so from it; why should the composers alone be sent away empty?" Four years later, he writes to Müller that he pities the preachers who must speak and have nothing to say, having as their subject "a sheaf which has been threshed for two thousand years." From the same period dates a remark to Zelter apropos of an *ecce homo* painting: "Everyone who looks at it will feel good, seeing someone who is even worse off than he is." And once, when he was accused of being a pagan, he replied: "I, a pagan? Well, I had Gretchen executed and let Ottilie starve to death; isn't that Christian enough for the people?"[55]

But in his *Geschichte der Farbenlehre*, under the heading of "Tradition," this same Goethe calls the Bible the book not only of the Jewish people but of all peoples, because it sets forth the history of one nation as a symbol for all the rest. "And as far as content is concerned, we should have to add very little to bring it completely up to date. Were one to append to the Old Testament an extract from Josephus, to continue the history of the Jews down to the destruction of Jerusalem; were one to insert a synopsis of the extension of Christianity and the dispersion of Judaism through the world after the book of Acts; were one, preceding the Revelation of John, to draw up a summary of unadulterated Christian doctrine according to the sense of the New Testament, in order to explicate and eluci- date the complicated exposition of the Epistles—then, in the immedi- ate present, this work would deserve to regain once more its old posi- tion not only as a universal book but as a universal library of all nations. Surely the higher the educational standards of the centuries become, the more it could be used for education, partially as a foun- dation, partially as a tool, obviously not by dilettantes, but by truly wise men." Finally, in the *Wanderjahre* (II/1) Goethe declared Christianity to be the "ultimate" religion because it represents an exalted culmination, which mankind can and must attain; Chris- tianity alone has opened to us "the divine depths of suffering."

But the detailed reasoning behind this is by no means Christian; it is very close to what Nietzsche called the Dionysian justification of life. According to Goethe's theory, Christianity transcends ancient ways of sanctifying life because it includes positively within itself what appears to go contrary to life. It teaches us to view as divine even what is repugnant, odious, and loathesome: "Lowliness and poverty, scorn and contempt, disgrace and misery, suffering and death"; it even teaches us to love sin and crime as ways by which to go forward. It is like "nature" in *Satyros:* both *Urding* and *Unding* (primal matter and impossibility; everything and nothing), a com- prehensive unity of contradictions. Life, we read in the fragment on nature, is "its most beautiful invention," and death "its device to have much life." Birth and the grave are one eternal sea.

Starting from this concept of nature as divine, Goethe interprets the genuineness of the Bible and its truth. But for him, the sun is no less true and quickening than is the appearance of Christ! "What is genuine except everything excellent which stands in harmony with purest nature and reason, even today serving for our highest devel- opment! And what is counterfeit except everything absurd, empty, dumb, everything which bears no fruit, at least no fruit of value! If the genuineness of a biblical document is to be decided by the ques- tion whether everything it tells us is true, then in a few points the genuineness even of the Gospels could be doubted. . . . And yet I consider the Gospels, all four, to be genuine; for there works within them the reflection of a majesty which proceeded from the person of Christ. It is of such a divinity as any the deity has ever assumed upon earth. If I am asked whether it accords with my nature to give him reverent worship, then I say, 'Completely!' I bow before him as the divine revelation of the highest principle of morality. If I am asked whether it accords with my nature to worship the sun, then I say once again, 'Completely!' For it, likewise, is a revelation of the most high, and in fact the mightiest which has ever been granted us mortals to perceive. I worship in it the light and creative power of God, whereby alone we live and move and have our being, and all plants and animals together with us."[56]

Thus Goethe was able to call himself an adamant non-Christian and at the same time avoid being taken for a pagan. What he worshiped as divine was the productive power of the entire world, against which war, plague, water, and flame can have no effect.[57] To this Dionysian world of self-destruction and rebirth Christ, also, belongs, whose teaching extended the realm of what is to be revered until it included even what is most repugnant. When, in the last month of his life, Goethe writes (speaking of the *Bacchae* of Euripides), seemingly in a strange anticipation of Nietzsche's idea of a crucified Dionysus: the piece provides a most fruitful comparison of a modern dramatic presentation of the suffering divinity in Christ with the ancient presentation of a similar suffering, thence to issue all the more powerfully in Dionysus.[58]

The internal consistency of this statement can be measured by the fact that in the *Ewige Jude*, a *Sturm und Drang* Christ, who has had his fill of crosses, utters the unchristian words: "O world full of wondrous complexity, full of the spirit of order, of casual wandering, thou endless chain of ecstasy and misery, thou mother who borest me even to the grave! Whom I, though present at creation, do not particularly understand."

Goethe's free and careless attitude toward Christianity, based upon the fact that he "had such true emotions,"[59] became a superficial and pale commonplace of the intelligentsia of the nineteenth century, who thought that they could claim Goethe as their leader because they thought their indifference reconciled differences. A typical expression of the *juste milieu* of this bourgeois-Christian cultural class, even during the First World War, was the popular formula "Homer and the Bible," both of which were carried in the rucksack. Until very recently, this humanism tinged with Christianity left its stamp upon the more or less freethinking speeches of Protestant school directors and pastors. Some biblical text would be discussed, illustrated with statements by von Humboldt, Schiller, and Goethe. Overbeck characterized this state of affairs perfectly: "It is the fashion for contemporary Christianity to give itself to the world in its own way, in the world of today no man of importance can behave in anti-Christian fashion without being claimed by Christianity with special preference. Among the Christians of modern observance, Goethe and Schiller, Feuerbach, Schopenhauer, Wagner, Nietzsche, and, naturally, their successors, must be content with this. . . . In actuality, we will soon be at the point with Christianity that all those great men will be much more familiar to us as devout Christians than as apostates from Christianity. If nothing more were needed for evidence of such an estimation than to pluck out of their writings the raisins of 'warm' tones, approving of Christianity, who would hesitate long before joining himself wholeheartedly to modern Christianity?"[60]

Hegel never viewed his "understanding" of Christianity as a negation, but as a justification of the intellectual content of the absolute religion. In his mind, the Christian doctrine of suffering and redemption was also determinative for speculative thought. A search through his works and letters for ironic invectives against Christianity would be in vain; when he writes polemic, it is directed solely against inappropriate conceptual forms, barren of ideas, as found in particular theological movements. In his old age particularly he made the express claim that his was a Christian philosophy.[61] His biographer could describe Hegel's philosophy justly as a "perennial definition of God": so greatly was it a philosophy grounded on the historical basis of the Christian religion.

However unambiguous to Hegel was his mediation between philosophy and Christianity, it perforce became ambiguous to an equal degree when this mediation became a point of attack. The critical component which was already present in Hegel's justification became free and independent as soon as the mediation disintegrated. Because the ambiguity present in Hegel's conceptual *Aufhebung* (exaltation or nullification) of religion could be interpreted in two ways, criticism, too, could take Hegel's justification as its point of departure. On the grounds of Hegel's mediation between philosophy and Christianity, it pressed for their differentiation and for a decision. The consequence of this process can be seen in the criticism of religion which passes from Strauss through Feuerbach to Bruno Bauer and Kierkegaard.[62] Along the way is revealed, together with the crisis of Hegelian philosophy, a crisis of Christianity.

Hegel did not see a crisis coming in the history of Christianity, while Goethe, in 1830, saw it plainly before him. For one must either hold fast to the traditional faith without allowing room for criticism of it, or surrender oneself to criticism, also surrendering faith. A third course is inconceivable. "Humanity is now caught in a religious crisis; how it will come through I do not know, but come through it must and shall."[63] They both saw the political crisis in the same way. The external impulse was provided by the July Revolution.

f   The End of the World
of Goethe and Hegel

In 1829, in a conversation concerning the state of Europe, Goethe said to a Pole named Odynic that the nineteenth century "is not just the continuation of the preceding one, but seems destined to be the beginning of a new era. For such great events as shook the world in the opening years of this century cannot remain without great consequences, even though the latter, like grain from seed, grow and ripen slowly."[64] Goethe did not expect them until the autumn of the century. The first consequence was the July Revolution of 1830, which shook all Europe, and gave all who experienced it cause to reflect. Immermann said that it was not explicable on the basis of physical need, but only as a spiritual force and enthusiasm, similar to a religious movement, although the motive force was not faith, but "politics." More soberly, L. von Stein concluded that it was the great event whereby industrial society came to power. The social truths which it made manifest concerned all Europe, and the doubt which attached to the victory of the bourgeois class concerned civilization in general. More than anyone else, Niebuhr felt the revolution to be epoch-making. His deeply resigned preface to the second edition of the second part of his *Roman History*, dated October 5, 1830, sees "all hopeful prospects" threatened by a destruction such as the Roman world underwent in the third century: annihilation of property, of freedom, of culture, of science. And Goethe agreed with him in his prophecy of a barbarism to come; it was, indeed, already at hand, "we are already in the midst of it."[65]

The symptomatic significance of the July Revolution was that it showed that the chasm of the great French Revolution had closed only in outward appearance; in reality the world stood at the beginning of a whole "Age of Revolutions," in which the masses were to win from the upper classes an independent political power.[66] Kanzler

Müller gives an account of a conversation with Goethe in which the latter said that he could reconcile himself to the new crisis only because he saw in it "the greatest opportunity for intellectual exercise" which could come to him at the close of his life.[67] A few months later, Goethe writes to Zelter that he finds it remarkable that after forty years the old frenzy should begin all over again. The strategy for such powers as remained should be to make the individual paroxysms harmless. "If we survive, there will be calm again for a while. More I cannot say."[68] More out of place than ever, there seemed to be present in this revolution an "unmitigated striving for absolutism—in this thoroughly conditional world."[69] He preserved his sanity through the study of nature, which remains constant in the midst of all change. When Eckermann came to bring him the first reports of the revolution, Goethe said to him excitedly: "Well, what do you think of this great event? The volcano has erupted, all is in flames, and it is no longer a transaction behind closed doors." But to Eckermann's amazement, by "this event" he did not mean the political news, but a discussion in the Paris Academy concerning the methodology of natural science.[70]

Goethe recognized clearly that the world began to undergo a drastic change about 1830, as a result of democratic leveling and industrialization. On October 23, 1828, he said to Eckermann on the subject of mankind: "I see a time coming when God will no longer have any pleasure in it; he will once more have to destroy everything to make room for a renewed creation." The basis of bourgeois society and its social life seemed to him to be destroyed, and he viewed the writings of St. Simon as the ingenious outline for a radical abolition of the existing order. What came to him from France in the way of modern literature he viewed as a "literature of despair," forcing upon the reader the very opposite of what men should be told for their own well-being.[71] "It is their satanic business to exaggerate to the utmost limit everything odious, everything loathsome, everything horrible, everything unworthy, along with the whole pack of the depraved." Everything is now "ultra" and "transcendent," in thought as well as in action. "No one knows himself any more, no one understands the element in which he lives and moves, no one understands the material which he shapes. There can be no talk of pure simplicity, but of simple nonsense there is plenty." Modern man transcends himself and overeducates himself only to remain fixed in mediocrity; he becomes more extreme and more common.[72] The last document revealing his insight into the currents of the age is a letter to W. von Humboldt, in which he justifies the seal of secrecy he put upon the second part of Faust: "Without question it would give me infinite pleasure to dedicate these very serious jests to my esteemed friends, widely dispersed, whom I gratefully acknowledge, while they are yet alive—to let them see them and to hear their replies. But the day is really so absurd and confused that I am convinced that the honest efforts with which I have labored so long on this strange edifice would be ill repaid; they would be driven upon the shore, lie there like a shattered hulk, only to be covered over by the drifting sands of time. Confusing theories for confused actions hold sway over the earth; I have nothing better to do than, where possible, to augment what is my own and has been left to me, to distill and redistill my own individuality, just as you, also, my esteemed friend, are doing in your castle." With these words, full of astounding firmness and resignation, Goethe's correspondence ends, five days before his death.

Hegel was irritated by the July Revolution no less than Goethe. With rage and horror he saw the onset of new dissensions against which he now defended the existing order as a genuine source of stability. In his last political writing, written in 1831 criticizing the English Reform Bill, he called the desire for reform a "disobedience" born of "courage from below." Accused of servility toward Church and State, he wrote to Goeschel on December 13, 1830: "At present the enormous interest of politics has swallowed up all others —a crisis in which everything previously dependable seems to become problematic. So little can philosophy stand up to the uncertainty, violence, and evil passions of this great unrest, I hardly think that it can penetrate into those circles which rest so easily; it must realize that—even for the purpose of bringing calm—it is only for the few." At the close of the preface to the second edition of the *Logik*, he expresses the fear that in a period politically so agitated there might be no room at all for the "passionless calm of purely thinking knowledge." A few days after finishing the preface he fell ill with cholera and died.

In their common opposition to "transcendence," Goethe and Hegel were still able to construct a world in which man can live with himself; but even their immediate pupils no longer found themselves at home in it, and misunderstood the equilibrium of their masters as the product of mere harmonization.[73] In Marx and Kierkegaard,[74] the mid-point from which Goethe's "nature" drew its life, the mediation in which Hegel's "spirit" moved, diverged once more into the two extremes of internal and external, until finally Nietzsche sought, by a new beginning, to retrieve antiquity from the emptiness of modernity and, with this experiment, vanished in the darkness of insanity.

The Origin of the Spiritual Development of the Age in Hegel's Philosophy of the History of the Spirit

I The Eschatological Meaning of Hegel's Consummation of the History of the World and the Spirit

1 The Eschatological Design of World History

For Hegel, the history of philosophy is not a process parallel to or outside of the world, but "the heart of world history." What dominates both equally is the Absolute in the form of "world spirit," the essence of which is movement, and hence history.[1] Not only does Hegel's work include a philosophy of history and a history of philosophy, but his entire system is historically oriented to an extent which is true of no previous philosophy. His philosophizing begins with historicotheological discussions of the spirit of Christianity vastly transcending the historical sense of Voltaire, Hume, and Gibbon. There follow historicopolitical writings and the first ethical systems, in which the unconditioned power of history is presented as "time which conquers all" and "primal destiny."[2] Here we read for the first time of the "world spirit," which has "knowledge of itself in every form, either crude or highly developed, but in any case absolute." In every nation it gives expression to a "totality of life."[3] Then follows phenomenology, as the history of the unfolding of the spirit and of the cultural stages of knowledge; here the systematic stages of thought and historical relationships are even more inseparable, since they have no empirically determined relationship, but rather interpenetrate.

The goal of this elaborate dialectical movement of the spirit, which lives in the element of history, is "absolute knowledge." It is attained through "recollection" of all spirits which have ever existed. This pathway of the eternally present spirit through the previous nature of history is not a detour to be avoided, but the only practicable way to the consummation of knowledge. The absolute, or spirit, not only has its external history, as a man has clothing, but is, in its deepest nature, as a movement of self-development, an entity which exists only by becoming. As a spirit which continuously surrenders and recollects, it is per se historical, even though the dialectic of becoming does not proceed in a straight line toward infinity, but rather goes in a circle, so that the end is the consummation of the beginning. When upon this path of progress the spirit ultimately achieves its full being and knowledge, or its self-consciousness, the history of the spirit is completed. Hegel completes the history of the spirit in the sense of its ultimate fulfillment, in which everything which has taken place hitherto or has been conceived is comprehended in a unity; but he completes it also in the sense of an eschatological end, in which the history of the spirit is finally realized. And because the essence of the spirit is the freedom of existing with itself, complete freedom is achieved with the completion of its history.

On the principle of the freedom of the spirit Hegel also constructs the history of the world, with a view toward a fulfilled end. In his philosophy of history, the most important stages in the self-liberation of the spirit are the beginning in the East and the conclusion in the West. The world process begins with the great oriental kingdoms of China, India, and Persia. After the decisive victory of the Greeks over the Persians, it continues in the Greek and Roman political edifices on the Mediterranean. It concludes with the Christian-Germanic kingdoms in the western part of the North. "Europe is identical with the West," and "represents the consummation of world history, just as Asia is the East and the beginning."[4] The sun, which rises in the East and sets in the West, is the universal spirit of the world. During this process, bitter struggles educate the spirit to freedom. "The Orient knew and knows only that *one* man is free, the Greek and Roman world that *some* are free, the Germanic world knows that *all* are free." The freedom peculiar to the Christian-Germanic world is no longer the arbitrary will of an individual despot, nor is it the freedom of freeborn Greeks and Romans, which depended upon slavery; it is the freedom of every Christian person. The history of the Orient is the childhood of the world process, that of the Greeks and Romans its youth and manhood, while Hegel himself—standing at the conclusion of the Christian-Germanic world—produces his philosophy "in the old age of the spirit."

In the Orient the substance of the spirit remains massive and uniform; the peculiar characteristic of the Greek world is the individual liberation of the spirit. A few important individuals produce a wealth of plastic forms; here we feel at home immediately, because we are upon the ground of the spirit, which independently claims for itself everything alien. The life of Greece is a true "act of youth": Achilles, the youth of poetry, opened it; and Alexander, the true youth, brought it to a close. In both we see individuality at its most beautiful and free, an individuality developed further in the struggle against Troy and Asia. Politically and spiritually, Greece is an anti-Asiatic power, and thus the beginning of Europe. This is reinforced by the nature of the land, which is not a uniform continental block, but lies scattered on many isles and peninsulas along the coasts of the sea. Here we do not find the physical bulk of the Orient; there is no single river linking everything, like the Ganges and Indus, the Euphrates and Tigris. Instead we have a complex land, dispersed here and there, well in accord with the nature of the Greek city-states and the agitation of their spirit.[5]

Because it lacked unity, this gifted land of individual persons was subjected to the political power of Rome, which was the first creation of an independent state or "political generality," and, in turn, of private individuals with specific rights in relationship to the state.[6] With its power to organize everything on an equal footing, the Roman Empire laid the groundwork for the Europe which was to come, penetrating politically and culturally the entire contemporary world. Upon the Roman roads the Greek cultural milieu moved everywhere; without them Christianity would never have been able to grow into a world religion.

The internal limitation of both the Greek and Roman world consists in the blind fate which, in antiquity, still remained beside the spirit, so that ultimate decisions were determined from without. In all "decisive" questions of life, the Greeks and Romans did not consult their own conscience, the "point of decision," but oracles and signs. Before Christ, man was not yet a fully independent and infinitely free personality; at this stage of history, man's spirit was not yet free to itself, for self-existence.[7]

The ultimate liberation of the spirit results from the irruption of Christianity into the heathen world. "With the coming of the Christian principle, the earth belongs to the spirit; the earth is circumnavigated, and, for Europeans, a sphere." The Christian world is a "world of consummation," for "the principle is fulfilled, and thus the end of days is complete."[8] Only the Christian God is truly man and "spirit" at once. The spiritual substance becomes the subject in an individual historical person. Thereby the unity of the divine and the human is finally brought to consciousness; reconciliation is given to man as the image of God. "This principle forms the axis of the world, upon which it revolves. The course of history leads up to this point and flows from it."[9] Thus for Hegel the European way of reckoning time has not only temporary and conditional significance, but absolute historical meaning. In one decisive moment the European world became Christian forever.

The spread of faith in Christ necessarily has political consequences: the Greek state was already a state of (democratic) freedom, but only for "good fortune and genius." With Christianity the principle of absolute (monarchic) freedom appears, in which man knows himself to be identical with the power to which he relates himself. The freedom of the Greeks depended upon slaves; Christian freedom is infinite and unconditional.

The history of Christianity is the unfolding of the "infinite power of free decision"; in Christianity it attains its full stature.[10] It extends from the acceptance of the Christian faith by the Germanic peoples, through the hegemony of the Roman Catholic Church, to the Protestant Reformation, which reconciles church and state, conscience and law. Luther was the first to bring to fruition the idea that man is intended to be free through his own agency.[11] Further consequences of the Reformation are the Enlightenment and, finally, the French Revolution. The liberation of the individual conscience from the universal authority of the Pope created the necessary condition for the human will to decide to construct a rational state, the principle of which would be the Christian idea of freedom and equality. For Luther, the content of the Christian faith was determined by revelation; through Rousseau's mediation, in the French Revolution the European spirit determined for itself the content of its goal.

In this last stage of the history of the European spirit, "pure free will" is finally produced, which itself both wills and knows what it wills. For the first time man stands "upon his head": the process of the world becomes identical with the intellectual process of philosophy. With this event we reach the conclusion of the philosophy of history, whose principle is "progress in consciousness of freedom." Thus for Hegel the so-called secularization of original Christianity —its spirit and its freedom—by no means signifies a reprehensible apostasy from its original meaning. On the contrary: it signifies the true explication of this origin through positive realization.[12] Just as the history of the Christian world is a progressive movement transcending antiquity, so it is also the true fulfillment of the "yearning" of the ancient world. The Greco-Roman world is *aufgehoben* (both "elevated" and "abolished") in the Christian-Germanic world. Hegel's basic ontological concept is thus doubly defined: as Greek and as Christian logos. On the other hand, it was completely foreign to his concrete sense of history to restore once more the connection between the ancient world and Christianity, seeking to return once more to an abstract origin, "either" in Hellenism "or" in Christianity.[13]

The ultimate basis of Hegel's eschatological system lies in his absolute evaluation of Christianity, according to which the eschatological end and fullness of time occurred with the appearance of Christ. But because Hegel displaces the Christian expectation of the end of the world of time into the course of the world process, and the absolute of faith into the rational realm of history, it is only logical for him to understand the last great event in the history of the world and the spirit as the consummation of the beginning. In fact, the history of the "idea" comes to an end with Hegel; in recollection, he understands all history "up to this time and from this time" as fulfillment of all ages. This is not contradicted by the fact that the empirical process, without principle, and therefore also without epochs, goes on infinitely, without beginning or end.

This historical consciousness of Hegelian philosophy entered into the education not only of his pupils and successors, but also of his opponents. Even Burckhardt continued to contain his thinking within the circumference of Hegel's view of history, consciously restricting it to the ancient and Christian worlds, although he recognized that the spirit of the ancient world is no longer our own, and that the modern struggle for power and profit is moving toward an interpretation of life which is independent of Christianity. In spite of this insight and his opposition to Hegel's "rational" schematization of the world, he, too, confirmed Hegel's eschatological conception. The last motif of Burckhardt's reflections on the history of Europe was the awareness that "Ancient Europe" is at an end.

2   The Eschatological Nature of the Absolute Forms of the Spirit

a   Art and Religion

The principle of consummation dominates the nature of the three absolute forms of the spirit: art, religion, and philosophy. Corresponding to the three epochs in the history of the world, there are three in the realm of art: the symbolic, the classic, and the Christian-romantic.

Because every way of looking at the world is a "child of its time," the age of genuine seriousness of Greek and Christian art is past. This end of art is not an accidental misfortune which befalls it from without by necessity of time and its prosaic meaning. It is the "product and progress of art itself," which bring it to an end when "everything has been brought out" and there is nothing more left which is internal and obscure, still striving for form. At this point, absolute interest in art vanishes. "But now when art has made manifest the essential world views within its idea, together with the general content belonging to these world views, then it has liberated itself from this content, which each time is meant for a particular people, a particular age. The real need to take it up once more arises only with the need to turn against the content which, up to this point, has been the only valid content; thus in Greece Aristophanes, for example, turned against his age, and Lucian rebelled against the entire Greek past, and in Italy and Spain, at the close of the Middle Ages, Ariosto and Cervantes began to turn against the nobility."[14] In our own time, the development of reflective thought has turned the substantial forms of art completely into a *tabula rasa*.[15] "No matter how excellent we continue to find the Greek images of the gods, no matter how estimable and perfect we continue to find the representations of God the Father, Christ, and Mary, it does not help; we no longer bow our knees."[16] No Homer or Sophocles,

Dante or Shakespeare, can appear in our time: "What has been sung so well, what has been so freely proclaimed, is proclaimed. These are materials, ways of looking at things and comprehending them, which have been sung through. Only the present is vital; everything else is pale and faded."[17]

Not only have particular subjects of art lost their interest, but the form of art in general has ceased to be the highest need of the spirit. For us, it is no longer the supreme way for truth to come into existence.[18] It is no use to yearn once more to appropriate world views of the past, to become Catholics, for example, like many of the romanticists, who want to "settle" themselves in order externally to fix their uncertain dispositions. "The artist must not even need to achieve purity in his own disposition, having to watch for the good of his own soul; from the very beginning, his great, free soul . . . must know and possess its goal, be sure of it, and rely upon itself." Today especially, the spirit of the artist needs a liberating education in which all "superstition and belief restricted to particular forms of viewing and representation are reduced to the status of mere aspect and instance, over which the free spirit has made itself master by refusing to see in them any per se sacrosanct conditions for artistic creation. Instead, it accords them value through the superior content which it finds appropriate and puts into them in an act of renewed creation."[19] Thus transcending itself, art is equally a return of man to himself, whereby it puts aside all concrete limitations to particular contents, to achieve its ultimate goal. It is in this sense of perfection that Hegel interprets the humor in the poetry of Jean Paul, and Goethe's universal humanity: his unbounded freedom with respect to the varying content of his particular activities, and the creedal nature of his literary output, whose saint is simply Humanus. "Here the artist receives his content from himself; he is the true spirit of man, determining his own destiny, observing the infinite variety of his own feelings and situations, contemplating and expressing them. To him, nothing is alien which can come to life in the heart of man."[20] Everything in which man can feel at home to any degree is a potential subject of this art which has become perfectly free.

In conclusion, we also have the form of religion. It is true that the form of its internal consciousness towers above the sensuous consciousness of art; but it, too, is no longer the supreme way for the spirit to dwell on earth. At the close of the tenth lecture on the philosophy of religion,[21] Hegel posed the question of the empirical

condition of the Christian religion at the present time, and interpreted the "signs of the time." For it "might occur to us" to compare
our age with the end of the Roman world, where reason took refuge
in the form of private well-being and private justice because a universal religious and political life no longer existed. In such periods,
the individual lets the world be just as it is in order to look after his
own well-being. What is left is the moral view of the world, the
desires and ideas of the individual without objective content. Then
the time was fulfilled; this could be the case once more, now, when
there is need for the justification of faith because the religious forms
which have hitherto been valid no longer hold. "How much," one
might ask, "of this content of the Christian faith will still be considered true?" The clergy, whose duty should be to uphold religion,
has itself fallen prey to rationalization: it propounds Christian doctrine on the basis of ethical motifs and external history. But when
the truth of Christianity is described solely in subjective and historical terms, "then it is all over" with it. "The salt has lost its savor";
what is left is merely skeptical "elucidation" and the arrogant bar-
renness of the educated classes, who cannot be teachers to the people, since such reflection is of no use to them. Thus Christianity
seems to be passing—but this would be to close with a "false note."

Hegel comes to terms with this consciousness of the historical
condition of Christianity by claiming that the passing is an "accidental event," concerning only the external aspect of the world,
from which he excludes the essential reconciliation. What is to become of the "historical present" must be left to the present to decide.
The false note is without significance to philosophy, for its task is
to establish an eternal kingdom of God; the Holy Spirit lives on in
the congregation of philosophy, which now takes over the office of
the priestly class in administering truth.

Just as critical reflection broke into art, so it has broken into
religion. It is a mode of thought which cannot be halted and must
be carried through to its conclusion, because it is the "absolute
judge" before which the truth of religion must prove itself. Just as
art now becomes "the study of art," so now also religion becomes
"philosophy of religion," the thinking spirit having passed the stage
of immediate faith and mere enlightened understanding.[22] The subsumption of religion into philosophy of religion is also a way of
taking refuge: religion takes refuge in philosophy. Rational thought,
which furnishes religious feelings and conceptions with a comprehended pattern of existence, must be recognized as the purest form

of the self-conscious spirit. The science of absolute knowledge has become a true "spiritual cult." "In such a way the two aspects of art and religion are united in philosophy: the objectivity of art, which has lost its outward sensuousness, has only exchanged it for the highest form of objectivity, the form of thought; and the subjectivity of religion is purified so as to become the subjectivity of thought. For on the one hand thought is the innermost, most individual subjectivity; and on the other, genuine thought, the idea, is the most impartial and objective generality, which can comprehend itself in its own form only through thinking."[23]

b Philosophy

Philosophy, too, finds itself at a point of consummation. In his lectures on the history of philosophy, at both the beginning and the conclusion, Hegel included his own standpoint of philosophical consummation, bringing the kingdom of thought to completion. According to his arrangement of the history of philosophy into periods, his own system stands at the end of the third epoch. The first epoch extends from Thales to Proclus, including the beginning and breakup of the ancient world. At its highest pinnacle of perfection, in Proclus, there takes place the ancient reconciliation of the finite and infinite, the divine world and the earthly. The second epoch extends from the beginning of the Christian era to the Reformation. In it, there occurs once more, at a higher level, the same reconciliation of the earthly and the divine, so that in the third epoch, Christian philosophy from Descartes to Hegel, the latter may perfect it.[24] The philosophical systems of this final epoch bring about, through rational thought, the reconciliation which previously only had been hoped for.[25] In principle, all are nothing else than more or less complete methods of unification; at their culmination stands Hegel's absolute system: the absolute Christian spirit, comprehending itself in its own element, reality, and recognizing it as its own. Thus the real world has become "spiritual" in the Christian sense.

In agreement with this system of epochs, Hegel's history of the spirit is not given a mere preliminary conclusion at a random point; it is "concluded," definitively and consciously.[26] On this historical basis, its logical form is not a verdict, but a "conclusion," a merging of beginning and end. Like the conclusion of the *Phänomenologie*, the *Logik*, and the *Encyklopädie*, this conclusion of the *Geschichte*

der Philosophie is not an arbitrary "we have arrived at this point,"
but rather a "we are at the goal"; it is an "outcome." Like Proclus,
Hegel unified the world of the Christian logos into the absolute
totality of the concretely organized idea, bringing to an end all
three epochs. With reference to Proclus, he states that such a unification of all systems in a comprehensive, total system is no mere
eclecticism, but a "deeper understanding of the idea," such as must
occur "from time to time," that is, epochally.[27] With Proclus, Hegel
continues, the world spirit stands at a great "turning point" before
the absolute break, that is, the irruption of Christianity into the
pagan world. For Proclus, the divine nature of reality was still an
abstract ideal, before it became earthly reality in the particular individuality of the God-man Christ. Only then was the longing of the
ancient world fulfilled. From that point on, the task of the world (to
be reconciled with the world spirit) was transferred to the Christian-
Germanic world. In a letter to Creuzer,[28] Hegel writes in a similar
vein of the "enormous stride" which was principally due to Proclus,
and formed the true turning point in the transition from ancient
philosophy to Christianity. "Now once more" it is time to take such
a stride. Thus it seems to him that nothing is more significant for the
age than Creuzer's new edition of Proclus.[29]

But what is the result of all this for Hegel's consummation of
Christian philosophy? Obviously this: it is a final step before a great
turning and break with Christianity. If this is so, Hegel's consummation of ancient and Christian philosophy is the same thing as was
Proclus' philosophy: a "destroying reconciliation." Its culmination
is contemporary with the onset of a decline, a time when "everything is in the throes of dissolution and struggling toward something
new."[30] Similarly, Alexandrian philosophy was the final flowering of
the foundering Roman Empire; nor were the fifteenth and sixteenth
centuries, the close of the second epoch, any different, during which
the Germanic life of the Middle Ages achieved a new form. "Philosophy begins with the annihilation of a real world; when it appears, painting its black picture, the freshness of youth, of vitality,
has already gone. Reconciliation is a reconciliation *not in reality,
but in the ideal world*. In Greece, the philosophers withdrew from
the affairs of state; they were idlers, as the people called them, and
fled into the realm of ideas. This is an important observation; it is
verified by the history of philosophy itself."[31] Even Hegel's philosophy of the state paints this black picture. It does not seek to re-
juvenate a world which has become "ripe"; its only desire is to con-

tinue to know. As such knowledge, it is an acknowledgment of and a reconciliation with "that which is." Thought is now completely alone within itself; and yet, at the same time, as organized idea, it comprehends the universe as a world which has become "intelligible," sensible, and transparent. All extant "objectivity" has become one with its "self-begetting." "It seems that the world spirit has succeeded in discarding all alien, objective existence; it finally comprehends itself as absolute spirit, begetting of itself everything which for it becomes objective, calmly keeping it within its power."[32] In this unity of objectivity and self-directed activity we find the conclusion of the fulfillment-consummation of the "modern" epoch. Only from this eschatological point of view can Hegel's conclusion of the *Geschichte der Philosophie* be understood in its full pathos and gravity: "The world spirit has now arrived at this point. The final philosophy is the result of all that have gone before; nothing is lost, all principles are retained. This concrete idea is the result of the struggles of the spirit through almost 2500 years (Thales was born 640 B.C.), of its most serious effort to become objective in respect to itself, to know itself: Tantae molis erat se ipsam cognoscere mentem." The ambiguity of Hegel's "consummation," meaning both fulfillment and conclusion, is proclaimed by the transformation of Vergil's "Romanam condere gentem"[33] into "se ipsam cognoscere mentem." This transformation says: the laying of the foundations of the Roman Empire then demanded the same effort as is now demanded for the laying of foundations in the domain of the spirit. With the "courage born of knowledge," Hegel writes an end to two and a half millennia, thus opening a new era. In fact, he pronounces the end of the history of the Christian logos. He himself says of art that it loses absolute interest as soon as "everything has been brought out"; its successors are compelled to rebel against the entire past. The same is true of philosophy, which is brought to an end in him, as a result of his consummation: with Hegel's history of the spirit an entire world of language, ideas, and culture comes to an end. Starting from this end point we have our own true *Geistes-Geschichte* (Spirit-History)—like a *lucus a non lucendo*.

Hegel did not express directly the eschatological meaning of the consummation wrought by him, but he did so indirectly. He proclaims it by thinking retrospectively, in the "old age of the spirit," on what has passed, and also by looking ahead to a possible new realm of the spirit, although in the process he expressly denies any actual knowledge. Scattered references to America, ever since the beginning of the century, thought of as the future land of freedom, admit the possibility that the world spirit might emigrate from Europe. "Thus America is the land of the future; in it, in the time lying before us, . . . the significance of world history will be revealed. It is the land longed for by all who are bored with the historical armory of ancient Europe. Napoleon is reputed to have said, 'Cette vieille Europe m'ennuie.' But so far, all that has taken place there is only an echo of the old world and the expression of an alien life; as a land of the future, it concerns us here not at all." Similarly, Hegel concludes a reference to the future importance of the Slavonic world (which he saw as an "intermediary" in the struggle between Christian Europe and Asia) with the statement that he is excluding this entire mass from his treatment. Up to the present it has not appeared as an independent force in the series of configurations assumed by reason. "Whether this will take place in time to come does not concern us here."[34] In a letter to one of his pupils, Baron von Yxküll, the content of which is preserved by Rosenkranz,[35] Hegel expresses himself with less reserve. Europe, he states there, has already become a sort of cage, in which only two sorts of men still appear to move about freely: those who are themselves turnkeys, and those who have found for themselves a place within this cage where they do not have to take action either for or against the bars. But when conditions are such that one cannot ally himself genuinely to the state of the world, it is more advantageous to live completely as an epicurean, remaining solitary as a private individual—a position that is admittedly that of an observer, but yet of great effectiveness. Hegel contrasts the future of Russia to this cage of Europe. The other modern states have apparently already attained the goal of their development, perhaps have already passed their peak, their condition has become stagnant. Russia, by contrast, bears within its womb an "enormous possibility for the development of its intensive nature."[36] Rosenkranz interprets this as a jest on the part of Hegel in order to cheer his Russian friend. This is most incredible. It is in this letter that he had a presentiment of the mood of the following age, having himself in his *Rechtsphilosophie* "painted a black picture."

Ten years later, his reconciliation with "that which is" was attacked by new estrangements due to the July Revolution. It is called into question by a "purposeless desire for innovation," against which he felt himself powerless to contend, while his closest pupils im-

ported the shock from political reality into his philosophy. The last
months of his life were embittered by a quarrel over University
politics with E. Gans, the subsequent editor of Hegel's *Geschichte
der Philosophie* and his *Rechtsphilosophie.* The latter's liberal interpretation of right stands at the beginning of the road which leads to
Ruge, Marx, and Lassalle.[37]

But the possibility of further progress leading to a new estrangement is already allowed for in Hegel's own historical consciousness,
and provided for. Philosophical knowledge about the substantial
aspects of a period has its locus, it is true, in the spirit of the period
in question; it is thus only "formally," as objective knowledge,
transcendent to the period. But at the same time, together with this
contrasting knowledge of the period, there is also postulated a
divergence which leads to further development: the divergence between knowledge and "that which is." From this follows the possibility, the necessity, of continual progress leading to new estrangements in both philosophy and reality. "Thus the formal divergence
is also a real, a true divergence. It is this knowledge which engenders
a new form of development."[38] Through the freedom of its form,
knowledge revolutionizes even its substantial content. The philosophy which perfects itself becomes the birthplace of the spirit, which
then presses on to a new, real configuration.[39] And, in actual fact,
Hegel's summation of the history of knowledge becomes the birthplace from which the intellectual and political developments of
the nineteenth century arise. A few years after Hegel's death, Heine,
at the conclusion of his *Geschichte der Religion und Philosophie in
Deutschland* (1834), tried to open the eyes of the French to the
very concrete revolution which might proceed from the Reformation and German philosophy: "It seems to me that a methodical
nation like us had to begin with the Reformation, could only there-
after engage in philosophy, and only after the perfection of philosophy go on to political revolution. This order I find quite sensible.
The heads which philosophy has used for reflection can be cut off
later by the revolution for whatever purpose it likes. But philosophy
would never have been able to use the heads cut off by the revolution if the latter had preceded it. But do not become anxious, you
German republicans; the German revolution will not take place any
more pleasantly and gently for having been preceded by the Kantian
critique, Fichtian transcendental idealism, or even natural philosophy. Through these theories revolutionary forces have built up
which only await the day on which they may break loose, filling

the world with horror and awe. Kantians will appear who want nothing to do with mercy even in the phenomenal world; they will plough up without pity the very soil of our European life with sword and axe, in order to eradicate every last root of the past. Armed Fichtians will arise, whose fanaticism of will can be restrained neither through fear nor through self-interest, . . . indeed, in the case of a social upheaval, such transcendental idealists would be even more inflexible than the early Christians, since the latter bore martyrdom on earth to attain heavenly bliss, while the transcendentalist considers martyrdom itself to be mere appearance: he is unassailable behind the trenchwork of his own thought. More terrible than all would be the natural philosophers, who would participate actively in any German revolution, identifying themselves with the very work of destruction. If the hand of the Kantian strikes swift and sure because his heart is not moved by any traditional reverence; if the Fichtian courageously defies all danger because for him it does not exist at all in reality; so the natural philosopher will be terrible, for he has allied himself to the primal forces of nature. He can conjure up the demonic powers of ancient German pantheism. That lust for battle will flame within him which we find among the ancient Germans; it does not fight in order to destroy, or in order to win, but merely to fight. Christianity—and this is its greatest accomplishment—moderated somewhat that brutal Germanic lust for battle; but it could not destroy it, and if ever that restraining talisman, the cross, is shattered, there shall arise once more . . . that mindless madman's rage of which the Nordic poets sing so much. That talisman is decaying; the day will come when it collapses miserably. . . . I warn you, Frenchmen, keep then quite still, and for God's sake do not applaud! We could easily misconstrue such an action, and, in our crude way, set you at rest somewhat brusquely. . . . I have good intentions toward you, and therefore I tell you the bitter truth. You have more to fear from Germany liberated than from the entire Holy Alliance, with all its Croats and Cossacks. . . . What you are actually charged with I never have been able to understand. Once, in a beer-cellar in Göttingen, a young old-German declared that revenge must be taken upon the French for Konradin von Stauffen, whom they had beheaded at Naples. Surely you have forgotten that long ago. But we forget nothing. You see, if it ever amuses us to pick a quarrel with you, we shall have no lack of cogent reasons. In any case, therefore, I advise you to be on your guard. No matter what hap-

pens in Germany, whether the Crown Prince of Prussia or Dr.
Wirth comes to power, keep yourselves always armed. . . . I have
good intentions toward you, and it frightened me mightily when I
recently perceived that your ministers intend to disarm France.
Since, in spite of your present romanticism, you are born classicists,
you are well acquainted with Olympus. Among the naked gods and
goddesses . . . you see a goddess who, although surrounded by
such gaiety and pleasure, nevertheless always bears a shield, and
keeps her helmet on her head and her spear in hand. It is the goddess
of wisdom."

The German revolution predicted by Heine did not break out
at that time, but what took place through Hegel's pupils has continued to have an effect down to the present day. A decade after
Heine's inflammatory warning, there appeared in one and the same
year, 1843, the following revolutionary works: Feuerbach's *Grundsätze der Philosophie der Zukunft*; Proudhon's *De la création de
l'ordre dans l'humanité*; B. Bauer's *Das entdeckte Christentum*; and
Kierkegaard's *Either–Or*. With the exception of Proudhon, they
were all either pupils or opponents of Hegel, who put his theory
into practice. Through their work it became clear that Hegel's
philosophical theology was really a culmination, a turning point in
the history of the spirit and the culture of ancient Europe. In place
of Hegel's mediation, there appeared the demand for decision, separating once more what Hegel had united: antiquity and Christianity,
God and the world, the internal and the external, being and existence. On the other hand, only a well-ordered system such as Hegel's
could be dissolved once more into its components. The critical
acuity of the left-wing Hegelians has its historical measure in the
completeness of Hegel's reconciliation. The reconciliation found
its most intelligible expression in his political and religious philosophy. Its destruction was the goal of his pupils' efforts, precisely because they were concerned with the "real" state and with "real"
Christianity.

3   Hegel's Reconciliation of Philosophy
With the State and the Christian Religion

Hegel's *Rechtsphilosophie*, which appeared at the same time as
the first lecture on the philosophy of religion, is the concrete realization of the abstract tendency to reconcile philosophy with reality

in all areas: political philosophy with politics, religious philosophy
with Christendom. In both areas Hegel achieves a reconciliation not
only with reality, but also within it, albeit "through comprehension."
At this high point of his effectiveness, he saw the real world as a
world "conformed to" the spirit. In return, the Prussian Protestant
State appropriated philosophy in the person of Hegel.[40] In the
preface to the *Rechtsphilosophie*, Hegel states "the relationship of
philosophy to reality" expressly and polemically. Here lies the
problematical point at which Marx and Kierkegaard met, in their
thesis that the purpose of philosophy is to become realized. In the
case of Marx, philosophical theory became the "brain of the proletariat"; in Kierkegaard's case, pure thought became the "existential
thinker," for existing reality seemed neither rational nor Christian.

Hegel's political philosophy is directed against the view that, in
reality, there has never been a rational state, that the true state is a
mere "ideal" and a "postulate."[41] Thus true philosophy, an "investigation of everything rational," is also the comprehension of what is
"present and real." It does not postulate something in another world,
an ideal state which is merely meant to exist and never does. He saw
the existing Prussian State of 1821 as a reality in the sense defined by
the *Logik:* an immediate union of internal being and external existence, a reality in the "emphatic" sense of the word.[42] Once this
"fruition of reality"—that is, ripeness for downfall—has been attained, thought no longer stands in critical opposition to reality.
Instead, it stands "opposite" reality, reconciled, related to reality as
the ideal to the real.[43] Reason which is conscious of itself (the
philosophy of the state) and reason as existing reality (the real
state) are united with each other; "in the depths" of the substantial
spirit of the age they are one and the same.[44] But what lies "between" existing reality and reason as self-conscious spirit, what still
separates the former from the latter and opposes reconciliation, this
Hegel declares—both apodictically and vaguely—to be the "fetter of
something abstract, not yet liberated to the point of being an idea."[45]
This *hiatus irrationalis* is bridged by his elucidation of the idea of
rational reality by means of differentiation between "appearance"
and "being," between "variegated exterior" and "inner drive,"[46]
between externally accidental existence and internal necessary
reality. Hegel excluded mere transitory, "accidental" existence from
the interest of philosophy considered as a knowledge of reality.
Later he was attacked with his own weapon in the charge of "accommodation" of things transitory. This adjustment to existing

reality in Hegel's comprehension of "that which is" is disguised by the fact that "that which is" covers both that which merely exists and also that which is truly real.

For an understanding of Hegel's system, his philosophy of religion is even more important than his philosophy of the state. It is not just one component of the whole system, but its spiritual center of gravity. Hegel's philosophy is "worldly wisdom"[47] and "knowledge of God"[48] together, for its knowledge justifies faith. He states that God had damned him to be a philosopher;[49] for him, the "language of enthusiasm" was identical with that of the "notion." Reading the newspaper stood on an equal footing with reading the Bible: "Reading the newspaper early in the morning is a kind of realistic morning benediction. One orients one's attitude toward the world according to God or according to the way the world is. The former gives the same assurance as the latter that one knows how one stands."[50] True philosophy is itself worship, though "after a peculiar fashion": the philosophy of history is a theodicy; the philosophy of the state, a comprehension of the divine upon earth; and logic, a representation of God in the abstract element of pure thought.

For Hegel, the philosophical truth of Christianity consisted in the fact that Christ effected a reconciliation of the estrangement between the human and the divine.[51] This reconciliation can come into existence for man, only because it has already taken place per se in Christ; but it must also be brought about through us and for us as individuals, in order that it may become the truth which it already is.[52] This unity of divine and human nature in general, which for Hegel was attested in the incarnation of God, was once more torn asunder by both Marx and Kierkegaard. Marx's determined atheism, his absolute belief in man as man, is thus in principle further from Hegel than from Kierkegaard, whose paradoxical faith presupposed the difference between God and man. For Marx, Christianity is a "perverted world"; for Kierkegaard, a worldless standing "before" God; for Hegel, being *in* the truth, grounded on the incarnation of God. Divine and human nature "in one man"—that is admittedly a hard, a difficult expression, but only so long as it is taken representationally and not comprehended spiritually. In that "grammatical monstrosity" the "God-man," it is made clear to man that the finite weakness of human nature is not irreconcilable with this unity.[53]

The reconciliation between the earthly and the divine, the "Kingdom of God,"[54] is viewed as a "condition," that is, a reality in which God reigns as the one and absolute spirit. To produce this reality methodically through philosophy had been the goal of Hegel as a young man.[55] In his history of philosophy it seemed to him that he had finally attained his goal. The "Kingdom of God" of the philosophy of religion is identical with the "intellectual kingdom" of the history of philosophy, and with the "kingdom of spirits" of the phenomenology. Thus philosophy as a whole represents the same reconciliation with reality as does Christianity through the incarnation of God; as the finally comprehended reconciliation, it is philosophical theology. It seemed to Hegel that the "peace of God" was brought about in a rational way through this reconciliation of philosophy with religion.

Since Hegel ontologically comprehends both the state and Christianity on the basis of the spirit as absolute, religion and the state have a corresponding relationship. He discusses this, taking into account their disparity and pointing out their unity. This unity lies in their content, the disparity in the varying forms taken by the same content. The nature of the state is "the divine will present," a spirit which unfolds into the real structure of the world; similarly, the Christian religion has as its content nothing less than the absolute truth of the spirit. Therefore religion and the state can and must come to agreement on the ground of the Christian spirit, even though, giving form to the same content, they go separate ways in church and state.[56] A religion of mere "heart" and "inwardness," hostile to the laws and institutions of the state and thinking reason, or merely remaining passive and allowing the temporal affairs of the state to take their course, does not bear witness to the strength of religious conviction, but rather to its weakness. "True faith is unconcerned with whether or not it corresponds with reason; it is without regard or reference to reason."[57] But this state of affairs is peculiar to "our age," and one might inquire whether it arises from a "real need" or an "unsatisfied vanity." True religion has no negative bent in regard to the existing state, but recognizes and affirms it, just as the state likewise recognizes "ecclesiastical confirmation." What to Kierkegaard's extremely polemic concept of faith seemed an abominable compromise was for Hegel an essential agreement.[58] "It lies in the nature of the case that the state should fulfill its task by providing the congregation with every aid for its religious function and guaranteeing it protection. Indeed, since religion is the factor which integrates the state in its deepest convictions, it may demand of all its citizens that they hold membership in a religious denomination—any denomination they like—for the state may not interfere in the content to an extent that would affect the inner nature of the representation. The state, which is highly developed in organization and therefore strong, can conduct itself all the more liberally in this matter, completely overlooking details which actually affect it, and putting up with denominations within it (of course, depending upon their number) which do not recognize religiously their immediate duties toward the state."[59] Philosophical insight perceives that church and state are at one in the content of truth when both stand upon the ground of the spirit. In the Christian principle of the absolutely free spirit, there is present the absolute possibility and necessity "that temporal power, religion, and the principles of philosophy should coincide. The reconciliation of universal reality with spirit, of the state with religious conscience, and also with philosophical knowledge, are all brought about."[60] Hegel's *Philosophie des objektiven Geistes* closes with the sentence: "The morality of the state and the religious spirituality of the state thus mutually guarantee each other."

With his understanding of Christianity as an absolute and at the same time an entity, connected historically with the world and the state, Hegel is the last Christian philosopher before the break between philosophy and Christianity. This break was perceived and made final from two opposite directions by Feuerbach and Kierkegaard. According to Feuerbach, any mediation between Christian dogmatics and philosophy must be denied in the interest of philosophy and of religion.[61] If Christianity is taken in its historically conditioned reality, and not as an unconditional "idea," every philosophy is necessarily irreligious, because it explores the world through reason and denies the miraculous.[62] In the same sense Ruge, also, declared that all philosophy from Aristotle on is "atheism,"[63] simply because it studies and comprehends nature and man. On the other hand, Christianity cannot seek to be merely one factor in the history of the world, a human phenomenon. "Philosophy and Christianity can never agree," begins an entry from Kierkegaard's journal. For if I want to hold fast something of the nature of Christianity, then the necessity of salvation must extend to the whole man, and thus also to knowledge. One can indeed conceive of a philosophy "subsequent to Christianity," that is, after a man has become a Christian; but then the relationship in question is no longer that of philosophy to Christianity, but of Christianity to Christian knowledge—"unless one desires that philosophy prior to Christianity or within it should arrive at the result that the riddle of life cannot be solved." But if this were the case, philosophy at the height of its perfection would involve its own downfall—no, it could not even serve as a transition to Christianity, for it would have to come to a halt with this negative result. "In fact, here gapes the abyss: Christianity views human knowledge to be defective by reason of sin, and set right by Christianity; the philosopher seeks, simply qua human being, to account for the relationship between God and the world; the result can indeed be said, therefore, to be limited, in the sense that man is a limited being, but at the same time to be the ultimate possible for man qua man."[64] The philosopher—judged from the Christian point of view—must either "accept optimism, or despair," because, as a philosopher, he does not know salvation through Christ.[65] In contrast to this "either-or," Hegel divinized reason after the manner of Aristotle, and determined the divine with reference to Christ!

Hegel's reconciliation in the element of philosophy between reason and faith, and between Christianity and the state, came to an end around 1840. The historical schism with Hegelian philosophy is in Marx's case a break with the philosophy of the state, and in Kierkegaard's with the philosophy of religion, and in the case of both with the unified structure of state, Christianity, and philosophy. This schism was carried out as much by Feuerbach as by Marx, and by B. Bauer no less than by Kierkegaard—but in different ways. Feuerbach reduces the essence of Christianity to sentient man, Marx to the contradictions of the human world, Bauer explains its appearance on the basis of the dissolution of the Roman world, and Kierkegaard, surrendering the Christian State, the Christian Church, and theology, in brief, all its historical reality, reduces it to the paradox of a despairing, decisive leap into faith. No matter to what they reduce the phenomenon of Christianity, they agree in destroying the bourgeois-Christian world, and thereby also Hegel's philosophical theology of reconciliation. To them, reality no longer appeared in the light of freedom to be at one with oneself, but in the shadow of man's estrangement from himself.

Clearly aware of the complete end of Hegel's Christian philosophy, Feuerbach and Ruge, Stirner and Bauer, Kierkegaard and Marx, the true heirs of Hegelian philosophy, proclaimed a "revolution" which absolutely negates the existing state and existing Christendom. Like the Young Hegelians, the Old Hegelians also comprehended the eschatological significance of Hegel's theory. They were so thoroughgoing that as late as 1870 they still viewed all the philosophies which had appeared since Hegel as the mere later history of his system, while the Young Hegelians undermined his system by means of his own method. In comparison with the Neo-Hegelians, they had the advantage of not failing to recognize the claim which is found at the end of the *Logik* and *Phänomenologie,* under "System" in the *Encyklopädie,* and in the "Conclusion" of the *Geschichte der Philosophie.*

II Old Hegelians,
Young Hegelians, Neo-Hegelians

1 The Preservation of
Hegelian Philosophy
by the Old Hegelians

It is characteristic of the division of the Hegelian school into a right wing, composed of Old Hegelians, and a left wing, composed of Young Hegelians, that this division did not result from purely philosophical differences, but political and religious ones. Its form grew out of the political division of the French Parliament, and its content out of divergent views on the question of Christology.

The differentiation was first made by Strauss,[1] and then amplified by Michelet;[2] it has continued ever since. Following Hegel's breakdown of the Christian religion into "content" and "form," the right wing (Goeschel, Gabler, B. Bauer)[3] accepted the former positively, while the left wing subjected the content to criticism, together with the forms in which religion appeared. With the idea of the unity of the divine and human nature, the right wanted to preserve the entire Gospel story; the center (Rosenkranz, and to a degree also Schaller and Erdmann) only a portion; while the left declared that, on an ideal basis, the historical accounts of the gospels could not be maintained either partially or *in toto*. Strauss counted himself among the left. In his lectures on the personality of God and the immortality of the soul,[4] Michelet (together with Gans, Vatke, Marheineke, and Benary) suggested a coalition of the center with the left. Among the "Pseudo-Hegelians" he counts Fichte, K. Fischer, Weisse, and Braniss. It is today very difficult to imagine the liveliness of the controversies on the question of the divine-human nature, the personality of God, and the immortality of the soul,[5] so familiar are we with the destructive outcome of the criticism of religion accomplished by Hegel's pupils. The debate, concerned with these theological questions, was no less significant for Hegel's continuing influence than that which stemmed from his theory of the state, as developed by Ruge, Marx, and Lassalle.

The majority of the editors of Hegel's works were Old Hegelians in the original sense of the school founded by Hegel, von Henning, Hotho, Förster, Marheineke, as well as Hinrichs, C. Daub, Conradi, and Schaller. They preserved Hegel's philosophy literally, continuing it in individual historical studies, but they did not reproduce it in a uniform manner beyond the period of Hegel's personal influence. For the historical movement of the nineteenth century they are without significance. In contrast with these Old Hegelians, the designation "Young Hegelians," or "Neo-Hegelians," arose.[6] To avoid any confusion, in the following pages the term "Neo-Hegelians" will be applied exclusively to those who have rejuvenated Hegelianism in our own period, "Young Hegelians" to the radical left among Hegel's pupils and successors, and "Old Hegelians" to those who preserved his historical way of thinking beyond the period of the revolution, through the entire century, each in his own free way. They can be called Old Hegelians because they were not inclined toward radical innovation. Seen from this point of view, Rosenkranz particularly, but also Haym, Erdmann, and K. Fischer were the real preservers of Hegelian philosophy in the period between Hegel and Nietzsche.

K. Rosenkranz (1805–1879), rightly called by Ruge the "most liberal of all the Old Hegelians," made an accurate evaluation of the historical state of philosophy after Hegel in his two unsurpassed monographs on Hegel.[7] We men of today, he says in his first account, written in 1844, seem to be merely "the gravediggers and monument builders" for the philosophers produced by the second half of the eighteenth century, who died in the first half of the nineteenth: "Are we equally capable of providing for the second half of our century a company of philosophic saints? Are there among our young men those whose Platonic enthusiasm and Aristotelian devotion to labor arouse them to unflagging efforts for the cause of speculative thought? Do our young men perhaps dream of

other crowns, . . . do they see perhaps the gleam of the higher goal
of action, as doers, is it their idea to bring about the ideals of
those philosophers?[8] Or should they allow themselves to sink into
indifference toward science and life, and, not seldom having pre-
maturely boasted themselves the victors of the day, find themselves
without sufficient strength for the future? Strangely enough, the
talents of our own day do not seem capable of enduring. They
quickly wear themselves out; after a few promising blossoms they
become unproductive, they begin to copy and repeat themselves at
the very point where, once the more inhibited and imperfect, one-
sided and violent experiments of youth have been overcome, a period
of powerful sustained effort should follow." And, with a side thrust
at those Young Hegelians such as Feuerbach, Marx, and Ruge, who
claimed to "realize" Hegel's philosophy, he speaks of those who, in
"self-fabricated pre-eminence of an ephemeral journalistic appoint-
ment to leadership," improvise reforms and revolutions in philosophy, of which they will never have any experience in their course
through history. "These cavaliers of impromptu speculation, stumbling about in the maze of their hypotheses, confuse the babble of
their beer-hall adventure with the serious discussion of legislative
assemblies, and the uproar of a critical brawl with the tragic thunder
of battle." In spite of all this, Rosenkranz had no reservations about
the dialectical progress of philosophy. Its emergence from its previous "alienation from the world" undeniably has extended and transformed its "relationship with reality." But even in this it was Hegel
who not only had asserted but also preserved the unity of theory
and practice, namely in the identity of notion with reality, and
through the explication of being in phenomenal existence. In contrast, post-Hegelian philosophy "once more" is falling into the
"one-sidedness" of abstract ontology (Braniss) and abstract empiricism (Trendelenburg). Both tendencies of disintegration are combined in the existential philosophy of Schelling. The reflex of this
abstract theory is the abstract practice of Feuerbach, which makes
palpability the criterion of reality: "Feuerbach is the most determined, the most brilliant opponent of Schelling, but he agrees with
him in avoiding the development . . . of his science into a system.[9]
He persists in asserting embryonic generalities; and thus he cannot
exert upon the further development of philosophy the influence
which one might expect in view of the energy of the criticism with
which he made his appearance. Like Schelling today, he does not
venture further into the study of nature or the state. He begins at

once with man as he lives and breathes; he has a mortal terror of all theories of being, potential being, and necessary being, of eternal being and imaginary being, etc., as though they were antediluvian phantoms. He therefore appears more accessible, more particular, more human, more domesticated than Schelling, who derives real pleasure from inventing processes within the *status absconditus* of the Godhead, and knows how to captivate people with the mysterious air of one who is initiated into primordial events."[10] All four parties, it is true, move in an aura of deceptive self-confidence in their victory; but they have not attained Hegel's concretely organized idea, in which all dichotomies (reason and reality, theory and practice, ideality and reality, thought and being, subject and object, idea and history) are already overcome in principle, and hence in reality. They all remain "abstract theologians," who merely draw upon concrete reality for examples,[11] disdaining to know and comprehend it. These extremes provoked by Hegel's philosophy must once more be submerged within it. This philosophy is now entering its second epoch, more permanent and free of the egoism of the schools. The task before us now is to execute its method throughout the particular realms of knowledge.[12] In this process, without special preference for one thing or another, the universe must be gone through with equitable justice.

But at this very moment Marx and Kierkegaard were directing their impassioned attacks against this tolerance inherent to all-inclusive knowledge. They fought against Hegel's all-sidedness within the one-sided element of thought, with the most dogmatic one-sidedness and intolerance based on "interest" in "real" (economic and ethical) existence.[13] Rosenkranz could account for the "immeasurable sympathy" which this faction of Hegelianism found among the younger generation only on the grounds that it was "immeasurably comfortable": "Everything that has happened up to now is nothing; we dismiss it. What we shall do next, we do not yet know. But all that will work itself out, once everything in existence has been leveled to make room for our creations. Young Hegelianism casts suspicion upon Old Hegelianism with the simple innuendo that the latter was seized with fear when confronted with the real consequences of the system, while the former, with its rare sincerity, was prepared to accept them. This makes the younger generation uncommonly happy. A show of courage looks good."[14] Rosenkranz appraises *Die heilige Familie* of Marx and Engels as merely a "clever book." And yet it was a precursor of *Deutsche*

Ideologie, with which not only Marx but German philosophy in general took leave of its belief in universal reason and the spirit. In Rosenkranz' view, the crisis of German philosophy did not affect its entire substance, but only the temporary relapse of Hegelian ontology into logic and metaphysics, and of the latter into a philosophy of nature and the spirit.[15] As a result of this separation, logic perished, and metaphysics regressed to the notion of "existence" or even "practical reality." Incapable of manifesting the notion itself as the true content of real events, they take the need for a metaphysical principle (which is still present) and transfer it to ethics. Ethical philosophy has become the rage, and is destroying both metaphysics and knowledge of the good through presumptuous, moralistic twaddle. Quite apart from his negative appraisal, Rosenkranz' description of the state of philosophy after Hegel in fact grasped the decisive traits, to the extent that they derived from Hegel.

Twenty-five years later, in his second monograph on Hegel, Rosenkranz once more described the intellectual situation of the period. He believed that he could demonstrate the weakness of all the actions taken against Hegel's system up to 1870: "Since it has suffered so many and various defeats (if one is to believe the talk of its opponents), it must have been pulverized into nothingness . . . and yet it remained the perpetual object of public attention. Its opponents continued to draw nourishment from polemic against it, the Latin nations continued to go further and further in their efforts to turn it aside; in short, Hegel's system is still the focus of philosophical agitation. Even now, no other system exercises such a universal attraction; even now, no other has turned all the rest against it to such a degree; no other is . . . so ready and willing to make use of all true progress of science."[16] Its opponents, old and young, never cease repeating their traditional polemic, but the public has become more indifferent to such attacks—this signalizes the victory of Hegelian philosophy: "In the great political struggles, in civil and international wars, in the ever-expanding economic efforts of the nations, the consciousness of the age was given a meaning against which the significance of conflicts of philosophical schools, not to mention the quarrels of a few philosophers, shrank into ephemeral insignificance. One must perceive clearly this transformation of our entire public life if one is to understand how greatly philosophy, too, has gained thereby, most of all Hegelian philosophy. It, more than any other, was dragged more deeply and dangerously into the un-

folding crisis."[17] A bit less confidently, he writes two years later
after a survey of the "philosophical catchwords of the present":
"At the moment, our philosophy seems to have vanished, but it has
merely become latent to the extent that it has to adjust the truth of
its principles to the immense wealth of new discoveries, which continue to mount at such an enormous rate." A process of dissolution
has set in, in which the epigones continue to battle each other. But
they deceive themselves when they speak as though the only question to be decided is whether Hegel or Schelling, Herbart or Schopenhauer, will gain the upper hand. Neither will one of the old
systems arise once more, nor will a completely new one appear, until
the process of dissolution is completed. "Everything has its time, and
when this has taken place, there may once more be a decisive step
forward of knowledge. This step forward will probably be connected with a further transformation of the entire contemporary
religious world view."[18] Rosenkranz did not realize that the decisive
step against knowledge and against Christendom had already been
taken in 1840. He himself, with indefatigable effort, preserved that
readiness to accept all true scientific progress which he ascribed to
Hegel's mode of thought. Even technology and the first world expositions, which Burckhardt found so appalling, were included by
Rosenkranz in the progress of "mankind"—as he now translates
"spirit"—conscious of freedom. Far removed from pessimistic perspectives, he saw in the universal spread of international commerce,
the book trade, and the press, an elevation of mankind to the level
of universality and "progress in the uniformity of our civilization."[19]
The sequestered life of bounded consciousness must now subject
itself to the "rationalism of the thinking spirit and its leveling process." To de Tocqueville, Taine, and Burckhardt, to Donoso Cortes
and Kierkegaard, this leveling was simply the evil of the age; to this
cultured disciple of Hegel it signified a reduction of the remaining
"particularities" to the general level of a spirit already seen from a
humanitarian point of view. He attached positive value to this leveling. In themselves, steam engines, railroads, and telegraphs are admittedly no guarantee of increasing cultural advance and freedom;
nevertheless, they must ultimately serve for the "humanization of
mankind," because universal laws, which have been discovered by
science and broadcast by the press so that they are common property, are working irresistibly toward that goal.[20] Just as the press and
world travel strengthen, from day to day, the self-consciousness of
mankind, making a reality of the declaration of human rights, so

also the new geographical discoveries and subsequent commerce have engendered a true cosmopolitan spirit. In oceanic trade we see the truth of "the ocean of the spirit"![21] In this way, with undeniable consistency, Rosenkranz put the events of the nineteenth century into philosophical order, according to the Hegelian principle.

A further preservation of Hegelian philosophy beyond the period of the revolution was also effected by the critical-historical study of Hegel made by R. Haym.[22] More radical than Rosenkranz, he turned resolutely against Hegel's system, drawing even more far-reaching conclusions from the historical change. Unlike Rosenkranz, he did not intend to reform Hegel's philosophy,[23] but merely to elucidate it historically. To Rosenkranz, Haym's historical criticism seemed an "unfortunate error" and a product of "bad temper." In place of political action, he wrote his book, "which happened to be about Hegel, and was thus doomed to be diseased." By this "disease" he meant the liberal tendencies of the time, to which Hegel appeared a reactionary. But in spite of this, the unusual bitterness of Rosenkranz' quarrel with Haym is not based upon their completely divergent positions, but upon repulsion of an all too close contact. The divergence in their attitudes toward Hegel's metaphysics, which Rosenkranz modified while Haym abstracted from it, reduces itself to the different way in which each brought Hegel's theory of the spirit into agreement with the changing times: Rosenkranz through cautious humanization, Haym through ruthless historicization. The language used by Rosenkranz goes back beyond Hegel and Goethe to the culture of the eighteenth century; the political passion and deliberately commercial form of expression used by Haym is already completely at home in the new century. On good terms with his time, he narrates not without pleasure the fall from pre-eminence of Hegel's system. He recalls the period when one was considered either an Hegelian or a barbarian, a contemptible empiricist: one must recall this period if one is to know what is really involved in the recognized domination of a philosophical system. That passion and assurance must be brought to mind with which the Hegelians of 1830 in absolute, deadly seriousness debated the question of what was to be the future content of world history, now that in Hegelian philosophy the world spirit had reached its goal, knowledge of itself. One must recall this, and then compare it with the modesty with which our Hegelians of today, even the strictest school, those most true to the system, allow themselves the thought that Hegel was "really not unproductive" for the development of philosophy. In contrast to the epigones of Hegelian philosophy, Haym confirms not only the decline of this one system, but the exhaustion of philosophy in general: "This one great house has fallen into bankruptcy only because this whole line of business has collapsed. . . . At the moment, we find ourselves in a tremendous and almost universal shipwreck of the spirit, and of belief in the spirit in general." An unprecedented revolution has taken place in the first half of the nineteenth century. "It is no longer an age of systems, no longer an age of poetry or of philosophy. Instead, it is an age in which, thanks to the great technological discoveries of the century, material seems to have come to life. The deepest foundations of our physical as well as our spiritual life are being torn up and remodeled through these triumphs of technology. The existence of the individual as well as of nations is set upon a new basis, forced into new relationships."[24]

The philosophy of idealism has not stood the test of time. "Interests" and "needs"—two concepts which characterized the polemic of Feuerbach, Marx, and Kierkegaard—have brought it down. It is more than refuted: it is condemned, by the real, objective course of the world and the law of "living history," which even Hegel himself recognized as the court before which the world is judged, even though it contradict the absolute claim of his system.[25] Therefore, the task of the present can be only to comprehend the historical position of Hegelian philosophy, not to determine a new system in "an unready age," clearly incapable of "metaphysical legislation." The positive side of this reduction of Hegelian philosophy to its historical elements is the referral of philosophical truth once more to its human origin, the "sense of truth," the "conscience and temper of man." Therefore the study of history, as "an intellectually stimulating discussion of human events" is the only legitimate heir of Hegelian philosophy. But to the extent that Haym subjects Hegel's philosophy to objective criticism, he carries out only an academic modification of those motifs of attack upon Hegel which had already been brought out radically by Feuerbach, Ruge, and Marx. That which Haym was the first to declare unhesitatingly, and to make the guiding principle of his presentation, was also the concern of Erdmann, Fischer, and Dilthey, whose criticism of "historical reason" stands at the end of the development which grew out of Hegel's metaphysics.[26]

In 1834, J. E. Erdmann began his monumental work on the history of philosophy from Descartes to Hegel, and finished it in 1853.

Better than any other, it preserves the penetrating power of Hegel's historical sense. The inauspiciousness of the time for a new edition, and the simultaneous appearance of Fischer's popular history of philosophy, led in 1866 to his publishing the two-volume *Grundriss der Geschichte der Philosophie*, the second edition of which appeared in 1870. In the excellent supplement (which he says took more work than the body of the text, because of lack of preparatory work), he discusses the period from Hegel's death to 1870 under the headings "Dissolution of the Hegelian School" and "Attempts at the Reconstruction of Philosophy." At the conclusion of his work, in which he calls himself the "last of the Mohicans" of Hegel's school, he asks whether this preponderance of the historical viewpoint over the systematic may not be in general a symptom of the decrepitude of philosophy. It is an undeniable fact that what little interest is shown in the study of philosophy no longer consists in philosophizing on one's own account, but in studying how philosophy has been conducted by others—like the preponderance of literary history over poetry, and of biographies over great men. In the case of Hegel, the historical viewpoint was itself systematic; but it has become typical of the philosophers following him that their systematic studies should be almost completely ignored, while their critical-historical works retain lasting importance, as in the case of Sigwart, Ritter, Prantl, K. Fischer, and Trendelenburg. Even within the systematic branch of philosophy the predominance of the historical element has become apparent. It could be stated as a general rule that the historical-critical portion of these works comprises more than half their bulk. Yet the comforting remark can be added that the history of philosophy is not far removed from philosophizing, and a philosophical presentation of the history of philosophy is itself philosophical. The matter of philosophy is basically indifferent, whether it be nature, the state, or dogma: "then why not, now, the history of philosophy?" "Thus in answer to the plaint that philosophers have become historians, I would make clear that the historians of philosophy themselves carry on philosophy. Here, too, perhaps, the lance which wounds can bring healing." The historical significance of this argument can be measured by the fact that even today, seventy years later, we clearly cannot do without it.[27]

While Rosenkranz still had a systematic basis which allowed him to "annul" the claims of the younger generation, Erdmann, with his historical point of view, had to content himself with depicting the process of dissolution of the Hegelian school as an historical datum. All the events after 1830 proved to him that "everything which seems so superbly joined together can be put asunder." From the historical point of view, he called Hegel the philosopher of the "restoration,"[28] in conjunction with the political restoration after the fall of Napoleon, and in contrast to Kant and Fichte, whose systems corresponded to the various phases of the French Revolution. Hegel restored what Kant and those after him had destroyed: the old metaphysics, the dogmas of the church, and the substantial content of the moral powers. But there is no more danger of Hegel's reconciliation between reason and reality putting the movement of history to rest than the reverse, that their dissolution be final. On the contrary, awareness of a job well done will give the spirit of mankind strength for new deeds: "But when there are to be deeds of great significance in the history of the world, the philosopher to comprehend them will not be lacking, nor the spirit which is to beget them."[29] With this "historical" perspective which looks beyond the period of dissolution, Erdman refers the "impatience of the present" to future ages. Our lustra are not equal to the centuries between the few, but truly decisive events in the history of the spirit, and Hegel still awaits his . . . Fichte![30]

The actual mediator in the renewal of Hegelianism in the twentieth century is K. Fischer, whose *Geschichte der neueren Philosophie* began to appear in 1852, at a time when Hegel was as good as forgotten in Germany. As a friend of D. F. Strauss, as well as through his relationship with F. Th. Vischer, Ruge, and Feuerbach,[31] and his criticism of Stirner,[32] he was well acquainted with the circle of Young Hegelians, and at the same time distant enough from their impassioned disagreement with Hegel that he could view Hegel's accomplishment with the neutrality of the historical chronicler. In contrast to Erdmann and his thesis of restoration, Fischer interpreted Hegel as a philosopher of "evolution," and declared him to be the leading thinker of the nineteenth century, which he thought to be characterized by biological theories of evolution (Lamarck, Darwin) and historical criticism based on the evolutionary view of history (F. A. Wolf, K. Lachmann, Niebuhr, Mommsen, F. Bopp, K. Ritter, E. Zeller). From 1818 to 1831, Hegel dominates his age through personal influence, and then until 1848 through his pupils who made critical use of his philosophy, and finally through the appropriation of his historical viewpoint on the part of academic history. The idea of development inspired by him characterizes not only the historical criticism of the Bible of the Tübingen school (F. Ch. Baur, Strauss),[33] but also the historical criticism of economics in Marx's *Kapital* (1868) and Lassalle's *System der erworbenen Rechte* (1861). Hegel also dominates the nineteenth century in the antitheses of A. Comte and E. Dühring, Schopenhauer and E. v. Hartmann.

In detail, it is true, much of Hegel's system may be untenable and deficient, but the essential fact remains that he was the first and only philosopher of importance to see history in the light of "infinite" progress. By this, Fischer no longer meant Hegel's notion, but the simple infinity of an endless continuum. The spirit is to raise itself "to infinity" through constant multiplication of the duties of mankind. Hegel's conclusion of the *Geschichte der Philosophie*, according to which the final philosophy is the result of all that have gone before, means nothing more to Fischer than that Hegel's philosophy, by virtue of its historical inclusiveness, is temporarily the ultimate philosophy, but at the same time the first in which the development of the "world problem" is now taken over by the history of philosophy.

Thus the preservation of Hegelian philosophy comes about through an historicization of all philosophy, making it into a history of philosophy. Corresponding to this retreat into known history, there is a withdrawal from the events of the day, which were accepted more or less resignedly after 1850. Trusting in the reason of history, Rosenkranz expected a "new stride" of the world spirit; Haym, greatly disillusioned by the "triumphant misery of reaction," subjected himself to the "judgment of the age"; and Erdmann, in defiance of the age, with careless irony set about the accomplishment of his historical task, while Fischer left the solution of the problems to "evolution." The historicism which developed out of Hegel's metaphysics of the history of the spirit[34] became the "ultimate religion" of the intelligentsia who still believed in education and knowledge.

The great accomplishment of the "historical school" and the historical studies of the spirit cannot blind us to the philosophical weakness of a philosophy reduced to its own history. What was meant by the "spiritual-historical world," from Haym and Dilthey on, is as far from Hegel's philosophical theology as was the mode of thought of the contributors to the *Hallesche Jahrbücher*. The concept of *Geistesgeschichte* (spiritual or intellectual history), which has come into vogue since 1850, has not much more than the bare words in common with Hegel's notion of "spirit" and "history." For Hegel, the spirit as substance and subject of history was the absolute and basic concept of his theory of being. Thus natural philosophy is just as much a spiritual discipline as are the philosophies of the state, art, religion, and history. This absolute spirit (absolute because identical with the absolute religion of Christianity) exists by knowing itself; it is an historical spirit to the extent that it has as its course the recollection of previous forms of the spirit. "Its perseverance in the direction of free existence, appearing in the form of chance, is history; but in the direction of its comprehended organization, it is the science of phenomenal knowledge; both together, comprehended history, comprise the memorial and Golgotha of the absolute spirit, the reality, truth, and certainty of its dominion, without which it would be solitary and lifeless." A great gulf separates the idea of an infinitely progressing "spiritual history" from the spirit-filled infinity. Hegel accorded to the human spirit the strength to open the sealed nature of the universe, revealing its riches and its depth;[35] but from Haym to Dilthey it was the more or less avowed conviction that the human spirit is essentially powerless vis-à-vis the political and natural world, because it is itself only a finite "expression" of "sociohistorical" reality. For them, the spirit is no longer the "power of an age," in itself timeless because it is eternal present; it is merely an exponent and mirror of the age. Thus philosophy becomes a "world view" and "interpretation of life," the ultimate consequence of which is the self-assertion of "particular, individual" historicity in Heidegger's *Sein und Zeit.*[36]

From a constructive point of view, F. A. Lange has evaluated impartially the scope of the post-Hegelian reaction, and presented it as a limitation to the "materialism" of the nineteenth century.[37] In the July Revolution he sees the end of the age of idealism and the beginning of a turn to "realism," by which he means the influence of material interests upon spiritual life. The conflicts between church and state, the sudden flowering of industries based upon scientific discoveries ("coal and iron" became the catchword of the age), the founding of polytechnic institutions, the rapid growth of transportation systems (the first railroad was put into operation in 1835), the sociopolitical creation of the customs union and the tradesmen's unions, but also the writings of the "Young Germany" opposition (Heine, Börne, Gutzkow), the biblical criticism of the Tübingen school, and the immense popularity of Strauss's *Leben Jesu*—all this together resulting in new audience for, and new importance given to those philosophical writings whose content lagged far behind their revolutionary impulse. In association with these events, "a theological and political crisis of Hegelian philosophy which for violence, scope, and significance has never been equalled in the course of history"[38] resulted.

On the dividing line between Old and Young Hegelians stood Michelet, active in many fields, the publisher of Hegel's *Geschichte der Philosophie* and the *Jenenser Abhandlungen*. His long life (1801–1893) connects original Hegelianism with the beginnings of modern Neo-Hegelianism, to which he himself was related through the person of A. Lasson (1832–1917).[39] In his eyes, also, the "pinnacle" and also the "test" of Hegel's system was the philosophy of history.[40] Yet he does not historicize Hegel's system radically, but leaves it grounded upon the absolute of the spirit. "The question of the century,"[41] which was the problem of bourgeois society, seemed to him soluble within the framework of the philosophy of the spirit. He wanted to introduce "science" into "life," in order to realize Hegel's thesis of the reality of the rational.[42] For what "is left" after Hegel is this: to elevate to reality the reconciliation in thought between the human and the divine, to allow Hegel's principle to permeate all areas of life. "And thus thought ceases to be merely the end result of a particular stage in the unfolding of the world spirit; as befits the discretion of old age, it also becomes the first principle, consciously serviceable for the achievement of a higher stage."[43] Philosophy, he writes five years later, in the style of the Young Hegelians, is not only the "owl of Minerva" which begins its flight at dusk, but also the "cockcrow" which proclaims the dawn.[44] With this twofold metaphor Michelet takes his place between Hegel and Marx, who likewise took over Hegel's symbol, but instead of supplementing it, turned it into its opposite.[45]

2   The Overthrow of Hegelian Philosophy by the Young Hegelians

> "There is nothing more illogical than absolute logic: it gives rise to unnatural phenomena, which finally collapse."[46]
>
> GOETHE

Through Rosenkranz and Haym, Erdmann and Fischer, Hegel's accumulated empire was historically preserved. The Young Hegelians divided it into provinces, undermined the system, and thereby made of it an historical force. The expression "Young Hegelians" first of all means merely the young generation of Hegel's pupils; in the sense of "left-wing Hegelians," it designates the radical party, revolutionary in respect to Hegel. At this time they were also called *Hegelinge* (Hegelists) in contrast to *Hegelitern* (Hegelites), characterizing the revolutionary tendencies of these youths. But at the same time, the differentiation betwen Old and Young Hegelians had also indirect reference to Hegel's differentiation between the "old" and the "young," which Stirner reduced to triviality. In Hegel's system of morality, the old are those truly called to govern, because their spirit no longer thinks individually, but only "universally."[47] As incarnate "indifference" to the various classes, they serve for the preservation of the whole. The elders, unlike the youths, do not live in a relationship of unsatisfied tension to a world which they find inappropriate, with "antipathy toward reality"; neither do they live in "conformity" to the real world. They are like old men, without any particular interest in this thing or in that, oriented to the universal and the past, which they thank for their knowledge of the universal. In contrast, the young adhere to the particular and are attracted to the future, seek to alter the world; out of harmony with the world as it is, they set up programs and put forward demands with the wild idea that their first job is to set right a world which has jumped the tracks. To the young, the realization of the universal seems apostasy from duty. Because of this bent for the ideal, the youth gives an appearance of having a more noble heart and being more selfless than the man who is active on behalf of the world, adjusting himself to the reason of reality. When compelled by necessity, youth takes the step of recognizing things as they are: a painful desertion to the life of the philistines. But they deceive themselves in viewing this circumstance solely as an external necessity and not as a necessity of reason, in which lives the wisdom of age, free from all the particular interests of the present.

In contrast to Hegel's evaluation of youth and elders, the Young Hegelians represented the party of youth, not because they were themselves real youths, but in order to overcome the consciousness of being epigones. Recognizing the fugacity of all that exists, they turned from the "universal" and the past in order to anticipate the future, to promote the "particular" and "individual," and negate that which exists. Their personal lives exhibit the same characteristic traits.[48]

Writing of Feuerbach, F. A. Lange somewhere remarks that he worked his way up out of the abysses of Hegelian philosophy to a kind of superficiality, possessed of more character than spirit, but without quite losing the traces of Hegelian melancholy. In spite of its numerous "consequently's," his system hovers in a mystic darkness which is not made more transparent by his emphasis on "sensibility" and "perceptibility." This characteristic is true not only of Feuerbach, but of all the Young Hegelians. Their writings are manifestos, programs, and theses, but never anything whole, important in itself. In their hands, their scientific demonstrations became sensational proclamations with which they turn to the masses or the individual. Whoever studies their writings will discover that, in spite of their inflammatory tone, they leave an impression of insipidity. They make immoderate demands with insufficient means, and dilate Hegel's abstract dialectics to a piece of rhetoric. The contrasting reflective style in which they generally write is monotonous without being simple, and brilliant without being polished. Burckhardt's conclusion, that after 1830 the world began to grow "commoner," is borne out not least by the language which now becomes current, which amuses itself with massive polemic, emotional bombast, and stark imagery. F. List is also an example. Their critical activism knows no bounds; what they seek to bring about is in every case and at any price "change."[49] And yet, for the most part, they were desperately honorable men, who devoted their effective existences to what they wanted to see realized. As ideologues of growth and movement, they establish themselves upon Hegel's principle of dialectical negativity, and upon the conflict which moves the world.

It is typical of their mutual relationships that each tries to outdo the other in a process of mutual cannibalism. They take the problem presented to them by the age and develop it to the extreme; they are deadly logical. United only against a common foe, they can dissolve their personal and literary ties with infinite ease, separate, and then, according to the measure of their radicalism, revile each other as "bourgeois" and "reactionary." Feuerbach and Ruge, Ruge and Marx, Marx and Bauer, Bauer and Stirner—they comprise pairs of hostile brothers, only chance determining the moment each will look upon the other merely as an enemy. They are "cultured men run wild," frustrated existences who, under the pressure of social conditions, translate their scholarly knowledge into journalese. Their real occupation is "free" pamphleteering, perpetually dependent upon patrons and publishers, readers and censors. The world of letters, as a vocation and means of earning a living, came into its own in Germany about 1830.[50]

Feuerbach considered himself "a writer and human being" in the distinguished sense.[51] Ruge had definite journalistic talent, Bauer lived from his writing, and Kierkegaard's life is conterminous with his "authorship." What unites him with the others, in spite of his passionate opposition to journalism, is the intention of seeking effect solely through his writings. The special calling which he ascribed to his "work as an author," namely, to be an author "on the boundary between the poetic and the religious," not only distinguishes him from, but unites him with the literary activity of the left-wing Hegelians, who moved along the boundary between philosophy and politics, or politics and theology. Through the efforts of these men, it became Hegel's paradoxical fate that his system, which like none previous demands "mental exertion," was popularized energetically and exerted an enormous influence. If Hegel's statement is true, that the individual man is positively free and really amounts to something only in the "generality" of a particular class,[52] then Feuerbach and Ruge, Bauer and Stirner, Marx and Kierkegaard were only negatively free, and amounted to nothing. When one of Feuerbach's friends attempts to get him an academic position, Feuerbach writes to him: "The more people make of me, the less I am, and vice versa. I am . . . something only so long as I am nothing."

Hegel felt himself free in the midst of bourgeois restriction. For him it was by no means impossible as an ordinary official to be a "priest of the Absolute," to be something and at the same time be himself. With reference to the life of the philosopher in the third epoch of the spirit,[53] that is, since the beginning of the "modern" world, he says that even the physical circumstances in which philosophers live are different from what they were in the first and second epochs. The philosophers of antiquity were "plastic" individuals, each framing his life according to his theory, with the result that philosophy as such determined also the position of the individual. In the Middle Ages, they were primarily doctors of theology who taught philosophy, and, as clerics, were separate from the rest of the world. In the transition to the modern world, they, like Descartes, continued to wander about, always in inner struggle with themselves and in external struggle with the conditions of the world. Since then, philosophers no longer comprise a separate class; they are what they are, in perfectly ordinary relationship to the state: officially appointed teachers of philosophy. Hegel interprets this transformation as the "reconciliation of the worldly principle with itself." It is open to each and every one to construct his own "inner world" independent of the force of circumstances which has materialized. The philosopher can now entrust the "external" side of his existence to this "order," just as the modern man allows fashion to dictate the way he will dress. The modern world is in fact this power of universal mutual dependence in the context of everyday life. The important thing, Hegel concludes, is "to remain true to one's purpose" within the context of the normal life of a citizen. To be free for truth and at the same time dependent on the state—to him, these two things seemed quite consistent with each other.

It is typical of Hegel that, within the "system of needs," he remained true to his purpose which transcended this system. Similarly, it was to be typical for all who came after him that for the sake of their purpose they withdrew from the common order. Because of the scandal caused in academic circles by his *Gedanken über Tod und Unsterblichkeit,* Feuerbach had to resign his position as *Privatdozent* at Erlangen, at best to continue to lecture privately "in a village which didn't even have a church." He only appeared once more in public, when in 1848 the students called him to Heidelberg. Ruge was even harder hit by the fate of revolutionary intelligence: constantly at odds with the authorities and the police, he immediately lost his teaching position at Halle. His attempt to found a free academy in Dresden fell through, and the *Jahrbücher für Wissenschaft und Kunst,* of which he was joint editor, had to cease publication after a few years of productive effectiveness. To avoid imprisonment for a second time, he fled to Paris, then to Switzerland, and finally to England. Because of his radical theological views, B. Bauer was removed from his teaching position and thus became an independent writer, and the center of the Berlin "independents." And yet the continual struggle with the necessities of life never so much as made a dent in his firm character. Stirner, who at first had been a schoolteacher, was reduced to miserable poverty, and finally scratched out a living by translating, and selling milk. Marx failed in his plan of gaining a lectureship in philosophy at Bonn. First he took over publication of the *Deutsch-Französische Jahrbücher,* among whose contributors were Ruge and Heine. Later, in Paris, Brussels, and London, he lived on scanty honorariums, newspaper work, subsidies, and credit. Kierkegaard could never make up his mind to use his theological degree to obtain a cure, "to settle himself in finitude" in order to "realize the universal." He lived "upon his own credit," like a "king without a country," as he called his life as a writer, and materially on the estate left him by his father, which was exhausted just at the moment that he collapsed from exhaustion in his fight against the church. Schopenhauer, Dühring, and Nietzsche, too, were only briefly in the employ of the state. After his abortive attempt to teach at the University of Berlin in competition with Hegel, Schopenhauer withdrew once again into private life, full of scorn for "university philosophers." Dühring was relieved of his instructorship for political reasons, and, after only a few years, Nietzsche withdrew from the University of Basel forever. He admired Schopenhauer, not least for his independence from state and society. All of them either withdrew from all connection with the existing world, or sought to overturn the existing order through revolutionary criticism.

The schism of the Hegelian school into right and left wings was made possible by the basic ambiguity of Hegel's dialectical *Aufhebungen* ("suspensions"), which could be interpreted conservatively and revolutionarily with equal ease. An "abstract" emphasis on one side alone was all that was necessary in order to arrive at F. Engels' statement, which characterized the entire left wing: "The conservatism of this point of view is relative; its revolutionary character is absolute" because the historical process is a movement of progress and thereby a perpetual negation of everything presently existing.[54] Engels demonstrates this revolutionary character with Hegel's statement that what is real is also rational. At first glance, it seems reactionary, but in truth it is revolutionary, because by "reality" Hegel does not mean simply that which happens to exist, but rather "true" and "necessary" being. Therefore, the apparently conservative thesis of the philosophy of right can be subjected to "all the rules" of the Hegelian system and be turned into its opposite: "All that exists is worthy of perishing."[55] Hegel himself, of course, did not draw this conclusion of his dialectics so sharply; instead, he contradicted it through the conclusion of his system and disguised its critically revolutionary aspect under a conservative dogmatic cloak. Therefore he must be freed from himself. Reality must be brought to the point of reason through methodical negation of all that exists. Thus both sides of the schism in the Hegelian school can be traced back to one source: Hegel united two principles in one metaphysical point—the reason of reality and the reality of the rational.[56] These were once more separated, into left and right, first in the question of religion, second in the question of politics. The right wing emphasized that only the real was rational, and the left wing that only the rational was real, while for Hegel the conservative and revolutionary components, at least formally, were given equal weight.

In regard to content, the methodical overthrow of Hegelian philosophy attacked first of all its character of being a philosophical theology. The battle was fought over the atheistic or theistic interpretation of the philosophy of religion: does the absolute have its real existence in God become man, or only in mankind?[57] In this struggle, Strauss and Feuerbach opposed the dogmatic remnant in Hegel's philosophical Christianity. At this point, as Rosenkranz says, Hegel's philosophy "within its own boundaries went through the epoch of sophistry," but not to be "rejuvenated," rather to reveal, in Bauer and Kierkegaard, the radical crisis of the Christian religion. The political crisis turned out to be no less important. It was revealed in the criticism of the philosophy of right, which Ruge began and Marx brought to a head. For both prongs of the attack, without themselves being aware of it, the Young Hegelians reached back to the theological and political writings of Hegel's youth, which had already stated quite bluntly the problems involved in measuring the bourgeois state and the Christian religion against the Greek *polis* and its popular religion.

Three phases can be discerned in the overthrow of Hegelian philosophy. Feuerbach and Ruge undertook to alter Hegel's philosophy to bring it into agreement with the spirit of the changing time; B. Bauer and Stirner brought all philosophy to an end in radical criticism and nihilism; Marx and Kierkegaard drew the extreme conclusions from the changed situation: Marx destroyed the bourgeois-capitalistic, and Kierkegaard the bourgeois-Christian world.

a   L. Feuerbach [58] (1804-1872)

Like all philosophers of German idealism, Feuerbach started from Protestant theology, which he studied in Heidelberg with Paulus and the Hegelian Daub. He writes home that the lectures of the former are a spider web of sophistries, a rack upon which words are tortured until they confess something which was never meant. Repelled by this "expectoration of a delinquent genius," he wanted to go to Berlin, where Schleiermacher and Marheineke, as well as Strauss and Neander, lectured. Philosophy is mentioned only in passing, but even in his first letter from Berlin he writes: "I am

resolved . . . to dedicate this semester primarily to philosophy, in
order to complete the prescribed program in philosophy in this
course of studies all the more thoroughly, and with more practical
use. Therefore I am attending Logic and Metaphysics and Philosophy of Religion with Hegel. . . . I am infinitely pleased with
Hegel's lectures, even though I am by no means resolved to become
a Hegelian on that ground. . . ." Having conquered his father's
opposition, he devoted himself entirely to philosophy, studied two
years with Hegel, and concluded his studies with the dissertation *De
ratione una, universali, infinita*,[59] which he sent to Hegel in 1828,
accompanied by a letter, in which he called himself the latter's
immediate pupil, who hoped he had made his own something of his
teacher's speculative spirit.

The revolutionary changes which Feuerbach later was to undertake in Hegel's philosophy already can be seen through the tangle
of Hegelian concepts in this letter of the twenty-four-year-old
Feuerbach. He excuses in advance the failings of his dissertation
with the statement that it is intended to be a "living" and "free"
appropriation of what he learned from Hegel. He already lays emphasis upon the principle of "sensuousness"; ideas should not remain
above the sensuous in the realm of the universal, but should descend
from the "heaven of their colorless purity" and "unity with themselves" to observable particularity,[60] in order to incorporate themselves in the definiteness of phenomena. The pure Logos demands
an "incarnation," the idea, a "realization" and "secularization." He
remarks in passing—as though he had a premonition of his own fate
—that with this "materialization" and "realization" he does not have
in mind any popularization of thought, or even a transformation of
thought into fixed observation, and of concepts into mere images
and tokens. He justifies the tendency to secularization with the
statement that it is "time for it," or, "what is the same thing," it is
grounded in the spirit of Hegelian philosophy itself, which is certainly not a mere academic subject, but the concern of mankind.[61]
The anti-Christian bent is likewise given clear expression in this
letter. The spirit stands at the beginning of a new "world period";
the important thing, if the idea is to attain full realization, is to
dethrone the "self"—this "only spirit which exists"—which has
dominated the world ever since the beginning of the Christian era,
thereby eliminating the dualism of sensuous world and supersensual
religion, as well as that of church and state.[62] "Therefore the important thing now is not the development of concepts in their uni-

versal form, in their withdrawn purity and self-contained existence; rather, the important thing is truly to destroy all previous historical ways of looking at time, death, this world, the next, I, the individual, the person, the person as seen beyond finitude in the absolute and therefore called absolute, namely God, etc., in which is contained the foundation of all history up to the present, as well as the source of all Christian conceptions, both orthodox and rationalistic. We must bore through to the very foundations of truth." All these are to be replaced by the insights contained in recent philosophy, even though they are only "entangled" there. Christianity can no longer be considered the absolute religion. It is only the antithesis to the ancient world, and has excluded nature from the spirit. Similarly excluded from the realm of the spirit, death—that natural event— is considered by Christianity to be the "most indispensable laborer in the vineyard of the Lord."[63]

How at home Feuerbach was in Hegel's thought, in spite of this more than "free" appropriation, is shown by his criticism (1835) of von Bachmann's *Antihegel*,[64] Hegel himself could almost have written it. In sixty-four pages, he does away with Bachmann's "concept-free" empiricism with a penetration and superiority completely in line with the philosophical criticism whose nature Hegel developed[65] and used upon all human understanding.[66] Feuerbach differentiates two kinds of criticism: that of knowledge and that of misunderstanding. The one enters upon the positive nature of its object, and takes the central idea of the author as a measure by which to evaluate; misunderstanding, coming from without, attacks what is philosophically positive; it is always concerned with other things than its opponent is concerned with, and where the latter's concepts transcend its own ideas, it understands nothing. Feuerbach points out to Bachmann that he did not in the least understand Hegel's theories of the identity of philosophy with religion, logic, and metaphysics, the subject and object, thought and being, notion and reality. Bachmann's criticism of Hegel's idea of God is gross persiflage; the superficiality and groundlessness of his objections to Hegel's "deepest and most exalted" idea is beneath all criticism.

In view of this academically correct use of the Hegelian categories, it is understandable that Rosenkranz could write seven years later: "Who would have thought that the Hegelian philosophy, which Feuerbach once defended with me against Bachmann in his polemic against the latter's *Antihegel*, would be so degraded in his hands!"[67] Feuerbach himself later explains his criticism of the *Anti-*

hegel with reference to Lessing's criticism of the opponents of orthodoxy. He says that he was only an "interimistic" defender of Hegel against an unphilosophic attack, and that it would be most premature to think that whoever writes against the opponents of something is himself unconditionally in favor of what is being attacked. Rather he had the *Antihegel* within himself, "but because he was as yet only half a man, I commanded him to remain silent."[68]

Feuerbach's own opposition appeared in the open only in 1839, with the publication, in Ruge's *Jahrbücher*, of an article: "On the Criticism of Hegelian Philosophy." In all important points this criticism is in complete agreement with the previously demolished criticism by Bachmann. Feuerbach, too, now negates absolutely the dialectical identity of philosophy and theology, of notion and reality, thought and being. What he had previously defended against Bachmann as Hegel's most exalted idea seems to him now "the nonsense of the Absolute." The absolute spirit is "nothing else than" the departed spirit of theology, wandering about like a ghost in Hegel's philosophy.

In 1840, Feuerbach once more took account of his relationship with Hegel. He calls Hegel the only man who ever caused him to learn what a teacher is. But what we have been as pupils never vanishes from our being, even though it may from our consciousness. Not only had he studied Hegel, he also taught others, convinced that it was the duty of a young lecturer to acquaint the students, not with his own opinions, but with the teachings of recognized philosophers. "I taught Hegelian philosophy . . . at first as a man who identifies himself with his subject . . . because he does not know anything different and better; later, as a man who differentiates and separates himself from his subject, giving it its historical due, but all the more anxious to grasp it properly." Thus he was never an absolute Hegelian, holding rather to the essence of Hegelianism, subjecting even the absolute system to the "law of universal finitude." "As a budding author, I took the point of view of speculative philosophy in general, and of Hegelian philosophy in particular, but only insofar as it is the final, most comprehensive expression of speculative philosophy."[69]

Twenty years later—in 1860—Feuerbach summarized his position in regard to Hegel for the last time. In contrast to the "heroes of the spirit," he calls himself a last philosopher, relegated to the uttermost limit of the realm of philosophy, beyond the intellectual exaltation of system. In a style that reminds us of Kierkegaard's polemic, he calls Hegel the paragon of the self-sufficient professional thinker, whose real existence is looked after by the state and therefore is meaningless to his philosophy. He put an historical halo upon the lecture platform: "The absolute spirit is nothing more than the absolute professor."[70]

But of what does the transformation, proclaimed by Feuerbach, of the philosophy perfected by Hegel consist? A memorandum from 1842–43 on "The Necessity of a Transformation" gives the most important points. Philosophy is no longer within the epoch which included the development from Kant to Hegel; in fact, it no longer falls primarily within the domain of history of philosophy, but rather the immediate course of world events. Therefore a "decision" must be made, either to continue along the old track or to open a new epoch. But a radical transformation is necessary; it is a "demand of the age," more precisely, of the age that is coming into the present from the future. "The period of breakdown of an historical world view is necessarily filled with conflicting demands: some think it necessary to preserve the old and banish the new, others think it necessary to realize the new. Which party recognizes the true need? The one which sees the need of the future—the anticipated future—the one which shares in forward progress. The need for preservation is something artificial, something itself evoked— reaction. Hegelian philosophy was the arbitrary unification of various existing systems, superficialities, with no positive strength, because it contained no absolute negativity. Only he who has the courage to be absolutely negative has the strength to create something new."[71] To race forward into an anticipated future was also the intention of Ruge, Stirner, Bauer, and Marx, because they all saw in the present only something temporary, not, like Hegel, something eternal. One and all, up to Nietzsche and Heidegger, they are "preparatory" philosophers.[72]

The initial impulse was given to this overthrow of Hegel's philosophy of recollection by Feuerbach's *Thesen zur Reform der Philosophie* and *Grundsätze der Philosophie der Zukunft*. The dwelling place of the spirit, we read in a letter written about this time, has collapsed; we must make up our minds to "emigrate"—an image which we shall meet again in Marx—taking with us only our private possessions. "The carriage of history is a confined carriage; just as it is impossible to get inside if the right moment is allowed to slip by, . . . so likewise if one wishes to go along, one may take along only what is absolutely necessary, what is one's own, but not all the furniture,"[73] a metaphor which, for its view of history, is reminiscent of Kierkegaard's image of the "defile" through which everyone must pass, and of the "one thing needful." "A man cannot concentrate himself too much; one thing—or nothing," says Feuerbach.[74]

Feuerbach criticizes Hegel from the viewpoint of the intended changes.[75] Of necessity, philosophy is now in a stage of "disillusionment." The illusion in which it has rested hitherto was that of self-sufficient thought, that the spirit could base itself upon itself, while nature—both the nature of the world and of man—is determined by the spirit. The anthropological presupposition of this "idealism" or "spiritualism" is the isolated mode of existence of the thinker as a thinker. Hegel, too, in spite of all "suspensions" of opposites was an extreme idealist, his "absolute identity" was in fact an "absolute one-sidedness" on the side of self-assured thought. Starting with "I am" in the form of "I think," the idealist views his contemporary world, his environment, in fact the whole world, as merely the "other side" of his self, as an "alter ego," with the emphasis on the ego. Hegel interprets the "other," that which I myself am not, as my "own" otherness, and thereby mistakes the specific independent existence of nature and other people. He builds his philosophy upon a self-conscious, purely philosophical foundation; he mistakes the non-philosophical beginnings or principles of philosophy. Therefore, Hegelian philosophy is subject to the same reproach as all modern philosophy after Descartes: the reproach of an unrepaired breach with the observations made by the senses, an immediate presupposition of philosophy. There is, of course, an unavoidable discontinuity which resides in the nature of science, but it is mediated by philosophy's ability to engender itself out of nonphilosophy. "The philosopher must insert into the text of philosophy what Hegel put in a footnote: that part of man which does not philosophize, which is against philosophy and opposed to abstract thought."[76] Thus the critical starting point for Feuerbach's inquiry into the "thou mediated by the senses" was the traditional point of departure of the philosophy of the spirit from *cogito ergo sum*.

The historical motive behind idealism's disparagement of natural sensibility as "mere" naturalness can be found in the origin of modern philosophy in Christian theology, the principle of which is called the pure "self" in the letter to Hegel. Thus Feuerbach's attack in the *Grundsätze* is directed against Hegel as a philosophical theologian. "Modern philosophy is a product of theology—it is nothing else than theology broken up and transformed into philosophy." "The contradiction inherent in modern philosophy, . . . that it is a negation of theology based upon theology, or a negation of theology which is itself a theology: this contradiction is particularly characteristic of Hegelian philosophy." "Whoever does not surrender Hegelian philosophy does not surrender theology. The Hegelian doctrine that reality is determined by the idea is only the rationalistic expression of the theological doctrine that nature . . . was created by God." On the other hand, "Hegelian philosophy is the last refuge, the last rationalistic support of theology." "Just as once the Catholic theologians became *de facto* Aristotelians in order to combat Protestantism, so now the Protestant theologians must become *de jure* Hegelians in order to combat atheism." "Thus in the highest principle of Hegelian philosophy we have the principle and result of his philosophy of religion, that philosophy does not invalidate the dogmas of theology, but rather establishes them through the negation of rationalism. . . . Hegelian philosophy is the last ambitious attempt to re-establish lost, defeated Christianity by means of philosophy, by following the universal modern procedure and identifying the negation of Christianity with Christianity itself. The much-lauded speculative identity of spirit and material, infinite and finite, divine and human, is nothing more than the accursed paradox of the modern age: the identity of belief and unbelief, theology and philosophy, religion and atheism, Christianity and paganism, at the very summit, the summit of metaphysics. Hegel conceals this contradiction by making of atheism, the negation, an objective component of God—God as a process, and atheism as one component of this process."[77]

But the infinite of religion and philosophy is and was never anything else than something finite, and therefore definite, but mystified—something finite with the predicate of being not finite, that is, *in*-finite. Speculative philosophy made the same mistake as did theology: it made predicates of the infinite out of predicates of finite reality simply through negating the definite predicate through which they are what they are. A philosophy like Hegel's, which derives the finite from the infinite, the definite from the indefinite, will never arrive at a true placing of the finite and definite. "The finite is derived from the infinite, that is, the in-finite, the indefinite, is defined, negated; it is admitted that the infinite is nothing without definition, that is, without finitude. Thus the finite is set up as the reality of the infinite. But the negative non-entity of the absolute remains in the background; the postulated finitude is thus always abrogated. The finite is the negation of the infinite, and the infinite the negation of the finite. The philosophy of the absolute is a contradiction." The beginning of a truly positive philosophy cannot be God or the absolute, nor "being" in itself without anything which is to be, but only what is finite, definite, and real. But, above all, mortal man is a finite reality for whom death is affirmative.

"This new . . . philosophy is the negation of all academic philosophy, although it contains within itself whatever truth there is in the latter, . . . it has . . . no language of its own, . . . no principle of its own; it is thinking man himself—the man who is and knows himself. . . ." But if this name of the new philosophy is translated back into that of "self-consciousness," the new philosophy is being interpreted in the sense of the old, is being set once more upon the old foundations. But the self-consciousness of the old philosophy is an abstraction without reality, for only the individual human being "is" self-consciousness.[78] To construct an "anthropological" philosophy, one determined by man, means for Feuerbach in the first place: take care for the sensuous basis of one's own thought, the mode of which is definite, sensuous observation which fills thought with meaning. In the second place: have regard for one's fellow man who confirms one's own way of thought, who is the epistemological partner in intellectual dialogue. Attention given to both aspects will take thought which moves independently, which is restricted to deductive logic, will open it to the world and set it right.

The first aspect, sensuousness, is never merely the essence of human senses, but also of nature and corporeal existence in general. Fischer has remarked[79] that, for Feuerbach, the senses were the third estate, hitherto scorned, which he elevates to total significance. Hegel, on the contrary, extols thought as having no need of sight and hearing. The true concept of "existence" derives only from sensuousness, for the real existence of a thing is proven by the fact that it encounters us palpably, that it cannot be thought of, imagined, and merely conceived.[80] This "sensualism" of Feuerbach is most readily apparent in his criticism of the Hegelian dialectic of soul and body.[81] In opposition to it, Hegel asserts that this, like all Hegelian "identities," is in actual fact only an "absolute one-sidedness." Hegel sees nothing in the ideas of those who think that man should not have a body, because the body demands care for the satisfaction of its physical needs, thus diverting man from his spiritual life and making him incapable of real freedom. "Philosophy must recognize that the spirit can exist for itself by relating itself to material partially as its *own* corporeality, partially as external world. The spirit must then take what has been so differentiated and restore it to unity through antithesis and resolution of the same. Of course there is a closer connection between the spirit and its own body than between the rest of the external world and the spirit. Because of this necessary connection between my body and my soul, the activity which the latter engages in vis-à-vis the former is not . . . merely negative. First, I must assert myself in this immediate harmony of my soul and my body. . . . I may not scorn my body and view it as an enemy. . . . If I order my life according to the laws of my bodily organism, my soul is free within its body." "Completely true," says Feuerbach, but Hegel continues immediately with: "Nevertheless, the soul cannot call a halt at this immediate unity with its body. The form of immediacy of that harmony contradicts the notion of the soul—its characteristic of being an ideality which refers itself to itself. In order to correspond to its notions, the soul must transform its identity with its body into an identity determined or mediated by the spirit, take possession of its body, make of it a compliant and well-adapted implement of its activity, transform it so that the soul may refer to itself within the body." The word "immediate," Feuerbach continues, is used innumerable times by Hegel; but what this word refers to, the immediate, is completely absent from his philosophy. He never gets beyond the logical notion, because from the start he makes the immediate into one component of what is most mediate: the notion. How could Hegel speak of an immediate unity with the body, since the body has no truth, no reality for the soul, since, according to Hegel, the soul is only a notion mediated through the suspension, the negation of corporeality, is itself, in fact, the notion? "Where can we find even a trace of immediacy?" asks Feuerbach, and he answers: "Nowhere. Why? Because, as everywhere in idealism and spiritualism, the body is only an object to the soul, an object even of the thinker, but not at the same time ground of will and consciousness. Therefore it is completely overlooked that we perceive what is corporeal before our consciousness only through a corporeality behind our consciousness which is not objective to us. . . ." Of course, the spirit forms and determines the body, and this to such an extent that a man who has a spiritual profession, and orders his way of life accordingly, his sleeping, eating, and drinking, at the same time also determines indirectly his stomach and circulation according to his will. "But seeing the one side, let us not forget the other side; let us not forget that, however the spirit consciously determines the body, it was itself unconsciously so determined by the body. For example, as a thinker I determine my body according to my purpose because constitutive nature, allied with destructive time, have organized me into a thinker; I am thus a thinker by *fate*. How and as what the body is determined, so the spirit is determined. . . ." Cause becomes effect, and vice versa. Thus Hegel's recognition of sensuous-natural corporeality is only true under the hypothesis of a philosophy of the spirit which builds upon itself. The idealistic notion of self-consciousness no more recognizes the independent reality of other men than it recognizes the reality of sensuous-natural corporeality.[82]

For Feuerbach, the fundamental exponent of sensuous-natural corporeality is that organ which is not mentioned by name in proper society, although by nature it has great significance in the history of the world, and exerts a power which dominates the world: the natural sexuality of man. The true "I" is not "a neuter 'it' " but, "a priori," either a feminine or masculine existence; thus, *eo ipso* fated to be a social being. Philosophy could abstract from the difference between the sexes only if it were limited to the sexual organs. But it permeates the *whole* man, including his specifically feminine or masculine perception and thought. Conscious of myself as a man, I recognize thereby the existence of a being different from me, a being which belongs to me and contributes to the determination of my own existence. Thus before I understand myself, I am grounded in the existence of others by nature. My thinking only makes me conscious of what I am already: a being, not ungrounded, but grounded upon another existence. Not "I," but "I and Thou" is the true principle of life and thought.

The most real relationship between I and Thou is love. "The love of another tells you what you are." "The truth speaks to us, not from within our own preoccupied self, but from another. Only through communication, only through the conversation of man with man, do ideas arise. Two human beings are necessary for the begetting of another human being, spiritually as well as physically. The unity of man with man is the first and last principle of philosophy, truth, and universality. For the essence of man is contained only in the unity of one man with another, a unity which is based upon the real difference between I and Thou. Even in thought and as a philosopher I am a man among others."

With this appeal to the love which unites mankind, Feuerbach, the critic of Hegel, comes remarkably close to the young Hegel, whose concept of the spirit had as its point of departure the suspension of differences within the "living relationship" of love. Later, however, Hegel was to use the entire strength of his thought to differentiate philosophically-concretely his concept of the spirit into its various attributes: "sensual," "perceptual," and "rational" consciousness; "desiring" and "reflecting," "servile" and "masterful," "spiritual" and "reasonable" self-consciousness. In contrast, Feuerbach's "love" remains a sentimental cliché without any definite attributes, although it is the unified dual principle of his philosophy, of "sensuousness" and the "Thou."

A further consequence of Feuerbach's radical transformation is the changed attitude of philosophy toward politics and toward religion. Philosophy is itself to become religion, and also politics, a kind of political world view which replaces the religion of the past. "For we must once more become religious; politics must become our religion, but it can only do this if we have something ultimate in outlook, something which will make politics into a religion."[83] But the ultimate for man is man. The thesis that philosophy comes to occupy the place of religion leads of necessity to the further thesis that politics becomes a religion; when the man, poor in earthly goods, replaces the Christian, the fellowship of work must replace the fellowship of prayer. With complete logic, Kierkegaard explains the resurgence of politics out of the disappearance of the Christian faith;[84] with equal logic, Feuerbach deduces the necessity of man's becoming political from his faith in man as such. "Religion in the usual sense is so far from being the bond of the state that it is rather the dissolution of the same." If God is Lord, man must rely upon him and not upon men. If, on the other hand, men form a state, they deny thereby *in praxi* faith in God. "Faith in God did not found the states, but despair over God." Subjectively, the origin of the state is explained by "faith in man as the god of man."[85] Apart from the Christian religion, the secular state naturally becomes the "essence of all realities," the "universal entity," and the "providence of man." The state is "man writ large," the state in relation to itself is "absolute man"; it becomes at once the reality and practical refutation of faith. "Thus practical atheism is the bond of the state," and "men now throw themselves into politics because they recognize that Christianity is a religion that robs man of political energy."[86] Feuerbach did not give up this conviction even after the failure of 1848, which convinced him that it was not the time and place for realizing the political world view. The Reformation destroyed religious Catholicism, but a political Catholicism arose in its stead. What the Reformation had accomplished only in the domain of religion must now be striven for politically: the transformation of the "political hierarchy" into a democratic republic. Feuerbach's actual interest was the concentration and extension of the power of the state as such, much more than the outward form of a republic. This is even more true of Ruge, Marx, Bauer, and Lassalle, and is shown by the circumstance that later they viewed Bismarck not as an enemy, but as a pacemaker along the road to their previous revolutionary goals.[87] In a letter written in 1859, Feuerbach says, "As far as German politics is concerned, our motto is famous: *quot capita tot sensus.* But Germany can never be put under one heading until it comes under the control of one head; and it will never come under the control of one head until someone has the courage to stand with sword in hand and proclaim: I am the head of Germany! But where is this union of heart and head? Prussia, to be sure, has the head, but not the heart; Austria has the heart, but not the head."[88]

Measured by the standard of Hegel's history of the "spirit," Feuerbach's massive sensualism must seem as a step backward in comparison to Hegel's conceptually organized idea, as a barbarization of thought which replaces content by bombast and sentiment. Hegel's final doubt, whether the tumult of his contemporaries and the "deafening loquacity" of vanity left any room at all for passionless knowledge, is drowned out by the verbose rhetoric of his pupils, who replaced philosophy with the interests of the day. Upon Hegel's friendship with Goethe follows the "idyl" between "Ludwig" (Feuerbach) and "Konrad" (Deubler),[89] whose ingenuous worship of the "great man" was thoroughly in conformity with Feuerbach's disposition, basically so inoffensive. And yet it would be a great mistake to suppose that, mounted upon the steed of a dead philosophy of the spirit, one could ride roughshod over the "materialism" of the nineteenth century. Feuerbach's effort to make Hegel's philosophical theology tangible and finite simply became the standpoint of the age. Now—consciously or unconsciously—it belongs to all of us.

b   A. Ruge (1802–1880)

More completely than Feuerbach, Ruge based the new philosophy of the new age upon the statement that "everything depends
upon history"; "it goes without saying," he adds as a good Hegelian,
"philosophical history."[90] But history is philosophical not only as
history of philosophy, but also, and primarily, as mere course of
events and consciousness of history. "True reality" is "nothing else"
than "consciousness of historical time," which is the "truly positive,
ultimate outcome of history."[91] The "historical idea of an age" or
the "genuine spirit of an age" is "absolute master"; the only thing
valid in history is "that which is the power of the age." The absolute
nature of the spirit is real only within the process of history, which
is determined in freedom by the "political entity," man.[92]

In contrast, the spheres of the absolute in Hegel's system are
mere attempts to absolutize history which is in itself absolute. "We
attain the absolute only in history, but in history it is attained at all
points, before and after Christ. Man is everywhere in God, but the
final historical form is also, as form, the ultimate; the future is the
limit set to everything historical. The form of religion is not perfected in Christ, that of poetry in Goethe, that of philosophy in
Hegel; they are all so far from being the culmination of the spirit
that their greatest glory lies in being the beginning of a new development."[93] Everything falls within history; therefore, whatever
is the "newest" philosophy is "truly positive," containing within
itself the future as its own living negation. "The historical spirit" or
the "self-consciousness of the age" corrects itself in the course of
history, which must also be the end of Hegel's system.[94]

Thus a title such as *Our System, or the Wisdom and Movement
of the World in Our Time*[95] has more than incidental reference to
the time. This "system" *is* itself a philosophy of time, of the age,
just as the wisdom and movement of the world are one. Thus the
fourth volume of Ruge's *Aus früherer Zeit* addresses the Germans
first of all by speaking of the "spirit of our time." In this work, following the pattern of Hegel's history of philosophy, he gives an
excellent popular history of the development of philosophy from
Plato to Hegel, concluding with the "critical development of philosophy and the spirit of the age." Here, also, he thinks of philosophic thought as a partner of the age, for the general spirit of the
age, together with its particular philosophy, forms one and the same

movement of the spirit. And in actual fact, no age has been so permeated with philosophy in all realms, including journalism, belles
lettres, and politics, as was this epoch, through the influence of the
Young Hegelians. It is an a priori of their philosophy that the spirit
of the age—which Ruge occasionally equates with "public opinion"
—always and necessarily "keeps pace" with the philosophical spirit
of the age. "This conscious unity of the world spirit and the philosophical spirit" is characteristic of our age.[96] But Ruge was firmly
convinced that the spirit of the age, by its very nature, was progressive, just as he was convinced that the course of time cannot be
turned back. No reaction can defraud the spirit of the age of its
power and logical conclusion. Referring to the *Jahrbücher* he published, he says, "The ultimate victory is victory in the spirit. Thus
when we speak of a position taken by the *Jahrbücher* toward history, and thereby (!) of its future course, particulars are furnished
by the public spirit, or, more accurately, the spirit which, though
present, is kept from being truly public. For it is an open secret that
the ostensible spirit of paid and guarded newspapers is not the real
spirit, nor the disinterested spirit of ancient learned academies, nor
the spirit capable of life."[97] Thus the truly present spirit of the age
is under certain circumstances a public secret; but under all circumstances it is this spirit which drives history forward to victory. The
"reason of the age" is easy to recognize; anyone can know it if he so
desires.

For all the Young Hegelians, the actual discoverer of the unity
between philosophy and time was none other than Hegel. To justify their radical historicization of the spirit, they appealed to
Hegel's preface to his *Rechtsphilosophie*, which says, "As concerns
the individual, each is a son of his time; and philosophy is their time
comprehended in thought. It is just as foolish to imagine that some
philosophy transcends its present world as to imagine that an individual can transcend his time."[98] Hegel drew a reactionary conclusion from the circumstance that no theory can transcend its own
time, opposing and rejecting any imagined "imperative," and refused
to construct a world upon the "yielding element" of "purpose," a
world which is not but should be. His pupils, on the other hand, on
the basis of the same identity between spirit and time but with their
eyes to the future, insisted upon what *should* be. They sought to
place philosophy at the service of the revolution, following the
progress of time. In spite of this contrast in orientation, which in the
one case looked to the past, in the other to the future, both held to

the thesis of the necessary unanimity of philosophical consciousness and historical fact.[99] For Hegel, the history of the spirit was the heart of world history. Similarly, the Young Hegelians took the "true" course of events as the criterion for the movement of the spirit; they took the measure of the very reason of history with an historical measuring rod.

As a result of the basic connection made between history and the spirit, Hegel's system was also used for reflection upon the age in which it was developed. In the case of Ruge, the conclusion is twofold: Hegelian philosophy is "contemporary" with the French Revolution, which exalted the free individual as the purpose of the state. Hegel does the same by showing that the absolute is the thinking spirit, and its reality the thinking individual. As a political program, the spirit of freedom lives in the Enlightenment and Revolution, as metaphysics, in German philosophy.[100] In Hegel, human rights attained philosophical self-consciousness; there can be no further development than their realization. The same philosophy which gained for the human spirit the highest dignity of absolute freedom is a contemporary of the "counterattack of the spirit of the past" against freedom in thought and political purpose. Thus Hegel was related to both the progressive and reactionary spirit of the age; insofar as he was the latter, he was untrue to his own principle, progress in consciousness of freedom. Therefore it is the task of the progressive spirit of the age to free Hegel's philosophy from itself by means of the dialectic method. According to Hegel's statement that "the present is uppermost,"[101] it is the absolute right of the age which has superseded him to defend his system critically against himself, in order to accomplish the principle of unfolding and freedom. Through negation, history unfolds the truth contained in Hegel's system. It does this by removing the still present contrast between "notion" and "existence" through theoretical criticism and practical revolution. The German revolution of 1848 is the practical aspect of this theoretical correction.[102]

The *Hallesche Jahrbücher für deutsche Wissenschaft und Kunst* (1838–1843)[103] were the literary organs for the theoretical groundwork of the practical revolution. After their forced removal from Prussia to Saxony, they were renamed the *Deutsche Jahrbücher*. Among their contributors were Strauss, Feuerbach, Bauer, F. Th. Vischer, E. Zeller, Droysen, Lachmann, J. Grimm, and W. Grimm. Ruge's assertion in the foreword to the fourth series is no overstatement: no other German scholarly periodical ever experienced such satisfaction, seeing its discussions become events which went far beyond the circle of theoreticians, becoming involved in all of life. To the present day, German philosophy has nothing comparable to this journal which could equal it in critical forcefulness, effectiveness, and influence upon political theory.

The criticism undertaken in the *Jahrbücher* is primarily concerned with religion and politics. Rosenkranz censured the brusque, "atheistic-republican" tone of Ruge's writings. To him the German atheists seemed awkward and childish in comparison to the well-mannered and well-educated followers of Holbach.[104] But compared to Bauer's radical overhauling of Strauss's and Feuerbach's criticism of religion, Ruge is extremely moderate, and Rosenkranz' last studies show that in this matter he was not far removed from Ruge: in his case, too, the unfolding of the spirit had been tacitly changed to the progress of mankind.

More decisive than Ruge's abolition of the Christian religion in a "humanized world of liberated men" is his criticism of the state and of politics. In an article in the *Jahrbücher* entitled "Politics and Philosophy," he differentiates the Young and Old Hegelians. The latter accommodate Hegel's philosophy to what exists, while the former translate the philosophy of religion and the philosophy of right into a "negating and postulating activism." Therefore the Young Hegelians are compelled to protest, on the one hand against Hegel's "modesty," which transfers political reality from the obvious present course of events to a state of affairs in ancient England which was no longer true even in his own time;[105] on the other hand, they protest against the "arrogance" of absolute philosophy, which seeks to be a "present-day apocalypse" through recollection of what has been, whereas philosophy actually merely begins the future through its criticism in the present. Instead of constructing an absolute state by means of the categories of logic, the present existence of the state must be criticized historically with reference to the immediate future. For only the spirit of the age, as it realizes itself, is truly comprehended reality, as Hegel himself teaches "in a hundred passages," although he avoided everything that might give offense to the church and the state.

Ruge's fundamental criticism of Hegel's philosophy of the state is contained already in his review of the second edition of the *Rechtsphilosophie*.[106] Its greatest merit he sees in the fact that Hegel made self-determining will the basis of his theory of the state, so that the state is the substantial will which knows itself and fulfills its knowledge, while at the same time it has its mediate existence in the free will and knowledge of the individual.[107] The great defect in the execution of this principle is that "Hegel does not expressly include history, with the effect of its entire content, in his philosophy of right, but rather puts it at the end"—in contrast to his aesthetics, the systematic development of which is thoroughly historical.

The precondition of developed history is of course the existing state, for all history is the history of states; but the state is already in itself an historical movement toward freedom, which is never present absolutely, but only as the act of liberation. Hegel exhibits only the static concept of the state, but not the idea of the state in movement, the motive force of which is history. The absolute system of freedom must now be followed by the historical system, the presentation of freedom both real and to be realized. "In place of the system of abstract and theoretically absolute development, we have the system of concrete development, which everywhere grasps the spirit in its history and places at the end of every history the demand of its future." Hegel's speculative contemplation must be awakened once more by Fichte's energy,[108] for his polemic against what "should" be leads to "forms of existence without concept" and thus to recognition of that which merely exists, without being in agreement with its true concept. For example, in Hegel's system the royal and governmental power, the national assembly and the bicameral system, are such forms of existence contradicting the spirit of history. Hegel has no faith in the majority, and hates all forms of election. But for Ruge, not to have faith in this means not to have faith in the spirit (of the age)! It is a stupid objection that the masses are dumb, and "respectable only in riots."[109] "In whose name then do they riot, and how does it happen that they conquer only in the name of the spirit of world history? How does it happen that the rioting of the masses turned out to be purposeless neither in 1789 nor in 1813, and the majority by no means to be wrong? To hold to the statement, *philosophia paucis contenta est judicibus*, represents a total failure to understand the spirit and its process. On the contrary, truth subjects the world en masse. . . . Those who are wise in their wisdom will never leave the majority for long, and when the prophets of a new spirit are in the minority to start with and . . . perish, then the acclamation, the exaggeration even, of their merits is all the more assured them among posterity. . . . The truth of the majority is not absolute, but on the whole it is the assurance of the spirit of the age, political or historical truth. And if only one individual in a National

Assembly knows the word of the spirit of the age and speaks it (and such will never be lacking), then surely only egoism and malicious caprice remains in the minority. The majority shares its relative error with the historical spirit and its assurance in general, which of course cannot prevent itself in turn from being negated by the future."[110]

The conviction of the truth of the masses is itself "virtue." This is the "discovery of our century," which eluded Hegel, although it is only a consequence of his system of thought, which includes the spirit in the world process. Hegel denied this truth on the basis of his own viewpoint, still not sufficiently historical. That is, contrary to his own principle, he doubted the power of the spirit; otherwise he would not have expended so much effort in excluding the mass of the electorate from his system of rights. In its place, he arrived at the establishment of the classes and the absurd stipulation of primogeniture. In reality, even the material interests of the masses cannot go against the unfolding of the spirit, because, ever, material progress is also spiritual progress if history is "all" and a product of the real spirit.

As in the case of Marx, Ruge's criticism of Hegel's philosophy of right[111] rests upon the principle of critical differentiation of metaphysical "essence" (*Wesen*) from historical "existence" (*Existenz*). The general essence of the state is identical with that of the spirit, and thus definable by the general categories of logic (universality, particularity, individuality) and the philosophy of the spirit (will and freedom); but the real state, to which Hegel refers in agreement with his thesis of the reality of freedom, is an historical existence, which therefore can be comprehended only historically and criticized only with reference to its substantiality. "In logic or in the study of the eternal process . . . there are no existences. Here existence, the thinker and his spirit, is the indifferent basis, because what this individual does should be nothing else than . . . the universal action (of thought) itself . . . We are concerned here with the universal essence as such, not its existence. In the natural sciences, the existence of the natural object is of no interest. Although . . . the processes which exist are the object of examination, they are nevertheless the indifferent, ever-recurring example of the eternal law and eternal behavior of nature in the course of its self-production. Only with the entrance of history into the realm of science does existence itself become of interest. The movement of history is no longer the cycle of recurring forms, . . . but rather it brings to light new forms in the self-production of the spirit. As this existence, the constitution of the spirit and the state in various ages is of scientific interest. The circumstances of its formation are no longer indifferent examples, but stages in this process. The peculiarity of these historical existences is important for knowledge of them; the matter of concern is this existence as such."[112] Therefore, just as dogmatic theology was criticized by Strauss, Hegel's absolute metaphysics of the state must be historically criticized. This criticism is also the only objective criticism, because it judges according to the course of actual events. The historical change from universal essence to individual historical existence is not yet present in Hegel's philosophy of right, which, therefore, has the same impalpable character as his phenomenology. "The Hegelian state . . . is no more real than the Platonic, nor will it ever become more real; for although it refers to the present-day state in the same way the Platonic did to the Greek, even calling it by name, it does not draw its conclusion from the historical process, and therefore has no direct effect upon the development of political life and consciousness. Here the French are far in advance of us: they are historical at all points. Among them the spirit is vital, and forms the world according to its own design."[113] In order to prevent historical criticism from appearing, Hegel makes metaphysical essences of historical existences, for example, giving a speculative demonstration of hereditary kingship.[114] But the true connection of the concept with reality is not the apotheosis of existence into concept, but the realization of the concept in actual existence. Even freedom never exists absolutely, but always relative to specific external circumstances of existence from which man liberates himself. Hegel remains on the side of the purely theoretical spirit and purely theoretical freedom, although he himself stated in the opening paragraphs of his philosophy of right that will is only the other side of thought, that theory is itself practice, and the difference between the two is merely whether the spirit turns inward or outward.[115] German philosophy discovered theoretically this practical side of theory, but practically it hid it. True science does not go back to logic, but out into the real world of history; "logic itself is drawn into history" and must allow itself to be comprehended as existence, because it belongs to the structure of this particular philosophy and the only truth is in fact historical. Even truth is always in motion, it is self-differentiation and self-criticism.[116]

Similarly, the theoretical one-sidedness of Hegel's philosophy of right can only be comprehended historically, and only historically justified. "Hegel's age was not very favorable for politics; it had no political journalism or public life whatever."[117] The spirit retreated into theory and renounced practice. But Hegel had learned too much from the Greeks and had lived through the great Revolution with too clear a consciousness to avoid seeing that the extant, dynastic state of bourgeois society, with police and civil service, by no means corresponded to the idea of a public community, a "polis." Thus his rejection of imperative demands grows out of a lack of logic, the roots of which lie deep in the Prussian-German situation in which Hegel lived. The systems of Kant and Hegel are systems of reason and freedom in the midst of irrationality and subjugation; but they were constructed in such a way that they both hid this incongruity.

Kant made the famous statement to Mendelssohn: "Of course I think many things with absolute conviction which I would never have the courage to say; but I shall never say anything that I do not think."[118] This divergence between public pronouncement and private thought rests upon the fact that, "as a thinker," Kant was as different from himself "as a subject" as was the public life of his time from the private, and the general morality from the conscience of the individual. A subject was not allowed to be a philosopher; therefore, he becomes a diplomat, but without losing his "self-respect." His limited viewpoint is historically the viewpoint of "Protestant narrow-mindedness," which knows freedom only as a question of conscience, because it separates private from public virtue.[119]

The case of Hegel is even more dubious, because his philosophy elevates the Kantian viewpoint on morality and moral responsibility to a universal and political code of ethics. Now, as a philosopher, Hegel did not have any similar conflict with the Prussian State; on the contrary, it confirmed him in his philosophy, and thus he could declare himself to be on the side of thought, on good terms with the state. But his agreement is only apparent; it could only last as long as the absolutism of the Prussian State was reasonable enough to recognize the reason in Hegel's system, while Hegel, for his part, merely had an interest in securing his absolute system of knowledge and making it a force within the life of the state. Although Hegel originally was no enemy of political activism and criticism of the state, he later restricted himself to the development of his theory as such. In his inaugural speech at Heidelberg, he declared his conviction that philosophy should not engage in political reality, in which the enormous interest during the period of the wars of liberation displaced all interest in knowledge.[120] To this, Ruge asks indignantly, "What is this supposed to mean?" and answers, "Nothing less than: 'Let us continue, gentlemen, from where we were before the revolution and the war, namely, in the furtherance of inner freedom, the freedom of the Protestant spirit or abstract theory, of which philosophy is the ultimate perfection.' Hegel perfected this form of freedom, bringing it to a climax; now it can only retreat."[121]

This restriction to the notion as such was bound to lead to conflict with reality; for, when a clear view of the essence of the state has been achieved, it is driven to confront reality as criticism. Theoretical freedom, in its private existence, was bound to discover, through censorship, that it is practically without value, because it is not itself public property. But the "practical passion" of true knowledge cannot be restrained. The conflict from which Hegel was preserved was reserved for his pupils, "and so it becomes clear that the age, or the attitude of consciousness toward the world, was radically altered." "The development is no longer abstract; the age has become political, albeit there is still much lacking before it is sufficiently political."[122] Nineteenth-century man, Ruge writes apropos of a criticism of the "aesthetic" period of German civilization, cannot do without "ethical and political passion."[123]

Transition from philosophical criticism to political activism and from narrow-minded conscience to broad-minded party loyalty typify Ruge's development.[124] Typical also is his forced retreat to the kind of historicism which no longer consciously makes history, but only writes history. Besides the publication of his own collected works, the last piece of work he performed in exile was a translation of Buckle's *History of Civilization in England*. The task of theoretical criticism and practical revolution against the existing order, which he introduced, was taken up and continued with absolute consistency by Marx.

c K. Marx (1818–1883)

When Ruge went to Paris after the banning of the *Deutsche Jahrbücher* and there founded the *Deutsch-Französische Jahrbücher*, it was Marx who provided most of the assistance with this journal. In it appeared in 1844 Marx's discussion of the Jewish question, the introduction to the criticism of the Hegelian philosophy of right, and an exchange of correspondence between Marx, Ruge, Bakunin, and Feuerbach. Soon afterward, Marx broke with

Ruge. The extremely harsh judgment passed by Ruge upon Marx as a person,[125] and the no less unfavorable opinion expressed by Marx about Ruge, do not alter the fact that they held principles in common, in their criticism of Hegel. The difference rests upon the fact that, in respect to scientific rigor and impact, Marx far surpassed the journalistic talent of Ruge. Of all the left-wing Hegelians, he was not only the most radical, but also the only one who was a match for Hegel in conceptual acuity and also in erudition. Ruge's rhetoric is an essential component of his writings; Marx's is only a means to an end, and does not weaken the forcefulness of his critical analyses. How well schooled he is in Hegel is shown less by his early writings referring directly to Hegel, which were influenced by Feuerbach, than by *Das Kapital*. The analyses presented in this work, although far removed from Hegel in content, are unthinkable without the incorporation of Hegel's manner of reducing a phenomenon to a notion.

As he grew older, Marx came to determine the actual course of history by the changes in material production, and to view the struggle of the economic classes as the sole motive force of all history. He thought he had settled accounts with his "former philosophic conscience," but basically the original dialogue with Hegel remained even after his transition to criticism of the economy. His first and also last criticism of Hegel begins with an antithesis to Hegel's consummation. The question which moves Marx in his dissertation concerns the possibility of a new beginning after that conclusion.

His dissertation of 1840–1841 on Epicurus and Democritus contains an indirect argument with the situation brought about by Hegel. Epicurus and Democritus are viewed in connection with Greek philosophy as perfected by Plato and Aristotle; an analogy is drawn to the dissolution of Hegelian philosophy by its materialistic and atheistic epigones. The introductory portion, discussing the relationships of classical Greek philosophy to the later philosophical sects, alludes to Marx's own relationship to Hegel. "Greek philosophy seems to encounter what a good tragedy should not encounter: a feeble ending. With Aristotle, the Macedonian Alexander of Greek philosophy, the objective history of philosophy in Greece seems to come to a halt. . . . Epicureans, Stoics, skeptics, all seem an inappropriate postscript, completely out of proportion to their mighty premises."[126] But it would be an error to assume that Greek philosophy simply lived out its life; history shows that the so-called decomposition products of Greek philosophy became the archetypes of the Roman spirit, the independent and intensive individuality of which is beyond doubt. And even if this was the end of classical philosophy, the death of a hero does not resemble the "bursting of a frog that has puffed himself up," but rather the setting of the sun, which promises a new day. "Furthermore, is it not a remarkable phenomenon that new systems appear after the Platonic and Aristotelian philosophers who made philosophy all-inclusive, systems which do not depend upon these previous ample intellectual forms, but rather, reaching further back, turn to the simplest schools: in physics, to the natural philosophers; in ethics, to the Socratic school?" Is, therefore, the need at this time, after the departure of classical German philosophy, for a similar concentration and simplification of philosophy, such as went from Athens to Rome? But how, after Hegel, can we achieve any point of view which neither copies him nor yet is completely arbitrary? Only through a radical disengagement from Hegel's all-inclusive philosophy, through a "suspension" of it which will also "realize" it. Philosophy is always at such a "nodal point" when its abstract principle has become totally concrete, as in the case of Aristotle and Hegel. Then the possibility of continued development in a straight line is interrupted; a full circle has been described. Two totalities now stand confronting each other: an all-inclusive philosophy, and, opposite it, the actual world of complete nonphilosophy. For Hegel's reconciliation with reality was not within reality, but only with it, in the element of comprehension. Now philosophy must itself "turn outward" and engage the world. As a philosophy of the state, it becomes a philosophical politics. Then philosophy, which in Hegel was conterminous with the intelligent world, turns directly to the really existing world, and against philosophy. This two-edged behavior is the consequence of the division of the entire world of theory and practice into two mutually exclusive totalities. Because it is two totalities which confront each other, the disunion of the newly developing philosophy is itself total. The objective universality of a perfected philosophy breaks down first into the merely subjective forms of consciousness of an individual philosophy which grows out of it. This tempest, in which everything wavers, follows upon such nodal points of all-inclusive philosophy with historical necessity. Whoever does not see this necessity would have to deny, as a logical consequence, that man can continue his spiritual life after such a philosophy. Only this theory makes comprehensible the appearance after Aristotle of Zeno, Epicurus, and Sextus Empiricus, and after Hegel of "the usually baseless, impoverished experiments of recent philosophy."[127]

In contrast to the other Young Hegelians, who only wanted to effect a partial reformation of Hegel, Marx gained from history the insight that philosophy itself was at stake. "The halfhearted ones"— meaning philosophers like Ruge—"at such times hold to a view contrary to that of all generals. They think they can repair the damage by a reduction in forces, by dissipation, by a peace pact with the real demands. When Athens"—that is, philosophy—"was threatened by devastation, Themistocles"—that is, Marx—"urged the Athenians to desert it completely, and to found upon the sea, upon a different element"—that is, upon the element of political and economic practice, which must now be understood as "what is"—"a new Athens"—that is, a completely new kind of philosophy, which is not even a philosophy, according to the old definitions. It should also not be forgotten that the age following such catastrophes is an age of iron, "fortunate if characterized by the clash of titans, miserable if like the centuries which limp along after great artistic epochs; these latter busy themselves with copying in plaster and copper what sprang from Carrara marble. But these are times of titans, these times which followed an all-inclusive philosophy and its forms of subjective development, for gigantic is the dichotomy which is their unity. Thus Rome followed upon Stoic, skeptical, and Epicurean philosophy. They are wretched times and inflexible, for their gods have died, and the new goddess has the dark shape of fate, of pure light or pure darkness. The colors of daylight are still missing. But the heart of the misery is that the soul of the age . . . satisfied with itself . . . cannot give recognition to any reality which has come into existence without its aid. The fortune in such misery is, therefore, the subjective form . . . in which philosophy, as subjective consciousness, relates itself to reality. Thus, for example, Epicurean and Stoic philosophy were the positive results of their time. Thus the nocturnal moth, when the universal sun has set, seeks out the lamp light of the individual."[128] The statement that the new goddess has the dark form of an uncertain fate, either of pure light or of pure darkness, refers back to Hegel's image of philosophy being carried on in the grey twilight of a world which has been completed. For Marx, this says: now, after the dissolution of the philosophy completed in Hegel, we cannot yet see with certainty whether this twilight is the evening twilight before the onset of a dark night, or the twilight of dawn before the awakening of a new day.[129] For Hegel, the senescence of the real world is concomitant with a final rejuvenation of philosophy. For Marx, who anticipates the future, a philosophy brought to completion is concomitant with the rejuvenation of the real world in opposition to the old philosophy. Through the realization of reason in the real world, philosophy as such is suspended, enters into the practice of existing nonphilosophy. Philosophy has become Marxism, an immediately practical theory.

In Hegel, the world was given philosophical form; in Marx, philosophy must become completely worldly. Hegel's system is seen as a single abstract totality, having as its other side a total irrationality. Its inner polish and self-sufficiency is broken; the "inner light" in Hegel's philosophy becomes a "devouring flame," reaching out; the liberation of the world from nonphilosophy is at the same time the liberation of nonphilosophy from philosophy. From the theoretical point of view, this new kind of philosophy does not yet transcend Hegel's system, but is included within it. Therefore, the new way of philosophizing is aware of itself only in contrast to the complete system; it does not yet understand that its own dissolution of Hegelian philosophy is the most appropriate realization of the latter. For Hegel's principle is also Marx's principle: the unity of reason and reality, and reality itself as a union of essence and existence. Therefore, Marx is forced to attack in two directions: against the real world, and against existing philosophy. This is so because he seeks to unite both in an all-inclusive totality of theory and practice. His theory can become practical as criticism of what exists, as a critical differentiation between reality and idea, between essence and existence. In the form of such criticism, his theory prepares the way for practical changes. On the other hand, one can argue backwards from the nature of the "revolution" to the historical character of Hegelian philosophy. "Here we see the *curriculum vitae* of a philosophy narrowed down to its subjective point, just as the death of a hero can be made to tell the story of his life."

Marx had such a radical understanding of the new situation that he could develop from a critic of the Hegelian philosophy of right to the author of *Das Kapital*. For this reason, he could better understand Hegel's "accommodation" to political reality than could Ruge. "It is conceivable that some accommodation or other could lead a philosopher to some inconsistency or other; he may even be aware of this himself. But he is not aware of the fact that the possibility of this apparent accommodation has its deepest roots in an inadequacy or an inadequate formulation of his principle itself. If a philosopher really accommodated himself in this way, his pupils must explain on the basis of his essential, inner consciousness what he himself saw in the form of exoteric consciousness."[130] Because Hegel's philosophy does not include the world of theory *and* of practice, essence *and* existence, it must necessarily compare itself with what exists and accommodate itself. The entire concrete content of what is to be comprehended is always predetermined for it by what—in the sense of that which exists—"is."

The dialectic of theory and practice forms the basis not only of Marx's criticism of the idealistic philosophy of the spirit, but also of his criticism of Feuerbach's materialistic philosophy. In the eleven theses on Feuerbach (1845), Marx designates the major defect of earlier materialism: it apprehended sensuous reality only under the form of "observation" (theoria), and therefore as an already present "object," but not as the product of the activity and practice of sentient human beings.[131] On the other hand, idealism, taking the subject as its point of departure, gave full weight to the latter's productive activity, but only in the abstract, as a spiritual framework. Neither spiritualism nor materialism understand "revolutionary," i.e., practical-critical, activity, which contributes most to the creation of the human world. The historical reason for Feuerbach's limitation to a materialism of mere observation lies in the barriers erected by late bourgeois society, a society of mere consumers who do not know that everything they consume is the historical product of common human activity, that even an apple is the result of trade and world commerce, and is not at all just suddenly "there."[132] It was Feuerbach's great merit within this limitation to dissolve the religious world into its secular basis, but without calling the latter into question either theoretically or practically. Feuerbach, too, "interpreted" this world alienated from man differently, namely, humanly; but according to him the primary task was to "transform" it through theoretical criticism and practical revolution.[133] With Marx, the will to change the world does not mean direct action alone, but at the same time a criticism of previous interpretations of the world, a transformation of being and consciousness; for example, the "political economy" is to be transformed both as actual economic system and as economic theory, for the latter is the consciousness of the former.[134]

Using Engels' procedure,[135] popular Marxism simplified the dialectical relationship between theory and practice by freezing it upon an abstract-material "basis," the relationship of which to the theoretical "superstructure" can be inverted with equal ease, as M. Weber showed.[136] If, on the contrary, Marx's original insight is adhered to, then even Hegel's "theory" can be seen as practical. For the deeper reason why Hegel allows the content of his comprehension to be advanced without seeking to alter it through "criticism" lies not only in what it "interprets," but in what it strives for as a practical goal. Hegel's comprehension sought to make its peace with reality. But Hegel could reconcile himself to the contradictions in the empirical world because, as the last Christian philosopher, he was in the world as though he were not of it. On the other hand, Marx's criticism of the existing order is not motivated by mere "desire for change." It has its roots in a Promethean rebellion against the Christian order of creation. Only the atheism of man with faith in himself must also see to the creation of the world. This atheistic motif of Marx's "materialism" is expressed in the theme of his dissertation on two classical atheists and materialists. For him, Epicurus is the greatest representative of the Greek enlightenment. He was the first among mortal men to dare to defy the gods of heaven. The philosophy of human "self-consciousness" acknowledges Prometheus as the most honored martyr in the philosophic calendar, against all the gods of heaven and earth.[137] The destruction of the Christian religion is the prerequisite for the construction of a world in which man is his own master.

Therefore, Marx's criticism of the Prussian State and Hegelian philosophy of the state begins with the statement that criticism of religion—the "prerequisite for all criticism" of the world— is essentially concluded. "It is therefore the duty of history, the beyond of truth having vanished, to establish the truth of this world. Philosophy is in the service of history. Its primary duty, once the sacred image of human self-estrangement has been unmasked, is to unmask self-estrangement in all its unholy forms. Criticism of heaven is transformed thereby into criticism of earth, criticism of religion into criticism of right, criticism of theology into criticism of politics."[138] Together with philosophy, economic criticism stands in the service of history. This is the starting point for an understanding of Marx's peculiarly "historical" materialism. His historical studies of the class struggles in France, the French Civil War, the Eighteenth of Brumaire, and the German bourgeoisie are not a mere by-product of his politico-economic analyses; they are an essential component of his basic conception of the entire human world as being historical.

In spite of his presupposition that philosophic theory stands in the service of historical practice, Marx's criticism is not directed, as one would expect, at immediate political reality, but rather at the Hegelian philosophy of the state: instead of at the "original," at a "copy." The reason for this apparently "idealistic" turn lies within historical reality. The German political situation in the forties is an "anachronism" within the modern European world, dating from the French Revolution. German history has not even caught up with what has taken place in France since 1789. "We have shared in the Restoration of the modern nations without sharing in their revolutions. We were restored; first, because other nations dared a revolution, and second, because other nations suffered a counterrevolution, the one time because our rulers were afraid, the other time because our rulers were unafraid. We, with our pastors in the lead, found ourselves in the company of freedom on the day of its burial."[139] Germany has experienced only one radical act of liberation, the Peasants' War,[140] and it came to grief in the Reformation, in which Germany's revolutionary past manifested itself "theoretically," i.e., religiously. But today, "when theology itself has come to grief, the greatest bondage of German history, our status quo, will come to grief in philosophy," that is, in Marx's historical practice of philosophic theory. Intellectually, the Germans have already anticipated their future history in Hegel's *Rechtsphilosophie*, the principle of which transcends the present state of affairs in Germany. "We are philosophical contemporaries of the present, without being its historical contemporaries. German philosophy is the ideal extension of German history. . . . Among the progressive nations, there is a practical dissociation from the modern conditions of the state. In Germany, where these conditions do not even exist, there is critical dissociation from the philosophical reflection of these conditions. German philosophy of right and the state is the only part of German history that stands on a par with the official modern present. The German people must therefore include this dream history in its attitude toward existing conditions; not only these conditions, but also their abstract extension must be subjected to criticism. The future of the German nation cannot restrict itself to an immediate denial of its real political and legal conditions, nor to an immediate execution of ideal conditions. In its ideal conditions, it possesses the immediate denial of its real conditions; and, in the view of its neighbors, it has almost outlived the immediate execution of its ideal conditions."[141]

To what extent this criticism makes Marx an Hegelian or Hegel a "Marxist" is shown by Hegel's exposition of the differing relationship between philosophy and reality in France and in Germany. He, too, states that the principle of freedom is present in Germany only as notion, while in France it has achieved political existence. "The reality which has come to the fore in Germany appears as an act of violence of external circumstances and reaction against it."[142] The French have a "feeling for reality, for action, for getting a thing done. We have all kinds of commotion within our heads . . . and the German head prefers to lie quietly with its sleeping cap on, operating completely within itself."[143]

From this difference, Hegel drew the following conclusion: these two forms, each one-sided, of theoretical and practical freedom must be comprehended concretely out of the "unity of thought and being," the basic idea of philosophy. In actual practice, with this speculative move, he did not place himself above particular reality, but rather on the side of German theory.

With regard to the relationship of philosophy to reality, Marx took up a twofold position: he opposed the practical demand of a simple negation of philosophy, and also the merely theoretical criticism of the political party. The one side believes that German philosophy does not belong to reality, and would like to abrogate philosophy without realizing it; the other side holds that philosophy can be realized without abrogating it. True criticism must do both. It is a critical analysis of the modern state, and at the same time a dissolution of previous political consciousness, the final, most universal expression of which is Hegel's philosophy of right. "Only in Germany was the speculative philosophy of right possible, this abstract, rapturous thought of the modern state, the reality of which remains in the beyond. . . . Conversely, the German idea of the modern state, abstracting from *real man*, was possible only because and to the extent that the modern state itself abstracts from real man, or satisfies the *whole* man in a way which is merely imaginary. In politics, the Germans have *thought* what the other nations have *done*. Germany was their theoretical conscience. The abstraction and arrogance of its thought always kept pace with the one-sidedness and modesty of their reality. Thus if the status quo of the German political structure expresses the perfection of the *ancien*

régime, . . . the status quo of German political theory expresses
the imperfection of the modern state."[144] Marx's dominant interest
in theoretical criticism of the philosophy of right is based on this
practical significance of the Hegelian theory for German history.[145]

The dialectical unity in Marx's evaluation of German philosophy
and reality differentiates him from both Old and Young Hegelianism, which still lacked the practical or material viewpoint necessary
for the comprehension of the real history of the world. In the draft
of a preface to the *Deutsche Ideologie*, Marx derides the "innocent
fantasies" of the Young Hegelians, whose revolutionary clichés
are received with awe and horror by the German public. The purpose of the *Deutsche Ideologie* was to unmask "these sheep who
think themselves wolves" and were so thought by others, as well as
to show that the boasting of these philosophers merely reflects the
wretchedness of conditions in Germany.

"As German ideologues report," begins the section on Feuerbach, "in recent years Germany has gone through an upheaval without parallel. The decay of the Hegelian system, which began with
Strauss, has developed into a world-wide ferment, into which are
pulled 'all the forces of the past.' In the universal chaos, mighty
empires have been formed only to vanish once more, heroes have
emerged suddenly only to be hurled back into the darkness by more
daring and more powerful rivals. It was a revolution in comparison
to which the French Revolution is a children's game, a world
struggle in the presence of which the battles of the diadochi seem
petty. The principals displaced each other, the heroes of thought
overthrew each other with unexampled rapidity, and in the three
years from 1842 to 1845, more was set in order in Germany than
had been in the previous three centuries."[146] But in actual fact, there
is no revolution at all, but only the "decay of the absolute spirit."
The various philosophic "entrepreneurs" who had previously lived
off the extension of the Hegelian spirit speedily formed new alliances; they squandered their inheritance in mutual competition. "At
first it was carried on in a way rather ordinary and without imagination. Later, when the German market was flooded and, in spite of
every effort, the wares were not popular on the world market, the
business was destroyed in the customary German way: mass production of outwardly attractive goods, reduction of quality, sophis-
tication of raw material, false advertising, sham purchases, bill-
jobbing, and a system of credit without any basis in reality. The
competition turned into a bitter struggle, which we now acclaim,

construing it as an historic revolution, producing enormous results and gains. To evaluate correctly this philosophical medicine show, which awakens a beneficent feeling of national pride even in the breast of a respectable German citizen, the local narrow-mindedness of the whole Young Hegelian movement, in order to display the tragicomic contrast between the real accomplishments of these heroes and the illusions entertained about these accomplishments, it is necessary to take a look at the whole spectacle from a standpoint outside of Germany."[147]

In contrast to French criticism, German criticism never left the realm of philosophy, even in its most radical efforts. "Far from subjecting their universal philosophical hypotheses to searching criticism, all their questions arose within the framework of one particular philosophic system, the Hegelian. There is a mystification not only in their answers, but even in the questions themselves. This dependence on Hegel is the reason why none of these recent critics even attempted a criticism of the Hegelian system, however much they all declared that they had transcended Hegel. Their polemic against Hegel and against each other is limited to the fact that each takes a page of the Hegelian system and turns it against the whole, as well as against the pages taken out by the others. At first, pure, undistorted Hegelian categories were taken, such as substance and self-consciousness; later, these categories were profaned with more secular names, such as 'species,' 'the individual,' 'man,' etc."[148]

The real accomplishment of German criticism is limited to the criticism of theology and religion, under which ethical, legal, and political ideas were subsumed. The Young Hegelians "criticized" everything by the simple expedient of declaring it "theological"; the Old Hegelians "comprehended" everything as soon as it could be reduced to Hegelian categories. Both parties are united by a common faith in the rule of universal notions; the one side attacks this rule as usurpation, while the other considers it legitimate. The Old Hegelians want to conserve the old consciousness, the Young Hegelians want to revolutionize it, both equally far from the true historical situation—whether the consciousness they insist upon is "human" (Feuerbach), "critical" (Bauer), or "egoistic" (Stirner). "This demand that the consciousness be altered gives way to the demand that existing reality be interpreted differently, that is, be granted recognition by means of a different interpretation. In spite of their purportedly 'earthshaking' words, the Young Hegelian ideologues are the greatest conservatives. The youngest of them have found the right form of expression for their activity when they state that they are only fighting against 'clichés.' But they forget that they themselves have nothing but clichés to oppose to these clichés, and that they are not attacking the real world when they merely attack the clichés of this world. The only results of which this philosophical criticism was capable were a few, one-sided clarifications of Christianity from the viewpoint of history of religions. All their other claims are merely further embellishments of their pretension of having furnished discoveries of historic import with these insignificant clarifications. It never occurred to any of these philosophers to inquire into the relationship between German philosophy and German reality, into the relationship of their criticism to their own material environment."[149] The boundary of their theory was historical practice; within this limitation, they went as far as possible without ceasing to continue to exist in philosophic self-consciousness.

In opposition to this entire German ideology, Marx developed his materialistic view of history, which has since determined the thought of non-Marxists and anti-Marxists more than they themselves realize. In respect to Hegel's spiritual world, it makes no basic difference whether *Geistesgeschichte* after Hegel is given a material interpretation based on the economic factors of production, in general sociological terms, or based on "sociohistorical reality," whether history is organized by classes or by races. They all, like Marx, would comprehend "the real life-process" and the "particular way of living"; these are not unconditional, but are the very precondition for a particular mode of thought. "A point of view is not unconditional. It proceeds from real conditions, it never leaves them for a moment. Its preconditions are human beings, not in some fantastic abstraction and seclusion, but in their real . . . process of development under specific conditions. As soon as this active life-process is described, history ceases to be a collection of lifeless facts, as is the case even with the abstract empiricists, or an imaginary action of imaginary subjects, as is the case with the idealists."[150] Marx declares this conditionality of all historical existence alone to be unconditional. Hegel's metaphysics of the history of the spirit is developed thereby to the most extreme position possible, made temporal, and placed in the service of history.

From this historical point of view, Marx sees all previous history in the role of mere "prehistory" leading up to a total transformation of the existing economic situation, the way in which men produce their physical and intellectual life. To this "nodal point" in the history of philosophy there corresponds a point of intersection in the history of the world between the future and the past. The only thing radical enough to be compared to Marx is the converse program of Stirner, whose book divides the entire history of the world into two sections, entitled "Man" and "I."

d M. Stirner (1806–1856)

Stirner's book *Der Einzige und sein Eigentum* has usually been considered the anarchic product of an eccentric, but it is in reality an ultimate logical consequence of Hegel's historical system, which —allegorically displaced—it reproduces exactly. Stirner himself admits this derivation from Hegel in his discussion of Bauer's *Posaune*. At the conclusion of his history of philosophy, Hegel himself summoned men to grasp the spirit of the age and bring it from obscurity into the light of day—each in his own place. Marx, too, saw Stirner's book as a study of history after the pattern of Hegel, and furnished evidence in detail.[151] Stirner's Hegelianism is disguised by his ascription of names to the Hegelian categories which are popular, and thus gives an impression of being more concrete, presuming himself thereby to be above the history of the "spirit."[152]

The "individual and his individuality" draws life from the belief that it is the beginning of a new epoch, in which each individual "I" becomes the owner of his individual world. For this revolution, Stirner returns to "creative nothingness." Starting from this point, he outlines the history of the "old" and "new" world of paganism and Christianity against an eschatological horizon: "I" am the new beginning. To the citizens of the old world, the world was a material truth, after which came Christianity; to those of the new, the spirit became supernatural truth, after which comes Stirner, following upon Feuerbach. The last offshoot of the "spiritual" history of Christianity is the political, social, and humane "liberalism" of the left-wing Hegelians, which Stirner overtrumps with his "alliance of egoists." Radical—that is, without roots—as he is, he has put behind him the "worldly wisdom" of the Greeks, the "theology" of the Christians, and the "theological insurrections" of the most modern atheists.

For two thousand years, man has been at work trying to profane the spirit which originally was holy. The Christian faith in the spirit which gives life reached its final and highest form in Hegel. The process which began at the close of the Catholic Middle Ages came to a climax in him. Luther sanctified all secular being through faith; Descartes, through foundation in thought; and Hegel, through speculative reason. "Therefore Hegel, a Lutheran, succeeded . . . in applying the notion to everything. In everything there is reason, that is, Holy Spirit."[153] But in light of the "perfect bagatelle" achieved by Stirner, the difference between Luther, Descartes, and Hegel shrinks to nothing. They all believed in something divine within man, they were not yet aware of completely ordinary man, just as he is, who is his own "I." Finally, the "man" of humanitarianism still seemed to be a divine truth; but he is only a "solemn cliché," which Stirner transcends with his "absolute cliché" of the individual as the end of all clichés. Therefore his point of departure is neither spirit nor man, but exclusively himself. At the utmost limit of a lost faith in the Christian spirit and the pagan world, Stirner's "I" creates its world out of nothing. And it becomes evident that man has no universal "destiny" and "duty" at all,[154] for the significance of the individual resides solely and uniquely in his own individual power of acquisition.

If one nevertheless inquires after a universal destiny of man, one is still within "the magic circle of Christianity," and within the state of tension between universal (divine) "essence" and individual (earthly) "existence." Christianity, which was as concerned as was antiquity about the divine, never achieved an unambiguous history within the world. The Christian had before his eyes the salvation of the world as the "end of days," or the salvation of man as the "goal of history"; neither saw history in the immediate "moment,"[155] which is the temporal locus of the "I." Only man as "I," freed from magic, neither a citizen of the Christian kingdom of God nor an official in Hegel's spiritual kingdom of the world, is per se the history of the world—"and that transcends Christianity!" The individual has no concern for the rest of the world, which lies at his disposal. "If I rely upon myself, an individual, I am grounded upon the transitory, mortal creator of myself, consuming myself, and I may say: I rely upon nothing." Thus Stirner ends his historical system, based on the consummation achieved by Hegel, on a note of extreme reduction of everything to the finite and temporal, no longer considering the general "species" of man as Marx, but only the "I."

From the standpoint of the materialistic conception of history, Marx tore into this system in his criticism, *Sankt Max*, as a "spiritual-history" which has become "phantom-history." Stirner confuses the "local outcome in Berlin," that the entire world "is sick and tired of Hegelian philosophy," with his "individual" world empire. "In the case of a provincial Berlin schoolmaster or writer, . . . whose activity is restricted to hard work on the one hand and intellectual pleasure on the other, whose world extends from Moabit to Köpenick and is boarded up behind the Hamburg gate, whose connections with this world are reduced to a minimum by his miserable position in life, it is unavoidable, in the case of such an individual, that he have an intellectual need to make his thought as abstract as his person and his life."[156] Such a thinker must let philosophy come to an end "by proclaiming his own lack of thought as the end of philosophy and its triumphant entrance into corporeal life," while in reality he was only "spinning upon his speculative heel."

Marx's purpose is to demonstrate positively that Stirner is merely the most radical ideologue of decayed bourgeois society, a society of "isolated individuals." What Stirner liberates himself from are not real-life situations, but merely intellectual situations. He himself never sees through them because he is trapped in the private egoism of bourgeois society. Therefore he makes of the private individual and private property an absolute "category" of the individual and property in general. In opposition to this thesis of the property of the "individual," Marx demanded an expropriation, in order to give to man as "a member of a species" the world as his own. Stirner and Marx philosophize against each other in the same desert of freedom: Marx's man, alienated from himself, must transform the entire existing world through revolution, in order to be at one with himself under the new order; on the other hand, Stirner's "I," having freed itself completely from everything, has nothing else to do than turn back to its own nothingness, in order to make use of the world just as it is, to the extent that it is serviceable to him.

e B. Bauer (1809–1882)

Bauer's literary work begins with a criticism of the accounts of the synoptic Gospels, and ends with a profusion of historical studies which treat the revolutionary movements of the eighteenth and nineteenth centuries in France and Germany.[157] His thought is completely historical, as is true of all the younger Hegelians. The highest stage of intellectual activity is the historical process. In contrast to the left-wing Hegelians, who wanted to continue the practice of philosophy, he proclaimed the final end of metaphysics; for his own part, he devoted himself to a permanent criticism the "purity" of which did not permit a practical application. He sought neither to "transform" the existing world, nor "make use of it" for his own purposes, but, rather, critically to illuminate the historical situation. Even his attitude toward Hegel's consummation is determined historically; the conclusion of the Christian-Germanic world is seen against the background of the rising power of Russia. In 1853, he wrote a study entitled *Russland und das Germanentum*, which anticipates some of Dostoevski's ideas. In it, he analyzes the historical position of German philosophy.

Kant's philosophic and political ideas move within the limits of the French Revolution, in which he saw the highest surety for the natural moral tendency of man to progress. He arrived at his view of the task of history on the basis of his knowledge of this revolution. Fichte flattered the pride of the Germans by representing them as the primal creative people, and linked the restoration of the rest of mankind to the self-assertion of their nature. Hegel's consummation of knowledge, as a recollection of past history, represents a conclusion. He excluded from his presentation the possibility of a break with all prior civilization, and did not allow the question of a new age to arise. "All these German philosophers who expressed most grandly and purely the views of their nation were thinking only of the West—for them, the East did not exist—there was no relationship for them between the Germanic world and Russia. And yet Catherine, as early as in the time of Kant, had brought this entire land mass under the power of a dictatorship which far surpassed in power, influence, and historical significance that of Charles V of Spain or Louis XIV of France."[158] The question of today is "whether the Germanic world will survive the downfall of our old civilization (for nothing is more certain than its downfall), or whether the Russian nation alone will determine the new civilization, whether the age that is beginning will be called the age of Russia, or the German name will stand next to the Russian."[159] "The German question and the Russian question are the only two vital questions of modern Europe, but the latter is already so precisely formulated that its answer must precede that of the other. It is supported by an organization so great that the power to which its conduct is subject can determine the moment in which it wishes to provide the answer and cut through the Gordian knot."[160]

In connection with the dissolution of Europe, Bauer evaluates "the end of philosophy"[161] as the natural conclusion of an historical development, as a transition to a new organization of the world, both political and spiritual. "Is it a mere accident that philosophy, to which the Germans have dedicated their best minds for the past eighty years, should collapse at the very moment in which Germany, with all its National Assemblies, congresses, and trade conferences, is seeking in vain for the locus of inner strength which would be necessary to organize it? Is it a mere accident that the conquering power with which philosophy subjugated all the individual sciences, moral as well as physical, should be completely destroyed, that the supremacy which it has hitherto exerted over all other sciences should be called into question in the very moment in which the nation that convulsed the West in the name of philosophy . . . has likewise lost its offensive power? . . . Is it a mere accident, finally, that in the very moment in which the spiritual supremacy of the metaphysicians has attained its culmination a nation is asserting its dictatorship over the continent, a nation to which, from the very beginning of its existence, the philosophic work of the West has remained alien, which holds no brief with the metaphysics of the West, and which—we mean the Russian nation—knows only one point of view, what is practical? No! There is no doubt: the catastrophe which has simultaneously befallen the entire European political system, constitutionalism as well as metaphysics, is an inwardly consistent event."[162] The universities, Bauer continues in detail, have lost their attraction, their professors of philosophy are mere repeaters of antiquated systems; they no longer produce a single new thought which could move the world as in the past. The universal poverty of the time, a spiritual and economic "pauperism,"[163] has destroyed all interest in metaphysical studies. With good reason the number of students enrolled at the universities declines each year, while the engineering schools are growing. Even the academies bear witness to the decline of general studies, since they are filling out their ranks with the most ordinary men. "The nations which seek finally to come into being through the subjugation of nature need only the engineer, who builds industrial firms on new and logical principles, or overthrows previously fearsome difficulties in the setting up of means of communication. He is the man in whom the nations in their practical struggle with space and time put their trust.

But they have neither the time nor the inclination to listen to philosophers quarrel over the concept of time and space, nor to interest themselves in the skill with which these same philosophers make the transition from idea to nature. And the governments? The standing armies are their philosophic schools, which have agreed for the present to instruct the nations in the only system appropriate to the age: peace and order. At the universities, they only put up with the teachers of the old metaphysics as one puts up with an old ruin beside a new establishment as long as pressing needs do not demand its demolition." "And Europe is right. It is only expressing what German criticism had stated and begun to carry out ten years earlier. If Europe has turned away from metaphysics forever, this same metaphysics has been destroyed forever by criticism. There will never again be a metaphysical system set up, that is, none which will claim a place in the history of civilization."[164]

Instead, imperialistic dictatorships will dominate Europe, through which the question "Russia or Europe?" will be decided. "The illusion of the March Revolution that the time has come in which the members of the family of nations, protected by the new principle of equal rights against previous influences in their self-determination, will constitute themselves independently and work together in peace (an illusion which has been expressed in the . . . experiments of individual governments, as well as in the idea of a Congress of Nations and in the deliberations of the peace congresses), this illusion, as all the others which determine the era of a new freedom since the downfall of previous barriers of personal activity, must be dissolved in the recognition of a power more rigorously applied. They will all suffer the same fate as the illusion which sees a complete solution in individualism, the result of the last sixty years of revolution, but is forced daily to discover that this individualism is only a temporary arrangement; it comprises only *one* aspect, and is bound by an iron law to its opposite, imperialism and dictatorship."[165] The destruction of the old alliances and classes has robbed the individual of his personal importance as a member of particular bodies, and subjected him to an "expanded system of centralization and the absolute power of the whole." "Work has been freed; but its liberation has resulted in a more powerful centralization which grasps with an iron arm all the individual existences which felt happy and protected in their previous seclusion, compelling them to submit or perish." Once again there will be a law over mankind, just as in the old "military-theological world" before the French Revolution, taking mankind into its protection and ordering its emotions, thought, and volition according to fixed standards. But we do not yet have the "historical science of law" which could grasp the popular spirit of the masses as did the old moral order. In this area, the natural sciences still maintain their lead. Between the anarchy which faces us and the form of society and government which is yet to come, our contemporaries are rootless individuals, anxiously asking, "What now?"—supposing that their dissatisfaction with today already contains the strength of the future.

In contrast to them, Bauer takes his stand upon his own "self-being," as the true philosophical standpoint in periods of radical change. When the political power of Rome collapsed, the Christians were the "party of the future" precisely because they avoided all political activity. Similarly, what is necessary now is refusal to become involved in the existing order and assertion of oneself against the powers of government as the nucleus of a new community. "Like the early Christians, all who bear within them an idea transcending the moment are absolute strangers to the affairs of state. Just as the Christians opposed their passive resistance to the momentary victory of the Empire and waited for their future, so now entire parties have withdrawn into passive resistance against the dominant moment."[166] At such turning points of history, positive creative power necessarily appears negative. Toward the existing state and religious tradition, Socrates boasted of his lack of knowledge,[167] the Christians were concerned for nothing beyond the salvation of the soul, and, at the end of the Middle Ages, Descartes bade man doubt everything which is not based on self-consciousness. But just these "heroic deeds of negation"[168] created new worlds. Similarly, the important thing now is to will nothing—of the old—in order to give mankind dominion over the world. For this man needs a new beginning based on his own strength, a beginning which—in contrast to the revolutions of 1789 and 1848—must not be involved in any of the dead elements.

With Hegelian faith in the "eternal course of history," Bauer destroyed the present in his critical-historical works, surpassing the negativity of romantic irony in the same way as Kierkegaard, but for a different purpose. This criticism is absolute because it recognizes nothing as being absolutely valid, even negating itself in its own critical process. It is therefore quite deliberately different from the previous philosophic, theological, and political criticism of

Feuerbach, Strauss, and Ruge, who all desired to be positive and were therefore forced to be one-sided, while Bauer analyzes the various nonentities with stoical equanimity. The basic theme of his historical criticism was the French Revolution as the beginning of a universal destruction. But his own peculiar critical accomplishment consisted in the "discovery" of the Christianity both represented and at the same time attacked by Kierkegaard. His critical nihilism, limited only by his faith in history, did not have an extended influence in his own day, but more than a century later came to life once more in a new "party of the future." Political writers of the circle of the "Resistance" took up Bauer's ideas and applied them to the present.[169]

f S. Kierkegaard (1813–1855)

If Kierkegaard is not taken as a mere "exception," but as an outstanding phenomenon within the historical movement of his age, it becomes clear that his "individuality" was not at all individual, but a widespread reaction to the contemporary condition of the world. A contemporary of Bauer and Stirner, of Marx and Feuerbach, he was above all else a critic of the events of his time, and his *Either-Or*, in matters of Christianity, was also determined by the social and political movement. "In times like these everything is politics," begins the foreword to his two observations on the "individual" (1847), which concludes with the statement that what the time demands, namely social reforms, is the opposite of what it needs, namely something absolutely firm. It is the misfortune of the present to have become mere "time," wanting nothing more to do with eternity. In the work which Kierkegaard in 1851 commended to the present for "self-examination," we read in the discourse on the outpouring of the Holy Spirit that today hardly anyone can be found who does not believe in the "spirit of the age," no matter how much he may otherwise be blessed with mediocrity and stand under the curse of paltry regard. "Even he believes, firmly and obstinately, in the spirit of the age." He considers the spirit of the age something higher than himself, although it cannot be higher than the age, over which it hangs suspended like marsh gas. Or he believes in the "world spirit" and the "human spirit" of the entire species, in order in this manner to be able to believe in something spiritual. And yet no one believes in the Holy Spirit, who would have to be conceived definitely; but in the light of the Holy Spirit all those other spirits are evil. In an age of dissolution a man is unstable; he therefore prefers to rely on something unsteady, the spirit of the age, in order with a clear conscience to be able to yield to every breath of the age.[170]

By seeing himself as a "corrective against the age," Kierkegaard viewed himself historically, and oriented his task according to the character of the age. The individuality of the existence which decides for itself for or against Christianity has a precise relationship to the universality of the anonymous public course of world history. The individual is to make known "that the author . . . knows how to express absolutely decisively with a single word the fact that he understands his age and himself in relationship to it," that he has comprehended the fact that it is a "time of dissolution," as Kierkegaard doubly emphasizes.[171] It is a conscious reference to the "development of the world," namely leveling of all decisive differences, which led Kierkegaard to emphasize the isolated individual, while the same historical circumstances, in the case of Bauer, produced the critical position of "self-being"; in the case of Stirner, the nihilistic position of the "individual"; and in the case of Marx, the socialistic position of the "member of a class."

This attitude toward his own age and toward time in general also determines Kierkegaard's relationship to Hegel's philosophy. He saw it as representative of the leveling of the individual existence in the universality of the historical world, of the "dispersion" of man in the "world process." Similarly, his attack upon Hegel's "system" is directed not only against systematic philosophy, but also against the system of the entire existing world, as the ultimate wisdom of which he saw Hegel's philosophy of history. His criticism of Hegel and the age begins with the concept of irony (1841),[172] the "absolute negativity" of which he propounds as the truth of subjectivity against Hegel's systematic and historical interpretations. In *Philosophical Fragments* he explicitly denies Hegel's "system of existence," for there could only be a system of existence if from it can be abstracted that which its very essence implies, the ethical existence of the individual. In this divergence of the system from the world resides the truth of individual existence, for which the history of the world is merely concurrent and accidental. But Hegel's speculative way of thinking has ruined the nineteenth century for this seriousness of existence. "It is perhaps for this reason that our age is displeased when it must act, because it has been spoiled by speculation; . . . thence . . . the many fruitless experiments

by which man attempts to become more than he is, men joining
themselves together in social groups in the hope of influencing the
spirit of history. Spoiled by continuous converse with the historical,
man seeks solely that which is significant, man concerns himself
solely for what is accidental, the historical issue, rather than what is
essential, what is innermost, freedom, morality."[173] In comparison
to ethical existence, the "quantitative dialectics" of history is mere
trimming. But the Hegelian refuses to be content with the subjectivity of existing. With a kind of magnificent unselfishness, he sees
in every age a moral substance and an idea, as though his own existence were metaphysical speculation and the individual were the
generation. He commands a view of entire forests by taking no
notice of the individual trees.[174]

In the natural world, the single individual stands in immediate
relationship to his species; whoever improves a breed of sheep affects
all the individuals of the species. But when the individual is a
spiritually defined human being, it would be foolish to suppose that,
for example, Christian parents automatically beget Christian children. The development of the spirit is an act of the individual himself, and therefore it does not suffice to be born in the nineteenth
century, for a man cannot achieve his full stature with the aid of
history and his generation. "The more the idea of the generation,
even in ordinary thought, gains the upper hand, the more terrible is
the transition to being an individual existing man, instead of belonging to the species and saying, 'We, our age, the nineteenth century.'
I cannot deny that this is extremely difficult, and therefore great
sacrifice is required not to reject it. What is an individual existing
man? Yes, our age knows only too well how little he is; but this
is the peculiar immorality of the age. Every age has its own; ours
consists perhaps not in pleasure and enjoyment, . . . but in an . . .
extravagant disregard for the individual. In the midst of all the
jubilation over our age and the nineteenth century is heard the note
of a secret disregard for human life: in the midst of the importance
of the generation, there reigns a despair over human life. Everything, everything seeks to be included, everyone seeks to deceive
himself historically in totality, no one wants to be an individual
existing man. Thence possibly also the many attempts to hold fast
to Hegel, even on the part of people who have seen the difficulties
in his philosophy. There is a fear that if anyone becomes an individual existing man he will vanish without a trace, so that not even
the daily papers, . . . much less historical philosophers, will take

any notice of him. . . . And it cannot be denied: without ethical or religious enthusiasm, a man must despair upon finding himself an individual man—but not otherwise."[175] The apparent courage of the generation hides the real cowardice of the individuals, who dare to live only in great mass activities, in order to be something. The individual confuses himself with the age, the century, the generation, the public, the mass of mankind.

Since Hegel omits the individual, his talk of progressive "becoming" is mere illusion. In fact, he understands world history as the conclusion of a "being" which has already come to be, excluding any real "becoming," to which belong action and decision.[176] Just as irrelevant to the individual existence as Hegel's recollection of the past is the prophecy of his pupils about the possible progress of the world. In all seriousness, it can mean nothing more than an amusement such as skittles or cards, says Kierkegaard at the conclusion of his criticism of the age.

He was able to confront his age with a decision only because he, too, participated in its events, even though negatively. He himself expresses the manner of his individual participation in a metaphor: his age appears to him like a ship under way, upon which he finds himself, together with other passengers, but having a cabin alone for himself. The bourgeois reality of this being alone was an isolated private life, which, however, does not prevent him from following the public events of the world.

He saw in his little Denmark, as in "a complete preparation," the downfall of the European "constitution," in the face of which he considered the "individual"—who happens to be the basis of Christendom—as the sole salvation of the age. The progress of the world toward complete leveling and the Christian imperative to exist before God as oneself both seemed to him to coincide like a fortunate accident. "Everything fits into my theory [of the individual] completely; people will soon see how *I* am the one who understood the age," Kierkegaard notes, with the pride of the exception which understands the rule precisely because it is the exception.[177] He signalized the "catastrophe" of 1848, and thought he could predict that, unlike the Reformation, this time the political movement would turn into a religious movement. Driven faster and faster by growing passion, all of Europe has wandered into problems which cannot be answered in the medium of the world, but only in the presence of eternity. How long the state of mere convulsion will remain cannot be guessed, but it is certain that eternity will once again be considered, when the race has become fully exhausted through suffering and loss of blood. "To obtain eternity once more, blood is necessary, but blood of a different sort, not that of a thousand slain sacrifices; no, the valuable blood of individuals, of martyrs, the mighty dead, who can accomplish what no living man who has sacrifices slain by the thousands can accomplish, what these mighty dead themselves were unable to accomplish alive, but only dead: to force a raging mob into obedience, precisely because this raging mob was able to slay the martyrs in their disobedience."[178] In this decisive moment of "sudden change," only martyrs will be able to rule the world, but not as ordinary earthly rulers. What will be needed then are sacred ministers, not soldiers and diplomats: "Ministers who can separate 'the crowd' and make it into individuals; ministers who would not make too great claims on studying, and would desire nothing less than to rule; ministers who, when possible, though powerfully persuasive, would be no less powerful in silence and patient suffering; ministers who, when possible, though trained to know the human heart, would be no less trained in withholding judgment and condemnation; ministers who would know how to use authority to make sacrifices with the help of art; ministers who would be prepared, trained, and educated to obey and to suffer, that they might relieve, caution, edify, calm, but also compel—not by force, by no means, no, compel through their own obedience—and above all, suffer patiently all the rudeness of the sick without being disturbed. . . . For the human race is sick, and, speaking spiritually, sick unto death."[179]

Thus in spite of his polemic against Hegel's process, the force of the age led even Kierkegaard to historical speculation and, against Marx, to an anticommunist manifesto. He went so far as to predict the danger which would come when the catastrophe broke: false prophets of Christianity will then arise, inventors of a new religion, who, infected with demons, will arrogantly declare themselves apostles, like thieves in the costume of police. Thanks to their promises, they will receive terrible support from the age, until it finally becomes clear that the age stands in need of the absolute, and of a truth which is equally valid for all ages. With this view toward a restoration of Christendom through martyr-witnesses who allow themselves to be slain for the truth, Kierkegaard is the contemporary antithesis to Marx's propaganda of a proletarian world revolution. As the actual strength of Communism, Kierkegaard saw the "ingredient" of Christian religiosity which it still contained.[180]

g Schelling's Connection
With the Young Hegelians

The many-pronged attack made by the Young Hegelians upon Hegel's system was promoted by Schelling in his last years, as he lectured on philosophy in 1841 in Berlin. Among his listeners were such varied contemporaries as Kierkegaard, Bakunin, F. Engels, and Burckhardt.[181] The polemic with which Schelling opened his "positive" philosophy was directed against Hegel's ontology as being merely "negative," comprehending merely potential being but not real being as it comes to the attention of thought. With this last event in the history of classic German philosophy begins the "philosophy of existence" which Marx and Kierkegaard developed in opposition to Hegel, the one externally, the other internally.

The term *existentia* was originally a scholastic concept, the opposite of *essentia*. In the Christian philosophy of the Middle Ages, everything created by God shared in this dichotomy, but not God himself. Of him, it is true to say that his being exists essentially, because his essence is characterized by perfection, which is itself characterized by existence. Only in God do essence and existence occur together or as one. The demonstration of this was the purpose of the "ontological" proof of God of Anselm of Canterbury, and the same line of argument was taken by Descartes, Spinoza, Leibniz, and Wolff. The first criticism to attempt a radical refutation was Kant's, on the grounds that the "existence" of a "concept" cannot be separated from the concept itself. In concept, one hundred real dollars and one hundred potential dollars are indifferentiable; what differentiates them—the positive quality of "existence"—lies outside their "whatness," their essence. This critical distinction between *what* something is and the fact *that* it is was once more suspended by Hegel. His logic defines the "real" as the "immediate unity of essence and existence, or the inward and the outward." Therefore what, according to the older view, characterizes only the being of God, Hegel applies to everything which is, everything that is "truly" or in the "emphatic" sense a reality. For it is "trivial" to contrast essence as something solely inward to reality as something solely outward. Rather, essential being, that which is real and has effect, is the "idea" or the "notion." In contrast to this equation of essence and existence, Schelling insisted once more upon the contrast between a "positive" and "negative" philosophy, but not in order to return to Kant, but to go beyond Hegel.[182]

Schelling's philosophical turning against Hegel's "rational" philosophy to a philosophy centered on existence had been expressed long before his philosophy of mythology and revelation in the preface to a work by Cousin[183] (1834) and in his Munich lectures on the history of modern philosophy,[184] but it was publicly discussed in numerous writings only after the Berlin lectures.[185] We meet all the motifs of his criticism also in Feuerbach and Ruge, Marx and Kierkegaard, as well as in Trendelenburg, to whose criticism of Hegel, Kierkegaard frequently refers.[186]

In Hegel's logical ontology, Schelling misses the justification for dialectical progress and the transition from idea to nature. Pure thought cannot result in true movement or in any vital perception of the world, because there is no empirical basis for the deliberate lack of preconditions in its immanent movement. The synthesis of "becoming" out of pure being and nothingness is an illusion. An "abstraction of an abstraction," such as pure and vacuous being, can never proceed from itself, go toward something, and return to itself, or even give itself up to nature. This can be done only by something that really is, something positive.[187] The further definition of being in the dialectical progress of becoming is possible for Hegel only because a more substantial being already exists and because the thinking spirit itself is already such. What unknowingly guides the progress of Hegelian logic is its *terminus ad quem:* the real world, in which science makes its appearance, the perception of which is already presupposed.[188] Without its interpolation, Hegelian being would remain unfulfilled as what it is, namely, nothing.[189] Primary, highest being is itself a particular being, even if only as the thought of an existing subject that thinks.[190] But Hegel's philosophy of reason seeks being without anything which is to be, its idealism is "absolute" to the extent that he does not even discuss the question of positive existence. Hegel completely removed all these a priori empirical data, which were thus accidental,[191] by substituting the logical notion for that which lives and is real. He hypostasizes this notion by the strange expedient of ascribing to it a self-movement which it does not possess. As soon as his system takes the serious step from the negative aspect of existence, that is, the merely logical, into reality,[192] the thread of dialectical movement is broken completely, and there remains a "wide, ugly ditch" between "whatness" and "thatness" (*Was-sein* and *Dass-sein*). "A second hypothesis becomes necessary: for some reason, apparently to interrupt the boredom of mere logical being, it occurs to the idea to disintegrate into its components, thereby giving rise to nature."[193]

Philosophy claims to have no presuppositions;[194] but its first pre-supposition is that the purely logical notion tends by its very nature to overthrow itself only to fall back upon itself. Thus something is *said* concerning the notion which can only be *conceived* of something living. The second fiction is the breaking off of the idea from itself in order to be determined upon nature, whereby the empirical data which were previously rejected return through the back door of the idea's unfaithfulness to itself. What Hegel factually proves is only that the purely rational part of reality is insufficient. His theory of being comprehends only the negative-universal aspect of being, the "non-inconceivable" and "non-preconceivable" portion without which nothing exists; but it does not include that whereby something exists, truly positive existence which contains the negative within itself.[195] In order to raise philosophy to this positive level, it is necessary to will what has being, "what is or exists." Instead, Hegel takes that which merely has being—the culmination of all logical notions—and makes of it pure being, which in fact is "nothing," just as whiteness does not exist without a white object.[196] Through this differentiation of the negative being of essence and the positive "having being" of existence, philosophy is confronted with one great final transformation. On the one hand, it will give a positive explanation of reality, without, on the other hand, depriving reason of its priority of being in possession of the absolute *prius* "even of the godhead."[197]

Hegel's notion of God, on the contrary, is one and the same with the creative force of the notion, the purely rational nature of which he denied.[198] As a result, the popularization of his ideas inevitably lead to the pantheistic-atheistic conclusions of his pupils. For if the absolute is not conceived as historical existence but as a process immanent to the notion, then the knowledge which man has of God becomes the only knowledge which God has of himself.[199] Thus the "deepest note of popularity" for this system is reached; it is astonishing only that it did not gain a following in the "mass of the public," even though it is probable that Hegel himself would not have been pleased by this dilution of his thought. All this derives from the single blunder of treating logical circumstances as though they were real.[200]

In the introduction to his Berlin lectures, Schelling formulated his starting with "existence" even more radically. Positive philosophy, unlike negative-rational philosophy, proceeds not from thought to being, but from "immediate being" to thought. Its thought is free because it is intentional thought, and its system is "a priori empiricism," whose point of departure is that which "blindly has being" or "immediately exists." The true path of man as a philosopher, and even of God, is to liberate the self from blindly encountered being, the "ecstatic," to "break away" from what blindly exists to true independence. What blindly exists "cannot help" existing; it is "accidentally necessary." "The entire world is this suspended, immemorial blind existence."[201] From the Hegelian point of view, Marheineke could just remark that Schelling actually confirms Feuerbach's theology, since he is content with "such trivial categories" as "literal" and "figurative."

In Schelling, the problem of being in the anti-Hegelian movement arrived at the point where Heidegger once more took it up. For who could deny that the "facticity" of *Dasein*, which lies in the brute fact of *Dass-Sein*,[202] that *Geworfenheit* and *Entwurf* correspond to "immediate existence" and "breaking away" from this necessary accident? The difference with Schelling lies in the fact that Heidegger erects upon Kierkegaard's basis a "system of existence" (*Dasein*) which lacks Schelling's tension between the negative and positive philosophy of "reason" and "existence." For him, the general "essence" (*Wesen*) of *Dasein* resides only and immediately in the "existence" (*Existenz*) of the individual,[203] which remains unaware of its origin and goal and has simply "to be" by accepting the innocence of *Dasein*—the "cannot help it"—as "guilt." For Schelling, the Hegelian "being" was a mere "potentiality for being," in the sense of a possibility, and stood in contrast to reality. For Heidegger, this potentiality for being becomes an ontological predicate, precisely of real existence (*Existenz*).[204]

Schelling was not alone in his opinion that Hegel's ontology lacked immediate reference to real existence and observation; the Young Hegelians agreed with him. His statement that Hegel only "affects" the real and transforms it into a "wasteland of being" agrees with the criticisms of Feuerbach, Marx, and Kierkegaard; the latter defends Schelling against Hegel because he, at least, made an attempt at putting a halt to the reflection of thought upon itself.[205] Therefore Schelling was justified in stating that it was superfluous to come to the defense of the Hegelian philosophy against him. Even those who took Hegel's part and opposed him "did so partially at least not in order to oppose positive philosophy; on the contrary, they themselves also wanted something of the sort. Only they were of the opinion that this positive philosophy would have to be erected on the basis of the Hegelian system and could not be erected upon any other; further, the Hegelian system lacked nothing more than their effort to continue it in a positive direction. This, they thought, could come about in a continuous progress, without interruption and without any turning back."[206] Contrary to this attempt, by 1832, Schelling had already become convinced that Hegel's philosophy could not be extended; it would have to be interrupted in order once more to return to the "course of true progress."[207] Ten years later, when he gave his lectures in Berlin, he could pride himself on having most of the Hegelians in his audience, after they had shown him every respect in public and in private: "The tension is unbelievable, and already . . . all precautions have been taken to see that the enormous pressure to get into the largest lecture room, itself relatively small, does not cause any difficulties."[208] But his assurance of victory was bitterly disappointed, while the revolutionary impulse of the Young Hegelians reached a high point in its polemic against Schelling's "latest attempt at reaction."[209] But a decade later, reaction had overpowered even the Young Hegelians and brought their "progress" to an end. The political and ecclesiastical reaction of the fifties pulled the historical rug out from under their philosophy, which was obligated to the spirit of the age, while Schopenhauer's view of the world achieved enormous, though delayed, effect, traceable less to its positive content than to its attitude of alienation from politics and history.[210]

"Pessimism" and "optimism" became the catchwords of the hour,[211] because they corresponded to the prevalent resignation and discontent, as well as to a desire for better times. In the process, it does not make any basic difference whether the "philosophy of misery" had its start in the misery of economic (Proudhon), universally human (Schopenhauer), or spiritual (in the Christian sense [Kierkegaard]), existence; whether the philosophy of misery or the "misery of philosophy" (Marx) was emphasized; whether the valuelessness (Bahnsen) or the "value of life" (Dühring) was asserted; or whether, further, its value was considered estimable (E. v. Hartmann) or "inestimable" (Nietzsche). All these phenomena have in common that existence itself was called into question. Schopenhauer in particular became the philosopher of the hour, "sitting like a speculative Job upon the ash heap of finiteness," thereby gaining the regard of Kierkegaard.[212] This world of suffering is produced by blind "will," and "idea" can give no better counsel than to cease to will.

The history of German philosophy has not recognized the full significance of this reaction, nor the preceding and basic revolution in spiritual and political life. For this reason, it has never achieved a true understanding of the history of the nineteenth century. In contrast to the antirevolutionary philosophers of the French Revolution, who came from the noble classes, the German philosophers of the age of the bourgeois reaction are without breadth of vision and without a fixed spiritual position. In the sixties, the opinion was prevalent that Hegel and his pupils had been passed by the return to Kant prepared by Schopenhauer, without awareness that this revitalization of Kant was connected with an inability to deal with those questions which had evolved from the dialogue with Hegel in the forties.

The customary "appendices" to the history of philosophy since Hegel indicate, by their external form, that "exhaustion" of the spirit, with reference to idealism, was considered as its disintegration, while the destructive force of the movement remained unrecognized. In his two-volume work on Hegel, K. Fischer disposes of Hegel in two lines; and, as late as the fifth edition (1916), Friedrich Überweg's *Grundriss der Geschichte der Philosophie* devotes only two pages to Engels and Marx. Even F. A. Lange's history of materialism does not mention Marx at all in the text, and in the list of sources only as the foremost scholar in the field of national economics. In spite of the review of his dissertation in the *Hallesche Jahrbücher*, Kierkegaard remained unknown, and the critical-historical dissolution of Christianity was left to a theology the dogmatics of which, analogously to systematic philosophy, had itself already degenerated into history of dogma and church history, comparative religion, and psychology of religion. The danger and importance of the radical philosophical and theological movement, of which the original Hegelians were well aware, was forgotten. It could appear that nothing significant had taken place between Hegel's death and the revitalization of Kant. Seen in the context of the real total course of the century, however, this apparently so unmotivated return to Kant can be explained: the bourgeois intelligentsia had ceased in practice to be an historically oriented class, thereby losing the initiative and impact of their thought. The philosophical movement of the forties comes to an end, together with the end of the political revolutionary movement. The return to Kant, in the way it took place, shows a retreat behind the limit of questioning which the Young Hegelians had reached in religious, social, and political matters.[213] In the history of Neo-Kantianism, the bourgeois-Christian world, the very foundations of which had been attacked, experiences an apparent revitalization, and only in the crisis of Neo-Kantianism did there arise the attempt to refurbish Hegel.

3 The Refurbishing of Hegelian Philosophy by the Neo-Hegelians

The principle of the refurbishment of Hegel was first and most clearly determined by B. Croce, through the distinction between a "dead" and a "living" portion of Hegelian philosophy.[214] The dead portion consists primarily of the natural philosophy, but also the logic and philosophy of religion; the living, the theory of the objective spirit, to the extent that its absolute systematic claim can be reduced to an historical claim. This division, which denies Hegel's system as a whole, is also true of the German revival of Hegel. But while in Italy the tradition of Hegelian philosophy continued uninterrupted because the questions contained in it were never made oversubtle, in Germany a deliberate revival was necessary, in the face of the general disapproval into which Hegel had fallen. Schopenhauer's prophecy[215] that the period of Hegel's fame would be a permanent blot on the escutcheon of the nation and an object of ridicule of the century was destroyed by Neo-Hegelianism: Schopenhauer's memory was preserved only through the mediation of Nietzsche, and, at the beginning of the twentieth century, Hegel, contrary to all expectations, seemed to be resurrected. Having gone for eighty years without a new printing, the *Logik* appeared in two new complete editions; Hegel's posthumous works were published, together with a commentary on his early works, a Hegel lexicon, and a literature on Hegel which already passed counting.[216] The new Hegelianism itself has become historically self-conscious and reflects its changes.[217] A Hegel Society and Hegel Congresses demonstrate the study of Hegel. But the matter in question is not the outward fact of this revitalization, but whether and how the present time answers the question, posed by the original Hegelians, of history and of time in general.

Dilthey above all understood historical consciousness as a problem of philosophy and of the spirit. In the process, his treatment of Hegel's philosophy of the historical spirit is of decisive importance. This is true both for his *Einleitung in die Geisteswissenschaften* (1883), which sought to be a criticism of "historical" reason, and for his later works on the structure of the historical world. More than all the other Neo-Hegelians together, Dilthey revitalized Hegel's historical mode of thought and made it productive for the present through his *Jugendgeschichte Hegels* (1905) and his systematic historical works. His dialogue with Hegel goes back into the sixties—in which also appeared Stirling's *The Secret of Hegel*—and continues through the last years of his scholarly life. A sort of midpoint is provided by his revision in 1900 of K. Fischer's work on Hegel.

As in the case of Haym, the critical criterion for Dilthey's distinction between what is permanent in Hegel's philosophy and what is transitory is historicity. He considers the nonsensical portion of Hegel's philosophy to be the contradiction between the historical consciousness of the relativity of all historical reality and the metaphysical conclusion of the system.[218] The self-contained form of the absolute system is incompatible with the "great, future-laden thought of development" and the "facts" upon which it is based. "How can this claim be maintained in the midst of the immense system of worlds, the multiplicity of forms of development which take place upon them, the limitless future which is hidden in the womb of this universe, continually marching forward to new structures."[219] In contrast to Fischer's evolutionary interpretation, however, Dilthey is certain that the developmental theory of the nineteenth century is not that of Hegel, but, rather, contradicts him.[220] Hegel's final systematization of nature and the spirit in the logical form of a syllogism presupposes a world which is no longer ours. "If the spirit is to attain to absolute knowledge upon this earth, then it must once more become the mid-point of the world; and in fact Hegel's entire natural philosophy is constructed from this point of view. The unfolding of the spirit upon earth must reach its conclusion in the principle of the discovery of the absolute philosophy, and Hegel's entire history of the world and history of philosophy is constructed from this point of view."[221] For Dilthey, the "foolishness" of such a claim is beyond doubt, because his idea of the "reality" of the world is measured by "facts" discovered by positive sciences, and not, as in the case of Hegel, by the philosophical notion.[222] "Through all Hegel's writings runs the hopeless struggle against the sciences of nature, man, and history."[223] This reference to Hegel's polemic attitude toward the procedure of the positive sciences is the more noteworthy in that Dilthey indicates thereby the groundlessness of any revitalization of Hegel which disguises the unbridgeable

gap between modern scientific consciousness and Hegel's speculative "science," forgetting that Hegel called the sciences the "edifice
of an understanding deserted by reason," whose unhindered expansion is inadmissible.[224] But if Hegelian philosophy is the only true
"science," it is necessarily different from Dilthey's *Weltanschauung*
doctrine, which undertakes merely to be the "expression" of metaphysical "needs." As a result of this radical difference in their criticism and evaluation of science and reality, Dilthey finds Hegel's
effort to comprehend the totality of the spiritual world, historical
"of itself," to contradict the explanatory principle of the absolute spirit. Hegel subordinates to the "real" historical world of the
human spirit an "ideal" realm of logical predicates which, being
timeless, are incapable of explaining a real development in space and
in time. In the nineteenth century, Hegel's philosophy came to grief
on this interweaving of a "chimerical" notion of a development not
temporally conditioned with what is real in time. Similarly, the attempt to accomplish the wrongly conceived task by means of dialectics is completely useless and must be discarded.[225] To conceive
this task aright and enable it to be accomplished, Dilthey reduces
Hegel's speculative "comprehension" of the notion of reality to an
analytic "understanding" of its most universal structures. Thus the
"logos" of what has being is transformed into a relative "meaning,"
and Hegel's ontology into an empirical analysis of reality.[226] All that
remains as the permanent portion of Hegelian metaphysics is the
"historical intentions" with their metaphysical-theological foundation removed, which is precisely the final portion of the system.
Hegel's lasting significance rests in his theory that the nature of
every phenomenon of life is to be understood historically.[227]

Besides logic and natural philosophy, Dilthey also considers that
the philosophy of religion has succumbed to the course of history:
the thesis of the absolute status of the Christian religion, which is as
central to Hegel's historical systematization of the spirit as is the
central place of the earth in the universe to his natural philosophy.
"What is imperishable in him" is rather the recognition of the
historical relativity of all truths, even religious and ethical. "Everything is relative, absolute is only the nature of the spirit itself, manifesting itself in all this. Nor is there an end to the knowledge of this
nature of the spirit, no final formulation, each is relative, each has
done enough if it has sufficed for its age. The relativity of the notion
of property logically led to the revolution of the social order; this
great doctrine also led logically to the relativity of the doctrine of

Christ."[228] But with this transformation of the absolute into history, which—because it makes everything else relative—itself acquires the nature of the absolute, Dilthey does not refurbish Hegel, but rather the Hegelianism peculiar to Ruge and Haym, whose criticism anticipates all the motifs of his occupation with Hegel. But in contrast to the radicalism of the Young Hegelians, Dilthey's historicization of Hegel's metaphysics has no revolutionary purpose. What he sought to put forward was ultimately only a philosophical "attitude" which had grown out of his "reflection upon the logic of historical consciousness." In him, the metaphysical passion of Hegel's spirit, revealing the depths of the universe, is reduced to a "reflection" which knows that the reigning "anarchy in all the deeper persuasions"[229] is to be removed neither through the refurbishing of an old metaphysics nor through the construction of a new one. Hegel's world, dominated by spirit, becomes "sociohistorical reality," in itself neither rational nor irrational, but in an indefinite way "significant." But the significance of the world is no longer based upon the world itself, but is the product of our attitude toward the world and our understanding of it. "We" do not import meaning into life from the world, but rather the contrary: "we are open to the possibility that meaning and significance only come into being in man and his history." The great "objective forces of human history"— the objective spirit of Hegelian philosophy—constitute the substance to which the individual must cling if he is to understand human life on the basis of himself, without dogmatic theology or metaphysics. That this answer to the problem of history is not really a philosophical answer, that in fact Dilthey's lifelong efforts to construct a philosophy on the basis of historical consciousness per se were brought to nought by the honesty of his knowledge, cannot hide the fact that he was the only productive refurbisher of the Hegelian position, precisely because he surrendered it.

The "revival of Hegelianism" was officially proclaimed by Windelband[230] in a speech in 1910. Today, its formulation can only produce a kind of amazement at the impoverishment of the spirit. Without any original reference to Hegel, this official revival takes place by means of a detour via a revived Kant. "If post-Kantian philosophy was forced to direct its conceptual work toward the development of the system of reason, it was in fact a necessary step forward which led from Kant, via Fichte and Schelling, to Hegel. The repetition of this process in the progress of the most recent philosophy from Neo-Kantianism to Neo-Hegelianism is not accidental, but is an objective necessity."[231] Like Kant before him, Hegel is now experiencing "in the alternation of generations the alternation of recognition." This progress in the return to Hegel means that Kant's critique of reason demands an historical basis, his critique of natural science must be expanded to the domain of "cultural science," the latter having developed so enormously in the historical sciences of the spirit. But in order to make an abstract study of the copious development of "rational values," Hegelian philosophy is necessary; it is best able to illuminate the principles of the spiritual world. "It is a hunger for a world view that has seized our younger generation; it seeks to be filled in Hegel." But Windelband avoids the question of what changes in the spiritual environment have begotten this attitude: "it suffices that it is present, exploding with elemental force!" The younger generation yearns to return from metaphysical desolation to "a spiritual basis for life"; this need is particularly well met by Hegel's universal philosophy of the historical spirit, which demonstrates a "total meaning of reality." In addition, there is the "evolutionary optimism" of his theory, whereby he gains the victory over Schopenhauer's pessimism and Nietzsche's boundless individualism. In this sense, the return to Hegel means a step forward. But Neo-Hegelianism must keep itself free from the "strange external trappings" and "metaphysical rashness" of the older Hegelianism; the dead husk must be discarded and the living kernel retained. But this fruitful kernel which remains is the insight that we participate in the reason of the world as a "species undergoing development." Today it is impossible not to see that this program is nothing but husk, and its concepts the clichés which an optimistic bourgeois class borrowed from Hegel, clichés which by no means display any "elemental" force of the spirit.

In basically the same way, but with emphasis on the Prussian element and the Protestant consciousness of freedom in Hegelian philosophy, G. Lasson[232] understood the task of Hegelianism to be a result of Kantianism. In his twofold capacity as Prussian Hegelian and pastor, he undertook the meritorious new treatment of Hegel's works. The weakness of the repeated path from Kant to Hegel is shown by J. Ebbinghaus.[233] Soon after his enrollment in the party of Hegel's "absolute" idealism, he went back once more to Kant, only to end up finally with Wolff.

Only R. Kroner seriously undertook Windelband's program, in his work *Von Kant bis Hegel* and in a *Kulturphilosophie*[234] organized along Hegelian lines. Kroner says: "To understand Hegel means to see that he simply cannot be transcended." That he never-theless could intend to refurbish Hegel for the present has its basis in his equation of the immediate task with that accomplished by Hegel.[235] The presuppositions of philosophy have altered in the meantime; but to master this upheaval the reclamation of the classical tradition is necessary, such as we see most perfectly incarnate in Hegel. Above all, Hegel attained the reconciliation of the secular and religious consciousness, overcame the antithesis between antiq-uity and Christianity, and forged a bond uniting the Greek with the German spirit.

During the war, Hegel's dialectical identity of the ideal with reality was patriotically simplified: "German idealism and German sense of reality," according to Lasson,[236] have revealed themselves overwhelmingly as a "miraculous unity" in Hegel's philosophy and in the world war. According to Kroner,[237] reality and the ideal pur-sue and accompany each other step for step in the German state. In this period the actual historical meaning of the academic refurbish-ment of Hegel revealed itself as the self-assertion of the Christian-Germanic, or more precisely the Prussian-Protestant self-conscious-ness, disseminated in battlefield editions of philosophy.

If this Hegelianism had really understood, as it proclaimed, that the presuppositions of our life and thought have basically altered, and Hegel's world is no longer our own, had it taken seriously its paren-thetic insight that Hegel's destiny was Feuerbach,[238] it would have had to recognize the apparent contradiction between the absolute and historical sense of Hegelian philosophy as being a contradiction only because we no longer believe in the absolute status of Chris-tianity and the spirit founded upon it. Hegel's eschatological sys-tem can be comprehended only on the basis of this hypothesis, but the idea of an infinite progress of spiritual history a priori sets aside the Christian consciousness of time, even as secularized by Hegel.

Therefore the actual inconsistency in Kroner's Hegelianism re-sides in his affirmation of the Christian nature of the Hegelian spirit while denying the conclusion of the history of the spirit which follows from it. He does not want to admit that Hegel's philosophy is in fact the consummation of the principle of Christianity, and that his mediation between antiquity and Christianity is not an "inherit-ance," but was already called into question a century before.

In order to resolve the contradiction between "system" and "his-tory,"[239] Kroner reads into Hegel a contradiction which is much too modern to be characteristic of Hegel, namely the contradiction

between historical limitation and unlimited "validity." Hegel suffered this contradiction with "magnificent unconcern." On the one
hand, he stated that every philosophy is its age grasped by thought,
and on the other the eternal absoluteness of the spirit. Kroner first
seeks to explain the unity of these two statements on the formal dialectical level. Hegel's considered insight unites both because history
is itself a work of the spirit. "History is not merely history, it is also
the productive spirit of mankind, it is the house . . . in which it . . .
resides, and which it continually constructs and reconstructs."[240]
Kroner sees his further development of Hegel in this light, and
hence misunderstands the conclusion which he represents. He himself remarks that Hegel's philosophy contemplates the past like no
other, conscious of an historical completion, and the subsequent
course of events seems to confirm this view all too well.[241] But instead of elucidating the supposed contradiction between system and
history in the light of this historical question, Kroner asks: what
right had Hegel to claim "absolute validity" for his system "in spite
of" this historical resignation? Hegel equated the truth of his system
with truth per se, at the same time thinking more in historical terms
than anyone before him, while on the other hand his history of philosophy belongs to the system. He resolved this contradiction by
making a systematic aspect of the historical in order to escape the
danger of historical relativism.

But historical relativism is a very modern problem (and now no
longer even modern); it did not exist at all for Hegel. His peculiar
accomplishment is not the transformation of the historical aspect
into a systematic one—Dilthey was the first to undertake this—but
rather the reverse: the joining of the systematic to the historical. It is
no accident that only after Hegel do we have an historical aspect of
the systems of philosophy, a so-called history of ideas and problems.
But in his case the historicization of philosophical truth is equally
far removed from both historicism and validity. The modern claim
for validity per se derives historically from pre-Hegelian philosophy, and is a postulate of Neo-Kantianism. And only when confronted with a postulated truth per se does its historicity collapse
into an historicism which relativizes validity. As a consequence, the
contrast of system and history is not resolved, as Kroner would like,
through "metahistorical" history and the formalistic argument that
the thesis of the historicity of the spirit is itself metahistorical because it seeks to "be true" for all epochs. If Hegel causes the eternal
to be manifest in the temporal, this is not the result of any formal

dialectics, but an intrinsic metaphysics of the Christian logos. In fact, as Kroner himself remarks,[242] his philosophy includes within itself the Christian consciousness of the "end of all things," because Hegel does all his thinking conscious of the absolute significance of the historical appearance of Christ. He lived in the "millennium," in which "we all shall meet again," "namely in reality—for in my thoughts I have long dwelt there."[243] Therefore not any present moment at all was for him "the highest," but only that which, like his own, is a "final link" in the "sacred chain" of the past, now appropriated by thought in its full extent. Not any present moment at all, as in the case of Hegel, is "both beginning and end" and "for this reason absolute," rather only the time which extends from Thales to Proclus, from thence to Hegel, makes it possible to write a period after the "now" of "up to now." Of course, Hegel says literally that "for now" the series of spiritual configurations has been concluded by his own work. But this does not mean "solely" "that his philosophy is the highest form attained up to now,"[244] as any "convinced" philosopher would have to assert of his system; the time intended here is the time of "from age to age,"[245] which Hegel counts in thousands of years, just as he measures the truth of systems according to the measure of their totality.[246] Only in every sacred moment, not in every moment, is there a spiritual "jolt" which alters from top to bottom the sum total of all that has gone before. And hence there is no interruption of Hegel's historical way of thinking in favor of a systematic way, but *after* Hegel there occurs a complete change in the spirit of the age, and consequently in systematic thought. Thus Hegel's statements concerning the history of the spirit hitherto do not simply have the innocuous meaning "that the present as such is not and cannot be the object of historical study."[247] The "simple truth" of such statements is that, aware of a conclusion, Hegel effects the consummation of the history of the spirit. But then it is no longer necessary to defend him against the charge that he viewed his own age as the end of history. It was obvious to Hegel that an empirical course of events continues indefinitely. In contrast, the history of the notion was indeed concluded in him. And so, in spite of his historical resignation, Hegel did not claim absolute validity for his system; rather, as a result of his historical knowledge, he was more the master of systematic thought than any before or after him. In his unification of all previous history, the accent does not lie on the "previous," accented by Kroner, as though no reference to the future were intended. Rather, the accent is on the entire "thus far now," that is, "finally," the world spirit has come; and this entirety is deliberate goal. Hegel left an open question as to what might proceed from it in the future; but because three epochs have now been concluded, and not because the present cannot be studied historically, did Hegel consider history, taken abstractly, to be ended. He, more than anyone else, encounters the present in an historical context based on the recollected past. It is no accident that his immediate successors carried their philosophy into an anticipated future, only to view their own period from that point of view as "historical" in the opposite sense of the word. While Hegel brought into the present what had been and had come to be in the past, the criticism of the existing order by the Young Hegelians brought into the present, from the opposite direction, the task of the future. In contrast, Neo-Hegelianism silences both the past and the future because it misunderstands the historical significance of the break with Hegel, and does not recognize that our own *Geistesgeschichte* (spiritual history) begins with the collapse of the Hegelian spirit.

Scholz, too, undertook to explain the supposed contradiction between the absolute and transitory significance of Hegel's system.[248] From the formal point of view there is an inconsistency which cannot be completely removed; but the absolute claim can be explained from the fact that Hegel lived in the consciousness of having grasped the absolute for the first time as it should be grasped if it is to have any influence on reality, namely, as "constantly relativizing itself." The absoluteness of his system would then consist in an absolute relativism, because Hegel—in contrast to Kant—represents the absolute as an ever-present spirit, immanent in reality.[249]

In the realm of natural philosophy, Scholz considers that this attempt failed completely; in the realm of the historical spirit it met with partial success, namely: if the proof of the meaningfulness of all events is interpreted as a hypothetical procedure, designed to overcome the difficulties which stand in the way of a belief in the meaning of history, even in Hegel's own consciousness. In any case, a basic evaluation of Hegel's meaning for the present has to proceed from the fact that he was the first to make philosophy aware of itself as the thought of time; this thesis affects the entire relationship of philosophy to the historical reality of our lives. This joining of the temporal character of philosophy to its substantial content guarantees the permanent importance of Hegel. Every philosophy is the self-consciousness of its age; but this does not mean that it is a mere mirror of its age, but rather that every generation must undertake the task of philosophy with new strength and in its own way, precisely because there is no *philosophia perennis* in any external sense of eternity. The positive consequence of the transitory nature of philosophy is its continual rejuvenation. The significance of this idea can be properly evaluated only when one remembers the previous state of affairs. "Prior to Hegel, no great thinker dared so courageously to put philosophy into the stream of life. They all stood on the bank, thinking it their job to build a bridge across it, for eternity. The few who thought otherwise were not great thinkers, but skeptics or relativists. Hegel's true greatness rests on his break with Eleaticism, without even dipping his fingers into skepticism or relativism in the definitive sense of the word. Fate was so kind to him that not even the shadow of such a thought ever appeared to him. His spirit was anchored so firmly to the absolute that his peculiar brand of relativism was a mere product of his great consciousness of absoluteness."[250] Thus philosophy becomes an eternally living activity, excluding any revival of past systems. The philosopher who is to do justice to this transitory nature must be the most persevering and productive spirit of his age, a man with the surest capacity for making distinctions in order to be able to differentiate what is valuable from what is worthless, and what is significant for the future from what is merely topical. Because Hegel combined the broadest view with the deepest critical ability, he was the first after Aristotle and Leibniz to achieve an attitude toward history which does not remain external to philosophy. By viewing the past as having an effect on the future, philosophy becomes the consciousness of the age, and continuity becomes the principle of the historical process (in Hegel's case, to an exaggerated extent, with which we cannot agree, because an absolute continuity contradicts the transitory character of philosophy). But one thing remains decisive: the grasp of historicity of the spirit, a concept to which Hegel gave a peculiarly German development.

The refusal of Hegel's philosophy, in contrast to that of Vico and Herder, to consider the future, even for a moment, is interpreted by Scholz as a mere renunciation of romantic speculation, a "sense of reality." The original Hegelians saw the eschatological conception of Hegel's system as the problematic basis of its inclusiveness; Scholz reads into the temporality of Hegelian philosophy a motif of limitless self-rejuvenation which cannot be derived from Hegel himself. He did his thinking in the "old age" of the spirit, which corresponds to the complete fulfillment of the spirit which has returned to itself. But for an evaluation of Hegel's significance, the decisive question is whether this boundary of his historical meaning is not completely borne out by the history of the German spirit subsequent to him. In this case, the actual significance of his metaphysics of the historical spirit lies in the fact that it brought to an end the epoch of "Germanic" philosophy as "Christian" philosophy.

J. Plenge was acutely aware of the epochal boundary which separates us from Hegel. It caused him to pose once more the question of Hegel's attitude toward history and to draw Marx into the study of Hegel.[251] His study once more opened the doors to the questions which had been asked a hundred years before by the Young Hegelians, particularly Bauer. It begins with the statement that it would be unworthy of Hegel merely to repeat philosophically what he had already said better. In his eyes, this would be the very death of the spirit, which lives only in overcoming new dichotomies. "He would ask us, was I not followed by a new antithesis, coming from without and within? Formally, as the empirical knowledge of a scientism broken up into separate disciplines. Materially, as the socialism of Karl Marx, which grew out of my own school, drew its sustenance from my dialectics, and developed into the irresistible course of the social adventure. You want to return to me as to the vehicle of a victorious universal affirmation; but you are too weak to reach me beyond these antitheses, instead of being brought to a halt by them—as though my period had been older and more finished than even I was willing to construe it."[252] Hegel and Marx both recognized the fundamental historical nature of all human life; it is our duty to make use of their design, without giving uncritical support to either.[253]

The way in which Hegel, and even Marx, viewed the system of our world was limited; only in the course of the nineteenth century did "eruption of energy" set in, which ultimately led to the World War and the upheavals following in its wake; Hegel could not foresee this at all, and Marx only insofar as it pertained to capitalism. The inventions of the nineteenth century, together with the organization of economic, social, and military structures which they made possible, opened for the first time a "world" which now included in actual fact all the historical nations of the earth. With reference to this new world, Plenge attempts to restructure the previous history of Europe and to determine Hegel's historical place from the standpoint of the present. The Christian Middle Ages, the

modern era, and the nineteenth century, with which once more a
new epoch begins, are the three subsidiary periods of an historical
era preceding the newly arrived "world-system" which begins with
the World War. In contrast, Hegel's conclusion of world history
with the Christian-Germanic world was still based upon a Europe
not yet aware of the historical significance of America and Russia,
nor the new dialogue with the East. "Between us and Hegel there
lies a period of history for which we do not have a generally recognized descriptive name. The 'Age of Capitalism' refers only to the
. . . continuing process of economic reform, . . . 'Bourgeois Society,' without the connotations . . . so illogically attached to the
word 'bourgeois,' is really too pleasant-sounding for such an explo-
sive event, and the future misunderstandings could easily be even
more dangerous, because a socialistic work-army would need at least
as much discipline and order as does the middle class. One solution
is to take the famous phrase applied by Goldberger to America at
the turn of the century . . . and extend it to the entire nineteenth
century: 'the century of unlimited possibilities'! This phrase well
describes the reaching out of mankind toward greater and greater
technical achievements, and the whirl of personal success for the
fortunate exploiters and profiteers in this rising market. But probably the best name for the demonic power of this evolutionary process, which transcends anything that has ever existed previously, is
'eruption of energy.' All the forces of the earth are unleashed; the
effect is to overwhelm mankind, to force our society into an incal-
culable transformation, beyond the control of any insight or of any
will, which finally . . . through the fault of everyone, if there is
fault, ends in world war and world revolution. In the process, the
picture of reality is extended by the results of science to immeasurable and yet calculated cosmic distances, . . . with the result that
everywhere the eternal equilibrium of unchangeable laws is lost. . . .
'Development' becomes untamed erupting energy which pays us no
regard. Human society is torn loose from all universal systems regulating its behavior, both orderly systems and systems assumed for the
sake of order; any consistent view of all reality is lost. There is no
longer such a thing as a world view. There are only sciences! Specialized sciences fitted into no comprehensive order of a total system. . . . The only principle in the background is an absolute faith
in science as a method which reaches a sure knowledge even of the
last things, leading to the tendency to conceive these last things as
an absolute force which man may use in his maintenance of society,

but whose product he is. Material . . . as energy! Friedrich List and Karl Marx both put their faith in force. This is the world of the real nineteenth century, of which Hegel had no idea, although it was coming into being under his very eyes."[254]

Through all the struggles of races and nations, peoples and classes, the overcoming of time and space, through the technification of the world, everywhere pushes forward to a consciously organized world system and to a "history of world organization," although it is impossible to know whether this tower of Babel, with its confusion of tongues, can be made a lasting creation. Hegel, in contrast, wanted to explain the absolute completely in the midst of the structure of his own world. In spite of the breadth and assurance of his gaze, his view of the world was still completely restricted to the Christian-humanistic historical entity, although even during his life the study of history began to transform the traditional picture, revising it in the light of newly discovered historical sources from the Orient.[255] This restriction to a central portion of the European domestic world has an even deeper basis in Hegel's philosophical position, namely, in his idea of the state and of religion. For Hegel, the French Revolution was *the* great event; but he intentionally overlooked the possibilities arising from it, even though in his own period it was obvious that the Age of Revolutions was just beginning. "He had no premonition of the bewildering influences which were to come upon Europe from all over the world. This is the fault of his method itself, for what dialectics has once dealt with indeed remains alive within it as a suspended component, but it never has a basically new effect in its own right." The ultimate basis for this closed character of Hegel's system lies in his attitude toward Christianity. "For Hegel, Christ is the revolutionary of his synthesis, unifying once and for all the world which stands at the point of utmost antithesis. Hegel viewed Christ without reverence or emotion . . . with deep scientific tension as the problem of problems, because in him the infinite becomes finite, because he, as 'one of these,' in his very human life, includes within himself the All, demonstrating conclusively the essential union of man with God."[256] In this, abstract logical process loses all its original, human power; actually, the Protestant State suffices for this historical purpose of the Hegelian world. On the basis of this total spiritualization and secularization of the Christian supernatural world, the transition from the period of actual Christianity to the modern era has no particular significance for Hegel; the modern era loses the impetus of historical progress which, in the stormy course of the nineteenth century, finally drives it to the First World War. The modern era becomes simply a fulfilled Christianity, completely aware of itself. "Hegel overlooks the transformation of the picture of reality into an entirely new dimensional structure and the incipient unification of all the civilizations of the earth into one single theater, which distinguishes the modern era, no matter how much it remains a subsidiary period in the course of Europe's decline, from all the human past and thereby from the beginning of the West European period with the age of 'Christendom.' Of course it remains true that the assurance of being superior to the world which typifies the modern era at its peak is built upon this same assurance of Christendom, subjected to God; this then grows into the frenzy of scientific superiority of the nineteenth century, enslaved to its own products!"[257] In contrast to the demands of his method, Hegel's historical system only apparently concludes with a complete reconciliation and systematization of the experienced antitheses. In reality, its political conclusion is a radical hostility between warring national states; its religious conclusion is a Protestantism split up into sects, itself still an irreconcilable opponent of Catholicism.

Hegel's achievement in the study of history, magnificent in spite of these limitations, was only corrected in the nineteenth century by F. List and Marx, both of whom, in contrast to the bourgeois historians, sought with a quick grasp to shape their assumptions concerning the meaning for the world of the new technical and socioeconomic advances. "Without overmuch concern for Hegel, List viewed the national state as the vehicle of history and provided it with the economic weapons with which to secure its equal rights with other nations, upon which the world system was to grow. Marx, the spiritual heir of Hegel, like List, considered economics and science to be the real job and basis for existence of mankind; just for this reason he saw them as the seedbed of class conflict and of class wars, which he considered would have to be undergone until the final world system of work was achieved. We take them both only as examples of the way the facts of the age shoved Hegel's system aside, showing more simple ways for thought. Simultaneously, there have been attempts to answer questions which Hegel had answered wrongly or not at all, or had not even seen—incomplete answers, in their one-sidedness lacking the scope for which Hegel strove."[258] It remains to be asked whether the basic concepts of Hegel's philosophy of history can be applied to the phenomena of the period of the world just beginning, e.g., the dialogue of the various cultures and the leveling process going on beyond this dialogue.[259] Against this possibility one would surely have to say that only as corrected by Marx can Hegel be used for a real understanding of the nineteenth century. "Above all, with a proper view of the basic truth discovered by Marx, one can see in the utilization and subjugation of all the forces of the earth and the reaction upon society of the instruments forged for this purpose an enormously powerful effect of the productive power of our human spirit, of which we are able to see only the immediate consequences. . . . But these, one and all, are other paths than Hegel took."[260]

In contrast to this sociological appropriation of Hegel, formulated in such a way that it might frighten off the casual reader, the academic Neo-Hegelianism of the twentieth century, totally derivative, shut its eyes to the historical insights of Marx and Sorel. It failed to understand the philosophical problem of the nineteenth century. The German intelligentsia became aware of so-called Marxism only through the political propaganda of National Socialism and its polemic staging.

In Germany, original Hegelianism was forgotten; the revival of Hegel came about through Neo-Kantianism. But in Russia the Hegelianism of the forties, in the form of nihilism, Marxism, and Leninism, underwent continuous development down to the present, and made history. In 1931, there were three congresses on the occasion of the centenary of Hegel's death: one in Moscow, and two others in Rome and Berlin. In spite of their mutual antipathy, they belonged together as had the Hegelian right and left of the previous century. As then, the greater degree of culture belonged to the epigones, the historical power to those who wanted progress and interpreted Hegel by means of Marx. But over one thing the idealistic and materialistic dialectics of both parties were agreed: the notion that they were able by a simple operation to separate the "dead" from the "living" portion of Hegel's philosophy and to use either the spiritual "content" or the dialectical "method" in isolation.[261] But the real sundering of what Hegel's mediation had joined together had already been accomplished, in opposite directions, by Marx and Kierkegaard. That these two dogmatic and mutually opposed critics of Hegel were both under the spell of his concepts demonstrates the power of the spirit which could produce such extremes.

III The Dissolution of Hegel's Mediations in the Exclusive Choices of Marx and Kierkegaard

1 The General Criticism of Hegel's Notion of Reality

The attack of Marx and Kierkegaard separates precisely what Hegel had unified; both overturn his reconciliation between reason and reality. Marx takes Hegel's political philosophy as the object of his criticism; Kierkegaard's attack is directed against his philosophical Christianity. The result is not only a dissolution of Hegel's system, but at the same time of the entire system of the bourgeois-Christian world. The philosophical basis of this radical criticism of the existing order is their quarrel with Hegel's notion of "reality" as "unity of essence with existence."[1] The attack is directed primarily against a single statement from the preface to the *Rechtsphilosophie:* "Whatever is rational is real; and whatever is real is rational."

It is difficult today to conceive of the serious struggle and enormous excitement which this sentence produced even during Hegel's lifetime. As heirs of the nineteenth century, we think of "reality" as "facts" and "data," of a realism which could arise only after the breakdown of the Hegelian Real-Idealism.[2] The immediate cause of this transformation in the notion of reality was none other than

Hegel himself, through his unparalleled elevation of the real, contemporary world as the content of philosophy. It is essential that philosophy give to the content of consciousness the form of thought and thus "reflect" upon reality; it is equally essential to realize that its content is none other than the content of the world or empirical reality. The degree to which philosophy corresponds to reality can even be considered an external touchstone of its truth. But not any and everything in existence is "reality" in the same sense and to the same degree; for this reason a distinction must be made between real existence and what is merely "transitory," "meaningless," "accidental," "ephemeral," and "rudimentary" existence. Such an accidental reality, which equally could not exist, does not deserve the "emphatic" name of a genuine reality.[3] As a result of this distinction between accidental existence and reality, Hegel could see in the dictum of the preface to the *Rechtsphilosophie* quite "simple" statements, while for his successors they were extremely ambiguous, depending upon whether the first or the second portion of the statement was emphasized, that is, whether the criterion of interpretation was taken to be the sole reality of the rational or the sole rationality of the real. But even E. Gans, the editor of the second edition of the *Rechtsphilosophie*, could find no fallacy in Hegel's statement; he defended it as a simple truth against the attacks which it had drawn. "Straightforwardly interpreted," it says no more and no less than that "in order to be true to its nature, what is truly rational continually takes form in the world, achieving actuality; and what truly exists in the world contains within the world the justification of an inherent rationality."[4] Hegel's statement is nevertheless by no means self-evident; this is proved by the simple fact that Hegel found it necessary to justify it, and particularly the way in which he did so. He appeals to both God and the world, in contrast to the theologians and philosophers who objected to the rationality of reality. This statement, says Hegel, must be immediately obvious to theologians because it is precisely the doctrine of God's dominion over the world, and philosophers must know enough to realize that "not only is God real, he is that which is most real; he alone is truly real." Thus—like the efficacy of the "idea"—the equation of reason with reality is based on a philosophy which is also a theology. Its ultimate goal is to bring about, through recognition of the conformity of God and the world, the reconciliation between "self-conscious reason" and "reason which has being," that is, reality. Ruge and Feuerbach, Marx and Kierkegaard, challenged the validity of Hegel's reconciliation between reason and reality in a way which anticipated the arguments from Haym to Dilthey.

Ruge took over Hegel's notion of reality as the union of essence and existence; precisely for this reason he could object to Hegel's development of this principle in political philosophy on the grounds that he had absolutized (in the sense of universal essence) particular historical forms of existence which in themselves are transitory. In this manner Hegel allowed reason to withdraw from present, real life, losing historical "interest" in these political forms as such.[5] He gives the reader two separate foundations: at times, he supports individual existence upon a universal essence; at others, he supports a universal essence upon historical existence.[6]

Feuerbach's criticism is not directed against the failure of the logical predicates in the face of historical existence, but against their inadequacy for empirical existence,[7] which for him was the criterion of what was real. As empirical existence, reality appears immediately as what it is; but for Feuerbach this immediacy means not merely "not-yet-mediated," as it does for Hegel, who defines being, with reference to the spiritual activity of mediation, as that which is *im*-mediate. By confronting being, within itself, as the immediate, speculative thought can apparently resolve the antithesis between real being and thought without difficulty.[8] In contrast to this excogitated immediacy of being, which is thought, Feuerbach asserts the positive and primary character of immediately empirical reality, which nevertheless is not something from which thought is absent or which is self-evident. Even more direct than empirical observation of objective reality, for which one must go outside of himself, is the mere subjective mental image of something, which can remain completely with what is imagined. In order that empirical observation may exhibit that which has being in its reality, there is need for a change such as that from the oriental dream world to Greek clarity, which allows us to view that which has being in its genuine form.[9] In contrast, the intellectual "observation" of Hegelian speculation is a constructive cogitation in identity with itself. It does not achieve this real world, but only the actualization of a theological, shadow world. Christian theology is also the basis for Hegel's thesis of the rationality of the real. "The identity of thought and being is . . . merely the expression of the divine nature of reason—the expression of the fact that . . . reason is the absolute essence, the embodiment of all truth and reality, that no antithesis to reason exists, that reason is all, just as in traditional theology God is all, i.e., all that is essential and truly has being."[10] Only empirical being, palpable to the senses, which is different from the thinking of a thought, attests like an incorruptible witness the true being as the independent reality of something which itself has being. But for the thinker as a thinker[11] there is no real being and no real existence, no *Dasein* and no perseity, although these all exist for the man who thinks empirically.[12]

With this concentration on existing reality as perceptible to sense, always having particular significant content, Feuerbach deliberately relinquishes ontological inquiry into undifferentiated being, such as is predicable equally of everything that has being.[13] For purely ontological thought, the empirically defined "this" is not essentially different from any other "this" or "that," because the logical form of "this" in every case is the same for all data of the senses.[14] Thus Hegel's dialectic of empirical certainty dissolves every really individual "this" in universal logic, although the logic is a mere word, "this" alone being an object. But just as the word is not the object itself, so an imagined or merely stated "this" is not an empirically real being, the existence of which for me is always a "practical" question. The mystery of being does not reveal itself to thought in universal terms, but to empirical observation with the senses, to sensitivity and passion. "Passion alone," says Feuerbach, agreeing with Kierkegaard, "is the token of real existence," because passion alone is really concerned whether something exists or not. For purely theoretical thought, this practical distinction is of no interest.[15] Even mere sensitivity has a fundamental and not merely empirical significance for the knowledge of being. The hunger which demands nourishment reveals in the sense of emptiness a corporeal understanding of the abundance characteristic of really existing being. Like love and passion, it is an "ontological proof" of an involved existence which is really concerned with "being." Only what effects a change in my situation, what is pleasant or painful, can show that it "is" there or is lacking. And only thought which allows itself to be interrupted by observation, sensation, and passion, rather than continuing on always within the confines of itself can comprehend, even theoretically, what "reality" is.[16]

Marx and Kierkegaard also directed their criticism of Hegel against the notion of real existence. Ruge is concerned primarily with the ethical and political existence of the body politic, Feuerbach with the sensuous existence of the corporeal human being, Marx with the economic existence of the masses, and Kierkegaard with the ethical and religious existence of the individual. For Ruge, historical existence reveals itself to "interest," understood politically; for Feuerbach, all real existence reveals itself to sense perception and passion; for Marx, social existence is revealed through empirical activity as social practice; and for Kierkegaard, ethical reality is revealed to the passion of inner activity.

The Russian and Polish Hegelians of the forties were also concerned with "reality." The existential motif of their disagreement with Hegel is expressed with an openness and directness which is peculiarly Slavonic. The classification of the Russian intelligentsia into "Westerners" and "Slavophiles" is determined philosophically by their adherence to Hegel and his pupils or to Schelling's attack upon Hegel. But Schelling's demand for a positive philosophy of reality is determined by Hegel's claim to comprehend reality as the sole content of philosophy; for this reason, both sides of the Russian dialogue with German philosophy were determined by Hegel. The best evidence of this is the letters of the Russians studying in Germany at the time: for them, "Germany" and "Hegel" are practically synonymous.

During his transition from the Western to the Slavonic orientation, J. W. Kirejewski[17] (1806–1856) developed the thesis that Western thought *in toto* lacked a full and complete relationship between the person, as an intellectual spirit, and reality. He saw the ultimate basis for this in the Western European relationship between church and state, between faith and knowledge, as it developed after the breach between Rome and Constantinople. The destructive ideas of the eighteenth century, with their incorrect view of Christianity, are the result of the exaggerated rationalism and fragmentation of Western European thought. In Hegel's philosophy, the universal European belief in the susceptibility of ideas and reality to organization reached a climax. But Hegel brought the systematization of the world on the basis of human self-consciousness to an insurpassable culmination, creating thereby the basis for Schelling's demonstration of the "negativity" of this mode of thought, alienated from living reality. "And so today the situation of philosophy in the West is as follows: conscious of the restricted sphere of validity of all rational abstraction, it cannot progress further in this direction; neither can it find another, different direction, precisely because all its strength has been used up in the completion of the old system of abstract rationalism."[18] In contrast, Russia has preserved the tradition of the ancient church in its monasteries and in the doctrines of the Fathers of the Greek Church; this tradition includes the concentration of all spiritual activity upon the whole, unfragmented individual. "Western man is incapable of comprehending a living relationship of all spiritual faculties, in which none acts without the other. He has no understanding of that peculiar equilibrium of soul which characterizes the individual brought up in the Orthodox tradition, determining even his external mien and gestures. Even amidst the whirlwind of fate . . . his conduct displays . . . a final depth of calm, a moderation, dignity, and humility which witness to an equilibrium of the soul, a deep inner harmony of feeling for life. In contrast, the European seems to be in a perpetual ecstasy, his appearances are officious, almost theatrical, he seems full of agitation in his inward and outward bearing, which he nevertheless exerts himself frantically to bring into artificial symmetry."[19] But if Europe will only surrender the principles of its untrue Christianity and return to the stage of pre-Christian thought, then, perhaps, it will be capable once more of receiving the true doctrine, which is neither allied nor opposed to reason.

M. Bakunin (1814–1876) interpreted Hegel's philosophy primarily as a "new religion," in the hope of solving all his personal problems through complete dedication to the "life of the absolute." He even sought to determine the course of his brothers' and sisters' lives on the basis of Hegelian philosophy. "Through the spirit everything lives, everything is brought to life. Only to a dead eye is reality dead. Reality is the eternal life of God. . . . The more alive a man is, the more he is permeated by self-conscious spirit and the more alive reality is for him. . . . *What is real is rational.* The spirit is absolute power, the source of all power. Reality is the life of this spirit; as a consequence, it is all-powerful. . . ."[20] In the introduction to his translation of Hegel's *Gymnasialreden,* he proclaimed the necessity of a reconciliation with reality, and explained Hegel's sentence to himself in a way that was radically optimistic; for to revolt against reality is the same as to destroy every vital source of life within oneself. "Reconciliation with reality is within . . . all spheres of life the great task of our age; Hegel and Goethe are the principal representatives of this reconciliation, this return from death to life."[21]

Starting from this point, V. G. Belinskij (1810–1848) drew further conclusions. He writes to Bakunin: "In the smithy of my spirit there has grown a peculiar meaning of that great word 'reality.' I look at the reality which I previously so despised, and tremble, . . . because I have come to understand its rationality, because I see that nothing must be removed from it, that no aspect of it must be criticized. . . ." "Reality! I repeat this word when I arise and when I go to bed, by day and by night, and reality surrounds me, I feel it everywhere and in everything, even within myself, in that new alteration which is noticeable in me from day to day." "Now I daily meet with practical people, and it is no longer hard for me to breathe in their company . . ." "I form my judgments of everyone not according to some preconceived theory, but according to the data given by himself, I know how gradually to enter into the proper relationship with him; therefore all are content with me, and I am content with all. I am beginning in conversation to discover interests in common with people with whom I previously thought I had nothing in common. I demand only what may be demanded of me, and for this reason receive only good and nothing evil. . . ." "Not long ago I discovered a great truth which (until now) had been unknown to me. . . . I recognized that there is no such thing as a fallen man, who has betrayed his calling. I no longer look down upon anyone who has ruined his life through a marriage, who has extinguished his reasoning power and his genius in his occupation; such a man has no guilt. Reality is a monster, armed with iron jaws: it seizes by force anyone who does not surrender himself freely and devours him."[22] In this Russian reinterpretation of Hegel's emphatic reality we find the passion peculiar to Belinskij, which caused him to reconcile the highway of reason, not with the "blue sky" of infinity, but with "garden variety" reality.[23] He ceased to be a romantic, and sought to serve Russian reality, up to and including an absolute recognition of Russian absolutism, which estranged him from all his friends and ultimately brought him to a crisis which finally forced him into opposition to Russian reality. Under the influence of Bakunin and Herzen, he went over to the side of the left-wing Hegelians. Two years after the letter just quoted, which he wrote to Bakunin, he cursed his base longing for a reconciliation with miserable reality. The human personality is more than all history, and Heine is more than all the "professional thinkers" who defend reality as it is.[24] I have long guessed that Hegel's philosophy is merely one thing among others, perhaps very important, but that the absolute nature of its conclusions is rot, that it is better to die than to accept them willingly. . . . For him, the subject is not an end in itself, but only a means for a momentary expression of the universal; and for him, the universal is a Moloch, for it flaunts itself in the subject and then discards the subject like a worn-out stocking. I have particular reasons for being angry with Hegel, for I feel that I was basically true to him when I made my peace with Russian reality. . . . All Hegel's chatter about morality is complete nonsense, for in the objective realm of thought there is no morality, just as there is none in objective religion. The destiny of the subject, the individual, the personality, is more important than the destiny of the entire world and more important than the health of the Emperor of China (i.e., Hegelian universality)."[25] The only true reconciliation with reality seems to him to be that which Ruge preached as the turning of theory into practice.[26] He viewed Hegelian philosophy, indeed, as the highest achievement of our culture, but at the same time as the means whereby this culture dissolves itself in transition to a new form which the world will take; to turn away from Hegel means revolt against philosophy in general.

The philosophy of Count A. Cieszkowski (1814–1894)[27] is basically no less Slavonic, but in its abstract discipline and the way in which it construes questions, it can scarcely be distinguished from German Hegelianism. In 1832, he studied at the University of Berlin, attending the lectures of Michelet, Hotho, Werder, Gans, Henning, and Erdmann. His impression of the Germans was that they were the most "synthetic" and at the same time "abstract" of peoples. "They have no sense at all of concrete life. In Germany, everything is met with healthy and powerful approval; but all these elements lack organic and harmonizing accord. Everything dissolves into particularities, and thus the total picture is itself something abstract, a chimera, a *caput mortuum*. Knowledge and life, ideality and reality, are separated from each other. There is a constant hither and thither."[28] Cieszkowski sought to resolve this mutual "alienation" of theory and practice, of knowledge and life in the Slavonic spirit through a "philosophy of action," based on a "Christianism" which was to bring Hegelian "logism" back to the original Logos of the Christ-word.[29] In Hegel's philosophy he saw a final state which could be overcome only by passage from the element of thought to the element of will, because only the will reveals a new future.[30] On the other hand, Hegel's consummation also motivates Cieszkowski's return to the origins of philosophy in the original stages of Greek philosophy,[31] to which Marx, Kierkegaard, and Lassalle also referred in contrast to the end reached by Hegel. His disagreement with Hegel centers on the latter's notion of "universality." The true spirit is not a universal and impersonal "thinking," but the spiritual activity of the "complete self."[32] For the most part, Hegel contrasted the universal to the particular and resolved both in real individuality —but occasionally he also contrasted the universal to the particular *and* the individual. Cieszkowski explains this terminological confusion thus: that in every case the universal remains dominant for Hegel, so that in spite of his protestations of arriving at the concrete "one," the individual is surrendered to universality and the subject to substance. According to Cieszkowski, the third way in which a resolution may be achieved between individuality and universality is through the perfect individuation of the spirit in the divine person. Only there does substance actually become subject.[33] In other words, Cieszkowski wishes to reach the Christian position within the framework of German philosophy of the spirit, a position which Kierkegaard developed in a paradoxical manner against the thinking of the universal. His goal is a philosophy of life in activity, which has God as the self, perfect in itself, freely creating from itself.[34]

From this standpoint there develops a far-reaching correction of Hegel's philosophy of history, which Cieszkowski expanded in his *Prolegomena zur Historiosophie*.[35] In contrast to Hegel's division of history into the Oriental world, the Greco-Roman world, and the Christian-Germanic world, he sets forth the following threefold division: Ancient world to Christ, Christian-Germanic world to Hegel, and, as the third, the future, which is a component of all historicity, not only in the case of prophets but in every case, because history is not a deterministic process, but a free and responsible activity. We stand at the beginning of future history; it will bring the synthesis of the pre-Christian and Christian forms of the world. In his writings he discusses the concrete question of the future world as the reform of Christianity and of political society.[36]

2 The Critical Distinctions of Marx and Kierkegaard[37]

a Marx

In his criticism of the Hegelian philosophy of right, Marx does not quarrel with Hegel's principle, but only with the concrete working out of what he, too, asserted: the unity between reason and reality, and between universal essence and individual existence. The essence of political existence is the *polis*-nature of the social

organism, the "political universality." Hegel is not to be blamed for
depicting "the nature of the modern state, . . . but for holding 'that
which is' to be the essence of the state."[38] He mystifies *empeiria*,
thereby turning the content of his idealistic exposition into "the
crassest materialism," justifying philosophically that which merely
happens to exist. His mediation between bourgeois society and the
state does not really remove the contradiction between private-
egoistic and public-communal existence; in fact, this very mediation
points up this contradiction as being unresolved. "Hegel's greater
insight lies in the fact that he perceives the separation between bourgeois society and political society as a contradiction. But his error
lies in being content with the appearance of a resolution."[39] In
reality, the "real man" of bourgeois society is the private individual
of the existing constitution, because the abstraction of the state as
such and that of private life are in themselves a contradiction.[40]
"Therefore if a man would act as a real citizen, would achieve
political importance and effectiveness, he must step out of his bourgeois reality, abstract from it, withdraw from this entire organization into his individuality; for the only existence which he will find
for his status as a citizen is his pure, unmixed individuality. Without
him, the existence of the state as an administration is impossible; and
without the state his existence in bourgeois society is impossible.
Only in contrast to these solely present social units, only as an individual, can he be a citizen of the state. His existence as a citizen of
the state is an existence which lies outside of his social forms of
existence, and is therefore purely individual."[41]

As a citizen of the state, the bourgeois is necessarily a stranger,
someone external, foreign to himself—just as foreign and external as
his private life remains to the state. His state is an "abstract" state
because it is a bureaucratic administrative power which abstracts
from the real, that is, private, life of its citizens, just as they as individual human beings abstract from it. The choice of a man to be a
member of a state remains necessarily an abstract choice so long as
the real situation of life presupposes a separation between public and
private realms.[42] As a private individual, separated from the public
universality of life, he is himself privately determined. In communistic society, the reverse is true: there, the individuals as individuals participate in the state as their *res publica*. Communism, as
Marx, the Hegelian, understood it, is the true resolution of conditions of existence which have no essence, the social identity of essential reason with the real existence of human beings existing as a

social organism. Hegel achieved this reconciliation only in the realm of thought; in reality, he took as the content of his description the historically conditioned contradiction between private-individual and public-communal existence.

This modern contradiction existed neither in antiquity nor in the Middle Ages. For the actual private individual of antiquity was the slave who had no share in the social organism, and who, therefore, was not a "human being" in the full sense of the word.[43] In the Middle Ages, every sphere of private life was at the same time public and corporate; the life of the people and the life of the state were identical, even though the individual man was not free. Only the French Revolution produced the abstraction of private life, together with the merely political state, conceiving the freedom of the bourgeois as a negative freedom from the state. But true freedom is a freedom of the highest social nature, in a "society of free men." And yet the sense for freedom left the world with the Greeks, and the sense for equality vanished with Christianity into the blue of heaven. Only a radical revolution of the existing conditions can produce a *polis* extended to become a cosmopolis, the "true democracy" of a classless society, realizing Hegel's philosophy of the state in the element of modern society. Only in the *polis* of the future can the world in fact become our own, the isomorphic "otherness" of our selves; in contrast, the bourgeois, private individual necessarily remains alien in his public world.

In complete contrast to this philosophic communism, Kierkegaard treated the private individual radically, as an "individual," opposing the inwardness of self-being to the outwardness of wholesale relationships. For him, the two unique prototypes of individual existence are Socrates in the Athenian *polis* and Christ against the entire world, consisting of both Jews and Gentiles.

b Kierkegaard

In the last pages of his *Concept of Irony*, Kierkegaard indicated that it was the "task of the age to translate the results of scientific knowledge"—meaning Hegelianism—"into personal life," to "appropriate" them personally. For it would be ridiculous for someone to teach throughout his whole life that "reality" has absolute significance and then to die without any further evidence of this validity than having proclaimed this wisdom. The negativity of irony is useful as a means of verifying reality; it teaches us "to make reality real" by giving it the appropriate emphasis.[44] After finishing his dissertation, Kierkegaard undertook the trip to Berlin in order to hear Schelling, expecting of the latter's positive philosophy an elucidation of reality which he did not find in Hegel. We read in one entry of the journal: "It makes me happy to have heard Schelling's second lectures—indescribably so. Long enough have I sighed, and my thoughts sighed within me. He spoke of the relationship between philosophy and reality; and, when he spoke the word 'reality,' my thoughts leapt for joy within me as did the child in Elisabeth's womb. I remember almost every word which he said from that moment forth. At this point, perhaps, clarity is possible. This one single word, which reminded me of all my philosophical torment and agony."[45] This expectation immediately gave way to disappointment: "My age does not allow me to assimilate drop by drop what I would scarcely open my mouth to swallow all at once. I am too old to listen to lectures, just as Schelling is too old to give them. His whole theory of 'potencies' betrays complete impotence."[46] An epigram in *Either-Or* reflects his disappointment with both Hegel and Schelling: "Listening to philosophers discourse upon reality is often just as misleading as seeing in the window of a secondhand store a sign which says: Pressing Done. If you bring your washing to have it pressed, you have been taken in. The sign hanging there is only there to be sold."[47] From this time on, there runs through Kierkegaard's works a more or less explicit polemic against philosophy's claim to comprehend reality through reason.

Unlike Marx, Kierkegaard sees Hegel's failure to come to grips with reality not in a failure to follow through with his principles, but in Hegel's deliberate equation of essence with existence. This prevents him from ever describing a "real" existence, but rather only an ideal "abstract existence." For the *essentia* of something, *what* it is, concerns its universal nature; *existentia, that* something is, concerns its particular individuality, the particular existence of you and me, for whom it is a matter of concern whether it is or not.[48] Kierkegaard's criticism of Hegel goes back to Kant's criticism of the ontological proof of God, in order to justify his differentiation between essence and existence as the "only honest way to think of existence."[49] But Hegel could not see that existence "spatiates" the analysis of being, because he did his thinking not as a man, but as one possessed of a particular talent, a professional thinker. He understood only the notion of being, but not its reality, which is always individual.[50] But the category of individuality is not one category among others, but the definition of all reality par excellence; for, according to Aristotle, the only thing which really exists is "this particular something," the individual thing which is present here and now.[51] Hegel's theory of the notion admittedly postulates individuality as the only thing that is real, but in indifferent mediation between the particular and the universal.[52] For him, individual reality is self-reflected particularity of the universal; thus the individual man is a particular instance of universal humanity, the essence of which is the spirit. Kierkegaard did not deny this universality of humanity, this common property of all mankind; but he considered it realizable only in the individual, in contrast to whom the universality of the spirit (Hegel) or of mankind (Marx) seemed to him without existential meaning.

Basically, Kierkegaard's polemic against Hegel's notion of reality only consists of variations of the one central idea that no "system" of existence can come to grips with reality and that a "paragraph" discussing reality within the system is an absolute protest against the system.[53] "If the last section of the logic is given the heading 'Reality,' the advantage is gained of giving the appearance that we have arrived in the logic at the highest point—or, if you will, at the lowest. But meanwhile we see the disadvantage: neither the logic nor reality is done any service—not reality, for the logic cannot make room for contingency, which is an essential part of reality—not logic, for when it has thought of reality it has taken into itself something which it cannot assimilate; it has anticipated what it is intended merely to predispose. The penalty shows up clearly: all investigation into what reality is becomes difficult, perhaps impossible for a time, because the word must be granted time to reflect upon itself, time to forget its mistake."[54]

The "contingent" or even "miraculous"[55] which Hegel excludes from the notion of reality consists precisely in the fact that anything whatsoever exists and that I exist at all.[56] It is this mere "existence" which comprises absolute "interest" in reality, while Hegelian abstraction demands that the philosopher, in fact, be disinterested.[57] The "interest" of metaphysics is the downfall of the immanence of the system,[58] within which being and nothingness are indifferent possibilities of pure thought. For, for the man who himself exists, existence is in itself a matter of greatest interest; "reality is his involved interest in existence." "What reality is cannot be expressed in the language of abstraction. Reality is an 'inter-esse' in the midst of the hypothetical abstract unity of thought and being."[59]

Thus Kierkegaard elevates the brute fact of existence to the status of decisive reality, transforming the universal problem of being into an inquiry into human existence; the actual problem is not *what* it is but *that* it exists at all. Similarly, the existential philosophy which derives from Kierkegaard no longer inquires into *essentia* apart from *existentia;* instead, existence per se seems to be solely essential.

Kierkegaard shares this grounding of reality in "interest" with Feuerbach, Ruge, and Marx, albeit the interest in the case of Feuerbach is sensuous, of Ruge ethico-political, and of Marx practical and social. Kierkegaard calls this interest "passion" or "ardor," and contrasts it to speculative reason.[60] The essence of passion is that, in contrast to the conclusive "termination" of Hegel's system, it compels a de-termination[61] which decides "either" one way "or" another. A decision par excellence is the *leap,* this "decisive protest against the inverse methodological process," namely, dialectical reflection.[62] The determined passion of a decision ready for this leap determines an immediate beginning, while the beginning of Hegelian logic truly starts not with the "immediate," but with the product of an extreme reflection: pure being in general, abstracted from all real existence.[63] With this definition of existence, Kierkegaard reduces the self-knowing realm of rational reality to the "only reality of which an existing person has more than mere knowledge," namely, the reality "that he truly is."[64] To thought, which is oriented historically, this may seem to be "acosmism"; but, it is nevertheless the only way to take the encyclopedic, fragmented knowledge of the age and guide it back to its origin, once again to receive a primary impression of existence.[65] But it would be a mistake to conclude that the existing person does not think at all but seizes knowledge like a Neapolitan beggar. Rather the thinker refers everything to himself because of his interest in an existence which understands itself, which participates in ideas but does not itself exist as an idea.[66] The task put before Greece was to attain the abstraction of "being"; now, the situation is reversed—the difficulty lies in arriving once more at existence upon the height of Hegelian abstraction. To understand oneself as one actually is was the Greek principle, and to an even greater degree the Christian principle; but ever since the victory of the "system," a man no longer loves, believes, and acts himself—he only wants to know what all this is.

Kierkegaard's polemical notion of real existence is directed not only against Hegel, but also as a corrective against the demands of the age. Individual existence, limited to itself, is (1) the only reality par excellence in contrast to the system; the latter includes everything on an equal footing, leveling differences (between being and nothingness, between thought and being, between universality and individuality) down to the even plane of indifferent being. It is (2) the reality of the individual in contrast to the historical universal (world history and the generation, the crowd, the public, and the age), which has no concern for the individual as such. It is (3) the inward existence of the individual in contrast to the external superficiality of circumstances. It is (4) a Christian existence before God, in contrast to Christianity made superficial in the spread of historical Christendom. And it is (5) above all, with all these characteristics, an existence which decides either for or against life as a Christian. As an existence which decides one way or another, it is the antithesis of "discretion" and of Hegel's comprehension, which have no place for an Either-Or.[67]

Shortly before the revolution of 1848, Marx and Kierkegaard gave to the demand for decision a language whose words even now press their claim: Marx in the *Communist Manifesto* (1847) and Kierkegaard in a "Literary Announcement" (1846). The one manifesto ends, "Proletarians of all lands, unite!"—the other ends with the demand that each work out his own salvation, otherwise any prophecy as to the future course of the world is bearable, at most, as a joke. But viewed historically, this contrast merely represents two aspects of a common destruction of the bourgeois-Christian world. Marx based his revolution of the bourgeois-capitalistic world upon the mass of the proletariat, while Kierkegaard, in his struggle against the bourgeois-Christian world, depends completely upon the individual. This corresponds to Marx's view of bourgeois society as a society of "separate individuals," in which every man is alienated from his "species," and to Kierkegaard's view of Christianity as a Christendom extended en masse, in which no one is a follower of Christ. But Hegel mediated these contrasts of existence, making of them one essence: bourgeois society and the state, the state and Christendom. Therefore, the selective decisions of Marx and of Kierkegaard are intended to emphasize the differences and the contradictions within that mediation. Marx's target is the alienation of man from himself produced by capitalism, Kierkegaard's is the alienation of the Christian from himself produced by Christianity.

3   Criticism of the Capitalistic World and Secularized Christianity

a   Marx

Marx analyzed the alienation of man in the realm of the state, society, and economy. The political expression of this alienation is the contradiction between bourgeois society and the state, its immediate social expression is the existence of the proletariat, and its economic expression the existence of our commodities as merchandise. Capitalism, private economy with private ownership, is the antithesis of communism, communal economy with communal ownership. But even the criticism of "political economy" is and remains oriented toward the totality of the historical world and the related form of human existence.[68] The inhabitant of the capitalistic world is alienated from himself because capital, merchandise, and paid labor are the objective expression of circumstances under which man as producer and consumer is not (in the Hegelian sense) "at one" or "free."

The difference between Hegel's "system of wants" and Marx's "criticism of political economy" is shown by the fact that Marx attacks as an *alienation* of man from himself what Hegel views as a positive component of all human activity: self-renunciation. The spirit—that universal essence of man—is an interpretation of itself within the world, and at the same time "self-recollection," that is, a return from renunciation to itself. The result of this movement of the spirit is a mediation at every stage between its own being and all other being, "a tendency to become proportionate to itself in the otherness of its own being." Starting from this universal structure of the spirit, which "ex-ists"[69] and renounces itself productively, generating the world, Hegel viewed the particular relationship between man and "object" as "property," which he describes in more detail as "possession," "use," and "renunciation."[70] An object fulfills its purpose by being utilized by others. This use is not external or foreign to the object itself; for it exists to be used, its entire existence is existence-for-a-purpose. The complete use of an object is the object itself, just as a field realizes its own peculiar being through its yield. Thus the substance of an object is its "externality," which is realized through use. When I have full use of it, I have it as "property." Just as in my relationship to an object, the totality of my personal self-manifestation and the total use of my human powers is identical with the self-manifesting life of the personality.[71] There follows, for Hegel, the following view of the renunciation of human activity: "Out of my particular physical and spiritual abilities and possibilities for activity, I can surrender individual productions and a temporary use to another individual, because, by this limitation, they acquire an external relationship to my totality and universality. Through the renunciation of *all* my time, made concrete through labor, and the totality of my production, I would make its very substance, my universal activity and reality, my personality, the property of another."[72] Hegel illustrates this difference between partial and total renunciation by the difference between the slave of antiquity and the modern domestic. "As a rule the Athenian slave may have had easier tasks and more intellectual work than our servants, but he was nevertheless a slave, because the entire scope of his activities was surrendered to his master." In contrast, Marx concludes from the system of production that really exists that even a "particular" activity can surrender the entire man, even though he be legally his own master since nobody compels him to sell his labor. Nevertheless the real existence of the "free" wage earner is less free than that of the slave of antiquity. Even though he is the owner of his own labor and has equal rights with the owner of the means of production, and surrenders only a particular kind of work for a particular length of time, he nevertheless becomes completely the slave of the labor market because his salable labor is the only thing which he in fact possesses and must surrender if he is to exist at all.[73] For Marx, the wage earner incorporates the universal problem of bourgeois society, the economic nature of which consists in the production of a depersonalized world of merchandise. The mercantile nature of all our commodities and the corresponding use made of human beings is not restricted to the sphere of economics; it defines every manifestation of human life, its mode of production, as a surrender, a sale. Even intellectual and spiritual production becomes merchandise, a book becomes an item in the book market.[74] "There is one great fact which is characteristic of the nineteenth century, and which no party can deny. On the one hand, industrial and scientific forces have been brought to life such as no previous era of history could dream of. On the other, signs of deterioration are evident, a deterioration which places the famous horrors of the last days of the Roman Empire in the shade. In our time everything seems pregnant with its opposite. Machines are endowed with the wonderful power of reducing human labor and making it more productive: we see how they lead to hunger and overwork. The newly released powers of wealth, by a strange quirk of fate, become sources of poverty. The triumphs of art seem to be bought at the price of character. Mankind becomes lord over nature, but man becomes slave of man or slave of his own base nature. . . . The outcome of all our inventions and all our progress seems to be that material forces acquire spiritual life, and human existence becomes a dumb, material force. This antagonism between modern industry and science on the one hand, modern misery and decay on the other; this contrast between the productive forces and the social conditions of our epoch is a fact, a palpable, overwhelming, and indisputable fact. Many parties may lament this fact; others may yearn to be rid of our modern capabilities in order thereby to be rid of our modern conflicts. Or they may imagine that such obvious progress in economics demands an equally obvious step backwards in politics for its consummation. For our own part, we do not mistake the crafty spirit which continues vigorously to produce all these conflicts. We know that the new powers of society, if they are to accomplish good work, demand *new men*. . . ."[75]

A phenomenological analysis of this universal problem is given in the first portion of *Das Kapital*, in which Marx exhibits the mercantile character of everything we produce. In merchandise he sees revealed the basic ontological structure of our entire physical world, its "mercantile form." It characterizes both the alienation of man from himself and the alienation of the world of things from him.[76] The sociocritical and also human point of this economic analysis, however, appears in *Das Kapital* only in passing remarks and footnotes. On the other hand, it lies at the very surface of the report on the debates *in re* the law dealing with theft of wood, published in 1842.[77] This contains the first, exemplary disclosure of that basic inversion of "means" and "end," or of "object" and "man," which leads to the alienation of man from himself. To be related to oneself as to something other, something alien, this extreme "externality" is what Marx in his dissertation called "materialism," describing himself as an "idealist" seeking to abolish this alienation. Parting with an object is self-alienation, because man does not exist for the object, but the object for him. What Marx seeks to show is the following: the wood which belongs to an owner and can be stolen is not mere wood, but a thing of economic and social, and therefore human, significance. As wood which exists in this context, it is not the same thing to its owner as possessor of private property as it is to the non-owner who takes it away. Therefore, a punishment which is to be humanly just as well as juridically correct cannot come about as long as the former thinks of himself merely as an owner of wood, having this "narrow-minded" view of himself, and the latter is also not considered as a human being, but as a person who has stolen wood. In either case, the man is characterized by a dead object, a "material power," something nonhuman, and "subsumed" under it, if he is not himself capable of controlling the products of his labor in their social context. But the man can be defined by mere wood because this wood is itself an objective expression of "political" circumstances. Therefore, "the idols of wood can conquer and men can be sacrificed to them." "Thus if wood and the owners of wood, as such, determine the laws, these laws will not differ at all except as to the geographical point at which, and the language in which, they are framed. This depraved materialism, this sin against the Holy Ghost of the nations and mankind, is a direct consequence of that doctrine which the government newspaper of Prussia preaches to the lawmakers: when considering a law dealing with wood, consider only wood and forests; do not attack the specific material problem politically, that is, in the context of the purpose and morality of the entire state."[78] When, by reason of certain social conditions, such a thing as wood can become a criterion for the being and behavior of men, things themselves become the measure of man through the reification of human self-consciousness.

Marx asks this same question in the *Deutsche Ideologie*. Here, too, he asks whence comes this "alienation" which comes between men and their own products, so that they no longer control "the mode of their mutual relationship," "their circumstances achieve an independent power over them," and "the power of their own life overcomes them"? How does it come about that within the involuntary "growth of individual interests into independent class interests, the personal conduct of the individual must become materialistic and alienated, existing as a power . . . independent of the individual"?[79] The answer is, through the division of labor. The entire manner of work that has existed up to the present must be abolished; it must give way to a total "independence." This transformation does not mean a cessation of the division of labor into mental and physical alone, but also an abolition of the opposition between city and country, which is merely "the crassest expression of the subsumption of the individual under the division of labor."[80] But it can be abolished completely only in a society which transforms human nature as well as the institution of property.

Thus *Das Kapital* also is more than merely a criticism of political economy; it is also a critcism of the human member of bourgeois society guided by capitalistic economy, the "economic cell" of which is the mercantile form assumed by all products of labor. What was originally produced for *use* is not immediately exchanged, as needed, to be utilized; instead it comes onto the market as an independent mercantile value, taking this detour from the hand of the seller, for whom it has merely exchange value, to the hand of the user as purchaser. This independent existence of an object intended for use in the form of merchandise exemplifies once more the universal fact that in the bourgeois-capitalistic world the product dominates man. To discover the process which led to this perversion, Marx undertook his analysis of the "objective appearance" of the modern social conditions of labor in the "fetish nature" of merchandise. As merchandise, an ordinary table is a thing both tangible and supertangible. What is tangible is only what it is, not as merchandise, but as an object intended for use. On the other hand, what it is as merchandise which costs money—because it costs labor and time—is on the surface an intangible social relationship. In this manner, it "not only stands with its legs upon the floor, but in comparison to all other merchandise stands upon its head, and from its wooden head develops worries, more miraculously than had its individual parts begun to dance." "Thus the mysterious nature of the mercantile form consists in one simple fact: it reflects back to men the social character of their own labor as an objective character of the products of this labor, as natural social characteristics of these things. Thus it also shows that the social relationship of the producer to the total labor is a social relationship of objects which exists independently. Through this *quid pro quo*, the products of labor become merchandise, tangible-intangible or social things. . . . It is only the particular social relationship of men among themselves which presumes to see here the phantasmagorical form of a relationship between things. Thus if we are to find an analogy, we must escape into the mists of the religious world. Here the products of the human brain seem endowed with a life of their own; they seem self-sufficient forms, related to each other and to man. The products of the human hand behave similarly in the mercantile world. I call this the fetishism which adheres to the products of labor as soon as they are produced as merchandise; it is therefore inseparable from the production of merchandise."[81]

But the producers of merchandise, that is, of objects of every sort which assume the form of merchandise, have dealings with one another only through the exchange of their merchandise as merchandise. Therefore, the relationships which lie behind this merchandise appear to the producers, not as labor relationships among men; these social relationships appear to them to be purely "objective" relationships among themselves as producers of merchandise. Conversely, the material relationships among the various items of merchandise acquire the character of quasi-personal relationships between self-acting mercantile units in a market which obeys laws of its own.[82] Man is not immediately aware of this perversion, for his self-consciousness is reified to an equal degree.

The fact that this perversion is historically conditioned is veiled by the definite *value* attached to merchandise, in the form of money.[83] Thus it appears possible to alter the price of the merchandise but not the mercantile character of commodities. In order to see that such an economic system, in which the products of labor become autonomous vis-à-vis the producer of them, is completely perverted, one must compare it with other social and economic systems. Whatever verdict one reaches about the "dark" Middle Ages type of personal dependence typical of that period, at least the social relationships of individuals in their various forms of labor appear in this context as their own personal relationships and not "in the guise of social relationships among objects."[84] Because "personal dependency relationships constitute the given social basis, labor and its products have no need to take on a fantastic form, differing from their reality. The natural form of labor, its particularity, and not (as in the system of mercantile production) its abstract universality, is here its immediate social form."[85] From this historical perspective, Marx develops the possibility of a future communistic social order, in order to contrast the "perspicuity" of its social relationships between the laborers and their products to the opaque perversion of the modern mercantile world. Thus the mercantile world can be abolished only through a radical transformation of the total concrete life-situation of man as he exists in society.[86] To this return of objects from their role as merchandise to their role as commodity, there corresponds the necessity for a return of reified man to the state of "natural" man, whose nature is to be entirely social. "If man is social by nature, he can develop his true nature only within a society; the power of his nature must not be judged against the power of the individual in isolation, but against the power of society."[87] From this fundamental postulate, Marx's proletarian socialism follows in the footsteps of Hegel's Aristotelian prototype: the *polis*, in which man is a political animal whose freedom is a personal integrity based on relationships with others.

b Kierkegaard

Kierkegaard protested passionately against this idea of social existence because he saw "in our time" every kind of association—whether in the "system," in "mankind," or in "Christendom"—as a leveling force. "It is out of the question that the idea of socialism and the community should become the salvation of the age. . . . The principle of association (which is valid at best in respect to material interests) in our time is not affirmative, but negative, an evasion, . . . a mirage whose dialectic is: by strengthening individuals, it enervates; the common bond gives strength of numbers, but ethically it is debilitation."[88] Socialism's great mistake was to suppose that the problem of equality is soluble in the medium of the world, whose essence is variety.

Kierkegaard's particular concern was not human equality, but Christian individuality in contrast to the "crowd." In contrast to "fantastic theories dealing with society," he sought once more to decipher the paled "original of individual human conditions of existence," for the confusion of the age can be countered only by giving the necessary "ballast" to human existence so that it may endure within the stream of time with roots in eternity. Kierkegaard, too, was concerned with the alienation of man, but not within the world—rather within contemporary Christendom which had declared its solidarity with the world and with the state.

In his pamphlets, which he entitled "The Moment," in which a decision was to be made for Christianity or the world, Kierkegaard drew the ultimate conclusions from his will to effect change.[89] With extravagant irony he protests against the "Protestant mediocrity" of the Christians of the established Church, mediating between the world and Christ, and also against Hegel's mediation between the state and Christianity. The first sentence of the first pamphlet begins with an ironic exegesis of Plato's thesis that philosophers should rule the state. "Somewhere in his *Republic*, as you know, Plato says, 'One can hope for justice only when those men come to power who have no desire to. . . .' This statement is also true for other situations where something (meaning Christianity) is intended to be taken seriously." The true politician and the true Christian can have no desire to rule because they know on the one hand what the state is, and on the other, what Christendom is. But in the so-called Christian State, the human becomes the "patron" of the divine. "How in the world," asks Kierkegaard, with an allusion to Hegel, "did such an absurdity ever occur to such a reasonable entity as the state"—to become "patron" of the divine? "Well, that is a long story; primarily, it is bound up with the fact that in the course of time Christianity has been accorded its true character—as the divine —less and less. Think of a statesman about the time of the appearance of Christianity in the world, and ask him, 'Quid tibi videtur? Don't you think that would be a good religion for the state?' Presumably he would think you were mad and not deign to give you an answer. But when people adhere to Christianity out of cowardly fear of what others will think, out of mediocrity, out of opportunism, the matter appears in a different light. In such a case it could truly seem that Christendom (having become a miserable creature . . . through its treatment at the hands of its adherents) should be very thankful for its protection through the state, since in this manner it still continues to be respected."[90] Man cannot become the patron of God, for true Christianity is nothing more nor less than following Christ, an absolute renunciation of the entire world. But the world exists for man primarily in the form of the state, and so the "moment" is aimed at the acknowledged lie in the apparent understanding between Christendom and the state. "Let us assume that the state employed one thousand officials who earned a living for themselves and their families . . . by opposing Christianity; that would indeed be an attempt, if possible, to make Christianity impossible. And yet this attempt . . . would be in fact far less perilous than what actually happens: the state employs one thousand officials who, as 'heralds of Christianity,' have . . . a pecuniary interest first in having people *call* themselves Christians . . . and second in having things remain as they are, so that these people do not get to know what in truth Christianity is. . . . And the effectiveness of this state of affairs is not described as opposing Christianity and for this purpose employing one thousand officials, fur-

nishing them and their families with a living; no, they 'proclaim'
Christianity, they 'extend Christianity,' they 'work for Christianity'!
. . . Is not this practically the most perilous thing conceivable for
the purpose of making Christianity impossible?"[91] This Christianity
of the State Church, or even of the people (as represented in Denmark by Grundtvig[92]), is the opposite of the truth proclaimed by
the New Testament. The extension of modern Christendom has
done away with Christianity. Hegel's reconciliation between church
and state turned into the religious revolt of Kierkegaard and the
social revolt of Marx.

In *18. Brumaire des Louis Bonaparte*,[93] Marx describes the era of
the bourgeois revolution by stating that its passions were without
truth and its truths without passion. Its world, completely prosaic,
continues to produce only by borrowing; its development is a constant repetition of the same cycle of tension and relaxation; its contrasts grow more and more violent, only to be reduced and resolved;
its history is without event, its heroes without heroic deeds. Its "supreme law" is "indecision." In his criticism of the present under the
heading of "leveling,"[94] Kierkegaard uses almost these same words
to describe this world barren of passion or decision; to the leveling
of significant differences he opposed their accentuation. As concrete
instances of this leveling, he analyzes that which reduces speech and
silence to irresponsible chatter, that which reduces private and public to private-public publicity, that which reduces form and content
to a formlessness without content, that which reduces concealment
and revelation to representation, that which reduces love and de-
bauchery to passionless flirtation, that which reduces objective
knowledge and subjective conviction to an unconvincing argument.
To the bankruptcy of this "world grown old," Marx opposed the
proletariat; Kierkegaard, solitary existence before God. The economic disturbances seemed to him to have merely symptomatic
significance: "They indicate that the European constitution . . .
has undergone a total change. In the future we shall have inward
disturbances—secessio in montem sacrum."[95] Even more decisive
than the economic, social, and political bankruptcy toward which
Europe is moving is its spiritual decline, its "confusion of tongues"
brought about by the high-speed press. The best solution would be
to silence the chimes of time for an hour; since this would presumably not succeed, he would address his contemporaries in the words
of the financial experts: "Economy, energetic and vigorous economy measures!"[96] that is, reduction of human existence to the ele-

mentary questions, to the bare question of existence as such; this was for Kierkegaard the other side of what Marx called the "secular question as to the value of life." Thus both criticisms are based on the same hostility toward the existing order: to Marx's secular criticism of the bourgeois-capitalistic world there corresponds Kierkegaard's equally radical criticism of the bourgeois-Christian world, which is as far removed from primitive Christianity as the bourgeois state is from the *polis*. Marx confronts the external, existential situation of the masses with a decision, and Kierkegaard the internal,[97] existential relationship of the individual to himself; Marx philosophizes without God and Kierkegaard before God—but these obvious contrasts have a common presupposition in their dissociation from God and the world. Both no longer look upon existence as Hegel did: as pure "ex-istere," as the appearance of an internal essence in the appropriate form of existence.[98] For Kierkegaard, it is a retreat to individual existence which makes decisions according to conscience; for Marx, it is an advance to a political decision of circumstances considered en masse. Because of an identical hostility toward Hegel's rational world, they separate once more what he had put together. Marx decides for a humanitarian, "human" world, and Kierkegaard for an otherworldly Christianity which, "humanly speaking," is "superhuman."

When intellectual history between Hegel and Nietzsche is understood in its systematic and historical logic, it becomes evident that Marx's economic analysis and Kierkegaard's experimental psychology belong together both conceptually and historically: they comprise *one* antithesis to Hegel. They comprehend "what is" as a world determined by merchandise and money, and as an existence shot through with irony and the "drudgery" of boredom. The "realm of spirits" of Hegel's philosophy becomes a phantom in a world of *labor* and *despair*. For Marx, a "German ideology" perverts Hegel's self-existent "idea," and for Kierkegaard, a "sickness unto death" perverts the self-satisfaction of the absolute spirit. For both, Hegel's consummation of history becomes the terminus of a prehistory leading up to an extensive revolution and an intensive reformation. His concrete mediations are converted to abstract decisions for the ancient Christian God and a new earthly world. In place of Hegel's active spirit, Marx substituted a theory of social practice, and Kierkegaard a reflection of inner activity; thus both consciously and deliberately deny *theoria* as the title of highest human activity. Far apart as they are, they are closely related to each other in their common attack upon the existing order,[99] and in escaping from Hegel. Whatever separates them also confirms their unity in the same fixation upon that total estrangement between the earthly and the divine which, at the turn of the nineteenth century, Hegel had taken as the point of departure for his reinstatement of the absolute as the highest form of union between opposites.

4   Estrangement as the Source of Hegel's Reconciliation

Hegel's reconciliation with "what is" itself developed out of the same thing which it gave rise to: a fundamental estrangement from the existing order. Hegel lived through this crisis together with Hölderlin; his tacit dissociation from the friend of his youth marks the beginning of his reconciliation with the world as it is. Hegel turned away from his "youth," whose essence is individuality and a merely idealistic generality. In the last sentence of the first version of his system, dated precisely September 14, 1800, Hegel decided in favor of a bold "agreement with the age," in order not to remain estranged from himself and from the world. But *if* such an agreement were "ignoble and base," Hegel confesses at this decisive turning-point in his life, the only thing left would be the "absolute One" of isolation and fixation, either upon the bare subjectivity of internal existence, or the strict objectivity of the external world. The ultimate and absolute would then be the self-estrangement of life, one and entire, into "absolute finitude against absolute infinity." For the estrangement per se, it makes no difference whether man considers himself absolutely independent or absolutely dependent upon a distant God, whether he views himself as an isolated individual or as an existence en masse, whether he is turned totally outward or totally inward; for each of these extremes already implies the other, and "the more independent and separate the internal becomes, so likewise the more independent and separate the external becomes."

Shortly after finishing the first draft of his system, Hegel writes to Schelling[100] that the "ideal of his youth" has become a "system," and he would like to obtain a university lectureship in order to exert some influence once more upon human life. By accepting an ordinary position he placed himself within the system of the existing world. But even during his early period in Frankfurt he still vacillated between the painful pleasure of estrangement and the power of reconciliation; not only did he not yet want to enter into an "alliance with the world," he even wanted to prevent it.[101] And even at the age of forty he claimed his bride as the "agent of reconciliation" between his "true inward self and the way I behave—too frequently—towards reality."[102] But in principle, as early as the turn of the nineteenth century, Hegel had already decided for the reality of the world as the "objective element."[103] From that point on he became implacably opposed, to the point of wrath and derision, to all those souls fragmented by romanticism, overcome by the "vertigo of the spirit," estranged from themselves and the world, glorious in their misery. From the fate of Hölderlin and then of the romantics he became convinced that it was more than personal misfortune not to "find oneself" and feel "at home" in any world: it was "untruth" and the cruelest "fate of being without a fate."

But nevertheless this estrangement remains as a "presupposition" of philosophy.[104] The other presupposition is unity as the predetermined goal. During his stay at Bern and at Frankfurt, Hegel experienced this twofold presupposition of the absolute as the primary "source of the need for philosophy." At the time he left Frankfurt, he explicated it in the context of the general condition of the world; and in the first Jena essays, he interpreted it abstractly as the "identity between identity and nonidentity."[105]

Hegel's crisis is not documented in reflection upon himself, but in his analysis of the "world crisis" in an epoch of transition.[106] The tendency, already decisive, to reach an agreement with the age is expressed first in a criticism of the existing order, because this criticism is the prerequisite for any agreement with "what is." In this description of the contemporary world crisis, which for a time remained unpublished, Hegel anticipated many features of that criticism which Marx later developed fully. On the other hand, the antitheses which Marx believed he discovered in Hegel's mediations are just those which Hegel reconciled. The mediating analyses of the philosophy of right proceeded from a criticism of the existing order which itself discovered the antitheses to be mediated. This made possible Marx's critical attack upon Hegel's justification of the existing order. Without the possibility of knowing anything of Hegel's criticism,[107] the young Marx in 1841 referred back from the Hegel of 1821 to the young Hegel of 1798—just as Feuerbach's religion of love and Bauer's criticism of Christianity actually go back to Hegel's early theological writings. The criticism of the Young Hegelians repeated the crisis which Hegel had gone through himself before overcoming it in his system. It is therefore no mere coincidence that Marx often describes the crisis of bourgeois society in the same way Hegel had already described it, before discovering how to "overcome" the "lost extremes" of morality in a state modeled after Plato and Rousseau, empirically the Prussian State.

As Hegel characterized the world crisis, all the phenomena of the age indicate that satisfaction is no longer to be found in the old life. But in order to "abolish what is negative in the existing world, in order to find one's place within it, in order to live," a transition must be found from "idea" to "life," from reason to reality. Particularly in the German Empire, the "ruling totality" has vanished as the source of all justice; it has isolated itself and made of itself something particular, rather than universal. Even the individual citizen is no longer a whole person when, as in the existing tension between church and state, he is "shattered" into two "fragments," into "one person for the state, another for the church."[108] Universality of life occurs only as an idea. What public opinion[109] has already decided upon, through loss of confidence, does not take much effort to be brought to the attention of everyone. (It was Marx's concern to bring this to the attention of the proletariat as a class.) The vanished "totality" of the whole must be restored. And in the philosophy of right, Hegel sought to demonstrate that the idea of this universal totality is also present as a reality. First, he discovered the contradictions. He sees such a contradiction in a man's restricting himself to a small, subservient world of personal possessions, in which mere "objects" become absolute—the world of the "philistine"[110] and of "merchandise"—and, corresponding to it, a transcendence in thought of this narrow world "reaching toward heaven"—in Marx's terminology, its "solemn completion" through the spirit of material conditions. In addition, he sees the correlated antithesis of poverty and luxury,[111] a constant theme of Marx. A better man rightly disdains this life, which is restricted on all sides, as is "offered" and "permitted" to him; but it does not suffice only to "imagine" true nature and make the content of the imagination one's constant companion, as did Hölderlin in "Hyperion." Man "must also experience what is imagined as something living," through the real resolution of existing contradictions. But this can come about only after things have come to a head, "when life as it presently exists has lost its power and all its dignity." According to Hegel, as according to Marx, the existing order is attacked and defeated not through external and internal violence directed against itself or the world, but through its "own truth." This truth, hidden within the present order and digging its grave, is the sought-for universal basis of right. For the sake of its own existence, even that restricted life must base itself on this, although it has disintegrated into abstract particularities, until a better life denies it the living right to make this claim. And time has already brought a hint of such a life. "The age is moving irresistibly toward the actions of great individuals, toward the movements of entire peoples, toward the way poets have represented nature and destiny. Through metaphysics, the restrictions are given their boundaries and their necessity in the context of the whole."[112]

In his essay upon conditions in Württemberg, Hegel, with the revolutionary passion of righteousness, concludes the necessity for change. The alienation which is conscious of itself is a consequence of the fact that it is possible to imagine and describe, to hope for and to bring about, other, better times, in contrast to "what is." Thus in times of alienation, "what is" is not an "eternal present," but a transitory form of existence, something which merely happens to be without true reality. Then to "comprehend" it means what it also meant to Marx: not a mere understanding, but criticism and transformation. "Universal and deep is the feeling that the structure of the state, as it now exists, is untenable; universal is the anxiety that it will collapse and injure everyone in its fall. With this conviction in one's heart, is this fear to become so powerful that it will be left entirely to luck what will be overthrown, what preserved, what will stand, or what will fall? Should one not himself desire to desert what is untenable? Calmly discover what must be termed untenable? In this evaluation, righteousness is the only criterion; the courage to practice righteousness is the only power that can eliminate completely what is insecure, with honor and glory, and bring forth an assured state of affairs. How blind are those who would like to believe in the continued endurance of institutions, constitutions, laws which no longer agree with the customs, the needs, the opinions of mankind, from which the spirit has fled; who would like to believe that forms with which understanding and feeling no longer are concerned are mighty enough to continue to comprise the bond of a people! All attempts to reawaken confidence in situations, parts of a constitution, in which people no longer believe, all attempts to gloss over the gravediggers with fine words not only cover their clever inventors with disgrace, but prepare the way for a much more terrible explosion, in which the demand for improvement is joined to revenge, and the deceived, oppressed masses take vengeance for this dishonesty. . . . But if an alteration is to take place, something must be altered. It is necessary to state such an obvious truth because the anxiety which must, differs from the courage which will. The men who are driven by the former feel and admit the necessity for change; but when it comes time to make a beginning, they exhibit the weakness of wanting to retain all that they happen to be in possession of, like a spendthrift who is under the necessity of limiting his expenses, but finds indispensable all of his wants which he is advised to cut out, is unwilling to give up anything, until finally his necessities, as well as his luxuries, are taken from him. A people, the German people, must not display such a weakness. Objectively convinced that a transformation is necessary, they must not be afraid to conduct an investigation in detail. Whoever suffers injustice must demand the removal of the injustice; whoever possesses undeserved goods must surrender them willingly."[113]

This breakdown of unity between the internal and the external, between private and public life, has the result that the whole is "without spirit," or, as Marx says (from Feuerbach's point of view), "inhuman." Thus for Hegel, as for Marx, the positive goal of the criticism of the existing order is the restoration of a spirit-filled (or human) unity in the whole of real life.

In spite of this summons to effect a transformation, Hegel's criticism is no Marxist manifesto. As a political writer, he seeks to comprehend "what is." Such a comprehension is the express goal of his next critical discussion apropos the German Constitution; it is permeated with melancholy resignation. Despite biting criticism, it seeks only to come to a better understanding of the present state of affairs, and even promote a "moderate toleration." Hegel disguises the ambiguity of this transition from criticism to understanding by eliminating the difference between the ideal and reality in the notion of the idea; he removes the contrast between what should be and what is, as "destiny," necessary being.[114] He explicates the proposition concerning understanding as follows: "The thoughts contained in this work can have no other purpose or effect in their public expression than the understanding of what is, and thus the promotion of a more tranquil view of the same, together with a moderate toleration in actual contact and in words. For it is not what is that makes us vehement and causes us suffering; it is what is not as it should be. But if we recognize that it is as it must be, that is, it is not arbitrary or accidental, we also recognize that it should be so."[115] But how does Hegel recognize what must be, and hence also what is as it should be? By claiming to understand what the purpose of the "world spirit" is.[116]

But the boldness with which Hegel bases his insight into what must be on the self-conscious spirit of history must be corrected by his own evaluation of the Germans, in the context of the previous quotation and with reference to the supposed necessities of politics. He says of the Germans that "on account of their notion," in other words precisely because they are so philosophical, they appear so dishonest as to admit the true nature of nothing. "Caught in an eternal contradiction between what they demand and what does not take place as they demand, they appear not only censorious, but, when they speak merely of their notions, insincere and dishonest. They include the idea of necessity in their notions of right and duty, but nothing comes of this necessity. They are themselves so accustomed to the fact that, on the one hand, their words always contradict their deeds, and on the other they attempt to make of the facts something quite different from what they really are, and to reinterpret them in the light of certain notions. But it would be completely misleading to try to learn about what usually happens in Germany from the notions of what should happen, namely, according to the laws of the state. For the dissolution of the state is most easily recognized when everything goes contrary to law. It would be equally misleading if the form derived from these laws were to be taken in truth for the basis and purpose of the same. For just on account of their notions the Germans appear so dishonest as to admit nothing as it really is, nor to present a thing to be either more or less than it really amounts to. They remain true . . . to their notions, but as a rule the facts do not agree; and thus whichever side would reap an advantage seeks to bring both together through words, by force of notions."

But Hegel's reconciliation itself contains the same dishonesty as is present in the censoriousness of which he accuses his fellow countrymen. It is not accidental that his criticism closes with a problematic accommodation. Both the challenge to the existing order and the accommodation to it are disguised by the ambiguity in comprehending "what is"; this can include that which merely happens to exist as well as what is truly real. Using as a bridge this fundamental ambiguity in the notion of reality[117] as "what is,"

Hegel progressed from estrangement to union, from youth to old age, and from the French Revolution, via Napoleon's rule, to the supremacy of Prussia.

Hegel went through the same course of progress in his relationship to the Christian religion as he did in his relationship to the state. The philosophical justification of the doctrines of Christianity is preceded by a criticism of theology and of Christianity which is matched only by Hegel's pupils. A letter written to Schelling in 1795 proclaims an unconcealed joy over the dilemma of Protestant theology, which thinks that it can restrain the "passion of dogmatics." "What you tell me of the theologico-Kantian (*si diis placet*) course of philosophy at Tübingen is not surprising. Orthodoxy stands immovable so long as its profession, bound up with secular advantages, is woven into the totality of the state. This interest is too strong to be given up so quickly. . . . If this bunch reads something which contradicts their convictions (if we would honor their verbiage by calling it this) and the truth, which they perhaps sense, they will say, 'Yes, that's probably true,' and then go back to sleep, and the next morning drink coffee and pour it into another's cup as though nothing had happened. Moreover, they will readily accept anything offered them which will help keep them in their routine. But I think it would be interesting to be as annoying as possible to the theologians who fetch the material of criticism for the strengthening of their Gothic temple, to disturb them in their antlike industry, to make everything difficult for them, to block every retreat until they can find no more and are forced to display their nakedness to the light of day."[118]

Not many years later, Hegel differentiated the spirit of Judaism and of Christianity from that of the Greeks, Romans, and Germans in a way which excludes the possibility of any dialectical mediation. Christianity has destroyed the sacred groves, declared native religious fantasy to be scandalous superstition, and given us in return the fantasy of a people "whose climate, whose law, whose culture, whose interest are alien to us, whose history has not the slightest connection with us." "A David, a Solomon lie within the imaginative power of our people; but the heroes of our fatherland lie buried in the historical studies of scholars: they are as interested in an Alexander, a Caesar, etc., as in the story of a Charlemagne or Friedrich Barbarossa. With the possible exception of Luther among the Protestants, who could be our heroes, since we have never been a nation?"[119] But even the Reformation, that unique event in the history of Germany with both national and religious significance, no longer lives in the memory of the people, but only in the annual recital of the Augsburg Confession, which bores everyone listening.[120] "Thus we have no religious fantasy native to our soil with relevance to our history, and we are completely without political fantasy; only here and there among the common people traces of a native fantasy remain alive, under the name of superstition, retaining a phantom memory of a hill once haunted by knights, or a house, by monks and nuns . . . poor, sad remains of an attempt at independence and an attempt at individuality; the entire enlightened class of the nation considers it their duty to stamp all this out completely. . . ."[121] Contrast the festivals of Athens, equally religious and political, in which the educated and uneducated could all participate because a year within the walls of Athens was sufficient to become acquainted with the cults, games, and festivals of the *polis*, with their history and organization. The biblical narratives, on the other hand, simply because of their dogmatic and historical content, of necessity remained alien to the free play of imagination, which operates best in the local context. It was no more possible to make Achaea the fatherland of the "Tuistonians" than it is to bring "Judaea" near to contemporary Germany. The gods, altars, sacrifices, and festivals of the Greeks and Romans had no "positive" meaning, no meaning externally definable and capable of being taught; but they sanctified all of everyday life, while we must force ourselves to read a moralistic meaning into the stories of the Bible, a meaning which usually contradicts our empirical hypotheses. How should the Christian have any occasion to pity the "blind" heathen? "One of the pleasantest sensations of Christians is to compare their own happiness and knowledge with the misery and blindness of the heathens; it is one of the commonplaces whither the spiritual shepherds delight to lead their sheep in the meadow of self-satisfaction and proud humility, to place this happiness directly before their eyes, in which process the blind heathen usually come off a poor second. . . . But we could quickly discover that we might better save our pity by a failure to discover among the Greeks those lacks which characterize our present practical reason—to whose charge much can be laid."[122]

But how can we explain the fact that this fantasy religion, rooted in the general life of the *polis*, could be supplanted by the positive doctrine of Christianity? "How could belief cease in gods to whom cities and empires ascribed their origin, to whom the peoples daily

offered sacrifice, whose blessing they implored upon all their business, under whose banner alone their armies were victorious, to
whom they gave thanks for their victories, to whom their happiness
dedicated their songs and their seriousness, their prayers, whose
altars, riches, temples, and statues were the pride of the peoples,
the glory of their art, whose worship and festivals were merely
the occasion for general rejoicing; how could belief in these gods,
woven into the web of human life with a thousand threads, be torn
loose from its context? . . . How strong must be the counterforce
which can overcome that force!"[123]

The answer which Hegel, as a young man, gave to this question
coincides with that given later by Bauer and Nietzsche: the penetration of Christianity can be explained only on the basis of the
decadence of the Roman world.[124] Only when the freedom of public life and its virtues collapsed and the Romans led merely private
lives[125] could a religion gain a foothold which had no use for political self-sufficiency and freedom, because it came itself from a people
of "the utmost depravity." "The doctrine of the depravity of human nature was conceived of necessity within the womb of this
depraved fragment of mankind, who were even compelled to despise
themselves from the moral point of view, although in other respects
they considered themselves the favorites of God. On the one hand,
it agreed with their experience; on the other, it satisfied their pride
by removing their guilt and finding a ground for pride even in the
feeling of misery. It made an honor of disgrace, it sanctified and
made eternal their incapacity by making a sin of the very possibility
of any strength."[126] To Romans fallen from power, who had saved
themselves from death through flight, bribery, and mayhem, who
had lost all self-respect, a religious attitude must have been welcome
which, under the name of passive obedience, converted impotence
and dishonor into honor and the highest of virtues—"through which
operation these men could look with happy wonder upon the contempt of others and their own feeling of disgrace and see it transformed into pride and glory." "And thus we see St. Ambrose or St.
Anthony, together with a crowd of people whose city is being
approached by a herd of barbarians, not hastening to defend it upon
the walls, but kneeling in the churches and the streets imploring the
divinity to turn aside their terrible misfortune. And why should
they have been willing to die fighting?"[127] Thus we read; it is a
theory which coincides with Bauer's and Nietzsche's thesis of the
origin of Christianity from the resentment of a slave morality.

Through this "reversal of nature," the divinity gained a "positivity" or "objectivity" which stands irreconcilably opposed to any living relationship with it. "In this manner, through its objective God, this spirit was revealed. Men began to know such an astonishing amount about God, as though many secrets of his nature, in so many formulas, had not been whispered, like other secrets, by one man into the ear of his neighbor, but shouted out to all the world, and children learned them by heart. The spirit of the age was revealed in the objectivity of its god, as he was placed, not in infinity, according to his measure, but into an alien world, in which we have no share, where we cannot settle by our own doing, but can at best beg or charm our way in, as man himself became a not-I and his divinity another not-I. It was revealed most clearly in the multitude of miracles it produced, which took the place of man's own reason in the realm of decisions and convictions. Worst of all, men fought, murdered, defamed, burned, stole, lied, and deceived, all in the name of this god. In such a period, the divinity must completely have ceased to be something subjective, being transformed completely into an object. The perversion of the maxims of morality follows easily and logically from this theory."[128] The capacity for such objective belief presupposes the loss of freedom and self-determination. Hegel views the legal spirit of Judaism as an extreme case of such a loss,[129] a spirit which Jesus sought to conquer with his religion of love. But even this battle against "positivity" did not achieve a complete "sense of wholeness," however much the living relationship of love had reduced the separation between the "spirit" and the "real." A further development was still necessary in order to achieve a "mating" between the divine and the human, to guarantee satisfaction to the yearning for this mating, and to make of religion a complete life. For, all the historical forms of the Christian religion have retained the basic principle of contrast and opposition. Both the union of the mystic with God and the connection of the Catholic and Protestant Churches with the course of the secular world have been unable to bring real life and worship into agreement: "between these extremes, found in the contrasting of God and the world, the divine and life, the Christian Church has described the circle backwards and forwards; but it is against its essential nature to find peace in an impersonal living beauty. It is its destiny that church and state, worship and life, piety and virtue, religious and secular activity can never be joined together."[130] It is

just this unification which Hegel later considered he had effected in
his philosophy of the spirit, whose truth is the "whole."[131]

After Hegel had turned away from Hölderlin's yearning after
the Greek situation of a beautiful harmony between religious and
political life, he undertook to build the "kingdom of God"[132] philosophically within the existing order of reality and to elevate dogmatic Christianity to the level of philosophical existence, in order to
guarantee to the human spirit that sense of belonging in the historical world which he considered the peculiar characteristic of Hellenism. Even in his early writings he considered that the task reserved for "our days" was a vindication of the treasures which had
been squandered on heaven as the property of mankind—"at least
in theory." But at that time he was still in doubt what age could
possibly possess the strength to assert this right and claim possession
of these treasures.[133] This doubt, more than justified, fell silent from
the moment that Hegel decided upon an understanding with the age,
so that "what should be" surrendered its claim under the rigor of
reality. By thus coming to terms with the existing world, even at
points where he disagreed with it, Hegel found a way out of the
revolutionary criticism of his youth. From this time forward, speculative mediation became the standard of his criticism. And just as he
could never have shared Marx's revolutionary determination for a
radical transformation, so he would also have rejected Kierkegaard's
demand for an "existing thinker"; for him, this was no problem. He
once called thought in an existential context merely "having life
and opinions," in the old-fashioned manner. He distinguished three
types: "A few men have life and no opinions; others only opinions
and no life; finally, there are some who have both, life and opinions.
The last are rarer than the first; as usual, the most common are those
in the middle."[134] Having life and opinions in equal measure, Hegel
was assured of his superiority both to the extremes and to mediocrity; in contrast, Marx and Kierkegaard went to the utmost extremes
in their total alienation from the existing order.

But such an alienation between subject and object cannot seek
to remain as it is, according to Hegel. By its very nature it is an
alienation between what was originally one and seeks to become
one again. Man must be able to act as a native in what is other and
strange, in order not to be a stranger to himself in the otherness of
the world outside. Hegel saw the Greek way of life as the great
prototype of such "existential indigenousness"—even when his bold
acknowledgment of "what is" forbade all yearning for the past.[135]

What makes the educated European feel at home among the Greeks is the fact that they made the world their homeland; they did not seek to go "above and beyond." They manipulated, transformed, and converted the substantial alien beginnings of their religious and social culture to such an extent that it became essentially their own. And this is just what philosophy is: "to be at home with oneself—that man be at home with his spirit, be no stranger to himself."

For Marx and Kierkegaard, the world in which Hegel felt "at home" had become alien. They were "above and beyond" it, or it was "absurd" and "transcendental," as Goethe had called the spirit of the coming century. Nietzsche especially was no longer at home anywhere; all was "transition" and "destruction." Even in the Greek way of life he could no longer recognize existential indigenousness and plastic meaning, but only tragic pathos and the spirit of the music inspired in him through Wagner's modernism.

The Philosophy of History Becomes the Desire for Eternity

IV Nietzsche as Philosopher of Our Age and of Eternity

> "One never goes further than not knowing where one is going."
>
> GOETHE (Maxims, 901)

The way which leads from Hegel to Nietzsche is marked by the names of Young Germany and of the Young Hegelians, who gave Hegel's system historical efficacy by undermining it. On the other hand, Nietzsche's historical efficacy can be judged by the fact that only very recently has an attempt been made to take Nietzsche's apparently disconnected aphorisms and put them together systematically according to a fixed plan.[1] In neither case is their effectiveness limited to philosophy as such; it permeates the totality of spiritual and political life. Hegel then, like Nietzsche today, was a password—which was not necessarily to be taken literally.

Nietzsche's historical place has usually been determined according to his relationship to Schopenhauer and Wagner, without regard for the disparity of their historical locus. Schopenhauer's moralistic evaluation and unhistorical view of the world still have their roots in the *ancien régime*, while Wagner's literary fervor derives from the revolutionary Hegelianism of the forties. Their effect upon Nietzsche is to be differentiated accordingly. That portion of Schopenhauer's thought which gained a positive place in Nietzsche's philosophy derives from natural philosophy: the vision of an eternal recurrence of what is essentially the same in the apparent flux of the historical world. In contrast, Wagner's reformatory plans had their effect upon Nietzsche's temporal will to the future. Nietzsche is related to the revolutionary criticism of the left-wing Hegelians not only through Wagner's relationship to Feuerbach, but also by his own literary attack upon D. F. Strauss, which reaches a logical conclusion with the *Antichrist*. In his criticism of Christianity, he concurs with B. Bauer, whose criticism of religion developed out of Hegel's philosophy of religion. And so, historically considered, the coincidence that Stirner's book appeared in the year of Nietzsche's birth seems as necessary as the connection between Nietzsche's attempt at a new beginning and the Nothing which is reached in Stirner. Nietzsche learned of Kierkegaard through G. Brandes, but it was too late for them to become personally acquainted. Nietzsche seems never to have concerned himself with Marx. A comparison of the two is nevertheless justified, because Nietzsche is the only man, after Marx and Kierkegaard, who made the decline of the bourgeois-Christian world the theme of such a fundamental analysis. The antithesis between his theory of recurrence and Kierkegaard's "reiteration" of Christianity is immediately convincing; the historical connection between Nietzsche's criticism of civilization and Marx's criticism of capitalism is less obvious,[2] because it is hidden at first by Nietzsche's own bourgeois status[3] and his lack of concern for social and economic questions. Heine must be included among the Young Hegelians in the extended sense; Nietzsche thought him so significant a figure that he did not hesitate to name Heine in the same breath as Hegel and himself.[4] Whatever abyss separates Nietzsche's anti-Christian philosophy from Hegel's philosophical theology and his "hammer" from Hegel's "speculation" is bridged by Hegel's pupils through a consequent series of revolts against the Christian tradition and bourgeois culture. At the beginning and end of this bridge stand Hegel and Nietzsche; the question is whether—beyond Nietzsche—there is any practicable path at all.

1   Nietzsche's Evaluation of Goethe and Hegel

In agreement with his demand for a decision between antiquity and Christianity, Nietzsche saw in Hegel an insidious theologian and in Goethe an upright hero. But at the same time, he was conscious of the affinity of their spirits and dispositions. "Hegel's mode of thought is not far distant from Goethe's (cf. Goethe on Spinoza): The will to divinize the universe and life, in order to find peace and happiness in observing and investigating them. Hegel seeks reason everywhere, before reason one may submit and be content. In Goethe, a kind of fatalism, almost joyful and confident, a fatalism which does not rebel, which does not weary, which seeks to form from itself a totality in the belief that deliverance comes only in the totality, where all seems justified and good."[5] To him, Hegel and Goethe, together with Napoleon, constitute a meaningful event for all Europe and an attempt to overcome the eighteenth century.[6]

The first image which Nietzsche had of Goethe was not without critical reservations; these, however, retreated more and more into the background. In the third *Unzeitgemässe Betrachtung*, after a description of the nineteenth century, he puts the question: in such a time of downfall and explosions, who will preserve the "image of man"? Three images have determined humanity in the modern era: the man of Rousseau, the man of Goethe, and the man of Schopenhauer; Nietzsche interprets himself in the "heroic life" of the last. From Rousseau there emerged a popular strength which led to revolutions; Goethe represents a power which is not so menacing, he observes and organizes, but does not lead to revolutionary overthrow. He hates everything violent, all discontinuity—that is, every action. And thus Faust the liberator of the world becomes a mere world traveler. All domains of life and nature, all past history, arts, mythologies, all realms of knowledge see the insatiable observer fly past, the deepest craving awakes and is appeased, even Helen cannot bring him to a halt—and now the moment must come for which his scornful companion has been lying in wait. At some random spot upon earth the flight ends, the whirl ceases, Mephistopheles is at hand. When the German ceases to be Faust, there is no greater danger than that he become a philistine and fall prey to the devil—only the powers of heaven can save him. The man of Goethe is . . . the theoretical man at his highest. He keeps alive upon the earth only by assembling for his nourishment everything great and notable . . . and living upon it, even though it is only a life from one appetite to the next. He is not the active man: rather, whenever at some point he becomes a part of the existing order of active men there is one thing certain, that no good will result, . . . in particular, no 'order' will be overthrown. The man of Goethe is a preserving and conciliatory force, . . . just as the man of Rousseau can easily become a Catilinarian."[7] Similarly, he says in his remarks about Wagner that Goethe was indeed a great learner and scholar, but his widespread network of rivers seems not to bring its forces together to the sea, but to lose at least an equal amount in its twistings and turnings. There is something nobly extravagant in Goethe's nature, while Wagner's (that is, Nietzsche's) course and current might perhaps terrify and frighten off.[8] But later, when Nietzsche himself attained a kind of perfection in *Zarathustra*, he silenced his previous reservations and acknowledged Goethe's way of life all the more positively. For it was not Goethe's fault that German culture lay down upon the Schiller-Goethe foundation as upon a sofa.[9] At the height of his powers, Nietzsche comprehended why Goethe, who wanted to be neither "a writer nor a German by profession," could never achieve the popularity of Schiller, but in spite of his fame remained isolated and was forced to disguise and defend himself from his admirers.[10] "He belongs to a higher genre of literature than 'national literatures' belong to: for this reason, his relationship even to his own nation is not that of life, nor of innovation, nor of obsolescence. He lived and continues to live only for the few: for the majority, he is only a fanfare of vanity which is sounded from time to time across the German border. Goethe, not only a great and good man, but a culture, Goethe constitutes for the history of the Germans an episode without issue; for example, who could point out anything of Goethe in the German politics of the last seventy years! (Albeit there certainly has been a bit of Schiller and perhaps even a little bit of Lessing at work there.)"[11] Goethe—we read in another passage—wrote over the heads of the Germans, because in every respect he stood far superior to them. "How could any people be equal to Goethe's spirituality in well-being and well-wishing."[12] His followers were only a small band of "the best educated, experienced by virtue of age, life, and travel, having outgrown the German nature: he himself would not have it otherwise." Far from "idealism," he looked upon this drifting of German civilization in his own way: "standing to one side, gently resisting, reserved, fortifying himself more and more upon his own, better course," while the rest of the world thought that the Germans had "quietly discovered a corner of heaven," as these very Germans were already beginning to exchange their idealistic civilization for industrial, political, and military undertakings.[13]

What exalted Goethe so far above all the lesser spirits was the fact that he not only desired freedom, but was in full possession of it. From the vantage of this attained freedom he could afford to promote what he himself despised and to be an advocate of the whole of life, its illusory truth and its true illusion. "In the midst of an age undisposed to realism, Goethe was a convinced realist: he said yes to everything that was congenial to him; he had no greater experience than that *ens realissimum* called Napoleon. Goethe conceived a man: strong, well-educated, physically skillful, self-possessed, respectful of himself. This man may dare to permit himself the entire scope and wealth of nature; he is strong enough for this freedom. He is a man of tolerance, not out of weakness, but out of strength, because he knows how to turn to his own advantage what would be the ruin of the average person's nature. A man to whom nothing is forbidden, except perhaps weakness, whether it be called vice or virtue. Such a free spirit stands in the midst of everything with a joyful and confident fatalism, firm in the belief that only the particular is reprehensible, that, in the context of the whole, everything is redeemed and affirmed—he no longer says no."[14] But, at the same time, this is the formula for Nietzsche's "Dionysian attitude toward existence"; and, in fact, the last aphorism of the *Wille zur Macht* seems to come from the same spirit as Goethe's *Fragment über die Natur*.

Nevertheless, Nietzsche's will to power is as different from Goethe's nature as the extreme from the moderate, seething power from ordered cosmos, desire from ability, and the destructive violence of attack from well-meaning irony.[15] This difference is especially clear in their attitudes toward Christianity. Once, it is true, Nietzsche remarks that the "cross" should be seen as Goethe saw it.[16] But he himself saw it quite differently: he wanted to teach men laughter instead of suffering, and called his laughter holy. Zarathustra mocks Christ's crown of thorns by crowning himself with a crown of roses.[17] These roses have no human or rational relationship to the cross; Zarathustra's "rose-wreath crown" is purely a polemic contrast to that of the crucified. This perversion is the final end of the symbol of the cross with roses, which derives from Luther! Goethe was not an anti-Christian, and was therefore the more genuine pagan; his "god" had no need to oppose any other, because by his very positive nature he was disinclined to any such denial. But that his consummation of freedom had no influence upon German civilization is as fatal as it is understandable. "The . . . Germans think they only have spirit when they are paradoxical, that is, unrighteous."[18] They may indeed believe in ideas, but they do not observe the phenomena;[19] therefore, their *Weltanschauung* is an ideological phantasy. In the nineteenth century, this lack of pure observation of the world brought to power the pupils of Hegel—uninfluenced by Goethe—and made them the "actual pedagogues of the Germans of this century."[20]

One such idea taken from Hegel's philosophy was that of "evolving" or "becoming." "We Germans are Hegelians, even if there had never been a Hegel, because (in contrast to all the Latins) we instinctively ascribe to evolution a deeper meaning and higher value than we ascribe to 'what is.' "[21] The German is by nature an Hegelian in not being content with the immediate aspect of phenomena; he "gets behind the appearance," and thinks there is scarcely any justification for the concept of "being." In this respect, Nietzsche says, Leibniz and Kant were also "Hegelians." More than in the rules of logic, German philosophy puts its faith in "credo quia absurdum," with which German logic makes its appearance in the history of Christian doctrine. "But even today, a thousand years later, we Germans of today . . . have an inkling of the truth, of the possibility of truth, behind the famous dialectical principles with which Hegel assisted the German spirit to gain its victory over Europe—'contradiction moves the world, all things are contradictory to themselves'—for we are pessimists, even in logic."[22] Nietzsche constructed his own paradox of the eternal return from the self-dissolution of nihilism, thereby consciously leading the logic of contradiction one step further, and once more developing a credo out of the *absurdum*.[23]

Nevertheless, Nietzsche's pessimistic logic is set apart by its radical criticism of Christian morality and theology, which he saw dominating Hegel's philosophy of history.[24] With this insidious theology, Hegel set his own initiative at nought, which consisted in the fact that he was already on the road to including even the negative—error and evil—in the total nature of being. "In conformity with the grandiose attempt which he made to persuade us finally of the divine nature of existence with the aid of our sixth sense, our 'historical sense,' " he became *the* great obstacle preventing a liberation from Christianity and its morality.[25] This philosophical historicism had the most dangerous effect upon German civilization, for it would be "terrible and devastating" if such a belief in the meaning of history were to lead to an idolization of the actual. "If every result contains within itself a rational necessity, if every event is the victory . . . of the 'idea'—then quickly kneel and go down the whole 'stepladder' of 'results' upon your knees."[26] For the fu-

ture, Hegel made History, as belief in the meaning of history, a substitute for religion.[27] This historicism, which developed out of
Hegel's metaphysics of the history of the spirit, became more
futuristic than the unhistorical world view of Goethe, who derived
the forms of development and life of mankind from observation of
nature.

2 Nietzsche's Relationship to the Hegelianism of the Forties

Nietzsche's starting point, historical philology, from the very
beginning gave him a different attitude toward history than Schopenhauer, for whose philosophical view of the world the study of
the natural sciences is basic. Nietzsche's final assessment of Hegel,
in spite of all his criticism of historical meaning, is not least determined by this opposition to Schopenhauer's unhistorical background. Through his "senseless rage against Hegel," Schopenhauer
led the entire last generation of Germans to break loose from the
context of German culture, "which culture . . . has been a lofti-
ness and divinatory acuity of the sense of history." But in this respect
Schopenhauer was impoverished, unreceptive, and un-German to the
point of genius.[28]

At the time Schopenhauer began his work, the sense of history
was represented most influentially in German philosophy by Karl
Fischer. In regard to the latter's history of recent philosophy, Schopenhauer says: "Incurably tainted by Hegelism, he constructs the
history of philosophy according to his aprioristic models; I, as
pessimist, am the necessary antithesis to Leibniz, the optimist. This
is derived from the circumstance that Leibniz lived in an age that
was full of hope, but I, in an age desperate and wretched: ergo, had
I lived in 1700, I would have been a spotless, optimistic Leibniz, and
he would be I, were he alive today!"[29] This is the madness wrought
by Hegelism, that is, the sense of history grounded in dialectics. And
he adds the remark that his pessimism arose between 1814 and
1818, and in the latter year—the year of the appearance of the first
volume of *Die Welt als Wille und Vorstellung*—was already "in its
finished state." But the years between 1814 and 1818 had been the
most hope-filled period in Germany; as a consequence, Fischer's
explanation is nonsense. But this rejection of the sense of history is
not contradicted by the fact that Schopenhauer's historical effect

began when the German intelligentsia had been prepared for it by the failure of the revolution. Feuerbach's letters, A. Herzen's reminiscences, and R. Wagner's autobiography furnish a clear picture of the degree of resignation suddenly provoked by Schopenhauer's success. As early as 1843, Schopenhauer was able to use this connection between his late success and the spirit of the age. He writes to his publisher that the latter should publish a new edition of his work, with the addition of a second volume, so that it might finally attract the public notice it deserved. This is to be hoped, "particularly at this time, now that the pretenses of the swaggering heroes, of the podium, which have gone on so long, are being unmasked more and more, and recognized in their futility; while at the same time the need for philosophy is felt more strongly than ever by a sunken religious faith, so that interest in philosophy has become vital and universal, but on the other hand there is nothing to satisfy this need."[30] But this is a propitious moment for a revival of his work; its coincidence with the completion of his work is providential. With satisfaction, he confirms that even Hegelians like Rosenkranz and the contributors to the *Hallesche Jahrbücher* cannot avoid acknowledging him.[31] On the other hand, the idea of any connection between his philosophy and Wagner's music was so far from him that he greeted the polemic against Wagner with joy: "Dr. Linder has sent me two very interesting issues of *Echo*. . . . In them the aesth. cossack criticizes Wagner very much along the lines of what I have said, and with great justice. Bravo!"[32] When, in spite of his negative response to two "singular documents of admiration" from the Zürich Wagner circle, he received from the "master" himself, "upon wonderful heavy paper," the *Ring of the Nibelungs* with a dedication, he remarked very laconically: "A series of four operas he wants to compose someday, probably the real work of art of the future: seems completely phantastic: only read the prologue: we shall see."[33]

Seventeen years later, Nietzsche, together with Wagner, declared himself to be a disciple of Schopenhauer, and dedicated *Die Geburt der Tragödie* to him as "exalted pioneer," a work which in fact derives from the spirit of Wagner's music. It appropriates to itself the Greek reminiscences and ultramodern revolutionary tendencies of Wagner's work *Die Kunst und die Revolution* (1849); basically, even when he declared himself to be "anti-Wagner," Nietzsche remained in the power of his opponent, whose superiority consisted not least in the fact that he knew how to "direct" and have an effect. Even Wagner's first musical experience had not been actually musical; the impression he received, as a boy, of Weber's production of *Der Freischütz* was: "Not an emperor, not a king—but to stand up and direct like that!"[34] To rule an orchestra, to intoxicate the crowd and move them, that was and remained the ambition of his theatrical career. Nietzsche, after he had turned his back on the "performer" and had seen through the "magician" with the acuteness of disappointed veneration, called him a commanding artist in an age of the democratic masses.

In the introduction to *Die Kunst und die Revolution*, Wagner cites a passage from Carlyle's description of the French Revolution as the third act of the history of the world: "If the second portion began eighteen hundred years ago, I believe that this will be the third portion. This is the . . . heavenly-hellish event: the strangest that has taken place for a thousand years. For it marks the escape of mankind into anarchy, into . . . the practice of being ungoverned—i.e., . . . into an invincible revolt against false rulers and false teachers—what I charitably interpret as a . . . search for true rulers and teachers. This occasion of erupting self-cremation . . . should be noted and examined by all men as the strangest thing that has ever taken place. Centuries of the same still lie ahead of us, several unhappy, sordidly agitated centuries . . . before the old has been completely consumed and the new appears in recognizable form."[35] Wagner's summons to a revolution in art found itself in complete agreement with this outcry of the aged Carlyle, and also with the consciousness of crisis of the Young Hegelians, which points forward to Nietzsche's epochal consciousness of the crisis in the history of nihilism. He then delineates how greatly Feuerbach's writings have enthralled him, particularly the notions of his philosophy of art. At that time he believed that he could see his own "artistic man" prefigured in Feuerbach's conception of human nature. "From this sprang a certain passionate confusion, which revealed itself as an overhastiness and unclarity in the use of philosophic schemata." Only subsequently did this "misunderstanding" become clear to him. Just as Nietzsche could later say that he had ruined his "Dionysian intuitions" through formulas taken from Schopenhauer and "fashionable modernism" by setting his hopes upon Wagner, from whom nothing was to be hoped, so Wagner also regrets that he introduced confusion, with Feuerbach's formulas, into his first essay. In both cases, the subsequent correction confirms the original dependence: that of Wagner upon the revolutionary fervor of the forties, that of Nietzsche upon that of Wagner. In the foreword to *Die Geburt der Tragödie*, written in 1886, Nietzsche himself points out that, in spite of its apparent Hellenism, this work is still a work of anti-Hellenism, intoxicating and obscuring as Wagner's music, "the confession of an 1830 Romantic under the guise of the pessimism of 1850"—a self-criticism which contains more truth than the conclusion of the foreword with the laughing, dancing Zarathustra. But while Nietzsche did not test his will to spiritual revolution in any political reality, Wagner took a personal part in this intoxicating drama, first of all in Leipzig in 1830; according to his own report, he joined in, like a madman in the destructions. Similarly, in 1849 he hurled himself, with Röckel and Bakunin, into the current of events in Dresden, which he greeted in writing with Feuerbach-Marxian phrases: "I desire to destroy the rule of the one over the other, of the dead over the living, of matter over the spirit; I desire to shatter the power of the mighty, of the law, and of property. Let man's *own* will be his master, his *own* desire his only law, his *own* strength his total property, for *the free man alone is sacred*, and *nothing* is higher than He. . . . And behold the hosts upon the hills, they lie silent upon their knees . . . rapture beams from their ennobled countenance, a brilliant gleam streams from their eye, and with the heaven-shattering cry '*I am a man*' the millions, the living revolution, *man become God*, pour down into the valleys and plains and proclaim to the whole world the new evangel of prosperity!"[36] In this period, Wagner was politically and spiritually as much a "freethinker" as Heine. Like Feuerbach's axioms for the "philosophy of the future," he wanted to design a "work of art of the future."[37] "The future of our educational institutions" is the theme of Nietzsche's lectures, in which he penetrated the aftereffects of the "desperate adolescents" of Young Germany.[38]

Wagner had by far the better sense of reality. He understood the problems of art as being the problems of public life, and explained the decline of Greek tragedy with the dissolution of the Greek *polis;* similarly, he viewed the spirit of the industrial enterprises of our great cities as being also the nature of modern artistic activity. He depicts the original and broken relationship between art and public life in terms that are taken literally from the Hegelian school —it would be possible to isolate the individual notions which derive from Hegel and Marx. Art arose originally from the "self-conscious universality" of life; the "god of 5 percent" is today the master and organizer of all artistic endeavors. The "heroes of the stock exchange" dominate the market of modern art, while, in contrast, Greek tragedy was the "free expression of a free universality." The tragedies of Aeschylus and Sophocles were "the product of Athens" —the modern theater is "a blossom in the morass of the modern bourgeoisie." Genuine art of the present must of necessity be revolutionary, because it can only exist at all in opposition to the existing order. "Out of its condition of civilized barbarism, true art can rise to its dignity only upon the shoulders of our great social movement: they both have a common goal, and both can attain it only when they recognize it in common." With regard to the epigraph from Carlyle, Wagner, at the conclusion, demands that the revolution in art must be just as radical as the overthrow of paganism by Christianity. "Thus Jesus would have shown us that we men are all equal and brothers, but Apollo would have given this great alliance of brothers the seal of strength and beauty; he would have led man from doubts of his own worth to the consciousness of his supreme divine power. So let us erect the altar of the future, in life as in living art, to the two most exalted teachers of mankind: Jesus, who suffered for mankind; and Apollo, who raised them to their joyous dignity!" In contrast to Wagner, who immediately translated the Greek god into a pseudo-Germanic god, Nietzsche, as early as *Die Geburt der Tragödie*, set Dionysus in the place of Christ, and finally exposed Wagner's Christian-Germanic hero as a typical instance of German misrepresentation. But originally he had planned to dedicate himself to the service of Wagner as a kind of chief propagandist of Bayreuth. His subsequent attack upon Wagner is comprehensible on the basis of this original admiration for him.

Following the impulse of Bayreuth, Nietzsche wrote the first of his *Unzeitgemässe Betrachtungen* about D. F. Strauss, a criticism of the "narrow-minded intellectual" (*Bildungsphilister*) which is already implied in Wagner's work of art of the future. This attack is directed against the "new belief" of Strauss; but, at the same time, it is a considerable step along the road to that liberation which Strauss had himself produced in the general consciousness of the age through his early writings against the old belief. Not even Nietzsche denies his respect for the young Strauss, who was basically "a man of strong and profound scholarly and critical character."[39] In *Ecce Homo* he boasted of having given expression to his own liberation through criticism of the "first German freethinker." A critic also understood this to be the point of his work, seeing its task as the production of a "kind of crisis and ultimate decision in the problem of atheism." But for this reason, Nietzsche also could feel more antipathy toward the "libres penseurs" seeking to improve the world, who had not the least notion of this decisive aspect of liberation, than toward their opponents. The difference between the religious atheism of Strauss and the anti-Christianity of Nietzsche is basically the same as Nietzsche pointed out in Wagner's notion of "sensuousness": Wagner indeed formulated it after Feuerbach's example, but then "readjusted his ideas," ultimately preaching an ecstatic "chastity."[40] Nietzsche's "atheism" also underwent readjustment and finally proclaimed a new faith. What nevertheless distinguishes the two transformations is the fact that Nietzsche never lacked character, as he accused Wagner, in reference to the latter's attitude toward the "Empire" and toward Christianity.[41] Wagner could not be unambiguous because his music sought to "mean" something that it was not in itself. "What does Elsa mean? But there is no doubt: Elsa is 'the unlimited spirit of the people'!" Throughout his life, Wagner was a commentation on an "idea" and without logical clarity. Among Germans, such clarity is a fault, namely, a lack of "profundity"; in Nietzsche's view, Hegel's influence is to blame for this. "Let us remember that during the period when Hegel and Schelling were seducing people's minds, Wagner was young. That he divined, that he grasped with his hands, what only a German takes seriously—'an idea'—implies something that is obscure, uncertain, ominous." Wagner understood this taste, he invented for himself a style which means "infinity," he conceived music as an "idea," and became the heir of Hegel. "The same kind of person who reveled in Hegel, today revels in Wagner; in his school, they even write like Hegel! The youth of Germany understood him better than any. The two words 'infinite' and 'meaning' were already enough; they somehow gave an incomparable feeling of well-being. . . . Wagner's genius at building castles in the air, his roving, rambling, and roaming through the clouds, his Everywhere and Nowhere—all are the same as Hegel used in his day to entice and to seduce!"[42]

Nietzsche had a direct connection with the Hegelian school through his relationship to B. Bauer. In him, we read in the retrospection of *Ecce Homo*, he had his most attentive reader after his attack upon Strauss. In letters to Taine, Brandes, and Gast, he lauds Bauer as his only reader, indeed as his "entire public," besides Wagner, Burckhardt, and G. Keller.[43] Nietzsche knew Bauer's *Zur Orientierung über die Bismarcksche Aera* (1880).[44] It is not known whether he was also acquainted with the theological writings of the forties. The probability cannot be rejected, especially since Overbeck followed, and in part reviewed, Bauer's work in criticism of religion.[45] However this may be, the correspondences between Nietzsche's *Antichrist* and Bauer's *Entdecktes Christentum* are so obvious that they at least indicate a subterranean movement in the course of the nineteenth century, and are no less informative than the correspondences between Bauer's criticism of Christianity and that in the early theological writings of Hegel.[46]

Stirner is nowhere mentioned in Nietzsche's writings; but Overbeck's witness proves that Nietzsche knew of him, and not only through Lange's history of materialism.[47] Stirner has often been compared with Nietzsche, to the point of asserting that Stirner was the "intellectual arsenal" from which Nietzsche derived his weapons.[48] Others consider Stirner a forger of clichés whose petit-bourgeois mediocrity is completely beyond comparison with Nietzsche's aristocratic status. Such evaluations do not touch upon the historical problem. Both can be separated by an entire world and yet belong together through the inner consistency of their radical criticism of Christian humanitarianism. And so it is easy to imagine that Nietzsche was so "economical," as Overbeck called it, with his knowledge of Stirner because he was both attracted to and repelled by him, and did not want to be confused with him.

Above all, they have in common a consciously epoch-making relationship toward Christianity, from which follows their idea of a "surmounting of man." It is no accident that the notion of the "superman" makes its first appearance in its particular philosophic sense in the circle of Stirner.[49] The superman was originally the God-man and Christ-man;[50] after Feuerbach's anthropological use, it changes its meaning: in relationship to the universally human, the superman becomes on the one hand *in*human, and on the other *more* than merely human. M. Hess[51] employed the words "superman" (*Übermensch*) and "brute" (*Unmensch*) in this sense, applying the former to Bauer and the latter to Stirner. Bauer's thesis, that in the Christian religion man worships "brutality" as his essential nature,[52] corresponds to Stirner's thesis that so long as Christ is the superman, man can not be an "I." Therefore, the surmounting of Christianity is identical with man's surmounting of himself. This connection between the *God-man* Christ, *man* of Christian anthropology, and the individual's personal "I," which is a "brute" in contrast to the former, corresponds to Nietzsche's no

less consistent connection between the death of God and man's
surmounting of himself for the goal of the superman, who van-
quishes both God and nothingness. By recognizing the full significance for the humanity of man in the "great event" of God's death,
Nietzsche also saw that for the individual man, possessed of a will,
the death of God is a "freedom for death."[53]

Nietzsche's passing remark that the actual pedagogues of the
Germans of the nineteenth century were the pupils of Hegel, has far
more significance than Nietzsche himself could know.[54] The road
which leads via the Young Hegelians from Hegel to Nietzsche can
be characterized most plainly with reference to the idea of the death
of God: Hegel based his consummation of Christian philosophy
upon the origin of the Christian faith in the death of Christ upon
the cross as the "truth" of "ungodliness";[55] Nietzsche used the end
of Christianity as the basis for his attempt to overcome the "mendacity of millennia" through a repetition of the origin of Greek
philosophy. For Hegel, the incarnation of God means a once for
all reconciliation between human and divine nature; for Nietzsche
and Bauer, it means that man in his true nature was broken. Hegel
elevates the Christian doctrine that God is "spirit" to the plane of
philosophical existence; Nietzsche declares that whoever said that
God is spirit took the longest step toward unbelief,[56] a step that can
be overcome only through the rebirth of a corporeal God.

3   Nietzsche's Attempt
to Surmount Nihilism

> "That is the new stillness that I learned: its din
> about me spreads a cloak about my thoughts."

If Nietzsche is declared to be the philosopher "of our time," the
question must be asked what meaning time had for him. Three
things can be stated with reference to his relationship toward time:
(1) As a European fate, Nietzsche is the first philosopher of our
"era"; (2) as the philosopher of our era, he is equally timely and
untimely; (3) as a last admirer of "wisdom," he is also a philosopher
of eternity.

1. In the last chapter of his last work, Nietzsche explained to the
world why he is a "fate" and a "man of destiny." "I know my lot.
One day a memory shall attach to my . . . name, the memory of a

crisis the like of which there never was on earth, of a profound collision of consciences, of a decision demanded against everything that had previously been believed, required, sanctified. I am not a human being, I am dynamite . . . I oppose as has never been opposed, and am nevertheless the opposite of a negative spirit. . . . With all that, I am of necessity also a man of destiny. For when truth enters the lists against the lie of millennia, we shall have convulsions, a spasm of earthquakes . . . the like of which has never been dreamed. Then the concept of politics will be completely dissolved in a war between spirits, all authority structures of the old society will be blown into the air—one and all, they rest upon a lie; there will be wars the like of which has never existed on earth. From my time forward earth will see great politics."

This *ecce homo*, branded as the fate of Europe, can appear as the megalomania of a diseased mind, but also as prophetic knowledge, as madness and as profound insight. In his mad insight, Nietzsche, the pensioned professor of philology, became the crucified god Dionysus, who must sacrifice himself to determine the spiritual fate of Europe. But at the same time he had the feeling that he was ultimately only a "buffoon"—"of eternities."

Conscious of being the first philosopher of his era and "something decisive and fateful" "between two millennia," Nietzsche could also say: his work has time. In 1884 he writes from Venice: "My work has *time*, and I want to avoid at all costs being confused with the task which stands before the present as *its* assignment. Fifty years from now a few perhaps . . . will have eyes to see what has been done through me. But at the moment it is not only difficult, but completely impossible . . . to speak of me in public without falling far short of the truth." Thus the proper time for Nietzsche's philosophic purpose is not his own, dominated by Wagner and Bismarck; what Nietzsche, the approved discoverer of "modernity" and prophet of an age-old doctrine, saw was seen by looking far into the future.

By looking backwards, Nietzsche foresaw the future appearance of that "European nihilism" which declares that after the downfall of the Christian belief in God, and thus also of morality, "nothing is true," but "everything is permitted." "What I am telling"—we read in the foreword of *Der Wille zur Macht*—"is the story of the next two centuries. I am describing what is coming, what can no longer happen any differently: the rise of nihilism. This story can already be told; necessity itself is here at work. This future speaks already through a hundred signs, this fate is announced everywhere; to this music of the future all ears are already tuned. Our entire European culture has long been moving with a torture of tension that grows from decade to decade, as though approaching a catastrophe: agitated, violent, precipitate, like a river rushing toward its end, no longer taking thought, afraid to take thought. In contrast, he who speaks here has done nothing previously other than taking thought: as a philosopher and hermit by instinct, who found his profit in apartness, in being an outsider, in patience, in hesitation; as a daredevil and explorer, who has already lost his way in every labyrinth of the future; . . . who looks back when he tells what is to come; as the first complete nihilist of Europe, who has lived through his own nihilism to its end—who has it behind him, beneath him, beside him." With masterful psychological skill, Nietzsche portrayed this European nihilism in its historical origin and its forms of appearance, in science and art, in philosophy and politics. The result of his fifteen years of taking thought was *Der Wille zur Macht*, conterminous with his theory of eternal recurrence.

Nihilism, as such, can have two meanings: it can be a symptom of final and complete downfall and aversion to existence; but it can also be a first symptom of recovery and a new will for existence—a nihilism of weakness or of strength. This ambiguity of nihilism as the origin of modernity is also that of Nietzsche himself: "The happiness of my existence, perhaps its individuality, lies in its destiny: to put it in the form of a riddle: as my father, I am already dead, as my mother, I still live and grow old. This double descent, from the topmost and bottommost rung on the ladder of life, both decadent and beginning, this if anything explains that neutrality, that freedom from prejudice in regard to the whole problem of life, that perhaps characterizes me. I have a finer sense for signs of inception and downfall than any other man has ever had, in this I am the instructor par excellence: I know both, I am both." Therefore in *Zarathustra* he left the question open which he really was: a promiser or a fulfiller, a conqueror or an inheritor, a harvest or a plowshare, a sick man or a man recovering, a fabricator or a truth teller, a liberator or a restrainer, because he knew that he was neither the one nor the other, but both together. This ambiguity of Nietzsche's philosophical existence also characterizes his relationship to time: he is of "today and yesterday," but also of "tomorrow and the next day and time to come." This knowledge of yesterday and of tomorrow enabled him to interpret his present philosophically.

As a "fragment of the history of [Christian] posterity," his philosophy is also a fragment of Greek antiquity. Nietzsche is thereby the philosopher, not only of the most recent period, but also of a most ancient period, and hence of an "age."

2. Because Nietzsche was "untimely" in his relationship to his period and to contemporary philosophy, and has remained untimely, he was and is also "timely," a philosophic criterion of the period. This is at any rate the way in which he interpreted the timeliness of his untimeliness. The foreword to the second of the *Unzeitgemässe Betrachtungen* closes with the statement that it is only as the "pupil of former ages," particularly the Greek, in which Western philosophy has its fountainhead, that he, "a child of his own time," could acquire such "untimely knowledge." As a classical philologist, he did not know what the purpose of an acquaintance with Greek antiquity could be except this: to work against his time, and thereby upon his time, and so perhaps to the advantage of a future time.

In his last *Unzeitgemässe Betrachtung* of 1888, on Wagner, Nietzsche explained his relationship to his time in more detail, as a "surmounting" of his time: "What does a philosopher demand first and last of himself? To surmount his time in his own person, to become timeless. What gives him his fiercest conflict to withstand? That which makes him a child of his time. Fine! I am as much a child of this time as Wagner, that is, a decadent: only I realized this, only I resisted it. The philosopher in me resisted it." The philosopher overcame in him the mere contemporary of his time, making Nietzsche thereby the philosopher of his time, who passed his "test" by refusing to be diverted from his "primary task" by the great political movement of Germany, nor the artistic movement of Wagner, nor the philosophic movement of Schopenhauer.[57] By surveying the rise and fall in the growth of European man, from Aeschylus to Wagner and from Empedocles to himself, in the entirety of historical time, he was able to look deep within his own time also.

Unconnected with this untimely conformity to his time which belongs to Nietzsche as the philosopher of his age is the particular actuality which he enjoyed in the changing perspective of his literary successors. If we survey the various modes of actuality gone through by Nietzsche in the course of forty years in the eyes of P. Gast, of G. d'Annunzio and A. Gide, of R. Pannwitz and O. Spengler, of Th. Mann and R. Musil, of G. Benn and R. Thiel,[58] we can see a very clear picture of the spiritual problems besetting the period following him. The same mutation is reflected in the philosophic literature on Nietzsche from Riehl to Simmel and from Bertram to Jaspers. But none of this is any longer "timely," if we mean by this that the inclinations of one's own time are the proper standard by which to measure understanding of philosophic goals. In such a case, in conformity with irresistible "progress" of each vanishing moment, the Nietzsche of the last and most recent period would alone be timely, as interpreted particularly by Klages and Bäumler. In his ingenious aversion to will and spirit, Klages divides Nietzsche and declares him to be an "orgiastic" philosopher of the "body" and the "soul," retaining the Nietzsche of Dionysian philosophy at the expense of the will to power and to nothingness. In his desire for battle, Bäumler interprets the Nietzsche of the will to power and to nothingness as an "heroic realist" and political philosopher, at the expense of the Dionysian philosophy of eternal recurrence. These are but two contrasting varieties of one and the same prejudice in the spirit of a time hostile to the spirit. They are both equally far removed from Nietzsche's entire philosophy of the will to nothingness and to eternity.

Even further from Nietzsche's battle against his own and every "period" is the interpretation which claims he is neither a philosopher of the will to power nor one of eternal recurrence, but that he is a random anthology of statements which happen to be attractive at the moment. Because Nietzsche develops his thought in a thousand aphorisms and not as a system, one can find in him in particular whatever one wishes: matters startlingly timely and matters amazingly untimely. A few brief examples can illustrate: at the conclusion of *Ecce Homo*, Nietzsche says that only in him does the war of the spirit become one with "great politics"; but he also says, at the very beginning of *Ecce Homo*, that he is the "last of the antipolitical Germans," and more German than any "Imperial" German of the day. These statements seem to contradict each other, but in reality they comprise one and the same thought. Precisely because Nietzsche represents the idea of great European politics, he can also call himself the last of the antipolitical Germans in respect to the contemporary affairs of Imperial politics, and say that to understand him at all one must have put behind him all "miserable talk of politics and national self-interest." Nietzsche says that war and courage have accomplished more great results in the world than love of one's neighbor; but he also says that the "greatest events" are not our loudest, but our "stillest hours." He attacks the "free press" spirit of liberalism, but in equal measure all "party spirit";

the mere idea of belonging to some party, "even if it were one's own," arouses his disgust. He criticizes the democratic spirit of bourgeois society; but also, under the title *Vom neuen Götzen* (*The New Idol*), he says that the state is the most callous of monsters, and out of its mouth proceeds the lie, "I, the State, am the people." He believes in the necessity of a return to barbarism and the "masculinization" of Europe, coining for it the phrase "blond beast"; but he also characterizes Wagner's heroes as brutes with an ecstatic sensuality, and his "Germanics," as "obedience and long legs." He speaks in favor of selective racial breeding, but no less against undeserved self-admiration in the madness of anti-Semitic racism.[59] He makes fun of the "land of culture" and "pure knowledge," and sacrifices the "cultured individual"; but also, as a cultured individual himself, he confirms the general "plebeianizing" of taste and the growth of barbarism. He demands that those who "command" should take precedence over those who "obey"; but at the same time he refuses to be "shepherd and dog of a herd," and states that the "German servant-soul" has been idealized in the military virtue of absolute obedience. He talks of the necessity of a "ruling caste"; but he knows that the "trainability" of men has grown to monstrous proportions because they have nothing to say to each other. Finally, he develops the "will to truth" as "will to power"; but he also says that one must never ask whether the truth will turn out to be advantageous or fatal, and that *Der Wille zur Macht* is a book exclusively for those who still enjoy thinking; but the Germans of today are no longer thinkers, something else impresses and pleases them.[60] If a man wishes to base a philosophy for "our time" upon Nietzsche, let him hear Zarathustra: "I am a rail by the river—grasp me who can—but I am not your crutch." In order to grasp a philosopher, one must above all grasp his thought; and for this, Nietzsche desired readers who still had time to think.[61]

3. Nietzsche's actual thought is a thought system, at the beginning of which stands the death of God, in its midst the ensuing nihilism, and at its end the self-surmounting of nihilism in eternal recurrence. This corresponds to the threefold transformation of the spirit in the first speech of Zarathustra. The "thou shalt" of the Christian faith is transformed into the liberated spirit of "I will"; in the "desert of his freedom" to be nothing, there takes place the last and most difficult transformation: "I will" becomes the eternally recurring childlike game of destruction and creation. "I will" becomes "I am," that is, in the totality of being. With this final trans-

formation of the freedom to be nothing into the freely willed necessity of an eternal recurrence of the same, there is fulfilled, for Nietzsche, his temporal fate as an "eternal fate." His *ego* becomes his *fate*. And *ecce homo*, this accident of existence, is meant to show that one "becomes" only what one already "is," because the highest constellation of being is necessity, in which accident and self-being coincide.

> Shield of necessity!
> Great constellation of being!
> —that no wish attains,
> that no "No" defiles,
> eternal "Yes" of being,
> eternally I am thy "Yes":
> for I love thee, O eternity!

Under the "shield of necessity," that is, of antique Fate, the accident of existence is once more in the totality of being.

The importance of eternity to Nietzsche's philosophy, and thus also of the decisive "moment" in which it shows itself once for all, can be seen in the fact that the third and fourth portions of *Zarathustra* conclude with a hymn to eternity, and *Ecce Homo* was intended to conclude with the poem "Glory and Eternity." But the problem of eternity, how it comes to mean eternal recurrence, is found in the way by which Nietzsche surmounted "time" with "man." It is a way of escape from the history of Christianity. Nietzsche calls it "the self-conquest of nihilism," which proceeds from the death of God. Zarathustra is the "victor over God and nothingness." On the basis of this essential connection between the "prophecy" of eternal recurrence and the "prophecy" of nihilism,[62] Nietzsche's theory assumes a double aspect: it is a self-conquest of nihilism in which the "victor and the vanquished" are one.[63] They are one as the "twofold will" of Zarathustra, the Dionysian "twofold gaze" into the world, and the Dionysian "twofold world" are one will, one gaze, and one world.[64] This unity of nihilism and recurrence derives from the fact that Nietzsche's will to eternity is the converse of his will to nothingness.

But how can one continue to will the classical necessity of thus-and-not-otherwise with the freedom of will which derives from Christian existence—unless through a willing of obligation, which unites both? This superhuman will is twofold in respect to time, because it continues to will what it is obligated to do, because it paradoxically unites the will to the future with the will to the past. The whole problem of Nietzsche's "ultimate" will is systematically and historically comprehended in this twofold will, which wills against itself. The solution of this problem is the subject of the chapter of *Zarathustra* entitled "Of Redemption," namely, from the past.

Zarathustra sees the surrender of the entire past, in two ways. Some reduce it to a preparatory symptom of their decadent present; and for others, past time comes to a close with "grandfather."[65] Neither way can redeem us from the past. "To redeem everything in the past and to re-create all 'it was' into a 'thus I willed it!'—that would be a redemption! Will, that is the name of the liberator and bearer of joy; so I taught you, my friends! But now learn this in addition: the will itself is still a prisoner. The will liberates; but what is the name of that which fetters the liberator? 'It was'—that is the name of the will's gnashing of teeth and solitary affliction. . . . That time does not run backwards, that is its wrath; 'Thus it was'— that is the name of the stone which it cannot roll away." But because the will which wills the future is incapable of taking revenge on what already is, what has already been willed and done, this life of will—and man *is* will, since no god tells him any longer what he "shall" do—becomes its own "guilt" and "punishment." Existence becomes "again and again its own act and guilt," precisely because it is *not* itself responsible for the accident of its existence, which has always come to be present prior to an act of will, but, as a will which has existence, wills to be responsible and yet is not *able* to be. And therefore the will becomes unwilling antipathy, rolling "stone upon stone" against the burden of the existence which has befallen it, until finally madness preaches: All perishes, and therefore all deserves to perish. Resentment over the past time of the deed already done devalues it to the status of something merely transitory, unless "the will should finally redeem itself," as in Schopenhauer's meta- physics, and "willing becomes unwillingness." In contrast, Zara- thustra's creative will says to the stone which is the burden of an existence designing itself in vain: "But I willed it so," and will con- tinue to will it through all eternity! But when did he speak thus? And when will it come to pass that the creative will to the future will replace the past? And who taught him to will to return in place of unwillingness, to bring happiness in place of bringing pain? Zarathustra answers this question as the teacher of eternal being. For, in willing the eternal recurrence of time and being, the will itself ceases to be a uniform movement into an endless infinity, and becomes a circle, willing both progress and return. It is this twofold will, which continues always to will what is forced upon it, that is meant by Nietzsche's "amor fati." In it the totality of time and being merge in a future, which has already been, of a being which is still becoming.[66] Thus Zarathustra's soul is the "most necessary," "plunging joyfully into accident"; but it can do this only because "all things have their currents and countercurrents, their ebb and flow," in it, as in the "highest mode of all that has existence,"[67] but "that is the very notion of the Dionysian"; and its formula is not merely the will to destiny, but to destiny as fate, "subjecting destiny to destiny."[68]

Nietzsche accordingly differentiated his teaching of redemption from the belief of the ancients in a destiny with power over both gods and men, and from the belief of the moderns in the freedom of will: "Formerly man believed in soothsayers and astrologers. And therefore it was thought, 'All is destiny! Thou shouldest because thou must!' Then again all soothsayers and astrologers were disbelieved: and therefore it was thought, 'All is freedom: thou canst because thou willest!' "[69] In contrast to these alternatives, Nietzsche wished to unite the willing of the individual with the cosmic imperative.

But how, in view of the modern freedom to will and to be able, should it be possible to recapture that ancient intimacy with what must be and cannot be otherwise, in order that the fate once written in the stars be transformed into an individual fate through a willing of necessity, so that the individual may finally say, "I myself am fate, and have determined existence since eternity," "I myself am among the causes of eternal recurrence"? For this, must not the new prophecy be itself this unity, first of that written in the stars of heaven, and second of that which comes from nothingness, which is the ultimate truth in the desert of freedom of the individual's ability? Therefore, is not the whole which it proclaims a "heavenly nothingness"? And does not this linking correspond also to the twofold way by which the twofold will comes to its twofold truth, namely, through a decision and an inspiration, the latter as true as the former? A decision made by the will, which at the utmost extreme of freedom prefers "to will nothingness rather than not to will," and an inspiration, in which being inspires what has been thus decided with itself: these together comprise the problematic approach to Nietzsche's twofold truth, which, as a teaching of the self-overcoming of nihilism, is his "credo quia absurdum."[70] This alone is truly "untimely," because it is a theory of time and being which completely transcends time. No one after Nietzsche reached this extreme point of conversion. The few who still asked after eternity turned to the "eternal" truths of the Catholic Church, spoke "of the eternal in man," became intoxicated with forgotten "images" of cosmic life, conjured with "codes" of being,[71] while the majority obeyed the summons of the time, which offered them the racial hardware of a political zoology as a substitute for eternity.

"Beyond man and time," Nietzsche sought to transcend the whole "fact of man" together with time, and escape the dereliction of the modern world. Then there happened what he had himself told of the sufferer who "bore his ashes to the mount" and "sought to reach his goal with *one* leap": "It was the body which despaired of the body—which groped about the last walls with the fingers of a maddened mind. . . ."[72]

Another, who did not seek to reach his goal with one "leap," but rather glorified the "sequence," did not construe eternity as a "possibility" of life,[73] but saw it present in every moment of his corporeal existence. For this reason, Goethe's phrasing of the question of "will" and "must" differed from Nietzsche's. By really living within the totality of all that has being and not transcending himself, he could achieve the insight that the entire circle of apprehension is included in the unification of "will" and "must." "Lessing, who had an aversion to restrictions, has one of his characters say: ' "Must" is forced upon no one.' A clever, cheerful man once said, 'Whoever wills gives himself a "must." ' A third, admittedly a learned man, added, 'Whoever understands also will,' "[74] namely, what he must. The insight of the thinker corresponded to the experience of his life: when Goethe received the news of the death of his only son, and had to bear double the burden of his old age, he wrote to Zelter, "I have no other concern than to retain my physical equilibrium; everything else follows of itself. The body must, the spirit wills, and whoever sees the necessary course prescribed to the action of his will need not deliberate much."[75]

Goethe developed this thought further with reference to Christianity and antiquity. On the occasion of Reformation Day, he writes to Zelter that the basis and foundation of Lutheranism is the absolute antithesis between law and Gospel, and the mediation between these two extremes. If necessity and freedom, with their distance and proximity, are substituted for these words, we see clearly that within this circle "everything is contained that can be of interest to man." In the Old and New Testaments, Luther saw the symbol of the great, recurring structure of the world: "On that side law, aspiring to love, on this side love, which strives against the law and fulfills it, but not by its own strength and power, but through faith, through exclusive faith in the all-powerful Messiah, proclaimed everywhere."[76] From this little bit, one can realize that Lutheranism does not oppose reason when the latter decides to view the Bible as the mirror of the world. Therefore, Goethe's projected Reformation power should begin with the "Thou shalt!" of the thunder upon Sinai, and conclude with the resurrection of Christ and the "Thou wilt."

Freed from considering the "exclusive" faith in the dogmatic truth of the Bible, in his essay "Shakespeare und kein Ende" Goethe discussed the same problem of "must" and "will" with reference to antiquity.[77] He lists the following antitheses between the old and the new: antique and modern, pagan and Christian, necessity and freedom, should and must. From the lack of co-ordination between the last two members derive the greatest and most numerous torments which can afflict man. When the consequent "dilemma" is slight and soluble, it provides the occasion for ridiculous situations; when it is great and insoluble, it begets tragic situations. In the literature of the ancients, the disproportion between what man *should* do and what he accomplishes is dominant; in that of the moderns, it is the disproportion between what he *wills* to do and what he accomplishes. What a man should do is imposed upon a man from without, what he wills to do he imposes upon himself. In the one case, all appears to be destiny, in the other freedom. The inescapable imperative, which is only whetted and hastened by counteraction of the will, is incarnate in the ancient law of city and of custom, as well as in the laws of the cosmos; its goal is the well-being of the whole. Willing, on the contrary, is free, and favors the individual. "It is the god of the new age," and here lies the reason why our art and character remain eternally separated from that of classical antiquity. Shakespeare's uniqueness derives from the fact that he combines the old and the new to an "extravagant" degree, establishing an equilibrium in the individual character between what is demanded and what is willed. Each character in his dramas "must"; but as a human being, each "wills." He succeeds in this unification because he does not cause an immoderate will to spring from within, but has it brought about by an external occasion. "It becomes thereby a kind of imperative, and approaches the ancient." In his heroes, Shakespeare combines the old and the new world to our joyous astonishment. And this is the point that we must learn in his school: instead of unduly exalting our "Romanticism," that is, our modernity, we should attempt to resolve within ourselves that apparently irresolvable antithesis, the more so because a single great artist has already accomplished this miracle.

How well Goethe's remarks on Shakespeare can be applied to Goethe himself can be seen from the fact that even a romantic saw Goethe's greatness as his ability to unite what is "essentially modern" with what is "essentially ancient."[78] Schlegel's only error lay in seeing in Goethe the first representative "of an entirely new artistic epoch," setting out to approach this goal. In the history of the nineteenth century, he was rather the last man to feel the difference between ancient and modern, as well as between pagan and Christian, to be a problem demanding a "decision." In doing this, Nietzsche was obliged to seek to recover the closed view of the Greek world at the apex of modernity "which is at its wits end," forcibly to unite his "I" with Fate. In contrast, Goethe's nature realizes antiquity within the area of the modern. Goethe visualized the contrast between the ancient and modern not only in great tragedy, but also in everyday life: "Card games, too, may be looked upon as a kind of literature; they, too, consist of these two elements. The form of the game, in combination with chance, takes the place of the imperative, precisely as the ancients knew it under the form of destiny; the will, in combination with the ability of the player, opposes it. In this sense, I would call whist ancient. The form of this game sets limits upon chance, even upon the will. With given partners and opponents, with the cards I happen to have in my hand, I must control a long series of chance events, without being able to escape them; in l'Hombre and similar games, the reverse takes place. In the latter case, a great many doors stand open to my will and hazard; I can refuse the cards that I receive, let them be put to various uses, discard them partially or *in toto*, call upon luck for aid, even reverse the procedure and derive the greatest advantage from the worst cards; and so this sort of game bears a thorough resemblance to the modern way of thinking and writing." Such an "easy-going" reflection is inconceivable in Nietzsche. The spell which fought on his side was, as he knew, "the magic of the extreme, the temptation which goes to extremities,"[79] but not the more gentle enchantment of equilibrium, which is unpretentious. To the radical,

Goethe is a compromise, because the radical—contrary to etymology —is without roots.

The "German spirit," whose history we have traced from Hegel to Nietzsche, was measured by a generation taught by Nietzsche according to what Nietzsche wished and what he opposed. Innumerable are the pamphlets, books, and speeches in which the Third Reich was called the "fulfillment" of Nietzsche. But no one who takes Nietzsche's work seriously, or "expounds" it, can fail to recognize that Nietzsche is alien both to the "national" and to the "social," just as, on the other hand, the spirit of "Bayreuth" is related to the instincts of more than Bismarck's Reich. To see the abyss which separates Nietzsche from his latter-day prophets, it suffices to read his writings against Wagner and his remarks on the Jewish question, and the converse question of what is "German," without editing or excerpting. But this does not contradict the obvious fact that Nietzsche became a catalyst of the "movement," and determined its ideology in a decisive way. The attempt to unburden Nietzsche of this intellectual "guilt," or even to claim his support *against* what he brought about is just as unfounded as the reverse effort to make him the advocate of a matter over which he sits in judgment. Both crumble before the historical insight that "forerunners" have ever prepared roads for others which they themselves did not travel. More important than the question whether Nietzsche's historical effect speaks for him or against him is the discrimination of spirits according to their relationship to the period in general. However much Nietzsche sought to make time eternal, he was nevertheless—from his attack upon Strauss to his attack upon Wagner—more of his own time than he desired to be, precisely because his stance toward it was polemical, untimely. As antagonist to Bismarck and Wagner, he moved within the circumference of *their* "will to power," and even his timeliness in the Third Reich rested upon the fact that it was the heir of the Second.

Nietzsche was unable to grasp an eternity which is immanent in time; when he glimpsed it for one moment, he was—"six thousand feet beyond man and time"[80]—without his faculties. Goethe's Werther was indeed timely, but Iphigenia and Tasso were not. The more dense and inclusive Goethe's environment became, the more all his relationships to his time were transformed into the concrete generalities of his spiritual gaze. Goethe can never become timely or untimely, because he is forever a pure spring of truth in the relationship of man to himself and to the world.

v The Spirit of the Age
and the Question of Eternity

1 The Spirit of the Ages
Becomes the Spirit of the Age

The phrase "spirit of the age," which during the forties became the watchword of progress, originally had nothing to do with the particular age and its pretended historicity. In Goethe's *Faust*, the "Spirit of the Ages" refers only to the past ages, with the skeptical comment that it is the gentlemen's (they are historians) own spirit in which the ages are reflected. From the same period as Goethe's outline for *Faust* comes Herder's essay on Shakespeare, at the conclusion of which Goethe is named as the friend whose duty it is to translate the genius of Shakespeare, whose world has already passed, into our language and the spirit of the present. Just as each great man philosophizes "within the great temper of his time," so every nation must invent its drama afresh according to its own history, "according to the spirit of the age, customs, opinions, language," and not imitate the past. Thus in opposition to a dead tradition, Herder appeals to the individual spirit of the age, the language, or the nation. For the "soil of time" cannot always produce the same thing in every age. But if, in a "time changed for the better or for the worse," a great man should create a drama just as great and original as those of Sophocles or Shakespeare, then, in spite of the changes of the time, he would accomplish the same thing: a representation or "historia" taken from the great book of world events.

Thus the spirit of the age refers to its own particular age, insofar as it means the individual right of the present in contrast to a tradition which is no longer effective. It is not in itself a temporal spirit; it is rather—analogously to the spirit of the people or of the language—always one and the same spirit of the whole "sphere of mankind," which assumes a particular mode of appearance in different ages and among different peoples.

The French Revolution, with its destruction of tradition, had an historicizing effect upon the consciousness of its contemporaries. Thenceforth the time of the present, in contrast to the entire "past," views itself expressly as belonging to the course of history, looking toward the future. Herder is also a superlative source for observing the way in which the spirit of the age becomes problematic. In the first and second collection of his *Briefe zur Beförderung der Humanität* (1793), the spirit of the age is presented with an awareness based upon reflection. Typically, this reflection begins with a criticism of the age, that is, a critical distinction between this particular, new age and all the former ones which have preceded it. "How does it happen . . . that, in comparison with the poetry of former times, our poetry has so little to do with public affairs? . . . Is the Muse now fallen asleep? Or does she have . . . something else to do, with the result that, not awakened by the spirit of the age, she does not hear the tumult about her?"[1] Therefore, Herder seeks to take note of what "the divine messenger, time," brings to us, and, following the example of Horace, who lived in an even more critical time, to break "the blossoming of the time." Of course, poetry must not seek to involve itself too greatly in the "conflicts of the age," for the "immediate historical situation" will soon be past; but as a "voice of the age" it follows the "spirit of the age,"[2] and often there moves within it even a "prophetic spirit of the ages." Such book and periodical titles as *The Spiritual Situation of the Age, Voices of Our Age, The Turn of the Age,* and *Between the Ages,* have their historical genesis in the peculiar consciousness of time produced by the French Revolution: only since then has the particular age been a final court of appeal.

But what exactly is this spirit of the age, so often appealed to and discussed? "Is it a tutelary spirit, a daemon? . . . Or perhaps a breath of fashion, the sound of an aeolian harp? It is thought first one thing, then another. Whence does it come? Whither does it seek to go? Where is its authority? Where its might and its power? Must it rule? Must it serve? Can it be controlled? Can we read about it somewhere? How can we learn to recognize it on the basis of experience? Is it the genius of humanity itself? Or its friend, herald, servant?"[3] It permeates all spirits: everyone, whether active or passive, is subordinated to it, it has all power, it sees all—like wisdom in the biblical Book of Wisdom (7:22). But only the Reformation, the sciences and arts, liberated it; the art of printing gave it wings. Its mother is abstract philosophy, and its father laborious "experiment." It is the totality of historical consequences; it is very ancient, and at the same time ever new. "It has gathered from former ages, it gathers from the present age, and it presses forward to future ages. Its power is great, but invisible; the prudent man observes and makes use of it; the imprudent man gives it credence, usually too late, only by virtue of its accomplished effects."[4] As the spirit of history, it both dominates and serves man; but those who actually control it are not the many, but the few who dare and suffer much. The fleeting fashion of the age is its counterfeit sister, with whom it occasionally enters into instructive association. A man can become familiar with it best through his own experience and through tales which are written in the spirit of their own particular age. Not least, as the spirit of *our* age, it is a herald of humanity; indeed, letters pertaining to the advancement of humanity were the occasion of Herder's reflection upon time and the age. As the spirit of our age, it is the spirit of the age of the "universal spirit" of a Europe "enlightened or in the process of becoming enlightened," the "European world spirit," both present and pregnant with future. As spirit, it is an aspiring movement, force, and effect which produces life; as spirit of the ages, it is interwoven with the sequence of historical circumstances; and, as the spirit of our age, it refers to the universal spirit of Christian Europe.

This humanity which determines the spirit of the age was still at work during the forties, but with an essential change. The spirit of the age of which the Young Germans and Young Hegelians speak no longer has the spiritual outline of Herder's humanity. Instead, apart from any particular content, it is a temporal movement of progress per se. Under the influence of Hegel's equation of philosophy with the thought of history, the spirit of the ages is transformed into the spirit of the age in the narrow sense of the word. The major components of this change of meaning must be examined.

In Hegel's early theological writings, that is, even before 1800, the revolution through which Christianity conquered the pagan world is included in the "realm of spirits,"[5] on the grounds that it was begotten by the "spirit of the age." This great transformation in the spirit of the age became the historical model for the epoch-making consciousness of the nineteenth century. Nevertheless, for Hegel himself, this talk of the spirit of the age does not mean a reduction to temporal terms of the spirit as such. In spite of all aprioristic schematization, this was brought about only through Fichte's lectures on the "characteristics of the present age" (1804–05). It achieved popularity through Arndt's *Geist der Zeit* (1805), in which "loathing for the present" takes refuge in the "spirit of the past" and "prophecy of what is to come." This work, together with Fichte's lectures, marks the beginning of that chain of historical criticism which extends to Marx and Kierkegaard, and further to Wagner and Nietzsche. Nevertheless, even for Fichte the "spirit of the age" is still basically an "eternal" spirit, and thus by no means temporally determined. But because Fichte saw his own age completely dominated by sinfulness, and undertook his criticism from this point of view, he was forced to set up a distinction within one and the same chronological period: within the same period, various ages can intersect; not all contemporaries of a particular age are a "product" of the actual character of the age.[6] Fichte makes the claim that his own observations on the present age are not a mere product of the age, but are raised above the ages and are beyond all time. But are they not then a meaningless dream set in a meaningless time, without significance for "true and real" time? But what is real time in contrast to the meaningless time of mere amusement? "A thing falls within true and real time when it becomes a principle, a necessary basis and source of new manifestations of time which have never before existed. Only then is it a truly living life, begetting of itself other life."[7] Thus the criterion for Fichte's criticism of the present age is the significance of the life of the present for the future; at the conclusion of his lectures, he believes that in the renewal of religious life he can recognize the true movement of the present toward the future.

From Fichte, the phrase "spirit of the age" enters the romantics' criticism of their period; finally, among the writers of the thirties and forties, it becomes a universal slogan. In the midst of the radical changes taking place between ages, all events are referred more and more consciously to the spirit of the "epoch," and the feeling of an epoch-making turning point between two ages grows; thus the final age as such becomes the destiny of the spirit.[8] This is what lends all talk of the spirit of the age that contemporary note which adheres to it even today. "It is characteristic," writes the author of *Epigonen*,[9] "that we speak always of the age, of *our* age. But where does it begin, and what is so special about it . . . ?" In Immermann's work, Münchhausen, the liar, in whom the Lord God enclosed all the "winds of the age," incorporates the universal spirit of his age, the reverse side of which is the expectation of a new age. But even in Immermann there still lives Hegel's consciousness that beneath the dazzling surface of the age there pulses an eternal world spirit which is only waiting to break through the shell in order to achieve present existence. The spirit of the age, incarnate in Münchhausen, is not the spirit of eternity, which "in silent abysses carries on its secret work," but rather "a silly clown" whom "the cunning old man"—Hegel's "craftiness of reason"[10]—has sent up "among the disorderly mob." This ambiguous sense of time, which separates the present into temporal and eternal components, as surface and depth, was lost in the Young Hegelians, together with the conservative aspect of Immermann's revolutionary criticism of the age. Their attitude toward time is made fast unambiguously to the two poles of a radical criticism of the existing order and a preparation for the future, which is not only hoped for and awaited, but actively willed. The spirit of the present age is given a progressive interpretation which looks to the future, as the spirit of the true direction of the age and thus of the spirit. Theoretical criticism and practical change transform the constant "planning," which Immermann sees as a characteristic of the age, into theoretically grounded action. In the forward movement of the age, history, as progress, is elevated to the status of ultimate arbiter even of the spirit; the spirit of Hegelian metaphysics is consistently made temporal.

Together with this conscious emphasis on time, there arise the substitutes for eternity which characterize the century of the spirit's final realization. Immermann composed "chiliastic" sonnets reminiscent of the Christian expectation of the millennium; their language sounds like an anticipation of George's poetry, and they also have an inner connection with George's proclamation of a new "kingdom."

Weary with bearing the yoke of the age and sick of contempt, he addresses the future king, about whose throne there weaves a wreath of arabesques, as the greatest individuals have desired.

> I gaze into our night and see the star
> Which gives the future ages their direction.
> When duties see its beauteous reflection
> They turn their thoughts to where their rulers are.
>
> Its day will come. But still that day is far.
> Before it all the present day's collection
> Of fables shows its foolish imperfection.
> Tomorrow's seed is planted by that star.

This future ruler in the fullness of time will not be a hero surrounded by war; neither will he be a prophet who will enslave man through the power of his word. He does not preach, nor does he teach mankind a prayer; "naught to the eyes he gives, and naught to the ears." He is an incarnate god and a magnificent human being.

The appreciation accorded to Immermann posthumously by F. Engels[11] shows how much even the radicals considered him a spokesman of his age. Engels' description of the *Memorabilien* and *Epigonen* comes to the conclusion that Immermann recognized the historical demands of the age, and that he himself should be reckoned among the "moderns," but that his Prussian sympathies, to an extent, closed his mind to the course of history. He concludes his essay with a reference to the youthful nature of the "new" age, whose touchstone is the "new philosophy." In contrast to the youth "of twenty-five years ago," as depicted by Immermann, the youth of today has gone through the school of Hegel. Many a seed within the system has sprouted and grown magnificently, and so the battle for the realization of freedom must be continued. In Marx, the chiliasm of the *Epigonen* and the passion for freedom of the Young Hegelians is transformed into the political eschatology of the *Communist Manifesto*. At the end of the dialectic of capitalism stands the totality of collective man, exercising control over production. But even this state of affairs is still a realm of poverty and need; only beyond it do we find the true "realm of freedom,"[12] the "kingdom of God" upon earth, as Hegel early called the goal of his work.[13]

Kierkegaard's Christian reaction derived from the same epoch-making consciousness. Time, whose affliction is transitoriness, stands in need of something absolutely secure, "for the more a man thinks he can do without the eternal, . . . the more he ultimately needs it."[14] In contrast to the "artificial apings" of eternity within transitory life, in his religious discourses Kierkegaard preaches the "expectation of an eternal salvation" and the "unchangeableness of God."[15] If man, who is subject to constant change, approaches this thought with complete seriousness, he will be plunged into anxiety and despair, but also given peace and blessedness. For man's effort to be himself despite an eternal changelessness is in vain. The time which is decisive for man is not eternity itself, but the "moment," in which time and eternity touch.[16] This is the actual time of "decision," because in it time, which hastens uniformly past, divides into the dimensions of future, past, and present. But if time is to be so differentiated, the moment must not be an atom of time, but rather an instant of eternity. Time as such has no real present; it exists only in the moment, as the salient point of decision. The Greeks could have no idea of this meaning of the moment, as more than something evanescent;[17] only Christianity, with its consciousness of sinfulness, could also produce the consciousness of transitoriness and eternity. From the Christian point of view, the moment is the reflection of eternity in time, "its first attempt to bring time to a halt." Here begins the history of the spiritual existence of the self. It was a moment in the strictest sense for Kierkegaard when he attacked the Church and confronted his time with the question whether it was ready to admit the seriousness of eternity. But historically viewed, his attack upon the existing order of Christendom had deeper roots in the spirit of the age and greater consequences for the future than his attempt to make time come to a halt before God.

And thus it is no chance coincidence, but is rather a natural consequence, that Heidegger drew purely secular conclusions from Kierkegaard's Protestant Christianity, blunting the point of his paradox.[18] Out of Kierkegaard's "sickness unto death," he retains only the death and eliminates the despair. Thus despair arising from being-in-the-world[19] becomes the self-assertion of existence (*Dasein*), and death becomes the highest authority of being which rests upon itself.[20] Together with this delimitation of temporal existence, time itself is brought to a stop by means of death. As the only certain and a priori secure point, death becomes the actual *nunc stans* of finite existence, so that time, when examined from the point of view of death, itself acquires the appearance of eternity and permanence.[21] The expectation of future nothingness as the only certain future of the being of the individual transforms Christian eschatology into its opposite: the death of this theory of being, no

longer Christian and yet still somehow Christian, is the last judgment of existence within the world, which—it knows not why—
must "be," simply by being "there" (*da; Da-sein*, "being there,"
"existence"). As the *always* presupposed goal, death takes over the
role of eternity in an existence which is resolutely fixed upon everything and nothing.[22]

What Goethe calls the "all too fleeting," and Hegel a "sandbar
of transitoriness" is in Heidegger's finite metaphysics of finitude the
rock on which eternity runs aground. This philosophy of transitoriness not only has a theological "background," it is in its very substance a theology without God, having "sprung" from Christianity
in a double sense. For this reason it was acutely aware of the ancient
relationship of being to time as perpetual present or "presence."[23]
But eternity as perpetual present is not only the basic Greek concept
of time, beheld in heaven, but also that of Hegel and Goethe.

2   Time and History
for Hegel and Goethe

a   *The Present*
as Eternity

> "Fortunately your talent is directed towards the
> tone, that is, towards the moment. Now, since a
> consistent sequence of moments is itself always a
> kind of eternity, it has been granted to you al-
> ways to be constant in the midst of everything
> transitory; you satisfy thereby both me and
> Hegel's spirit, insofar as I understand it."
>
> Goethe's last letter to Zelter,
> March 11, 1832.

HEGEL   Hegel's first analysis of time[24] is a paraphrase of
Aristotle's discussion of time. In harmony with the Greek view of
time, Hegel also describes it as the "now" (νῦν). The now has an
"enormous right," because only the present truly "is," in contrast to
what is already past and what does not yet exist. The individual,
finite now is nevertheless only a point in time which "stands opposed" to the infinite whole of time, which is an eternal circle. In
the dialectical movement of time, in which the future becomes the

past, while the present, always passing, presses onward to the future, the different aspects of time are reduced to a perpetual present, which comprehends within itself both past and future. The true present is the eternity which is immanent in time. "Only the present is; before and after are not. The concrete present is the outcome of the past, and is pregnant with the future. The true present is thus eternity."[25] The important thing is, therefore, "in the outward form of what is temporal and transitory to recognize the substance which is immanent and the eternal that is present."[26] "Hic Rhodus, hic saltus!" Care for the future, on the contrary, vanishes in the "ether" of the absolutely free consciousness.[27] And because the truth of "Cronus, who begets all and destroys what he begets," is the eternal present, and Hegel does not measure time by what is finite and transitory, the "notion" is the power of time, and time is not the power of the notion.[28] The totality of the stream of time is not itself *in* the temporal process; a moment of the process can be forced into it, but never the totality of time, which is beyond process. In the infinite duration of eternity the limitation of what is transitory to a portion of time is suspended, that is, elevated, preserved, and abated.

What is true of time also characterizes the *spirit* of the history of the world; it is simply "present." "It is not already past, nor is it yet to come; it is completely now." "The spirit has within itself all the stages of the past. The way the spirit lives in history is to be a cyclic recurrence of various stages. . . . When we are dealing with the idea of the spirit and see all of world history merely as its manifestation, then we are dealing only with what is present, no matter how great the past through which we wander. Philosophy deals with what is present, what is real."[29] According to Hegel, the spirit's relationship to time consists simply in the fact that it must "expound" itself in time as well as space, not in any innate temporal quality of the spirit, arising from time and falling into its power.[30]

This concept of time was already surrendered by Hegel's pupils. At odds with their own time and the existing order of reality, they constructed their present according to the pattern of the future. In Hegel's speculation, they no longer saw philosophic theory, but only an apostasy from historical practice. The question of eternity is left to a theology which has seen its day, and philosophy is made over to the consciousness of the age. The relationship between the spirit and time is decided unambiguously in favor of time. Motives similar to those of the Young Hegelians led Heidegger, also, in his criticism of the Hegelian analysis of time,[31] to eliminate eternity as being of no consequence and to ascribe all importance to historical existence as such, limited absolutely by death. The reflection of death in finite existence is the "moment." When judged on this basis, Hegel's "now" seems to be nothing more than an accidentally present point in the continuum of time, far removed from any existential understanding of time as it grows ripe. Heidegger attempts to explain Hegel's "vulgar" understanding of time as arising historically from the "irruption" of classical ontology, which measures time in terms of space and "world time." On the other hand, it can be seen that the concept of time claimed by Heidegger as being "primitive" has its primitive home in the Christian evaluation of the *saeculum* or "world time," even though Heidegger himself only hints at this origin of his concept of time in passing,[32] leaving this historical substance of existential ontology in the background. Thus he can say that it is in vain to seek to explain the "ecstatic" phenomenon of the moment and the priority of the future on the basis of the "flattened" now and "accidentally present" (*vorhanden*) present. But the question remains whether an analysis of time oriented according to Kierkegaard's "moment," which reduces the present to a time merely "accidentally present," contains a truer understanding of time than Hegel, who, still following Aristotle, comprehended the totality of time, and, as a philosopher, was free of anxiety over his own "ability to be whole." Only if Hegel had sought to be "momentarily" for his own time[33] could one say that he had leveled the now and accommodated "world time."[34]

The true crux in Hegel's analysis of time is not that he thought of eternity, but that—in spite of his study of Aristotle's *Physics*—he no longer saw it as it was primitively seen by the Greeks, in the circling constellations of the heavens and the real "ether," but rather ascribed it to a spirit, in the notion of which the Greek and Christian traditions are inextricably entangled. As philosopher of the Christian-Germanic world, Hegel understood the spirit as will and freedom. For this reason, the relationship of the spirit to time, which he views in the Greek fashion as an everlasting present and recurrent cycle, remains in fact a contradiction and a riddle, solved only by Hegel's pupils in favor of freedom of the will, for which the future is primary. But even for Hegel the liberation of the spirit effected by the irruption of Christianity was the absolutely critical point in the history of the spirit. In Hegel's philosophy, this historical moment in the growth of the Christian spirit is considered one with the eternal present of the Greek view of the world.

GOETHE   At the level of words, Goethe's view of time is identical with Hegel's concept; but the way by which Goethe arrived at the view that the eternal is immanent in time is as different from the way in which Hegel arrived at the same idea as Goethe's sense of nature is different from Hegel's intellectual speculation. In innumerable passages Goethe sings the praises of the present and the moment, not the violently "decisive" moment, but rather the moment in which eternity appears of its own accord. Nothing should be anticipated, nothing regretted. Once, when a toast was proposed to reminiscence, he declared vehemently that he did not approve a reminiscence: whatever we experience of any importance must enter at once into our inner self and live within us eternally, shaping our lives. Man must learn to appreciate the present and the condition of the moment, because every condition, indeed every moment, is infinitely valuable: "it is the representative of eternity as a whole."[35] The archetype of a perpetual present was for Goethe the being of nature, whose generation and passing revealed itself to him as a metamorphosis of something ever constant. Morphology in particular taught him to see the "eternal in the transitory." Hegel's description of "spirit" is true of Goethe's "nature": "Everything is always present in it. It knows no past and future. The present is its eternity."[36] "Nature is always Jehovah: what it is, what it was, and what it will be." In poetic perfection there unfold from the same thoughts three poems from *Gott und Welt.* "The eternal makes advance in all: For all to nothingness must fall, If it persists in standing still," ends the poem "Eins und Alles." "Nothing to nothingness can fall! The eternal makes advance in all, And therefore live your life in joy," begins "Das Vermächtnis." "Nor time, nor power can ever mutilate a form which life continues to create," we read in "Urworte."

This view of the totality of time[37] is true not only for God and the world, but also for the life of man: here, too, the present is all. "All love refers to the present; something that is pleasing to me in the present, appears to my mind's eye when absent, awakes the desire for its renewed presence; the fulfillment of this wish is accompanied by a lively enjoyment, the continuation of this joy by a pleasure which is always the same. This is what we actually love, and it follows that we can love whatever can come into our presence. To say the final word: the love of what is divine is always striving to realize in the present that which is highest.[38] Such an exalted realization of man in the totality of the world is expressed by the poem which is called "the present" and concludes with "eternity."[39]

Not only the present, in which eternity resides, but also the fleeting moment is infinitely valuable.[40] Even the value of the past depends upon the seriousness with which the present moment is encountered, whereby what is transitory is preserved for the future. For this reason Goethe commended diaries of all sorts. "All the same we value the present too little, . . . discard most things in order to be free of them. A daily review of what has been achieved and experienced has the effect of making a man aware of his activity and contented with it; it leads to conscientiousness. What is virtue except what is truly suitable for every occasion? In such a daily diary, errors and mistakes come to light of their own accord, the illumination of the past profits the future. We learn to value the moment when we treat it at once as an historical moment."[41] It is also a kind of eternity when man gives to moments, as they vanish away, the logical order of a "series," thus remaining constant in the face of what is transitory. With the desire to unite his view of eternity in time with the Christian, Goethe wrote to Countess Stolberg, after he had recovered from a deadly sickness, "To live long means to outlive many things: men whom we have loved, hated, ignored; kingdoms, capitals, even forests and trees which we sowed and planted in our youths. We outlive ourselves, and are completely thankful if only a few gifts of body and spirit are left to us. We can take pleasure in all this that is transitory if only the eternal is present with us in every moment; the transitoriness of time causes us no suffering."[42] A "supreme moment" in which eternity resides is also the final word of Faust as he dies. In this conviction Goethe considered himself at one with Hegel, as his last letter to Zelter shows.

Nevertheless, Goethe's sense of nature rejected the belief in the reasonableness of history, which teaches that the eternal presence of "what is" is revealed primarily in the history of the world and as spirit. The deeper reason for his antipathy toward the world of history lay in his insight that Christianity had effected a separation between the natural world and the "idea." "The ideal was merely religious, Christian."[43] Their evaluations of the historical world accordingly diverge. Hegel holds to the idea of world history as an emanation of the spirit, whose absolute nature is grounded upon Christianity. Goethe views the course of the world as an emanation of nature, which is itself reason. Their attitudes toward history reveal the difference between their apparently identical conceptions of time.

b Hegel's Philosophy of History and Goethe's View of the Course of the World

Etymologically *Geschichte* ("history," "story," "event") means the same as *Geschehen* ("happening," "event"). In Greek, *historein* means "to inquire after something" or "to investigate something," and by report and description to give information about what has been inquired after and investigated. The two basic meanings of *Geschichte* and history have been covered over and assimilated by many secondary meanings.[44] The meaning of history has traveled so far from its original meaning that among modern historians reflection upon the history of "historicism" has almost replaced the investigation of events. The first historians of the West did not study the "Rise of Historicism"; they were explorers, with their eyes and ears open, and told us in exemplary fashion what they had seen themselves and learned through others. What is meant by "world history" since Hegel's time is as remote and abstract as this original meaning of *historia* is concrete and natural. Ever since Hegel, world history, in contrast to *historia*, seems to be precisely what one has *not* seen and experienced, inquired after and investigated for himself. And yet the events of each single day, everyday history, show us on a small scale something of world history on a large scale. Before any universal history, the daily papers transmit every day the events of the world; our own time in particular can flatter itself that it is daily experiencing world history on a grand scale. But together with world history as a whole, which passes us all by without regard, there is also another kind of event, which attracts less attention but, for all that, is none the less real: the unpretentious events in the course of man's daily life, and the uniform events of the course of the natural world.

A trivial example may clarify: the front page of every newspaper contains a large-scale report of world history as a whole; a few pages later, the reader finds stories reported which are small, less remote from everyday life, such as news of the social life of the city. And finally, in a corner, stands the daily weather report. Anyone who has not become dulled through habitual reading of the paper will have to ask the following question: What have these three spheres of life in common, large-scale world history, the small events of daily life, and nature, whose course is neither trivial nor imposing? The simple fact that man must live in the midst of nature, his environment, and world history, determines the way philosophy must approach the events of the world.

Hegel delivered his lecture on the philosophy of history in the years 1822–23 and 1830–31. The introduction explains the principle of his study: the unfolding of the spirit, and also of freedom, in stages. The spirit, which, as world spirit dominates history, is negative vis-à-vis nature; that is, progress in the unfolding of the spirit toward freedom is progress in liberation from subjection to nature. In Hegel's philosophy, therefore, nature as such has no independent positive significance. It is not the ground of the history of the world, but only its geographical terrain. The natural relation of land and sea, the configuration of the coasts, of the mountains and plains, the course of rivers and the form of mountains, rain and drought, hot, cold, and temperate climate—it is true that all of these have an influence upon the historical life of man, but it is never absolutely determinative. To the "natural type" of a particular "locale," there corresponds the type and character of the people living there, because the spirit displays itself in time *and* space. Hegel frequently developed these correspondences between the world of nature and the world of the spirit in great detail.[45] In principle, nevertheless, nature was for him merely the natural "arena" of the spiritual events of the world. For Goethe, nature is the key for understanding these events.

Furthermore, the everyday life of mankind is without substantial significance for Hegel's idea of world history. It is true that every individual has a value which is independent of the "tumult of world history"; and the interests and passions which dominate the "small circles" of human life are the same as in the great theater of the world. But world history moves upon a higher plane than that of everyday life, whose ethical criteria do not obtain for political events. Of course, it can happen that a single individual who personally opposes the historical progress of a universal idea stands on a higher moral level than one who commits a crime which serves as a means to the end of historical order. But in such conflicts, both parties stand "within the same circle," namely, the universal course of events; and it is ultimately absurd to make moral demands of historical actions and oppose politics with morality.[46] The absolute right of the world spirit transcends all particular rights. Within the movement which involves the "world as a whole," individuals are only means to the end of this whole.

Therefore, for Hegel the only really valuable individuals are those who are "historic," who bring to fruition the great universal purposes of world history by representing a "national spirit" and an "idea" destined to dominate. For example, Hegel considered Napoleon such an individual. When the latter arrived in Jena in 1806, Hegel wrote in a letter, "I saw the Emperor—that soul of worldwide significance—riding on parade through the city. It is indeed a wonderful sensation to see such an individual, who here, concentrated at one point, sitting upon a horse, encompasses the world and rules it." Even Napoleon's downfall only corroborates this historical view. In 1816, Hegel writes to Niethammer, "The more universal affairs of the world . . . give me most occasion for more universal observations, which the individual and proximate, however interesting, only remove from my mind. I am convinced that the world spirit has given our age the command to advance. Such a command must be obeyed. This state marches forward irresistibly, like the closed ranks of an armored phalanx, with a motion as imperceptible as that of the sun, through thick and thin. Innumerable light-armed troops of both sides surround the flanks, most of whom have no idea what the battle is about; their heads are battered as by an invisible hand. No deception can bring about delay; it can reach as far as the shoelaces of this colossus, and smear a bit of polish or of mud on them, but cannot undo them, much less take off his divine shoes with the . . . elastic soles, or even the seven league boots, once they have been put on. The safest (inwardly and outwardly) course is probably to keep the giants advancing always in sight. In this way one can hold one's ground, and edify the entire company of zealots by helping spread pitch to snag the shoes of the giant, amusing oneself the while by giving an assist to the solemn confusion." The reaction against Napoleon was well described by the Jacobins: *la vérité en la repoussant, on l'embrasse.* It stands within the same sphere as that against which it reacts, and ultimately puts its seal upon the events it presumed it detested the most. As far as the fuss of the "personal ants, fleas, and bugs" is concerned, the "kindly creator" meant it only for jests, sarcasms, and malicious sport, without having any appreciable effect upon the proportion of good or evil. Hegel has a lofty conception of world history as a history of national spirits, states, and historic individuals who carry out the "notion" of their age. For Goethe, too, Napoleon was a "compendium of the world," but because he did not systematize on the basis of an idea, but rather lived by intuition, he saw in Napoleon not only a mere "agent of the world spirit," but an inconceivable "phenomenon," a "demigod," a completely extraordinary man who emerged from the "abyss."

If the principle behind the events of the world is neither nature nor the everyday life of man, but rather "idea" and "spirit," then it must be asked upon what Hegel bases this "ideological" history of the world, and in what relationship it stands to the immediate experience and intuition of real life.

The basic phenomenon of historical life is *change*, the perpetual succession of nations, states, and individuals, of birth and death, of vigor and decay, initiating and destroying. The noblest and the basest, actions of heroism and outrages—nothing remains constant. And in all this process we recognize something of ourselves: human activity and suffering. The "self-seeking" of individual men, together with that of entire states and empires is the "most potent" influence. Immense labors turn to dust, and the smallest events produce the greatest historical consequences. Periods of energetic freedom and abundant wealth alternate with periods of miserable dependence and wretched poverty. An unprejudiced view of this play of human passions and sufferings, irrationality and violence, provides neither a basic idea nor a rational goal in the history of the world. It is a "confused heap of rubble" and a "shambles" upon which the fortune of peoples, states, and individuals is sacrificed. It is just this "immediate" view of history which makes Hegel ask why, for what purpose, this all takes place. Hegel believes that, as a Christian philosopher, he can answer this question by secularizing the Christian doctrine of providence and converting the salvation story of Christianity into a secular theodicy, for which the divine spirit is immanent in the world, the state is an earthly god, and all history is divine.

In contrast to historical empiricism and "emotional reflection" upon it, the task of the philosophy of history is to discover the "principle" which permeates all change. By using the "eye of the notion" to obtain a rational view of the world, it recognizes the rational content of world history, although not in every individual, "accidental" existence, but in the world "as a whole." According to

Hegel, the rational principle of the world consists in its perpetual "progress in consciousness of freedom," knowing that freedom is "producing a world" here. Hegel's philosophy of history traced this process consistently from the Oriental world through the Greco-Roman world to the Christian-Germanic world. At the end stands the liberation effected in Europe by the French Revolution.

This metaphysical historicism of the Hegelian system replaces the vanished doctrine of providence of the Christian religion. Even today, as faith in the meaning of history, this historicism is the religion of the "educated," whose skepticism is not vigorous enough to live entirely without faith; it is the cheapest sort of substitute. For what is cheaper than the faith that over the long course of history everything that has ever happened, with all its consequences, must have a meaning and a purpose! Even those who know nothing of Hegel continue to think today in the Hegelian spirit, to the extent that they share his admiration for the power of history, using "world history" to disregard the demands and miseries of the day. Only such an honest thinker as Burckhardt was free of the fascination which Hegel exerted on his successors. The actual pupils of Hegel converted his metaphysics of history into an absolute historicism; that is, they retained merely this historical aspect of the absoluteness of the spirit which unfolds historically, and made the events of the age into the supreme power over even philosophy and the spirit. The "historical idea of an age" or the "genuine spirit of the age" is exalted by Ruge to the position of a supreme master which is right in every case. For—he concludes from Hegel[47]—the "spirit" is real only in the world process which is brought about by the actions of men. For Hegel's pupils, the "historical spirit" or the "self-consciousness of the age" is the criterion of what is true and what is false, because only history in the course of time reveals what is the truth of the age, through its success. But if "everything falls to history," the history of the world and of the spirit is in principle full of promise, for its principle is progress toward the future, which is the essence of time. Thus the Young Hegelians transform Hegel's retrospective and reminiscent historicism into an historical futurism; they desire to be more than the consequence of history, they want themselves to be epoch-making and thus "historic."

As a result of the political reaction to the events of the forties, this active historicism of the Young Hegelians died down, and from Haym to Dilthey, historicism was content to water down Hegel's metaphysics of the history of the spirit into a "spiritual history" without metaphysics. But the Fascist revolution which emerged in Italy and Germany after the First World War led to a revitalization of the activistic historicism of the forties. Those who were historically educated felt it at first to be only negative, an "antihistoricism."[48] But already in Nietzsche it was revealed as a will to the future, and only for this reason was it so critical of "historical" culture. As was the case a century previously, the desire is to be consciously "historical," to engage in more than "antiquarian" retrospection. What leading statesmen do and preach today is done with the desire and awareness of being a priori "historic"! Men think in terms of centuries and millennia. Not a week passes without someone delivering an "historic" speech, that is, a speech which—in contrast to a commemorative speech—commemorates the future, because it is assumed that only the centuries to come will appreciate what we do today. The future is trusted to give historical right and historical justification to the actions and events of the present; man is convinced that history is the last judgment. Even in this perverted use of the word "historic" can be heard the solemnity given it by Hegel. When man engages in extravagant historicism, it makes no real difference whether he is retrospective or expectant, tired of the past or greedy for the future.

However extravagant Hegel's systematization of history as "progress in consciousness of freedom" appears in light of its immediate, empirical aspect, the reason it could become so popular lies in its own kernel, from which the Christian theological hull can be stripped off.

The outline of the Hegelian system consists in its measuring the course of history according to temporal progress; that is, on the basis of the final stage, it argues backwards to those preceding as necessarily leading to it. This orientation toward an historical sequence presupposes that the only valid aspect of world history is that which has many consequences, that the sequence of world events should be evaluated according to the rational principle of its success. But success is not only the highest court of appeal for Hegel's historical theory; it is also a constant measure of everyday life, where the assumption is likewise made that the success of something proves its superior right to that which is unsuccessful. Thus the popular kernel of Hegel's speculation lies in the universal conviction that only what is succcessful is proven right. Through Darwin's theory of evolution, in the nineteenth century this belief also received an apparent support in the realm of nature. Under the influence of economic competition, Darwin discovered the law of "natural selection," according to which the higher species of animals arise through the survival, in the "struggle for existence," of the fittest over the less fit. Hegel's philosophy of history and Darwin's biological theory[49] both started from what is empirically successful, and argued backwards to the supposed necessity and inner right of its appearance. Their admiration of historical and biological forces led to an idolization of whatever force happened to be victorious.[50] Whatever, on the other hand, vanished from the memory of history because it was destroyed or remained unsuccessful, was, according to Hegel's formula, an "unjustified existence."[51]

"Success," says a German proverb, "crowns the master." "Success," says Nietzsche, with equal right, "has always been the greatest of liars."[52] Success is in fact an indispensable criterion of human life, but it proves everything and nothing: everything, because in world history as in everyday life only that which is successful remains, and nothing, because even the greatest popular success proves nothing of the inner worth and true "historical greatness" of what has actually been successful.[53] Things wretched and stupid, baseness and madness, have often had the greatest success. It is quite remarkable when a victorious power proclaims the fame and honor of those it has conquered and not merely the ostensible right of its own successful power. Never has an historical power come to be without violence, injustices, and offenses; but for good or ill, offended mankind accustoms itself to every change, while world history "gathers great treasures at our expense."[54]

Whoever has really experienced a slice of world history, rather than merely knowing it through hearsay, speeches, books, and newspapers, will have to come to the conclusion that Hegel's philosophy of history[55] is a pseudotheological schematization of history arranged according to the idea of progress toward an eschatological fulfillment at the end of time; it does not correspond at all to visible reality. The true "passion" of world history does not reside only in the sonorous and imposing "quantities" with which it deals, but also in the silent suffering it brings upon men. If there is anything in world history to be admired, it is the power, the patience, and stubbornness with which it continues to re-create mankind after all losses, destructions, and injuries.

The way in which Goethe looked at history is far removed from Hegel's schematization, not because Goethe was a "poet," and Hegel a "thinker," but rather because Goethe's pure human disposition was as open to nature and the everyday life of man as to the great events of the world. Through his position at the court at Weimar, he experienced world history at much closer proximity than did Hegel. The historical events with which Goethe came in contact were the coronation of Emperor Joseph II in Frankfurt (1764), the Seven Years' War (1756–63), the death of Frederick the Great (1786), the outbreak of the French Revolution (1789), the German campaign in France (1792), the Battle of Jena and the end of the Holy Roman Empire of the German Nation (1806), the Assembly of Princes at Erfurt and the parley with Napoleon (1808), the burning of Moscow (1812), the Prussian wars of Independence (1813–14), Napoleon's downfall (1815), Metternich's ascendancy, and finally the Paris, July Revolution (1830). "I have the great advantage . . . of having been born at a time when great events were the order of the day, which continued throughout my long life, so that I was a living witness of the Seven Years' War, next the separation of America from England, then the French Revolution, and finally the whole Napoleonic era until the downfall of its hero and the subsequent events. I have arrived thereby at quite different conclusions and insights than will be possible for all those who are now being born, who must appropriate those great happenings through books which do not understand them."[56]

That historical event with which Goethe not only came in contact, but against which he was forced to direct his entire life, was the French Revolution, to whose outbreak he was all the more sensitive for having just returned from Italy in order to settle at Weimar. Only a few passages in his works and letters betray the degree to which this historic cataclysm of the existing order upset his inner peace through its perceptible effect upon human conditions. "You can well imagine that the French Revolution was also a revolution for me. For the rest, I am studying the ancients, and following their example as well as may be done in Thuringia," we read in a letter to F. H. Jacobi.[57] In the midst of dissolution he clung to his studies "as to a spar in a shipwreck," and tried to master this "most terrible of all occurrences" through literature, with an effort which he called "boundless." "When I look back over the many years, I see clearly how dependence on this immense object so long devoured my poetic ability to almost no result; and yet it made such an impression upon me that I cannot deny, when I still think of continuing *Die natürliche Tochter,* this remarkable production takes shape in my thoughts, even though I do not have the courage to give myself over to working it up in detail."[58]

Forty years later, looking back over what he had accomplished, Goethe distinguishes himself from the younger generation by the criterion of this event, so decisive did he feel that historical discontinuity in the thoughts and affairs of men.[59] None of his revolutionary dramas was successful, but only his description of the campaign in France.

One sentence is usually quoted from this classic representation of a period of war, a sentence which sounds very Hegelian. It refers to the bombardment of Valmy: "A new epoch of world history begins at this place, today; and you can say that you were there." But the proper meaning of this sentence can be understood only in the context of what follows, which shifts the historical accent to the entirety of real and banal everyday life: "In these moments, when no one had nothing to eat, I claimed a bite of bread from what had been acquired earlier today; furthermore, of the wine, which yesterday had flowed so freely, enough was left to fill a brandy bottle. . . ."[60] In another passage, where Goethe returns once more to his statement, he continues in the same fashion: "But this is the way man lives, especially in war; he is satisfied with what is unavoidable, and tries to fill the intervals between danger, deprivation, and dismay with pleasure and amusement. The same was true here. The oboists of Thadden played 'Ça ira' and the 'Marseillaise,' while one bottle of champagne after another was drained."[61]

These two remarks are much more characteristic of the mood, tone, and content of the description than the isolated historical statement. The persuasive truth of Goethe's account rests upon the complete fairness with which he depicts soldiers and civilians, peasants and nobles, revolutionaries and emigrants, friends and enemies, leaders and followers, excitement and boredom, exertion and fatigue, hunger and thirst. He describes the entire course of the real life of men in the midst of war's confusion in the proper mixture; he neither glorifies the story in monumental terms nor trivializes it critically; he views it without prejudice, as a phenomenon.

The prejudice to which world history as a whole can seduce us consists in viewing this history in the abstract, without the realities of human life and real situations, as though it were a world in itself without relevance to people that act and are acted upon within it. Goethe was not guilty of such philosophic abstraction. He does not construct "national spirits" as incarnations of absolute "principles," but rather tells quite graphically how he felt the desire to eat in that historic moment of the bombardment of Valmy. After Goethe's return from Bohemia, when the "Holy Roman Empire of the German Nation" came to an end, he confesses that at that moment he was more disturbed by a quarrel between his attendant and his coachman than by that important, but vague and distant, event.

Similarly, he confesses in a letter to Zelter that the "Jeremiads" of the world, after Napoleon's victory in the Battle of Jena, seemed to be mere "empty clichés," although they were occasioned by great evils. "When someone bewails what he and his surroundings have suffered, what he has lost and is afraid of losing, this I hear with sympathy, am glad to talk of it, and glad to give comfort. But when men lament some great thing that is supposed to be lost, which no man in Germany has set eyes on once in his life, much less worried about, then I must conceal my impatience in order not to be impolite or appear as an egoist."[62] A short while before the battle, when Goethe's friends were enthusiastic and could think of nothing but war songs, Wieland asked him why he was so quiet. Goethe replied that he had also composed a war song, which, to the unwilling amazement of the others, he recited: *Vanitas! Vanitas! Vanitas!*[63]

During Napoleon's campaign in Russia, he wrote to C. F. von Reinhard: "The world is larger and smaller than is thought. . . . Whoever moves, touches the world; and whoever remains still, is touched by it. For this reason we must always be ready to touch or to be touched. That Moscow has been burned does not matter to me. History will have its story to tell in the future. Delhi was destroyed only after conquest, but it was the conquest of the conquerors; Moscow is destroyed after conquest; but it is that of the conquered. Were I a speaker, it would provide me with much amusement to develop such an antithesis. But now when we come back to ourselves, when in such an immense, enormous misfortune you have lost brothers and sisters and I have lost friends, who were close to my heart, then of course we feel the times we live in, and how serious we must be if we are to be gay after our former fashion."[64] The statement about Moscow may seem cynical, but cynicism is usually only the grosser manifestation of a truth, which in this case is the fact that world history loses all true meaning when we do not come back from it to ourselves and what is nearest to us.

But where Goethe views world history in its own power, disregarding man, it does not appear to him as "reason," but as a phenomenon of nature. In 1802, on the occasion of reading an historicopolitical work, he wrote to Schiller, "Taken as a whole, it presents the frightful aspect of brooks and streams which, by natural necessity, rush together out of many heights and through many valleys, until finally they bring about the overflowing of a great river and a flood, in which all are destroyed, those who saw it coming as well as those who were unsuspecting. In all this monstrous experience there is nothing to see but nature: nothing of what we philosophers would be so happy to call freedom. We shall wait and see whether Bonaparte's personality will amuse us further with this glorious and dominating appearance."[65] But even Napoleon was looked upon by Goethe not as a step towards freedom, but as a natural phenomenon at war not only with princes and peoples, but also with the very elements, eliminating everything standing in the way of his great plan: "At every moment he is pursuing his purpose. Whatever stands in his way is cut down and removed, even if it were his own son. Other princes and great men give themselves over to numerous aversions and diversions; he loves everything that can serve his purpose, however much it is at variance with his individual mood. He is like a good conductor who, while everyone has his favorite instrument which he prefers, knows how to make use of them all in his orchestra without love and without hate. Therefore, the end result is the same, and an individual has no advantage, whether he is loved or hated by him. He certainly has no love for the Duke of Weimar, and yet this does not disadvantage the latter. Similarly, those whom he loves derive equally little advantage from the fact. He lives at all time within an idea, within a purpose, within a plan; and one must beware coming in its way, because on this point he shows no indulgence. In short, Goethe let it be known that Napoleon directed the world according to the same laws by which Goethe directed the theater."[66]

He admired Napoleon's "enormous understanding of the world" and his more than human will, which clearly and decisively subordinated everything to his political purpose. For him, Napoleon was the incarnation of the two great powers through which everything of consequence and permanence in the world comes to pass: "force and consequence." Consequence, the consistent pursuit of a goal, represents for Goethe in the realm of human caprice what universal "reason" is for Hegel.[67] "But consequence, unyielding, strict consequence, can be applied even by the most insignificant, and will seldom fail of its purpose, since its silent power grows without

ceasing over the course of time. Where I cannot act with consequence, cannot exert continuous influence, it is advisable not to seek
to act at all. To do so would be only to disturb the natural evolutionary course of things, which brings medicine for its own
wounds, without being able to guarantee its taking a more favorable
course." Force, nevertheless, "easily becomes unpopular, incites
counteraction, and is actually given only to a few favored individuals."[68] He knew that "absolute activity," of whatever sort, must
lead to "bankruptcy," while "flexibility coupled with a firm will"
conquers in the end over mere violence.

> Freedom is never gained by mere desiring:
> Who would have all, must be o'er all the master,
> His victory teaches strife to those aspiring;
> His cunning makes the others' cunning vaster;
> Thus force and treachery arise untiring,
> The world at rest is pregnant with disaster.
> The birth-pangs make humanity aghast,
> Threatening each day as though it were the last.[69]

But the human sum and final truth of world history is shown as
much in peace as in war, because the human condition as such remains constant throughout all change. In the provocative conversation which Goethe had with the historian Luden, he says, "And
even if you were able to study and examine all the sources, what
would you find? Nothing else than a great truth which has long
been known, for whose confirmation one does not have far to look—
the truth that men have been miserable in all lands and in all ages.
Men have always been troubled and worried; they have tortured
and martyred each other; they have made their brief lives bitter for
themselves and for others, and have been unable either to see or to
enjoy the beauty of the world and the sweetness of existence which
the world offers them. Only a few have been comfortable and
happy. The majority, having experienced life for a while, would
rather leave the scene than begin over again. That which gave or
gives them still some hold on life was and is only fear of death. Thus
it is today; thus it has always been; thus it will probably always be.
That is simply the lot of man. What further evidence do we
need?"[70] When Luden replied that the life of individual men is not
the historical life of peoples and nations, Goethe answered, "It is
the same with nations as with individuals. Nations consist of individ-

uals. They, too, come to life like individuals, behave as strangely, though for a somewhat longer time, and likewise die either a violent death or a death brought about by old age and fragility. The total misery and total woe of individuals is the misery and woe of nations."[71]

It is extremely characteristic that Goethe did not owe this unusual humanitarianism of his historical view, which was more rigorous than sympathetic, to any study of the history of the spirit, but rather to his study of nature, which he felt to be "true," "solid," and "orderly" in every phenomenon. His familiarity with plants and bones, with stones and colors, developed in him the patience and attentiveness which does not construct systems and does not gain knowledge by force, but rather allows phenomena to reveal their own secrets, letting them speak for themselves. It is not a mere escape from politics and world events, but rather an essential portion of Goethe's positive nature, when in the midst of the French Revolution he occupies himself with the metamorphosis of plants, during the campaign in France, with the phenomena of color, and during the July Revolution, with morphology, and when he was more concerned with the scientific dispute between Cuvier and Geoffroy Saint-Hilaire than the political cataclysm.[72]

In nature he recognized a law of change such as cannot be demonstrated in the course of world history; for this reason he saw his "primary phenomena" in nature rather than in history. While Hegel had a "spiritual" conception of history, in agreement with Christian theology, which was his point of departure, and saw in nature only the "otherness" of the idea, Goethe saw reason and ideas in nature as such, and found in it an approach to the understanding of man and of history: "Without my studies in the natural sciences, I should never . . . have come to know men as they are. In no other realm can one so easily observe pure intuition and thought, the errors of the senses as well as of the mind, weaknesses and strengths of character. Elsewhere, everything is more or less flexible and insecure, and can be more or less controlled; but nature has no sense of humor, it is always true, always serious, always rigorous, always right, and mistakes and errors are always on the part of man. It scorns the inadequate, surrendering itself and revealing its secrets only to the man who is prepared, honest, and pure."[73]

Kanzler Müller once expressed astonishment when a pupil of Hegel left jurisprudence for the study of the natural sciences. Goethe answered laconically, "From his study of law, he could gain nothing more than insight into the wretched condition of man; therefore he turned to nature."[74] We read again, "For almost a century now the humanities have no longer influenced the minds of the men engaged in them; it is a real piece of good fortune that nature has intervened, drawn the essence of the humanities to itself, and opened to us the way to true humanism from its own side."[75]

Following this road from nature, which is both individual and orderly, to the realm of human caprice, Goethe clung to his scientific insight into the law of change: in all that lives, there takes place a constant alteration of forms, a metamorphosis of what remains the same. "When one views the doings and activities of men over the course of millennia, a few universal formulas can be recognized, which have always exerted a magical power over entire nations as well as individuals; these formulas, eternally recurring, eternally the same under a thousand various embellishments, are the secret gift to life of a higher power. Each man translates these formulas into his own peculiar language, accommodates them in a variety of ways to his own restricted circumstances, and, in the process, often adulterates them so that their original meaning can scarcely be recognized. But again and again this meaning reappears unexpectedly, now among this people, now among that, and the alert investigator can put together out of such formulas a kind of alphabet of the world spirit."[76]

Goethe did not decree this alphabet of the world spirit as a "principle" of the spiritual world, but rather observed it in the primary phenomena of the natural world and tested it in the realm of history, to the extent that it could be tested. For he knew that the action and counteraction of men, which comprise the history of the world, are to an extent "incommensurable" with the notion, because law and chance may work at cross purposes, while Hegel was forced to eliminate chance in order to maintain his philosophicotheological schematization. Goethe saw the foundation for such an explanation in the historian's ability to derive an advantage from the uncertainty which is present in everything historical.[77] In spite of the limitless scope of all historical activity, one can observe in it a universal law. As a totality, the history of the world moves in cycles which rise like a spiral, as the past recurs with analogous situations. "The circle of man's course is definite enough; notwithstanding the standstill brought about by barbarism, it has gone through its cycle more than once. Even if a spiral movement is ascribed to it, it still returns again and again to the region through which it has already passed. In this way, all true views and all errors are repeated."[78]

Burckhardt's view of world history was formed according to Goethe's view of the events of the world; for this reason, he is the only modern historian to see it as it is. But in comparison to Goethe, even Burckhardt remained an Hegelian, because he did not view nature immediately, but rather through the mediation of art, and presupposed the distinction between "nature" and "spirit," between study of nature and study of history, which had been made a commonplace by Hegel, Ranke, and Droysen. All historical realms of learning which deal with the spirit suffer from this discontinuity between nature and spirit,[79] which originates with Descartes. Therefore, Goethe's bitter struggle against the natural science of Newton is in agreement with his ironic attitude, which reached the level of satire, toward the current official historical disciplines. It was not the result of mere "antipathy,"[80] but rather of the firm conviction that world history, viewed purely historically, is the most "absurd" thing under the sun,[81] "a tissue of nonsense for the higher thinker."[82] The work of the historian is not only uncertain, thankless, and dangerous,[83] it is a "mishmash of error and violence," a "refuse can and junk pile; at best a government project." What History transmits is, like any newspaper story, a distortion of the truth, composed of wishful thinking and tendentiousness, special pleading and stupidity, cowardice and lies. How much does even the best historical study give us of the real life of a people, and how much of this little bit is true, and how much of what is true is certain?[84]

In our own time, two paths have been taken to escape this historical skepticism. In their effect, they both belong together, and both avoid Goethe's insight into the seriousness of the problem of historical epistemology. Some have rejected in advance any knowledge of historical truth by diverting their poetic enthusiasm to "heroes," transforming world events into a "myth" or a "legend."[85] Others have made a virtue of necessity by stiffening their subjective standpoint into a dogma, and their distaste of objective knowledge into the will to "decide" and "judge." In contrast to these modern escapes from the difficulties of historical knowledge, Goethe insisted that physical and ethical phenomena be studied as purely as possible, that is, as they are. Consequently, Goethe's oft-quoted statement about the "rewriting of history" had a very different meaning for Goethe than that usually read into it.

This phrase about "rewriting" history comes from Goethe; but he himself uses it as something "someone has said." The passage in question, from one of his letters, refers to Sartorius' historical study of the rule of the Ostrogoths in Italy. In context, it reads: "Someone has said that world history must from time to time be rewritten. When has there been an epoch that made this as necessary as does the present one? You have provided a superb example of how it should be done. The hatred of the Romans for the victor, even when he was kindly, presumption upon outmoded privileges, the desire for a different state of affairs without having anything better in view, irrational hopes, haphazard undertakings, alliances with no prospect of benefit, and whatever else is the unhappy retinue of such times—you have described all that magnificently, proving to us that such things really happened in those days."[86]

Thus for Goethe the rewriting of the past by no means had the now current sense of a self-assertion of the present; on the contrary: it meant a justification of the past. It describes everything just as it "really" took place in those days. This claim to historical objectivity is only apparently contradicted by the circumstance that Goethe's agreement with Sartorius' description of a time long past contains a tacit reference to his own time, since Goethe, thinking of the victors and vanquished of a former age, was also thinking in his letter of 1811 of the supine reaction of the Germans to Napoleon's rule. The experiences of the "present epoch," which necessitate the rewriting, do not influence it, but rather make possible for the first time a proper understanding of what took place then; for what is taking place now reminds us of what has taken place before. History repeats certain basic forms of human destiny "with a thousand various embellishments," and it must therefore be rewritten "from time to time," because it is only under analogous circumstances that the fantasies, wishes, hopes, and undertakings of past ages can appear as they really were. Goethe's concrete mode of thought was so far from any polemic attitude toward objective knowledge of historical truth in favor of an evaluating subjectivity that he discarded the writing of history precisely at the point where it seemed to him to be "dishonest," because it was subjectively based.

Even more clearly than in the letter to Sartorius, Goethe expressed his views on the rewriting of history in his history of color theory (at the conclusion of the third section): "That world history must be rewritten from time to time is not doubted in our day. But such a necessity does not arise because much of what took place has been discovered only later, but because new points of view are given, because he who lives in time which goes forward is brought to new vantage points from which the past can be surveyed and evaluated in a new manner. The same is true for the sciences." In particular, the eighteenth century, which might be called "self-satisfied," should be re-examined in this light, because it did many an injustice to the preceding ages! "Skepticism and debunking" led to the same result in this century: "an arrogant self-sufficiency," a rejection of everything that cannot be taken in at a glance, and a suspicious lack of forbearance for "daring but unsuccessful efforts." Goethe accuses the historians of the eighteenth century of a lack of "thoroughness and fairness" in their evaluation of other people and other ages; for this reason he thought it necessary to submit the works of this period to a rewriting. Goethe's sense of justice resists the "exorcism" of the Enlightenment, which banished the "spirit" together with the "ghosts," but by no means—as was the case with the exorcists of rewriting—historical and human justice toward other men and ages.[87]

It was Nietzsche's questioning of the value of truth in general, and the usefulness of historical truth in particular, which gave to the phrase "writing history" that activistic meaning which transforms it into an easy justification for every arbitrary reordering of the past. "Only with the utmost power of the present may you interpret the past: only through the most powerful exertion of your noblest traits will you discover what in the past is great and worthy of being known and of being preserved,"[88] said Nietzsche. But this is not a claim for any self-righteous superiority of the present as such. Instead, it replaces an "objectivity" which has become dubious, because it is equally tolerant of everything, with a higher objectivity, namely, justice, which judges.[89] Nietzsche's followers strayed far from this sense of justice. Feeling themselves to be "architects of the future," they thought they were automatically possessed of those noblest traits without which the message of the past cannot be deciphered. They thought they could hold up an empty scholarship and an outworn culture through indisputable "evaluations," through "response," "reorganization," "revolution," and existential "decision." German history from Charlemagne to Bismarck, the history of Christianity, the history of philosophy, art, and literature: all were "rewritten," that is, told in a way they had never been, but which corrresponded to the "historical self-consciousness of the twentieth century."[90]

The same Goethe who described so bitterly and sarcastically the inadequacies of historical study, himself opened new and progressive ways in the realm of history. In the historical portion of his theory of color, he provided a standard for the treatment of "spiritual history" by discussing a series of scientific discoveries and concealments with reference to the character and way of thought of human beings, but not abstractly as a history of mere ideas and opinions. For he understood the actual history of realms of knowledge as the conflict of the individual with immediate experience and mediated tradition, because in the last analysis it is the "individual" who can "open himself to a more inclusive nature and a more inclusive tradition."[91] In addition, his sketch of Winckelmann shows marvelously how even art can be treated historically from the standpoint of man; and particularly in *Dichtung und Wahrheit*, he showed how an individual man caught in the action and counteraction of his historical environment develops into a man whose life is of significance for the entire world.

> Let vanish all the fleeting mystery!
> In vain you search for counsel there.
> For virtue lies within past history,
> Enshrined in deeds beyond compare.
>
> And thus what lives in perpetuity
> Gains power from what comes after it;
> Reflection source of continuity,
> Alone brings man eternal benefit.
>
> This is the question's sole solution
> Which seeks our other fatherland;
> What's constant in our earthly constitution
> Fulfills eternity's demand.

These verses contain whatever "historical sense" Goethe had. But in his old age, after finishing the *Wanderjahre*, and forty years after the French Revolution, he looked back upon all that had taken place, and was forced to conclude that, as a result of the cataclysm of the existing order, the younger generation was incapable of producing a life work which of itself would endure and have a lasting effect. He writes to Zelter: "I must now attempt to see, day by day and hour by hour, what remains to be done in order to assist the healthy growth of what has been begun and give it practical security. There are many excellent young people, but the idiots all want to begin at the beginning, independently, . . . without help, ineffectually, and work to do justice to what is unattainable. I look upon this course of events since 1789 and know what could have been accomplished if someone had intervened out of unmixed motives, and everyone had not tried to hold on to a peculium of his own. It is fitting now, in 1829, that I have a clear vision of the future, perhaps state it publicly; but even if I succeed, it won't help. For what is true is simple and gives men little to do; what is false gives plenty of opportunity for wasting time and strength."[92]

It is easy to miss seeing that what is true, to the extent that it has made itself heard in Germany during the past century, can be seen in Goethe and not in more recent figures. It is usually not understood that the exception to the ordinary is not what is conspicuous by excess and deficiency, but what is completely normal.

In Goethe's house at Weimar, his existence in time made itself visible and palpable in space. At a seemly distance from it there stands the Nietzsche Archives, to which a pretentious hall was added, somehow appropriate to the early style of *Zarathustra*. It is intended to promote the expansion of the "Nietzsche movement," the growth of "Zarathustra's way of life," and the "somehow" related creative forces of Young Germany.[93] The Nietzsche Hall of the Third Reich is Nietzsche's "Bayreuth," by which Wagner took revenge on Nietzsche. The other Germany, older in years, can be seen in the ordinary house of Goethe.[94]

Part Two

Studies in the History of the Bourgeois-Christian World

1 The Problem of Bourgeois Society

> "This man cares for himself and for his family
> . . . and at the same time he also labors for the
> common good. . . . On the one hand he is called
> *bourgeois*, on the other, *citoyen*. Townsman and
> citizen of the nation, the one as much a formal
> townsman as the other."
>
> HEGEL

Rousseau's writings contain the first and clearest statement of the human problem of bourgeois society. It consists in the fact that man, in bourgeois society, is not a unified whole. On the one hand, he is a private individual, and on the other, a citizen of the state, for bourgeois society has a problematic relationship to the state. Ever since Rousseau, the incongruity between them has been a fundamental problem of all modern theories of the state and society. The totalitarian states of the present day are an attempt to answer Rousseau's question: How can man, who is by nature himself something entire, be brought into conformity with the completely different entirety of the *société politique?* A true conformity between the two seems impossible; and therefore, in the education of an individual, the decision must be made whether to bring up an *homme* or a *citoyen*, a human person or a citizen of the state. "Celui qui dans l'ordre civil veut conserver la primauté des sentiments de la nature ne sait ce qu'il veut. Toujours en contradiction avec lui-même, toujours flottant entre ses penchants et ses devoirs, il ne sera jamais ni homme ni citoyen; il ne sera bon ni pour lui ni pour les autres. Ce sera un de ces hommes de nos jours, un François, un Anglais, un bourgeois: ce

ne sera rien."[1] Thus the human problem of "our days" is the fact
that the modern bourgeois is neither a citizen in the sense of the
ancient *polis*, nor a whole man. He is two things in one person; on
the one hand, he belongs to himself, and on the other, to the *ordre
civil*. The Christian origin of this distinction is made plain by Rousseau's appeal to the untainted "nature" of man in the Christian conception of Paradise and the Fall. *Emile* begins with the distinction
between the way man was when he left the hands of the Creator of
all things and what has become of him ever since he left this original
order and entered society.

1   Rousseau:
Bourgeois and *Citoyen*

> "Le patriotisme et l'humanité sont deux vertus
> incompatibles . . ."
>
> *Lettres de la Montagne*

In the *Contrat Social*, Rousseau demands an "aliénation totale de
chaque associé avec tous ses droits à toute la communauté," a complete renunciation of the individual on behalf of the community, the
prototype of which is the ancient *polis*. But in his *Confessions*, the
same Rousseau acknowledges his individual personal identity after
the fashion of Augustine. This contrast between the Christian and
classic tradition is characteristic of all European culture. It is expressed in Rousseau by the either-or of (Christian) "humanité" and
(classical) "patriotisme"; we see it in the contrast, characteristic of
the modern bourgeois, between "homme" and "citoyen."
    The first and second *Discours*[2] (1750 and 1754) are both a
criticism of modern civilization, but are completely opposite in
respect to their positive goals. The first treatise gives us the picture
of a complete and unified citizenry, after the example of Spartan and
Roman patriotism; the second describes a Golden Age, analogous to
the Christian myth of Paradise. The one glorifies the true *citoyen*,
the other, the original *homme;* these are the two archetypes of a
nonbourgeois mankind. The first attempt at a resolution of this
antinomy is contained in the *Discours sur l'Economie*. But even
here the rights of man are not identical with the duties of the citizen.
The possibility of harmonizing them is the problem of the *Contrat
Social* and *Emile* (1762). For this harmonization to be possible, the

private will of all individuals (*volonté de tous*) must be identical with the common will of the whole (*volonté générale*), which is something other than a mere will of the majority. But at the same time the "volonté générale" must be identical with "conscience divine," the religious conscience of the individual. Finally, the unity of the political community with the Christian religion, and of patriotism with humanitarianism, is to be guaranteed by a "religion civile."[3]

The rigor with which Rousseau develops the antinomy from the very outset compels him to seek a solution at the very point where the problem arises: in the relationship between the state and religion. In the *Contrat Social*, he argues as follows:[4] Initially, every political order justifies itself by religion, and each religion is for its part restricted to the state within whose boundaries its cultus is observed. The destiny of the state stands and falls with that of its gods. This relationship of harmony was altered with the entrance of Christianity into the ancient world. It separated religion from politics and proclaimed a heavenly kingdom above all earthly dominion. And ever since Christianity itself became political in the form of the Roman Catholic Church, Europe has been living in a schism between state and church, empire and papacy. The man who belongs to a Christian church cannot be a full and complete citizen of the state, for his religious conscience opposes his political conscience. Rousseau accordingly distinguishes two kinds of religion: first, the religion of "man," which has no national boundaries and no particular form of worship and corresponds to Emile's confession of faith; and second, the national polytheistic state religions. He judges Catholicism to be a compromise between both, while the religion of man is said to be true Protestantism. The attitude taken by the state toward religion depends on its usefulness; that of the individual man depends on its truth. The result is that the universal religion of man is true, but useless, and the particular heathen state religions are useful but not true. Rousseau attempts to reconcile this opposition in a *religion civile*. In the dogmatic sense, it is neither the religion of Christian revelation nor a heathen state religion, but the religion of the citizen as man or man as citizen. Yet even here, Rousseau's reconcilement is only apparent. At one moment he supports the religion of mankind which transcends all national peculiarities, and in the next, the most exclusive nationalistic education and national religion. The *religion civile* which is intended to combine the advantages of both remains a mere program and compromise. When Rousseau was attacked for his attitude toward Christianity and compelled to defend his position in the *Lettres de la Montagne,* he was bound to come to grief: "Le patriotisme et l'humanité sont deux vertues incompatibles dans leur énergie et surtout chez un peuple entier." Whoever wants both attains neither the one nor the other. Similarly, he finally despairs of any possibility of "conformité" between the "volonté générale" and public power. He compares the resolution of this question to the squaring of the circle, and calls it the "abîme de la politique dans la constitution de l'état."

In his drafts of constitutions for Corsica and Poland, Rousseau addresses himself once more to the idea of a citizenry completely along classical lines, in which the *polis* is everything and the individual nothing. To these marginal young nations he does not recommend the *contrat social* and *religion civile,* but the classical idea of the citizen. But when he comes to speak of the great ancient states of Europe, he does so in a spirit of resignation. The concluding question of *Emile* remains unsolved: how can something right and whole be made of the modern bourgeois? In his scheme for Poland, he gives expression to his yearning for a sound mankind, but at the same time he descends into the abyss of his private existence, finally to conclude with the despairing *Rêveries d'un Promeneur Solitaire.*

Scarcely eleven years after his death, Rousseau had a following without precedent in the French Revolution, which he foresaw but would not abet. He himself was afraid of that for which his writings gave others courage. To him, the truths which he pronounced seemed ominous, because it was in vain to seek to stop up the springs of evil and bring men back to their original equality when their hearts have been corrupted once for all. He writes to the King of Poland: "There is no longer any remedy except a great revolution which would be almost as terrible as the evil which it could heal, which it would be a crime to seek to bring about." In *Emile,* we read: "You depend on the present order of society without considering that this order is subject to unavoidable revolution. . . . We are approaching a critical situation, and the century of revolutions. I consider it impossible that the monarchies of Europe should be able to endure any longer." Despite this fear, Robespierre prepared his great speech, in which he proclaimed as national religion the religion of bourgeois humanitarianism described in *Emile,* in the very house Rousseau had lived in. Similarly, in 1788 Marat proclaimed the *contrat social* in a public garden in Paris; it thereupon became the bible of the Assembly. "C'est la faute à Rousseau,"

Napoleon said of the French Revolution, whose chasm he sought to fill in.[5]

The Revolution was immediately preceded by the polemic of Sieyès with the provoking title *Qu'est-ce que le tiers état?* (1789). The expression "third estate" already indicates the problem of the society which preceded it: in comparison to the first two estates, the nobility and clergy, this numerical designation has no particular content of its own. It is first of all only a denial of the privileged estates of the feudal system. A critical contemporary of Sieyès defined it therefore as "the nation, minus the nobility and clergy." The positive goal of this denial of all previous tradition was the production of a constitution which would rest upon the sovereign social will of citizens with equal rights. In contrast to Rousseau, Sieyès did not want an absolute democracy, but rather a representative democracy, making use of the majority principle and a single legislative assembly of representatives of the people. For him, the "volonté générale" becomes a "volonté commune." For the first time, total political power is accorded to the middle class, to which Sieyès himself belonged.

His work begins with three questions, to which he gives three brief answers. 1. What is the third estate?—Everything! 2. What has it been hitherto?—Nothing! 3. What does it demand?—To become something! Then the revolutionary means are explained which must be used if this nothing is to become everything. The third estate has a right to this because it performs "useful labor," while the clergy and nobles are useless usufructuaries of its labor. It includes the farm labor of the peasants, the processing of raw materials by the hand workers, the mediating work of the merchants and the higher educated classes (teachers, officials, lawyers, etc.). It is itself already a "complete nation." Sieyès means the same by "la nation" as Rousseau does by "le peuple." The community of individuals united in the third estate rests upon its community of "interest," which also furnishes the basis for equal political rights. This typifies the economic nature of bourgeois society which ever since—for Stein, Hegel, and Marx—has determined it, down to the present.

In the same year came the "déclaration des droits de l'homme et du citoyen." It is even today the basis of all democratic states. The distinction between *homme* and *citoyen* is conspicuous in the title. It implies that man is conceived in opposition to his status as a citizen, and that the rights of man vis-à-vis the state are of more concern than the duties of the citizen. Thus the declaration of human rights is much more liberal than the *contrat social*, which demands a renunciation of all the rights of man in favor of the community. As G. Jellinek has shown,[6] the prototype of this foundation of human rights upon freedom and equality is the Christian idea that all men, as creatures of God, are born equal, and that no one, as likeness of God, has a prerogative over his equal. The French Revolution is a distant consequence of the Reformation and its struggle for freedom of belief. The *Civitas Dei* upon earth becomes the social contract, Christianity becomes the religion of humanitarianism, the creature of Christianity becomes natural man, the freedom of each individual Christian becomes the freedom of the citizen within the state, and religious conscience becomes the "libre communication des pensées et des opinions." As a consequence of this origin in Christianity, the very first basic principle ("Les hommes naissent et demeurent libres et égaux en droit") is incapable of harmonization with the pagan theory of the state, which postulated that "by nature" there are free men and slaves. On the other hand, to make effective its claim for the forming of man, the totalitarian state must logically do battle with both the rights of man and Christianity, because it is a hindrance to the equation of *homme* with *citoyen*. But in actual fact Napoleon's dictatorship brought an end to freedom and equality except for legal equality, and bourgeois society soon brought forth a new inequality between the third and fourth estates.

2   Hegel:
Bourgeois Society
and Absolute State

> "The principle of the modern states has this enormous power and depth: it causes the principle of subjectivity to perfect itself to the independent extreme of personal individuality, and at the same time brings it back to substantial unity, thus preserving this unity within itself."
>
> *Rechtsphilosophie*, 260

Hegel experienced three great political events: in his youth, the French Revolution; as a grown man, Napoleon's world rule; and finally, the Prussian wars of liberation. These events also determine the transformations of his political thought: from a radical criticism of the existing order, through the recognition of Napoleon, to justification of the Prussian bureaucratic State. His *Rechtsphilosophie*, published in 1821, contains both a theory of bourgeois society (*homme* as bourgeois) and of the state (*citoyen* as citizen of the state). Like Rousseau's *Contrat Social*, it is based upon two traditions: that of the ancient *polis* and the idea of freedom of Protestant Christianity. Plato's state and Rousseau's social contract (of which Hegel took the idea of the rights of man, but not that of the duties of the citizen) are the two postulates upon which Hegel elevates the reality of the Prussian State to a philosophical existence. The means whereby he accomplishes the harmonization is the dialectic mediation between the individualistic principle of bourgeois society and the totalitarian principle of the state, between individual particularity and political totality.

According to Hegel, the principle of the French Revolution is the freedom of the rational will which forms the world as though it were its own. In his philosophy of history,[7] he describes the revolutionary power of the ideas of the French Revolution with the solemn words, "For as long as the sun has stood in the firmament with the planets revolving about it, it has remained unseen that man stands upon his head, that is, upon his thoughts, and constructs reality accordingly. Anaxagoras was the first to say that νοῦς rules the world; but now man has finally come to realize that thought is meant to rule spiritual reality. It was a glorious sunrise. A feeling of exaltation reigned at that moment, an enthusiasm of the spirit filled the world with awe, as though a real reconciliation between the divine and the world had finally taken place." Even as the State Philosopher of Prussia, Hegel celebrated the anniversary of the Revolution.

In his philosophy of right, he analyzes the limitations of the reconciliation. To Rousseau belongs the honor of having made the rational will the principle of the state, but he nevertheless failed to recognize the true relationship between state and society. He was unable to achieve a positive resolution of the contradiction between the "volonté de tous" and the "volonté générale," because he understood the will of the whole as the common will of individual citizens, but not as something truly general.[8] As a consequence, union in a state was reduced to a mere social contract whose basis remained the capricious acquiescence of individuals. This resulted in consequences destructive of the self-sufficient totality of the per se rational state. Thus the French Revolution had been right in demolishing a state which no longer corresponded to the idea of freedom, but it did not furnish any new foundation. By reason of deficient principle, it effected an enormous revolution, but did not organize a new community. It confused the state with bourgeois society by defining the state in terms of mere protection of private property and personal safety. The ultimate purpose of the state is held to be the particular interests of its individual members, but not the true general interest of the state itself. It seems to be left to the bourgeois to choose whether or not to be a member of the state.

Thus Hegel's criticism of bourgeois society is directed against the liberal conception of the state as a mere means to an end, an attitude classically represented in Germany by W. von Humboldt. Bourgeois society, according to this theory, is a mutual association or a "system" of "needs," and its principle is individualism. In it, every citizen defines his own purpose. Everything else is nothing to him insofar as it cannot be made a means to *his* end. Each individual is free and at the same time dependent upon all others, for the well-being or ill-being of each is interwoven with that of all others and is secured only in its economic context. For bourgeois society, the state is merely based upon "need" or "mutual understanding"; that is, it has no substantial meaning of its own; it is merely a "formal" union and generality *above* the particular interests of the individuals making it up.

Despite this, the nature of the state also enters into the constitution of bourgeois society, because even for its particular ends the latter is dependent upon the universal whole of the state.[9] Willy-nilly, the individual member of bourgeois society is educated behind his back to the generality of his personal interests. Bourgeois society, lost in its extremes (e.g., poverty and wealth), is forced against its will to become the true state as an absolute community. Because the state is itself substantial, objectively filled with spirit, and moral, the individual is possessed of substance, objectivity, and morality only to the extent that his life is "general," that is, political.[10]

This idea of the state, which is the critical criterion for Hegel's analysis of bourgeois society, is only apparently the result of a dialectical development of modern society.[11] In reality, it springs from quite a different source: the *polis* of classical antiquity. It serves Hegel as a model because in it the public community was in fact also the substance of personal life and destiny. This introduction of the ancient idea of the *polis* into modern society does not lead Hegel to a negation of the principle of bourgeois society, but rather

to its "suspension." He uses the ancient ideal of the state as a criterion for his criticism of bourgeois society, but also uses the individualistic principle of this society as a criterion for the mere substantiality of the ancient community. In principle, Hegel wants both
aspects of freedom: the indefinite "I will it" and the delimiting
willing "of something" definite.[12] He seeks to combine freedom's
option with its substance. Therefore, his criticism of Rousseau's
social contract corresponds to an inverse criticism of Plato's state.
In comparison with modern society, the ancient state has the advantage of substantial universality; but as a state it is "merely" substantial, and the individual person is not yet "let loose" and "liberated" or emancipated.[13] The ideal of the Platonic state contains
injustice against the "person," to whom it allows no freedom,[14]
because Plato excludes from the state all private individuality for the
sake of maintaining traditional morality.

The new principle, which is higher and which defeated the
ancient state, the Platonic state could not withstand; it is of Christian origin. It is the principle of the "infinitely free personality," of
every individual man as such. Christianity made this principle of
historic importance by placing every human being equally in a
relationship with God.[15] Upon this Christian principle rests, according to Hegel, the "irresistible power" of the idea of freedom belonging to the French Revolution. "There is no idea so generally known
to be liable to the grossest misunderstandings, and therefore really
subject to them, as the idea of 'freedom,' nor is there any idea
bruited about so unthinkingly. Since the 'free spirit' is the 'real'
spirit, to misconstrue it leads to the most monstrous practical consequences. . . . Whole continents, Africa and the Orient, have never
shared this idea, nor do they share it now; the Greeks and Romans,
Plato and Aristotle, even the Stoics did not share it; on the contrary,
they knew only that man becomes truly free through his birth . . .
or through strength of character, education, philosophy. This idea
came into the world through Christianity, according to which the
individual as such is of infinite value as an object and end of the
love of God, and is thus intended to have an absolute relationship to
God as spirit, having this spirit dwelling within."[16]

The political consequence of this principle is the modern European state, whose task it is to reconcile the principle of the *polis*—
the substantial generality—with the principle of the Christian religion—subjective individuality. In this dialectical harmonization of
two opposing powers Hegel sees, not the peculiar weakness, but

rather the strength of modern states! The generality of the *polis* is of no value without the particular willing and knowing of the individuals, and the individuals are of no value when they do not themselves will the general will of the state. The modern state can afford to allow subjectivity to develop to the self-sufficient extreme of particularity because this extreme, for its own part, is able to bring subjectivity back to the substantial unity of the state (§260). Hegel considered this synthesis not only possible, but actually accomplished in the contemporary Prussian State. The contrast between private and political life, as well as between the bourgeois and the *citoyen* seemed to him, in the "general case," to be reduced to a difference completely encompassed by the totality, and to be suspended.

Hegel thought that property, possessions, the family, and marriage were safeguarded according to the sense of bourgeois society. Only at the edges of the philosophy of right do the problems appear which determine the future development of bourgeois society: the question of how to control the poverty brought about by wealth (§244 ff.), the progressive division of labor (§198), the necessity of organizing for the masses forcing their way upward (§290 and 301 ff.), and—"after the fifteen year farce" of the restoration of the French monarchy—the collision with "liberalism," with the increasing claims of the will of "the many" and its empirical generality, which now seeks to rule by force of numbers.

Hegel's pupils and successors put asunder what he had so skillfully joined together, and demanded decisions in place of his mediations. While Hegel everywhere sought the mean, the Young Hegelians became radical and extreme. The extremes of bourgeois society, which in Hegel's system of needs are reduced to aspects of a total whole, become self-sufficient, and drive toward a dialectic that no longer fits within the framework of Hegelian dialectics. Marx decides against the state of bourgeois society and in favor of a communistic community; Kierkegaard, against the existing relationship between church and state and in favor of a restoration of primitive Christianity; Proudhon, against the existing state and in favor of a new democratic order; Donoso Cortes, against atheistic democracy and in favor of a Christian dictatorship; Stirner, against the entire previous history of mankind and in favor of a "union" of egoists.

Halfway between Hegel and Marx stands Lorenz von Stein, whose theory of bourgeois society is an historical analysis without a basis in history. His concept of the state is still completely Hegelian, but his concept of society is already influenced by the rise of the industrial masses. Ever since the state surrendered its legitimate authority in the French Revolution, it has been able to achieve its own ends, power and freedom, only by advancing those ends of society based upon profit. It is thereby drawn into the social movement and must attempt to extend citizenship to the working classes. Its actual purpose is to make all citizens into free and equal persons; but because participation in government is determined by property and education, the state itself becomes a phenomenon of the dominant order of society, which itself is the "source of all freedom and lack of freedom." It is still a political unity, but no longer above, but rather in the midst of the bourgeois society which fulfills it. Its life consists in the continuous development and resolution of the conflict between social and political forces. At the moment, the latest stage of this dialectic, after the "political society" at the time of the Restoration, is the "industrial society" since 1840. But Stein holds fast, on the one hand, to Hegel's idea that history is progress toward freedom, and recognizes on the other that the principle of modern society, divided into unequal classes, is mutual dependence; he therefore concludes with the question whether freedom is in fact opposed to state and society.[17]

3 Marx: Bourgeoisie and Proletariat

> "The abstraction of the state as such belongs only to the modern era, because the abstraction of private life belongs only to the modern era."
> *Werke*, I, 1, 437

Marx and Hegel both analyze bourgeois society as a system of needs, whose morality is lost in extremes and whose principle is egoism. The difference between their critical analyses consists in the fact that Hegel's suspension preserves the difference between particular and general interests, while Marx suspends the difference in the sense of removing it, for the purpose of producing an absolute community with communal economy and communal ownership. As a result, his criticism of Hegel's philosophy of right is directed primarily against the relationship between state and society. Hegel is

right in feeling the separation between private and political existence to be a contradiction; but he is wrong in supposing that he has
really suspended, that is, removed it. His mediations only disguise
the existing contrast between the privately egoistic and publicly political existence of the bourgeois. The modern citizen, as bourgeois,
is not a *zoon politikon;* as a citizen, he is abstracted from himself
as a private individual. Marx points up this contradiction everywhere in Hegel's philosophy of right and develops the implied problem to the utmost limit, thereby going beyond Hegel, on the one
hand, and reverting on the other to Rousseau's distinction between
homme and *citoyen.* He is a follower of Rousseau who has been
trained by Hegel, for whom the universal estate is neither the petit
bourgeois (Rousseau) nor the bureaucrats (Hegel), but the proletariat.[18]

On the basis of the social movement which arose after the
French Revolution, Marx discovers that the "droits de l'homme"
are not universal human rights, but bourgeois privileges. "The
droits de l'homme, are as such distinct from the *droits du citoyen,* the
rights of the citizen. Who is the *homme* as distinct from the
citoyen? Simply the member of bourgeois society. Why is the member of bourgeois society simply termed 'man,' why are his rights
called the 'rights of man'? How can this fact be explained? On the
basis of the relationship between the political state and bourgeois
society, on the basis of the nature of [*sc.,* purely] political emancipation."[19] The declaration of human rights presupposes the private
individual of bourgeois society, that is, the bourgeois individual, to
be the truly real *homme,* because it is still engaged in the struggle
against feudalism. "Here man is far from being conceived as a member of a general class; rather the life of this class itself, society, is
conceived as a framework external to the individuals, a restriction
upon their original independence. The only bond holding them together is . . . need and private interest."[20] Therefore the "political" emancipation of the French Revolution must be completed by
a "human" emancipation. This must have the effect of making the
individual human being as such a member of the social community.
Then there will disappear both the state, which abstracts from man
and is therefore itself abstract, and the private individual of bourgeois society, who is abstracted from the state. Only then can
Hegel's statement that "ultimate freedom" is "ultimate community"
become true.

The agent of this emancipation is the fourth estate, which Marx
describes in exactly the way Sieyès described the third: it is nothing,

and must become everything. But its nothingness is no longer referred to the nobility, but rather to the newly come to power bourgeoisie, which is the "commander of the industrial armies." In
respect to the bourgeoisie, the mass of the proletariat is simply the
"universal estate," which has no particular interests of its own, but
rather represents the universal interests of mankind. What was for
Hegel still the portion of the people that "does not know what it
wants," and which he expressly called "the many" in contrast to
"all," to them, Marx ascribes the self-consciousness of seeking to
become a whole. From the standpoint of the proletariat, he characterizes the bourgeois as the representative of class interests, the
capitalistic entrepreneur and owner of production facilities, by
which means he keeps the wage earner dependent. At the same time,
Marx emphasizes the revolutionizing power of the entrepreneurial
bourgeoisie.[21] In the course of a century, it has created by itself
more plentiful and colossal productive might than all previous generations put together. Through the exploitation of nature, industrial
technology, railroads, ships, industry, physics, and chemistry it has
opened and civilized entire continents, and brought about an enormous increase in population. On the other hand, Marx believed that
the lower middle class of the petit bourgeois would necessarily be
reduced to the level of the proletariat, because it could not keep pace
with the productive power of large-scale capitalism.[22] He had a
decided respect for the upper middle class; the petit bourgeois he
despised as utopian and reactionary.

4   Stirner:
The Individual "I" as the
Common Ground of Bourgeois and
Proletarian Man

> "The principle of the bourgeoisie is neither noble
> birth nor common labor, but mediocrity: a little
> birth and a little labor; that is, interest-bearing
> property."
>
> *Der Einzige und sein Eigentum*

The extent of the devaluation in Germany of the Declaration of
Human Rights during Marx's time is clearly shown by Stirner's

Der Einzige und sein Eigentum (1844). In it, not only does the member of bourgeois society and the proletariat reach a nadir, but man as such loses all value. Stirner reduces the idea of bourgeois humanitarianism to the "I" which claims as its own property everything it can acquire. The French Revolution did not liberate bourgeois society; on the contrary, it begot an obedient citizen, dependent on the state for protection. This mediocre citizen lives on security and legal integrity. The "social liberalism" of the proletarian working class is just as limited as this "political liberalism" of the bourgeoisie. The only difference is that the one makes itself subject to the state and property, the other to society and labor. The ultimate form of faith in mankind is the "humane liberalism" represented by Bruno Bauer. He recognizes neither the bourgeoisie nor the working class; he merely criticizes unflinchingly all forms of establishment and every particularity. The man possessed of this critical consciousness is indeed clothed only in rags, but he is far from being naked like the "I" who is rid of everything.

With this, his individual "I," Stirner considered himself above every social limitation, whether proletarian or bourgeois. Marx nevertheless demonstrated to him in the *Deutsche Ideologie* that the social truth of his "individual" is the decadent bourgeoisie. "The sole thing which he has to his credit is against his will and without his knowledge: he is the expression of the German petit bourgeois of today, whose aspiration is to become bourgeois. It was completely logical that, narrow-minded, timid, and prejudiced as these bourgeois are, "the individual" should swagger into the world as their philosophical representative, equally gaudy, bragging, and impertinent. It is quite in agreement with the circumstances of the bourgeoisie that they want nothing to do with their theoretical braggart, nor he with them, that they are in mutual disagreement and that he must preach his own peculiar egoism: now perhaps Sancho will see the umbilical cord which connects *his* 'union' with the Customs Union."[23] Stirner absolutizes bourgeois egoism, the private individual, and private ownership, making them into general "categories" of egoism, the individual, and ownership. From the sociological point of view, he is the most radical ideologist of bourgeois society, which is per se a society of "isolated individuals." What Stirner frees himself from is not real conditions of existence, but merely conditions of consciousness which he himself cannot see through because he is engrossed in private egoism as the principle of bourgeois society. His thought, as well as his actual life, stood at the extreme limit of his world, which had lost its substance and become disillusioned.

5   Kierkegaard: The Bourgeois-Christian Self

> "Emperors, kings, popes, Jesuits, generals, diplomats have hitherto been able to rule the world at a decisive moment; but from the time of the institution of the fourth estate it will develop that only martyrs can rule the world."
>
> *The One Thing Necessary*

Kierkegaard follows Stirner as the antithesis of Marx. Like Stirner, he reduces the entire social world to his own "self." But at the same time he finds himself in absolute opposition to Stirner; instead of grounding the individual upon creative nothingness, he places the individual "before God," the creator of the world. His criticism of the present, which appeared in the same year as the *Communist Manifesto*, is therefore directed both against emancipated "mankind" elevated by Marx to the status of a fundamental principle and against a "Christendom" emancipated from the imitation of Christ. His basic concept of the individual is a corrective to the "mankind" of Social Democracy and the "Christendom" of the liberal intelligentsia. For the principle of association is not positive, but negative; it weakens the individual human being through an enormous merger. Only as an individual self can a man now realize his universal humanity, but not by becoming a member of a class (Marx), or on the contrary by abstracting from the concrete world he lives in (Stirner). In the former case, says Kierkegaard, men would all become equal laborers in a factory, wearing the same clothing and eating the same food from a common pot; in the latter, man loses all his concrete identity by being stripped to complete nakedness.[24] In neither mode of existence does he, as an individual, himself realize the universal nature of man.

Kierkegaard put forward this "universality" of the human self as a demand, without himself being able to realize it. Throughout his life he remained an outsider, at the utmost limit of bourgeois society, because he could not bring himself to engage in a profession and "settle down with the finite" through marriage. Only literarily did he give the inward nature of his self a social existence, in the figure of "Assessor Wilhelm," who represents the "ethical." It is the task of this moral philosopher to justify the generality of normal human life to an aesthetician. This expressly characterizes the concrete self of Assessor Wilhelm as bourgeois. "Although he is himself his own goal, this goal is nevertheless something external; for the self that is the goal is not an abstract self which would be at home anywhere, and therefore nowhere, but a concrete self that stands in active association with this particular environment, these circumstances of life, this world order: it is a self not merely personal, but social, bourgeois."[25] This self which is bound up with the world realizes itself in a bourgeois profession and a bourgeois marriage, but in such a way that all external circumstances are to be made internal. To the objection of the aesthetician that such an internal appropriation of external circumstances has objective limits which spell its downfall, he replies that even need and poverty could hold nothing against him, "were he even to dwell in three small rooms." "With God's help," even under these limitations (a minimal existence, which nevertheless still remains bourgeois) a man can succeed in transforming the external into something internal; as Luther rightly said, no Christian ever died of hunger.

This justification of bourgeois-Christian existence, which hovers between ethical seriousness and aesthetic irony, is nevertheless made relative through Kierkegaard's critical insight into the dissolution of both the bourgeois and Christian worlds. The blame for the whole present state (1848) of the European world must be borne by a "conceited, semieducated bourgeoisie, demoralized by the flatteries of the press," which supposes that as the "public" it can rule. "But perhaps never before in history has nemesis been seen to come so speedily; for in the same instant, at the same stroke, that the bourgeoisie made a decided effort to grasp power, the fourth estate arose. Now people will of course say that it is *they* who are guilty, but that is not true: they are only the innocent victims left in the way, who are shot down, execrated; and this is called self-defense, even is self-defense in a certain sense: self-defense, because the bourgeoisie overthrew the state."[26] While in former ages recognized authorities could rule the world, ever since *all* have sought to be equal it has become impossible to rule, in the true sense of the world, with secular means. Therefore, Kierkegaard's political demand is purely and simply that rule be carried out with absolute authority. But at such moments the actual government of the world is no longer in the hands of secular ministries, but of martyrs, who conquer by allowing themselves to be slaughtered for the truth. The archetype and prototype of the Christian martyr is Christ, crucified by the mob, that truly "individual" God-man. Only in his presence can the problem of human equality be solved; but not in this world, whose nature is to contain more or less inequality.

6   Donoso Cortes and Proudhon: Christian Dictatorship from Above and Atheistic Reordering of Society from Below

> "Proudhon is the opposite of what he appears to be: he supports freedom and equality, and in reality builds the foundation for despotism."
>
> CORTES, *Der Staat Gottes*

> "L'homme est destiné à vivre sans religion."
>
> PROUDHON, *De la création de l'ordre dans l'humanité*

To the radical Protestant reaction of Kierkegaard against the leveling of mass democracy, there corresponds, at the same time, in Spain the radical Catholic reaction of Donoso Cortes to the socialistic movements in France. Cortes was himself an important statesman of an ancient Catholic noble family. He describes bourgeois society in exactly the same terms as Kierkegaard and Marx: as an undifferentiated "clasa discutidora," without truth, passion, or heroism. It eliminates hereditary nobility, but does nothing to combat the aristocracy of wealth; it accepts the sovereignty neither of the king nor of the people. Hatred for the aristocracy drives it to the left, and fear of radical socialism to the right. The opposite of its wordy indecisiveness is the decisive atheistic socialism of Proudhon. In contrast to him, Cortes represents the political theology of the counterrevolution, to which the French Revolution, which declared man and the people sovereign, appeared as a revolt against the created order. But because the time of Christian kings is coming to an end and no one any longer has the courage to rule by other means than through the will of the people, there is only *one* remedy left: dictatorship by the government from above in order to prevent the dictatorship of revolution from below. "If it were necessary to choose between freedom, on the one hand, and dictatorship on the other, there would be no difference of opinion. . . . But that is not the question. In reality, freedom does not exist anywhere in Europe. . . . The necessary choice is between the dictatorship of revolution and the dictatorship of government."[27] Cortes chose the dictatorship of government, because it is less oppressive and shameful, and comes from purer realms, and because the dictatorship of the saber is to be preferred to the dictatorship of the dagger, as being more noble. He summarizes the experience of the revolution as follows: "I looked about, and saw the bourgeois societies grown sick and fragile, all human circumstances complicated and confused. I saw the peoples intoxicated with the wine of rebellion, and freedom vanished from the earth. I saw tribunes crowned, and dethroned kings. No play ever contains such violent transformations and upheavals, such advancements and degradations. Then I asked myself the question, Does this confusion perhaps result from allowing the basic principles of morals and order, preserved in the sole possession of the church of Christ, to be forgotten? My doubt was turned to certainty when I realized that today only the Church provides the image of an ordered society, that it alone is the calming element in the general tumult, that it alone is inwardly free, that only in it does the subject obey with love properly constituted authority, and authority on its part proves itself just and gentle in its orders, that it alone is the school from which proceed great citizens, since it possesses the art of life and the art of death, of life which produces the holy, and of death which begets martyrs."[28]

Proudhon, too, was an opponent of the bourgeoisie, but for different reasons than Cortes: he hated them with the rage of the parvenu who would like to re-form the world; Cortes despised them with the passion of the man for whom they were the gravediggers of all sacred tradition. Proudhon declared that the time of theology and Christianity was past; Cortes, that there was no social and political salvation outside the Catholic Church, because only the Christian God completely reveals what man is, thereby also founding a human society.[29]

On the other hand, only a world grounded upon Christianity could become radically atheistic and make the attempt to constitute itself by its own power, and rule itself. Cortes saw such presumption of man in the French Revolution and its "philosophic civilization," and to counter it he recommended dictatorship from above. In another way, his great opponent Proudhon confirms the Christian schema of history. At the conclusion of his criticism of religion,[30] written in 1843, he recalls in this "last hour" of the Christian religion the good deeds and noble inspirations which proceeded from it. It laid the foundation of human society, gave to the modern nations their unity and personality, sanctioned the laws of the state, and, even in the nineteenth century, filled magnanimous souls with zeal for truth and justice. In 1860, when Proudhon substantiated the "dissolution sociale," he saw this unequaled crisis of European history as one which wrote an end to the phenomenon of Christianity: "Toutes les traditions sont usées, toutes les croyances abolies; en revanche, le nouveau programme n'est pas fait, je veux dire qu'il n'est pas entré dans la conscience des masses; de là ce que j'appelle *la dissolution*. C'est le moment le plus atroce de l'existence des sociétés. Tout se réunit pour désoler les Hommes de bien: prostitution des consciences, triomphe des médiocrités, confusion du vrai et du faux, agiotage des principes, bassesse des passions, lâcheté des mœurs, oppression de la vérité, récompense au mensonge. . . . Je me fais peu d'illusions et je ne m'attends pas, pour demain, à voir renaître dans notre pays, comme par un coup de baguette, la liberté, le respect du droit, l'honnêteté publique, la franchise de l'opinion, la bonne foi des journeaux, la moralité du gouvernement, la raison chez le bourgeois et le sens commun chez le plébien. . . ." "*Les tueries viendront et la prostration qui suivra ces bains de sang sera effroyable*. Nous ne verrons pas l'œuvre du nouvel âge; nous combattons dans la nuit; il faut nous arranger pour supporter cette vie sans trop de tristesse en faisant notre devoir. Aidons-nous les uns et les autres; appelons-nous dans l'ombre et chaque fois que l'occasion s'en présente, faisons justice. . . ."[31]

7   A. de Tocqueville:
The Development of Bourgeois Democracy
Into Democratic Despotism

> "There are three men with whom I spend some time each day: Pascal, Montesquieu, and Rousseau."

De Tocqueville's study of American democracy appeared between 1830 and 1840; his historical analysis of the *ancien régime* and the French Revolution was published in 1856. Personally, his attitude toward the events of his period was in complete balance. "I came into the world at the close of a long revolution which destroyed the old State and founded nothing permanent. When I began my life, aristocracy was already dead, and democracy not yet born. Thus my instinct could not lead me blindly to choose the one or the other. . . . Since I belonged myself to the ancient aristocracy of my fatherland, I neither hated nor envied it, nor had I any particular love left for it when it was destroyed; for one allies himself willingly only to what is alive. I was near enough to it to know it well, and far enough from it to be able to evaluate it without passion. I can say the same about democracy." Because of this neutral position between two ages, he had a "goût de tête" for democratic institutions, and also an "instinct aristocratique" against them.[32] Like Burke and Gentz he was neither a determined opponent of the French Revolution, nor its friend. And because he possessed in the *ancien régime* a criterion by which to evaluate the Revolution, his attitude toward it could be remarkably clear.

The great problem of his studies is the tension between freedom and equality. The emancipation of the third estate brought about a leveling and equalization, but the question is whether bourgeois democracy also makes men free. By freedom, de Tocqueville means not merely independence, but the dignity of the man responsible for his own acts, without which there is neither true command nor true service. The first enthusiasm of the French Revolution was not only for equality, but also for free institutions; but it very quickly lost its passion for freedom, retaining only that for equality. Both are not of the same age, nor have they always worked toward the same goal, although for a moment they appeared equally open and powerful. The striving for equality is older and more permanent. Equality had long been the goal of the Christian church, of trade and commerce, of fiscal economics, of the invention of printing and firearms, of the colonization of America, and finally of the literary Enlightenment. Younger and less lasting is the belief that men can become equal only through freedom. When Napoleon made himself master of the Revolution, freedom abdicated in favor of equality. He was dealing with a nation in which all law, custom, and morality had been dissolved. This allowed him to carry out a despotism in a form much more rational than had ever previously been possible. "After, in the same spirit, he had formulated and passed all the laws which were to order the myriad relationships of citizens among themselves and to the State, he could create all executive power at the same time and so subordinate it that, taken all together, it was merely a simple, great governmental machine, whose motive power he alone was." While every individual over-valued his own worth and independence, the public order as a whole was tending toward a "political pantheism" which robbed the individual of his existence. A superb administrative machine assured Napoleon's power within France, and his military genius outside it. But men became indifferent to their destiny, far removed from all grand sense of citizenship such as distinguished the ancient *polis* democracies, in which it was precisely the constraint of the *polis* which produced the most extreme individuality. In the ancient *polis*, in the medieval corporate states with their manifold corporations and rights, and likewise in the tyrannies of the Italian Renaissance, there lived more personal and political freedom than in modern "despotic democracy." A democracy loses all its value if it only makes men equal without producing freedom. For in a democracy, freedom is the only counterpoise to leveling, uniformity, and centralization. In America and England, democracy has succeeded in creating genuinely free institutions;[33] because of their completely different origin, the democracies of the continent of Europe did not understand how to make use of freedom. It was their fate to push onward to despotism, in accord with their own origin.[34] The ancient aristocracy had forged a great chain out of the citizens; its manifold links reached from the peasant to the king. Democracy broke asunder this legitimated structure of particular classes and rights, isolated each from the others, made them all equal and thereby ripe for subjection by one despotic central power. So the Revolution succeeded in making of the "free" *citoyen* "something less than a human being."

Together with collecting all social forces, the despotism which proceeds from bourgeois democracy also increases retroactively the isolation of the individuals. It opposes all free co-operation in thought or action. "Since in such societies men are not linked together by classes, castes, guilds, or tribes, they tend too greatly to care only for their own affairs . . . and restrict themselves to a dull egoism in which every public virtue suffocates. Despotism, far from opposing this tendency, makes it irresistible, for it robs the citizens of all shared goals, all mutuality, all necessity of consulation, all opportunity for acting in a social framework. They were already inclined to isolate themselves: it cuts them off, immures them in private life."[35] But the greatest evil of democratic despotism is not subjection to a leveling central power, but the injustice of this sub-jection. For the French Revolution made men far too independent, enlightened, and skeptical to continue to believe in the *right* of an absolute but illegitimate power. What Sieyès failed to understand was that the struggle against the nobility and clergy not only de-stroyed their particular privileges, but tradition in general, the "mother of right." The consequence of this destruction of tradition is the "doctrine of necessity," which puts all too high a value on the unity of the nation, and all too low a value on the individual man.

Toward the end of his life, de Tocqueville, the aristocrat, had the feeling of being "an obsolete worshiper of freedom," while his democratic contemporaries wanted to have a master, and made of "readiness for slavery" a "basic element of virtue." In Germany, J. Burckhardt continued de Tocqueville's line of thought about de-mocracy, drawing the outlines a bit more clearly so as to cause his contemporaries "at least to subject their subordination to a critical examination."

Tocqueville was of the opinion that bourgeois democracy was essentially aimed at security and well-being, mediocrity without human greatness. About 1830, he writes in his memoirs, the victory of the middle class to the exclusion of the nobility and the lower classes was already complete and final. It forced its way into all public offices and accustomed itself to living by the profit motive and public funds. The result was a rapid expansion of the average wealth. The character of the middle class became also the intellec-tual attitude of the government of the first bourgeois king. "It was an active, diligent, often dishonest spirit; occasionally, because of vanity and egoism, bold with fainthearted temperament; moderate in all things, except the desire for an easy life; in a word, mediocre; a spirit which, if combined with that of the people or of the nobility, would have been able to accomplish miracles, but by itself, capable of producing nothing more than a government without virility and greatness. The master of all society to an extent that had never been possible for the nobility, . . . the middle class, as soon as it took over the government, took on the appearance of a private under-taking. It entrenched itself behind its power, and soon afterwards behind its own egoism. Its representatives cared more for their private affairs than for affairs of state, more for their personal com-forts than for the greatness of the nation."[36] Together with this emphasis on private comfort, there appeared also a powerful tend-ency to level everything to an average, as private good was combined inextricably with public good: little splendor and little misery, but an average prosperity; little original knowledge and little gross ignorance, but a general semiliteracy; little hate and little love, but relatively permanent customs. Thus de Tocqueville, fulfilling Goethe's prediction of the demeaning of a middle-class culture, depicts those men, orderly but average, timid and egoistical, of the middle class, which had just acquired political power.[37] In such a world, a dwarf, if only borne by the wave of the democratic masses, could reach the summit of a mountain which a giant standing dry on the shore could never climb. The mediocre condition of bourgeois democracy makes truly historic greatness impossible. And therefore in such a period, everything is healthy which advances the ideal of individuality, of the responsible person; and everything is dangerous which increases the power of the generality, of the genus and species.[38]

Sorel, too, at the end of the nineteenth century sought to exert influence upon the working class within democracy, but against its bourgeois character, following the course outlined by de Tocqueville. While de Tocqueville's experience in America had convinced him that democracy of necessity lacked virile passion and martial virtues, it was just these which Sorel sought to couple with Social Democracy. The sum purpose of his historical and sociophilosophical studies can be expressed by the question: How, after the decline of bourgeois ideals and illusions, can modern society be renewed?

8   G. Sorel:
The Nonbourgeois Democracy
of the Working Class

> "Plus je réfléchis à ces questions, plus je me persuade que le travail peut servir de base à une culture qui ne ferait pas regretter la civilisation bourgeoise. La guerre que le prolétariat doit conduire contre ses maîtres est propre . . . à développer en lui des sentiments de sublime qui font aujourd'hui complètement défaut à la bourgeoisie."
>
> *Les illusions du progrès*

Sorel concludes his *Réflexions sur la violence*, which made him the tutor of Mussolini, with a "Pour Lenin." Its concluding sentences are: "I am now an old man, whose existence depends on the smallest accidents; but nevertheless, before I go to my grave, I may yet see the humiliation of the proud bourgeois democracies which today [1919] exult so cynically"—so great was his scorn for the bourgeois society of modern democracy. In contrast to it, he admired the middle class of old, which accomplished productive work proportionate to its real circumstances. But an upper stratum of consumers arose from the productive middle class and came to power; instead of the manly virtues of discipline and renunciation they cultivated humanitarian illusions and intellectual aberrations; he therefore denied the bourgeoisie all the virtues which he ascribed to the class-conscious working class.

In Sorel's study, four stages can be distinguished in the development of the bourgeoisie: 1. The prerevolutionary bourgeoisie of the eighteenth century. It occupies an independent position because it consists primarily of royal officials and functionaries. As a subordinate class, it developed no aptitude for ruling. Sorel calls it a "classe de commis." 2. The revolutionary bourgeoisie of the end of the eighteenth century. It represents the "illusion du progrès" and consists of dilettantes who have learned to do nothing properly. Their spokesmen are literati who dabble in politics, and the Encyclopedists who can talk about everything and nothing, because they are not intellectual workers and scholars. Their character is "arbitrary" and their "audacity" an irresponsible "temerity." They have no respect for historical tradition, are without intellectual training, and are basically sentimental. 3. The disillusioned bourgeoisie after 1850 under Napoleon III and Bismarck. Their revolutionary myth has faded. The new captains of industry are realistic and interested in large-scale capitalism; they take over the leadership in this industrial epoch of the acquisitive bourgeoisie. 4. The "cultured" bourgeoisie at the end of the nineteenth century. Their representatives are the epigones of revolutionary literature: political poets like P. Claudel, G. d'Annunzio, and M. Barrès. This same overrefined bourgeoisie which is "ultra-policée" and seeks to live in peace can also develop on paper an enthusiasm for war. "Les cochonneries viennent tout naturellement sous la plume des écrivains qui prétendent introduire des imitations de la tragédie et de l'épopée mythologiques dans les aventures de la vie bourgeoise."[39] They are artists, not to be taken seriously either in their political actions or in their religious conversions. In contrast to this decadent bourgeoisie, without the energy of capitalism, Sorel entrusted the task of history to the revolutionary energy of class-conscious trade unions, a task which the bourgeoisie can no longer fulfill. He did not look upon the proletariat either in sympathy or indignation as a class of the exploited, but as a reservoir of sound instincts and creative power needing only proper selection and leadership to become capable of founding and ruling free institutions, and comprising a "classe de maîtres." Nietzsche's ideas on "master-morality,"[40] applied to Marx and Proudhon, typify his thought historically. He wanted to give to the revolutionary trade unions martial virtues in place of the illusions of progress of the third estate. The virtues of the modern army of labor are martial virtues because, like war, they demand a unity of all strength, extreme exertion, patience, and readiness for sacrifice. The elite of the workers creates a "civilization de producteurs." It is the hero-class of our epoch in its progress toward rational domination of the world, not vulgar but sublime,[41] because it knows what pain and exertion are, while the bourgeois seeks only painless pleasure. The intellect of the bourgeois floats abstractly far above the material conditions of life; the spirit of the productive worker, on the other hand, like the spirit of good architecture, is united technically with the purposes and demands of real life.

In his reflections upon power, Sorel expresses the conviction that only a great war awakening every energy will bring to power the men who have the will to rule and the capacity to govern, or a great extension of power of the proletariat, which can eliminate the "platitudes humanitaires" of the bourgeoisie as well as of parliamentary socialism. But when the philosophy of violence was triumphant in reality between 1914 and 1918, Sorel did not see a confirmation of his views in the war, but instead a victory for democratic ideals, for industry and plutocracy. "Jamais on ne vit une telle soif de carnage chez les gouvernements et autant de servilisme chez les peuples qui se laissent entraîner dans des guerres, dont la fin s'éloigne chaque jour," he writes to B. Croce in 1915. As far as the bourgeois spirit is concerned, it is invincible, because it appeals to nearly every base instinct of man. When Sorel died, in 1922, he, like Flaubert and Proudhon, was resigned to the "triumph of mediocrity"[42] and base nature of human passions. He was deeply convinced that the natural course of all history is decay, and that movement in the other direction, toward human greatness, is an artificial movement, wrung from the general movement of decay. Not only did he fight against democracy, but also quite as much against the state which had been transformed into a "Church," which uses public force to control people's conscience, guide their spirit, and reduce them to equality.[43]

9 Nietzsche:
The Human Herd and Its Leader

> "These same new conditions which lead on the average to a . . . general degradation of man to a common mean, a useful, hard-working, . . . handy herd animal, are extremely well adapted to providing an origin for exceptional individuals of the most dangerous and attractive nature. . . . The democratization of Europe is at the same time a spontaneous arrangement for the breeding of tyrants."
>
> *Werke*, VII, 207

As a critic of the existing world, Nietzsche was to the nineteenth century what Rousseau had been to the eighteenth. He is a Rousseau in reverse: a Rousseau, because of his equally penetrating criticism of European civilization, and in reverse, because his critical standards are the exact opposite of Rousseau's ideal of man. Recognizing this relationship, Nietzsche saw in Rousseau's image of man "the greatest revolutionizing force of the modern era," which had also exerted a decisive influence upon the formation of the German spirit through Kant, Fichte, and Schiller.[44] At the same time, he terms him a "monstrous birth at the threshold of the new age," an "idealist and canaille" in one person. His concept of equality set the unequal equal, and brought to power a slave morality. His democratic-humanitarian ideals counterfeited the true nature of man, which is not humanitarian, but rather a "will to power."

Bourgeois democracy is without substance; it is the "historical form of the decay of the state," while radical socialism promotes despotism. Both movements together reduce man to a member of a herd. Both the intelligentsia of the propertied classes and the uneducated class of laborers without property are caught up in this leveling process, and therefore no longer provide a foundation for the renewal of civilization. A short note written in 1873 casts a glaring light on the situation as seen by Nietzsche in the midst of the national prosperity following the victory over France: the intelligentsia and intellectuals must be sacrificed, for the money and goods economy of the propertied classes has become mean and contemptible. Thoughtless and stupid, they have no idea of the danger which threatens them from the quarter of the working class. On the other hand, even the uneducated classes have been affected by the leaven of contemporary universal education, and are far distant from any genuine popular culture. If the working classes should convince themselves that they can easily excel the proficiency of the educated and propertied, then, says Nietzsche, "we are finished." He continues, "But if this does not happen, then we are really finished."[45]

In *Zarathustra*, Nietzsche ridiculed this entire world of decayed humanity, and shaped the image of the "last man." His antitype is the superman. As a philosophic concept to overcome nihilism, this idea has no immediate social content and political meaning; but it becomes concrete indirectly, in Nietzsche's historical reflections upon outstanding "exceptional men," and in his idea of future *Herrenmenschen* ("master-men"), whose task it is to give a goal to the existence of the herd-men of democracy.

The democratic leveling of the masses, resulting in a degradation of man, and also the breeding of a master caste, which leads to the exaltation of individual men—these belong together like the two faces of a coin. A posthumous note states that Zarathustra's hatred for the democratic system of leveling is "only a front." In reality, he is pleased that the world has finally "come so far," for only now can he carry out his task, namely, the education of a master caste which renounces its own pleasure and comfort, allowing these to the lowest in the new hierarchy.[46] The "mediocrity" of the majority is the necessary condition for the existence of "exceptions"; together with the "herd-animal," there develops also the "leader-animal." "And would it not actually be a kind of goal for the democratic movement, its redemption and justification, if someone should come who would make *use* of it, so that finally its new . . . order of slavery . . . might gain that higher form of masterful, Caesar-like spirit: men who might support themselves on this society, involve themselves in it, raise themselves by means of it? . . . The face of Europe today gives me much hope: a bold master race is forming there upon the surface of an extremely intelligent herd. . . . The same conditions which further the development of the herd-animal also further the development of the leader-animal."[47] Referring to Napoleon and Bismarck, he says: "A man who has developed and preserved a strong will, together with a great spirit, has better prospects than ever before. For in this democratic Europe, the capacity of men to submit to training has become very great. Men who learn easily, who submit easily, are the rule: the herd-animal, extremely intelligent, has been prepared. Whoever can command will find those who *must* obey."[48] Democracy brings forth a tractable mass in the hands of "large-scale politics." By this, Nietzsche meant a farseeing plan including all of Europe, determined by the question of the future masters of the earth. He thought primarily of Russia and Germany, but not of the Anglo-American world. The new masters of the earth shall "replace God" for the unbelieving masses. Like Napoleon, they will be men of the people, and at the same time stand above them in absolute self-confidence, as lawgivers and men of violence both. Under their leadership, the laboring masses will learn to feel like soldiers and carry out their orders.

No less instructive than this idea of the future masters of the earth, who will make use of democracy's leveling as a means to an end, is the opposite possibility, that the government of the world will fall into the hands of the "mediocre," because in a "mesquin age" they will be the survivors of the future. "In an agitation so extreme in both its tempo and means, such as our civilization presents, the human center of gravity is moved. . . . Under such circumstances, the center of gravity of necessity belongs among the *mediocre:* mediocrity, as the surety and vehicle of the future, consolidates its position against the rule of the mob and the eccentrics (both usually in league). This produces a new opponent for the exceptional man, or a new temptation. Assuming that he does not accommodate himself to the mob and sing songs to please the instinct of the disinherited, he will have to become 'mediocre' and 'conservative.' . . . Once again . . . the whole spent world of the ideal gains a talented spokesman. . . . Result: mediocrity acquires spirit, appeal, genius, it becomes entertaining, it seduces. . . ."[49]

II The Problem of Work

In the nineteenth century, work and education became the substance
of the life of bourgeois society. No previous century ever disseminated education on such a grand scale, at the same time developing
such energy of work. Burckhardt ironically called it the "century
of education"; Marx subjected its system of work to criticism. Work
became the mode of existence of the "wage earner," and the "possession" of education became the privilege of the "educated." Yet
there appears an essential unity in this allotment of work and education to two separate classes: it became the goal of the worker to
gain for himself the privileges of bourgeois education, while the
educated could not avoid calling themselves "intellectual workers"
in order to prevent their privilege from seeming an injustice. The
perplexity of the bourgeois intelligentsia in Germany became
clearly apparent after the war when—following the example of the
Russian workers' councils—they established an "intellectual" workers' council which gave itself the task of healing the breach between
proletarian work and bourgeois education. The reduction of this
opposition was also one of the pre-eminent tasks of National Socialism, which brought young students into contact with the people in
work camps, and permeated the mass of the wage earners with
political ideology, a derivative of bourgeois education. Both the

separation of work and education, making of them two extremes, each implying the other, and their reduction to a mean of "popular culture" bear witness to two aspects of the same situation: work is no longer in a position to contribute to the education of man as such.

It has not always been as natural as it is today for every man, whether he be merchant, physician, or writer, to term his occupation "work." Work has gained its social respectability only very gradually. In the Christian conception, it was originally not in itself a meritorious accomplishment, but the wages and punishment of sin.[1] Man must work by the sweat of his brow ever since he has been condemned to labor through his guilt. As a severe, accursed imperative, work means essentially need, affliction, and misery. Biblical man does not enjoy the "fruits" of the "blessing" of work; instead, he atones through work for violating the fruit of paradise. Even Pascal still maintained that work merely proves the emptiness of worldly activity, which presents the illusion of being busily filled, using this diversion to distract man from the misery of his existence.[2] Only in Protestantism did there develop that regard for secular work which is represented classically by Benjamin Franklin. But even the complete secularization of the Christian tradition, which took place in the eighteenth century, was in opposition to the teaching of the Church. It brought about the acceptance of the bourgeois estimation of work, which has dominated ever since, as an accomplishment which provides life with significant content. Now man enjoys with a clear conscience the fruits of the work he has done.[3] It becomes the preferred road which leads to satisfaction and success, acclaim, gratification, and riches.[4] Not only *must* the man of the bourgeois epoch work, he desires to work, for a life without work would seem to him not worth living, lived "in vain." He thinks of work not merely as an ascetic activity which preserves him from the vices of boredom and intemperance by forcing order upon his activity; he also sees it as that which leads to a successful conclusion, with independent, constructive meaning. It becomes a source of all earthly proficiency, virtue, and happiness. In this purely secular evaluation of work, the Christian estimation of it only appears in the emphasis laid on its meritorious difficulty, which allows a hint of the conception of the curse to shine through. Similarly, freedom from work is considered a quasi-paradisiacal condition, although continuous leisure produces a state of deadly boredom in the man whose life is determined by work. The two basic meanings of work, on the one hand misery and toil (*molestia*), and at the same time accomplishment (*opus, opera*), show up also in the history of its meaning. Originally, "labor" means primarily the hard work of agriculture and therefore working in dependent servitude. But at the same time the work which oppresses the farm laborer and for which he receives his daily wage is also a creative accomplishment, like that which produces other works.[5]

This double meaning does not describe its entire nature, however. Work is rather simply part of human existence, to the extent that there is any activity at all in the world. It was the full, original meaning that Hegel ascribed to it. According to him, work is not a particular economic activity,[6] to be contrasted, say, to leisure or play, but the basic way in which man produces his life, thereby giving form to the world. Hegel comprehends this movement between selfness and otherness under the completely universal notion of the spirit; for him, therefore, work is neither physical nor intellectual in a particular sense, but spiritual in the absolute ontological sense. On the other hand, it only becomes clear from the point of view of Hegel's philosophy of the spirit how Marx and Engels, in their disagreement with him, could arrive at the paradoxical assertion that the German labor movement is the heir of classical German philosophy.

1 Hegel:
Work as Self-Renunciation
in Forming the World

> "Ora et labora! Pray and curse! In other contexts, cursing is when you say, 'Damn!'; but in religion all these otherwise separate things are joined together. The earth is cursed, and thou must earn thy bread by the sweat of thy brow! To work means to destroy or curse the world."
> HEGEL (Rosenkranz, *Hegels Leben*, p. 543)

Hegel discussed the theme of work three times: in the Jena lectures, in the *Phänomenologie*, and in the *Rechtsphilosophie*. In the lectures of 1803–04,[7] he describes its spiritual character as being primarily a "negative attitude" toward nature. Work is not an instinct, but a product of "reasonableness," a "mode of the spirit."

No animal works by the sweat of his brow; it satisfies its wants immediately from nature. Man, on the contrary, is distinguished by his producing bread indirectly, using nature only as means.[8] This "mediation" between needs and their satisfaction comes about through work, which for its part is mediated through the means of tools and machines. Work is a "middle term" between man and his world.[9] As a movement of mediation, it is not negative in the merely destructive sense; it is, rather, a fashioning or "forming," and therefore positive destruction of the world which is present by nature. In contrast to the drive of animals, which satisfies its greed simply by devouring the object and thus making it vanish, and therefore must always "begin again from the beginning" without producing anything permanent, a work, spiritual human work, is constructive by means of tools; by the process of formation, it produces something permanent, that is, something which stands by itself.[10]

Natural, individual skill is not sufficient to accomplish such work. The individual acquires the skill necessary for work only by learning universal laws of work, whereby he overcomes his "natural unskillfulness." Work turns the subjective activity of the individual into "something other" than it seems at first glance, namely, into a "universal," because it has been learned according to universal laws. Each new invention of better tools and more efficient methods of work not only comes about in opposition to already extant customs and rules, but also produces something new, to the benefit of all men. Just as work is one of the distinguishing characteristics of man, so it also, as a manifold and complex activity, begets problems which are peculiar to the spirit.

The tool, by means of which man opposes his activity to nature, is an "existing, rational middle term" between the worker and that upon which he works; it is the constant in the process of work. Its function is to remove man from any living connection with nature by putting a distance between him and the immediate destruction of the object. But the tool is itself still an inert thing, with which I act only formally, making myself a "thing."[11] Only the machine, which is a self-sufficient tool, is a perfect mediator of work. Through it, nature is deceived by man, as he causes it to work for him. But this deception has its revenge upon the deceiver: the more he subjugates nature, the lower he himself sinks. "By using machines . . . to manipulate nature, he does not escape the necessity for work, but only defers it, removes it further from nature, no longer confronts nature as one living being confronting another. Instead, this negative vitality vanishes; the work that he is left with becomes itself more mechanical. He succeeds in reducing work for the whole, but not for the individual. Rather he increases it, for the more mechanical work becomes, the less value it has, and the more he must work in this fashion."[12] In the course of the nineteenth century, this work, mediated by machines, became the general fate. Together with the isolation of the work performed, it increases the quantity of what is shaped by the work. The value of work decreases proportionately as the quantity of production increases. "Work becomes even more absolutely dull, . . . the skill of the individual becomes infinitely more limited, and the consciousness of the factory workers is reduced to complete apathy. The connection between the type of work performed and the whole unending mass of needs increases incalculably, becoming a blind dependence, so that a far-distant operation often restricts the work of a whole class of men who satisfy their needs by its means, making it superfluous and of no use. Just as the assimilation of nature becomes more convenient through the introduction of intermediaries, so these stages of assimilation are infinitely divisible, and the large quantity of conveniences makes it once more absolutely inconvenient."[13]

Originally, work satisfied the immediate needs of the individual, but it becomes abstract and universal, that is, no one produces what he himself needs. Instead of working toward the reality of satisfying his specific needs, everyone works for the universal possibility of satisfaction in general. It is impossible for a man to satisfy his needs except by collaborating in the total satisfaction of everyone's needs, without regard for his own particular needs. For example, he works to produce a luxury in order to meet his basic needs for food and clothing. He does not work to satisfy his concrete needs, but to satisfy the "abstraction" of a general need. Thus the value of work no longer resides in what it produces, but in the fact that it enables a man to satisfy his own needs indirectly, through the universal interdependence of all work. The dialectical antithesis of this generalization of work into a system is the specialization of work, just as the simplification of work to particular jobs leads to the multiplication of jobs. Work becomes simpler, more monotonous, and more specialized, because each individual produces one individual article, and more complicated, because this diffusion of a concrete whole into a process with many divisions and subdivisions leads to an endless number of restricted specializations. The more man frees himself from the concretion of nature, the more he controls nature, the more he also becomes dependent upon nature; for the more an individual's knowledge becomes restricted to the production of one abstract article, the less capable he must be of satisfying all his other needs.[14]

The concrete reality of work, the "materially existing notion," the process of becoming more and more abstract and universal, but also more "spiritual," is money—"a great invention." It is the "potential satisfaction of all needs," whereby the abstract value of all merchandise becomes real. Money can be used to stand for all needs because it is an abstraction from everything particular, because it reduces everything to a common denominator by virtue of its spiritual unity and universality. "Need and work, raised to this level of universality, constitute in themselves . . . an immense system of solidarity and mutual dependence, a self-activating life of what is dead, moving to and fro with a blind, elemental motion, and, like a wild animal, demanding constantly to be controlled and held in check."[15]

The type of work performed also distinguishes the manners and thought of the working classes, divided by Hegel into three sections: farmers, hand workers, and merchants.[16] The work of the farmer has not attained the level of spiritual abstraction, but remains elementary and concrete. It is intimately bound up with the natural conditions of the basic needs of life. Although the work of the farmer, like all work, is a negative activity, it is so only to a limited degree. For the farmer still lets nature work directly for itself by using earth and sky, warmth and cold, rain and drought as natural forms of assistance in tilling the soil. His attitude is, therefore, determined more by faith in nature and the labor of his family than by confidence in the legal institutions of bourgeois society. Because the success of his work is to a large extent dependent upon the gifts and chances of nature, the work of his hands does not produce anything independent, such as the hand worker produces. The latter's bourgeois occupation forms the transition to abstract work and the "knowledge of the universal." By imposing form upon nature, the hand worker makes of it an independent work, whose form, through the work of his hands, has a self-sufficiency which is based upon the self of the work which forms it. What the object upon which he works is by nature, is restricted to the natural material, which is more or less serviceable and workable. This independence from nature develops in the class of hand workers a consciousness of law which is positive in comparison to that of the farmer, who asks of the law only that it not disturb him. Even further removed from the nature of things is the merchant class, which imposes form on nothing, only exchanging what has been formed by others through the abstract means of money. The "spiritual" aspect of work is most purely expressed in the movement or exchange of finished goods. The work of the merchant class is free of all immediate connection with need and use. The object of its work is split into the two spiritual abstractions of article of commerce and money. An object no longer has value in itself, but only according to the "meaning" that it can have for someone, according to its derived value, which is "hard cash." Money, the medium of exchange, is more than a medium of work: it is a "formal principle of reason," something spiritual because it is abstract and universal. It is the essence of the spirit to be able to abstract from everything that immediately exists, even from its own being.[17] The attitude of the merchant is therefore this "rigor of the spirit," whose legal expression is strict laws of exchange. He builds factories upon the misery of an entire class, no matter what destruction is entailed.

Hegel's primary insights into the nature and problem of work which were sketched in these manuscripts, not intended for publication, were partially systematized in later works. The *Rechtsphilosophie* discusses work as the first component of the "system of needs." The work of bourgeois society is to supply particularized means of satisfying minutely defined abstract needs.[18] Here the essence of work is made clear: man only "is" insofar as he is productive; he must produce himself and his world because his entire existence is completely mediating and mediated. In this process of productive work there develops "culture," theoretical as well as practical: diverse forms of knowledge, the ability to imagine means suited to particular ends, the ability to comprehend complicated universal relationships. All this arises in consequence of the differentiation of needs, means, and work. Work is culturally educative in that it accustoms men to being busy in general[19] and to having regard for the will of others. It teaches objective physical activity and universally applicable skills; it disciplines man and raises him to the universal level of the spirit. In contrast to the barbarian, who is essentially lazy, the man who works is both cultured and culturally productive by virtue of his needs. But work can have this educative effect only because it is itself a form-giving activity on the spiritual level, capable of making abstractions.

The *Rechtsphilosophie* was written twenty years after the Jena lectures.[20] In it, Hegel no longer treats the peculiar problem of work, which derives particularly from the intervention of the machine, as an unsolved problem. Instead, he touched upon it only in the positive context of spiritual progress, which is brought about by the fact that division of labor causes work to grow more abstract. Similarly, he recognized as "nodal points" in the development of modern society the problem of organizing the newly developed "masses"[21] and the question of regulating the extremes of poverty and wealth.[22] But he does so with a marginal reference to the still very promising possibilities in emigration to America.[23]

Within the scope of the purpose of his system, which was to mediate contradictions, Hegel was extremely realistic and far-sighted. This is shown by the first paragraph of his *System der Bedürfnisse*, in which he treats the new science of political economy with a philosophic seriousness equaled only by Marx. Just as in the philosophy of history, so also in the science of economics, Hegel sees rational necessity in the midst of an apparently random confusion of arbitrariness and indigence. It is therefore a science which does honor to thought. If Marx had been able to see the critical expositions of the Jena lectures and the commentary on Stewart's *Political Economy*,[24] he would have been able to develop his own statement of the problem, out of Hegel's, much more directly than he was able to on the basis of his study of the *Phänomenologie*. The Hegelians Rössler and Ruge occupy a middle position between Marx's concept of work, which is economic, but philosophically based, and Hegel's, which is purely speculative.

2   C. Rössler and A. Ruge: Work as Appropriation of the World and Liberation of Man

Following Hegel, Rössler views work as a process of "appropriation,"[25] which springs from the freedom of the active spirit. It is part of the moral definition of the man who sets himself a goal. There are two modes of appropriation. The first affects a direct alteration of nature for the sake of the individual, as in the assimilation of nourishment. It is restricted to individual forms of life, and is not generally communicable. This mode of appropriation is shared by men and animals. The other is communicable, because it is mediated by organs of another order: tools and machines. The indirect organs of appropriation can be used equally well by every individual; they are exchangeable and communicable. They transform nature into a world which belongs to man, and is suited for his use. The production of the means for this appropriation of the world is called work in the highest sense. It transcends all individual needs, and its energy lies in the continuous subjugation of natural drives, in respect to which work essentially represents discipline. Their satisfaction does not consist in a separate pleasure, but in the realization of the power of appropriation itself, whose free activity transcends every goal which has been attained and every stage in the subjugation of the world. The historical development of work as a spiritual and moral power of appropriation takes place only in Christianity. All the pre-Christian religions knew work only as a subordinate means for achieving other ends, but not as an end in itself. But even within Christianity, Protestantism alone gave work the freedom to become "infinitely progressive productivity," making it a worthy ethical component of the whole of human life. It comes to full flower in the "community of work" which is bourgeois society. The result of the free mutual exchange of work is "universal intrinsic values"; in spite of their material nature, they do not contradict the spiritual nature of man, which is proved precisely by its permeation of what is material.[26] In contrast to the individualistic life-context of the family, bourgeois society, by means of work, creates also an "appropriation of the personality"; it makes of each individual, even if not in his totality, a collaborator, working toward the common ends of production for society. In spite of his polemic against the "ridiculous aberration of socialism," Rössler hoped for a "universal freedom and education" based upon the sharing of work.

In his study of the history of philosophy,[27] Ruge was even more decisive in making work the outcome of the history of the spirit. Plato, Aristotle, and Hegel brought about great revolutions, but fear of the practical consequences made them set a limit to their liberation of the spirit of progressive dialectics of thought before reaching the realm of social castes, guardians, and classes. The actual history of the spirit and its liberation has removed this bar, and made work a universal principle. It is one with education, because it is itself educative by its very nature. "We know now that there is no form of work which is degrading, that work alone furthers man's freedom. Hegel himself . . . showed how, through work, the slave becomes master of his master. If all work is to be ennobled, it is only necessary to develop the proper notions and see what work is, what it accomplishes. Every day it re-creates mankind." It is a "self-bearing god," who makes "man out of man."[28] Ruge organizes the history of philosophy from the standpoint of the universalization of work. Its highest attainment is the Aristotelian polity, but understood as bourgeois society, democratically organized. He sees the Republic of the United States of America as the ultimate realization of this ideal of a *polis* in which every citizen acts spontaneously as a worker. This creative character of work was comprehended by Hegel only to a very limited extent, and by Aristotle not at all. "Although Aristotle sees very well the necessary function work fulfills for the state, he fails to recognize its creative character and the nobility of the way in which it educates and liberates the world. He fails to recognize that it brings to pass the subjection and transformation of the external world and the human world, that it does this not as mere life, but with a rational spirit, as liberator of itself. The worker is not an animal, but an intelligent man. Work is no longer infected with the idea that it is demeaning when it is seen and understood in its creative activity, which permeates everything. Through the work of hand workers and artists, the spirit achieves itself in its otherness; through science, in its own element. But in the case of the state, Aristotle omits both. For him, the work of civil society is beneath the state, that of philosophy above it; but in reality the former is its heart, the latter its head."[29] For Aristotle, not every man is a member of the state, and thus a man in the true sense; there is still only a class of fully enfranchised citizens. "The Aristotelian state is not yet a community involving all its members in the struggle for freedom; it is only the superstructure of full citizens who do no work, but make all the others work for them, in order to carry on war, art, science, and affairs of state. For him, 'slavery' and 'work' are still synonymous. He does not yet possess the civilizing, dignifying concept of work which subjects nature. Time has brought forth this concept, but not yet put it into effect. The difficulty lies in constituting the state of bourgeois society, based on need, as a state based on freedom, making of the substructure a superstructure, that is, making it the only structure. As long as the state, as the domain of freedom, confronts the state of necessity—the domain of slavery of labor and industry—the totality will lack the basic principle: that the work of each individual has as its end the whole, and the whole has as its end the good of each worker, so that there are only workers and no drones; for 'only what is active is free.' "[30] Work is the liberating activity of thinking man; as such, it is the most important confirmation of man's peculiar being, it is "the sole source of salvation and blessing." Modern society in particular is based upon it, and is therefore the first truly "human" society. "Only the worker produces bourgeois, that is, human, society; all the culture of nature and the spirit is his work; he is the *father of mankind*."[31] Intellectual or abstract work is also a kind of work, the kind in which man best exercises his peculiar abilities.

Ruge emphasizes this universal significance of work in contrast to the narrow economic concept of work. The principle of economics is merely value, and its abstract form, money; but the principle of society based upon work is not the mere production of value, but the production of value as a means toward the "production of man and his own in the natural world." "All value which the worker produces is produced only in order to produce man, . . . bodily and spiritually." Thus the real meaning of socialism, as opposed to national economics, lies in the fact that the latter stops with the system of egoistical needs, while the former mediates between particular and universal interests, setting the common spirit as its goal. Economics ignores the spiritual and human side of bourgeois society because it analyzes only the external relationships which exist between capitalists and workers. But Hegel also fails to recognize the spirit of bourgeois society when he omits the real universal class from his theory of the three classes. The working class includes both the first and the third class, "because both theoretical learning and farming are included in the notion of work."

3   Marx:
Work as Man's Self-Alienation
in a World Not His Own

Marx concentrated his analysis of work upon the problem of economics, as the expression of the real conditions of life. At the same time, he based it critically upon the universal notion of work in Hegelian philosophy. This leads to a twofold criticism: of classic national economics, and of Hegelian philosophy. What remains for Ruge an humanitarian program is carried out by Marx with scien-

tific thoroughness. The best source for insight into the original connection between his economic theories and Hegelian philosophy is
his 1844 manuscript dealing with national economics and philosophy.[32] It, together with the *Deutsche Ideologie*, is the most significant event in the history of post-Hegelian philosophy.

a   The Criticism of the
Abstract Classical Notion of Work

Marx's criticism of classical economics (A. Smith, J. B. Say,
Ricardo, Mill)[33] begins with the thesis that this new science of
economics is the theoretical expression of the actual movement and
energy of capital and modern industry. On the other hand, it also
accelerates and justifies the development of industry by making
industry more conscious of itself. It is the great discovery of Smith,
the "Luther of Economics," that the essence of what is apparently
objective private property is human work, which creates all value.
But the more radically and cynically it reduces all values to the
work which creates value, analyzing paid labor from the standpoint
of the profitable use of capital, the more it leads of necessity to a
criticism based on the criterion of the working man in society rather
than capital and labor as independent entities. Marx accepts Feuerbach's view of man,[34] interpreting the essence of man as the ability
to live and produce in society.[35] It follows that in the system of
capitalism the worker is a man who has lost his own self, is alienated from himself, existing only as merchandise or capital. As soon
as it occurs to capital, as in the case of reduced demand, no longer
to be "for the worker," the worker is no longer "for himself"; he
is out of work and gets no pay, because his only existence is as
worker. "The existence of capital is *his* existence, his *life*, since it
determines the content of his life in a completely arbitrary way."[36]
Instead of achieving his own individual existence through the work
which he performs, the worker, alienated from himself, produces
not only merchandise but also a kind of depersonalized form of himself. But it is the necessary paradox of the capitalistic world that it
produces a devaluation of the human world proportional to its
utilization of the world of objects, reducing the major portion of
mankind to the abstract status of "labor." Thus, for Marx, work is
no longer abstract in the Hegelian sense of a positive universality of
the spirit, but in the negative sense of an abstraction from the
totality of concrete man, who seeks to perform his work as an inte-

grated human being. This abstraction reaches its extreme in the fact that the worker, instead of expressing (*äussern*) his life in productive fashion, is compelled, if he is to find work at all, to sell (*veräussern*) himself, to alienate himself, in his work.[37] His life becomes a mere livelihood; work serves only to prevent the privation of bare existence. An animal is coextensive with its whole active life; but man, who deliberately and consciously produces a world, is reduced to a subhuman level when he can understand his humanity only in the animal functions of eating, drinking, and procreation, and consider himself an animal in his compulsion to work.[38] His spiritual essence, freely willed activity, becomes economic activity, a mere means whereby the elementary needs of physical existence can be satisfied. Instead of being truly himself within the context of his work, the worker is truly himself, or free, only outside of this context.

Classical economics ignores what the worker is apart from his work. It relegates this portion of man to physicians and courts, to religion and politics. For it, the needs of the worker are reduced to the need to preserve his capacity for work so that he can produce merchandise. Wages, therefore, are part of the necessary expenses of capital, and must not exceed the bare minimum necessary. Classical economics, the science of wealth, is also a science of saving, or, briefly, "economy." Its basic ascetic dogma is to relinquish everything that does not serve to increase capital. It replaces what man concretely *is* and is capable of with abstract "means"[39] and "credit,"[40] the only mode of acquisition in a system of private ownership. This poverty of needs is the result of the alienated wealth of the economy which degrades human nature by increasing unreal needs. But this perversion of the meaning of production for the man who has possessions can be seen only in reference to the man who has nothing; for its expression upwards is as refined, ambiguous, and disguised as its expression downwards is coarse, direct, and undisguised. But in actual fact, industry speculates upon the refinement of needs by effecting a coarsening of them. Within progressive civilization, it produces a progressive barbarization.[41]

The connection between work and capital, as well as between poverty and wealth, is confirmed by the controversy between the two parties of classical economics: the one (that of Malthus) commends luxury and deplores economizing; the other (that of Ricardo) seeks economy in place of luxury. This contradiction is reconciled by the confession of the former that its only purpose in promoting luxury is in order to encourage work, and of the latter that its support of economy is based on the desire to increase wealth. Both demonstrate that basically capital and labor belong together, like two hostile brothers. If the worker is himself an item of capital, the capitalist is also a slave to his work, which serves to multiply profit. In both cases, the moral principle of classical economics is the utility of unconditional acquisition and production; virtue is ascetic work.

The capitalistic method of producing life gives the best demonstration of its full consequences in the matter of money.[42] Money has the characteristic of being a universal medium by which a person can acquire anything which he does not already have. It is therefore the disinterested intermediary between needs and their satisfaction, between life and its necessities, the mediator pure and simple. But because it is *the* means of life, it ceases to be a means and becomes an end. Money is too good for nothing and too bad for nothing; it substitutes for and confuses all natural relationships by setting a fixed monetary value upon them. "Money is the *real* spirit of all things," while Hegel's logic presents merely the "money of the spirit," the spiritual value of everything that has being.[43] As the alienated wealth of mankind, it is the most universal means of binding together and separating a world alienated from itself. Instead of setting human abilities freely in motion and enriching them, everyone speculates upon the possibility of tempting his neighbor to economic ruin through the generation of new needs. Every new product is a new potential for mutual deceit and pillaging. But the poorer man becomes, humanly speaking, the more he needs money to master his alienated being. The only real product of classical economics is the need for money.[44] This tendency of production is necessarily boundless, because quantity is the only quality of money, and by its very nature it has no limit. By its very nature, this is most obvious in the case of money considered in the abstract; but it is already present in the work which is performed for money. It is an activity which abstracts from the total man, making of an expression of life an alienation of life, of objectification a de-objectification, and of realization an abstraction. It perverts all the human sense.

The task resulting from this system of capital and labor is the reunification of human nature through the ending of man's alienation from himself, the two sides of which are the objective world and man objectifying himself in work. It is concerned not only with economic life, but with all the aspects of man's life, his sight and hearing, his feeling and thought, his will and his love, because every way in which he behaves toward something is an historically determined way of appropriating the human world.[45] Marx's outline of a solution for this problem is completely determined by his disagreement with Hegel.

b Criticism of the Abstract Notion of Work in Hegelian Philosophy

Hegel was unable to solve the problem of alienation because he abstracted from the *particular mode* of production and contented himself with generalities about common "needs." In agreement with its theological origin, the philosophy of the spirit took no account of the natural sciences and the industries they had made possible, failing to recognize that man becomes depersonalized through industrial work, without expressing himself positively. And yet it is industry that is the "open book" dealing with human abilities, depersonalized and alienated. It is the most conspicuous anthropology, the most accessible realm of history; hitherto it has been viewed only superficially, because it has not been seen in the context of the real nature of man.[46] Because Hegel sees man as "spirit," and nature merely as the otherness of the idea, he was able to define work only as a formal spiritual behavior.[47] His idealistic abstraction of the flesh and blood worker corresponds to the materialistic abstraction of classical economics, which deals with man merely as abstract labor. Both ignore the total humanity of man as he really is by nature.

Since Hegel takes as his starting point the absolute activity of the logos, the categories of the particular parts of his system are ontological categories, defining a universal essence of work, for example, at the expense of its real forms of existence. Mere universal categories, they are indifferent to all particular content; they can therefore be applied to anything.[48] Crucial for an understanding of Hegel's viewpoint on work is the phenomenology, in whose various forms one and the same movement appears again and again: the dialectics of consciousness and self-consciousness. By means of this "intellectual construction," whose principle is a double negation, Hegel ingeniously transcends real human expression and alienation, depersonalization and estrangement. The phenomenological movement therefore comes to an end with absolute knowledge. "Thus the entire history of alienation and the entire withdrawal of alienation are nothing but the history of the production of abstract, that is, absolute, thought."[49] Estrangement, which is the actual concern of alienation and its abolition, is conceived as the difference between per se and *pro se*, between consciousness and self-consciousness, between object and subject, within which the real, material contrasts vanish. "All other contrasts and motions of these contrasts are merely the manifestation, the hull, the exoteric form of these contrasts which alone are of interest, which comprise the sense of the other, profane contrasts. It is not that human nature becomes depersonalized, in contrast to itself; rather, the fact that it becomes depersonalized in contrast to abstract thought should be considered that fixed nature of alienation, which must be abolished." From the standpoint of the spirit, depersonalization, as such, must be considered behavior which does not accord with the spiritual nature of man.[50]

Like alienation, the appropriation of human abilities, considered as mere objects, is simply a movement of thought. The reappropriation of human nature, which alienation has depersonalized, abolishes the depersonalization, but not the alienation. "The vindication of the objective world for man . . . therefore this appropriation, or insight into this process, is brought forward by Hegel in such a fashion that materiality, religion, political power, etc. are spiritual objects; for only the spirit is the true essence of man, and the true form of the spirit is the thinking spirit."[51]

Just as appropriation and alienation are spiritualized and emptied of reality, *what* man appropriates through work and *what* alienates him from himself is nothing real and independent, but rather an abstraction which is derived from all particular objects and is indifferent to them, which alienates self-consciousness from itself. What this self-consciousness knows is that the world of self-sufficient objects which confronts man positively is of no value. In this negation of positivity, self-consciousness proves to itself the nonobjectivity of its own nature. Man is a nonobjective, spiritualistic being. Instead of returning to man our historically determined world of real objects, as self-generated, Hegel dialectically equates the object of consciousness with self-consciousness. He considers self-consciousness the true nature of man, and therefore the reappropriation of his alienated, objectified nature appears as a return of the self to itself, which can take place without much expense, once the "hostile estrangement" of the objective world has been reduced to an "indifferent strangeness." Hegel's self-consciousness flatters itself with the illusion that its active knowledge in its otherness has reconstituted the self, because it knows nothing of any real externality; it knows only a recoverable alienation of itself.[52] But the fact that self-consciousness is at one with itself in its *own* otherness means that man possesses his true human nature in the existing order of law, politics, and economics. The merely theoretical abolition of alienation in practice leaves the alienated objective world exactly as it is. Hegel's apparent criticism, which formally denies the existing powers while actually assuming their content is a false positivism,[53] a philosophical dissolution and restoration of empirical reality. Hegel can view the process of alienation of the self as a gaining of the self because his conception of the entire process of negation is merely formal. For him, the movement of emanation and return is a circular autotelic process. What he describes is not a human process at all: it is a divine process within man, and its actual subject is absolute Idea.[54]

A corporeal man, "breathing an atmosphere of natural forces," relates himself to a world of real objects. On the basis of his criticism of Hegelian "spiritualism," Marx developed this "materialistic" view of history as the only true "natural history." "Material" in this context does not refer to an "economic basis," but rather the physical, objective existence of real men and things.[55] The first formulation of historical materialism as a "naturalistic humanism" is determined by the criticism which takes as its starting point, not the absolute spirit, but "anthropological nature."[56] Within this world of our natural senses, man, too, is an objective being. Only as a natural, corporeal being can he incorporate real, physical objects into his being, using them as a means of expressing his life. "A being which does not have its nature external to itself is not a natural being, it does not partake of the essence of nature. A being which has no object external to itself is not an objective being. A being which is not itself an object for a third being has no relationship to its object, that is, it does not enter into objective relationships, its existence is not objective. A nonobjective being as a *nonbeing*."[57] Thus when man objectifies his natural abilities and makes them external to himself, he is ever so much under the influence of the given objective world and its forces. Therefore, real abolition of alienation cannot come about in a nonobjective or spiritualistic fashion, but only through an "objective action" which alters the existing conditions.

In spite of this basic rejection of the "standpoint" of Hegel's phenomenology, Marx's criticism is positive, recognizing Hegel's distinctions, retaining them, and furthering their realization. "Hegel's phenomenology is . . . its own hidden, unperceived . . . criticism; to the extent that it portrays the alienation of man—even if man appears only in the form of the spirit—it contains within itself all the elements of criticism, frequently prepared and worked out in a manner which far transcends the Hegelian standpoint. The 'unhappy consciousness,' the 'honest consciousness,' the struggle of the 'magnanimous and abject consciousness,' etc., these individual sections contain, though in alienated form, the critical elements of entire spheres, such as religion, the state, bourgeois life, etc."[58] The greatness of Hegel's phenomenology lies in its comprehension of "man's self-generation"[59] as a process, of depersonalization as alienation, and of appropriation as the abolition of this alienation; in short, its understanding of the universal nature of work and the human world as its result. "Hegel occupies the standpoint of modern economics. He sees work as the essence . . . of man,"[60] even though he sees only the positive side of alienation and abolishes its negative side idealistically. Thus Hegel views work as man's development in "proseity," but within the context of alienation. Aside from this positivism of idealistic speculation, Hegel achieved an abstract understanding of the essential action of man as he generates himself in the world; within his speculative system, he made "distinctions which reach the nub of the matter."[61] He had an "estranged insight" into the real depersonalization, estrangement, and reappropriation of man. But a real reappropriation can come about only through the "destruction"[62] of the estranged condition of our objective world. This incidental modification, which turns "abolition" into destruction, differentiates Marx methodologically from Hegel, and to this extent represents a basic divergence; for the rest, he takes over Hegel's categories and preserves them, in material form, even in *Das Kapital*.[63]

"Communism," too, is constructed according to the concepts of Hegelian philosophy. It is intended as the realization of the dialectical unity between independent action and depersonalization which is the outcome of Hegel's history of philosophy.[64] It is the practical way in which man, living in society, keeps the entire objective world

in subjection, as self-generated, and also remains himself in his otherness. Thus according to Marx's idea, it is not only the expropriation
of private property, but also the "vindication of real human life as
man's property,"[65] a total return to himself of man who has become
a stranger to himself within the objective world which he has gen-
erated. The expropriation of private property is only one consequence of the general appropriation of the world. Therefore, Marx
distinguishes a false and a true communism.[66] He criticizes the
theories (such as that of Proudhon)[67] which attack the existing
distribution of wealth by equalizing differences through an increase
in wages or seek to bring about equality through equal distribution.
Such partial reforms do nothing to alter the basic relationship of
man to the world, the devaluation of the human world through the
high value attached to the world of things. Such a theory would
destroy everything that cannot be shared equally by everyone in
the form of private property. Not only would it fail to abolish the
definition of man as a "worker," it would extend this definition to
all men and leave capital the only power dominating society. True
communism, on the other hand, as Marx, the Hegelian, conceives it,
is a reappropriation of human nature at the stage of development
which civilization has attained in capitalism. Within this context, it
is the "genuine resolution of the conflict between . . . existence
and essence, between depersonalization and independent activity,
between freedom and necessity, between individual and species. It is
the riddle of history solved."[68] Therefore communism, understood
in its totality, alters not only the social and economic situation of
man, but also his political, legal, religious, ethical, and scientific behavior. The man who lives in a communistic society does not possess objective reality in the form of ownership common to private
capital, but rather through the fact that all objects are for him a
positive, depersonalized objectification of himself. He is the man to
whom the world indeed belongs, because its manner of production
does not alienate him, but establishes him.[69]

Marx developed these ideas in his 1844 manuscript, but they
remained temporarily unpublished; even in the form of *Das Kapital*
they exerted no influence on German philosophy. Nevertheless, they
made history like no other theory ever has: the Marxism of Lenin
and the Russian worker-state have their spiritual basis in Marx's disagreement with Hegel. In the further development of his analysis
of appropriation and estrangement, Marx treated the problem of
work more and more in a narrowly economic fashion, defining work

in connection with wages and profit[70] as the social substance of merchandise. This concept of work, limited to the specialized realm of economics,[71] calculates the "quantity of work" and out of its relationship to capital derives the notion of "surplus value." But we must not forget that the original basis of this much-discussed economic theory is the much-neglected disagreement of Marx with Hegel's philosophy of the spirit.

After Hegel and Marx, German philosophy never again discussed the theme of work in its full scope and significance. The analysis of work became the prerogative first of economics and then of sociology, which explored endlessly the particular relationships between work and all conceivable phenomena, such as knowledge;[72] in spite of its obligation to Marx, it forgot its debt to Hegel. Except for E. Dühring, no one made any attempt to provide a philosophical basis for the economic and social problem of work. Finally Engels, in his *Anti-Dühring* and at the conclusion of his study of Feuerbach, drew the conclusion from Marx and Hegel that the labor movement was the true heir of German philosophy, because the labor movement alone understood that work is the "creator of all culture and civilization," and its history is the key to the entire history of mankind. However repugnant this statement might appear to bourgeois philosophy, it was not without foundation. Ever since the turn of the century it has been the basic weakness of bourgeois education that it has been the education of an educated class, building a wall of separation against the working class and losing the spiritual horizon for the universal problem of work.[73]

4   Kierkegaard:
The Meaning of
Work for the Self

Kierkegaard was discussing the problem of work at the same time as Marx, but in such a way that he kept the question within the framework of bourgeois-Christian ethics. He treats the problem of work in connection with the growth of the "personality"; but this individualism of the self should not be misconstrued. Even though every isolated individual may have his teleology within him, still the individual cannot be separated from his relation to bourgeois life, as though, in the "abstract sense," he should and could be self-sufficient. His self is absolutely concrete; therefore, by concentrating on itself it can never relate negatively to the surrounding world. It moves "away from itself, through the world, back to itself."[74] This movement of alienation and recollection is thus defined in Hegelian terms; its Christian reality consists in the fact that it is an "act of freedom," through which the individual may stand *above* the conditions, such as marriage and work, *in* which he nevertheless remains. As a concrete individual, every man must first of all eat and drink, find clothing and shelter, or, in a word, "exist." But in order to exist, so and so much money is needed per year, the "nervus rerum gerendarum." "Money is and will remain the absolute condition for life," argues the aesthetician against the "moralist." But the latter is not content; assuming that a person has neither income nor capital, scarcely a hat for his head—what then? The aesthetician shrugs his shoulders and says, "That is of course another matter; ultimately there is no other way than to find work." But what is the sense of placing a creature, intended to exercise dominion over the world, in this life, if he must work himself to death for his daily bread? "Is this human treatment of a human being?" Is the only purpose of life to assure a miserable sustenance and then to improve it and so on, finally to die, just before attaining ample sustenance? "This consideration could be developed into a proof of human immortality. As follows: it is the destiny of every man to achieve ample sustenance; if he dies before this, he has not achieved his destiny and must therefore (says everyone's private suspicion) achieve it in another world; if, on the contrary, he has achieved ample sustenance, and thus achieved his destiny, it cannot be his destiny to die and thus lose this ample sustenance; it must rather be that he amply enjoy it: ergo man is immortal. This might be called the Popular Proof or the Proof from Substance and Sustenance."[75]

Against this irony of the aesthetician, the moralist replies: work is the duty of man. As such, it is not a burden, but an ethical moment. It is neither a burdensome compulsion, nor reward and pleasure, neither is it an imperfection of human existence; it is rather a peculiar form of human perfection, in contrast to animals and plants, which neither must nor can work. "The lower a human life stands, the less necessity there is to work; the higher it stands, the more this necessity presents itself. The duty of working in order to live expresses the universal aspect of human nature, even in the sense that it is a manifestation of freedom. Through work, man becomes free; through work, he becomes master over nature; through work, he shows that he is more than nature."[76] More beautiful than the sight of a lily growing in the field[77] is the sight of a man who gains what he needs through his own work, preserving his human dignity in the struggle for food. "What gives this struggle such a high educative value is the fact that the prize of victory is so small, in fact nonexistent: the struggle goes on only so that man may continue the struggle. The greater and more extrinsic the reward of the struggler becomes, the more surely he may rely on all the ambiguous passions that have their abode in man: ambition, vanity, pride. These are motivations of enormous power, which can carry a man far. Whoever struggles to earn his bread soon notices that these passions leave him in the lurch: . . . when all his effort suffices merely to gain the bare necessities, how can the reward stimulate him to continue his efforts? If he has no other source of strength, he is lost. You see, this is why the struggle for bread educates and ennobles man: it gives him no possibility of being deceived about himself. If he can see nothing higher in this struggle, then it is really a wretched, miserable situation to have to continue the struggle so as to be able to eat by the sweat of one's brow. But for this very reason this struggle forces man to see something else in it. If a man does not want to be discarded in this struggle, he must see in it a struggle for honor, a struggle, which brings greater honor the lesser the reward is. Thus, although one indeed struggles for sustenance, in reality he is struggling for himself."[78] Therefore it is not mere necessity which compels man to work; he does the necessary work because he seeks to work as a man. For this reason he seeks a "nobler name" for his work, one which will describe its relationship to his life and that of others, at the same time denoting it his joy and dignity.

Thus viewed and performed, the work through which a man is nourished has at the same time a deeper significance for his personality: it is the man's vocation, whose fulfillment brings satisfaction and through which he acquires an essential relationship to his fellow human beings. Work is common to all mankind; its universal human meaning causes the differences between various talents to vanish. Both the greatest and the least can prove themselves true in their vocation. The work of a man's vocation regulates his life, preventing him from emancipating himself from the rest of mankind. It relieves him of the effort of trying to build his life from the ground up, like the man with no vocation. The man who performs regular work is not dependent upon a particular talent in order to accomplish something in the world. Everyone can do his proper task; and to this extent it is true that "in essence every man accomplishes equally much."[79] Whoever in this fashion makes work a part of his life, both spiritually and intellectually, is far removed from the aesthetic view which "refuses to put a yoke upon Pegasus," preferring to make work a pleasure through the development of a particular talent. The aesthetician, who sees in work only the trivial destiny of the crowd, is blind to its educative importance for mankind.

Kierkegaard, who had an inherited income, was clearly aware of the problems involved in his exceptional mode of existence. "You, of course, have no cause to complain, since you do not have to work for your sustenance; nor would I advise you to discard your wealth so as to be placed in this necessity: all such experimentation is mere foolishness, and leads to nothing. In the meantime, in my view, you will have to acquire the necessities of life in another fashion. To be able to live, you must become master of your innate melancholy. To that extent, I can apply that statement of the old man to you: you were brought betimes to the school in which you must learn to work for your living."[80] Just as man cannot live on mere money, neither can he live on melancholy alone; and Kierkegaard knew very well, with his "art of existing," that the inwardness of his melancholy "spiritual existence" was bound to something as external as money: "That there are publishers, that there are men whose entire existence expresses the fact that books are merchandise and an author a merchant, is a completely immoral state of affairs. To the extent that pecuniary interests enter into a spiritual relationship (such as that of an author), that he . . . receives honoraria, etc., the man who establishes the spiritual relationship is also forced to establish a monetary relationship, to involve himself in pecuniary matters, not in the least for the sake of some potential pecuniary advantage, . . . but so that there can be some shame in the transaction. If the monetary relationship is established in such a way that it is the source of gain for another person only, it easily becomes insolence. . . . The insolence lies in viewing the spiritual production quite without reservations as merchandise. Thus the public, through money, gains power over the publisher, the publisher, through the monetary relationship, over the author. . . ."[81] Thanks to this insight into the connection between spirit and money, Kierkegaard was able of his own accord to make the following remark, both serious and paradoxical: "For my becoming a writer, the blame must be laid essen-

tially upon my melancholy and my money."[82] His innate melancholy isolated him, turned him inward, and set him before the
boundary of the religious, but his money made possible for him the
life of a man of private wealth.[83] Shortly before his death he made
clear to himself the remarkable correspondence which existed between the exhaustion of his spiritual existence and of its material
means: a few months before he collapsed, he withdrew from the
bank the last installment of his inheritance, which had been de-
posited there without interest.[84] Thus even he, Marx's exact opposite, proves the latter's insight into the connection between capital,
labor, and the totality of human existence.

5   Nietzsche:
Work as the Dissolution of
Devotion and Contemplation

In Nietzsche's occasional thoughts on the position of work in
the life of man, work is no longer a power which contributes to the
formation of the world and the education of man; it is felt only as a
pressure and a burden. But if the basic characteristic of work is its
difficulty, and if in spite of all will to accomplish it has no purpose
of its own, then man will free himself from the burden and seriousness of work by plunging into light pleasures whenever he no longer
has work to do. In his flight from work to pleasure, the worker has
no chance for recuperation; the pressure of work and the search for
pleasure are merely two aspects of one and the same situation. By
way of contrast, Nietzsche defends contemplation, which takes its
time and allows itself leisure. "There is an Indianlike . . . wildness
in the way the Americans strive for money: and the breathless pace
of their work—the real vice of the New World—has already begun
to inflame ancient Europe with the wildness, to spread over it a
thoroughly amazing lack of spirit. Every man is ashamed to be calm;
long reflection almost causes pangs of conscience. Men think with
their watches in hand, the way one eats lunch, with one eye on the
exchange list. Everyone lives like a man about to be late for something. Better to be doing something than to be doing nothing: this
principle is a noose to put an end to all culture and all good taste.
And just as all manner of forms are destroyed by this pressure of
work, so the feeling for form itself . . . is destroyed. . . . There

is no longer the time or the energy for ceremony, for the byways of courtesy, for all esprit of amusement, in short, for any *otium*. For life which is hot on the trail of profit always forces the spirit to the point of exhaustion, in constant pretending, outwitting, or anticipating. The real virtue of today is being able to do something in less time than it takes anyone else. And so only rarely are there hours of permissible honesty, but in them a man is tired; he wants not only to let go, but to lie down and collapse. This propensity now influences the writing of letters: the style and spirit of letters are always the real index of the time. If there is still any pleasure in society and the arts, it is the pleasure of slaves who have been worked until they are weary. Oh, the restrictions on joy among our people, educated and uneducated! All clear conscience stands on the side of work: any disposition toward joy calls itself need for recuperation, and begins to be ashamed of itself. It is necessary to preserve one's health —such is the excuse if one is discovered on a jaunt in the country. It might soon reach the point that no one could give in to a disposition to the *vita contemplativa* . . . without self-reproach and a bad conscience."[85] The inclination toward contemplation had its roots in both the ancient and the Christian ethos. In antiquity, it was considered dignified and noble to cultivate leisure, and as long as the Church determined the norms of life, the *vita contemplativa* was assured of the precedence given to meditation and devotion, above all secular activity. Only the tireless industry of the modern world destroyed the old proportion between *otium* and labor, Christian recollection and the bustle of the secular world, until finally Sunday became a day of boredom, no one having anything to do. The modern drive to "make the most of one's time" with the fetish of industriousness has done more than anything else to lead to lack of faith and the breakup of the religious life. "Among those who, for example, live their lives today in Germany apart from all religion, I find men of many sorts, . . . but particularly a majority whose religious instincts have been destroyed by industriousness: they no longer have any idea of what religions are for, and only register . . . a kind of apathetic amazement at their own presence in the world. They feel that there are already plenty of claims upon them . . . whether made by their business, their pleasure, not to mention their fatherland and the newspapers . . ."[86] The same thing that is true of these enormously busy people is also true of scholars,[87] for even scholarly investigation has become one component in the machinery of unceasing labor.

Work has lost its curse ever since the bourgeois-Christian world
—to use the title of a much-read anthology of Carlyle—began to do
"work" in order to avoid "desperation," and to speak of the "blessing of work." "In this glorification of work, in this inexhaustible
talk of the 'blessing of work,' I see the same thought in the background as in the praise of beneficial impersonal activities on the part
of the community: fear of everything individual. The basic feeling
today is . . . that such work is the best police, that it keeps a check
on everyone and is a powerful restraint upon the development of
reason, cupidity, and the desire for self-sufficiency."[88]
One of the classic eulogists of work in the nineteenth century
was E. Zola, who proclaimed in an address to youth: "I had only
one faith, one source of strength: work. I was held up only by that
immense task I had laid upon myself. . . . The work of which I
speak is regular work, a lesson, a duty which I have assigned myself
to make some progress in every day, even if only one step forward.
. . . Work! Consider, gentlemen: work forms the only law of the
world. Life has no other purpose, there is no other reason for existence, we all come into being only in order to do our share of the
work, and then vanish." Only rare spirits like Nietzsche and Tolstoy
recognized the false ardor and hidden nihilism which are characterized by this estimation of work.[89]
In the course of the nineteenth century, work was elevated to
the position of being an end in itself. By no means was it limited to
the "industrial society" of the bourgeois epoch; it is even more characteristic of the "people" of the totalitarian state, which confronted
them with an apparent goal which in actual fact could not be anything but war. The German "labor front," which even harnessed
leisure time for the purposes of work through "strength through
pleasure," created an organizational system of labor such as can be
compared only with that of the army. The political purpose of this
labor "front" was the construction of a totally martial state through
the complete militarization of life. This development, too, was predicted by the author of the *Wille zur Macht:* "From the future of
the worker: workers should learn to feel like soldiers: an hono-
rarium, an allowance, but no wages."[90] But Nietzsche saw the "training" of the masses only as a means toward higher ends; for this
reason he could ask, with reference to the "slavery of the present":
"Where are those *for* whom they work?"

III The Problem
of Education

> "That it might still be possible for a man to
> receive an education purely through his own
> motivation—that has long been out of the ques-
> tion. The demands of the time are too great, men
> cannot simply be left to themselves, they need a
> universal mold so that at least everyone can fit
> into the turbulence called modern life."
>
> BURCKHARDT (to Kinkel, 1846)

The humanistic ideal of education was outlined in Germany by
W. v. Humboldt and realized in the universities. Today it is no
longer in a defensive position. Even the much-discussed question of
the choice between humanistic or political education has long been
a dead issue. The intelligentsia were made to realize that their non-
political education was no match for the attack of the state; and the
state boasted of being able to do without the "intellectuals," which
of course did not prevent the new political education of the *Reich*
from living off the remnants of the old, as is demonstrated by every
sentence and the entire vocabulary of its manifestoes, speeches, and
documents. For Hegel, the problem of a choice between humanistic
and political goals was simply nonexistent; he still thought it obvious
that "humanistic" education was just what educated the individual
for his life in the *polis*.

1   Hegel's
Political Humanism

The five addresses delivered by Hegel between 1809 and 1815, when he was Rector of the Nürnberg Gymnasium, present briefly and simply a complete picture of his idea of education.[1] It is as far removed from an external compulsion to bring politics into education as from the aristocratic educational individualism of von Humboldt. The fact that a man can only educate himself was the assumption behind the fact that he must educate himself to take a share in the community, in the context of traditional language and custom which are not only mine, but everyone's. Self-education is education by which the individual raises himself to the universal nature of the spirit. This basic principle lies behind all five addresses. The first discusses particularly the study of the ancient classics and the significance of grammatical and linguistic studies for education as such. The second develops the concept of discipline, and discusses the connection between moral and scholarly education. The third places the school between the family life of the child and the public life of the adult. The fourth illuminates the study of the classics with respect to the education of man that makes him an integrated whole. The fifth characterizes the problematic position of contemporary education as the struggle between the ancient and traditional, on the one hand, and the new on the other.

As a task of the secondary school, education is limited at first to the study of what is taught. True studying is distinguished from mere passive learning and self-willed argumentation. The teacher must so educate his pupil that the latter may learn to think for himself in the learning of something else. "The restraint of idle chatter is an essential condition for all education and all learning. One must begin by comprehending the thoughts of others, renouncing his own ideas." This combination of learning with independent thought converts the former into genuine study. The test of whether a person has really made something his own in the learning process is whether he can apply it in new and different cases.[2] The achievement of this goal is the pedagogical goal of instruction, which must be educational in itself and therefore has no need of external pedagogy.

Hegel explains the advantage of becoming Rector of a new educational institution by the fact that it is founded upon older institutions, and thus continues a tradition which guarantees permanence. The principle of the older institutions, which forms the basis for faith in the new one, is humanistic education. "For several millennia this has been the soil upon which all culture has stood, from which it has sprouted, and with which it has been in continuous contact." "The preservation of this soil is important; equally essential is the modification of the situation in which it previously was." What is old must be put in a new relationship to the whole in order that its essential components may be preserved. Hegel uses Latin as an example. It has fallen into disfavor because it allowed important areas of learning of bourgeois life to be neglected; but it does not follow that mere study of current events can replace the study of the Greeks and Romans. The material studied is not what educates, neither in the case of Latin nor in the case of discussion of everyday affairs. It is the education of the man himself that is valuable, in and of itself. "But let us assume that what is excellent is in general the proper point of departure: then the basis for all higher study is and must remain the literature of the Greeks primarily, and next, that of the Romans." Only in the study of the perfect works of antiquity does a man receive the "profane baptism" "which gives the soul its first unforgettable feeling for good taste and knowledge." A man must give himself completely to the ancients, receive "bed and board" from them, in order to absorb their atmosphere, their ideas and customs, even their errors and prejudices, and to become at home in this world, which is the most beautiful that has ever been.[3] The ancient world provides the noblest sustenance in the noblest form for education; no other people produced as much that was original, excellent, and versatile as did the Greeks, whose plastic virtue was free from the "moral ambiguity" of the Christian world.

Its wealth is incorporated into its language, and so the study of the ancients must be above all a study of their languages. But a true acquisition of a strange language cannot take place directly. The acquisition of something strange demands an estrangement from what is one's own. A man must be able to achieve a certain distance from himself if he is to bring nearer to himself what is strange and different. Not only does education need a subject upon which to work, but there must be something alien about this subject in our encounter with it. "Estrangement is a necessary condition for theoretical education; education demands, to this end, that the student occupy himself with something that is not immediate, something alien."[4] This "demand for separation" is expressed by the drive

which is especially typical of youth: to break away from what is
familiar and search for oneself far off, because what is distant and
strange exercises the most fascination on the learning capacity of
the individual. "Upon this centrifugal drive of the soul is based . . .
the necessity that the soul make for itself that divorce which it seeks
by its very nature and condition, and give to the young spirit a
strange, distant world. The dividing wall which accomplishes the
separation for education . . . is the world and language of the ancients. But that which keeps us apart also contains all the starting
points and threads which lead to a return to ourselves, an amicable
relationship, and the rediscovery of ourselves, but ourselves, according to the true universal nature of the spirit."[5] Thus true appropriation is not an assimilation of what is strange, preserving no distance;
it demands, rather, that a person go forth from himself. The only
educated man is he who appropriates the other in its otherness. It
follows that even the "mechanical" aspect of learning a foreign
language is more than a necessary evil. "What is mechanical is what
is foreign to the spirit; the spirit takes an interest in digesting what
has been fed it undigested, in coming to understand this lifeless
object that has been given it, in making it its own." The same is true
for grammatical studies, which are an excellent means for educating
the spirit precisely because of their abstraction. Just as the notion of
"being" in general is already present in every grammatical "is," so
linguistic forms in general contain the logos of things.[6] The educated man must be able to think concretely; but only he can think
concretely who can make distinctions within the great mass of ideas
and abstract from empirical material.[7] The study of grammar is an
"elementary philosophy" because it acquaints us with simple abstract
entities, the "vowels of the spiritual." These three strange things—
the ancient world, its language, and systematic grammar—comprise
the educative force for humanistic studies by separating the human
spirit from itself and thus freeing it for its true end. But the basic
principle of a scholarly education is also the principle of behavior
worthy of a human being; this latter demands equally that a man
achieve a certain distance from himself. "A scholarly education in
general has the effect on the spirit of separating it from itself, lifting
it above its immediate natural existence, the sphere of bondage to
emotions and drives; it places the spirit within the realm of thought.
Thus the spirit achieves consciousness of its own reactions to external influences, reactions that are otherwise constrained and instinc-
tual. This liberation means control over immediate impressions and

emotions; it is the formal basis for all moral actions."[8] Therefore, military training also has an educative influence upon the spirit; it counters natural distraction and laziness, forcing a man to be alert and carry out the orders of others with precision. Education is, in fact, not limited to this or that peculiar subject: a man who is "educated in other areas" has the ability to gain an understanding of every knowledge or skill with which he is as yet unacquainted. Education is universal, precisely because it is not a "general education" in the sense of superficial juxtaposition of many particulars.[9]

But because the effectiveness of bourgeois educational institutions does not extend to the entire scope of human existence, limiting its attention, rather, to man as a pupil, it is the task of schools to mediate between the private particularity and the public universality of life. The school presupposes that the pupil comes to it already with a certain amount of knowledge, and, on the other hand, that he must later establish himself in the world outside the school. It mediates between life in the family and life in the world, which is common to all.[10] The world to which the pupils must be educated is not a private world, but a *res publica* or *polis*. Man's place in it is not determined by his individual particularity, but by the extent of his contribution to one of its objective spheres. Thus the aim of education is to develop the individual through renunciation of his peculiarities and to incorporate him into the "objective element" of the common world, in contrast to the particular personal relationship of the family, out of which it is the job of the central portion of an individual's education to lead him. The world in which the educated man achieves a "universal self-existence" is characterized by Hegel as a "system of universality," in which individuals count only to the extent that they accommodate themselves to it. What is brought about by the schools is the capacity of the individual to participate in public life.[11] This was the purpose of that education according to whose example we called ours "humanistic." In the modern situation, the great public conditions upon which the cohesion of the bourgeois moral order rests have been removed beyond our sight and participation. In the *polis*, they were present and immediate because the absoluteness of the state rested upon the independent participation of the individuals. In our modern condition of isolation, brought about by overeducation, the "inner life of the whole," as an abstract spirit, is no longer a concern of the individual. "Every individual receives only a fragmented share; he is granted a restricted sphere, over which stands the soul . . . which brings all these . . .

particular movements . . . into a unity. No one has a feeling for
the whole, nor an active view of it."[12] The vocational class to which
we dedicate ourselves is more exclusive than among the ancients; but
it is therefore all the more important for us to preserve at least the
idea and notion of a "complete life." The best guide to this end is
study of the humanities. "They give us a familiar idea of man as a
whole. The kind of freedom which existed in the ancient states, the
inner unity of public and private life, of public consensus and private
opinion, implies a great familiarity with the great interests of
individual humanity, the most important pillars of public and private action, the powers which bring about the rise and fall of
nations. These thoughts appear as natural reflections upon everyday
objects of an ordinary present, thoughts which, in our educational
system, do not enter into the circle of our life and action. Thus
laws and duties appear to us in living form as customs and virtues:
not in the form of reflections and principles according to which we
must frame our lives as according to precepts imposed from above."[13]
In order to keep alive before him this basic idea of a noble life, considered as a whole, in order to secure an "inner place" to which he
can retire from the isolation of our real life, a man must study a
classical curriculum and learn from the Greeks and Romans.

In Hegel's actual attitude toward the world, however, the recognition of "what is" outweighed all criticism of the existing order
according to the educational standard of the ancients. His feeling
for reality repudiated the "eternal youths" who wanted to overthrow the existing order. They proclaim their "lack of education"
by their unwillingness to give up their personal selves and enter into
reality. If they belong to the upper classes, says Hegel—as though
with a premonition of his revolutionary pupils—they band together,
construct idle programs of how the world should go according to
their view, in order to smash a "hole in the order of the world."

2   The Young
Hegelians

a   Ruge's Politicization
of Aesthetic Education

Ruge drew the most definite conclusions concerning the consequences for education from the "politicization of the age." He

utilized Hegel's political educational ideal as a basis for a self-sufficient education which would withdraw from public life. His thought is as follows. The politicization of education seems at first to be a destruction of the free domains of knowledge and fine arts. But yet the Greeks were "political" through and through, while at the same time, poetic, philosophic, and free. But in their case, the arts and sciences did not possess that "ingenuousness" which is peculiar to our situation; the apparent freedom of our arts and sciences rests upon private isolation from the common life of the public.[14] The "overeducation" which proceeded from this isolation, creating "Alexandrian" scholarship, demands a thorough reformation. The only exception is the natural sciences: they do not have as their object of study any "historical modes of existence of the spirit." By contrast, the march of time means the death of existing philosophy, theology, and jurisprudence; history robs them of their former material. "With the Greek gods, Greek theology dies; with the Greek State, Greek jurisprudence; together with the Holy Roman Empire there perished an immense juristic world, a true paradise . . . for legal scholars." Likewise the poetic genre of scenes of nature, love, family, and village life vanishes as soon as the newly awakened sense of politics gives literature historical themes. To outmoded education must also be reckoned the other side of popular literature, that is, romanticism. Together with it, classicism is condemned by the verdict of history. As a consequence of their restriction to the historicopolitical situation in Germany, even Goethe and Schiller withdrew "egoistically" to their inner selves, Goethe in a spirit of renunciation, Schiller in a spirit of challenge, but both unable to give political reality to their poetic ideals.[15] That portion of "former" education which survives Ruge's radical criticism as belonging to the "new" literature is limited to the names of a few political literati such as Herwegh and Hoffmann von Fallersleben.

It is stated one degree more plainly in the last volume of the *Jahrbücher*[16] that the age of "blasé theoreticians" and the illusion of abstract philosophy are past. Faith, knowledge, and poetry, the "absolute" sphere of Hegel's system, are not suspended in the air somewhere above the state; they are themselves a public concern and a necessary component in the spiritual organization of political freedom. The true religious question does not lie in reservations of "conscience" or in "good will"—which is as powerless as it is estimable—but in the secularization of religion, science, and art on the part of the state as the public totality of our common life. A blasé education lacks great historical goals, and is therefore self-satisfied. "The philosophy which loses sight of its radical goal, like the general education of purely private individuals, always runs into danger of condemning itself to destruction through mere self-reflection and idle movement within its own subjectivity. The jokes and stale humor of great cities which always lie in wait for a suitable opportunity to break forth and sparkle, the idolization of all genius and fame, empty enthusiasm for dancing girls, gladiators, musicians, athletes—what does all this prove? Nothing more than a blasé education, lacking all sense of real labor toward great goals, . . . nothing more than the frivolousness of formal knowledge and formal talent. A man must be able to despise all these gifts and all this skillfulness if he is not to be caught up in this same senseless maelstrom, insipid and lifeless. Amuse yourselves with your supercleverness, pass the time away, if you have reached the point of being able to join in the game and shine at it; then reflect upon this dandelion consciousness, in which you have achieved everything, including the insight that you are unable to advance beyond this satiation and ennui. But do not get the idea that you are whole human beings, even if you have yourselves shot to relieve the ennui. The same phenomena which are produced by the overeducation typical of life in the capital also arise out of self-sufficient philosophy. Its illusion is the same as that of general education, that a formal theorizing is a form of the spirit and an end in itself." Ruge's description of the blasé consciousness simplifies Hegel's analysis of the world of "estranged education,"[17] but without bringing the "spirit-forsaken surface" of this merely overclever education beyond itself to absolute knowledge. He does not abolish it, but seeks to destroy it politically. If it is to be destroyed, it must become entangled in the practical problems of political activity, which seize each individual by the scruff of the neck and tear him loose from his overeducation. This reform of consciousness does not mean the ruin of the arts and sciences, but rather gives them popular roots. It begets first of all a "real and powerful" learning. The spirit of learning must acquire a truly vital content in public life, so that self-consciousness becomes consciousness of the world, and liberalism "democratism," which erases the dividing line between the educated and uneducated. "The problems of the age must be in the possession of the people, they must be problems for the people, if they are to have real life in this world. The notion of the 'people' is the abolition of the barriers between caste and class, not only the illusory ones between peasant and noble, bourgeois and aristocrat, . . . but also the real barriers between those who have knowledge and those who do not have it. Much more can be accomplished in this direction than appears at first glance." In place of the abstruse intellectual world of a lifeless education, of a police which stands removed from bourgeois life, of a judiciary which is suspended mysteriously above all, and a military system completely isolated from the life of the people, there must arise a community both spiritual and political, within which all the contradictions of outworn liberalism will vanish. The following practical problems result: "1. The Church must be transformed into a school, organized into a real means of educating the people which will absorb the entire mob. 2. The military system must be merged completely into this educational system. 3. The people, educated and organized, must be allowed to rule themselves and administer justice themselves, in public life and in public courts."

Upon the accomplishment of this reform, even the caprice of frivolousness embodied in Heine[18] will be reduced to a mere aspect of the real spirit. For true freedom is not the "spiritual freedom" which grew out of Protestantism and romanticism, but political freedom, which includes freedom of spirit and of education. "The spirit is a political spirit, and all men . . . are political beings." The state is not a private affair; it is a *res publica*, it is "the concern which concerns everything."

Ruge saw his program as the German fulfillment of the French Revolution. Even during the reaction, he set his hope upon Prussia, whose mission in Europe was to bring into being a Germany which would be a great power. He prophesied that the political education which he preached would lead to an "attitude," then to a "character," and finally to political "action."

b Stirner's Reduction of Humanistic and Scientific Education to Self-Revelation of the Individual

At the same time as Ruge, Stirner took up the theme of the false principle on which our education is based, in an essay on humanism and realism.[19] His point of view is not political freedom, but the absolutely "personal" freedom of the individual "I." Like Kierkegaard, Stirner formulates truth as nothing else than the "revelation of the self." This includes the "discovery of the self." In contrast to Kierkegaard, he understands this growth of the self as an

"extreme abstraction or exemption from all authority."[20] In education, the authority structure has been expressed by the fact that
down to the Enlightenment, higher education was the exclusive
property of scholars and priests. It was in the hands of the humanists
and clergy because only the classics and the Bible were considered
truly educational and edifying. And education in Latin and Greek
made one master over the masses of the laity. Ever since the French
Revolution and the Declaration of Human Rights, this exclusive
education came into conflict with the demand for universal education. An education was sought which would have real influence upon
bourgeois life, which would abolish the humanistic distinction between scholar and layman. "The comprehension of the past, as
taught by humanism, and the apprehension of the present, which is
the goal of realism, only leads both to power over what is temporal.
Only the spirit which comprehends itself is eternal," that is, the
unity and omnipotence of the "I" which educates itself for its own
ends. Neither ancient humanism nor modern realism had any idea of
this freedom. Through the spread of universal education, the scholar
who had been through higher education was transformed into a man
with a one-sided education; the man with the realistic, scientific
education became a "practicer" without ideas, an "uncultured in-
dustrialist." The reverse of this educated industrialism is dandyism.
In order to overcome these contradictions, the educational system as
such must die, to be resurrected as "will." For whoever seeks to
preserve his knowledge will lose it, but whoever surrenders his
knowledge will gain it. The end and, at the same time, the eternity
of knowledge consists in its once more becoming "simple and immediate," by begetting itself anew in every action as impulse and as
will. It is then no longer an external possession of knowledge, but
rather a knowing which has become one with me, which has personal existence. Instead of acquiring knowledge from without, a
person should achieve self-revelation: "Knowledge, however scholarly and deep, or however broad and intelligible, remains merely
a possession, like property, so long as it has not vanished into the
invisible point of the 'I,' to break forth once more . . . as will.
Knowledge experiences this transformation when it ceases to refer
solely to objects, when it becomes a knowledge of the self, or, in
case this seems clearer, becomes . . . a self-consciousness of the
spirit. It then is converted, so to speak, into the drive, the instinct
of the spirit, an unconscious knowledge. Everyone can have at least
an inkling of this when he compares it with the way he himself

sublimates so many diverse experiences into the simple feeling which we call a sense of time: all the diffuse knowledge deriving from those experiences is concentrated into a momentary knowledge, which determines his actions in an instant."[21] This momentary, immediate, and vital knowledge today would be called "existential." In it all estranged education "shrinks together." It corresponds to the existential concentration of the entire world upon the particular, individual "I."

c Bauer's Criticism of
the Cliché of the "Universal"

As a keen observer who held himself above the "movement," Bauer, from the very beginning, saw through the shallowness of both the personal and political involvement of education and knowledge with "life," making it the object of a critical historical study.[22] The flood of philosophical periodicals,[23] pamphlets, and lectures on the reform of the universities and the necessity of a political education which filled the German classrooms between 1842 and 1846 he described with the pertinent formula of "pauperism" and the subsequent "simplification of concepts."[24] These two phrases say everything "that has been important (since Gutzkow)." The formulas in which this pauperism expresses itself are: the "organization" of education, man as a political "member of a class," "participation in the state." But Ruge did not evaluate correctly this participation in the "cliché of the universal." His impassioned challenge, by "force of endless repetition," had already transferred the citizens of Germany into the realm of action. What Ruge "sought to pour out over the sinful world in one great stream," was allowed to trickle out "drop by drop upon the stone of the existing order," to hollow it out all the more surely.[25]

While everyone was proclaiming that philosophy and theoretical education were finally permeating the actual conduct of life, Bauer established that the scientific education which had become so "vital" was not any education at all. The universities had long ceased to be the arena of historical conflicts, while the radicals—knowing less of the history of science than of anything else—proclaimed at the top of their lungs the appearance of a superficial compilation as an event of decisive importance, and rejoiced over the stilted phrases addressed by a politically motivated professor to students in a torchlight procession, announcing the victory of the "popular interest."[26]

The reduction, particularly of history, to the "interests of the present," with its gross violations of documentary history, provided a proof of the superiority which these simple concepts helped the new "popular philosopher" achieve over the "dry material" of history.[27] "Those who were studying spoke of a 'destiny' of the universities when it was already fulfilled, of the 'river of history,' when it no longer flowed through the canal of the universities, . . . of science, when it had been . . . dissipated and its particles dispersed . . . into a vague gas."[28] The talk was all of the "whole" which each must serve, of the "political knowledge" which no one could evade. To make learning come alive, an intellectual commerce was demanded between the teacher and the learners, without the realization that the medium of exchange, learning itself, was no longer present.[29] "The scholastics . . . were plainly opposed to this doctrine of participation in the state; all philosophic systems were popular in comparison to this university lecture on the nature of the subject citizen. . . . The ingenious mystics must look with awe upon this transcendence of the theory of self-surrender, which far surpasses the edifice of their doctrine of the exaltation of the individual to the universal."[30]

In reality, it was of no use at all to the "political monks" to offer art and science as a sacrifice to the state, seeking to please the state by calling a political education the "only truly human" education. "The state took no heed of their assurances, declared its duty to be the defense of itself and its own against the encroachments of science, and guarded against surrendering itself as common property to universal education." Thereupon the radical intelligentsia accosted the state with even greater demands, trying to embarrass it, if at all possible. "But at this point, when the claims made upon the state had reached a maximum and the dependence of the individual had been exalted to an absolute principle, radicalism was finally cut off by the real state and transferred to a new area, where it could cultivate exclusively the vagueness which had condemned its political demands to sterility, without regard for political success, where it could honor dispassionately the omnipotence . . . of the whole, and where it could preach selflessness to better effect than in the realm of politics."[31]

Bauer's attempt to illuminate the origin and destiny of the modern liberal movements in a series of historical studies remained an isolated undertaking; it ran into violent opposition not only from Marx, but from everyone. Then, as today, such criticism was called "sterile," "abstract," and "confused," because it did not become involved in "real life." The arrogance of Bauer's criticism, it was said, fell under the power of a sophistry which estranged it from the concerns of the people. The vital thing was not criticism, but rather a "reconstruction" in which is realized the sum of everything toward which history was tending.[32]

3 J. Burckhardt on the Century of Education and G. Flaubert on the Contradictions of Knowledge

In 1846, the same year in which Bauer wrote his critical history of the situation in Germany, Burckhardt wrote a letter to G. Kinkel, who himself played a not inconspicuous part in the radical movement. In it, he expressed the opinion that the nineteenth century would some day be called the "educated" century, for today, no matter how stupid an individual might be, he was the target of so many sparks of widespread education that only a Hercules could cut off all the heads of this hydra. "A while back each man was a fool unto himself and left the world in peace; now, on the other hand, everyone thinks he is educated, constructs a patchwork *Weltanschauung*, and preaches away at his fellow men. No longer is there any desire to learn, much less to keep silent, least of all to let someone else follow his own course of development. The whole thing is diabolical." This universal education daily builds up a shell of conventional opinions, that is, errors, within which entire classes of society move in false enthusiasm.[33] Feeling this hopelessness of his age, Burckhardt decided to flee to the South to escape them all: "the radicals, Communists, industrialists, intellectuals, pretenders, thinkers, abstractionists, absolutists, sophists, political fanatics, idealists, -ians and -ists of all kinds."[34] Forty years later he saw in the general condition of an education constantly becoming more inclusive and common the confirmation of his former conviction that the education in modern cities was producing only "force-fed mediocrities."[35] In opposition to this "compulsory leveling," he defended, as the lesser evil, the breach between the educated and uneducated which came into existence with the breakup of the Middle Ages.[36]

The real compendium of problems having to do with education is Flaubert's unfinished masterpiece *Bouvard et Pécuchet*.[37] While in Germany the epigones of classical education were writing novels after the pattern of *Wilhelm Meister,* about 1850, Flaubert conceived the plan of laying out a "dictionnaire des idées reçues,"[38] a documentary history of human stupidity which would be an ironic "glorification historique de tout ce qu'on approuve." After he finished the *Temptation of St. Anthony,* in which this saint was tempted by all the beliefs and superstitions that have ever assailed mankind, he set about to arrange and analyze the present state of chaos in scholarly education. Two kindly and cautious townsmen, honestly concerned about their higher education, are at their country estate, which they were lucky enough to acquire. They wander through the entire maze of collected knowledge—from gardening, chemistry, and medicine to history, archaeology, politics, pedagogics, and philosophy—only to return finally to their writing and produce extracts out of the books they studied in vain. In the style of high comedy the whole work passes through the realm of estranged education, finally ending with the absolute knowledge that our entire education is without foundation. "Doctrines that have lived for centuries are explained in ten lines, developed, and disposed of by confrontation with other doctrines which are elucidated and destroyed with equal acuity and vitality. On one page after another, in one line after another, an idea rises up; immediately there arises another idea which knocks the first to the ground, only to fall mortally wounded by its neighbor."[39] In a sketch at the conclusion of the work, Pécuchet paints a dark picture of the future of man; Bouvard a bright picture. According to the former, the end of the human race, which has become more and more inferior, is approaching in a general process of decay and decomposition. There are three possibilities: "1. Pantheistic radicalism may destroy every connection with the past, with an inhuman despotism as a consequence. 2. In the case of a victory for theistic absolutism, the liberalism which has controlled mankind since the Revolution will perish, with a consequent upheaval. 3. The convulsions which have been taking place since 1789 may continue; without deciding between the two alternatives, the oscillations will drag us along. Then there will be no more idealism, religion, or morality. Then America will have conquered the world." In the view of the latter, Europe will be rejuvenated by Asia, undreamed modes of travel will come into being, with submarines and balloons, new sciences will grow up which will enable man to place the forces of the universe in the service of civilization and, when the earth is used up, migrate to other planets. Evil will come to an end together with want, and philosophy will become religion.

4   Nietzsche's Criticism of Education, Present and Past

The discoveries which Burckhardt made at the beginning of the social movements became the property of Nietzsche after 1870 in the context of the national state. At a distance of thirty years, they both saw the coming of a "civilized barbarism" which reached its full growth with the unification of these two tendencies of the nineteenth century.[40] Even the *Bildungsphilister* (narrow-minded intellectual), whom Nietzsche saw and attacked in Strauss, is by no means extinct; he has, rather, become a wholesale phenomenon: the politically trained man with the prescribed world view.[41]

Under the heading "Former German Education," Nietzsche describes the "dull gleam" which illuminated the "nobly distorted gestures" of education as incorporated in Germany particularly in Schiller, Humboldt, and Schleiermacher, but also Schelling and Hegel. The "galactic gleam" of this education, nevertheless, was immediately laid aside. "When the Germans began to become objects of interest to the other nations of Europe . . . it was on account of an education which they no longer possess, which, in fact, they shook off with a blind eagerness as though it were a disease, and yet they had nothing better for which to exchange it than political and nationalistic madness. Of course this had the effect of making them objects of even greater interest to the other nations than they had been by virtue of their education: that may be their satisfaction!"[42]

He considered the Bismarckian State an "extirpation of the German spirit on behalf of the German Empire," Bismarck himself, a "fraternity student," and the "Era of Bismarck," an era of "Germany's increasing stupidity." Bismarck constricted the German spirit to a nationalistic spirit, forced the Germans into international politics, heaped up for them a monstrous empire and power, and caused the German people to sacrifice their ancient virtues, giving them instead a "parliamentary education" and making a mockery of their reputation as a nation of thinkers.[43] In Nietzsche's judgment, nevertheless, within the given situation of Germany, Bismarck was relatively "great," precisely because he did not cling to German education, but was in his own fashion more intelligent than the contemporary German scholars. The Germany which he created is not a picture of high culture and taste, but "a great quantum of inherited and acquired virtue," a large potion of industriousness, patience, and willingness to obey—which, of course, does not exclude the possibility that political power will spoil the Germans. "The Germans—once they were called the nation of thinkers: today do they think at all? Today the Germans are weary with intellectual matters, today the Germans mistrust the spirit, politics devours all serious interest in really spiritual things. *'Deutschland, Deutschland, über alles'*: I'm afraid that was the end of German philosophy. . . . Are there German philosophers? Are there German poets? Are there good German books? These are the questions foreigners ask me. I blush, but with the boldness characteristic of me in desperate straits, I answer, *'Yes, Bismarck!'* "[44] Nietzsche's attitude toward Bismarck was of necessity ambiguous,[45] because he himself sought to achieve a union of the "spirit" with "politics" and the will to power; when his madness finally erupted, he invited the leading statesmen of Europe to a conference in Rome. The concept of politics was to be absorbed in a "war of the spirits"; the criterion for the seriousness of a philosophy was to be the fact that statesmen could declare their allegiance to it.[46] But as long as the spirit is mere education, and politics is without thought, those philosophers are relatively best who, like Schopenhauer, do their thinking apart from the state, and those statesmen are relatively best who, like Bismarck, have no understanding of philosophy.

What Nietzsche saw in 1873 were "symptoms of the atrophy of education," brought about by the fragmentation of knowledge, the struggles for power among nations, the wealth and pleasure economy of the educated classes. "Everything assists the coming barbarism, art as well as science. Whither shall we look? . . . Since we really have no method of defense, and everyone is in the same position—what is to be done? Try to warn the forces that are still present; form an alliance with them; while there is still time, restrain the classes from which the danger of barbarism threatens. But all alliances with the 'educated' must be rejected. That is the greatest enemy because it hinders the physicians and seeks to deny the sickness."[47] The educated classes, we read further on, must be surrendered; the men who know what is necessary will have the best feeling for what can be their wisdom. But the danger is that the uneducated classes will catch the fever of contemporary education and make this pseudo-education universal. No one is able truly to overcome the degeneration of education, which produces on the one hand scholarly specialization and on the other a journalistic general education.[48] Each complements the other in producing one and the same lack of education; scientific rigor gets along quite well with lack of judgment and barbarism of taste in all other matters. Both standpoints are right to a certain degree because no one is capable of reaching the point where both are wrong.

"Education shrinks daily because hurry increases daily," is the theme of the lectures on the future of German educational institutions (1871–72).[49] They are an attempt to describe the point from which, beyond journalism and specialization, the problem of education can be solved. The thesis which Nietzsche uses to develop his treatment of the question is: "In the present, two tendencies dominate our educational institutions, which were founded originally upon other principles. They are apparently divergent; their effects are equally deleterious, and in the long run, ultimately the same. On the one hand, there is the drive toward the greatest possible extension of education; on the other, the drive to reduce and weaken it. In agreement with the former drive, education is to be provided for ever-widening circles; following the other tendency, education is expected to surrender its highest claims to glory, and subordinate itself to another form of life, that of the state. These fatal tendencies of expansion and reduction should lead to hopeless despair if it is not sometime possible to assist the victory of two contrary tendencies that are truly German: the drive towards a restriction and concentration of education as the counterpart to enormous expansion, and the drive towards the strengthening and self-sufficiency of education as the counterpart to its reduction."[50] The second *Unzeitgemässe Betrachtung* is an application of this thesis: it discusses the limitless extension and weakening of education brought about by historical knowledge. Several chapters of *Zarathustra* are an echo of this early criticism of education, "Of the Land of Education," "Of Undefiled Knowledge," and "Of Scholars": "Without either faith or superstition, they are a motley picture of all that has ever been believed; like mills they labor to grind the grain that others have sown." Between the education of today and that of yesterday, Nietzsche sought a way back to the true requirements of primitive education, that is, one which forms or educates man in the totality of his corporeal humanity.[51] Thus his criticism of the existing education is first and last a criticism of existing humanity.

IV The Problem of Man

> "An animal which was able to speak said, 'Being human is a prejudice which does not afflict us animals, at least.'"
>
> NIETZSCHE

1 Hegel:
Absolute Spirit as
the Universal Essence of Man

The spirit is Hegel's basic principle.[1] As the "absolute," it is also the true universal essence of man. Only the presupposition of the "inner universal," the spirit, enables one to recognize the external particularities of men.[2] But the "omnipotent age and its culture," that is, the epoch of the Enlightenment, led to man's disinclination to recognize "God or the absolute." Its absolute standpoint is, rather, "man and mankind." Philosophy, nevertheless, cannot halt at this empirical mankind and its superficial ideality, relinquishing the absolute "for the sake of its beloved mankind." What is usually called "man" is merely a "determinate finite object," not "the spiritual focus of the universe." As a consequence of the distinction between the sensuous and supersensuous world, the latter is merely "an escape from the former"; man is a material being, covered with an immaterial whitewash. "Suppose that the ideal of art were to bring a look of yearning into the eye of a common face, a timid smile onto its lips, but it was a forbidden art to represent the gods, who are above all, yearning and melancholy. . . . In similar fashion, philosophy is supposed to represent, not the ideal of man, but only the abstraction of empirical mankind, with all its limitations. It is supposed to bear the stake of absolute antithesis immovably imbedded within it. As it makes clear its limitation to what is sensuous, . . . it is to adorn its surface with a façade of the supersensuous, by pointing in faith to something higher."[3] The empirical and absolute essence of man "should" coincide, but cannot, so long as the philosophy of the Enlightenment pours the speculative idea of reason in a "human form." The "perennial consideration of man" has the effect of giving the word "humanity" the meaning of "whatever is vulgar." In contrast, Hegel emphasizes that it is only the spirit that "makes man man."[4] This sentence occurs on the first page of the philosophy of religion, giving an external indication of the fact that Hegel's notion of the spirit is not intended anthropologically, but theologically, as the Christian Logos. It is thus "superhuman."[5]

Hegel's criticism of the merely humanistic definition of man presupposes that only the Christian religion, which is the absolute religion, produced the absolute (i.e., spiritual) definition of man, namely, through its doctrine of the incarnation of God.[6] As "Son of God" and "Son of Man," Christ belongs to the human race in general, not to "a particular nation." Ever since, there has existed, therefore, the universal, true, spiritual notion of man. "The Greeks, otherwise so well educated, knew neither man nor God in true universality; the gods of the Greeks were merely the particular forces of the spirit, and for the Athenians the universal God . . . was still the hidden God. For the Greeks, there was a similar chasm between them and the barbarians, and they as yet had no knowledge of man as such, in his infinite value and infinite rights. . . . The Christian religion is the religion of absolute freedom; only the Christian has a valid conception of man as such, in his infinity and universality."[7] Thus it follows from Hegel's definition of man that, for him, man as a finite being was no problem at all, because the ultimate appeal of his absolute philosophy was to something more than merely finite and human. Only "at the name of the infinite does illumination come to the spirit." He claimed to know with absolute certainty what makes man man, because the Christian God, who is spirit, is included speculatively in his notion of absolute spirit. Hegel brings to an end the truly metaphysical definitions of man, which

define him from the standpoint of something absolute. Starting with
Feuerbach, man was considered anthropologically, from the conditional standpoint of the finite individual. Only this individual man,
based upon himself, gives rise to an actual problem of man.

But if by his very essence, man is divine spirit, what meaning
can Hegel see in the ordinary, humanistic idea, which sees man as
nothing more than man? Hegel refers to it at one point in the
Rechtsphilosophie, in the context of an analysis of the spirit of
bourgeois society. "In law, the object is the person; in ethics, it is the
subject; in the family, the member; in bourgeois society, the citizen
(conceived as bourgeois). Here, from the point of view of needs, it
is the concrete object of description that is called 'man'; thus, only
here do we speak of man in this sense."[8] Thus, the only entity
defined by the notion of "man," in the strict sense, is the bourgeois,
the subject of needs, a mere particularity in comparison to his inner
universality. Man, in the sense meant by later philosophy—Feuerbach, Ruge, Marx, Stirner, and Kierkegaard—is discussed by Hegel
only within the framework of bourgeois society! Of course, he did
not simply deny the validity of the concept of "man in general" and
"as such" in the realm of law and society, but his recognition of it
was based on man as the possessor of civil rights; precisely at this
point, we see his eminently realistic outlook. He says that every
human being is first and foremost a man, whatever his race, nationality, faith, class, or calling; this simple humanness is by no
means a "superficial, abstract" quality. But the actual significance
of this quality consists in the fact that "bourgeois civil rights accorded to an individual bring into being . . . his personal feeling
for his self-existence as a *legal* person within bourgeois society";
they also produce the "necessary compromise between disposition
and conviction."[9] He nevertheless defends himself against any abso-
lutizing of this definition, which concerns man as man. For even
though every individual may be equal to every other simply by
virtue of his "humanness" (quite apart from whether he is an Italian
or a German, a Catholic or a Protestant), such self-consciousness is
nevertheless "defective" when it becomes established—"for example,
as cosmopolitanism"—and confronts the public life of the state as a
fundamental, independent entity. In Hegel's philosophical theology,
the universal definition of man's essence is, and remains, that man is
spirit (Logos), understood in the Christian sense, not merely a human being with earthly needs.[10] This onto-"logical" definition of

man, on Christian postulates, is the "notion" of man. To it is subordinated the fact that as a subject of earthly needs, with particular civil rights, he is "ideally" a human being.

This traditional connection between the idea of man and the Christian doctrine of the incarnate God led also to the exaltation of man as a self-sufficient being, in opposition to the Christian religion. But if the notion of man and humanity was originally connected with Christianity, then mere humanness is called into question as soon as it loses its Christian foundation. At first, the nineteenth century believed it possible to replace Christianity with humanity and humanism (Feuerbach, Ruge, Marx), but with the result that faith was finally lost in humanity (Stirner, Kierkegaard, Nietzsche). A further consequence of the doubt in a humanity emancipated from Christianity is the present "dehumanization" of man.[11] The inner logic of this development can be traced step by step in the characteristic representatives of the historical movement of the nineteenth century. Its actual author was Feuerbach.

2   Feuerbach: Corporeal Man as the Ultimate Essence of Man

Feuerbach's entire work was directed toward converting the absolute philosophy of the spirit into a human philosophy of man. But the immediate task (1843) is not to "represent" man in positive fashion, but first of all to "extract" him from his idealistic veil. The necessary task is: "to derive from the philosophy of the absolute, that is (philosophical) theology, the necessity for a philosophy of man, that is, anthropology, and base the criticism of the philosophy of man on criticism of the philosophy of God."[12] The important thing at the moment is to make man the object of philosophy, and philosophy the concern of mankind.[13]

In contrast to philosophical theology, whose basic principle is the infinite, Feuerbach demands the "true position" of finitude for the philosophy of the future. The starting point of true philosophy is, therefore, no longer God or the absolute, but finite, mortal man. "All speculation about right, the will, freedom, personality, without man, apart from man, or even beyond man is speculation without unity, without necessity, without substance, without foundation, without reality. Man is the existential form of freedom, of personality, of right. Man alone is the ground and basis of the Fichtean 'I,' the ground and basis of the Leibnizian monad, the ground and basis of the absolute."[14] The term "man" means in general only man with his needs, perceptions, and emotions, man as a person in contrast to his spirit. A distinction should therefore be made between what someone is "as a human being" and what he is, for example, as a philosopher, an artist, a judge, etc.—his social aspect in general. But by a theoretical dissociation of the characteristics of man from humanness as such, Hegel absolutized abstract quantities. Following the fundamental meaning of humanness, Feuerbach criticizes Hegel's particularistic definition of man. He takes up the previously cited passage from the *Rechtsphilosophie;* where Hegel says that it is possible to talk of man "in this sense" only within the framework of bourgeois society, Feuerbach continues polemically: therefore, in reality, where Hegel speaks of the legal "person," the ethical "subject," the family "member," he is always speaking of one and the same human being, though each time in a difference sense. For it is one of man's basic characteristics that he can be defined first in one way, then in another. The subject of all possible predicates is, and remains, man, as he lives and breathes.[15]

Feuerbach associates this humanization of philosophy with the Protestant tradition, which, in the realm of religion, carried out a humanization of God. He himself goes one step further, declaring the true essence of the Christian religion to be no longer God incarnate as man, but man as such. For Feuerbach, this leads directly to the complete dissolving of religious and philosophical theology in the "universal science" of anthropology. The Christian dogma of the Trinity and Hegel's dialectical trinity is replaced by the principle of the essential unity between I and Thou, between man and his fellow man.[16]

But what makes this human being a man, what comprises the actual content of emancipated and self-sufficient humanity, Feuerbach, with his abstract principle of concrete man, was unable to develop beyond sentimental clichés. Engels' statement in his work on Feuerbach is justified: "The same Feuerbach who on the one hand . . . preaches immersion in the concrete becomes abstract through and through as soon as he comes to speak of any intercourse between human beings at any level above the sexual. He sees only one side of this intercourse: ethics. And here we are struck once more by the astounding poverty of Feuerbach in comparison with Hegel. The latter's ethics or theory of morality is his philosophy of right, encompassing three parts: 1. abstract right, 2. morality, 3. morals, the last including the family, bourgeois society, and the state. Here the content is as realistic as the form is idealistic. The entire area of right, economics, and politics is included here beside morality. With Feuerbach, the exact reverse is true. He is realistic in form, using man as his point of departure, but he has nothing to say of the world in which this man lives, and so man remains the same abstract man that was the subject of the philosophy of religion."

What is the meaning, then, of Feuerbach's proclaimed emphasis upon man "as man," if not merely that man, once raised to the level of being the basic principle of philosophy, is no longer subject to any higher court of appeal which could help in defining him? Man becomes of necessity relative to man when the absolute has its "ground and basis" only in him. The next steps to a philosophy erected on Feuerbach's foundations were taken by Ruge and Marx.

Building on Feuerbach's foundation, Ruge made of the sentimental remnant of Christian humanity a "system" both ambitious and popular, pointing up the necessity for the destructive criticism of Stirner and the constructive criticism of Marx.[17] Instead of recognizing in Hegel's particularistic definition of man the implicit criticism of mere humanity, Ruge drew the opposite conclusion in his criticism of paragraph 190 of the philosophy of right: "of course" only bourgeois society is "human"; in it, every citizen is a worker.[18] This is the actual, universal state of man. Ruge sees the decisive "progress" made by our world beyond the ancient *polis* in this universal distribution of work. He gives a sociopolitical content to Feuerbach's sentimental private notion of humanity. "Philosophy and revolution" are to beget together the system of "humanism." "Out of the heavenly 'philosophy of the spirit,' philosophy developed the earthly freedom of living men." Liberated man and the humanized world are the realized philosophy of the spirit and freedom of Hegel. The political form of true humanity is the Social-Democratic State, because it presupposes the unity and quality of men, no longer, it is true, before God, but before the law. The proof of the system of humanism would be that even Negroes are human beings! "Do you believe that Negroes are human beings? You in Germany probably believe it, for you do not have any Negroes, but there are plenty of men who deny it, namely, those who have Negroes."[19]

3 Marx:
The Proletariat as
the Possibility of Collective Man

At the outset, Marx was a colleague of Ruge; in a letter to the latter, he stated that he considered his task to be "to make man of man." For man, as he "walks and talks," is a producer of merchandise, basically estranged from himself. In this plan for recapturing "true man," Marx identifies himself at first with the "realistic humanism" of Feuerbach.[20] Accordingly, *Das Kapital* contains a polemic like that of Feuerbach and Ruge, though only parenthetic, against Hegel's particularistic definition of man.[21] Marx compares man in bourgeois society to merchandise. Like the latter, he has a dubious, "ambiguous character": a "value form" and a "natural form." As merchandise, something is worth so and so much money; what it is by its natural constitution is indifferent in respect to its mercantile value. Random items of merchandise can have completely different values, and yet the same natural constitution. Similarly, the individual human being in this mercantile world, considered in his bourgeois "value form"—for instance, "as a general or a banker," a man defined and classified according to his objective form of activity—is very important both to himself and to others; but the individual human being "simply" as such—in his natural form, so to speak—is "insignificant." Here Marx refers laconically in a note to paragraph 190 of Hegel's *Rechtsphilosophie*. This reference is to be interpreted as follows. Hegel makes much of man as such, as subject to certain needs and endowed with civil rights. This theoretical limitation reflects an actual deprivation of spirit and dehumanization in the existing conditions under which mankind lives at present, for this theoretical isolation corresponds to an actual abstraction from man as such.[22] Such modes of human existence are abstract because they abstract from man per se; Marx thinks particularly of the bourgeois or proletarian, of the worker, whether engaged in mental or physical labor, and of the universal division of bourgeois society into two complementary and contrasting modes of human existence: the private individual, with his private morality, on the one hand; and citizen of the state, with his public morality, on the other. All these forms of human existence are partial; man as such, as a totality, is lacking in them. Since he achieves his identity only in a particularity, he achieves this particularity only in respect to another: his professional existence is distinguished from his family life, his private life is distinguished from its public circumstances. In such a society, man "as such" has no basic part to play, but rather the particular definite "something" that a man is by virtue of his social position and achievement. This is essentially determined by economic conditions, which Hegel calls "needs." Thus the latter's definition of man *in concreto*, as a bourgeois, is the appropriate theoretical expression of an actual "dehumanization" of the existing conditions of life in the modern bourgeois-capitalistic world, a sign of man's estrangement from himself.

Thus Feuerbach and Marx share the observation that Hegel's philosophy of the spirit contains man only as a particularity, but not as the human whole which is basic to philosophy. But Feuerbach's "man," also, is in reality only a bourgeois, a private individual without public social existence. In contrast to Feuerbach and Hegel, Marx attempts to discover the full and complete meaning of that bourgeois particularity which, in Hegel's philosophy of the spirit, stands equally revealed and concealed. He seeks to explain the apparently obvious fact that—to the member of bourgeois society— the bourgeois is considered as a "human being," while in reality he is merely a bourgeois. In order to free this particular historical human being from his particularity and abolish the estrangement of man, Marx demands an emancipation which will be not only economic and political, but also "human." This does not consider man as an "ego" and "alter ego" (Feuerbach), but rather the world in which man lives. Each man *is* the human world, because he is essentially a "member of a social species," a *"zoon politikon."* For this reason, Marx's criticism of bourgeois man is developed as a criticism of bourgeois society and economics, without losing its basically anthropological significance.[23] Nevertheless, as long as the individual is not a member of a social species or *zoon politikon*, and thus does not participate in the state as his *res publica*, the bourgeois private individual can appear to be true man. If the mere private individual is to be abolished at the same time as the mere citizen of the state, it will be necessary to carry through a radical revolution in the whole structure of private and public life. "Only when the real individual man reincorporates in himself the abstract citizen of the state, when he, as an individual man, becomes at the same time a generic man in his empirical life, in his individual work, in his individual condition, when he recognizes that his 'forces propres' are social forces and organizes them accordingly, no longer separating himself from the power of society in the form of political power—only then will the emancipation of man be complete."[24]

Marx turns to the proletarian to bring about this final liberation of man from the merely political state of bourgeois society and to bring into being communistic man, who is identical with the society in which he lives. The proletariat is a society which has an absolute duty because of its absolute opposition to the existing order. Only the proletariat, the complete privation of humanity, is capable of achieving once more the unity and completeness of man. It is from this exception to bourgeois society that Marx creates his ideal of a new, universal man, purely human.[25]

The introduction to the criticism of the Hegelian philosophy of right already contains the statements: "The proletariat, as a particular class, is the dissolution of society." It is a particular class, but not as one class within bourgeois society; it is a society outside of existing society. This is what enables it to exert a positive influence on the dissolution. In the proletariat, so understood, Marx's philosophy found its natural weapon, while the proletariat found in Marxism its intellectual weapon. "The head of this emancipation is philosophy, its heart the proletariat."

Considered objectively, the proletariat and propertied bourgeoisie both evidence the same estrangement, but the one class is happy and contented in its estrangement without being conscious of it, while the other represents estrangement which is conscious of itself and therefore abolishes itself. Only the proletariat develops a critical and revolutionary class consciousness out of the situation which is common to all. It is just this fact which makes the proletarian class less dehumanized than the bourgeois: its dehumanization is obvious, not in a concealed form.[26] The proletariat, in its own living conditions, "comprehends within itself the dehumanized extreme" of the living conditions of the other social spheres. For this reason, it is the key to the problem of the whole of existing society, which it must liberate together with itself. In the *Deutsche Ideologie*, the universal significance of the proletariat is developed in more detail, in the context of the extension of modern world trade. "Only the proletarians of the present, completely excluded from all independent activity, are in a position to . . . achieve their open-minded independence of action, which consists in the appropriation of a totality of productive power. . . . In all previous appropriations, a mass of individuals remained subsumed under one single instrument of production; in the appropriation of the proletarians, a mass of instruments of production must be subsumed under each individual, and property among all. There is no other way to subsume the universal commerce of today among individuals than to subsume it under all of them."[27]

Thus the proletariat has an historic role to play and a fundamental significance for the whole process, not because they are "gods," but because they incarnate the generic nature of man in the extremity of estrangement. The secular world has alienated the entire life of the wage earner; he is no longer even a human being, but the seller of his labor. This particular class has a universal function. The proletariat is conscious that he is merchandise; trade is thereby seen to be human destiny, and economics becomes the "anatomy" of bourgeois society. The proletariat is the "universal class," representing no particular limited interests. When it liberates itself, it will mean the end of the private human existence of the bourgeois as well as of private property and private capitalistic economics: in short, all distinction between the private and public spheres. This distinction will be replaced positively by the universality of a mode of existence which is common to all, a community with communal ownership and a communal economy. Marx's ideal of democracy is the *polis* which has been transformed into a *cosmopolis*, a society of free men, whose individual member is not a bourgeois, but a *zoon politikon*.

But if we ask what it is that makes this individual a human being, we are shown no new essence of humanity, but only a radical execution of the principle of bourgeois society. It is simply production as such (though in anticapitalistic fashion) which makes the individual human when his general essence consists merely in the fact that he is a "subject of needs."[28] In contrast to this whole bourgeois-proletarian world, Stirner, in desperation, rashly "staked his life on nothingness," in order to replace man, still appearing in objective form, with his featureless "I."

4 Stirner:
The Individual "I"
as the Proprietor of Man

Stirner's ultimate aim is to show that the exaltation of man to the status of a supreme creature is nothing but one last disguise for the Christian belief in a human incarnation of God. "To man, man is the supreme creature—so says Feuerbach. Only now have we discovered man—so says Bruno Bauer. Let us take a closer look at this supreme creature and this new discovery." This is the epigraph of the first section, entitled "Man," while the second deals with the "I."

Of course the Christian God, who is Spirit, has become more and more tenuous; all that remains is the "spirit of mankind." In reality, however, the primitive starting point of Christianity returns in this complete humanization: man considered purely in himself, who, as Christ, was the superhuman origin and goal of history. As the claim for supremacy is transferred increasingly to man as such, "I" am forced to discover that this absolute man remains as foreign to me as was the former absolute God or Spirit.

But what is the "I" to do once man, too, has died? Its activity is nothing but a continual "squandering" and disposal of the self and its own world. It is not "my" task to realize the universal essence of man, but only to satisfy myself. As an "I," a man no longer has a "vocation" and a "destiny"; he "is" whatever he *can* be at any particular moment, no more and no less.[29] In the individual, the proprietor returns to the "creative nothingness" from which he was born. "If I rely upon myself, as an individual, I rely upon the transitory . . . creator of myself, who is self-consuming."

Feuerbach, Bauer, and Marx sought to establish man in general, and ignored man as he really is; for the only real man is the individual human being as he lives and breathes, here and now, in this or that particular form. Like the high priests of the French Revolution, they believed in the truth of man in general, and therefore followed the principle of beheading some individuals for the good of mankind. The spirit which possesses these critics of the spirit is admittedly not an absolute spirit, the Holy Spirit, but rather the spirit of humanity. This completely generalized humanity, nevertheless, is as different from the real "I" as is a universal ideal from the individual, transitory existence which I am.

To the disciples of universal man, this nihilistic "I" must seem to be egoistical and "in-human." In actual fact, the individual egoist is everyone, because everyone is concerned for himself above all else. Stirner no longer "dreams" of freedom and emancipation, but "decides" for individuality.[30] As an individual "I" he lives neither in the bourgeois state nor in communistic society—neither the heavy cords of blood nor the light threads of humanity bind him—but in the "association" of egoists. Only they, precisely because of their superiority, are his equals. The "I" is the nihilistic end of Christian humanity, whose last man is "in-human" just as its first was "superhuman." The "I" enjoys life, unconcerned with the *idée fixe* of God and mankind.

5 Kierkegaard: The Solitary Self as Absolute Humanity

Stirner's theory of the individual is contemporaneous with Kierkegaard's basic idea of the "solitary individual" who "is unsatisfied with himself before God." Both have ceased to believe that the mankind which they saw about them was fully human, and that the Christianity of the modern world was fully Christian. Stirner's "I," which relies on nothingness, is an attempt to break out of the Christian circle which began with the preaching of Christ and ended with the discussion of man. Kierkegaard, on the other hand, seeks to recapture the beginning as though eighteen hundred years of Christian history had never taken place; his goal is once more to be contemporary with the "absolute humanity" of primitive Christianity which—humanly speaking—is "inhuman."

To Ruge, humanism was the "consummation" of Christianity; for Stirner, humanism was the ultimate form and end of Christianity; for Kierkegaard, true Christianity is the very opposite of what it had become in the course of time: humanitarianism and education. "Once the protest against Christianity (and this was just at the moment when it was plainest what Christianity is, and the protest was made by the heathen whose vision was most acute) was that it is misanthropic; but now, Christianity is humanitarianism! Once Christianity was a stumbling block to the Jews, and to the Greeks, foolishness; now it is education!"

Kierkegaard's notion of the "individual" is the basis of both his anthropology and his Christianity; for this reason, his criticism of the present is directed as much against the "mankind" exalted to a first principle by Feuerbach, Ruge, and Marx as against a "Christendom" emancipated from God. His individual is a "corrective" to the mankind of Social Democracy and the Christendom of the liberal intelligentsia. In the face of the historical movement of the world, whose goal is an undifferentiated leveling, what is needed now is the resolute isolation of the individual, the exaltation of individuality above the extant social and Christian order.

All universal systems—whether of the spirit (Hegel) or of mankind (Marx)—in their preoccupation with the great course of history forget "what it means to be a human being. Not human beings in general, but what it means for you and me and him, each for himself, to be human beings."[31] "Pure mankind," on the contrary, is a purely "negative association," serving to submerge the individuals who have their own existence in the uniform bustle of the crowd. "It is out of the question that the ideal of socialism and community will be the salvation of our age. . . . In our time . . . the principle of association . . . is not affirmative, but negative, an escape, a distraction, a mirage. Its dialectic is to enervate individuals by strengthening them; it strengthens them in numerical association, but ethically, that is a source of weakness."[32]

Kierkegaard's polemic is directed basically against Hegel's "system" and the association of "mankind." On the other hand, he did not fall victim to Stirner's idea of a naked "I" which forfeits what is universally human in renouncing mankind as a universal. "If man in general is external to me, in the course of my life I can follow only this one method: divest myself of everything particular about me. This uncontrollable passion to abstract from oneself is not so very uncommon. A certain sect of the Hussites thought that a person can become a normal human being only by going naked like Adam and Eve in paradise. There are more than a few these days who preach the same doctrine in respect to spiritual and intellectual matters: a person becomes a normal human being by divesting himself of everything particular until, so to speak, he is completely naked. But that is not the real state of affairs."[33] Instead, he assigns himself the task—without himself being able to carry it out—of realizing as an "individual self" the "universality" of humanity.[34]

The "I" which has become a self is not an isolated abstraction; its entire life is a concrete expression of what is universally human. It makes of itself an apparently quite ordinary human being, who realizes the "universal" in marriage, vocation, and work. The man who truly exists is a "thoroughly individual human being without others like him, but at the same time he is man in general."[35] He is "autodidact" and "theodidact" both.

As a man who has his existence before God, who realizes the universal, he does not live as "others" live. "It would be a deification of the most trivial kind of mediocrity to see in life as it is ordinarily lived that which is universally human. The exception which realizes, with increased intensity, the universal, at the points where it is able to realize it, stands much higher. . . . But the man who has become exceptional in the nobler sense . . . will always admit that it would be far better to absorb the universal completely into his life."[36]

The man who is considered exceptional is for the most part, nevertheless, only an insignificant exception to the general rule, a man who is conscious of himself as a person who can do something or other better than everyone else. "One man can swim the canal, another knows twenty-four languages, a third can walk on his hands, etc. All this, *si placet,* can be admired. But if the individual in question is considered great in any universal sense . . . admiration is a delusive attitude. . . ."[37] For this reason Kierkegaard addresses himself to every man, but as an individual—just as Nietzsche addresses himself to "all and to none."

Just as a double meaning attaches to the "individual," so also there are two separate aspects to the problem of human equality. Men are equal before the extramundane God, but unequal in the world which they all share, which is the element of dissimilarity. Within the world, one man is preferred above another; before God, each man is a neighbor to his fellow man.[38]

Thus there are characteristically three "exceptions" which determine the universal essence of man in the midst of the disintegration of the existing order: the mass of the proletariat which is excluded from bourgeois society (Marx), the "I" which excludes itself from all social intercourse (Stirner), and the self which excludes itself from Christendom (Kierkegaard). These three exceptions, in the midst of the disintegration of bourgeois humanity, continue to determine the universal essence of man.

There are, nevertheless, difficulties which stand in the way of any restoration, whether of "true man" (Marx's ideal), the "naked I" (Stirner's ideal), or the "true Christian" (Kierkegaard's ideal). These difficulties are all the greater because every man can believe that he is a "human being" just as he is, even though he is merely a bourgeois; or that he is an "I" just as he is, although he is only a man possessed of the spirit of mankind; or that he is a "Christian" just as he is, although he is only a worldly member of Christendom. Anciently, says Marx, it was still evident whether a man was free, because there were still slaves; in primitive Christianity, says Kierkegaard, it was still clear whether a man desired to be a follower of

Christ, because there were still Jews and pagans who resisted Christianity. For the restoration of man, Marx postulates a generic man whose existence is absolutely social; Stirner postulates an "I" who is absolutely egoistical; Kierkegaard postulates a religiously isolated self, who is said to represent "absolute humanity" in contrast to Marx's principle of association and Stirner's principle of isolation. Marx's end is communistic man who no longer owns anything as a private individual; Stirner's, an "in-human" man whose humanity is merely one attribute among others; Kierkegaard's end is Christ, the superhuman measure of man throughout all ages.

This marks the end of the radical attempts at redefining man, a chain which began with Hegel. The breakdown of the radical intellectual movement corresponded to the post-1850 political reaction, during which Schopenhauer became influential.

Only Nietzsche, with different presuppositions, restated the question once more: what is this "undetermined" being, "man"?

6   Nietzsche:
The Superman as
the Transcendence of Man

"This is our suspicion which keeps recurring, . . . our question which no one . . . may hear, our sphinx beside which yawns more than one abyss . . . : I believe that everything which we in Europe today are wont to honor as the values of all those honorable things called 'humanity,' 'humaneness,' 'sympathy,' and 'pity' may indeed have a certain immediate value as a moderation and weakening of certain basic drives which are both strong and dangerous; but in the long run it means only the depreciation of the entire species called 'man'—its reduction to mediocrity . . ."[39]

Nietzsche developed his criticism of modern man as a protest against this humanitarianism of a secularized Christianity, which distorts the "measure of man." Its conclusion was a demand for a "transcendence of man" which would annul the entirety of Christian humanitarianism; man seemed to him transcended by the "superman." This is the answer to the cry of distress of the "most loathsome" man, who is the murderer of God, and of the "higher" man, higher because he can despise himself, while the "final" humanitarian man of the present can no longer despise himself, being for that reason despicable. He is the antipode of the superman, whom Nietzsche created "at the same time." "The earth has grown small, and upon it skips the final man, who makes all things mean. His race can no more be exterminated than can the flea; the final man lives longest. . . . No longer is there wealth and poverty: both are too burdensome. Who still desires to rule? Who to obey? Both are too burdensome. One herd, without a shepherd! Everyone wants the same thing, everyone is equal: if anyone feels differently, he goes of his own accord to the madhouse."

But why is a transcendence of man necessary in the first place? The answer—as in the case of Stirner—is based on the traditional connection between Christianity and humanity, between God and man. Stirner's individual "I," which creates itself out of nothingness, and Nietzsche's superman, who creates the hammer of the theory of recurrence in order to transcend the purposeless existence of mankind—these two are the extreme consequences of the problems involved in Christian anthropology.

The internal connection between Christianity and humanity is expressed in Nietzsche's case by the appearance of the superman when God is dead. This death demands of the man who wills himself, to whom no God says what he must do, that he transcend man at the same time as he is freed from God. Thus man forfeits his traditional place as a being ordered between God and the brutes. He must rely on himself as upon a rope stretched over the abyss of nothingness, extended into emptiness. His existence—like that of the tightrope walker in the foreword to *Zarathustra*—is essentially in danger, danger is his "vocation"; only in danger do we find the "destiny" of man which has become problematical! Happiness, reason, virtue, justice, civilization, compassion[40]—the whole essence of traditional humanity is no longer relevant for Nietzsche's redefinition of man's destiny.

In spite of this criticism of humanity as "soft and degenerate," Nietzsche was far removed from undervaluing man for the purpose of political regimentation. "Now almost everything on earth is under the control of the most gross and evil powers, the egoism of profiteers and military dictators. In the hands of these latter, the state, like the egoism of the profiteers, makes an attempt to reorganize everything according to its own principles, to restrain all these hostile powers. That is, it wants men to engage in the same idolatry toward it as they formerly did toward the Church. With what success? We shall find out; at any rate we are still living in the full flood of the Middle Ages: the ice is melting, and the stream is sweeping all before it. Floe is piled upon floe, all the shores are flooded and endangered. . . . There is no doubt that there is more danger to everything human when such periods are approaching than during the actual collapse and ensuing maelstrom. Anxious expectation and greedy exploitation of the moment call forth all the cowardly, self-seeking drives of the soul. . . . Who now, in the midst of these dangers of our age, will dedicate himself to serve as watchman and cavalier for humanity, for the inviolable, sacred temple-treasure gradually accumulated by all the races of man? Who will support the image of man when all feel within themselves only the worm of self-seeking and a cringing anxiety, and have fallen so far from that image that they are mere animals or even mechanical robots?"[41]

Nietzsche sought to support such an image of man by combating radically the Christian idea of humanity, as well as the ideal of unity and equality of men; in order to do this he went back to antiquity, when the difference between the birth of a free man and of a slave was made legitimate "by the order of nature." But because it is impossible to destroy the historical influence of Christianity by a retreat into the past, the question asked by Nietzsche remains—precisely on the basis of his criticism of humanity.[42]

But do we have any criterion at all for the unity and equality of men, which would measure more than relative similarities between the various races, nations, and individuals? Are we not completely without any standard of comparison by which we might set up a definition of man which would be universal, not merely "particular" or "individual"? The eccentric measure of Christian humanity, which destroyed the cosmos of the Greeks, seems to be giving way to a new uniform discipline of man, in the face of whose concrete power what remains of humanity seems only to give the appearance of being a "man without attributes."[43] And yet humanity is not a "prejudice" which can be discarded. It belongs to the nature of man, even though humanitarian "humanity" and its reactionary counterpart, intolerance which assumes the air of heroism, both equally fail to understand the nature of man: his misery and his greatness, his fallibility and his steadfastness.

Goethe says of tolerance that it is a state of mind in transition to "recognition"; the latter constitutes "true liberality."[44] He himself attained this maturity of recognition to a greater extent than any other German. It is an attitude which is equally far removed from

both forcible appropriation and rejection of what belongs to someone else. Confident in himself, he accepted those who thought and
acted differently. One of his maxims deals with association between
people: "Books are like new acquaintances. At first it gives us great
pleasure to encounter general agreement, to feel a friendly contact
at some important point of our existence. But with a closer acquaintance, differences become apparent; the important thing then for
sensible conduct is not to retreat at once (as one is apt to do in one's
youth), but to hold fast to the points of agreement and achieve a
clear understanding of points of dispute, without seeking to come
to an agreement on them."[45] Goethe praised an Englishman, L.
Sterne, as an exemplary exponent of the recognition of all that is
human. "This high, benevolent irony, this fairness of judgment, this
even temper in the face of offensiveness, this equanimity in all vicis-
situdes, and whatever other related virtues there may be were a
commendable education for me; in the last analysis it is these habits
of mind which bring us back from all false steps along the way of
life."[46] To see what is human and to recognize it seemed to him a
middle course between attention to errors or to truths, which
"waver to and fro" among men. One might think here of "idiosyncracies." "This is what constitutes the individual and makes the
general specific. In the midst of what seems most strange and wonderful, there always appears a bit of understanding, reason, and good
will which charms and fascinates us."[47] This "human side of man"
was most sensitively discovered and encouraged by Sterne. Goethe
was grateful for the edification he received from observing Sterne's
"free spirit,"[48] knowing full well that it would not do to translate
Sterne's Shandyism directly into German.[49] But even his own final
word on the meaning and significance of his life and work is, "the
triumph of the purely human," which of course the morbid enthusiasm of the high-flown poets of the German nation, who
"drown him in clichés," cannot see. Within the German nation, says
Goethe in his conversation with the Russian Count Stroganoff, a
spirit of "sensual exaltation" holds sway, which is foreign to him;
therefore the Count is not far from right in asserting that Germany
did not understand what Goethe was attempting to do in his life and
work: to bring the human side of man to recognition, free of the
distortions which disfigure it, particularly in Germany.[50]

"Let us stop, therefore, at the word 'humanity,' with which the
best writers, both ancient and modern, have associated such noble
ideas. Humanity is the character of our race; but we have it only as

an hereditary potential, and must be educated to it. We do not come into the world fully possessed of it. . . . Humanity is the treasure and prize of all human effort, the art of our race. Education to it is a labor which must be continued without cease, or we sink back . . . into brutality. Does the word 'humanity' disfigure our language? All civilized nations have appropriated it for their speech; and if our letters should come into the hand of a stranger, they would at least seem harmless: no honorable man would willingly have written letters for the promotion of brutality" (Herder, *Briefe zur Beförderung der Humanität*, Third Collection).

v The Problem of Christianity

> "All the possibilities for a Christian life, the most
> single-minded and the most superficial, the . . .
> silliest and the best thought out, have been tried
> out: it is time to discover something new."
>
> Nietzsche

The historical world which gave rise to the "prejudice" that everyone with a human countenance has, simply by virtue of that fact,
the "dignity" and "destiny" of being human is not in the first instance the world (now fading away) of mere humanity, which had
its origin in the "uomo universale" and also "terribile" of the Renaissance; it is rather the world of Christianity, in which the divine man
Christ is the measure of man's relationship to himself and to his
neighbor. The image which converted the *homo* of the European
world into a human being is basically determined by the idea which
the Christian has of himself as the image and likeness of God. Thus
the statement that we are "all" human beings is restricted to the
conception of humanity produced by Christianity in association
with the Stoics. Indirect evidence of this historical circumstance in
regard to human nature is the fact that anthropology becomes a
problem only when Christianity begins to vanish from the world.
But the vanishing of Christianity within the European world is not
least a consequence of the critical movement which reached its
extreme limit in the last century.

Philosophical criticism of the Christian religion began in the
nineteenth century with Hegel and reached its climax with Nietzsche. It is a Protestant movement, and therefore specifically German; this holds true of both the criticism and the religion at which
it was directed. Our critical philosophers were all theologically

educated Protestants, and their criticism of Christianity presupposes its Protestant manifestation. Criticism, that is, discrimination, can be exercised with reference to what unites things or what separates them. These two formal possibilities for critical discrimination also describe the concrete relationship between philosophy and religion in this last phase of philosophical criticism of the Christian religion. The two extremes of unification and separation are represented by Hegel's philosophical theology and Nietzsche's anti-Christian philosophy. The decisive turning point from Hegel's reconciliation to Nietzsche's break with Christianity is characterized by the criticism of religion which came from the left-wing Hegelians. If we are to understand this turning point in its historical setting, we must be aware above all of the ambiguity of the way it built upon Hegel.

1   Hegel's Transcending of Religion by Philosophy

Hegel's philosophical writing begins with his early theological works: *Volksreligion und Christentum, Leben Jesu, Die Positivität der christlichen Religion*, and *Der Geist des Christentums und sein Schicksal*. These works do much to illuminate the course of Hegel's philosophical development. Written in the last decade of the eighteenth century, they remained unpublished until W. Dilthey's study of Hegel's early life, *Die Jugendgeschichte Hegels* (1905), led H. Nohl to edit and publish the manuscripts in 1907; later (1929 and 1938), T. Häring wrote a commentary on them. The Young Hegelians knew nothing of them. It is all the more remarkable to observe in retrospect the extent to which Hegel himself as a young man anticipated the criticisms of the Young Hegelians.[1] The content of these fragments is an exposition of Christianity; only as a translation of Christianity from the positive form of religion into the form of philosophy can Hegel's interpretation be understood, in its own terms, as a criticism of the Christian religion.

The dominant theme of this critical (i.e., discriminating) exposition of the Christian religion is the question whether it is possible to restore the "totality" of "life" which is estranged within itself. Hegel considers the historical task of Jesus to have been the restoration of inner totality in opposition to the "positivity" (*Gesetztheit*) of the Jewish religion of law (*Gesetz*); this was to be accomplished through a religion of "love" which would overcome the "law."[2] In the "living relationship" of love between man and God, but also between man and man or between I and Thou, this legally determined opposition is abolished, this separation of one entire life into hostile opposites. This one life, once more unified within itself, is the only true life because it is the only total life or mode of being; life which is not unified is not genuine being. Genuine being is always unified being, and the unification is brought about through the living relationship of love, in which each individual becomes himself only through another. "Unification and being are equivalent"; there are as many modes of being as there are of unification. The linguistic expression of this specifically Hegelian notion of being is the copula "is."[3] Therefore the methodology of Hegel's *Leben Jesu* is to attempt to demonstrate that every form of "positivity," that is, every determinacy which is purely external and objective, can be abolished by the concept of the living relationship of love, a precursor of the mediating movement of the spirit. Thus, Hegel put a philosophical interpretation upon the miracle stories of the New Testament by abolishing their positive miraculous element, that is, the miraculous aspect of Eucharistic doctrine. Viewed objectively or from without, that is, apart from any living relationship with it, the bread distributed by Jesus is "mere bread" and the wine which is passed, "mere wine"; but "each is something more." This "something more" does not consist in a mere allegorical addition to the real bread and wine; Jesus' body and blood are really indistinguishable from the bread and wine. It is not only as though both were the same, or somehow comparable; rather, what at first appears so different is inextricably united. Only to the "understanding," which comes from without, to the "perception" of the senses, are the bread and body, the wine and blood, distinguishable and comparable; this does not hold true for the spiritual apprehension of the bread and wine, for the inner relationship. When both are received not only physically and materially, but also, in the presence and name of Jesus, are received spiritually and intellectually, these objects are by their very nature more than mere objects of physical enjoyment: they are a spiritual communion become objective. This "love become objective, this subjectivity which has become an object . . . becomes once more subjective through the act of eating." Thus in the eating of the bread and wine, when the spirit really comes to life, the objectiveness of the objects "vanishes," giving place to the subject. Considered as objects, they are "mystical," things both sensuous and supersensuous.

The mere "positivity" of the objects vanishes; this means a return to the "subjectivity" or "ideality" which originally constituted them. This retrogression to primitive origins Hegel later discussed systematically as the "subjectivity" of "substantiality." These two basic concepts of Hegel's philosophy of the spirit correspond to the contrast between "ideality" and "positivity" expressed in his early theological writings, the abolition of mere positivity by being raised to its subjective ideality. Thus religion is not spiritually real and philosophically comprehended as "positive" religion, but only in the abolition of its "mere" positivity. All inflexible positivity is "disgraceful," whether in the realm of religious objects and laws or—as in the case of Kant—of moral laws. In every case Hegel's aim is to transform "dead contrasts" into "living relationships," in order to restore the totality originally present. Thus he sees Jesus as a "man who sought to restore man in his totality" by combining within himself, the God-man, both the human and the divine.

In his treatise, *Glauben und Wissen* (1802), directed against Kant, Jacobi, and Fichte, Hegel followed out the program of his theological writings: he attempted to abolish the "positive" contrast between faith and knowledge by raising both to a unity at once higher and more primitive. If we know nothing of God and can only believe in him, if reason is incapable of "having knowledge of God," then neither genuine faith nor true knowledge can exist, but only the dead contrast (a product of the Enlightenment) between faith and knowledge. In Hegel's opinion, the "contemplative philosophy" deriving from Kant came to a halt with this inadequate conclusion. "Our civilization has brought our age so far beyond the old contrast between reason and faith, between philosophy and positive religion, that this opposition of faith and knowledge has acquired a totally new meaning; it has now been transferred to a position within philosophy itself. Anciently, reason was claimed as the handmaid of faith; against this claim philosophy has indomitably asserted its absolute autonomy. Now these ideas or modes of expression have vanished. Reason, if the entity which gives itself this name is indeed reason, has achieved a position of such power within positive religion that even an attack by philosophy upon the positive aspects of religion, such as miracles, is considered outmoded and obscure. A further consequence of this power was that Kant's attempt to revivify the positive form of religion by interpreting it in light of his philosophy was doomed to failure, not because this attempt altered the particular meaning of those forms, but because they no longer appeared to deserve this honor."[4]

Thus Hegel criticizes religion, not through a critical distinction between religious faith and philosophical knowledge, but through a criticism directed only against the "positive form" assumed by religion even within contemplative philosophy. The goal of this criticism is a radical abolition of an improvement upon this positive form through a philosophical transformation of "positive" Christian religion. The outcome of this absorption of religion into philosophy is Hegel's philosophy of religion. In his lectures, he expressly treats religion and philosophy as one. True philosophy is itself "worship": "It is frequently . . . heard that every attempt to comprehend the plan of providence is presumptuous. This must be viewed as a consequence of the idea, which has almost become a universal axiom, that man can have no knowledge of God. And if theology itself arrives at this desperate position, refuge must be taken in philosophy if any knowledge of God is to be had. . . . If there is to be no knowledge of God, the only realm which remains to interest the spirit is the realm of the ungodly, the limited, the finite. Of course man must be content with the finite; but it is an even higher necessity that he have a Sabbath in his life, in which he may transcend his workaday affairs, in which he may devote himself to what is truly genuine and come into awareness of it."[5]

At the very outset of his lectures on the philosophy of religion, Hegel therefore states that there is something misleading about this expression; it simulates an objective situation, as though religion were the object of philosophy in no other sense than that in which space is the object of geometry. "The content, the need, the interest" of philosophy is, however, completely identical with that of theology. "The object of religion, as of philosophy, is the eternal truth of its own objectivity: God, nothing but God, and the explication of God. In explicating religion, philosophy only explicates itself; in explicating itself, it explicates religion. Like religion, it is definable as an occupation with this object; it is the thinking spirit which permeates this object, the truth. Vitality and enjoyment, truth and purification of subjective self-consciousness in and through this occupation."[6]

The "difficulties" and reservations which stand in the way of this equation derive, according to Hegel, only from the fact that religion and philosophy are forms of worship, but each in its own particular way, so that it can appear as though they were in fact different things. Their unity, on the contrary, has been sanctioned historically since time immemorial. The Church Fathers, Hegel shows, were Neoplatonists and Aristotelians; some were even converted to Christianity by their philosophic study. On the other hand, Christian systematic theology could come into being only through the acceptance of philosophy. All of scholastic philosophy was identical with theology; "natural theology" was still a proper object of Wolff's philosophy. The problem of the difference between them reduces from a problem of content, which is the same for both, to a problem of form.

Hegel distinguishes three forms. The same spiritual content can appear in the form of merely casual, subjective feeling, in the form (already more objective and appropriate) of sensuous imagination, and finally in the philosophical form of thought, which is universal by its very nature. This final form is the form most appropriate to "spiritual" content. Only in this form is the content (God or the absolute) truly comprehended; only here does it attain its proper form. "God is essentially in the process of thought." A theology like Schleiermacher's, on the other hand, which takes feeling to be the ground of believing knowledge of God, and "merely describes emotions," necessarily remains stranded in the fortuitous realm of empirical events. This is the "worst" form in which a content can be given: "Of course everything spiritual, all content of consciousness, everything that is the product or object of thought, particularly religion and morality, must also exist in man in the mode of feeling; this is its immediate form. But feeling is not the source from which this content comes to man; it is only the mode and manner in which man discovers it within himself. It is the worst form, a form which he shares with the brutes. . . . When content comes through feeling, everyone is reduced to his own subjective point of view. . . . If someone says that there is religion in his feeling and someone else says that he cannot find a god in his feeling, each is right. If the content of divinity—the revelation of God, the relationship between man and God, God's being in its relationship to man—is reduced in this fashion to mere feeling, it is restricted to the standpoint of individual subjectivity, discretion, caprice. In fact, all truth which per se has existence has been done away with."[7]

Even as understood through images of the senses, this content does not genuinely attain its proper form; it is only imagined, rather than being understood and comprehended. Only in the philosophy of religion is the form of mere feeling and imagination transformed into that of conceptualization. The foolish objections to this necessary transformation of positive religion into philosophy can be reduced to the statement that philosophy discards the forms which belong to the realm of the imagination. Ordinary thought is not aware of this distinction; its understanding of the truth is bound to these limitations, and it assumes, therefore, that the content is itself being taken away.[8]

But in reality this "translation" of religious content into another form does not mean its destruction, but rather a transformation which is at once an improvement. It is to the greatest advantage of religion that its spiritual content be retranslated in this fashion. The final sentences of *Glauben und Wissen* are a culmination of this exaltation of religion to the level of "philosophical existence"; they transform the death of God into a "speculative Good Friday." The historicoempirical "feeling" that God himself is dead, this infinite grief "which forms the basis for the religion of the modern era," must be comprehended as a "component" of the "ultimate ideal," namely as a component of absolute freedom![9]

This distinction, and the consequent exaltation of religion out of the form of feeling and imagination into that of the notion, are the means by which Hegel accomplishes his positive justification of the Christian religion, and at the same time his criticism of it. The ambiguity of this distinction forms the background for all post-Hegelian criticism of religion; it even produced the breakdown of the Hegelian school into a left and right wing. The questions which were the bone of contention in the thirties had nothing to do with Hegel's attitude toward the state and toward history, but rather toward religion: whether he viewed God as a person or a process, and immortality as universal or personal.[10] Ecclesiastical orthodoxy declared Hegel's translation to be non-Christian because it destroyed the positive content of the faith; the Young Hegelians, on the contrary, were offended by Hegel's retention of dogmatic Christianity even in the *form* of his concept. Rosenkranz thought he could draw the conclusion from this opposition[11] that the truth lay in Hegel's mediating position, and that it was precisely its attitude toward Christianity which gave it "a special promise for the future." This turned out to be the case, but in a different way than Rosenkranz supposed. The historical consequence of Hegel's ambiguous "translation" was an absolute destruction of Christian philosophy and of the Christian religion.

2   Strauss's Reduction of
Christianity to Myth

Strauss's life of Jesus, published in 1835,[12] was a product of the
Hegelian philosophy of religion under the influence of Schleiermacher. It marked an application of this philosophy to religion,
while Hegel, in contrast, had come to philosophy from theology
and his own life of Jesus. Hegel's thesis formed the mid-point of
Strauss's theological thought: what religion in itself knows only in
the form of imagination is raised by philosophy to the form of concept. The dogma of Christianity indeed contains truth, but the form
is inappropriate to the content it expresses. But precisely this fact
prevents its immediate translation from its historical setting in the
church into conceptual form. On the other hand, whoever follows
the Hegelian right wing in transcending the brute facts of history
to the idea only to retreat from the idea back to the brute facts
merely makes a pretense of critical freedom. Together with this
rejection of orthodox speculation, Strauss seeks to demonstrate from
Hegel's own works that Hegel was himself by no means opposed to
criticism of the Gospel narrative. Quite the contrary: Hegel's philosophy of religion itself contains such a criticism in its surrender of
historical fact to the form of imagination.[13] The methodological
difference between Hegel and Strauss consists in the fact that Hegel
elevates religious imagination to the level of a notion, while Strauss
reduces it to a freely created myth. The end result of his mythological exegesis[14] of Christian doctrine was: "mankind is the incarnate
God." This statement is already implicit in Hegel, in that he, too,
understands the incarnation not as an isolated historical fact but
rather as a manifestation of the absolute—that is to say, the spirit.
The reduction of religion to subconscious mythopoeic fantasy sup-
posedly explained faith at the same time it was explaining the miracle
stories of the Bible; for faith, to Strauss as to Feuerbach, is essentially
a faith in the miraculous—nor is this less true for Kierkegaard.[15]

In his last work, *Der alte und der neue Glaube* (1872), Strauss,
influenced by scientific positivism, pushed his conclusions to the
limit, giving up Christianity together with Hegelian philosophy.
His "new" faith is an ethics of "modern" man, tinged with religion.
The first question put to the old faith, "Are we still Christians?" is
answered negatively. The second, "Do we still possess a religion?"
he answers half affirmatively. The third and fourth, "How do we

apprehend the world?" and "How should we order our lives?" are answered in the "modern" spirit of scientific progress, and with two characteristic "supplements" ("by our great poets and musicians"). The "new" faith consists in a "further development" of Christianity in the direction of "humanism." Having spent his entire unhappy life trying to write a life of Jesus, Strauss concludes, when confronted by this insoluble problem, with skeptical enjoyment of civilization.[16] "God" is replaced by the "cosmos" or the "universe." Strauss's course of development from theology to philosophy, and thence to positivism, is signalized by the fact that in the first volume of his work he still called himself Doctor of Philosophy and Tutor at the Evangelical Seminary, but in the second volume only Doctor of Philosophy, although even in the process of writing the first volume he realized that everything he wanted to do in the realm of theology could only be "perilous labor."

It is difficult today to have more than a vague idea of the passionate arguments pro and con that swirled about Strauss's *Theologie;* this self-dissolution of Protestant theology with the aid of Hegelian philosophy seems far removed from that which is going on today. In his period, however, the "old faith and the new faith" had the effect, according to contemporary witnesses, of "a spark in a powder keg," an effect both enormous and liberating.

3 Feuerbach's Reduction of the Christian Religion to the Nature of Man

The same is true of Feuerbach's *Wesen des Christentums* (1841). In his study of Feuerbach, F. Engels writes: "It is necessary to have experienced personally the liberating effect of this book to have any conception of it. The enthusiasm was universal: we all became disciples overnight. Marx's enthusiastic welcome of the new interpretation as well as the extent . . . of its influence upon him can be read about in *Die Heilige Familie.*"[17]

In contrast to the criticism of B. Bauer in Strauss, Feuerbach's "essence" of Christianity is not a critical destruction of Christian theology and Christianity, but an attempt to preserve the essential part of Christianity, specifically in the form of a religious "anthropology." This corresponds to what differentiates Feuerbach from the other two: "Concerning my relationship to Strauss and Bruno Bauer, together with whom I am continually being named, I should like to point out . . . that the difference between our works . . . is already indicated by the difference between their subjects. The object of Bauer's criticism is the Gospel narrative, that is, Biblical Christianity or rather Biblical theology. Strauss concerns himself with Christian doctrine and the life of Jesus, which can also be included under the heading of Christian doctrine, that is to say, dogmatic Christianity or rather dogmatic theology. My concern is with Christianity in general, that is, the Christian religion, and consequently only Christian philosophy or theology. For this reason I draw most of my quotations only from such writers who approached Christianity not merely as a theoretical or dogmatic object, not merely theology, but religion. My chief object is Christianity as a religion, as the . . . immediate essence of man."[18]

He is further removed from Bauer, however, than from Strauss, for only Bauer remained an Hegelian in his role as critic. Strauss and Feuerbach changed from being Hegelians to being humanistic "materialists," thereby giving up philosophy as they previously had understood it. Their criticism reduces to a more or less unsystematic anthropology.

Feuerbach abolishes the "theological essence" of religion in favor of its true, anthropological essence, reducing it to precisely that nonspiritual form which Hegel attacked as being mere "feeling." This is what Feuerbach sought to restore as its essential form—essential because immediately intelligible to the senses. For him, the transcendence of religion is grounded upon the immanent transcendence of feeling. "Feeling is the human essence of religion." "Feeling is your inmost power, and yet at the same time a power distinct and independent of you. It is *in* you and *beyond* you: it is your most personal nature, which takes hold of you as though foreign to you, in short, your God. How then would you distinguish some other objective essence from this essence within you? How would you transcend your feeling?"[19] Feuerbach distinguishes himself accordingly from Hegel's criticism of the theology of feeling: "I do not censure Schleiermacher . . . for making religion a matter of feeling, but only because theological prejudice prevented him from drawing the necessary conclusions from his standpoint, for not having the courage to see and to admit that objectively God is himself nothing but the essence of feeling, if, subjectively, feeling is the central aspect of religion. In this respect I disagree so little with Schleiermacher that he actually serves to confirm the statements I have made on the basis of the nature of feeling. For this very reason Hegel failed to penetrate the peculiar essence of religion: as an abstract thinker, he did not penetrate the essence of feeling."[20]

The most universal axiom of Feuerbach's criticism of religion is: "Anthropology is the secret of theology," that is, the primitive essence of religion is the essence of man. Religion is an "objectification" of man's primitive essential needs; it has no particular content of its own. Properly understood, the knowledge of God is man's knowledge of himself, but knowledge which is as yet unaware of its own nature. "Religion is the first, indirect self-consciousness of man," a detour taken by man on the way to finding himself. Man first transfers his own essence to a point external to himself, before he finds it within himself. "Religion, at least the Christian religion, is the conduct of man toward himself, or, more correctly, toward his own essence; but it is conduct toward his own essence as though toward a foreign essence. The divine essence is nothing else than the human essence, or, better stated, the essence of man, isolated from the limitations of the individual, that is, real, corporeal human being, that is, viewed and revered as another, individual essence, distinct from the viewer. Thus all the attributes of the divine essence are attributes of the essence of man."[21] The divine spirit which is perceived or believed is the same as the perceiving spirit—so we read in Hegel.

The "development" of religion therefore consists positively in the fact that man "denies more to God and accords more to himself." Protestantism is traveling in this direction, because it is the religious expression of the humanization of God: "The God who is man, that is to say, the human God: Christ—he alone is the God of Protestantism. No longer, like Catholicism, does Protestantism concern itself with what God is in himself, but only with what he is for man. For this reason it no longer has any speculative or contemplative inclinations, such as belong to Catholicism. It is no longer theology, it is essentially only Christology, that is, religious anthropology."[22]

The critical distinction between religion and philosophy, as anthropology, is based exclusively on the character of "images." That is to say, religion itself takes the objective images constructed by man as though they were not images, but rather self-sufficient "things." Hegelian philosophy, on the other hand, takes them as mere constructs of the imagination, images which as such are without truth. But Feuerbach does not, like Hegel, wish to translate the images into "thoughts" (thereby philosophically justifying the dogmas of religion); neither does he wish to leave them as untranslated, imagelike objects. He seeks instead to view these images "as images" of the manifestation of the essence of man. Theology is transformed thereby into "psychic pathology." All religious ideas are translated back into their foothold in the senses, from which they originally proceeded: the symbolic bread into palpable bread, the symbolic wine into real wine. "In all truth I replace the sterile water of baptism with blessing of real water." This simplification of religious ideas to "their simplest elements, which are immanent in man," is admittedly trivial; but why should not the truth of religion, like truth in general, be ultimately a complete triviality? While Hegel was still concerned with demonstrating the inner agreement between philosophy and the dogmas of Christianity, Feuerbach seeks to demonstrate both more and less: that philosophy is in itself a religion when both are reduced to anthropological terms. "For this reason . . . modern philosophy, unlike the ancient Catholic philosophy and modern Protestant scholasticism, can no longer succumb to the temptation of proving its agreement with religion via its agreement with Christian dogmatic theology. Instead, begotten of the essence of religion, it has within itself the true essence of religion; in and of itself, as philosophy, it is religion."[23]

On the other hand, the historical dissolution of the Christian religion was as sure for Feuerbach as it later was for Nietzsche. It is opposed to the entire situation of the modern world. Christianity is negated even by those who continue to believe firmly in it, who deceive themselves into not seeing that Christianity is no longer determined by the Bible or the symbolic books and Church Fathers. It is denied in life and in science, in art and in industry, "because man has appropriated everything human, with the result that Christianity is deprived of all power to oppose."[24] But if in practice, man and work have replaced the Christian and prayer, theoretically the essence of man must replace the divine. Christianity has been reduced to a Sunday affair, it has vanished out of the everyday life of man because it is nothing more than an *idée fixe* "which stands in glaring contrast to our fire and life insurance companies, our railroads and steam engines, our warehouses full of art and gems, our war colleges and business colleges."[25] Feuerbach perceived this contrast in exactly the same way Kierkegaard did; but the latter drew the equally logical, but exactly opposite, conclusion: that science, and natural science in particular, is simply irrelevant to the religious situation.[26] Both agreed in recognizing that the contradiction between Christianity and the scientific, political, and social interests of the world were unreconcilable.[27]

But the "hypocrisy" of a Christianity within the modern world did not have the same enormous significance for Feuerbach as for Nietzsche and Kierkegaard. His attack upon Christendom is much less spirited.[28] It does not resemble a deathblow, but rather a well-intentioned effort to keep Christianity within the limits of "humanity" by means of that critical "reduction" which made philosophy into religion: "I am far from ascribing . . . merely a subordinate significance to anthropology, a significance ascribed to it only so long as a theology stands above and beyond it. By degrading theology to anthropology, I rather exalt anthropology to theology. . . . Therefore do not take the word 'anthropology' . . . in the sense of Hegelian philosophy, or of any previous philosophy whatever, but in an infinitely higher and more universal sense."[29]

Hegel still belongs to the "Old Testament" of philosophy, for his philosophy is still based on the standpoint of theology. His philosophy of religion is the last great attempt ever made to "resolve" (ambiguously) the conflict between Christianity and paganism, between Christian theology and Greek philosophy. Hegel is the culmination of the ambiguity of the modern age, which equates the negation of Christianity with Christianity. "All previous philosophy comes within the period of the decline of Christianity, the negation of Christianity, which sought at the same time to be the establishment of Christianity. Hegelian philosophy disguised the negation of Christianity under the contradiction between idea and thought, that is, it negated Christianity by postulating it. It disguised the negation further behind the contradiction between the beginnings of Christianity and its finished form. . . . A religion is preserved only when it is preserved . . . in its original meaning. At the outset, religion is fire, energy, truth; to start with, every religion . . . is absolutely rigorous; but in the course of time it becomes dulled, loses its firmness, . . . falls prey to the fate of custom. In order to mediate this practical contradiction between religion and backsliding, recourse is had . . . to tradition or modification."[30] In contrast to this seminegation, we now have a complete, conscious negation. It marks the beginning of a new age and the necessity for an absolutely non-Christian philosophy, which will be itself religion.

But Feuerbach's very claim that philosophy is itself religion brands his "atheism"—as Stirner reproached him—as a "devout" atheism. But he did not consider this accusation true. His only aim was to remove the "subject" of religious predicates, God; he had no designs upon the predicates themselves, when interpreted in their proper human sense.

"Therefore the only true atheist, that is, atheist in the usual sense, is the man for whom the predicates of the divine essence, such as love, wisdom, righteousness, etc., mean nothing, but not the man for whom only the subject of these predicates means nothing. To deny the subject is by no means the same thing as denying the predicates in themselves. The predicates have their own, independent significance; their content forces man to recognize them: they show themselves to be true immediately through their own existence; they are self-verifying, self-demonstrating. Goodness, righteousness, wisdom are not made chimerical simply because God is a chimera; neither are they made truths by the truth of God. The concept of God is dependent upon the concept of righteousness, of goodness, of wisdom. A God who is not good, not righteous, not wise, is no god at all, but the reverse is not true."[31]

Thus Feuerbach was no "ordinary" atheist; or rather he was, to the extent that atheism is usually precisely what Feuerbach claims to stand for: a retention of the Christian predicates while discarding their subject!

The fact that his criticism of religion was accused of religious devotion is typical of the entire confused and paradoxical movement following Hegel: what one man thought to be atheism, his neighbor discovered to be theological, religious, and Christian. Strauss thought Bauer a "parson," Feuerbach was considered by Stirner to be a "devout atheist," Marx considered Bauer a critic only in the realm of theology. Stirner thought he outdid them all, but—together with the "holy family" (Bauer)—Stirner was given the appellation "Church Father" and "St. Max" by Marx. In Stirner's "nothingness" Feuerbach still perceives a "divine predicate," and in his "individual 'I' " the "Christian salvation of the individual."[32] Everyone seeks to point out a remnant of Christianity in everyone else, a circumstance which holds true of all criticism of Christianity which is still polemically determined by its opponent. Historically, Feuerbach derived the possibility for this interchange from the separation of the Gospel from the Jewish religion of Law. In contrast to the positivity of Judaism, Christianity is already a "religion of criticism and freedom." "In contrast with the Israelite, the Christion is a . . . free spirit. Times change. What was still religion yesterday is no longer so today, and what is today considered atheism, is tomorrow considered religion."[33]

Feuerbach's humanization of theology belongs to the history of Protestantism because he derived the principles of his criticism of religion from Luther. In the fourteenth chapter of *Das Wesen des Christentums*,[34] which discusses faith, he quotes a statement made by Luther: "You receive from God to the extent that you believe in him. If you believe it, it's yours; but if you don't believe it, it's not yours." "Just as we believe, so it befalls us. If we take him for our God, of course he won't be our Devil. But if we don't take him for our God, then of course he won't be . . . our God." Interpreting, Feuerbach continues: "Thus if I believe in a God, I *have* a God; that is, belief in God is the God of man." For "if God is the object and manner of my belief, what more is the essence of God than the essence of belief?" In believing in God, man believes in himself, in the divine power of his belief. God is an essence *for* man, he is essentially *our* God,[35] and belief in him is thus a religious expression of "the self-certainty of man." The world of faith is a world of "unlimited subjectivity!" In a special treatise, *Über das Wesen des Glaubens im Sinne Luthers* (1844), Feuerbach actually sought to demonstrate the identity of Luther's concept of faith with the "essence of Christianity." The essential point of Luther's concept of God is the denial of Catholic positivity; positively, it is the assertion that Christ exists only in so far as he exists for us, that he is only real as the object of our faith. "If God sat all alone in heaven," Feuerbach quotes from Luther, "like a bump on a log, he would not be God." He continues, "God is a word whose meaning is only seen in man." "In faith, God is the 'thou' of man." In this fashion, Feuerbach proceeds from Luther's internal or existential understanding of faith to an anchoring of the Lutheran "correlation" between "what is God's" and "what is man's" to the particular end which is man, and to the thesis that God "presupposes" man because the theological essence of religion is also its anthropological essence.[36] In principle, Feuerbach's interpretation is already implicit in Hegel, who also sees the liberating event of the Reformation as being Luther's victorious conclusion that man's destiny must come to pass "within man himself," even though he still considered its content as being something given from without, by revelation.[37] In *Protestantismus und die Romantik* (1839–40), A. Ruge formulated the danger which, of necessity, followed: "The principle of romanticism . . . consists in the fact that, in the Protestant process of self-appropriation, the subject retains only what is properly its own, the 'I,' which carries out the appropriation; thus it comes to a halt at the stage of negating what is universal and objective." Feuerbach's criticism of religion could not be, nor did it attempt to be, conclusive, but merely something preliminary, whose consequences nevertheless would follow immediately. Its basic conceptions, he thought, would remain valid, but "not in the way they are here spoken, the only way they could be spoken under the conditions presently obtaining."

4   Ruge's Replacement of Christianity by Humanity

In his criticism of religion, A. Ruge starts from Hegel and covers much the same ground as that covered by Feuerbach. In Hegel (according to Ruge) we see a man struggling with the faith he has been brought up in, first justifying it, and then discarding it. He emphasizes that in Christianity the absolute spirit is known after human fashion, but forgets his own insight in giving philosophical existence to Christian dogmatic theology and the God of the Jews.[38] The only proper procedure was pioneered by Feuerbach, in his demonstration that theology is "nothing else than" anthropology. "Humanistic religion"[39] alone solves all the riddles of the past, culminating the development from Hellenism to Christianity. "Popery and Lutheran dogmatics destroy the idea of Christianity. The religiosity of the Reformation, the ethical enthusiasm of the Revolution, the serious-mindedness of the Enlightenment, philosophy and socialism, on the other hand, are real extensions of the Christian principle of humanity."[40] This principle is immanent and universal, whereas Christ remained transcendent and unique. The ultimate goal of religious development is the replacement of Christianity by humanity.

Ruge's popular *System der Religion unserer Zeit* is meant as a derivation of the religion of humanism from the historical religions; in its style, as in its content, it is a precursor of Strauss's "new faith." But even in this humanistic attenuation Ruge's program is a direct consequence of Hegel's spiritualization of Christian ideas by raising them to the level of notions. Not only the political journalism of the Left, but even such a scholarly Old Hegelian as Rosenkranz, ten years after Ruge's work, expressed the view that the Christianity spiritualized by Hegel was about to reach its "consummation" in modern humanity and civilization![41]

5   Bauer's Destruction of
Theology and Christianity

The striking and significant personality of Bruno Bauer was the intellectual center of the Berlin "free spirits."[42] At first, even Marx and Stirner were under the influence of his radical criticism. He was an ascetic and stoic. His last works came into being in a cell which he had made out of a stall in the country near Berlin; he was known as the "hermit of Rixdorf."

His theological work, which cannot be evaluated here, at once expired under public judgment; even Overbeck felt compelled to defend himself against it. A. Schweitzer made the following summary of his impression of Bauer's achievement: "We do not recognize as great those men who ironed out problems, but those who discovered them. Bauer's criticism of the Gospel narrative is worth a dozen good lives of Jesus, because—as we are only beginning to recognize now, a half century later—it is the most brilliant and most complete repertory of the difficulties in the life of Jesus that exists. Unfortunately, the superior, all too superior, attitude in which he developed the problems made his thought ineffectual for the theology of his day. He filled up behind him the passageway he had driven into the mountain, so that a whole generation was kept busy rediscovering the veins which he had already hit upon. They had no idea that the abnormality of his solutions was grounded in the intensity with which he had grasped the questions, and that he had become blind to history because he had been too good an observer. And so his contemporaries thought him a dreamer. But in his dreams ultimately there lies hidden a deep insight. It had never dawned on anyone else in this grandiose manner that the history of primitive and early Christianity was not the simple consequence of the message of Jesus, that it was more than a doctrine put into practice, much more; that the life of the world soul entered into union with the life of that personality as its body, the citizens of the Roman Imperium, lay in its death throes. No one after Paul grasped so powerfully the mysticism of the suprapersonal *sōma xristou*. Bauer translated it into history, and made the Roman Imperium the 'Body of Christ'."[43]

Bauer completed his early studies in Berlin under Marheineke (the first editor of Hegel's *Rechtsphilosophie*),[44] Schleiermacher, and Hegel, in philosophy and theology. His literary career began with a criticism of Strauss's *Leben Jesu*. As editor of a journal for speculative theology, he was at first a representative of Hegelian orthodoxy. His critical attitude toward Hegel is first announced in two works which appeared anonymously: *Die Posaune des Jüngsten Gerichts über Hegel den Atheisten und Antichristen. Ein Ultimatum* (1841), and *Hegels Lehre von der Religion und Kunst* (1842), which he wrote in collaboration with Ruge. Bauer's criticism of Christian theology is characterized completely by the manner in which he takes his departure from Hegel. More radically than Strauss and Feuerbach, he quarrels with Hegel's philosophy of religion. He conceals the result ironically, making it all the more powerful. In the guise of an orthodox pietist, he shows, "from the standpoint of faith," with many quotations from the Bible and from Hegel, that it was not just the radical Young Hegelians who were "atheists": their father was one already, under the cloak of a philosophical justification of dogmatic theology. "Oh, the poor and wretched souls who let themselves be taken in when it was whispered to them that the object of religion as well as philosophy is the eternal truth in their own objectivity, God and nothing but God and the explication of God; the poor souls who heard with joy that religion and philosophy coincide, who thought they could preserve their God when they heard and accepted that religion is the self-consciousness of the absolute spirit." These poor souls have ears and hear not, eyes and see not. For what is plainer than the fact that Hegel's explanation of religion effects its destruction, although the Christian framework of the destruction makes it seem as though he, too, were talking of the one living God who was before the world was, and who in Christ revealed his love to man. Hegel's passionless intellect is acquainted solely with the universal of the world soul, which becomes conscious of itself in man. Ingenuous pupils like Strauss saw this as "pantheism"; but it is thoroughgoing atheism, which replaces God with self-consciousness. Hegel indeed speaks of this substance as a subject, but he does not mean an individual, particular subject that created heaven and earth; quite the contrary, he requires a whole hierarchy of spirits, innumerable subjects, in order that in the course of time this substance can finally become conscious of itself, in Hegel.[45] The conclusion of his train of thought is not substance, but "self-consciousness," having as its essence the universality of substance. To this irreligious self-consciousness Hegel ascribes the attributes of the divine. But the credulous could not see through his devilish cunning, and have failed to recognize that Hegel is a revolutionary, a greater revolutionary than all his pupils put together: he carries out a radical dissolution of all conditions of substantiality.[46]

The deception is compounded—Bauer seeks to point out to the "devout"—by Hegel's polemic against Schleiermacher's "theology of feeling." In reality, Hegel's criticism of feeling was not in the least directed against subjectivity as such, but only an inadequate form of it. For Hegel, religion is not less a product of spiritual self-consciousness than are art and science. Therefore Bauer warns the "well-disposed" against Hegel's magical "reconciliation" of the thinking spirit with religion: ". . . how many have been bewitched by this magic word . . . which was all the rage a few years ago, . . . diverted from the true God and brought into atheism! What humbug! According to Hegel, the reconciliation of reason with religion consists in realizing that there is no God and that the 'I' is only contemplating itself in religion, while it . . . supposes that it is contemplating a living, personal God. Realized self-consciousness is a tour de force whereby the 'I' views its double in a mirror and finally, having thought of the image for thousands of years as God, discovers that the image in the mirror is itself. The wrath and punitive righteousness of God are accordingly nothing more than the 'I' making a fist and threatening himself in the mirror; similarly, the grace and mercy of God are nothing more than the 'I' extending its hand to its mirror image. Religion considers this mirror image to be God, philosophy destroys the illusion and shows man that there is no one behind the mirror, and therefore that it is only the reflection of the 'I' toward which the 'I' has directed its actions."[47] Bauer's next work was *Hegels Lehre von der Religion und der Kunst;* in part, it is identical with the *Posaune,* but much of it dares to go even further. In it he rouses the "devout" with all the stylistic and technical means at his command (italics, boldface, and pointing fingers), reinforcing the irony of his attack upon Hegel with a warning against his own theological writings.

Philosophy and religion cannot be combined. On the contrary, faith must banish the arrogance of the notion if it is not itself to be banished by the latter. The difference between Voltaire's attack upon the Bible and Hegel's dissolution of religion is only apparent; basically they are both doing and saying the same thing, the Frenchman with wit, the German with pedantic seriousness. Hegel, indeed, surpassed his prototype, because he puts forth his blasphemies with calm deliberation, giving them a sustained force through philosophical arguments. He is imperturbable, because he no longer has any feeling for faith. "Voltaire still feels the first passion . . . of hate, and rages when he . . . attacks the men who are intimate with God. Hegel, on the other hand, disposes of the matter in complete tranquility by means of a philosophical category; his transgression costs him no more effort than drinking a glass of water."[48] In Voltaire's school Hegel also learned that the Jews are a people disunited and rejected; the mythology of the Greeks seems to him much more human, more free, and more beautiful than the Bible. Hegel's thoughts on the New Testament correspond to what he has to say about the Old Testament; and Jehovah, who "being One seeks to be All," in his view does not achieve the spiritual universality which lies beyond "limitation." Together with Oriental religion, Hegel contemns the Christian revelation, because it has not yet advanced to the atheistic self-sufficiency of the subject. He even ventures to assert that culpability is the "glory" of noble characters, because he is thinking of the heroes of Greece rather than the Christian saints. In place of martyrdom, he glorifies atheistic tragedy, whose major conflict is by no means Christian: the conflict between members of a family or state. According to Hegel, the Orientals were unaware that the spirit of man is free per se. This may be, but they did well enough for all that. According to Hegel, all the devout are Orientals, Syrians, and Galileans— "but they are still quite right in not wanting to be free in this atheistic sense. We do not want to be at one with ourselves, but at one with God."[49] The spirit must yearn, hope, mourn, and lament, but Hegel says, *Hic Rhodus, hic saltus,* that is, he wants to dance, to dance right here in this world! Hegel most clearly reveals his hatred of Christianity in his aesthetics—in general, his attack on sacred history is from the direction of aesthetics—where he bluntly admits that he will not bend his knee before Christ and Mary. He despises all humble adoration, he seeks constantly to spread "self-consciousness," and make the whole world his possession. Self-consciousness and reason are everything to him; he negates everything else as being an "alien" power, not yet liberated and become a notion. To him, the freedom to be at one with oneself is the means and the end of history. For the Christian, however, there can be only *one* historical power: the power of God; only *one* end: the glory of the Lord; and therefore only *one* means to this end: Christ, the *one* mediator between God and man.

What will Hegel's mediation do about this unique, truly liberating mediator? In order to exclude him, Hegel must explain the Holy Scripture mythologically. At bottom he is even more radical than Strauss, for Strauss only assumes that individual myths are contained in the New Testament, while according to Hegel the whole thing is mythological simply because it is religion presented in religious terminology and images.[50] Nor is that enough: in the Greek myths and epics he finds a work of creative individuality which freely makes tradition its own, but in the narrative of the Gospels a restricted development of a preordained tradition, a "purely external creativity."

But if mythology is the art which gives the divine human form and man his free humanity, in another respect sacred history is not mythological, because its scope is limited to the deeds of God and the bondage of mankind. For this reason, according to Hegel, the biblical historians could never form a work of art, because the worthlessness and depravity of man and the uniformity of the activity of the One gave them no possibility for any spiritual movement involving real collisions and their free human resolution. "Where the One is All, and the others all slaves, all possibility of history and the historical point of view is radically excluded."[51] On the other hand, sacred history must not be understood symbolically, because what is divine must retain its strict individuality; Jehovah experiences the fate of man, including death. This is symbolic only to the extent that all natural and human phenomena are made significant in the Bible, not for their own sakes, but because of their relationship to the Lord. From Hegel's standpoint, the sacred narrative of the Bible is a hybrid of Oriental and Occidental ideas, a cloudy mixture of symbolism and mythology. If it should be asked whether the story is to be understood mythologically in the trivial sense meant by Strauss,[52] because the narrative does not always correspond to the pretended course of events, the master would only laugh at the wretched framing of the question, he, the great juggler with the "two-edged sword" (Heb. 4:12) of the word of God, which he appears to swallow so that it will no longer frighten anyone!

In this fashion, Bauer reads his own destruction of theology into his exposition of Hegel, in order to demonstrate that it is the only legitimate consequence of his philosophy of religion. He himself points out to the "devout" that he is a much more dangerous pupil of Hegel than is Strauss. Strauss made many concessions to the biblical narrative by making a distinction between pure myth and historical myth, seeing a basis of actual fact in the latter. In his "madness," Bauer goes much further: he asserts that the Gospels themselves are an artificial product of theology.[53] "Strauss discusses the question whether the Gospel narratives are legendary, . . . Bauer searches in them for traces of deliberate reflection and theological pragmatism. On account of the weakness of his principle, and since he still acknowledges the presence of much historical data in the Gospels, Strauss is finally compelled . . . to ask whether the miracle described in the narrative is possible. . . . Bauer, on the other hand, never asks this question . . . and believes he can do without it, because he breaks up the narratives . . . by showing them to be a product of reflection. He is so positive of this that he even recognizes the presence of more miraculous elements in the Gospels than does Strauss: these literary miracles are his favorite topic, because he can dismiss them easily as mere creations of unthinking pragmatism."[54]

At that time, Bauer was planning a "Journal for the Study of Atheism and the Mortality of the Finite Subject."[55] To him, even Strauss seemed "a Hengstenberg" (i.e., an orthodox reactionary) "within the realm of criticism." He, on the contrary, was that "Atheist and Anti-Christian" as whom he describes his teacher to the devout. He makes ironic use of the image of the theologian from Ecclesiasticus 14:22–24 to describe himself: like him, he goes after her, pries in at her window, hearkens at her doors, lodges near her house, and sets his children under her shelter, in order finally to overthrow the innermost sanctuary and compromise the entire edifice of theological wisdom as though it were an ordinary dwelling. He even declares that theological exposition of the Bible *must* be "Jesuitical," because the expositor presupposes the eternal truth of Scripture, but also has his own educational background and human nature, which presume postulates which must be supported in the face of the former, although they contradict the biblical postulates. Besides his modern education, the theologian has apologetic interests; he must harmonize the old-fashioned Bible with his modern barbarian education—something that is possible only when both are falsified.

Bauer's ideas had no effect upon contemporary theology and philosophy; even in the case of Overbeck it is questionable whether Bauer's analysis of the "theological consciousness" was an immediate

influence upon his attitude toward theology. Only for one critical
moment did Bauer's radicalism exert any influence upon his immediate contemporaries. After Bauer's overly violent criticism of his
Leben Jesu, Strauss withdrew completely from association with him;
at first, Feuerbach was thought to be the author of the *Posaune*, but
he rejected Bauer's work because it seemed to him to *support* Hegel,
whereas Ruge recommended it to him as the most complete break
with Hegelianism.[56] From the very beginning, a gulf separated
Feuerbach from the "Berlin sophists"; but Ruge compared Bauer's
critical accomplishment with that of Voltaire and Rousseau. He
declared Bauer to be a "messiah of atheism" and the "Robespierre of
theology."[57] But even he soon began to have reservations, for Bauer's
strength only appeared in denial, because he failed to understand the
social or political nature of human existence. Historically and politically, his "system of frivolity" led nowhere. Later, in the *Anekdota*,
Ruge attempted to define Bauer's "negativity" more precisely. Bauer
had indeed succeeded in making clear his own inconsistency by
banishing Hegel's atheistic consistency, but without being able to
give a firm foundation to this new turn. "It is not enough to point
out that the progress of today already existed in the past; what is
new must stand on its own feet; for all exegesis of something new
on the basis of what is old is a distortion, it is the error of Hegelian
ambiguity and its double meaning, the error of the philosophy . . .
which reads itself into the historical Christian world view, thereby
misunderstanding both that particular stage of spiritual progress and
itself."[58] Bauer's *Posaune* is actually a logical consequence of Feuerbach, but one which appears to take a backward step for the sake
of polemic. Ruge's final verdict, which dates from 1846, is basically
identical with that of Marx and Stirner: Bauer is the "ultimate
theologian," a total heretic who pursues theology with theological
fanaticism, and for precisely this reason is not free of the faith
against which he fights.[59]

Bauer's direct criticism of the Christian religion is contained in
*Entdecktes Christentum, Eine Erinnerung an das achtzehnte Jahr-
hundert und ein Beitrag zur Krise des neunzehnten* (1843).[60] Its
basic thesis, that Christianity developed out of the decline of freedom in the Roman world, looks backward to Hegel's early works
and forward to Nietzsche's *Genealogie der Moral*. He no longer
seeks to humanize the "essence" of Christianity, but to demonstrate
its "inhumanity," its paradoxical contrast to all that is natural to
man.[61] For him, Christianity simply is the "misfortune of the world."

It made its appearance when the ancient world could no longer hold itself together, exalted this misfortune to the essence of man, and made suffering his sure fate. But man is by nature free, he can and must prove his freedom, even in the face of death. He is himself his own lawgiver, even when he makes himself believe that he must make himself subject to an external law. God is man estranged from man, but no longer in the same sense as Feuerbach. For Feuerbach, this estrangement meant only a reversible objectification of the essence of man in the image of religion; for Bauer, it is a complete loss of the self, which can only be reversed by total de-Christianization. For this reason, complete liberation from religion is more than a mere liberation: it represents a complete and final break, a deliberate and conscious freedom from all religion. Not the least expression of this freedom is that even criticism of religion brings itself to an end. "The French Revolution failed, among other reasons, in letting itself be driven . . . to employing the police power against religion and the Church, a power which the privileged classes had formerly employed against their opponents. . . . But things are different now: self-consciousness has achieved assurance of its freedom, and, at the crucial moment, will even allow to those who are not free the freedom of remaining so. Freedom is not forced upon them. With freedom the world will be overcome. After the crisis, history will no longer be religious, will no longer be Christian; but toward those who stand at the outskirts of the civilized world, desiring to retain their gods, it will exercise the generosity of scorn. After Tarentum had been taken, Fabius' soldiers asked him what should be done with the plundered statues of the gods, he answered, Let the Tarentinians keep their angry gods. . . . Let the Christians keep their angry gods!"[62]

6 Marx's Explanation of Christianity as a Perverted World

The criticism of religion which we have been studying took a new turn with Marx, and came to an end with Stirner. In *Die Heilige Familie, oder Kritik der kritischen Kritik, gegen B. Bauer und Consorten* (1844–45), written in collaboration with Engels, Marx turns against Bauer, with whom he had previously worked. In this polemic he ranges himself completely on the side of Feuerbach's "realistic humanism," on the grounds that Feuerbach's communism of "I and Thou" has caught a glimpse of man as he really is, even though it has not yet recognized him in "practice" as a social generic being. Bauer's antithesis between "self-consciousness" and "mass" seems to him, on the contrary, to be a piece of bad Hegelianism built upon Feuerbach. For the "self-consciousness" on whose basis Bauer criticizes the "mass" is no longer the total and absolute subject of Hegelian philosophy, but a finite, anthropological subjectivity which claims absolute significance. In Marx's eyes, Bauer remains a "theologian" and an "Hegelian," whose discussion of the Jewish question was critical only so long as this question was theological, but became noncritical as soon as it began to become political. Judged by the standards of social and political reality, Bauer's absolute "self-consciousness," like Stirner's "unique individual," is an ideological absolutization of the principle of bourgeois society, whose determining class is the individualistic middle class, and whose real principle is "egoism." What Marx attacks in Bauer, and even more forcibly in Stirner, is therefore the sociopolitical postulates and consequences of "self-consciousness." These are apparent in Bauer's antithesis; for his opposition to the "mass" is determinative for his "self-consciousness," just as the "crowd" is determinative for Kierkegaard's "self-being."[63]

"Absolute criticism speaks of 'truths which are a priori self-validating.' In its critical naïveté, it invents an absolute 'a priori' and an abstract, unchangeable 'mass.' In the eyes of absolute criticism, there is as little difference between the 'a priori' of the mass of the sixteenth century and the 'a priori' of the mass of the nineteenth century as there is between these masses themselves. . . . Because *the* truth, like history, is an ethereal subject, divorced from the material mass, it does not address itself to empirical man, but to the 'innermost soul,' it does not impose itself . . . upon the gross body of man, but 'infiltrates' throughout all his idealistic intestinal tract." "On the one side stands the mass, the passive, spiritless, nonhistorical, material element of history; on the other stands the spirit, criticism, Bruno & Co., the active element from which all historical action proceeds. The act of transforming society is reduced to the intellectual activity of critical criticism."[64]

With polemic directed specifically against Bauer's "last judgment" upon Hegel, Marx concludes his criticism of Bauer with a "critical last judgment" in the style of the *Posaune*, and with an "historical epilogue": "As we found out later, it was not the world, but the critical journal which perished." According to Marx,

Bauer's self-sufficient, merely "critical" criticism had only one real accomplishment: it made plain through empirical application the idealistic nature of Hegelian "self-consciousness."

For the criticism of religion, more important than the polemic against Bauer is Marx's disagreement with Feuerbach's reduction of theology to anthropology. For Marx, this is only the preliminary to a further criticism of the conditions of human life themselves. From this point of view, he considered Feuerbach's criticism of religion an incontestable "outcome." "For Germany, criticism of religion essentially has been brought to a close, and the criticism of religion is the prerequisite for all criticism," reads the first sentence of the introduction to the criticism of Hegel's philosophy of right. In spite of this, Marx's advance to criticism of the political world is not content simply to accept the criticism of religion which has already been accomplished; in this progress toward criticism of the earthly world, he also gains a new standpoint for criticism of the "heavenly" world of religion. Religion becomes a component of the theory of "ideologies."[65] But religion can show itself to be an ideology only when the world as such has become secular. But under precisely these circumstances there is need for a criticism of the existing world as such, that is, a distinction between how it is and how it should be. "The man who has found only the reflection of himself . . . in the fantastic reality of heaven will no longer be inclined to find only the semblance of himself, a nonhuman, where he seeks and must seek his true reality."[66] On the other hand, the existence of a world which transcends this world is comprehensible only on the basis of the real deficiencies of this real world.

If one assumes, with Feuerbach, that the religious world is only a shell surrounding the earthly kernel of the human world, one must ask: why is this kernel surrounded by an alien shell, how does there come to be any superstructure of a religious, ideological world? With this question Marx not only goes beyond Feuerbach's criticism of religion, but also goes back before it. According to him, all criticism of religion which does not ask this question is uncritical. For "it is in actual fact much easier to find analytically the earthly kernel of religious cloud-castles than to reverse the process and, examining particular, real (i.e., sociohistorical) conditions of life, develop their religious forms. The latter is the only materialistic, and therefore the only scientific method," in contrast to the abstract materialism of natural science, which excludes the historical process from consideration.[67] Thus while Feuerbach's only concern was to uncover the so-called earthly kernel of religion, the important thing to Marx is to proceed in the other direction, analyzing historically the conditions of life on earth and discovering what needs and contradictions within the secular circumstances make possible and demand religion. The goal is to explain why the secular basis comes into conflict with itself, giving rise to a world which differs from this earthly world. This Feuerbach was unable to explain, for he was still convinced that it is the "essence" of man, something essential in man, which expresses itself in religion, albeit "indirectly." Marx had to be able to answer this question, which was no question at all to Feuerbach, if indeed this world was to be basic in every instance, and religion nonessential. This leads to the following criticism: "Feuerbach takes as his point of departure the fact of religious self-estrangement, the bifurcation of the world into religious and secular aspects. His work consists in resolving the religious world into its secular basis. But the fact that the secular basis comes into conflict with itself and defines for itself an independent kingdom in the clouds can only be explained on the basis of the internal divisions and contradictions of this secular basis. Thus it is necessary to understand the contradictions of this world in itself as well as to revolutionize it. Thus, for example, once the earthly family has been discovered to be the secret behind the Holy Family, the former must itself be abolished both in theory and in practice."[68]

As a consequence, Marx goes beyond Feuerbach's statement that "man makes religion," but not conversely; he continues: "And further, religion is the self-consciousness . . . of that man who has either not yet gained his true self, or already lost it." "His true self," that means his self in its secular social environment. For this reason, Marx does not see religion as a mere "objectification" of human existence, but as a "reification" in the sense of "self-estrangement." Religion is a perversion of the world,[69] a perversion which remains necessary so long as the social aspect of human nature does not achieve true reality. Thus the struggle against religion of the beyond is indirectly a struggle against the world of here and now, a world so fashioned that it demands to be supplemented and transfigured by religion. And conversely "religious misery" (i.e., misery in the religious sense) is "both the expression of real misery . . . and protest against it." Religion is the "soul of a heartless world," the "spirit of unspiritual circumstances," and the "illusory sun which moves about man as long as he does not move about himself." Therefore the abolition of the illusory "salvation" of religion is positively the promotion of earthly "happiness."[70] By means of the will to happiness, Marxist Socialism leads to an "atrophy" of religion, but it does not allow itself to be sucked into the "adventure of a political war against religion."[71]

Thus the "positive" element of Marx's criticism of religion does not consist in the humanization of religion (Strauss and Feuerbach), nor in its mere repudiation (Bauer), but in the critical demand that the circumstances be abolished which lead to the birth of religion. These circumstances belong to the universal social realm. "Once the beyond of truth has vanished, it is the task of history to establish the truth of the here and now." Once the "sacred image of human self-estrangement" has been unmasked, criticism must unmask the *same* self-estrangement in its unholy, profane, economic, and social image, and revolution must transform it. This alone can transform what has up to now been a criticism of religion and theology into a criticism of right and of politics, that is, of the human commonwealth or *polis*.

The meaning of "atheism" is similarly transformed. It ceases to be a theological position and becomes really atheistic, that is, it dissolves in a temporal shaping of earthly existence. The Marxist atheist does not believe in any god; he believes in man. His battle is no longer against gods, but against idols. In *Das Kapital*, Marx showed that one of these idols of the modern capitalistic world is the "fetish-nature" of merchandise, the mercantile form assumed by all modern commodities. The fetish of merchandise demonstrates the predominance of "things" over the "men" who produce them, the degree in which creative man is dependent upon his own creatures. It is this predominance which must be destroyed, not any power which religion has over man. "Just as in religion man is dominated by the product of his own mind, so in the capitalistic system of production he is dominated by the product of his own hand." Modern man no longer exercises immediate control over the world of his own creation; it encounters him with a kind of autocracy, because the work of his own hands has been lost to him because of the private nature of the means of production in our economic system. The work of his own head and his own hands has grown over his head and out of his hands. And more, the modern world of man, which has become completely earthly, is once more creating myths. "Up to now, it was supposed that the growth of the Christian myth under the Roman Empire was possible only because printing had not yet been invented. Just the reverse is true. The daily newspaper and the telegraph, which disperses its inventions in a moment over the entire surface of the earth, fabricate more myths . . . in one day than formerly could be constructed in a year."[72] Therefore, more is necessary than a mere theoretical reduction of theology to "self-consciousness" or "anthropology"; what is needed is an ever-renewed criticism of the human condition itself.

7 Stirner's Systematic Destruction of the Divine and the Human

In his review of Bauer's *Posaune*, Stirner remarks that Hegel's pupils have done nothing really new. "Shamelessly enough," they had merely drawn aside the transparent veil in which the master had occasionally wrapped his statements.[73] Stirner considered Bauer's work to be such an unveiling; its radicalism was not anything unique, but a universal characteristic of the Germans: "The Germans are the first and foremost exponents of the historical vocation of radicalism; they alone are radical, and they alone justly so. There are no others so relentless and ruthless; not only do they bring about the collapse of the existing world so that they may themselves stand fast, they also bring about the collapse of themselves. When Germans demolish, a god must fall, a world must pass away. To the Germans, destruction is creation, the pulverization of the temporal is eternity."[74] In this fashion Bauer destroys the Hegelian world spirit, the Christian God, the church, and theology. He is "free and intelligent" in a fashion impossible for the religious man.

Stirner seeks to outdo Hegel's pupils by discovering once more something "religious," something that transcends man, in that to which Feuerbach, Bauer, and Marx reduce the essence of religion: in man, in self-consciousness, in human nature. He seeks an *idée fixe* which will transcend the real, individual human being represented by each unique "I."

The positive portion of his book discusses the "I" and its "uniqueness." It has as its epigraph, "At the beginning of the modern age stands the God-man. At its end, will only the God in the God-man pass away, and can the God-man really die if only the God in him dies? This question was neither asked nor answered during the time that the work of the Enlightenment, the vanquishing of God, was being brought to a victorious conclusion, in our own time. It was not noticed that man had killed God only himself to become the sole God in heaven. The beyond *above us* has been done away with, the great undertaking of the men of the Enlightenment has been completed. But the beyond *within us* has become a new heaven . . . : God has been forced to make room, not for us, but for man. How can you believe that the God-man has died until not only the God, but also the man has died?"

God has been vanquished by the religious criticism of Strauss, Feuerbach, and Bauer; but man remains to be vanquished, because God has always determined what man should be. But what concerns me is neither the divine nor the human, nothing at all universal, but only what is uniquely mine, because "I" am always an "individual" with my particular "property." I may be a Christian or a Jew, a German or a Russian, have the consciousness of being a "citizen" or a "worker," or even merely a human being; as "I," I am more than all of this, because only "I" can appropriate it for myself.[75]

In Hegel's philosophical theology, the incarnation of God means the unity existing between human and divine nature; Feuerbach reduces the essence of God to man, the highest essence; for Marx, Christianity is a perversion of the world. Finally, Stirner recognizes that the "mankind" which has been exalted to the status of highest essence is the ultimate attenuation of the God-man: the God has died, but not the man.

Strauss, Feuerbach, Bauer, and Marx all took as their basis the critical distinction between theology and anthropology; Stirner transforms this into a more inclusive distinction between universal definitions of the essence of man, both theological and anthropological, and the ability of the individual. The essential distinction is not whether this or that is essential to man, but whether a man relies on nothing but himself. "Understandably, there can be meaningful argument over what is to be accorded the honor of being the highest essence only when even the most bitter opponents concede each other the major point, that there *is* a highest essence, deserving of cultic service. Suppose that a man were merely to smile sympathetically at the whole controversy over a highest essence, as a Christian smiles at the verbal duel between Shiites and Sunnites . . . : he would consider the hypothesis of a highest essence to be invalid, and on this basis the whole argument would be a pointless game. It makes no difference at all to him whether the One God or the Three-in-One, the Lutheran God or the *être suprême*, or even no God at all, but only man, is considered to be the highest essence. He denies the very existence of a highest essence; for in his eyes these servants of a highest essence are all religious men: the ranting atheist no less than the most devout Christian."[76]

Feuerbach still grasped at the entire content of Christianity, with the strength of despair, "not to discard it, no, rather to seize it for himself, to . . . exert one last effort to drag it from its heaven and keep it forever. Is this not a gesture of complete desperation, a gesture of life and death, and is it not at the same time the Christian yearning . . . for the beyond? The hero's purpose is not to enter the beyond, but to draw the beyond to himself and force it to become the here and now! And has not all the world cried out ever since . . . that the important thing is the here and now, that heaven must come down to earth and be experienced here?"[77]

This reduction to nonreligious man has been completed in political, social, and humanistic "liberalism"; but for Stirner this goal, once attained, is only the starting point for the process of overcoming the distinction between what man essentially should be and what in fact he is. For the ancient world, he says, the "world" was truth; for the Christian, "spirit" was truth, and this spiritualized world is brought to an end in the left-wing Hegelians, with their faith in the spirit of "mankind." But for the future world, as Nietzsche says, "nothing is true"; everything is permissible, because in this world the only truth is what the individual can appropriate for himself without becoming estranged from himself. From this point of view, that of the "I," human truth is nothing more and nothing less than what the individual can in fact be. This also determines Stirner's attitude toward the Christian religion: he does not attack it, neither does he defend it, but rather leaves it to the individual to decide to what extent he can appropriate such an entity and "utilize" it for himself.

In his reply to Stirner's attack,[78] Feuerbach attempted to show that it is impossible to be a "human being" and say anything at all about human beings without making distinctions: between essential and nonessential, necessary and accidental, potential and real. For man is never a perfectly simple being, but always one with internal distinctions. The religious difference between God and man goes back to "distinctions which occur within man himself." In the very process of comparing ourselves with others, we also make distinctions within ourselves. At all times man is transcending himself

within himself. Every moment of life has something transcen-
dentally human; "therefore men always want to be and to have more
than they are and possess." And thus there is also an essential distinction between the various things that I possess: "There is that which
is mine and which can be gone without myself being gone, and there
is that which is mine and which cannot be gone without myself
being gone also."

In his reply, Stirner sought to explain[79] that his complete
"egoist" is not an "individual" determined by content, nor an
absolute principle, but rather, considered in its content, an "absolute
cliché," properly understood, the "end of all clichés." The "egoist"
is a formal definition of the "potentialities of unique, individual
appropriation," both of the self and of the world. From this point
of view, the distinction between what is essential and what is nonessential to a person, who makes each his own in a different fashion,
is itself no longer essential. It can appear to be an essential distinction
only so long as man remains fixed to the universal ideal of man. This
is the only criterion by which the existing distinctions between
various things that are mine can be distinguished as essential or nonessential. For example, Feuerbach considers that love for a "sweetheart" is *eo ipso* superior to love for a "courtesan," as well as more
human, on the grounds that a man can satisfy his "full and complete" essence only with a sweetheart. He is not proceeding, Stirner
says, from the particular potentialities for appropriation open to the
individual, but from a preconceived ideal: that of "true" love, of the
"essence" of love, on the basis of which one woman is to be distinguished from another, as courtesan or sweetheart. But in respect
to his uniqueness, as this particular man with this particular woman,
a man can belong totally to himself, can satisfy himself, as much or
as little with a so-called courtesan as with a so-called sweetheart.
What at any given moment can really become my own cannot be
distinguished in advance on the basis of a universal ideal; it is only
shown by actual appropriation. But whatever can really belong to
a man belongs to him neither essentially nor accidentally, but
uniquely and therefore by nature.

By thus denying the substantiality of all self-differentiation,
Stirner eliminated not only the theological distinction between what
is human and what is divine, but also the anthropological distinction
between what I am "intrinsically" and what I am "accidentally."
For his own part, he presupposes as an ideal only the "absolute
cliché" of the "I."

8 Kierkegaard's Paradoxical Concept of Faith and His Attack Upon Existing Christendom

Stirner's cliché of the "unique individual" and Kierkegaard's concept of the "individual" both illustrate the same question, asked in religious and profane terms. The problem of their common radicalism is the nihilism which arises from extreme isolation. For Stirner, it is the careless nihilism of "I entrust my cause to nothing" —namely, to nothing other than myself. For Kierkegaard, it is the melancholy nihilism of irony and boredom, of anxiety and despair.[80] Kierkegaard's analyses of these phenomena have all the same function: to make man dependent entirely on himself, thereby confronting him with nothingness, and in this fashion to force him to take a stand, to make a decision: "either" to despair (actively through suicide and passively through madness), "or" to dare to make the leap of faith. In this *salto mortale*, man comes to stand, not before nothingness, but before God, who created being out of nothingness. Stirner, on the other hand, declares himself to be the nothingness which is itself creative.

In one passage in *Either-Or*,[81] Kierkegaard says that today (1843) there are more than a few to be found who, with an unbridled passion of abstraction, unclothe themselves to the point of complete nakedness in order to become normal human beings. This passage could refer to such a man as Stirner. It is doubtful, nevertheless, whether Kierkegaard was acquainted with Stirner's book. Nor does he mention Bauer in his works. In spite of this, it is very improbable that Kierkegaard should have known nothing of him and of his circle, the more so since the left-wing Hegelians, during Kierkegaard's stay in Berlin, were carrying on their controversy with Schelling, which was also Kierkegaard's concern at that time.[82] We have concrete evidence only of his relationship with Feuerbach.

Kierkegaard realized fully that Feuerbach's dissolution of theology was a logical consequence of Hegel's inclusion of Christianity in the history of the world spirit. He cites Feuerbach's statement, in *Das Wesen des Christentums*, that anthropology is the secret of philosophy. The occasion is a polemic against Hegel's transformation of Christianity's "existential proclamation" into a metaphysical doctrine,[83] and he ranges himself on the side of Feuerbach. Like

Feuerbach, he is persuaded that Hegel's equation of the divine and the human is the contradiction of the modern age, an age which cleverly reconciles lack of faith with faith, and Christianity with paganism. "Modern speculative philosophy seems almost to have performed the feat of having gone so far beyond Christianity, or so far in its understanding of Christianity, that it has just about returned to paganism. That no one prefers paganism to Christianity is not surprising at all; but to discover that paganism is the supreme expression of Christianity is an injustice, both to Christianity, which is made something other than it was, and to paganism, which is not made into anything that it was. Speculation has achieved a complete understanding of Christianity, and at the same time declared itself to be the supreme manifestation of Christianity. In the process, it made the remarkable discovery that there is no beyond, that 'above' and 'beyond' are the dialectical narrow-mindedness of a finite intellect."[84] Kierkegaard's relationship to Feuerbach is characterized not only by their common opposition to Hegel, but also by a kind of sympathy Kierkegaard had toward Feuerbach's attack upon existing Christianity. "Börne, Heine, Feuerbach, and similar writers are most interesting subjects for an experimenter. They often are very well informed about religious matters; that is, they are absolutely sure that they want nothing to do with religion. They show up thereby to advantage in comparison with the systematizers, who have no understanding of religious matters, . . . but are always unhappily engaged in trying to explain them."[85] On the other hand, the true nature of Christianity can be perceived no less clearly from an absolutely anti-Christian standpoint than from an absolutely Christian standpoint. To demonstrate this thesis, Kierkegaard invokes Pascal and Feuerbach. "Thus I have understood religion experimentally. That I have also understood it correctly I perceive from the fact that two experts who start from contrary principles have an identical conception of the relationship of religion to suffering. Feuerbach, who embraces the principle of health, says that the religious life (particularly the Christian life) is a continuous story of suffering; it is necessary only to observe the life of Pascal—that is enough. Pascal says exactly the same thing: 'Suffering is the natural state of the Christian' (just as well-being is the natural state of sensual man). . . ."[86] The journals express the matter in fundamental terms: writers like Feuerbach, who comprise a "final formation of freethinkers," can be quite beneficial to Christianity. Basically they are defending it against the Christians of today, who no longer know that it is not humanitarianism and progress, but a perversion of the world. "Et ab hoste consilium," concludes a reference to Feuerbach's significance for an understanding of Christianity in a world which calls itself Christian, but is a negation of Christianity.[87]

More important than Kierkegaard's tactical evaluation of Feuerbach is the return of both of them to Luther's criticism of Catholic positivity, from the standpoint of individual appropriation. Just as Feuerbach invokes Luther for his dissolution of the Christian faith, so Kierkegaard derived from Luther his concepts of "training" and "recapitulation." "Take away the appropriation of what is Christian, and what is left to Luther's credit? But open him up, and feel throbbing in every line the strong pulse of appropriation. . . . Did not the papacy possess objectivity and objective definitions and objective objects to spare? What was missing? Appropriation, inwardness."[88] From Luther's "pro me" and "pro nobis," Feuerbach argues that the essence of faith is man trusting in himself; Kierkegaard translates them as "appropriation" and "subjectivity." Just as Feuerbach sees Protestantism as the religious mode of the humanization of God, says Kierkegaard, so the danger of Protestantism is that it will become a Christianity "in the interests of mankind," a "reaction of humanism against Christianity." This is apt to happen as soon as it seeks to exist for itself, and become a "norm" instead of a "corrective."[89] Kierkegaard wants to avoid this danger, while he himself pushes the principle of appropriation to its extreme limit. He is compelled therefore to develop the "Christian ideality" as a "paradox," that is, within the extreme tension of a relationship with God in which the particular mode of appropriation retains the disproportion of his alien object.[90] In this paradoxical relationship between the divine and the human, the accent lies on appropriation on the part of subjective inwardness. God is truth, but this truth is present only to the faith of a man who has his existence before God. "When a concrete individual lacks faith, then neither does God exist, nor is God present, albeit God, eternally understood, is eternal."[91] Thus Kierkegaard takes Hegel's statement that God is essentially present only "in the process of thought," because the spirit perceived is the same as the spirit which perceives, and transforms it by means of Feuerbach's axiom of the anthropological essence of Christian truth, arriving at the existential thesis that God is present only in and to the subjectivity of a particular individual "relationship with God."

With this basic concept of existential theology, Kierkegaard destroyed the objectivity of historical Christianity. His criticism of a Christianity which has become secularized in church and state, theology and philosophy, is a criticism of a Christianity which has become "positive" and therefore estranged; his criterion is the inwardness of individual appropriation through an existing subjectivity. With this thesis of the "subjectivity of truth"—subjective to the point of complete negation of all objective existence, and at the same time true in a completely independent sense—Kierkegaard stands exactly on the borderline of that correlation between God and man which Feuerbach fixed upon man.[92] Historically considered, therefore, Feuerbach's reduction of the Christian religion to the "feeling" of sensual man is merely the prelude to Kierkegaard's existential experiment, through which he seeks to abolish historical distance by means of internal "contemporaneity," and recover primitive Christianity, at the end of its process of decay, by means of particular individual existence.[93] His spiritual power exalts religious feeling to an antirational "passion."[94] "To objective vision, Christianity is a *res in facto posita;* its truth then is questioned, but purely objectively. The modest subject is too objective not to take up an external position, or even automatically to assume that it is itself among the believers. This objective understanding of truth can mean: 1. historical truth, 2. philosophical truth. Viewed as historical truth, truth must be discovered through a critical examination of various accounts, etc.; in short, in the same fashion as any other historical truth is discovered. If philosophical truth is in question, then the question concerns the relationship between a theory which has been posited historically and recognized to be valid and eternal truth. Thus the subject, inquiring, speculating, and apprehending, is seeking after truth, but not after subjective truth, the truth of personal appropriation. This subject, which investigates, is interested, but not to an infinitely personal degree, not with passion."[95]

In spite of this emphasis upon "passion," the decisive contrast between Hegel and Kierkegaard is not in the polemic attitude taken by impassioned subjectivity toward objective reason, but rather in their conception of the relationship between history and Christianity. To Kierkegaard, the relationship between eternal truth and process of history was a dilemma which he sought to resolve by dialectical paradox. Hegel located the absolute of Christianity in universal history, so that there could never be any disparity between the two. Kierkegaard, on the contrary, considers the contradiction involved in basing "eternal salvation" upon historical knowledge; therefore he must favor the subjectivity of individual appropriation of Christianity in opposition to its historical spread, erecting a concept of history which ignores the objective power of history and perverts the sense of history. This history, subjectivized for the purpose of appropriation, leads to two concepts of "historicity": the existential-ontological of Heidegger, and the existential-philosophical of Jaspers.

Kierkegaard's appropriation has the task of "removing eighteen hundred years as though they had never existed," of becoming inwardly "contemporaneous" with primitive Christianity. But this is possible only if the Christianity which has existed for centuries ceases to become a universal historical reality and becomes an individual possibility, a kind of "postulate." "In this fashion, of course, God becomes a postulate, but not in the popular idle sense of this word. It rather becomes clear that the only way in which an existential human being can come into a relationship with God is for dialectical antithesis to bring passion to the point of despair, so that God may be grasped under the category of despair (faith). Thus the postulate is by no means arbitrary: it is self-defense. Thus God is not a postulate; but rather, the existential human being postulates God—a necessity."[96]

It is not possible to come into possession of the independent, objective truth of Christianity, "absolute" in the literal sense. The "nodal point" of its absoluteness rests in "absolute relationship" to it. In the moment of decision, the objective existence of Christianity throughout eighteen hundred years is, as an "argument in favor," worth "precisely nothing"; but as a "deterrent against," it is "superb." For if truth resides in appropriation, the objective validity of Christianity merely shows that it is indifferent to the subject, to me as a person.

In the framework of such a definition of truth, how can any distinction be made between madness and truth, if both can evidence the same "inwardness"?[97] An impassioned anti-Christian would be no more and no less "true" than an impassioned Christian; so, too, every other impassioned existential involvement would, as such, have its own truth.[98] Kierkegaard took note of this dilemma, but gave voice to it only in passing. He assures his thesis through the restriction that a distinction must be made between the impassioned inwardness "of infinity" and merely "finite" inwardness. But can inwardness as such be judged by this criterion? The "infinity" of Christian inwardness is not self-validating, on the basis of its own subjectivity; it is validated by its object: the infinity of God. But if this is the case, the inwardness of "real" infinity, that is, impassioned relationship to God, can be distinguished from a relationship to something finite, which, as an impassioned relationship would be as madness, only by reference to God; such distinction runs counter to individual passion, which is always finite. If, on the other hand, impassioned existence were really the "ultimate," and objectivity merely "evanescent," then of necessity there would also vanish the possibility of any distinction between finite and infinite inwardness, and thus between madness and truth. In fact, Kierkegaard drew this conclusion by locating truth in the realm of inwardness: "When one inquires objectively after truth, one reflects objectively upon truth as an object to which the inquirer stands in a relationship. It is not the relationship upon which one reflects, but rather the fact that it is the truth, that which is true, to which he stands in a relationship. If that toward which he stands in a relationship is only the truth, that which is true, the subject is within this truth. When one inquires subjectively after truth, one reflects subjectively upon the relationship of the individual. If only the 'how' of this relationship is true, then the individual is within truth, even if it stands in relationship to an untruth."[99]

The question of God's existence remains indifferent if the "only" matter of importance is that the individual stand in relationship "to something," "that his relationship is in truth [i.e., subjectively] a relationship to God." Thus the path to truth is itself truth;[100] the maximum objectivity attainable along this path is "objective uncertainty." Whether his own relationship to God is objectively (i.e., from God's point of view) a true relationship, no man can ever be assured. For a human being whose "existence" is in faith, the "highest" truth is precisely this objective uncertainty in his individual appropriation. According to Kierkegaard, therefore, a man can pray to God "in truth" even though he is actually worshiping a pagan idol; conversely, a man can pray to an idol "in truth" even though he is in a Christian house of God, worshiping the true Christian God. Truth is the "inward" *how*, not the "external" *what*. But Christian subjectivity is concerned, not with "any object at all," but with true Christianity; this must be so if truth is not to be madness. For this reason, the truth of faith consists in more than mere subjective appropriation: this appropriation must also "hold fast to objective uncertainty" as such. Thus the objectivity of faith is not grounded in itself; as a deterrent, it is constitutive for the truth of individual appropriation. Both together make faith a "paradox." "If the subjectivity of inwardness is truth, then truth, objectively defined is a paradox. The fact that truth, objectively, is a paradox shows in turn that subjectivity is truth; for objectivity repels, and this repelling, or its expression, is the tension and dynamometer of inwardness."[101] Thus subjectivity is the true path to truth which is in itself eternal, but necessarily paradoxical to an existential human being; it attracts only by repelling.

A consequence of the subjectivity of Christian truth is the form in which it is conveyed. "When I realized this, it became clear to me at once that, if I were to convey anything of this, my presentation must remain in indirect form. If inwardness is truth, then a conclusion is mere booty with which a man should not load anyone else down; to convey a conclusion is unnatural intercourse between man and man. Each man is spirit, and truth is precisely the independent act of appropriation which prevents a conclusion."[102] The truth of Christianity is an existential miracle or a paradox, a man who is also God; therefore, in truth, this truth can be conveyed only paradoxically, not directly. It must be conveyed in such a fashion that the recipient is brought into his own relationship of appropriation toward what is conveyed, but not to the one who conveys it to him. The truth of "Christian maieutics" rests upon the subjectivity of the existential human being. Its origin and goal is a truth which is transmittible only indirectly, because it must be appropriated independently. The process of conveying it reduces to a mere "attention-getting," so that appropriation is made possible for everyone as an individual. "To attract attention, without authority, to what is religious, what is Christian: that is the definition of all my literary activity, considered as a whole."

Kierkegaard recognized that the same contradiction lies in the indirectness of the process of conveying as in the existentialization of a nevertheless postulated truth.[103] He has this indirectness conclude in directness: a "witnessing" to truth. "The conveyance of what is Christian must ultimately conclude with an act of witness; maieutics cannot be the ultimate form. From the Christian point of view, truth does not reside in the subject (as Socrates conceived); it is a revelation which must be proclaimed. Maieutics has its place in Christianity precisely because most people live under the impression that they are Christians. But since Christianity is Christianity, the maieutician must become a witness."[104]

Kierkegaard himself did not appear as a "witness to the truth," although it was his deepest inclination "to have himself martyred for the truth." But this was permitted only to an "apostle," not to a "genius."[105] His own Christian vocation was therefore to be a "religious writer," living on the borderline between poetry and religion. The religious discourses he published under his own name he viewed not as sermons, but as Christian "discourses" in "edifying style."[106] Therefore his attack upon existing Christianity should not be seen as a consequence of his literary vocation, but as an eruption of his desire to become a witness. In a striking attack, he denied the representatives of the Danish Church the right to be considered witnesses to the truth without representing Christian truth with apostolic authority. Kierkegaard made his appearance only in the name of "human honesty": "I will risk my life for this honesty. On the other hand, I am not saying that I am risking anything for Christianity. Suppose for a moment, suppose that I should literally sacrifice my life: it would not be a sacrifice for Christianity, but only for my desire for honesty."[107]

Like his attack upon Pastor Adler,[108] this attack remains extremely ambiguous. It was launched from a position within Christianity, a position which he represented throughout the attack as being true, even though he did so "without authority," as he never tires of declaring. Kierkegaard had already conceived this ambiguous attack in his inquisitorial polemic against Adler, in deliberate contrast to other, less offensive possible attacks, such as that of Feuerbach. "In the total sense," to be a critic like Feuerbach was "a bit stupid." Such angry men attack Christianity, "but they place themselves outside it, and for precisely that reason do no damage." "No, the angry man must see to it that he has a different plan of attack, that, like a mole, he may appear suddenly in the midst of Christianity. Assume that, instead of attacking Christianity, Feuerbach had gone about his business more cunningly; assume that he had made his plan in demonic silence, and had then appeared and proclaimed that he had received a revelation; and assume now that, as a criminal can stick to his lie, he had held to this unflinchingly, while at the same time cleverly spying out all the weakness of orthodoxy, which he was far from attacking, but rather sought only to hold up to the light with a certain candid naïveté; assume that he had done this so cleverly that no one had seen through his cunning: he would then have brought the most extreme embarrassment upon orthodoxy. In the interest of the existing order, orthodoxy fights to preserve the illusion that we are all Christians, that the land is Christian, and that our congregations are made up of Christians. A man takes up a position outside of Christianity and attacks it. If he were to win, the congregation would have to pull itself out of its comfortable routine, . . . would have to confront the decision to give up Christianity."[109] And—"however strange it may appear"—Kierkegaard recognized that he could participate in an impassioned rebellion against Christianity, but not in official compromise.[110] This evaluation of Feuerbach reflects the questionable nature of Kierkegaard's own attack, which admittedly did not invoke a personal revelation, but was deceitful in apparently attacking existing Christianity from without, while able to do so only because it had taken a position within Christianity, on the borderline between anger and apology.

Kierkegaard's own Christianity must be questioned on the basis of this attack upon existing Christianity. It is as ambiguous as the consideration of whether a man in pain should "take aspirin" or "have faith"![111] The phenomenon which led Kierkegaard to decide in favor of the Christian interpretation of suffering was his innate "melancholy," which he knew to be an "unhappy affliction," brought about by a disproportion between the "psychic and the somatic," which come into dialectical contact along a common border. "I have therefore asked my doctor whether this disproportion in my constitution between the physical and the psychic might be cured, so that I might realize the universal. He expressed his doubts. I asked him whether he thought that the spirit was capable of transforming or transfiguring such a basic misproportion through the will. He expressed his doubts. He would not even advise me to exert all my will power, of which he had some notion, since I might tear the whole asunder. From that very moment I made my choice. That sad disproportion, together with all the suffering it occasions, (which doubtless would have driven to suicide the majority of those who would have had spirit enough to comprehend all the misery of suffering), I have viewed as my thorn in the flesh, my limitation, my cross. . . . With this thorn in my foot, I leap higher than anyone whose feet are whole."[112] This relationship of tension between soul and body gave Kierkegaard's spirit the enormous power with which he transcended his own nature. His Christianity was an

escape from despair, "exactly as Christianity was a desperate expedient when it came into the world, and will forever remain such
for every individual who really accepts it."[113]

The extent to which Kierkegaard's "decision" was a problem to
him is shown by the following statement: "If my melancholy has
somehow led me astray, it must be in making me view as sin and
guilt what was perhaps only wretched suffering and temptation.
This is the most terrible of mistakes, the signal for maddening torture; but even if I have gone too far, it has served me in good
stead."[114] Nietzsche's criticism of Christianity began at precisely
this problematical point of choice and decision, with moralistic
Christian "value-interpretation" of suffering.

9   Nietzsche's Criticism of
Christian Morality and Civilization

According to Nietzsche, sin and guilt are not phenomena proper
to human existence as such; they are only what they signify. Their
only existence is in the consciousness of sin and guilt; their being is
a state of mind, and as such, an interpretation of being which can be
either true or erroneous. There exist various "causalities of suffering," dependent upon the conscious attitudes in which man is accustomed to view himself. The Christian interprets his suffering on
the basis of sin, that is, he searches for an intelligible basis for his
discomfort; "reasons make things easier," and "if a man knows the
why of his life, he can put up with any how." Following such an
explanation of suffering, Christianity has produced a world of sin
out of a world without any feelings of sin. It has made the "sick"
man a guilty "sinner." "The appearance of the Christian God . . .
has produced the maximum of guilt feelings upon earth. Assuming
that by now we are moving to the contrary direction, one might
conclude . . . from the irreversible decrease in faith in the Christion God that there were already a considerable decrease in human
consciousness of sin. Indeed, the conclusion is inescapable that the
complete and final victory of atheism should free mankind from all
these feelings of being guilty vis-à-vis their origin, their *causa prima*.
Atheism and a kind of second innocence go together."[115] Nietzsche
reverses once more the revaluation of the pagan world brought
about by Christianity, viewing the consciousness of sin as the "most
important event in the history of the sick soul" and the "most disas-

trous trick of religious interpretation." In contrast, he sought to recover the "innocence" of existence; his goal was once more to unite eccentric human existence with the natural cosmos of ever-recurring life, beyond good and evil. But the "Dionysian" view of life could be developed only in the polemic form of a criticism of Christianity, whose morality he declared to be "against nature." In order to give this criticism an historical foundation, he made the paradoxical attempt to recapture antiquity at the extremity of modernism. The anti-Christian purpose of his veneration of the Greeks is a consequence of his early study of classical philology; it is already implicit in the rough draft of *Wir Philologen*.

If the *Antichrist* is viewed in the context of Nietzsche's total development, it is far from being a primitive *skandalon;* still less is it a "rediscovery of primitive Christianity."[116] It is the culmination of a line of criticism which began with the *Unzeitgemässe Betrachtungen*. In this final attack, Nietzsche is much more deeply involved than in the earlier work because, in his isolation, he had worked himself further and further into a role in which he was forced to overextend himself.

Nietzsche's personal Christianity was shaped by his pietistic environment. In his informative studies on Nietzsche, E. Podach[117] has argued persuasively for the decisive influence exerted by Nietzsche's mother on his later attitude toward Christianity. The essays and poems written by Nietzsche as a young man show that from the very beginning his religiosity had something secondhand and forced about it. The Christianity which he first encountered within his family was too weak to do more than arouse antipathy and suspicion within him, a distrust which became intensified when directed later against Wagner's "Parzifal Christianity." It was the "homeopathy of Christianity," its modest "moralism," which he originally questioned and attacked. To him, Christianity was no longer an active faith, overcoming and yet ruling the world; it was only Christian civilization and morality. He formulated his criticism as a fivefold "No!" the second of which includes all the others: "My recognition and isolation of the traditional ideal, the Christian ideal, even where it has been degraded by the dogmatic form of Christianity. The danger of the Christian ideal rests in its sense of values, in what can do without abstract expression: my struggle against latent Christianity [e.g., in music, in socialism]."[118] He saw the Christian religion as an "ebbing tide" after an enormous innundation. "All the possibilities of Christian life, the most serious and the most idle, the

. . . most frivolous and the most considered, have been tried out. It is time to discover something new if we are not to go through the whole cycle once more: obviously it is difficult to escape the whirlpool once it has spun us around for a few thousand years. Even ridicule, cynicism, and enmity toward Christianity have lost their vitality. It is like an ice sheet during a thaw: everywhere the ice is broken, dirty, dull, full of puddles, treacherous. It seems to me that the only appropriate response is a careful, considered withdrawal: I honor religion thereby, though it is a dying religion. . . . Christianity will very shortly be ripe for a critical history, an autopsy."[119] To Nietzsche's mind, the "death of God" was a datum whose significance lay less in the fact itself than in its nihilistic consequences. The essential elements of his criticism of this Christianity without God are already contained in the introductory sentences of an essay written in 1862, which otherwise fits completely into the mold of the traditional humanization of the "essence" of Christianity.[120] The way in which Nietzsche's interest in Strauss manifested itself is also characteristic of his attitude toward Christianity. What attracts and occasions his criticism is not the Christianity of the church and of theology, but its secular metamorphoses, the "amusing mendacity" represented by primitive Christianity within the modern world: ". . . with melancholy caution I wander through the madhouse world of centuries, now called Christianity, the Christian faith, the Christian church—I hesitate to blame mankind for its psychoses. But my sentiment changes suddenly and breaks forth as soon as I come to the modern era, to our age. Our age knows. . . . What yesterday was merely sick, today is unseemly: it is unseemly today to be a Christian. Here my revulsion begins. I look about: there is not a hint left of what formerly was called 'truth,' we can no longer stand to hear the mouth of a priest even mention the word 'truth.' Anyone with even the least claim to integrity today must know that with every sentence a theologian, a priest, a pope speaks, he not only errs, he lies. It is no longer possible for him to lie 'innocently' or 'in ignorance.' . . . Everyone knows this; and yet everything stays the same. What has become of our last feelings of decency, of self-respect, when even our statesmen, otherwise a very unprejudiced sort and thoroughly anti-Christian, still call themselves Christians and go to communion? . . . *Whom* then does Christianity deny? *What* is meant by the 'world'? Being a soldier, a judge, a patriot; defending oneself; keeping one's word; seeking one's own advantage; being proud. . . . Every action of every moment, every instinct, every estimation which is acted upon today is anti-Christian. What a monster of perfidy modern man must be not to be ashamed of being called a Christian!"[121]

Like Feuerbach and Kierkegaard, Nietzsche attacked Hegel as the last great representative of this separation between our secular world and the Christian faith. Two things reach their culmination in him: the tendency toward a radical criticism of theology, which derives from Lessing, and at the same time the romantic desire to conserve it. Hegel was therefore the roadblock par excellence in the way of "straightforward atheism," "in accordance with the grandiose attempt which he made to persuade us of the divine nature of existence with the aid of our sixth sense, the 'sense of history.' "[122] In contrast to this roadblock in the way of straightforward atheism, Nietzsche considered his task to be "the production of a kind of crisis and ultimate decision in the problem of atheism."[123] He believed that the atheism of the future was prefigured in Schopenhauer's "pessimism." With increasing urgency and fullness of detail he developed it as the problem of the self-vanquishing of European "nihilism."

This tendency toward "absolutely honest" atheism also typifies Nietzsche's criticism of German philosophy as being half theology. Kant, Fichte, Schelling, Hegel, but also Feuerbach and Strauss, are all (according to Nietzsche) still "theologians," "priestlings," and "Church Fathers." "The Germans immediately understand what I mean when I say that philosophy has been contaminated by theological blood. The Protestant pastor is the grandfather of German philosophy, Protestantism its *peccatum originale*. . . . It is only necessary to say the words 'Tübingen School' to understand what German philosophy is at heart: insidious theology."[124]

The reverse side of Nietzsche's insight into the Protestantism of German philosophy was his quick eye for the philosophical atheism of Protestant theology. It had taken to itself the scientific atheism of philosophy, but only half way, so that it remained half theology and half philosophy. Thus the "decline of Protestantism": "theoretically and historically, it is not a whole. Because of the actual preponderance of Catholicism . . . Bismarck understood that Protestantism no longer works."[125] As children of Protestant preachers, says Nietzsche (describing himself also), too many German philosophers and scholars have heeded their fathers, "and consequently no longer believe in God," "and so German philosophy may be considered a perpetuation of Protestantism."

Nietzsche also viewed his own "immoralism" as a perpetuation of the Protestant tradition of Christianity; he, too, is a final fruit from the tree of Christian morality. "Of itself this tradition honestly compels a denial of morality"—the philosophical suicide of Christian morality is totally self-willed. First, in the Reformation, Christianity perished as Catholic dogma; now it is perishing as morality, and we stand at the threshold of this event. But one final question of veracity remains: "What is the meaning of all will to truth?"[126] For the present, the ultimate framework within which the question of truth can truly be asked is "absolutely honest atheism." "Everywhere else where the spirit today goes about its work rigorously, powerfully, and without counterfeiting it has no use for any ideal (the popular term for this abstinence is 'atheism'): the one exception is its will to truth. But this will, this remnant of idealism, is . . . the ideal itself in its most rigorous intellectual formulation, completely esoteric, bare of all decoration, not so much a remnant as a core. Thus absolutely honest atheism . . . is *not* opposed to this ideal . . . ; it is only one of the last phases of its development, one of its ultimate forms and internal consistencies; it is the awesome catastrophe of two thousand years of training for truth, which finally prohibits the lie of belief in God."[127] There can be no doubt: the growing self-consciousness of the will to truth is bringing the downfall of morality, "that great play in a hundred acts which is in store for the next two centuries of Europe, the most terrible, most dubious, and perhaps also the most promising of all plays. . . ."

In this breakdown of previously accepted values, man is forced into "unexplored" and "undiscovered" territory, no longer possessed of any land where he can be at home. Our apparent civilization has no permanence, because it is erected upon conditions and conceptions which have already almost vanished. "How could we be at home in this today! We are ill-disposed toward all ideals which might furnish a home . . . even in this delicate time of transition; as far as their 'realities' are concerned, we expect no permanence of them. The ice which still bears our weight today is already very thin: the south wind is blowing, we ourselves, we homeless ones, assist in breaking the ice and other all too thin 'realities'. . . . We 'conserve' nothing, neither do we seek to return to any past, we are not at all 'liberal,' we do not work for 'progress,' we do not even need to stop our ears against the economic sirens of the future. . . . We modern men are too motley a bunch by race and descent, and are therefore little subject to the temptation . . . to participate in

mendacious glorification of our own race. . . . In a word, we are
. . . good Europeans, the . . . overabundant and overobligated
heirs of thousands of years of the European spirit: as such, we have
also outgrown Christianity. . . ."[128]

How little Nietzsche had outgrown Christianity is shown not
only by his *Antichrist*, but also by its counterpart: the theory of
eternal recurrence. It is an avowed substitute for religion; no less
than Kierkegaard's Christian paradox, it is an escape from despair:
an attempt to leave "nothing" and arrive at "something."[129]

10　Lagarde's Political Criticism of Ecclesiastical Christianity

Contemporaneously with Nietzsche, Lagarde and Overbeck
were carrying on a criticism of Christianity which was less striking
but no less penetrating: Lagarde, with an eye to politics; and Overbeck, with reference to theology.

In 1873, Nietzsche's first *Unzeitgemässe Betrachtung* appeared.
In the same year, Lagarde published his theologicopolitical pamphlet
*Über das Verhältnis des deutschen Staates zu Theologie, Kirche
und Religion;* its outline dates back to 1859. Like all of Lagarde's
Deutsche Schriften, this treatise is distinguished by its penetration
into the internal connection between theology and politics. His
rejection of existing Christianity is as scholarly as it is absolute; its
radicalism surpasses that of Strauss, whose study of the life of Jesus
(the product of an "honorable demand for knowledge") was expressly recognized by Lagarde.[130]

Lagarde's criticism denies that either of the branches of Christendom possess any portion whatever of evangelical Christianity. But
it is directed primarily against German Protestantism, whose historical instability is grounded on its very nature as a mere reformation of Catholic dogma. "All the statements made by Catholic dogma
about God, Christ, and the Holy Spirit, that is, everything that is
most repugnant to the modern mind, remained untouched by the
Reformation. The quarrel between the Protestants and the Church
concerned solely the way in which the salvation of the human race
from sin and its consequences, . . . which had been accomplished
in Jesus Christ, could be appropriated, and certain institutions which
rendered more difficult the appropriation of this salvation in the
way the Reformers considered correct, and which the Protestant

side therefore felt compelled to do away with."[131] Even the "conscience" claimed by Protestantism has meaning only within the context of the historical situation of the Catholic Church. Luther's attack on particular points presupposes the existence of the whole. When Protestantism finally was given complete recognition at the Peace of Westphalia in 1648, it lost the last remnants of its inner strength, which it had possessed only by virtue of its opposition to the dominant Church: "it was given solemn permission to live, thereby losing its last pretext for life." What today is called "Protestantism" is neither evangelical nor reforming; it is merely a faded remnant.[132] The "liberation" which it is popularly supposed to have produced is not a product of its excellence, but of its internal "solubility." On the other hand, the process of decomposition to which it fell prey resulted in the liberation of Protestant Germany from all the obstacles in the way of its natural development, which were contained in the Catholic system and those portions of it preserved by Protestantism. The political reshaping of Germany was not a consequence of the Reformation. It is ascribable solely to the circumstance that in Brandenburg and Prussia the Hohenzollern set up a State which could stand on its own feet, whose "exigent existence"—"its need somehow to exist"—of necessity went beyond its own borders.[133] By the same token, our classicists are not in the least Protestant, if we mean thereby the doctrines of the Reformation.[134] A high priority attaches to the abolition of the Protestant clergy, because they have no sense for what is "spiritual"—Nietzsche says, for what is "holy." The clergy are merely a "theologically tinged projection of political velleities." By the abolition of celibacy and the denial of the priesthood, Protestantism made it impossible for sensitive souls and the sons of good families to become clergy and live in service of the Church.[135]

The basic trouble with the Church is that it accepted for itself the basic principle of Judaism:[136] it took as the goal of its religious life something that had already taken place in the past instead of something which continues to take place in the present. In its more primitive form, the Church "with an admirably correct instinct" rectified this evil through the sacrifice of the Mass, in which the historical fact is continually repeated. "The sacrifice of the Mass is the strength of Catholicism. The Mass alone makes Christianity (I do not say, 'the Gospel') a religion; and only a religion, not a surrogate for religion, can absorb the human heart. The eternal spirit of man is not content with something that has taken place. Immersion in the past is not religion but sentimentality. Consciousness of the immanent temporal life of eternal forms vanishes as the memory, growing every year weaker, of primeval unrepeated events is exalted to the status of a religion. Our religion then becomes an opinion, a judgment, a belief, an idea, rather than a way of life; until we give up this deadly point of view, no improvement in our condition is possible. We need the presence of God and the divine, not their past. Therefore Christianity is no longer a live option for us: neither Protestantism, nor, because of the unacceptability of its doctrine of the Mass, Catholicism, can provide this presence for us."[137] Both Churches are a distortion of the Gospel. Vis-à-vis the state, all the religious communities of today are at the point of death. "The sooner they are let alone, the sooner they will die out; for their life, of whatever sort, is artificial, preserved only by the attention devoted to them and their own mutual antagonism."[138] In a later treatise, written in 1878, Lagarde prophesied that the future would show that all of Protestant history after the Reformation is not a development of Christianity, but rather an attempt to create something new, "to the extent that it was not based, on the one hand, on the universal principle of inertia and decay, or, on the other, upon the nationalistic drive of the Germanic peoples, freed from the oppression of the Roman Church." Protestantism is no more primitive Christianity than is Jesuitism. The future course of both is clear. "Jesuitism must seek to remake the Church whose business it conducts, and which has been destroyed by German nationalism, into a universal Catholic Church rather than a Roman Catholic Church. . . . The Germanic peoples, on the other hand, must relate religion to their nationalism: for Protestantism has become what it is only through the Germanic temperament of those who joined it, and hostility to Rome is the natural position of those who fight, not as Christians, but as Germans. Universal religion in the singular and national religions in the plural, those are the programs of the two opponents."[139]

Lagarde supplements his historical criticism of the Christian Churches and their theology with his outline of a "religion of the future." The movement which is called upon to form a national religion has a twofold task. It is to utilize the ethical and religious views of Christianity, in particular of the Catholic Church, and to make use of the "national idiosyncracies of the German people." In order to make the dogmas of the Church "religiously practical," they must be purified of all "Jewish poison." On the other hand, the dogmas contained in the fluid form of the sacraments must be retained, because in the sacraments divine power mysteriously effects salvation under the veil of earthly things.[140] But thought will have to be taken for a corporeal locus for the sacraments, within which they can work effectively. This body, says Lagarde, will come into being of its own accord if the spirit is not prevented from doing its work. Temporarily, the important thing is to prepare the way by removing obstacles.

He gives more definite expression to the negative side of the "Germanic temperament" which is to be realized in the national church of the future. It is essentially anti-Jewish, but not anti-Christian, so long as the pure Gospel is taken as the doctrine of Christ. Pure Germanicism cannot be found among the educated classes of the present day. The Germany which is officially recognized is as un-German as the classical literature taught in the schools, which is either cosmopolitan or modeled on Greek or Roman examples. In contrast to Hegel's scholastic education, Germany is characterized truly by Grimm's German mythology, independence of spirit, love for solitude, and the uniqueness of the individual. "Whoever knows the signature of the new German Empire, will know when he reads this, with tears in his eyes, how German this Empire is."[141] What is "good" is not a German concept, but rather what is "genuine." But who can penetrate the profusion of civilization to reach the primitive level, since the life of the individual is more and more under the control of bureaucracy, and despotism masquerades as freedom?

The Germany which Lagarde longed to see "has never existed," it is an ideal both vain and powerful. If it is to be approached, all illusions must be destroyed, all "Judeo-Celtic theorems" about Germany must be left behind. "The indispensable conditions for the existence of religion are honesty and veracity. If, therefore, Germany is to have a religion, all the alien rags in which Germany is wrapped must be put aside. They have done even more than individual self-deception to make Germany a liar to its own inmost soul. Palestine and Belgium, 1518 and 1789 and 1848 simply do not concern us. We have finally become strong enough to hold the door of the house against aliens; let us also discard everything alien which we have within the house. When that has been done, the real work can begin."[142] But this work demands an "heroic deed, in the age of paper money, stock-market manipulation, party-controlled newspapers, and universal education." And the question is whether it is still possible in 1878 to carry out what . . . should have been done in 878!

Lagarde describes the religion of the future as German "piety." As a "guide" for it, he calls for another kind of theology besides the one which already exists, a theology which will deal with the universal history of religion. "It will provide an understanding of religion as it gives a history of religions."[143] Its goal is to discover a national religion, which can be neither Catholic nor Protestant, but exclusively German: "a life of intimate relationship with the almighty creator and redeemer, majestic dominion over everything not divine." "We should not be humans, but children of God; not liberal, but free; not conservative, but German; not credulous, but devout; not Christians, but evangelicals; the divine, living incarnate in each of us, and all of us united in one growing circle."[144] This national German religion corresponds to the "divinely willed essence of the German nation."

In its own time, Lagarde's criticism of Christianity had only a small sphere of influence. It subsequently became operative in the religious program of the Third Reich, which likewise sought to erase a thousand years of German history and reduce Christianity to a specifically German "piety."

11 Overbeck's Historical Analysis of Primitive and Passing Christianity

Because of his connection with the historical criticism of F. C. Baur, Overbeck counted himself a member of the "Tübingen School," although only "allegorically." With regard to the course of development of German criticism of religion from Hegel to Nietzsche, the following attitudes can be isolated from his works: toward Nietzsche, whose first *Unzeitgemässe Betrachtung* appeared at the same time as Overbeck's *Christlichkeit der Theologie* (1873), toward Lagarde and Strauss, toward B. Bauer and Kierkegaard, and, indirectly, toward Hegel.

The first chapter of *Die Christlichkeit der Theologie* discusses the general relationship between theology and Christianity. In contrast to Hegel, it attempts to show that not only modern theology, but the science of theology from the very beginning, has been opposed to the primitive meaning of the Christian faith. Primitive Christianity was a faithful expectation of the end of the world and the return of Christ. As such, it had an "unambiguous antipathy" toward all scientific knowledge; this antagonism between faith and knowledge cannot be reconciled after the manner of Hegel, it is "absolutely irreconcilable." "Thus all theological activity, to the extent that it brings faith and knowledge into contact, is irreligious; no theology can ever arise unless there are other interests present besides the religious."[145] The destiny of Christianity certainly gives no occasion to conceive any more conciliatory relationship between faith and knowledge. A religion which lived in expectation of the *Parousia*, so long as it remained true to itself, could not seek to develop a systematic theology and a church. The fact that this took place so rapidly is based not in Christianity itself, but in its emergence into the world of pagan culture, which it was unable to destroy and in which it therefore sought support, although until the time of the Reformation it never lost sight of its enmity toward the world and the state.

The battle between faith and knowledge was fought in the very infancy of Christianity, when Gnosticism destroyed all the assumptions of the infant faith, and transformed it into a metaphysics. But the defeat of Gnosticism meant only a new covenant with the worldly wisdom represented most powerfully by Alexandrianism. "The simple faith in redemption through Christ might have withdrawn within itself all the more energetically; instead, a Christian theology was set up as true Gnosis beside the Gnosis . . . which had been declared false. In this theology, particularly through the newly determined Christian Canon, at least a certain portion of the Christian tradition was protected by faith against the attacks of knowledge; but it was considered imperative to rise from the level of faith to that of knowledge. A sure proof of the antagonism between knowledge and the purely religious interests of faith is the fact that even in this moderate form scientific knowledge gained a foothold in the Church only by force. It secured its position only under the keenest scrutiny, and was always in danger of coming under accusation each time heresy reared its head. In fact, it remained the hotbed of unceasing conflicts with the faith of the community. The very beginning is typical of the whole course of development, as represented at the turn of the third century first by Clement of Alexandria and then by Origen."[146] The original contrast between the Christian faith and theological knowledge later became clear with the vanishing of the illusion that dominated the Middle Ages, that theology is the positive apologetic aspect of the

Christian faith. From the moment that Protestant theology borrowed the methods of historical and philosophical criticism from the
secular sciences, theology was doomed to become the grave digger
of Christianity. Whoever engages in theology for any purpose beyond that of theology itself must recognize that it is "part and
parcel of the secularization of Christianity, a luxury which it allows
itself but which, like all luxuries, can be had only for a price."[147] The
only real task of theology is to make Christianity problematical as a
religion, whether the theology is critical or apologetic and liberal.
Critical and historical study can indeed destroy religion, but not
reconstruct it. Nothing was further from Overbeck's mind than
Hegel's "exaltation" of the Christian religion to the level of conceptual existence. His basic distinction between the history of the
"origin" of Christianity and the history of its "decay" means that,
with reference to the "development" of Christianity, Overbeck is
unalterably opposed to Hegel's progressive and optimistic schema.
To him, as to Lagarde, Protestantism does not mean the consummation of Christianity, but the beginning of its dissolution. The productivity of the Christian church comes to an end with the
Reformation, which has in itself no religious meaning, but is defined
totally in terms of protest against the Catholic Church. It is an "absurd" consequence of disdain for the otherworldly nature of Christianity to conclude that the first fifteen hundred years of the Christian faith are a disguising of its real nature.[148] But this is precisely the
conclusion of Hegel's schema, which sees Christianity as engaged in
a progressive "realization," that is, secularization. In Overbeck's
opinion, Pascal was the last real Christian in the modern world; he
assigns Luther to the same category as Nietzsche and Denifle.

Overbeck's attitude toward those like Vinet, Lagarde, and
Kierkegaard, who turn against the existing order in the name of
Christianity, is as negative as his attitude toward Hegel. By denying
theology the right to speak for Christianity, he denied himself the
same right. "Thus I confront the situation quite differently than, for
example, does Kierkegaard, who attacked Christianity although he
spoke for it. I refuse to attack it even though I myself stand aside
and speak as a theologian, even though that is just what I would
rather not be. Kierkegaard speaks under the paradoxical pretense of
being a reformer of Christianity; I would not consider doing so, but
neither would I consider reforming theology, which I claim as my
vocation. I acknowledge its worthlessness in itself, and am not inclined to deny its present state of dilapidation; I am opposed to its

basic principles. For the moment, I would have no reservations about letting Christianity completely alone."[149] He recognized the "vulnerable spot" in Kierkegaard's attitude toward Christianity: "The manner of his attack is insincere, rhetorical, and paradoxical"; "he merely affects the disguise of an assailant." "It appears as though Kierkegaard were relying solely on himself and letting fly his attack upon Christianity, but he does so only after he has taken up a firm position within Christianity. He has no excuse for attacking Christianity; in a sense, even less excuse than those whom he attacks. An inferior representative of Christianity is always better qualified to criticize it than one who is irreproachable, even if only in his own eyes."[150]

Overbeck's attitude toward B. Bauer can be seen in his review of Bauer's *Christus und die Cäsaren*.[151] In four long sections he analyzes the "incredible" theories which Bauer has once more, after thirty-five years, laid before the public without the slightest qualification. This represents a steadfastness which would be impressive if total lack of scientific support did not make it untenable. He concludes by stating that despite all criticism of Bauer's thesis that Christianity and Stoicism derived from one and the same source, Bauer's position is "not far from the truth." The total failure of his work is therefore all the more regrettable. The extent to which Greco-Roman paganism contributed to the growth of the Church has been greatly underestimated; "a goodly number of paradoxes" are necessary to untangle the early history of the Church. These paradoxes must be put forward; but they must be given a form which makes it possible gradually to reach the point of well-founded conviction, instead of remaining at the stage of mere extravagance. Apart from these reservations, theologians should not be "dissuaded" from reading the book. It is an arbitrary assemblage of material that Bauer has given us, but it is nevertheless material which should give us frequent occasion for fruitful reflection. The parallelism between Stoicism and Christianity can be pursued a thousand times more productively, more sensitively, and more profoundly than Bauer has done. This would give rise to observations and problems of which Bauer had not the slightest hint.

When these critical remarks are compared with Overbeck's own thoughts on the relationship between Christianity and the ancient world, more weight is given to the basically favorable conclusion of this criticism, so severe in detail. Overbeck himself never ceased to stress the "classical" nature of Christianity, denying that it was an absolute "innovation." He contrasted both the ancient world and Christianity to the modern world.[152] He asserted indirectly the "family relationship" between Christianity and the ancient world through the thesis that our understanding of Christianity has diminished proportionately as the ancient world has vanished from our lives.[153] In *Die Christlichkeit der Theologie*, he states that Christianity is the form in which the ancient world has been embalmed for preservation down to our own time. Because Christianity is itself a part of the ancient world, a "modern" Christianity is a contradiction in terms. The ties connecting Overbeck's theological position with Bauer's are even closer than he himself realized. It was Bauer who had anticipated Overbeck's discovery of the necessary "Jesuitism" of the "theological mind,"[154] the antithesis between the Bible and contemporary culture.

Overbeck several times defended the critical theology of Strauss against the presumptions and illusions of apologetic and liberal theology. Strauss's declaration that secular culture and Christianity are irreconcilable is irrefutable. It does not depend on the apparent cosmopolitanism and actual parochialism of the culture which Strauss in his old age supported as the "new faith." Strauss was also right in his recognition of the fateful significance inherent in the idea of a "life of Jesus." But it is erroneous to suppose that a truly critical theology must lead to a negation of Christianity. Without supporting Christianity, such a theology can protect it "against all the theologies which think they are supporting it by accommodating it to the world. Indifferent to its peculiar point of view, they turn it into a dead, desiccated orthodoxy which removes it from the world, or reduce it to the secular level, where it vanishes. Critical theology can prevent such theologies from peddling an unreal thing to the world under the name of Christianity, a thing from which the very soul has been removed: the negation of the world."[155] Strauss fails to recognize the excessive humanity of Christianity. He seeks to put Christianity completely out of mind; with all his talk of "human feeling," "national feeling," and "littleness," he forgets "that we are human"![156] If we compare what Strauss has to say about the state and about war, about penal authority and about the working class, with the appropriate Christian parallels, for example, from Augustine, there is no doubt that we shall find the latter incomparably more profound and at the same time more human, and therefore more true. Christianity has dealt conclusively with the kind of culture represented by Strauss. If Christianity is to be overcome, it must be by a culture higher, not lower, than that which Christianity overcame. In a few sober sentences, this criticism of Strauss's *Bekenntnis* says everything that Nietzsche in his *Unzeitgemässe Betrachtung* said with the exuberance of youth, and without a fair assessment of Strauss's historical achievement.

Through his early work, Strauss did the science of theology a considerable service. But it is wrong to suppose that Christianity consists of a series of dogmas and myths which must be either accepted or rejected, in whole or in part. Its heart and soul is faith in Christ and his return, and the end of the world as it now exists. "As is true of the apologetic and liberal theologians whom we have studied in this respect, Strauss thinks that he has finished with Christianity when he has destroyed critically a series of its basic dogmas, particularly the Church's conception of its early history. But he skims over the ascetic outlook of Christianity with two or three disparaging and very marginal remarks."[157] Christianity is by nature eschatological, and therefore ascetic. Only the man who is well aware of this can achieve a proper standpoint from which to evaluate the "way of life" which Strauss suggests after Christianity has been done away with.

Overbeck took issue with Lagarde's work as soon as it was published. Both possess the same disinterested scholarly attitude. That of Lagarde is permeated by a desire for rhetorical effect, while Overbeck is characterized by a calm sobriety that is almost superhuman. He neither wanted to nor could educate the Germans; but he wanted to be clear in his own mind with reference to theology and Christianity.

Overbeck discusses Lagarde's suggestion that the existing theological faculties be reduced to denominational seminaries, and be replaced at the universities by a theology whose task is to teach the history of religion in order to prepare the way for a German religion. Overbeck objects that such a purely historical view of the history of religions is not a theology at all, and should therefore fall within the discipline of philosophy. If Lagarde wants his new theology to occupy an independent position, he can support it only on the basis of its practical task, which it shares with denominational theology. "But this is just what is dubious: whether a task of this kind can really be found for Lagarde's theology. He himself points to one by saying that the new theology should be the 'guide leading to a German religion.' But theologies have always followed after their religions; and they have been further behind, the more energetic and undisputed were the original forces behind these religions. It is unexampled that they should precede a religion, and hardly to be expected that something of the sort might yet take place."[158] In reality, Lagarde's theology will not prepare the way for a new religion. The hopelessness of its ultimate goal and the overwhelming power of history in all scholarly pursuits of the present will cause it very rapidly to lose sight of its goal and immerse itself in the historical material—a prediction which has proven true for all denominational theology wherever the content of what has been called "dogmatics" has in fact been only comparative religion with a Protestant flavor.

Thirty years after writing *Die Christlichkeit der Theologie*, in the preface to the second edition, Overbeck discusses his relationship to Nietzsche. He says there that Nietzsche's influence was the most powerful he had encountered in the course of his life. Nietzsche himself is an "extraordinary man, extraordinary even in bearing misfortune." There is no better proof of Nietzsche's extraordinary quality than the friendship of so circumspect and reserved a man as Overbeck. Overbeck states that he cannot actually say that even in Basel he learned "wisdom" from Nietzsche; neither can he say that he, who was seven years older, followed him unconditionally on his "voyage of exploration," letting himself be deflected from his own course. But his friendship toward Nietzsche was very much present when he penned his "abdication from the fraternity of theologians." This parallels Nietzsche's dedication of his first *Unzeitgemässe Betrachtung* to Overbeck. Even in later years, Overbeck followed Nietzsche's voyage of exploration to the end with loyal attentiveness, unperturbed by the aspects of it that must have been terrifying and even repugnant to him. His posthumous notes and his correspondence with Nietzsche bear witness to the fact that, if he did not join in Nietzsche's attack upon Christianity, he at least went along with it in his own way, by furnishing his friend with occasional scholarly references for the criticism of Christianity. Nietzsche's attempt to "overcome God and nihilism" failed; but Overbeck never recognized this fact as an argument against the attempt. Despair had seized Nietzsche on his journey, so that he deserted his ship. This happened long before his madness erupted. "No one has ever arrived at the goal of voyage that I have in mind; Nietzsche's failure was no greater than that of all the rest. What forsook him was fortune, which has smiled more favorably upon others I know, who have been more fortunate. He failed; but his failure was such that he is

no better and no worse an argument against the voyage he undertook than are castaways against sailing the sea. A man who has
reached his haven will be the last to deny his shipwrecked precursor
the name of an equal. With reference to Nietzsche, the same is true
of the more fortunate seafarers, who at least have managed to stay
afloat in their craft on their aimless journey."[159]

The question Overbeck asked with reference to Christianity
did not concern Christian "morality." Unlike Nietzsche, he saw its
ascetic character as a superior form of human life. His question concerned the relationship between primitive Christianity, which renounced the world, and the history of the world. The most interesting aspect of Christianity is its impotence, "the fact that it cannot
rule the world" because the wisdom of its life is a "wisdom of
death."[160] If a serious historical study is made of Christianity, the
only conclusion can be that it has undergone a "decline" from its
"nonhistorical" origin, although the decline is inextricably entangled
with "progress" throughout the course of history. Like transitoriness, permanence is a basic concept of all historiography; similarly,
all historical manifestation of life must be either old or young. In
spite of Kierkegaard's demand for "contemporaneity," two thousand years of Christianity cannot simply be erased, least of all by a
theology which is itself completely penetrated by the historical
mode of thought. "Christianity has had a long life. It can no longer
occupy the same position it occupied at the beginning, after all the
events that then lay before it, and now lie behind it!"[161] Christianity
existed originally as Gospel, denying all history and presupposing
an "hyperhistorical" world—"neither Christ himself nor the faith
which he founded have had historical existence under the name of
Christianity"[162]—but this "prehistoric embryo" has lived its life in
the history of a church, which is bound to the world. The world
would not be convinced that God loves man.[163] "When it lost its
faith in the *Parousia*, primitive Christianity lost its faith in its own
youth." This contrast between the eschatology of primitive Christianity and the future-oriented mood of the present is fundamental.
"It is, perhaps, the basic reason behind the gulf separating Christianity from the present." Our present age works to prepare the
future; nothing is further removed from it than belief in an imminent
end of the world. Now that Christianity has grown old in the sense
of becoming decrepit, its age is no longer an argument for its permanence, but only its most dubious aspect.[164] The "eternal" existence
of Christianity can be defended only *sub specie aeternitatis*, that is,

from a point of view which has no concept of historical time. The eternity of Christianity can never be guaranteed by history. Purely historically, all we have is proof that Christianity is worn out.[165] To the serious historical viewpoint, its age is a "deadly" argument. Christianity cannot control the course of history, which everywhere reaches out to its limits. Therefore history is an "abyss in which Christianity has been catapulted quite against its will."[166] Before the time of Constantine, it seemed "as though Christianity would outlast civilization; today the converse is true." "Prometheus seems to have been proven right; the fire that he stole from heaven is not what he was supposed to have been given."[167]

The final conclusion of Overbeck's historical viewpoint is his contesting of the Christian chronology. His denial of its significance puts him in opposition to Hegel, who was the last person to maintain it seriously. But it does not place him on the side of Nietzsche, whose *Ecce Homo* claimed to begin the "first day of the year One" with September 30, 1888, "according to the false chronology."[168] According to Overbeck, the Christian chronology would have been justified only if Christianity had introduced a "new" age. But this is not the case; "for originally it spoke of a new age only under circumstances that never took place: the existing world must perish and yield to the new. For a moment, this was seriously expected; this expectation has continued to make its appearance, but only fleetingly. It has never become a permanent historical fact. This alone would have been able to furnish the real basis for a significant chronology, corresponding to the facts of reality. It is the world that has prevailed, not the Christian expectation."[169] The possibility of conceiving this moment as a turning point grew out of the earlier existence of an eschatological expectation of the end. This alone gives the Christian chronology a claim to be taken seriously. But in actual fact the old has not passed away, the new has not arrived; it remains one of the major problems of the history of Christianity how it came to terms with this disappointment of its original expectation. Overbeck attempts to answer this question by transforming the primitive Christian expectation of the return of Christ into an "ascetic theory and practice of life," "which is in fact a metamorphosis of the primitive Christian faith in the return of Christ. It is based upon the continued expectation of this return, and therefore continues to view the world as ripe for destruction. It moves the faithful to withdraw from the world in order to be ready for the appearance of Christ, which threatens to come at any moment. The expectation of Christ's return became untenable in its primitive form. . . . It was transformed into the idea of death, which as early as Irenaeus, is said always to accompany the Christian. It became the *memento mori*, the Carthusian formula which gives a more profound summation of the ultimate wisdom of Christianity than does the modern formula, 'let nothing intrude between man and his primary source.' This seems to contain a hackneyed expression . . . of negation, until one remembers that, in the eyes of Christianity, it is the world itself which 'intrudes.' "[170]

When Christianity was granted official recognition by the state, the ideal of martyrdom was lost. It was replaced by the *martyrium quotidianum* of monasticism. From the fourth century to the Reformation, everything great and vital in the Church proceeded from the cloister. But Catholic theology long ago lost the pureness of vision necessary for a proper evaluation of the significance of monasticism; Protestant theology never had it.

The inner nucleus of Overbeck's own theological existence is a conduct of life and wisdom of death which are ascetic in a broader sense. The ultimate purpose of his theology was to demonstrate scientifically that modern Christianity was the "finis Christianismi."[171] For him, too, the wisdom of death replaced the expectation of the future. For us men, death is the most vexing of riddles, but far from being the key to its own solution. "Precisely because death makes the riddles of the world most vexing to us, it should be the last thing in the world to serve to make life difficult for us. Let us rather respect death as the most unambiguous symbol of our community, in the silence which he inescapably imposes upon us all as our common lot."[172] To the Christian view of death he preferred that of Montaigne and Spinoza, because it is less affected. A *memento mori* can easily be conceived which would benefit life by the light of day by its ability to banish deception and disperse the shadows which lie upon life and distort it. But death, chosen by one's own free will, seemed to him to lie at the limit of "what can be discussed rationally among men." Overbeck did not reject it. His reflections may sound un-Christian, but when he was concerned with having the proper attitude in thinking about death, the first thing that occurred to him was a reference to the resignation of the Thirty-ninth Psalm.

Overbeck did not decide against Christianity or in favor of secular education or "culture."[173] Any man who esteems the Either-Or for its own sake, confusing what is radical with what is extreme, will achieve only uncertainty in his attitude toward the world and toward Christianity. And within this apparent external ambiguity there lies hidden a more unequivocal radicalism than in Nietzsche's dogmatic attack. Nietzsche's antagonism can be reversed, just as Dionysus can become the Crucified. Overbeck was fully aware that religious problems must be placed upon a completely new foundation, "even at the cost of what has up to now been called religion."[174] "The religious development of man down to the present day represents a disastrous aberration; it must be brought to an end" —"at least so long as the solution to the religious confusion of our time is sought in the area of the Bible and the theological conflict which rages about the Bible, and we do not make up our minds to find that solution completely apart from the Bible! This will not happen until we humans recognize that we go forward only by losing our foothold from time to time; we live our lives under conditions which do not permit us to evade this experiment. Furthermore, the Bible itself should help us to see this. Its own narrative provides us with the supreme example of this phenomenon. The transition from the Old Testament to the New does not differ from such a loss of foothold. Its success was complete, but correspondingly slow and laborious."[175] This loss of foothold Overbeck took as his own position between culture and Christianity. To perform his function he lacked the necessary criticism of theology and Christianity, "the spur of a genuine hatred for Christians or religion"; but he also lacked the absolute affirmation of the secular world which makes the atheism of Strauss, Feuerbach, and Bauer so superficial. This twofold lack is Overbeck's human and scholarly advantage; it distinguishes him from all the other assailants and apologists, like Nietzsche and Kierkegaard. His "caution" with regard to Christianity consisted in avoiding the "twofold danger" of a sterile routine relationship or an unconsidered battle of extermination. "Either course must be avoided. Christianity must be given an end more worthy and less pernicious."[176] He numbered himself among the unbelievers by subordinating theology to philosophy and disputing its right to be called Christian. But he was conscious that the courage and tenacity to do so grow best out of a view of life such as that of Christianity, which increased the demand for honesty "probably at least as much as it reduced its actual appearance among men."[177] Even in his early writings he rejected the overhasty ruthlessness with which Strauss broke the fetters of the old faith, the more so because the present gave no cause to think poorly of the Christian view of life or to consider itself superior. It is rather of inestimable value "that at least the name of 'Christian' hover over this whole calamitous period as a kind of categorical imperative, condemning it."[178]

And so it is comprehensible that Overbeck's judgment upon Christianity, particularly German Christianity,[179] which condemned it to death, expressed neither satisfaction nor regret; it simply described the process as a matter of record.[180] His historical position is based on the fact that without Christianity, European civilization would not be what it is, nor would Christianity, without its connection with that civilization.[181] Overbeck belongs more, not less, to the history of their union and conflict than do those who think to solve the problem of Christianity by means of a simple "decision." The truly decisive contrast to their mere decisiveness is a critical analysis which gives neither a simple "yes" nor a simple "no." "The unique and significant aspect of Overbeck's elucidation of the relationship between Christianity and culture is the fact that it does not give any solution. All solutions would come into conflict with his basic axiom. Overbeck's merit consists in having demonstrated the impossibility of any solution, at least of any solution which man as he is today could contrive by his own efforts."[182] Even his admiration for Nietzsche was not based on the latter's apodictic statements, but on the way in which he preserved his "courage to face the problem," an attitude inconceivable apart from the "skepticism" which goes hand in hand with historical knowledge.[183] On the other hand, Nietzsche prized Overbeck's "gentle firmness" and balance.

Whoever will take the trouble to pursue Overbeck's train of thought will perceive in the labyrinth of his sentences, so full of reservations, the straight and daring line of an absolutely honest mind. He elucidated the problem which Christianity presents for us. In the typical figures of the nineteenth century, he made clear the abyss separating us from Christianity.[184] Since Hegel, and particularly through the work of Marx and Kierkegaard, the Christianity of this bourgeois-Christian world has come to an end. This does not mean that a faith which once conquered the world perishes with its last secular manifestations. For how should the Christian pilgrimage *in hoc saeculo* ever become homeless in the land where it has never been at home?

Bibliography

The following articles by the author are partially based on the same material as this book:

"Feuerbach und der Ausgang der klassischen deutschen Philosophie," *Logos* No. 3 (1928).
"Max Weber und Karl Marx," *Archiv für Sozialwissenschaft und Sozialpolitik*, Nos. 1–2 (1932).
"Kierkegaard und Nietzsche," *Deutsche Vierteljahrsschrift für Literaturwissenschaft und Geistesgeschichte*, No. 1 (1933).
"Die philosophische Kritik der christlichen Religion im 19. Jahrhundert," *Theologische Rundschau*, Nos. 3–4 (1933).
"L'achèvement de la philosophie classique par Hegel et sa dissolution chez Marx et Kierkegaard," *Recherches Philosophiques* (Paris, 1934–35; 1935–36).
"Zur Problematik der Humanität in der Philosophie nach Hegel." *Festschrift für F. Toennies (Reine und angewandte Soziologie)*. Leipzig, 1936.

Recent events caused the author to emigrate, making impossible a complete cognizance of the relevant literature. Most of the works of the Young Hegelians were never republished after their first appearance, and so for the most part the author had to restrict himself to those books and periodicals from the forties which he had already assembled and excerpted during his period as private lecturer at Marburg. Special thanks for the procuring of important works is due to Professor K. Ishiwara and Professor S. Takahashi, of the Imperial Tohoku University in Sendai.

TRANSLATOR'S NOTE   All quotations appearing in this book are the translator's renderings of the author's quotations, which were themselves taken from the following editions:

Collections

FEUERBACH, L. *Sämtliche Werke*. Vols. I–X. Leipzig, 1846, etc.
GOETHE, J. W. VON. Cotta Edition. 40 vols. 1840.

———. *Gespräche.* Edited by Biedermann. 5 vols. Leipzig; 2nd edition, 1909.

———. *Maximen und Reflexionen.* Edited by M. Hecker. Weimar, 1907.

HEGEL, G. W. F. Original edition, unless otherwise specified.

KIERKEGAARD, S. *Werke.* Vols. I–XII. Jena, 1909, etc.

MARX, K. *Marx-Engels Gesamtausgabe.* Part I. Vols. I–V. 1927–1932.

NIETZSCHE, F. W. *Werke.* 16 vols. Large and small 8°.

Individual Works

BAUER, B. *Das entdeckte Christentum, eine Erinnerung an das 18. Jahrhundert und ein Beitrag zur Krisis des 19.* Zurich, 1843. New edition by E. Barnikol. Jena, 1927.

———. *Die Posaune des jüngsten Gerichts über Hegel den Atheisten und Antichristen. Ein Ultimatum.* (Anonymous.) Leipzig, 1841.

———. *Vollständige Geschichte der Parteikämpfe in Deutschland während der Jahre 1842-46.* Vols. I–III. Charlottenburg, 1847.

BAUER, B., and E. BAUER. *Briefwechsel 1839-42.* Charlottenburg, 1844.

BAUER, B., and A. RUGE. *Hegels Lehre von der Religion und Kunst, vom Standpunkt des Glaubens aus beurteilt.* (Anonymous.) Leipzig, 1842.

ENGELS, F. *Feuerbach und der Ausgang der klassischen deutschen Philosophie.* Stuttgart; 5th edition, 1910.

FEUERBACH, L. *Ausgewählte Briefe von und an L. Feuerbach.* Edited by W. Bolin. 2 parts. Leipzig, 1904.

———. *Briefwechsel und Nachlass.* Edited by K. Grün. 2 parts. Heidelberg, 1874. (Abbreviated in Notes *Br.*)

———. *Briefwechsel zwischen L. Feuerbach und Ch. Kapp 1832-1848.* Edited by A. Kapp. Leipzig, 1876.

———. *Grundsätze der Philosophie der Zukunft.* Edited by H. Ehrenberg. Stuttgart: Frommanns Philos. Taschenbucher, 1922.

HEGEL, G. W. F. *Briefe von und an Hegel.* Edited by K. Hegel. 2 parts. Leipzig, 1887. (Abbreviated in Notes *Briefe.*)

———. *Theologische Jugendschriften.* Edited by H. Nohl. Tübingen, 1907.

HESS, M. *Sozialist. Aufsätze 1841-47.* Edited by Th. Zlocisti. Berlin, 1921.

KIERKEGAARD, S. *Angriff auf die Christenheit.* Edited by Dorner and Schrempf. Stuttgart, 1896.

———. *Der Begriff des Auserwählten.* Translated by Th. Haecker. Hellerau, 1917.

———. *Das Buch des Richters.* Translated by H. Gottsched. Jena, 1905.

———. *Das Eine was Not tut.* Translated by H. Ulrich. Zeitwende. Vol. I. Munich, 1927.

———. *Kritik der Gegenwart.* Translated by Th. Haecker. Innsbruck, 1914.

———. *Tagebücher, 1832-39.* Edited by H. Ulrich. Berlin, 1930.

———. *Die Tagebücher.* Translated by Th. Haecker. Vols. I and II. Innsbruck, 1923.

———. *Über den Begriff der Ironie.* Translated by H. Schaeder. Munich, 1929.

KÜHNE, W. *Cieszkowski, ein Schüler Hegels und des deutschen Geistes.* Leipzig, 1938.

MARX, K. *Der 18. Brumaire des Louis Bonaparte.* Edited by Rjazanov. Berlin, 1927.

———. *Das Kapital.* Vols. I–III. Hamburg; 6th edition, 1909.

———. *Zur Kritik der politischen Ökonomie.* Edited by K. Kautsky. Berlin, 1930.

RUGE, A. *Die Akademie.* (*Philos. Taschenbuch,* Vol. I.) Leipzig, 1848.

———. *Aus früherer Zeit.* Vol. IV. Berlin, 1867.

———. *Briefwechsel und Tagebuchblätter.* Edited P. Nerrlich. 2 vols. Berlin, 1886. (Abbreviated in Notes *Br.*)

———. *Unser System.* 3 vols. Leipzig, 1850. New edition by Clair I. Grece. Frankfurt, 1903.

STIRNER, M. *Der Einzige und sein Eigentum.* Leipzig: Reclam, n.d.

———. *Kleinere Schriften.* Edited by H. Mackay. Treptow bei Berlin, 1914.

TSCHIZEWSKIJ, D. *Hegel bei den Slaven.* Reichenberg, 1934.

General Works on the Nineteenth Century

CROCE, B. *Storia d'Europa nel Secolo Decimonono.* Bari. 1932.

FRIEDELL, E. *Kulturgeschichte der Neuzeit.* Vols. I–III. Munich, 1931.

SCHNABEL, F. *Deutsche Geschichte im 19. Jahrhundert.* Vols. I–IV. Freiburg, 1937.

TREITSCHKE, H. VON. *Deutsche Geschichte im 19. Jahrhundert.* Leipzig; 8th edition, 1919.

Studies on the German Spirit
in the Nineteenth Century

BALTHASAR, U. VON. *Apokalypse der deutschen Seele.* 3 vols. Munich, 1937 etc.

HECKER, K. *Mensch und Masse, Situation und Handeln der Epigonen.* Berlin, 1933.

PLESSNER, H. *Das Schicksal deutschen Geistes im Ausgang seiner bürgerlichen Epoche.* Zürich, 1935.

STERNBERGER, D. *Panorama oder Ansichten vom 19. Jahrhundert.* Hamburg, 1938.

Since this book first appeared, the following works on the same subject have been published:

CARROUGES, M. *La mystique du surhomme.* Paris, 1948.

KOJÈVE, A. *Introduction a la lecture de Hegel.* Paris, 1947.

LUBAC, H. DE. *Le drame de l'humanisme athée.* Paris, 1945.

LUKACS, G. *Der junge Hegel.* Zürich, 1948.

MARCUSE, H. *Reason and Revolution.* New York, 1941.

Translations of works mentioned in
Löwith's *From Hegel to Nietzsche*

BAUDELAIRE, C. *Fusées. Intimate Journals.* Translated by Christopher Isherwood (Hollywood: M. Rodd, 1947).

BERDAYEV, N. *Wahrheit und Lüge des Kommunismus. Problème du Communisme.* Paris, 1933.

CHAMBERLAIN, H. S. *Grundlagen des 19. Jahrhundert. The Foundations of the 19th Century.* Translated by J. Lees. New York, 1911.

CROCE, BENEDETTO. *Storie d'Europe nel Secolo Decimo. History of Europe in the 19th Century.* Translated by H. Furst. New York, 1933.

ENGELS, F. *Anti-Dühring. Herr Eugen Dührings Revolution in Science.* Chicago, 1935.

———. *Der deutsche Bauernkrieg. The Peasant War in Germany.* Translated by M. J. Olgin. New York, 1926.

———. *Feuerbach und der Ausgang der klassischen Philosophie. Ludwig Feuerbach and the Outcome of Classical German Philosophy.* London, 1934.

ERDMANN, J. E. *Grundriss der Geschichte der Philosophie. A History of Philosophy.* Translated by W. S. Hough. New York, 1890–92.

FEUERBACH, L. *Gedanken über Tod und Unsterblichkeit.* "La Mort et l'Immortalité," *Qu'est-ce que religion d'après la nouvelle philosophie allemande.* Paris, 1850.

FISCHER, K. *Geschichte der neuern Philosophie. History of Modern Philosophy.* Translated by J. P. Gordy. New York, 1887.

FLAUBERT, G. *Oeuvres comp. The Complete Works of Gustave Flaubert.* New York, 1904.

FREUD, S. *Unbehagen in der Kultur. Civilization and Its Discontents.* Translated by Joan Riviere. London, 1930.

———. *Die Zukunft einer Illusion. The Future of an Illusion.* Translated by W. D. Robson-Scott. London, 1928.

FRIEDELL, E. *Kulturgeschichte der Neuzeit. A Cultural History of the Modern Age.* Translated by C. F. Atkinson. New York, 1930–32.

GOETHE, J. W. VON. *Complete Works. The Works of Johann Wolfgang von Goethe.* Philadelphia, 1901.

———. *Conversations of Goethe with Eckermann.* Translated by J. Oxenford. New York, 1930.

———. *Letters to Zelter (Briefe an Zelter)*. *Goethe's Letters to Zelter.* Translated by A. D. Coleridge. London, 1887.

———. *Maximen und Reflexionen*. *The Maxims and Reflections of Goethe.* Translated by Bailey Saunders. New York, 1893.

———. *Wilhelm Meisters Wanderjahre*. *Wilhelm Meister's Travels.* Translated by Th. Carlyle. Boston, 1902.

GROETHUYSEN, B. *Die Entstehung der bürgerlichen Welt und Lebensanschauung in Frankreich. Origines de l'esprit bourgeois en France.* Paris, 1927.

HEGEL, G. W. F. *Ästhetik. The Philosophy of Fine Art.* Translated by F. P. B. Osmeston. London, 1920.

———. *Geschichte der Philosophie. Lectures on the History of Philosophy.* Translated by E. S. Haldane and F. H. Simson. London, 1892–96.

———. *Logik. The Logic of Hegel.* Translated by W. Wallace. Oxford, 1892.

———. *Phänomenologie. The Phenomenology of Mind.* Translated by J. B. Baillie. New York, 1931.

———. *Rechtsphilosophie. Hegel's Philosophy of Right.* Translated by S. W. Dyde. London, 1896.

———. *Vorlesungen über die Philosophie der Religion. Lectures on the Philosophy of Religion.* Translated by E. B. Speirs and J. B. Sanderson. London, 1895.

———. *Vorlesungen über die Philosophie der Weltgeschichte. Lectures on the Philosophy of History.* Translated by J. Sibree. London, 1902.

HEIDEGGER, M. *Kant und das Problem der Metaphysik. Kant et le problème de la métaphysique.* Paris, 1953.

———. *Sein und Zeit. Existence and Being.* Chicago, 1949.

HEINE, H. *Lutezia. Lutèce.* Paris, 1892.

HUMBOLDT, A. VON. *Briefe an Varnhagen von Ense. Letters of Alexander von Humboldt to Varnhagen von Ense.* Translated by F. Kapp. New York, 1860.

JASPERS, K. *Nietzsche, Einführung in das Verständnis seines Philosophierens. Nietzche; introduction à sa philosophie.* Paris, 1950.

———. *Vernunft und Existenz. Reason and Existenz.* Translated by W. Earle. New York: Noonday, 1955.

JELLINEK, G. *Die Erklärung der Menschen und Bürgerrechte. The Declaration of the Rights of Man and of Citizens.* New York, 1901.

KIERKEGAARD, S. *Angriff auf die Christenheit. Attack upon Christendom.* Translated by W. Lowrie. Princeton, 1944.

———. *Ausgewählte christliche Reden. Christian Discourses.* Translated by W. Lowrie. London, 1939.

———. *Concept of Dread.* Translated by W. Lowrie. Princeton, 1944.

———. *Concluding Unscientific PS.* Translated by D. F. Swenson. Princeton, 1953.

———. *Drei fromme Reden.* In *For Self-Examination & Judge for Yourselves! & Three Discourses.* Translated by W. Lowrie. Princeton, 1944.

———. *Either-Or.* Translated by D. F. Swenson and L. M. Swenson. Princeton, 1944.

———. *Kritik der Gegenwart. The Present Age.* Translated by A. Dru and W. Lowrie. London, 1949.

———. *Vom Leben und Walten der Liebe. Works of Love.* Translated by D. F. Swenson and L. M. Swenson. Princeton, 1946.

———. "May a Man Be Martyred for the Truth?" *The Present Age and Two Minor Ethico-Religious Treatises.* Translated by A. Dru and W. Lowrie. London, 1949.

———. *Die Tagebücher. Diary.* Translated by G. M. Andersen. New York: Philosophical Library, 1960.

———. *Tagebücher. The Journals of Søren Kierkegaard.* Translated by A. Dru. London, 1938.

KRONER, R. *Die Selbstverwirklichung des Geistes. Culture and Faith.* Chicago, 1951.

LANGE, F. A. *Geschichte des Materialismus. The History of Materialism.* Translated by E. C. Thomas. London, 1925.

LENIN, V. *Über Religion. Religion.* London, 1931.

LUBAC, H. DE. *Le drame de l'humanisme athée. The Drama of Atheist Humanism.* Translated by E. M. Riley. London, 1949.

MARCUSE, H. *Hegels Ontologie und die Grundlegung einer Theorie der Geschichtlichkeit. Reason and Revolution: Hegel and the Rise of Social Theory.* London, 1941.

MARX, K. *Der 18. Brumaire des Louis Bonaparte. The 18th Brumaire of Louis Bonaparte.* New York, 1935.

———. *Der Bürgerkrieg in Frankreich. The Civil War in France.* Translated by E. B. Bax. New York, 1903.

———. *Die Heilige Familie. The Holy Family.* Translated by R. Dixon. Moscow, 1956.

———. *Das Kapital. Capital.* Translated by Dona Ton. London, 1938.

———. *Das kommunistische Manifest. The Communist Manifesto.* New York, 1933.

———. *Zur Kritik der politischen Ökonomie. A Contribution to the Critique of Political Economy.* Translated by N. Stone. London, 1904.

———. *These über Feuerbach.* "Theses on Feuerbach" in F. Engels, *Ludwig Feuerbach and the End of Classical German Philosophy.* Moscow, 1949.

MEINECKE, F. *Die Entstehung des Historismus. El Historicismo y su Génesis.* Mexico, 1943. *Le Origini dello Storicismo.* Florence, 1954.

NAPOLEON, L. *Memorial de Saint-Helene. Memoirs of Napoleon.* London, 1929.

NIETZSCHE, F. *Die Fröhliche Wissenschaft. The Joyful Wisdom.* London, 1918.

———. *Jenseits von Gut und Böse. Beyond Good and Evil.* Translated by H. Zimmern. New York, 1924.

———. *Unzeitgemässe Betrachtungen. Thoughts out of Season* in *The Complete Works of Nietzsche.* London, 1909–13.

———. *Der Wille zur Macht. The Will to Power.* Translated by A. M. Ludovice. New York, 1924.

———. *Zur Genealogie der Moral. The Genealogy of Morals.* Translated by H. B. Samuel. New York, 1924.

PODACH, E. *The Madness of Nietzsche.* Translated by F. A. Voigt. London, 1931.

ROSENKRANZ, K. *Die Pädagogik als System. The Philosophy of Education.* Translated by A. C. Brackett. New York, 1903.

ROUSSEAU, J. J. *Contrat Social. The Social Contract.* London, 1913.

———. *Émile. Emile.* Translated by B. Foxley. London, 1933.

SCHWEITZER, A. *Goethe. Goethe.* Boston: Beacon, 1949.

SEILLIERE, E. *Der demokratische Imperialismus. L'Impérialisme Démocratique.* Paris, 1907.

SIMMEL, G. *Philosophische Kultur. Mélanges de Philosophie Relativiste, Contribution à la Culture Philosophique.* Paris, 1911.

SOREL, G. *Reflexions sur la violence. Reflections on Violence.* Translated by T. E. Hulme. New York, 1941.

STIRNER, M. *Der Einzige und sein Eigentum. The Ego and His Own.* Translated by S. T. Byington. New York, 1918.

TOCQUEVILLE, A. DE. *Das alte Staatswesen und die Revolution. The Old Regime and the Revolution.* Translated by S. Gilbert. Garden City, 1955.

———. *Demokratie in Amerika. Democracy in America.* Translated by H. Reeve. New York, 1904.

TREITSCHKE, H. VON. *Deutsche Geschichte. Treitschke's History of Germany in the 19th Century.* Translated by E. Paul. New York, 1915–19.

VERGIL. *The Aeneid.* Translated by E. F. Taylor. New York, 1933.

WAGNER, R. *Die Kunst und die Revolution.* "Art and Revolution" in *Richard Wagner's Prose Works.* Translated by W. A. Ellis. London, 1893–99.

———. *Das Kunstwerk der Zukunft.* "The Art-Work of the Future," in *Richard Wagner's Prose Works.* Translated by W. A. Ellis. London, 1893–99.

WEBER, M. *Ges. Aufsätze zur Soziologie und Sozialpol. Essays on Sociology.* Translated by H. H. Gerth and C. W. Mills. New York, 1946.

———. *Wirtschaft und Gesellschaft. The Theory of Social and Economic Organization.* Translated by A. M. Henderson and T. Parsons. New York, 1947.

Chronology

Goethe   1749–1832
Hegel   1770–1831
Schelling   1775–1854

Schopenhauer   1788–1860
Nietzsche   1844–1900

Pupils of Hegel

L. Michelet   1801–1893
K. Rosenkranz   1805–1879
A. Ruge   1802–1872
L. Feuerbach   1804–1872
M. Stirner   1806–1856

D. F. Strauss   1808–1874
B. Bauer   1809–1882
S. Kierkegaard   1813–1855
K. Marx   1818–1883

1806   Goethe, *Faust I;* Hegel, *Phänomenologie.*
1831   Goethe, *Faust II;* Hegel, preface to the 2nd edition of the *Logik.*
1841   Marx, *Dissertation über Demokrit und Epicur.*
       Kierkegaard, Master's Thesis, *Über den Begriff der Ironie.*
1842   Feuerbach, *Wesen des Christentums.*
       Comte, *Cours de Philosophie Positive.*
1843   Feuerbach, *Grundsätze der Philosophie der Zukunft.*
       B. Bauer, *Das entdeckte Christentum.*

Kierkegaard, *Either-Or*.
Marx, *Kritik der Hegelschen Rechtsphilosophie*.
Proudhon, *De la creation de l'ordre dans l'humanite*.
1844 Stirner, *Der Einzige und sein Eigentum*.
Kierkegaard, *The Concept of Dread*.
1846 Marx, *Deutsche Ideologie*.
Kierkegaard, *Concluding Unscientific Postscript*.
1847 Marx, *Das kommunistische Manifest*.
Kierkegaard, *May a Man Be Martyred for the Truth?*
1867 Marx, *Das Kapital*, I.
1868 Burckhardt, *Weltgeschichtliche Betrachtungen*.
1880 Dostoevski, *The Brothers Karamazov*
(XI, 4: "The Hymn and the Mystery").
1881 Nietzsche, *Eingebung zum Zarathustra*
(IV: "Das trunkne Lied").

Notes

EDITOR'S NOTE   References in the notes, unless otherwise indicated, are to editions or individual works cited in the Bibliography, from which quotations have been taken for this book.

Part I   Introduction: Goethe and Hegel

1   In the course of the nineteenth century, the culture of Germany, which had culminated in Hegel and Goethe, was discovered to present certain problems. The purpose of this section is to give an introduction to the intellectual history of the nineteenth century by studying these problems. It differs in this regard from previous treatments of the same theme, whose authors still presuppose the validity of German Idealism.

Cf. K. F. Goeschel, *Hegel und seine Zeit, mit Rücksicht auf Goethe* (Berlin, 1832); R. Honegger, "Goethe und Hegel," *Jahrbuch der Goethe-Gesellschaft,* XI (1925); J. Hoffmeister, *Goethe und der deutsche Idealismus* (Leipzig, 1932); J. Schubert, *Goethe und Hegel* (Leipzig, 1933); H. Falkenheim, *Goethe und Hegel* (Tübingen, 1934).

2   Cf. Hegel's account to his wife of his visit to Goethe, *Briefe,* II, 280.

3   *Heidelberger Enc.,* 221; *Enc.,* 317 ff.

4   *Goethe-Jahrbuch,* XVI (1895), 68 f.

5   Letter of January 5, 1832.

6   Conversations with Eckermann, March 21, and March 28, 1827.

7   *Gespräche,* III, 426 f.

8   *Briefe,* II, 31 f.

9   Cf. Goethe's letters to Zelter of June 7, 1825 and January 27, 1832; also the conversation with Eckermann of March 12, 1828.

10   *Gespräche,* III, 414.

11   *Briefe,* II, 249.

12   Letter to Zelter of August 13, 1831.

13   Letter to Zelter of March 11, 1832.

14   The first formulation of the principle of Hegelian philosophy is contained in the *Theologische Jugendschriften,* p. 348, and the *Abhandlung über die Differenz des Fichteschen und Schellingschen Systems,* I², p. 246. On the concept of the "mean," cf. *Jenenser Realphilosophie,* I, 203 ff.

15 *Gespräche*, III, 428. On the concept of the "mean": *Wilhelm Meisters Wander-jahre*, II, 1 (Cotta edition, XL, 189), and *Geschichte der Farbenlehre*, XXXIX, 437. Cf. G. Simmel, *Goethe* (1923), pp. 90 ff.

16 Hegel's *Ästhetik*, X/1, 2nd edition, pp. 83 ff.; and Goethe's conversation with Eckermann of January 29, 1826.

17 Best discussion in Simmel's book on Goethe.

18 Letters of August 23, and August 31, 1794; cf. *Der Sammler und die Seinigen*, XXVII, 215.

19 *Bedenken und Ergebung*, XL, 425 f. For Goethe's estimation of Kant, cf. *Gespräche*, II, 26; also the letter to Voigt of December 19, 1798 and the letter to Herder of June 7, 1793.

20 Cf. Hegel, *Enc.*, 70, on the third attitude of thought toward objectivity.

21 *Einwirkung der neueren Philosophie*, XL, 421.

22 *Anschauende Urteilskraft*, XL, 424 ff. Cf. Hegel, I², pp. 39 ff.

23 *Gespräche*, IV, 44, 337; cf. *Geschichte der Farbenlehre*, XXXIX, 187.

24 *Briefe*, II, 47; *Maximen und Reflexionen*, Nos. 261 and 809.

25 *Briefe*, II, 145.

26 *Gespräche*, II, 524; III, 327 ff.

27 *Bedeutende Fördernis durch ein einziges geistreiches Wort*, XL, 444 f. Cf. *Briefe von und an Hegel*, II, 248; *Gespräche*, III, 85; IV, 104; *Maximen und Reflexionen*, No. 657.

28 *Enc.*, 377, Zus.

29 The most important of the relevant letters, in temporal sequence: G. to H., July 8, 1817 (*Briefe*, II, 7); H. to G., July 20, 1817 (*Goethe-Jahrbuch* [1891], pp. 166 ff.); G. to H., October 7, 1820 (*Briefe*, II, 31); H. to G., February 24, 1821 (*Briefe*, II, 33); G. to H., April 13, 1821 (*Briefe*, II, 47); H. to G., August 2, 1821 (*Goethe-Jahrbuch* [1895], pp. 61 ff.).

30 Letters of March 5, and March 29, 1821 to Graf Reinhard, and of March 10, 1821 to Schultz.

31 Conversation with Eckermann of October 18, 1827.

32 Letter of July 20, 1817.

33 It is not accidental that this expression, like the preceding "transubstantiation," points to the Christian realm of ideas, with which Hegel was familiar through-out his life. Goethe separated himself from this sphere, particularly in the question of revivification and transformation.

34 *Briefe*, II, 36.

35 *Briefe*, II, 37.

36 *Briefe*, I, 94.

37 Conversation with Eckermann of September 1, 1829.

38 Letter to Seebeck, November 28, 1812; cf. *Gespräche*, I, 457.

39 See in the following Chap. V, par. 2b.

40 Zelter's letters to Goethe of December 2, 1830, December 14, 1830, and May 19, 1831.

41 This word derives from the Latin *contignatio*. It means literally "a joining together of two different things by means of beams, conjoining."

42 Goethe's letter to Zelter of June 1, 1831.

43 Goethe's letter to Zelter of June 9, 1831.

44 *Gespräche*, IV, 283.

45 Cf. XI, 201 (2nd edition, p. 277).

46 Cf. Hegel, XVII, 227, 403.

47 In his interpretation, Lasson proceeds on the false supposition that Hegel's medal also depicts a rose in the midst of a cross. The error probably is due to his having seen neither the original nor a copy of the medal. Further, in his criticism of the statements of Goethe and Hegel, he disputes the theological significance of the cross. Its philosophical significance overshadows its religious significance. This is understandable: Lasson was himself both a pastor and an Hegelian, and therefore was automatically attracted to Hegel's philosophical Christianity. As a result, there is no question in his eyes that Hegel has the "more profound" conception of the relationship between philosophy and theology. Even if the cross *were* a theological symbol, the rose in the midst of the cross of the present would signify "that philosophy stands at the center of theology, glorifying and perfecting it. The two female figures mentioned by Goethe can have only 'contrast' as their mutual relationship." For Lasson, such a contrast is a priori a defect, because he shares Hegel's ideal of mediation. Lasson is in error also when he asserts that Luther's crest showed a rose "in the midst of a cross." This error is obviously related to his similar error in regard to Hegel's medal. In both cases, Lasson read the statement from the preface to the *Rechtsphilosophie* into the material. (G. Lasson, *Beiträge zur Hegelforschung* [1909], pp. 43 ff.: "Kreuz und Rose, ein Interpretationsversuch.")

48 I², p. 153; XII, 235; XVII, 111 ff.; *Enc.*, 482.

49 VIII², p. 19; cf. IX, 416 ff. and p. 437; XV, 262.

50 VIII, 89, and the conclusion of paragraph 552 of the *Enc.*; cf. Hegel's *Rede zur Reformationsfeier*, XVII, 318 ff.

51 *Gespräche*, IV, 443; cf. his *Gedicht zur Feier der Reformation: Dem 31. Oktober 1817.*

52 *Gespräche*, IV, 283.

53 *Gespräche*, IV, 261. Cf. the brilliant interpretation by F. Rosenzweig in *Der Stern der Erlösung* (2nd edition, Berlin, 1930), part III, pp. 22 f. and p. 34.

54 See H. A. Korff, *Geist der Goethezeit*, I (1923), 275 ff.; and E. Seeberg, "Goethes Stellung zur Religion," *Zeitschr. f. Kirchengeschichte* (1932), pp. 202 ff.

55 Letter to Herder of May 1775; to Lavater of June 22, 1781 (cf. letter to A. v. Stolberg of April 17, 1823); to Herder of September 4, 1788; *Gespräche*, I, 202; to Zelter of April 28, 1824; to Müller of August 16, 1828; to Zelter of January 18, 1829; *Gespräche*, II, 62.

56 *Gespräche*, IV, 441 f.

57 *Gespräche*, IV, 334.

58 *Gespräche*, IV, 435. Cf. Nietzsche's *Wille zur Macht*, Aph. 1052.

59 On Goethe's Christianity, cf. F. Overbeck, *Christentum und Kultur* (Basel, 1919), pp. 142 ff.

60 W. Nigg, *F. Overbeck* (Munich, 1931), p. 58.

61 XVII, 111 ff. Cf. K. Rosenkranz, *Hegel's Leben*, pp. 400 f.

62 See Part II, Chapter V.

63 *Gespräche*, IV, 283.

64 *Gespräche*, IV, 152. After the Congress of Vienna, Metternich stated even more pointedly, "I secretly believe that the old Europe is at the beginning of its end. I am determined to perish with it; I shall know how to do my duty.

The new Europe, on the other hand, is still to come; between the end and the beginning there will be chaos."

65 *Gespräche*, IV, 317, 353; also letter to Adele Schopenhauer of January 10, 1831. For a description of 1830, see Dilthey, *Ges. Schr.*, XI, 219.

66 Cf. J. Burckhardt, *Ges. Schr.*, VII, 420 ff.; and A. de Tocqueville, *Autorität und Freiheit* (Zürich, 1935), pp. 169 ff.

67 *Gespräche*, IV, 291.

68 Letter to Zelter of October 5, 1830.

69 *Maximen und Reflexionen*, No. 961.

70 Conversation with Eckermann and Soret, July 2, 1830; *Gespräche*, IV, 290; V, 175.

71 Letter to Zelter of June 18, 1831.

72 Letter to Zelter of June 7, 1825; cf. *Gespräche*, III, 57, 500 ff.

73 "Youth Without Goethe" (the title of a lecture given in 1931 by M. Kommerell) is a phenomenon a century old. As early as 1830 Goethe was attacked and suspected, rejected and reviled, by the "younger generation." This resistance to a consummate humanity unites contemporaries as disparate as W. Menzel and Börne, Schlegel and Novalis, Heine and Kierkegaard. See V. Hehn's excellent discussion *Goethe und das Publikum*; H. Maync, *Geschichte der deutschen Goethebiographie* (Leipzig, 1914); P. Kluckhohn, *Goethe und die jungen Generationen* (Tübingen, 1932).

74 To Kierkegaard, Hegel and Goethe remain only "titular kings." In the journal entry of August 25, 1836, we read: "When Goethe had supplied a transition to the ancient world, why did his age not follow him, why did it not follow when Hegel did the same . . .? Because they both had reduced it to an aesthetic and speculative development; but political development also had its romantic development to undergo, and so the whole modern romantic school is made up of—politicians." H. Opel, "Kierkegaard und Goethe," *Deutsche Vierteljahrsschrift für Literaturwiss. und Geistesgeschichte*, No. 1 (1938).

I The Eschatological Meaning of Hegel's Consummation of the History of the World and the Spirit

1 See H. Marcuse, *Hegels Ontologie und die Grundlegung einer Theorie der Geschichtlichkeit* (Frankfurt a. M., 1932). On Hegel's equation of philosophy with the history of philosophy, see particularly *Philosophie der Geschichte*, ed. Hoffmeister (1938), pp. 34 f.

2 *Schriften zur Politik und Rechtsphilosophie*, ed. Lasson (Leipzig, 1913), p. 74.

3 *Ibid.*, p. 409.

4 IX, 97, 102.

5 *Ibid.*, p. 234.

6 *Ibid.*, p. 290.

7 *Ibid.*, p. 248, 263.

8 *Die Germanische Welt*, ed. Lasson (Leipzig, 1920), pp. 762 f.

9 IX, 331.

10 *Ibid.*, pp. 332, 346.

11 *Ibid.*, p. 418.

12 Cf. L. Michelet, *Entwicklungsgeschichte der neuesten deutschen Philosophie* . . . (Berlin, 1843), pp. 304 f.: "The goal of (Hegelian) history is the secularization of Christianity."

13 IX, 342.

14 X/2 (2nd edition), pp. 231 f.; X/3, pp. 579 f.; see B. Croce, *Ultimi Saggi* (Bari, 1935), pp. 147 ff.

15 *Ibid.*, p. 232. Cf. Goethe, *Gespräche*, I, 409.

16 X/1 (2nd edition), p. 132; cf. X/2, p. 230. See also B. Bauer, *Hegels Lehre von der Religion und Kunst*, pp. 222 ff.: "Die Auflösung der Religion in der Kunst."

17 X/2, p. 236.

18 X/1, pp. 13 ff., 132. Cf. *Phänomenologie*, ed. Lasson (Leipzig, 1907), pp. 483 f.

19 X/2, pp. 233 ff.

20 X/2, pp. 235, 239 f. Cf. Goethe, *Gespräche*, II, 51; III, 106, 493.

21 *Vorlesungen über die Philosophie der Religion*, ed. Lasson (Leipzig, 1929), III, 229 ff. This pessimistic remark is dated August 25, 1821, about the same time as the letter to Yxküll (Rosenkranz, *Hegels Leben*, p. 304), in which the same awareness of being at the end of an epoch is expressed openly.

22 X/1, pp. 129 ff. Cf. Marx, III, 165.

23 X/1, p. 134.

24 XV, 253 ff. (New edition, 1938, pp. 251 ff.)

25 XV, 294.

26 XV, 690. Cf. F. Rosenzweig, Part I, pp. 9 ff.

27 XV, 34, 95 f.

28 *Briefe*, II, 52.

29 Cf. Feuerbach, *Grundsätze*, par. 29; L. Michelet, *Hegel, der unwiderlegte Weltphilosoph* (Leipzig, 1870), p. 2.

30 XIII, 67.

31 XIII, 66 ff. (Italics are the author's.)

32 XV, 689; cf. X/1, p. 124.

33 *Aeneid*, i, 33.

34 *Vorlesungen über die Philosophie der Weltgeschichte*, ed. Lasson, pp. 200, 779. Cf. A. Ruge, *Aus früherer Zeit*, IV, 72, 84. Fichte was one of the first to consider emigrating to America (letter to his wife, May 28, 1807).

35 Rosenkranz, *Hegels Leben* (Berlin, 1844), pp. 304 f.; and also in Prutz, *Historisches Taschenbuch* (1843). Cf. D. Tschizewskij, *Hegel bei den Slaven*, p. 148.

36 Cf. Napoleon, *Memorial de Sainte-Hélène*, entry of November 6, 1816; A. de Tocqueville, *Demokratie in Amerika*, end of Part I; Heine, *Lutezia*, IX.

37 See A. Ruge, *Aus früherer Zeit*, IV, 431 ff.; also K. Fischer, *Geschichte der neuern Philosophie*, VII, 200. Cf. Dilthey, *Ges. Schr.*, IV, p. 256.

38 XIII, 70, 118; cf. XIV, 276 f.; *Briefe*, I, 194: "Theoretical work, I became daily more and more convinced, accomplishes more in the world than does practical work; when the realm of ideas has been revolutionized, reality can no longer resist."

39 B. Bauer interpreted this passage as an expression of revolutionary progress, criticizing the existing order (*Die Posaune des Jüngsten Gerichts* . . . , pp. 79 f.); more moderately, in a discussion of one of Cieszkowski's works, L. Michelet derived the form to be taken by the practice of history from Hegel's principles (W. Kühne, *Cieszkowski*, p. 64).

40 See Hegel's inaugural speech at Berlin, *Enc.*, ed. Lasson, p. lxxii. An illuminating article on "Das historisch-statistische Verhältnis der Philosophie in Preussen und Deutschland," by Rosenkranz, *Neue Studien*, II (Leipzig, 1875), 186 ff.

41 VIII², pp. 7 ff.; XIV, 274 ff.

42 *Logik*, ed. Lasson, II, 156; *Enc.*, 6.

43 VIII², p. 20.

44 Cf. Marx I/1, pp. 612 f., for the contrary view.

45 VIII², pp. 18 f.

46 VIII², p, 17; XI, 200 f.; *Enc.*, 6; *Enc.*, 24, Zus. 2; *Enc.*, 213, Zus.; *Enc.*, 445, Zus.

47 *Enc.*, 552; IX, 440.

48 XI, 5, 15; *Die Vernunft in der Geschichte*, pp. 18 f.

49 *Briefe*, II, 377.

50 Rosenkranz, *Hegels Leben*, p. 543. Cf. Hegel's *Geschichte der Philosophie* (1938), pp. 220 f.

51 XII, 228 ff.; *Phänomenologie*, p. 529.

52 XII, 209, 228, 235; *Enc.*, 482. Cf. Michelet, *Entwicklungsgeschichte der neuesten deutschen Philosophie* . . . , p. 304. For Hegel, all realms of the spirit are "only the forms in which God ever has and ever will become man."

53 XII, 238 ff. Cf. Kierkegaard, IX, 73 ff. for the contrary view.

54 XII, 244. Cf. also Kierkegaard's satirical sketch of the "Kingdom of God," XII, 98.

55 *Briefe*, I, 13, 18.

56 *Rechtsphilosophie*, 270; *Enc.*, 552.

57 Rosenkranz, *Hegels Leben*, p. 557.

58 Hegel's polemic is directed against Jacobi and Schleiermacher, but it also applies to Kierkegaard, who takes Schleiermacher's "feeling" and exalts it to "passion," opposing it to reason. For Kierkegaard's polemic concept of Christianity, see particularly XII, 29, 47 ff.

59 *Rechtsphilosophie*, 270.

60 *Enc.*, 552. "Religious conscience" means to Hegel the Protestant conscience, which he sees as the union of morality and religion.

61 "Über Philosophie und Christentum, in Beziehung auf den der Hegelschen Philosophie gemachten Vorwurf der Unchristlichkeit" (1839), I, 42 ff.

62 "Über Philosophie und Christentum" (1839), II, 179 ff.

63 *Br.*, I, 269.

64 *Tagebücher*, ed. Ulrich, pp. 128 ff.; cf. pp. 264, 463 f.

65 "That God could create beings free with respect to himself, that is the cross which philosophy cannot bear, on which it has remained suspended." This is Kierkegaard's evaluation of the philosophy of freedom from Kant to Hegel (*Tagebücher*, ed. Ulrich, p. 338).

II Old Hegelians, Young Hegelians, Neo-Hegelians

1 *Streitschriften zur Verteidigung meiner Schrift über das Leben Jesu*, No. 3 (1837). Cf. Th. Ziegler, *D. F. Strauss* (Strassburg, 1908), p. 250.

2 *Geschichte der letzten Systeme der Philosophie in Deutschland*, Part II (Berlin, 1838), pp. 654 ff.; also, *Hegel, der unwiderlegte Weltphilosoph* (Leipzig, 1870),

pp. 50 ff. Cf. Rosenkranz, *Hegel als deutscher Nationalphilosoph* (Leipzig, 1870), pp. 311 f; J. E. Erdmann, *Grundriss der Geschichte der Philosophie* (Berlin, 1870), 329.10, 336.2, 337.3.

3 Originally Bauer supported the orthodox interpretation of Hegel's philosophy of religion; *pace* the Erlangen dissertation of M. Kegel (Leipzig, 1908), his transition to the radical criticism of religion of the left-wing Hegelians has not yet been explained.

4 See the reference in W. Kühne's monograph on Cieszkowski, pp. 84 ff.

5 The initial impetus was given by Feuerbach's *Gedanken über Tod und Unsterblichkeit* (1830). Apart from works by Strauss, the following appeared between 1830 and 1840: F. Richter, *Die Lehre von den letzten Dingen* (1833–34); *Die neue Unsterblichkeitslehre* (1833), in which Feuerbach's *Gedanken* are derived directly from Hegel; J. E. Erdmann, *Vorlesungen über Glauben und Wissen als Einleitung in die Dogmatik und Religionsphilosophie* (1837); K. F. Goeschel, *Von den Beweisen für die Unsterblichkeit* (1835); *Beiträge zur spekulativen Philosophie von Gott und den Menschen und von dem Gottmenschen* (1838); J. Schaller, *Der historische Christus und die Philosophie* (1838); K. Conradi, *Christus in der Gegenwart, Vergangenheit und Zukunft* (1839); L. Michelet, *Vorlesungen über die Persönlichkeit Gottes und die Unsterblichkeit der Seele* (1840); and Cieszkowski's criticism of the latter in *Gott und Palingenesie*, Part I (1842). Cf. J. E. Erdmann, *op. cit.*, p. 335; also Rosenkranz, *Neue Studien*, II, 454.

6 Thus in Krug's 3. *Beitrag zur Geschichte der Philosophie des 19. Jahrhunderts: Der Hallische Löwe* [meaning Leo's attack on the "Hegelites"] *und die marzialischen Philosophen unserer Zeit* (1838), p. 5. See also Eisenhart's polemic, *St. Georg, Ein Versuch zur Begründung des Neuhegelianismus* (1838).

7 *Hegels Leben* (Berlin, 1844); *Hegel als deutscher Nationalphilosoph* (Leipzig, 1870). On the following, see also, *Neue Studien*, IV, "Zur Geschichte der neueren deutschen Philosophie, besonders der Hegelschen" (Leipzig, 1878); *Neue Studien*, I and II (Leipzig, 1875); *Aus einem Tagebuch von 1833 bis 1846* (Leipzig, 1854); *Politische Briefe und Aufsätze, 1848 bis 1856*, ed. P. Herre (Leipzig, 1919).

8 A "philosophy of action" was contained in Cieszkowski's *Prolegomena zur Historiosophie* (1838); see W. Kühne's monograph, *op. cit.*, pp. 25 ff.

9 Cf. *Neue Studien*, II, 460 ff.; also K. Fischer, "Feuerbach und die Philosophie unserer Zeit," which appeared in Ruge's small philosophical collection *Die Akademie*, pp. 128 ff.

10 *Hegels Leben*, pp. xix f.

11 Marx also reproached Stirner for the same thing: he uses the concrete world only for examples to give an appearance of substance to the abstract skeleton of his system—"just as in Hegel's *Logik* it makes no difference whether an atom or a human being is used to elucidate the concept of 'proseity'" (V, 261 f.).

12 A. Schwegler published the *Jahrbücher der Gegenwart* (1843 to 1848) in order to answer this need. The contributors included E. Zeller and F. Th. Fischer. L. Noack had the same purpose in publishing the *Jahrbücher für spekulative Philosophie und die philosophische Bearbeitung der empirischen Wissenschaften* (1846 to 1848), later called *Jahrbücher für Wissenschaft und Leben*. Here were published the studies of the *Philosophische Gesellschaft*, founded

in 1843 by Michelet. These two publications replaced the *Jahrbücher für wissenschaftliche Kritik*, founded in 1827 by Hegel and Gans.

13   See Rosenkranz, *Aus einem Tagebuch*, p. 116. Cf. also Marx, III, 153 ff; Kierke-gaard, VII, 46; Feuerbach, X², p. 142.

14   *Aus einem Tagebuch*, pp. 140 f. Cf. *ibid.* the admirable descriptions of Ruge, Feuerbach, Bauer, and Stirner, pp. 109, 124; 140; 110 f., 113; 112, 116, 132. It is typical of them all that, as genuine sophists, they had mastered the art of "saying commonplaces in language which seems marked with genius," each outdoing the other (pp. 133, 141).

15   Cf. *Neue Studien*, II, 124 ff.: "Die Metaphysik in Deutschland 1831 bis 1845."

16   *Hegel als deutscher Nationalphilosoph*, p. 317; also in the Michelet Jubilee Volume, which appeared at the same time: *Hegel der unwiderlegte Weltphilosoph*.

17   Rosenkranz, *op. cit.*, pp. 316 f.

18   *Neue Studien*, II, 568.

19   *Neue Studien*, I, 548. Cf. Burckhardt's remark on Rosenkranz' discussion: "Reading it is like being forced to go to church on a rainy Sunday afternoon" (Letter to Preen, October 3, 1872).

20   *Neue Studien*, I, 413.

21   *Ibid.*, pp. 464 f.

22   R. Haym, *Hegel und seine Zeit* (Berlin, 1857); cf. Rosenkranz' criticism, *Neue Studien*, IV, 375 ff. See also Haym's *Feuerbach und die Philosophie* (Halle, 1847), and Feuerbach's reply, *Br.*, I, 423 ff.

23   See Rosenkranz, *Kritische Erläuterungen des Hegelschen Systems* (1840); *Die Modifikationen der Logik* (1846); *System der Wissenschaft* (1850); *Meine Reform der Hegelschen Philosophie* (1852). For a criticism of the *Modifikationen*, see Lassalle, *Die Hegelsche und Rosenkranzsche Logik* (1859). 2nd edition (Leipzig, 1928).

24   *Hegel und seine Zeit*, pp. 4 ff.

25   Haym, *op. cit.*, pp. 7, 444 ff.

26   See Dilthey, *Ges. Schr.*, XI, 224 ff.

27   See F. Meinecke, *Die Entstehung des Historismus* (Munich, 1936), I, 5.

28   See in what follows K. Fischer's evolutionary theory. Cf. D. Sternberger, *Panorama oder Ansichten vom 19. Jahrhundert*, Chap. 4, "Das Zauberwort 'Entwicklung.' "

29   *Versuch einer wissenschaftlichen Darstellung der Geschichte der neueren Philosophie*, Vol. III, 3, p. 557.

30   See Part I, Chap. II, Sect. 2, b of this work for Ruge's goal of bringing Hegel's speculation once again to life by means of Fichte's energy.

31   See Fischer's discussion of Feuerbach, *loc. cit.*, and also Ruge's letters to Fischer.

32   O. Wigand's *Epigonen* (1848), V, 277 ff.; Stirner's reply is in *Kleinere Schriften*, pp. 401 ff.

33   See Dilthey, *Ges. Schr.*, IV, 403 ff.

34   In his history of German philosophy, E. Zeller says of the criticism of Hegel's schematization of history: "If the historiography of today is no longer satisfied with scholarly research and evaluation of traditions, with the compilation and pragmatic explanation of facts, but is rather concerned primarily with understanding the sweeping principle behind events, with comprehending the large-

scale course of history and the spiritual powers which determine it, this progress is due not least to the influence exerted by Hegel's philosophy of history
upon even those who never belonged to the Hegelian school."

35 Inaugural address at Heidelberg.
36 See the article by E. Grisebach, "Interpretation oder Destruktion," *Deutsche
    Vierteljahrsschr. für Literaturwiss. und Geistesgeschichte*, No. 2 (1930), pp.
    199 ff.
37 *Geschichte des Materialismus*, II (3rd edition; 1877), 72 ff.
38 K. Rosenkranz, *Hegel als Deutscher Nationalphilosoph*, p. 312.
39 See W. Kühne, *Cieszkowski*, p. 349. For a picture of later Hegelianism, see
    Michelet's periodical *Der Gedanke* (1860 to 1884).
40 L. Michelet, *Entwicklungsgeschichte der neuesten deutschen Philosophie, mit
    besonderer Rücksicht auf den gegenwärtigen Kampf Schellings mit der
    Hegelschen Schule* (Berlin, 1843), pp. 246, 304. See also the discussion of
    "Das Verhältnis der geschichtlichen Entwicklung zum Absoluten," published
    in Noack's *Jahrbücher* (1846), pp. 99 ff.; (1847), pp. 150 ff., 223 ff.
41 Noack's *Jahrbücher*, No. 2 (1846), pp. 90 ff. Cf. *ibid.*, "Über das Verhältnis
    der Stände," No. 1 (1847), pp. 113 ff.; also Michelet's discussion of a socio-
    philosophical treatise by Cieszkowski, referred to on pp. 179 ff. of W. Kühne's
    monograph.
42 *Entwicklungsgeschichte der neuesten deutschen Philosophie*, pp. 315 ff., 397 ff.
43 *Geschichte der letzten Systeme der Philosophie*, II, 800 f.
44 *Entwicklungsgeschichte der neuesten deutschen Philosophie*, p. 398.
45 See pages 106 ff. below.
46 Goethe, *Maximen und Reflexionen*, No. 899.
47 *Schriften zur Politik und Rechtsphilosophie*, ed. Lasson (Leipzig, 1913), pp.
    483 ff.; *Enc.*, 396, Zus.; *Phänomenologie*, ed. Lasson (Leipzig, 1907), p. 310.
48 For a witty and informative description of the Young Hegelians, see the open
    letter to L. Feuerbach by von Reichlin-Meldegg, Professor of Philosophy at
    Heidelberg, *Die Autolatrie oder Selbstanbetung, ein Geheimnis der junghegel-
    schen Philosophie* (Pforzheim, 1843).
49 See K. Hecker, *Mensch und Masse*, pp. 80 ff.
50 For the social history of the German literati, see W. H. Riehl, *Die bürgerliche
    Gesellschaft*, Book 2, Chap. 3 (8th edition, 1851), pp. 329 ff. Cf. also A. de
    Tocqueville, *Das alte Staatswesen und die Revolution*, Book 3, Chap. 1
    (Leipzig, 1857); G. Sorel, *Les illusions du progrès* (Paris, 1927), pp. 83 ff., 107,
    179.
51 See Feuerbach's treatise *Der Schriftsteller und der Mensch* (1834), III³, pp.
    149 ff.
52 *Rechtsphilosophie*, 6 Zus.; 7, Zus.; 207, Zus.; *Philosophische Propädeutik*, pp.
    44 f., in *Schr. zur Politik u. Rechtsphilosophie*, p. 475.
53 XV, 275 ff.
54 F. Engels, *Feuerbach*, p. 5.
55 Cf. M. Hess, *op. cit.*, p. 9; also A. Herzen, *Erinnerungen*, I (Berlin, 1907), 272.
56 Cf. Michelet, *Entwicklungsgeschichte der neuesten deutschen Philosophie*, pp.
    315 ff., 397 ff.
57 See K. Fischer, *Feuerbach und die Philosophie unserer Zeit*, pp. 148 ff. Accord-
    ing to Fischer, the only question is "whether the supermundane God should
    be buried in logic or anthropology."

58 Cf. F. Lombardi's study, *L. Feuerbach* (Florence, 1935), which presents the historical parallels in Italian Hegelianism (Spaventa, Tommasi, Labriola, De Sanctis).

59 See Lombardi, *op. cit.*, pp. 37 ff.

60 *Br.*, I, 215. Schelling criticized Hegel for the same reason: the latter's "notions" are an "insult" to images of the senses, because he never brings them down to the realm of sense perception (*Werke*, Part I, Vol. X, p. 162).

61 II, 413.

62 For Feuerbach's awareness of his epoch-making significance, see the introduction to the *Todesgedanken* (1830): "Whoever understands the language spoken by the spirit of history cannot avoid the realization that our present age is the capstone of a great period in the history of mankind, and thus the point of departure for a new life."

63 *Br.*, I, 214 ff.

64 II, 18 ff.

65 Hegel, XVI, 33 ff.

66 *Ibid.*, pp. 50 ff.

67 *Studien*, Part V, 3rd series, p. 326. See Feuerbach, *Br.*, I, 238, 241. In his second monograph on Hegel (p. 313), Rosenkranz states that Feuerbach's polemic against Hegel "had its greatest success among all those who had not got beyond the first third of his *Phänomenologie* and the first volume of his *Logik*."

68 *Br.*, I, 390.

69 *Br.*, I, 388 f.

70 I, 256; *Br.*, II, 120. Cf. Rosenkranz' criticism in *Studien*, Part V, 3rd series, pp. 325 ff.: "Hegel, der Fakultätsphilosoph, und Feuerbach, der Menschheitsphilosoph" (1842). See also the description of Hegel's "pure proseity" in D. F. Strauss, *Ausgewählte Briefe*, ed. E. Zeller (Bonn, 1895), p. 8.

71 *Br.*, I, 407. On "need" as the root of both philosophy and religion, cf. I, 207 ff.

72 Cf. K. Hecker, *Mensch und Masse*, pp. 29 ff., 77 ff.

73 *Br.*, I, 349.

74 *Br.*, I, 365.

75 Feuerbach's criticism of Hegel is contained in the following works: *Hegels Geschichte der Philosophie* (II, 1 ff.); *Kritik der Hegelschen Philosophie* (II, 185 ff.); *Über den Anfang der Philosophie* (II, 233 ff.); *Vorläufige Thesen zur Reform der Philosophie* (II, 244 ff.); *Grundsätze der Philosophie der Zukunft* (II, 269 ff.); *Der Spiritualismus der sog. Identitätsphilosophie oder Kritik der Hegelschen Psychologie* (X², pp. 136 ff.); *Kritik des Idealismus* (X², pp. 164 ff.); *Br.*, I, 387 ff.

76 Cf. Kierkegaard, VII, 30 ff.

77 II, 262; Grundsatz 21; cf. *Br.*, I, 407 f.

78 II, 264 ff.; Grundsatz 54.

79 *Die Akademie*, pp. 158 ff.

80 Grundsatz 24 ff.; cf. *Br.*, I, 95 ff.

81 X², pp. 136 ff. For a criticism of Feuerbach's sensualism, see J. Schaller, *Darstellung und Kritik der Philosophie Feuerbachs* (Leipzig, 1847), pp. 28 ff.

82 X², pp. 164 ff.; Grundsatz 41, 59, 61 ff.; see also the author's *Das Individuum in der Rolle des Mitmenschen* (Tübingen, 1928), pp. 5 ff.

83 *Br.*, I, 409.

84 *Angriff auf die Christenheit,* p. 457.
85 *Br.,* I, 410. Cf. Engels: "The essence of the state, as of religion, is mankind's fear of itself."
86 *Br.,* I, 411.
87 See Ruge, *Br.,* I, xxviii; *Br.,* II, 32, 41 f., 55, 271 f., 285, 290, 350, 404, 410 f.; Engels, *Feuerbach,* p. 1; Engels' letter to Marx of August 15, 1870 (*Werke,* III/3, 349 f., 351). Cf. Lagarde, *Deutsche Schriften* (Göttingen, 1892), p. 82; P. Wentzke, *1848, Die unvollendete deutsche Revolution* (Munich, 1938).
88 *Br.,* II, 59.
89 *Br.,* I, 215 ff.
90 *Br.,* I, 216; *Br.,* II, 165.
91 *Br.,* I, 186.
92 *Br.,* I, 300.
93 *Hallesche Jahrbücher für deutsche Wissenschaft und Kunst* (1840), p. 1217.
94 *Ibid.,* p. 1243.
95 *Unser System, loc. cit.*
96 *Br.,* II, 51, 68; *Aus früherer Zeit,* IV, p. 126.
97 *Hallesche Jahrbücher* (1841), Foreword, p. 2.
98 Cf. X/2 (2nd edition), 229; XIV, 275 (New edition [1938], pp. 39 f., 72, 125, 148 f.).
99 Cf. XV, 535, 685. K. Korsch, *Marxismus und Philosophie* (2nd edition; Leipzig, 1930), pp. 60 ff.
100 *Aus früherer Zeit,* IV, 12, 16.
101 XV, 686.
102 *Aus früherer Zeit,* IV, 599.
103 See Ruge, *Aus früherer Zeit,* IV, 443 ff.; Rosenkranz, *Hegel als deutscher Nationalphilosoph,* p. 315; *Aus einem Tagebuch,* pp. 109 ff.; J. E. Erdmann, *Grundriss,* II, 340; *Reichls philosophischer Almanach* (Darmstadt, 1924), pp. 370 ff.
104 *Aus einem Tagebuch,* p. 109; also Ruge, *Br.,* I, 271 f.
105 This refers to Hegel's criticism of the English Reform Bill.
106 *Hallesche Jahrbücher* (1840), pp. 1209 ff.
107 *Rechtsphilosophie,* 257 and 265, Zus.
108 See note 30, Chap. I, *supra.* For Ruge's return to Fichte, see W. Kühne, *Cieszkowski,* p. 41. Kierkegaard's relationship to Fichte is discussed in E. Hirsch, *Kierkegaardstudien,* II, 471 ff. Feuerbach's relationship to Fichte is discussed in R. Haym, *op. cit.,* pp. 23 ff.
109 Cf. Hegel's *Rechtsphilosophie,* Sections 316–318. The transition from Hegel to Ruge with reference to estimation of public opinion is discussed in an article by Rosenkranz, *Studien,* Part II (Leipzig, 1844), pp. 222 ff. The subject of public opinion is said to be the "spirit of the people" or the "free people."
110 Cf. Marx on "spirit" and "the masses," III, 249 ff.; also Gutzkow, *Die geistige Bewegung* (1852). The true course of the spirit of the age, served equally by the army and the electorate, is the disciplining of the spirit of the masses. The "art of subordination" appears to become historical.
111 *Hallesche Jahrbücher* (1842), pp. 755 ff. (Reprinted in *Aus früherer Zeit,* IV, 549 ff.).
112 *Aus früherer Zeit,* IV, 571 ff.; cf. Feuerbach, *Grundsätze,* p. 28.

113 *Aus früherer Zeit,* IV, 575; cf. Hegel, IX, 439, and XV, 552 f.; Marx, I/1, pp. 608 ff.

114 For the contrary view, see Rosenkranz, *Hegel als deutscher Nationalphilosoph,* pp. 148 ff. The progressive character of Hegel's *Rechtsphilosophie* is demonstrated with reference to contemporary conditions in Germany.

115 *Rechtsphilosophie,* Sections 4–7.

116 *Aus früherer Zeit,* IV, 581 f.

117 *Ibid.,* pp. 550 ff.

118 *Ibid.,* pp. 559 ff. See also Dilthey, *Ges. Schr.,* IV, 285 ff.

119 Cf. also Marx's criticism in V, 175 ff.

120 See Hegel's inaugural addresses at Heidelberg and Berlin.

121 *Deutsche Jahrbücher für Wissenschaft und Kunst,* V (1843), 6.

122 *Aus früherer Zeit,* IV, 570.

123 *Die Akademie,* p. 125.

124 See the article on "Kritik und Partei," *Deutsche Jahrbücher,* V (1842), 1177 ff.

125 Ruge, *Br.,* I, 343 f.; cf. Feuerbach, *Br.,* I, 358, 362.

126 I/1, p. 13.

127 I/1, p. 132.

128 I/1, pp. 132 ff.; cf. Hegel, XII, 224.

129 Like Marx, Immermann also used the image of "twilight" to describe the crisis: "It is still twilight, and the boundaries of the forms of knowledge are critically indistinct. When illumined by the light of day they will show their distinct shapes, each in its own place" (*Memorabilien, Die Jugend vor 25 Jahren: Lehre und Literatur*). But as early as 1815, in his *Ahnung und Gegenwart,* Eichendorff used the image of an uncertain twilight to describe his age: "Our age seems to me to resemble a vast, uncertain twilight. Light and shadow assume strange shapes and battle each other violently. The outcome is uncertain. Dark clouds interpose ominously, uncertain whether they bring death or grace. Below them the world lies spread in silent expectation. Comets and strange signs in the heavens are seen once more. Spirits wander once more through our nights. Fabulous sirens, as before a thunderstorm, appear again above the surface of the sea and sing. Our children take no pleasure in careless, easy play, in happy relaxation, as did our fathers; the seriousness of life has gripped us early."

130 I/1, pp. 63 ff.; cf. III, 164.

131 V, 533 (first thesis on Feuerbach).

132 V, 31 ff.

133 For Marx's evaluation of Feuerbach, cf. III, 151 ff. From Feuerbach's point of view, the difference between Marx and Feuerbach consists in Marx's reassertion of Hegel's doctrine of the objective spirit against Feuerbach's anthropology. He repudiates Feuerbach because the latter took as the basis of his philosophy an abstract man, that is, man apart from his world. Hegel's *Rechtsphilosophie* brought to light this world of political and economic conditions. Feuerbach's only uncontested merit lies in his reduction of the absolute spirit to human terms. But Feuerbach's concrete definition of human nature, as a naturalistic generic entity, indicates to Marx that he "pushed Hegel aside" without "overcoming him critically." Feuerbach constructed a "man" whose reality reflects only the life of the bourgeois private individual.

Like the actual life of the bourgeois private individual, his theory of "I and Thou" reduces to the private relationship between isolated individuals. He does not realize that not only the circumstances of life that are apparently "purely human," but also the most primitive objects of sense perception, are predetermined by the universal social and economic conditions of the world. Marx destroyed Hegel's concrete analyses on the basis of their philosophical claim; but he was able to make use of them against Feuerbach, and conversely he was able to understand Hegel's principles from Feuerbach's anthropological point of view. He defends Hegel against Feuerbach because he has grasped the decisive significance of the universal; he attacks Hegel for casting a veil of philosophical mystery over the universal relationships of history.

134 See K. Korsch, *Marxismus und Philosophie*, pp. 102 ff.; also E. Lewalter, "Versuch einer Interpretation des 1. Teiles der Deutschen Ideologie," *Archiv für Sozialwiss. und Sozialpol.*, No. 1 (1930), pp. 63 ff.

135 F. Engels, "Vier Briefe über den historischen Materialismus," Marx–Engels, *Über historischen Materialismus*, ed. H. Duncker, Part 2 (Berlin, 1930), pp. 138 ff.

136 See the author's "M. Weber und K. Marx," *Archiv für Sozialwiss. und Sozialpol.*, Nos. 1 and 2 (1932), especially pp. 207 ff.

137 I/1, pp. 10, 51; cf. pp. 80 f., 110 ff. against Plutarch's "theologizing mentality" in his polemic against Epicurus. On the history of modern materialism, see III, 302 ff.

138 I/1, p. 608.

139 I/1, pp. 608 f.

140 See Engels, *Der deutsche Bauernkrieg*, ed. H. Duncker (Berlin, 1930).

141 I/1, pp. 612 f.

142 XV, 535.

143 XV, 553.

144 I/1, p. 614.

145 See below, Part II, Chap. I, Section 3.

146 V, 7.

147 V, 7 f.

148 V, 8.

149 V, 9 f.

150 V, 16. On criticism of Hegel's concept of "self-presupposition," cf. V, 245 ff.

151 See K. A. Mautz, *Die Philosophie M. Stirners im Gegensatz zum Hegelschen Idealismus* (Berlin, 1936). Remarkably, this work treats Marx's analysis of Stirner's Hegelianism as though it did not exist, although it is the only work which provides documentation for the thesis of the author.

152 V, 109 ff., 118.

153 *Der Einzige und sein Eigentum*, p. 111.

154 *Kleinere Schriften*, p. 369.

155 The inspiration for Stirner's motto probably was Goethe's poem "Vanitas vanitatum vanitas." Kierkegaard, too, was acquainted with it. In his *Journals* (ed. Ulrich, p. 145), he describes it as being "very interesting," because it is the nihilistic "summation of life" of a very great individuality.

156 V, 243.

157 We know of the following works by Bauer:
Theological and philosophical works:

Zeitschrift für spekulative Theologie, 5 vols. (Berlin, 1836–37).

Herr Dr. Hengstenberg, Ein Beitrag zur Kritik des religiösen Bewusstseins (1839).

Die evangelische Landeskirche Preussens und die Wissenschaft, anon. (1840).

Kritik der evangelischen Geschichte des Johannes (1840).

Die Posaune des jüngsten Gerichts über Hegel . . . anon. (1841).

Hegels Lehre von der Religion und Kunst . . . anon. (1842).

Die gute Sache der Freiheit und meine eigene Angelegenheit (1842).

Kritik der evangelischen Geschichte der Synoptiker, 3 vols. (1841–42).

Das entdeckte Christentum . . . (1843).

Die Apostelgeschichte, eine Ausgleichung des Paulinismus und des Judentums innerhalb der christlichen Kirche (1850).

Kritik der Paulinischen Briefe, 3 parts (1851–52).

Philo, Strauss, und Renan und das Urchristentum (1874).

Christus und die Cäsaren, der Ursprung des Christentums aus dem römischen Griechentum (1877).

Das Urevangelium und die Gegner der Schrift Christus und die Cäsaren (1880).

Political and historical works:

Die Denkwürdigkeiten zur Geschichte der neueren Zeit seit der Französischen Revolution (1843).

Die Septembertage 1792 und die ersten Kämpfe der Parteien der Republik (1844).

Geschichte der Politik, Kultur und Aufklärung des 18. Jahrhunderts, I–II (1843–45).

Geschichte der konstitutionellen und revolutionären Bewegungen im südlichen Deutschland in den Jahren 1831–34, 3 vols. (1845).

Geschichte Deutschlands während der Französischen Revolution (1846).

Vollständige Geschichte der Parteikämpfe in Deutschland während der Jahre 1842–46, 3 vols. (1847).

Der Fall und Untergang der neuesten Revolution (1846–50).

Die bürgerliche Revolution in Deutschland seit dem Anfang der deutsch-katholischen Bewegung bis zur Gegenwart (1849).

Der Untergang des Frankfurter Parlaments (1849).

Russland und das Germanentum (1853).

Einfluss des englischen Quäkertums auf die deutsche Kultur und auf das englisch-russische Projekt einer Weltkirche (1878).

Zur Orientierung über die Bismarcksche Ära (1880).

158 *Russland und das Germanentum*, pp. 1 f.

159 *Ibid.*, pp. 7 f.

160 *Ibid.*, Section II, pp. 83 f.

161 *Ibid.*, pp. 44 ff.

162 *Ibid.*, pp. 45 f.

163 Cf. the sections on "pauperism" and the "university movement" in the 3rd portion of Bauer's *Vollständige Geschichte der Parteikämpfe*.

164 *Russland und das Germanentum*, pp. 47 ff. Cf. also the author's *Burckhardt*, pp. 159 ff., 233 ff.

165 *Ibid.*, Section II, p. 76.

166 *Ibid.*, p. 77.

167 Cf. Kierkegaard's positive exposition of "absolute negativity" in *Der Begriff der Ironie*.

168 *Russland und das Germanentum*, p. 121.

169 See E. Niekisch and O. Petras, *Post Christum* (Widerstands-Verlag, 1932–35).

170 XI, 61 f. (*Angriff auf die Christenheit*, pp. 76 f.).

171 X, 93 (*Angriff auf die Christenheit*, p. 473). Cf. VII, 59; *Tagebücher*, I, 58 ff. and II, 367; *Kritik der Gegenwart*. See also J. Wahl, *Études Kierkegaardiennes* (Paris, 1938), pp. 172 f.; the description of this epoch in Cieszkowski, *op. cit.*, p. 444.

172 *Der Begriff der Ironie*, pp. 204 ff.

173 VI, 214 f.

174 VII, 7, 30 f., 51 ff.

175 VII, 51 f.; cf. pp. 42 f.

176 VII, note 6.

177 *Tagebücher*, I, 324, 328; *Der Begriff des Auserwählten*, p. 30; *Angriff auf die Christenheit*, p. 475.

178 *Das Eine was not tut*, p. 4; *Der Begriff des Auserwählten*, pp. 273 ff., 170 ff. on the nature of authority.

179 *Ibid.*, p. 6.

180 See also N. Berdayev, *Wahrheit und Lüge des Kommunismus* (Luzern, 1934).

181 Kierkegaard, *Tagebücher*, I, 169 ff.; Marx-Engels, *Ges. Ausg.*, I/2, 173 ff.; Burckhardt's letter to Kinkel of June 13, 1842.

182 On Kant, *Kritik der reinen Vernunft* (Reclam, pp. 468 ff.), cf. Schelling, *Werke*, Part II, Vol. I, pp. 285 ff., and Vol. III, p. 46.

183 *Werke*, Part I, Vol. X, pp. 212 ff.; cf. Part II, Vol. III, pp. 80 ff.

184 X, 126 ff.

185 In the single year 1843 the following appeared: L. Michelet, *Entwicklungsgeschichte der neuesten deutschen Philosophie mit besonderer Rücksicht auf den gegenwärtigen Kampf Schellings mit der Hegelschen Schule* (Berlin); Ph. Marheineke, *Zur Kritik der Schellingschen Offenbarungsphilosophie* (Berlin); K. Rosenkranz, *Über Schelling und Hegel, ein Sendschreiben an P. Leroux* (Königsberg); *Schelling* (Danzig); cf. also *Aus einem Tagebuch*, pp. 80 ff., 97 ff.; Chr. Kapp (anon.), *Schelling, ein Beitrag zur Geschichte des Tages* (Leipzig).

186 Trendelenburg, *Logische Untersuchungen*, I (Leipzig, 1840), 23 ff. On Trendelenburg's attitude toward the Hegelians, see the data in W. Kühne, *Cieszkowski*, pp. 128 f.; cf. Kierkegaard, VI, 67, 194; VII, 1, note; *Tagebücher*, I, 314 f.; Pap. VI A, p. 145. See also Ruttenbeck, *Kierkegaard* (1929), pp. 79 ff. Ruttenbeck's admirable reference to Kierkegaard's position within the circle of Hegel's opponents (pp. 57 ff.) does not make full use of the assembled material; the historical uniqueness of this movement cannot be pinned down by such vague terms as "irrationalism," "subjectivism," and "realism."

187 Cf. Kierkegaard, V, 78; VI, 67.

188 Cf. Marx, III, 169 f.

189 Cf. Kierkegaard, VI, 196.

190 Cf. Kierkegaard, VII, 1, 30 ff.

191 Cf. Kierkegaard, V, 4.

192 Cf. Kierkegaard, V, 3 ff.; VI, 193 ff., 206.

193 Schelling, *Werke*, Part I, Vol. X, pp. 212 f.

194 On criticism of the dialectics of beginning, cf. Kierkegaard, VI, 194 ff., and Feuerbach, Grundsatz 26.
195 Schelling, *op. cit.*, p. 214; cf. p. 143.
196 *Ibid.*, p. 215, note; also Schelling's letter to Weisse of November 3, 1834; on criticism of the Hegelian concept of being, see Feuerbach, Grundsatz 24.
197 *Ibid.*, p. 216; on "whatness" and "thatness" or essence and existence, cf. Section II, Vol. III, pp. 57 ff., 70 ff., 90 ff., 163.
198 *Ibid.*, p. 127; cf. Feuerbach, Grundsatz 24.
199 Cf. Hegel, XIII, 88; also Feuerbach, Grundsatz 23.
200 *Ibid.*, pp. 160 f.
201 As evidenced by agreeing accounts of Michelet, *op. cit.*, pp. 174 ff., 195, and Marheineke, *op. cit.*, pp. 20 ff., 36 ff., 41.
202 *Sein und Zeit*, Section 29. The conclusion of Heidegger's inaugural dissertation on Duns Scotus (Tübingen, 1916, p. 241) supports the argument that his existential ontology is still determined indirectly by disagreement with Hegel.
203 *Sein und Zeit*, Section 9.
204 On reality and potentiality in the existential sense, cf. Kierkegaard, VII, 17 ff.; VIII, 12 ff. Only one inadequate attempt has been made to work out the historical connection between Heidegger's philosophic position and that of both Kierkegaard and Marx: the essays of M. Beck and H. Marcuse in the special issue devoted to Heidegger's *Sein und Zeit* of *Philosophische Hefte*, No. 1 (Berlin, 1928).
205 VII, 33; cf. V, 14, 55.
206 *Werke*, Section II, Vol. III, pp. 90 ff.
207 *Aus Schellings Leben in Briefen*, III (Leipzig, 1870), 63.
208 *Ibid.*, p. 173.
209 See Marx-Engels, *Ges. Ausg.*, II, 173 ff.; F. Engels, *Schelling über Hegel* (1841); *Schelling und die Offenbarung* (1842); *Schelling, der Philosoph in Christo* (1842). In the summer of 1841, A. Ruge met Schelling, and felt more than a little flattered by the latter's praise of the *Jahrbücher*. Scarcely six months later he had to admit in a letter to Rosenkranz that Schelling had "stuffed him with lies" (*Br.*, I, 174, 236, 272 f.).
210 See also Nietzsche, I, 487 ff.; X, 297, 304, 348. Schelling's account of Metternich is an interesting document bearing on this turn to philosophy: "At this time I heard from a reliable source of a confidential letter of Prince Metternich, in which he expresses with heart-rending grief his disgust with affairs of State. The powerful man, who has grown old and grey in the most important political activities . . . wishes for nothing more than to be able to devote his life to philosophy. Who would have imagined it? But the age is moving in this direction of its own accord; the ultimate decision which will lead us forth from the need, mediocrity, and meanness of the present will be a decision of the spirit" (*Aus Schellings Leben*, III, 197).
211 See Rosenkranz, *Neue Studien*, II, 571 ff.: "Die philosophischen Stichwörter der Gegenwart"; also H. Vaihinger, *Hartmann, Dühring, und Lange* (Iserlohn, 1876), in which the connection of Dühring and Hartmann with the Hegelian school is indicated.
212 See *Tagebücher*, II, 244, 344 ff., 351 f., 367.
213 See K. Korsch, *Marxismus und Philosophie*, pp. 57 ff.
214 *Cio che e vivo e cio che e morto della filosofia di Hegel* (1907); German

translation, 1909. For the history of Italian Hegelianism, see the Bibliography of the essay by E. Grassi, "Beziehungen zwischen deutscher und italienischer Philosophie," *Deutsche Vierteljahrsschr. für Literaturwiss. und Geistesgesch.*, No. 1 (1939). On De Sanctis, see B. Croce, *Saggio sullo Hegel* (Bari, 1913), pp. 363 ff.

215 *Parerga und Paralipomena*, Vol. II, Chap. 20.

216 More than fifty studies are discussed in J. Brecht's "Bericht über die Hegelforschung von 1926 bis 1931," *Literarische Berichte aus dem Gebiete der Philosophie*, ed. A. Hoffmann (Erfurt, 1931).

217 See H. Levy, "Die Hegelrenaissance in der deutschen Philosophie," *Vorträge der Kant-Gesellschaft* (1927); H. Glockner, "Krisen und Wandlungen in der Geschichte der Hegelianismus," *Logos*, XIII (1924–25).

218 *Ges. Schr.*, IV, 187.

219 *Ibid.*, p. 219.

220 *Ibid.*, pp. 244 f., 248 f.

221 *Ibid.*, pp. 219 f.; cf. p. 246.

222 *Ibid.*, p. 218.

223 *Ibid.*, p. 220, 223.

224 XVI, 47 f.

225 *Ges. Schr.*, IV, 229 f. Dilthey considered that Trendelenburg had already demonstrated the emptiness of Hegelian dialectics.

226 *Ibid.*, pp. 227 f.

227 *Ibid.*, pp. 249, 254.

228 *Ibid.*, p. 250; cf. V, xxii ff.

229 VIII, 175 ff.

230 *Präludien*, I⁵, pp. 273 ff.

231 *Ibid.*, p. 279.

232 *Was heisst Hegelianismus?* (1910).

233 *Relativer und absoluter Idealismus* (1916).

234 *Von Kant bis Hegel*, Vols. I and II (Tübingen, 1921 and 1924); *Die Selbstverwirklichung des Geistes* (Tübingen, 1928). On what follows, cf. "System und Geschichte bei Hegel," *Logos* (1931); "Bemerkungen zur Dialektik der Zeit," *Verhandlungen des 3. Hegel-Kongresses* (Tübingen, 1934), pp. 153 ff. For a criticism of Kroner's Hegelianism, cf. S. Marck, *Die Dialektik in der Philosophie der Gegenwart*, Vol. I (1929).

235 Vol. II, p. x.

236 *Was heisst Hegelianismus?* (1916).

237 *Idee und Wirklichkeit des Staates* (1930).

238 H. Glockner, *Hegel*, I, xv ff.; "Krisen und Wandlungen in der Geschichte des Hegelianismus," pp. 346 f.

239 For an idea of how the first Hegelians conceived the question of the relationship between history and the absolute, see the discussion of these themes in Gabler, "Über das Verhältnis der geschichtlichen Entwicklung zum Absoluten," *Noacks Jahrbücher*, No. 4 (1846), pp. 99 ff.; also No. 1 (1847), pp. 150 ff., and No. 2, pp. 223 ff.

240 *System und Geschichte*, pp. 248 ff.

241 See Kroner's speech at the opening of the second Hegel Congress, 1931.

242 *Von Kant bis Hegel*, II, 505.

243 *Briefe*, I, 141.

244 *Von Kant bis Hegel*, II, 506, note.
245 Hegel, XV, 34, 95 f.
246 Hegel, XVI, 174.
247 *System und Geschichte*, p. 256.
248 "Die Bedeutung der Hegelschen Philosophie für das philosophische Denken der Gegenwart," *Vorträge der Kant-Gessellschaft* (1921).
249 *Ibid.*, pp. 31, 39, 59.
250 *Ibid.*, p. 46.
251 *Marx und Hegel* (1911); *Hegel und die Weltgeschichte* (Münster, 1931).
252 *Marx und Hegel*, p. 13.
253 For Plenge's positive criticism of Marx, see the summary on pp. 9 f.
254 *Marx und Hegel*, pp. 35 ff.
255 See the instructive article by W. Kaegi, "Voltaire und der Zerfall des christlichen Geschichtsbildes," *Corona*, Vol. VIII, No. 1.
256 *Ibid.*, p. 65. Cf. also S. Marck, *op. cit.*, I, 57.
257 *Ibid.*, p. 66.
258 *Ibid.*, p. 70.
259 Cf. Lenin's critical estimation of Hegel's philosophy of history: this is the most obsolete aspect of Hegel, and has been replaced by Marx. "Aus dem philosophischen Nachlass Lenins," *Marxistische Bibliothek*, XXIII, 175.
260 *Ibid.*, pp. 71 f.
261 See Kroner's addresses at the opening of the 2nd and 3rd Hegel Congresses; also A. W. Lunatscharski, "Hegel und die Gegenwart," *Das neue Russland* (Berlin, Nov., 1931). With reference to Croce's distinction between what is dead and what is vital in Hegel, L. states: "We, too, in our own fashion, have distinguished the once from the other."

III   The Dissolution of Hegel's Mediations in the Exclusive Choices of Marx and Kierkegaard

1 *Logik*, ed. Lasson, II (Leipzig, 1923), 156 ff.
2 See *Jenenser Realphilosophie*, I (Leipzig, 1932), 214 ff.
3 *Enc.*, Sect. 6; cf. Sect. 24, Zus. 2; Sect. 213, Zus.; Sect. 445, Zus.
4 VIII², p. x.
5 *Vide supra*, Part I, Chap. II, Sect. 2, b.
6 Cf. Haym, *Hegel und seine Zeit*, pp. 368 ff., 387 ff., 462.
7 *Vide supra*, Part I, Chap. II, Sect. 2, a.
8 Grundsatz 24.
9 Grundsatz 43.
10 Grundsatz 24.
11 Grundsatz 51.
12 Grundsatz 26.
13 Grundsatz 27.
14 Grundsatz 28.
15 Grundsatz 33 and 28; also *Werke*, I, 256.
16 Grundsatz 48; cf. II, 258; Marx, III, 161.
17 In 1830 Kirejewski heard Hegel in person, and spent much time in the company of E. Gans. His most important discussions have appeared in German

translation in *Drei Essays* (Munich, 1921): "Das 19. Jahrhundert" (1832); "Über den Charakter der Zivilisation Europas und ihr Verhältnis zur Zivilisation Russlands" (1852); "Über die Notwendigkeit und Möglichkeit einer neuen Grundlegung der Philosophie" (1856).

18 *Drei Essays*, p. 114.
19 *Drei Essays*, p. 121.
20 D. Tschizewskij, *Hegel in Russland*, in the volume *Hegel bei den Slaven*, pp. 193 ff. This excellent presentation and analysis (of which I make grateful use in what follows) revealed for the first time the entire extent of Hegel's historical influence. Cf. also B. Jakowenko, *Ein Beitrag zur Geschichte des Hegelianismus in Russland* (Prague, 1934); A. Koyre, "Hegel en Russie," *Le monde slave*, II (1936).
21 Tschizewskij, *op. cit.*, p. 196.
22 *Ibid.*, p. 222.
23 Cf. in Chapter 7 of Gogol's *Dead Souls* the hymn to the poet of everyday life.
24 *Russische Meisterbriefe*, ed. K. Nötzel (Munich, 1922), pp. 177, 179.
25 Tschizewskij, *op. cit.*, p. 226.
26 See the correspondence with Ruge, Marx-Engels, *Ges. Ausg.*, I/1, p. 566.
27 For the following, see the monograph by W. Kühne, *loc. cit.*, which treats in detail the relationship of Cieszkowski to Michelet; I am grateful to be able to utilize this source.
28 W. Kühne, *op. cit.*, p. 429.
29 *Ibid.*, pp. 264 ff.
30 *Ibid.*, pp. 28 f., 43 f., 65 f.
31 *Ibid.*, p. 73.
32 *Ibid.*, pp. 22, 45, 98.
33 *Ibid.*, pp. 93 ff., 96.
34 *Ibid.*, p. 110.
35 *Ibid.*, pp. 13, 25 ff. See also B. Croce, *Saggio sullo Hegel* (Bari, 1913), pp. 149 ff.
36 *Ibid.*, pp. 89 ff., 251 ff.; 14, 161, 179 ff., 347.
37 The following comparison between Marx and Kierkegaard is also intended as a corrective to the comparison of Nietzsche and Kierkegaard, which up to the present has been considered the only meaningful and fruitful comparison. The author himself contributed to this comparison before he saw the historical connection with Marx in its full scope. See the author's *Kierkegaard und Nietzsche* (Frankfurt, 1933); K. Jaspers, *Vernunft und Existenz*, 1st lecture (Groningen, 1935); A. Bäumler, *Studien zur deutschen Geistesgeschichte* (Berlin, 1937), pp. 78 ff., 244 ff.; J. Wahl, *Études Kierkegaardiennes*, pp. 207 ff., 429 ff.
38 I/1, p. 476.
39 I/1, p. 492.
40 I/1, pp. 437, 499.
41 I/1, p. 494.
42 I/1, p. 538.
43 I/1, p. 437.
44 *Über den Begriff der Ironie*, p. 274.
45 *Tagebücher*, I, 169 (= Pap. III A, p. 179). Cf. the no less expectant excitement of such a prudent scholar as Rosenkranz: "Schelling's inaugural address is here. I have devoured it. If he fulfills only half of what he promises, he will

finish his course infinitely greater than when he began it. He possesses to the highest degree the art of keeping people in suspense. His desire is to 'push mankind beyond its previous knowledge.' If he succeeds, he is more than a philosopher: he is the founder of a religion." And further: "Throughout the year, Schelling and more Schelling. Well, he deserves it. How a great man can stir up a commotion! From the realm of serious struggle for truth to the realm of base passions . . . he has aroused excitement everywhere. When Gabler was called to succeed Hegel, he was the subject of conversation for four weeks. Then nothing more was heard of him. Now months and months have gone by, and still all the papers, journals, and brochures are full of Schelling. All Berlin is forced to change its views. Many an Hegelian secretly engages himself in diplomatic parley, asking himself whether Schelling may not be more correct than Hegel, and whether he should not go through a public conversion." *Aus einem Tagebuch,* pp. 79 f. and 107 f.; cf. Engels, II, 173 f.

46 *Tagebücher,* I, 176.
47 I, 29.
48 *Tagebücher,* II, 127 f.
49 *Tagebücher,* II, 86. Cf. Feuerbach, Grundsatz 22 and 25, and Hegel's criticism in *Logik,* ed. Lasson, I, 74 f.; XII, 368 ff.
50 VI, 207; VII, 3, 27 ff. Cf. Feuerbach, Grundsatz 24.
51 VII, 1. Cf. Feuerbach, Grundsatz 28.
52 *Logik,* ed. Lasson, II, 238 ff.; *Enc.,* Sects. 112–114; *Rechtsphilosophie,* Sect. 270, Zus.
53 VI, 206.
54 V, 3 f.
55 VI, 196.
56 VII, 15; III, 180 f.
57 See Hegel's *Logik,* ed. Lasson, I, 74.
58 V, 14, note.
59 VII, 13. Cf. *Kritik der Gegenwart,* p. 54.
60 Epigraph to *Either-Or,* I; V, 15; VI, 272 ff.; VII, 3, 47; *Tagebücher,* I, 170; *Kritik der Gegenwart,* pp. 5 ff., 43.
61 VI, 196 f., 265. In Kierkegaard's categories, determined passion is distinguished from vacillating irony, the endless cycles of boredom from the reverie of melancholy.
62 VI, 190.
63 VI, 196 ff.; V, 10, note.
64 VII, 15.
65 VII, 41.
66 VII, 16, 25, 27 ff.
67 VII, 5; cf. also Hegel's *Schriften zur Politik und Rechtsphilosophie,* p. 368, and I², p. 131.
68 In the criticism of political economy this connection is expressly emphasized: "As in all of the historical social sciences, so in the construction of economic categories it must always be remembered that . . . modern bourgeois society is a given fact, and that these categories therefore . . . are expressions of forms, limitations, often merely individual aspects of this particular society;

even from the scientific point of view, economics by no means begins only where it is explicitly discussed" (*Zur Kritik der pol. Ök.*, p. xliii).

69 *Enc.*, Sect. 123, Zus.
70 *Rechtsphilosophie*, pp. 41 ff.
71 *Ibid.*, Sect. 61.
72 *Ibid.*, Sect. 67 and Zus.
73 *Kapital*, I⁶, pp. 130 ff.; also I/1, pp. 251 ff.
74 Cf. K. Hecker, *Mensch und Masse*, p. 62.
75 *Die Revolution von 1848 und das Proletariat* (1856).
76 On the following, see G. Lukacs, *Geschichte und Klassenbewusstsein* (Berlin, 1923), pp. 94 ff.
77 I/1, pp. 266 ff.
78 I/1, p. 304.
79 V, 25 ff.
80 V, 21 ff., 39 ff.,; cf. Engels, *Anti-Dühring* (11th edition; Berlin, 1928), pp. 312 ff.
81 *Kapital*, I⁶, pp. 38 f.
82 For an attempt from the aesthetic point of view to develop the problem of this objectification as the "tragedy of civilization," see G. Simmel, *Philosophische Kultur* (3rd edition; Potsdam, 1923), pp. 236 ff.
83 On the fetish nature of interest-bearing capital, see *Kapital*, III/1, pp. 339 ff.
84 For Marx, it goes without saying that this is only a "mask," which in every case conceals the dominant interest of production: *Kapital*, III/2, pp. 326 f.
85 *Kapital*, I⁶, pp. 43 ff.
86 See Marx's letter to Engels of June 22, 1867.
87 III, 21, 117, 307 f.; *Zur Kritik der pol. Ök.*, p. xiv; *10. These über Feuerbach*. On criticism of "generic man," see Stirner's *Der Einzige und sein Eigentum*,. and also B. Bauer, *Vollständige Geschichte der Parteikämpfe*, Vol. II, Chap. 4; Vol. III, pp. 30 ff., 185.
88 *Kritik der Gegenwart*, p. 54; cf. *Tagebücher*, I, 315 f.: "The 'mass' is actually what I have taken for the goal of my polemic." Cf. Immermann's *Memorabilien*, I (1839): "In truth our age furnishes a strange spectacle in regard to energy. There is a well-known passage where Schiller develops the dichotomy between the spirit of individuals and the spirit of their fraternization. Today a parody could be made from the opposite point of view: where many work together, there appears a giant, which, when the associates are observed individually, dissolves into a swarm of dwarfs. This is one of the most outstanding points of transition from the subjective period to the objective."
89 See F. C. Fischer, *Die Nullpunkt-Existenz* (Munich, 1933), pp. 203 ff.
90 XII², pp. 17 ff.; cf. Feuerbach's criticism, which is equally sarcastic, I, 98 ff.
91 *Ibid.*, pp. 5 ff.
92 "This Grundtvigian nonsense about 'nationality' is . . . a step backward toward paganism. It is incredible with what mad fanaticism Grundtvigian candidates state their case. Th. Fenger says, for example, that no one can be a true Christian except through 'nationality.' Christianity, whose goal was to eliminate the deification of nationalities rampant in paganism!" "This 'participation in everything' is a figment of the imagination." "In his younger days, he spoke for ancient, ancestral, primeval, pre-primitive Christianity; now, in his old age, he has been decked out as a first-rate pillar of the Establishment."

"It has anyhow come to this, that what is now called Christianity is precisely what Christ came to supplant. It has come to this particularly in Protestantism, particularly among the disciples of Grundtvig. They are, precisely—Jews. . . . Their superstitious faith in ancestry is genuinely Jewish. Further, they imagine that they are God's chosen people. . . . That is Jewish optimism . . . and is passed off as the Christianity of the New Testament!" (*Buch des Richters,* pp. 177 ff.).

93 Cf. the study of Marx in C. Frantz, *Louis Napoleon* (1852), reprinted by F. Kemper (Potsdam, 1933).

94 Cf. K. Hecker, *Mensch und Masse,* pp. 96, 113; Immermann, *Epigonen,* I, (1830), 10.

95 *Tagebücher,* I, 328.

96 *Tagebücher,* I, 64.

97 On the relationship between externality and internality, see Hegel's *Logik,* ed. Lasson, II, 150 ff., 156, 169; *Enc.,* Sects. 139 ff. Kierkegaard, I, 3 f., 21; IV, 253, 409, 444 f. Marx, III, 160 ff.; V, 26 ff.

98 *Enc.,* Sect. 123, Zus.

99 See Kierkegaard, IX, 74 ff.

100 *Briefe,* I, 26 ff.

101 F. Rosenzweig, *Hegel und der Staat,* I (Munich, 1920), 73 ff.

102 *Briefe,* I, 321.

103 XVI, 171.

104 I², pp. 168 ff., 173; XIII, 66; cf. XVI, 47.

105 I², p. 246; *Theolog. Jugendschr.,* p. 348; *Vorlesungen über die Philosophie der Religion,* ed. Lasson, I, 240 ff.

106 Rosenkranz, *Hegels Leben,* pp. 88 ff. Also, Haym, *Hegel und seine Zeit,* pp. 62 ff.; cf. Dilthey, *Ges. Schr.,* IV, 122 ff.

107 Marx would have been able to acquire an indirect idea of this, but only after 1844, from Rosenkranz' monograph on Hegel. In a lecture delivered in Frankfurt in 1932, G. Lukacs attempted to furnish a Marxist reconstruction of the commentary by Hegel on Stewart's *Political Economy* mentioned there (p. 86). As far as I know, this lecture has remained unpublished.

108 Rosenkranz, *op. cit.,* p. 88; cf. Marx I/1, pp. 585 ff.

109 Cf. on the contrary Hegel's later estimation of public opinion in *Rechtsphilosophie,* Sects. 315 ff. Cf. Rosenkranz, *op. cit.,* p. 416.

110 See *Jenenser Realphilosophie,* II, 249, margin. Cf. *Philosoph. Proprädeutik,* Sect. 56.

111 Cf. the resolution of this contradiction in *Rechtsphilosophie,* Sects. 190 ff., 241 ff.; cf. IX, 200, where emigration is mentioned as a means of eliminating the contradiction.

112 Rosenkranz, *op. cit.,* p. 90.

113 *Ibid.,* pp. 92 ff. (= *Schr. zur Politik und Rechtsphilos.,* pp. 151 ff.).

114 In 1795 Hegel expected the transformation of the existing order through the "spread of ideas as to how everything *should* be" (*Briefe,* I, 15). That is, he still equated ideas with ideals, contrary to the "indolence of the people in power," who always accept everything "exactly as it is" (cf. *Briefe,* I, 194, and the poem "Eleusis").

115 *Schr. zur Politik und Rechtsphilos.,* p. 5.

116 See XV, 95 f.

117 Haym, *op. cit.*, pp. 368 ff., 387 ff., 462.
118 *Briefe*, I, 11 f.
119 *Theolog. Jugendschr.*, p. 215; cf. Lagarde, *Deutsche Schriften* (Göttingen, 1892), p. 183.
120 Thirty years later, on Reformation Day, Hegel gave an address in Latin.
121 *Theolog. Jugendschr.*, pp. 215 f.; on the following, cf. Rousseau, *Contrat Social*, IV, 8.
122 *Ibid.*, pp. 219 f.
123 *Ibid.*, p. 220.
124 Cf. Gibbon, *The Decline and Fall of the Roman Empire*, Chap. 15.
125 *Theolog. Jugendschr.*, pp. 71, 223, 229 f.; cf. *Schrf. zur Politik und Rechtsphilos.*, pp. 472 f. This description of private life, for which security of person and property is the highest goal and death the most terrible event, contains *in nucleo* the later analysis of bourgeois society. On the basic significance of the fear of death for the spirit of bourgeois society, see Leo Strauss, *The Political Philosophy of Hobbes* (Oxford, 1936), pp. 57 f., 105 f., 122 f.
126 *Theolog. Jugendschr.*, p. 225; similarly in *Geschichte der Philosophie*, XV, 116 f. Cf. Wellhausen's distinction between ancient Israel and post-exilic Judaism, on the basis of which Wellhausen was enabled to sketch ancient Israel in the same way Hegel sketched the Greek *polis*. See the Marburg dissertation of F. Boschwitz, *J. Wellhausen, Motive und Massstäbe seiner Geschichtesschreibung* (Marburg, 1938), pp. 26, 35 ff.
127 *Theolog. Jugendschr.*, p. 229.
128 *Ibid.*, p. 228. Cf. Part II, Chapter 5 of the present work for Bauer's interpretation of the Hegelian philosophy of religion according to the principle of subjectivity.
129 *Ibid.*, pp. 245 ff.
130 *Ibid.*, p. 342.
131 *Enc.*, Sect. 552.
132 *Briefe*, I, pp. 13, 18.
133 *Theolog. Jugendschr.*, pp. 225, 71.
134 Rosenkranz, *op. cit.*, p. 557.
135 XIII, 171 ff., XVI, 139.

IV Nietzsche as Philosopher of Our Age and of Eternity

1 See A. Bäumler, *Nietzsche der Philosoph und Politiker* (Liepzig, 1931); the author's *Nietzsches Philosophie der ewigen Wiederkunft des Gleichen* (Berlin, 1935); K. Jaspers, *Nietzsche, Einführung in das Verständnis seines Philosophierens* (Berlin, 1936); K. Hildebrandt, "Über Deutung und Einordnung von Nietzsches System," *Kantstudien* (1936).
2 Hints of the historical connection between Nietzsche and Marx can be found in H. Fischer, *Nietzsche Apostata* (Erfurt, 1931), pp. 13 ff.; see also E. Troeltsch, *Der Historismus und seine Probleme* (1922), pp. 26, 497 ff., and W. Schubart, *Europa und die Seele des Ostens* (Luzern, 1938), pp. 195 f.
3 See Overbeck's remark in *Christentum und Kultur* (Basel, 1919), p. 287.

4   X, 253, 264; XV, 35.
5   XV, 211 f.
6   XV, 218; cf. XIV, 178; X, 279 ff.
7   I, 426 f.; cf. III, 264; XIII, 335.
8   I, 510 f.
9   X, 250; VIII, 129.
10 VIII, 13.
11 III, 128, 265 f.
12 III, 89.
13 IV, 179 f.; VIII, 111 ff.
14 VIII, 163 f., and also "Beschreibung der Wohlgeratenheit," XV, 12 f.
15 See the letter to Zelter of December 25, 1829; on Goethe's irony, see E. Franz, *Goethe als religiöser Denker* (Tübingen, 1932), pp. 62 ff.
16 XV, 272; VIII, 50, 165.
17 VI, 428 ff.; cf. XII, 383; VII, 315, and the early poem "Vor dem Kruzifix."
18 Letter to Zelter of July 27, 1828.
19 *Gespräche*, III, 504.
20 Nietzsche, III, 90.
21 V, 300 ff.
22 IV, 7 f.
23 See the author's book on Nietzsche, p. 81; Jaspers, *Nietzsche*, pp. 317, 325.
24 XV, 439 f., 442.
25 V, 301.
26 I, 353 ff.
27 On Hegel's influence on H. Taine, see VII, 225; also Rosca, *L'influence de Hegel sur Taine* (Paris, 1928).
28 VII, 145.
29 *Schopenhauers Briefe*, ed. Griesebach (Leipzig), p. 300.
30 *Ibid.*, p. 77.
31 *Ibid.*, p. 78, note, and p. 82. The review appeared in Vol. IV, No. 2, pp. 29 ff. Schopenhauer mentions here also an essay which appeared in the *Pilot* in May, 1841, "Jüngstes Gericht über die Hegelsche Philosophie," whose author speaks of him "with most appropriate approbation." This presumably refers to an article on Bauer's *Posaune*. As another "very well stated" presentation of his teaching on the part of an Hegelian, Schopenhauer mentions De Sanctis' work, *Schopenhauer und Leopardi* (1858–59).
32 *Schopenhauers Briefe*, p. 266; cf. p. 128.
33 *Ibid.*, p. 285.
34 See K. Hildbrandt, *Wagner und Nietzsche im Kampf gegen das 19. Jahrhundert* (Breslau, 1924), p. 9.
35 Cf. F. Engels' appreciation of Carlyle's *Past and Present* (1843), Marx–Engels, *Ges. Ausg.*, II, 405 ff.
36 Quoted by K. Hildebrandt, *op. cit.*, p. 44; cf. R. Huch, *M. Bakunin* (Leipzig, 1923), pp. 103 f., 113 ff., 116 f., 119 f.
37 Wagner was living in Zürich at the time as a political exile, and attempted to have Feuerbach called there. He dedicated to Feuerbach *Das Kunstwerk der Zukunft* (1850); cf. Nietzsche's criticism of Wagner's *Musik ohne Zukunft*, VIII, 191 ff.
38 IX, 412. Cf. Ruge's remark that he had been told "quite drily" that all his

writings stemmed only from the fact that he had had no success at the University! (*Br.*, I, 289)

39 I, 250.
40 VIII, 197 ff.; cf. VII, 403.
41 XIV, 168.
42 VIII, 33 f.
43 *Ges. Br.*, III, 201, 274; likewise in P. Gast, *Br.*, IV, 81 f. On Nietzsche's first *Unzeitgemässe Betrachtung*, see Bauer's *Philo, Strauss und Renan und das Urchristentum* (Berlin, 1874), particularly pp. 16 ff. On G. Keller's relationship to Feuerbach, which brought about his rejection of Nietzsche's attack upon Strauss, cf. A. Kohut, *Feuerbach* (Leipzig, 1909), pp. 230 ff.
44 *Ges. Br.*, IV, 54; cf. p. 94 and the letters from P. Gast to Nietzsche (Munich, 1923–24), I, 220, 225; II, 162.
45 Cf. C. A. Bernoulli, *Overbeck und Nietzsche* (Jena, 1908), I, 441.
46 See the present work, Part II, Chapter 5. Cf. D. Tschizewskij, "Hegel et Nietzsche," *Revue d'histoire de la philosophie* (Paris, 1929), pp. 338 ff.; E. Benz, "Nietzsches Ideen zur Geschichte des Christentums," *Zeitschr. für Kirchengesch.*, Vol. LVI, Nos. 2/3 (1937).
47 C. A. Bernoulli, *op. cit.*, I, 135 f., 148 ff., 238 ff., 427 ff.; cf. Ch. Andler, *Nietzsche*, IV, 166 ff.
48 Thus E. Barnikol in his new edition of Bauer's *Entdecktes Christentum*, p. 79.
49 See Tschijewskij, "Hegel et Nietzsche," pp. 331 ff.
50 *Zeitschr. für die deutsche Wortforschung*, Vol. I, No. 1 (1900), pp. 3 ff., 369 ff.
51 M. Hess, *Sozialistische Aufsätze*, pp. 149, 188 ff.
52 *Das entdeckte Christentum*, Sect. 12.
53 See the author's book on Nietzsche, pp. 36 ff.
54 A family relationship has also been discovered through a study of correspondence with Ruge: Ruge's wife was born Agnes Nietzsche, belonging, like Nietzsche, to the third generation of Gotthelf Engelbert Nietzsche (1714–1804). See Ruge, *Br.*, I, 19, 23, 43.
55 Hegel, I², p. 153; *Phänomenologie*, ed. Lasson, p. 483; XI, 352 ff.
56 VI, 456.
57 XIV, 348.
58 D'Annunzio, *Per la morte di un distruttore*; A. Gide, "Nietzsche," *Jahrbuch der Nietzsche-Gesellschaft* (Munich, 1925); R. Pannwitz, *Einführung in Nietzsche* (Munich-Feldafing, 1920); G. Benn, *Nach dem Nihilismus* (Stuttgart, 1932); R. Thiel, *Generation ohne Männer* (Berlin, 1932), particularly the chapters on Thomas Mann and St. George. See also G. Deesz, *Die Entwicklung des Nietzschebildes in Deutschland*, Bonn dissertation (1933).
59 *Fröhl. Wiss.* Aph. 377; cf. letter to Overbeck of March 24, 1887: "Enclosed a strange fact, which comes more and more to my attention. I have gradually come to have some 'influence'—all underground, of course. Among all the radical parties (Socialists, Nihilists, Anti-Semitists, Christian-Orthodox, Wagnerians) I enjoy an amazing and almost mysterious esteem. . . . In the *Antisemitische Korrespondenz* (which is only sent privately, only to 'trusted party members'), my name appears in almost every issue. Zarathustra, the divine human being, has bewitched the anti-Semites; they have their own anti-Semitic interpretation of him, which has given me a good laugh. In passing: I

made the suggestion to the 'competent authority' that a careful list be made up of all German scholars, artists, writers, actors, and musicians of Jewish or partially Jewish descent. This would be an outstanding contribution to the history of German civilization, and also to its *criticism.*"

60   XIV, 420; cf. *Ges. Br.,* I, 534.
61   *Ges. Br.,* I, 515.
62   On the following, see the author's book on Nietzsche, pp. 36 ff.
63   XVI, 422.
64   VI, 203 ff., 210; XV, 80; XVI, 515, 401 f.
65   VI, 295 f.
66   VI, 206 f.; cf. XVI, 201, 409; XIV, 219; *Wille zur Macht,* Aph. 617 and 708.
67   VI, 18, 304; XV, 96.
68   XV, 48, and the poem "Letzter Wille."
69   VI, 294 f.
70   *Vorrede zur Morgenröte,* para. 3 and 4. On Nietzsche's theory of recurrence, cf. the remarkable parallel in the Russian philosopher Strachov, cited in Tschizewskij, *Hegel bei den Slaven,* pp. 327 ff.
71   See H. Ball, *Die Flucht aus der Zeit* (Munich, 1931); Th. Haecker, *Schöpfer und Schöpfung* (Leipzig, 1934); M. Scheler, *Vom Ewigen im Menschen* (Leipzig, 1923); L. Klages, *Der Geist als Widersacher der Seele* (Leipzig, 1929); K. Jaspers, *Philosophie,* Vol. III (Berlin, 1932).
72   VI, 42 f.
73   X, 233 ff.; see the author's work on Nietzsche, pp. 83 ff.
74   *Maximen und Reflexionen,* No. 542; cf. the beginning and conclusion of the letters to Zelter of January 15, 1826 and January 21, 1826.
75   Letter to Zelter of November 21, 1830.
76   Letter to Zelter of November 14, 1816.
77   See also the Shakespeare Address of 1772, in which he says that all Shakespeare's pieces "revolve about the secret point which no philosopher has yet seen or defined, in which the individuality of the ego, the pretended freedom of our will, collides with the necessary course of the whole" (Weimar Edition, I/37, p. 133).
78   F. Schlegel's letter to his brother of February 27, 1794.
79   *Wille zur Macht,* Aph. 749; cf. Nietzsche's self-criticism in *Ges. Br.,* IV, 75 ff., 345, 355.
80   XV, 85.

V   The Spirit of the Age and the Question of Eternity

1   *Briefe zur Beförderung der Humanität,* I, 11.
2   Cf. Herder's essay of 1795, *Homer ein Günstling der Zeit.*
3   *Briefe zur Beförderung der Humanität,* II, 14.
4   *Ibid.,* II, 15.
5   *Theolog. Jugendschr.,* p. 220; cf. pp. 228, 229.
6   Fichte, *Werke,* 6 vols., ed. Medicus, Vol. IV, pp. 407 f.
7   *Ibid.,* p. 639.
8   On the equation of "all-powerful time" with "eternal destiny," see also

Goethe's "Prometheus" fragment (1773) and Hegel's work on the German Constitution (1802), *Schr. zur Politik und Rechtsphilos.*, p. 74. In Hölderlin's poem "Zu lang schon waltest über dem Haupt mir . . ." the "God of time" is said both to awaken the spirit of man and also, even more, to make it tremble.

9 Immermann, *Die Epigonen*, Part I, Book I, Chap. 8; Book II, Chap. 10. Cf. F. Gundolf's lecture on Immermann in *Romantiker*, n. f. (Berlin 1931); also K. Hecker, *Mensch und Masse*, pp. 72 ff.

10 See also *Epigonen*, Part I, Book II, Chap. 4 ("Die Weltgeschichte ist das Weltgericht").

11 Marx-Engels, *Ges. Ausg.*, Part I, Vol. II, pp. 111 ff., 126 ff. See also the articles on Immermann in *Hallesche Jahrbücher*, II (1839), and III (1840).

12 *Kapital*, III/2, 2nd edition, p. 355.

13 *Briefe*, I, 13.

14 *Angriff auf die Christenheit*, p. 458.

15 "Über die Geduld und die Erwartung des Ewigen," *Religiöse Reden*, translated by Th. Haecker (Leipzig, 1938), pp. 65 ff., 181 ff.

16 V, 78 ff.; VII, 48. Cf. the author's work on Nietzsche, pp. 64 ff., 153 ff. on Nietzsche's concept of "noon and eternity."

17 V., 79, note; p. 84, note.

18 See G. Kuhlmann, "Zum theologischen Problem der Existenz," *Zeitschr. für Theologie und Kirche* (1929), pp. 49 ff.; also the author's article in *Theol. Rundschau*, No. 5 (1930), pp. 334 ff.

19 See Kierkegaard, III, 180.

20 On Heidegger's anticipation of death, cf. Kierkegaard, VI, 242 ff.

21 Cf. J. Wahl, *Études Kierkegaardiennes*, pp. 465, 468, 470.

22 *Sein und Zeit*, Sect. 53.

23 *Kant und das Problem der Metaphysik* (Bonn, 1929), pp. 231 f.

24 *Jenenser Logik*, ed. Lasson (Leipzig, 1923), pp. 202 ff.

25 *Enc.*, Sect. 259, Zus.

26 Preface to *Rechtsphilosophie*.

27 XI, 4.

28 *Enc.*, Sect. 258.

29 *Die Vernunft in der Geschichte*, ed. Lasson, p. 166.

30 See Heidegger's reversal of the Hegelian thesis at the end of Section 82 of *Sein und Zeit*.

31 *Sein und Zeit*, Sect. 82.

32 *Ibid.*, Sect. 68a, and conclusion of Sect. 81.

33 *Ibid.*, Sect. 74.

34 In contrast to Heidegger's terminology, in ordinary German usage (as in Hegel and Goethe), *Dasein* means precisely what Heidegger means it not to be, namely, "being present."

35 *Gespräche*, III, 36 f. On the following, cf. F. Rosenzweig, *Der Stern der Erlösung*, Part III, pp. 36 ff.; also E. Staiger, *Die Zeit als Einbildungskraft des Dichters* (Zürich, 1939), pp. 101 ff.

36 *Fragment über die Natur*.

37 See stanza five of the poem "Vermächtnis."

38 *Maximen und Reflexionen*, No. 388.

39 Cf. Goethe's correspondence with M. Willemer, ed. Hecker (Leipzig, 1915), pp. 42 f., 312 f.

40 See *Gespräche*, III, 446; cf. IV, 160 f.
41 *Gespräche*, III, 421.
42 Letter of April 17, 1823; cf. stanza five of "Vermächtnis."
43 *Gespräche*, I, 495.
44 See J. Henning, "Die Geschichte des Wortes Geschichte, *Deutsche Viertel-jahrsschr. für Literaturwiss. und Gesitesgesch.*, No. 4 (1938).
45 *Die Vernunft in der Geschichte*, ed. Lasson, p. 191; also A. von Humboldt's ironic remark: "Of course this Hegel is for me a forest of ideas, . . . but to a man like me, who crawls like an insect on the ground and is held in check by his own differing nature, an abstract statement of completely false facts and views about America and Indies seems only repressive and alarming. . . . I would forgo the 'European beef' which Hegel on page 77 says is so superior to the American, and live among the weak, powerless (unfortunately twenty-five feet long) crocodiles." *A. von Humboldts Briefe an Varnhagen von Ense* (1860), pp. 44 f.
46 *Rechtsphilosophie*, Sects. 337, 345.
47 *Vide supra*, II, 2, b.
48 B. Croce, *Ultimi Saggi* (Bari, 1935), pp. 246 ff. on "antistoricismo."
49 It is significant for the historical connection between the two theories that an Hegelian like Marx could see in Darwin a materialistic dialectician, and dedicate *Das Kapital* to him.
50 Cf. Nietzsche, I, 223, 353 f.; X, 273 f. The best example of the theory of historical success is the victory of Christianity over the ancient world. Not only Hegel, but almost all historians accept the facts that the historical success of Christianity, its expansion throughout half the world, its permanence and its power furnish at least indirect proof of its spiritual superiority. For the contrary view, see Nietzsche, I, 340, 368; X, 401. Also Kierkegaard, VI, 140 ff. Precisely because they took Christianity seriously, both of them rejected the "evidence of centuries."
51 See J. Burckhardt, VII, 26, 198, 205.
52 See L. Klages, *Die psychologischen Errungenschaften Nietzsches* (Leipzig, 1926), Chap. 6.
53 See the chapter on "Historische Grösse" in Burckhardt's *Weltgeschichtliche Betrachtungen*.
54 Goethe, *Gespräche*, II, 159.
55 See the author's *Meaning in History: The Theological Implications of the Philosophy of History* (Chicago, 1949).
56 *Gespräche*, III, 74.
57 Letter of March 3, 1790; cf. *Annalen*, Vol. XXVII, *op. cit.*, pp. 9, 19 f.; *Gespräche*, III, 61 f.
58 Goethe, XL, 446.
59 Letter to Zelter of January 2, 1829; see Tieck, *Goethe und seine Zeit* (1828); also Gutzkow, *Über Goethe im Wendepunkt zweier Jahrhunderte* (1835).
60 Goethe, XXV, p. 61.
61 *Ibid.*, p. 225; cf. Vol. XXVII, 46, 226.
62 Letter to Zelter of July 27, 1807; cf. *Gespräche*, I, 491 ff.
63 *Gespräche*, I, 449.
64 Letter to Graf Reinhard of November 14, 1812; cf. letter to Ch. L. F. Schultz of May 31, 1825; *Gespräche*, III, 489.

65 Letter to Schiller of March 9, 1802; cf. *Gespräche*, I, 494 f.
66 *Gespräche*, I, 546 f.; cf. III, 491 ff.; IV, 94 f.; also "Timur" in *West-östlicher Diwan*.
67 Cf. Hegel's statement: "But if you are awake, you will see everything and call everything by name. This is reason, this is domination of the world" (Rosenkranz, *Hegels Leben*, p. 540).
68 *Gespräche*, IV, 476; cf. II, 49; III, 96 f., 492; letter to Beulwitz of July 18, 1828.
69 *Des Epimenides Erwachen*, epigraph.
70 *Gespräche*, I, 434 f.
71 *Gespräche*, I, 435; cf. letter to Zelter of September 4, 1831, to Reinhard of September 7, 1831.
72 *Gespräche*, IV, 290; V, 175; conversation with Eckermann of August 2, 1830.
73 *Gespräche*, IV, 69; cf. II, 40.
74 *Gespräche*, II, 572.
75 *Gespräche*, II, 6.
76 *Gespräche*, II, 419; cf. p. 416; III, 155; IV, 275; letter to F. Mendelssohn-Bartholdy of September 9, 1831.
77 *Geschichte der Farbenlehre*, XXXIX, 59.
78 *Ibid.*, 1; cf. *Gespräche*, II, 632; IV, 51.
79 See Burckhardt's characteristic regret that Goethe "was preoccupied with botany" at the expense of his tragedy of *Nausicaea* (XIV, 176), and that he set limits to the nature of the spirit (VII, 18); cf. Dilthey, *Ges. Schr.*, VII, 88 ff.
80 F. Meinecke, "Goethes Missvergnügen an der Geschichte," *Berliner Sitzungs-berichte* (1933); *Die Entstehung des Historismus*, II (1936), 480 ff. Meinecke's ability to include Goethe in the origins of "historicism" is comprehensible only when one realizes that his theme is not the historicism which derives from Hegel, but the individualization of man's attitude toward life. On what follows, cf. E. Cassirer, *Goethe und die geschichtliche Welt* (Berlin, 1932); H. Cysarz, *Goethe und das geschichtliche Weltbild* (Brünn, 1932); A. Schweitzer, *Goethe* (Munich, 1932).
81 *Gespräche*, III, 489.
82 *Gespräche*, III, 137.
83 Letter to Zelter of March 27, 1824; cf. *Gespräche*, II, 571; *Maximen und Reflexionen*, No. 271; letter to F. H. Jacobi of July 7, 1793.
84 *Gespräche*, I, 433 ff.
85 Cf. the section on "Geschichte und Politik" in Gundolf's *Goethe*, where he asserts that history had merely "symbolic truth" for Goethe. Its only value was to convey "images" of events, to arouse the imagination, and develop character through great deeds and figures, all without regard to "empirical accuracy." Historical and philological criticism was mistrusted. But it is only necessary to refer to Goethe's conversations with Luden, to his relationship with F. A. Wolf and his estimation of Niebuhr (letter to Niebuhr of April 4, 1827), to realize that this explanation of history according to the criterion of "poets and heroes" does not agree at all with Goethe's seriousness and sense of reality.
86 Weimar Edition, IV/22, p. 28; cf. *Tagebücher*, IV, 183 f., and the letter to Zelter of October 11, 1826.
87 Good examples of rewriting of German history (besides the publications of the *Reichsinstitut für die Geschichte des neuen Deutschlands*): H. Schwarz,

Grundzüge einer Geschichte der artdeutschen Philosophie (Berlin, 1937); E. Seeberg, *Meister Eckhart* (Tübingen, 1934); H. Mandel, *Deutscher Gottglaube von der deutschen Mystik bis zur Gegenwart* (Leipzig, 1930); etc.

88 I, 336.

89 I, 330 ff.

90 See the symptomatic address of H. Freyer, *Das geschichtliche Selbstbewusstsein des 20. Jahrhunderts* (Leipzig, 1937).

91 *Geschichte der Farbenlehre*, XXXIX, 4, 61.

92 Letter to Zelter of January 2, 1829; cf. the letter of March 23–29, 1827.

93 R. Oehler, *Die Zukunft der Nietzschebewegung* (Leipzig, 1938).

94 Immermann, *Memorabilien*, "Fränkische Reise: Goethes Haus":

"A Jove principium, in Jove finis"

In an open space, brought to life by a fountain, there can be seen a two-story house, covered with a coat of reddish-grey paint, the windows surrounded by black frames. It seems spacious, but no more so than the average residence of a well-to-do townsman. We step through the doorway, and stand in an entrance hall made bright and cheerful by a yellowish paint. We climb up the steps, which are provided with side pieces of massive masonry; broad treads lead upward on the gentlest of inclines . . .

In the upper hall, the figures of Sleep and of Death, as well as a colossal head of Juno, stare at us out of niches in the wall. Views of Rome, hanging above the steps, recall that land after leaving which, as he used to say, he had never again been truly happy.

A narrow little room, painted yellow, appears. Here he dined with his guests. The walls are covered with Meyer's drawings of antique or Poussinic objects; behind a green curtain he kept the water color of Meyer's "Wedding of Aldobrandini," which he considered his most valuable treasure. The rooms to the right and left, also, are furnished solely with articles which belong to this artistic period and movement. There is . . . nothing that was not devoured in the period of his education, and nothing of a later period was permitted to enter. Moved, we survey the poor, small objects with which the great man grew up.

To the right, off this room, we look into the so-called Deckenzimmer. . . . To the left lies his blue reception room, and beyond it the so-called Urbino room, named after the picture of a Duke of Urbino which he brought from Italy. . . . At the door to his reception room, we are greeted by his friendly "Salve!" . . .

These are the rooms to which others were admitted during his lifetime. To his workroom, with the exception of his most intimate friends, Coudray, Riemer, Müller, Eckermann, he admitted no one . . .

Death removed the ban laid by the master; we could go at will through the tiny communicating chambers, directly through the house, to the study and workroom. We stopped for a moment in one of the small chambers; it is the one in which he took his meals when he was alone with his children. A leafy canopy in front of this room gives it a green tinge; one step takes the visitor to the garden in which Goethe used to enjoy watching the sun during his free hours. In the corner stands a summerhouse in which he kept his scientific apparatus.

In the entrance hall to the museum, in cabinets and under glass, I saw steps, stone, conchylia, petrifacts—in short, everything that was the object of his scientific studies. I found everything kept very clean, and arranged with a certain elegance. A door opened on the right; I looked into the library. It might appear rather small in comparison to the resources that were available here. Goethe purposely did not collect many books, since the libraries of Weimar and Jena were open to him. In order to prevent the accumulation of whatever objects might seem to him unnecessary, he gave away most of the things sent to him from far and near as soon as he had read them.

Now the secretary of the library, Kräuter, who had been Goethe's scribe, . . . opened the door to the workroom, and I saw a moving sight. . . . This small, low, tasteless green room, with dark serge window shades, shabby window sills, frames beginning to decay, was the place from which such a stream of brilliant light had poured forth! I was deeply moved; I had to compose myself in order not to fall into a reverie which would have robbed me of my power of vision.

Nothing has been moved from its place; Kräuter insists religiously that every scrap of paper, every pen shaving remain in the place where it lay when the master passed away . . .

Every spot here is holy ground. The thousand objects with which the room is filled bespeak the nature and activity of the spirit. Round about the walls run low cabinets with drawers, in which various pieces of writing were kept. Above them are repositories in which Goethe placed whatever occupied him at the moment. . . . He read standing, he wrote standing, he even devoured his breakfast standing at a high table. He recommended similar behavior to everyone in whom he took an interest; it would lengthen a man's life, as would holding the hands behind the back, so that, as he put it, the chest was kept from all narrowing and compression.

Let us examine more carefully this venerable work-place! Left, by the door, hangs a kind of historical diary. Each year Goethe placed in the first column the personages and institutions which in his opinion showed promise of making history; in the following columns he noted whether and to what extent they fulfilled their promise. He had great expectations of Jackson; but his behavior toward the Indians was subsequently given a black mark.

A cardboard pyramid which he made himself, which now stands in a repository, is remarkable as a monument to a psychological game. Goethe wanted to determine more closely the relationship between the various faculties of the soul. The world of the senses seemed to him to be the basis of all the rest; he therefore showed it as the base of the pyramid, which he colored green. Fantasy was given a dark red side, reason yellow, wisdom blue.

Beside it lies a hemisphere of cardboard, painted black, on which Goethe loved to make bright sunshine light up with all the colors of the rainbow by means of a glass sphere full of water. He could occupy himself with it for hours on end, particularly after the death of his son; it was one of his greatest pleasures to produce this brilliant spectrum so energetically.

He was completely happy whenever he encountered a natural phenomenon. There stands a small bust of Napoleon, made of fused opal, which Eckermann had brought him from Switzerland; it confirmed aspects of his theory of color, and gave him real delight. He rejoiced like a child over the bottle that is shown us in the other table. It had been full of red wine; it had been lying on its side, and when Goethe accidentally held it to the light he saw in it the most beautiful crystalline patterns of precipitate, in the shape of flowers and foliage. He called his friends together enthusiastically, showed them the phenomenon, had a burning candle brought, and ceremoniously impressed his device in sealing wax upon the cork, lest any accident disturb the bottle. The bottle remained in the room ever since.

Napoleon gave him information in the realm of light; but he also was to Goethe a demon in that dark region into which no ray of light from the upper world penetrates. On the day of the battle of Leipzig, a plaster figure fell from the nail that was holding it; a piece of the edge broke off, without any damage to the countenance of the hero. In a niche there still hangs the damaged figure; parodying Lucian, Goethe inscribed on the image in red letters the verse:

Scilicet immenso superest ex nomine multum.

Here is also the original manuscript of the Roman Elegies . . . also the first version of Götz . . .

Goethe had an immoderate love for neatness. It disturbed him that the little perpetual calendar which he used would not stay clean through the year, and so with his own hands he made a cardboard case for it.

In the midst of the room stands a large round table. At it sat the copyist to whom Goethe dictated while walking ceaselessly about the table. Work began at eight in the morning, and often lasted until two in the afternoon, with no interruption.

In the evening, when Goethe withdrew (as always in his latter years) to this quiet room, his servant would look at his eyes, to see whether they were friendly and alert. If he sensed in them a desire for information and companionship, he would silently move the easy chair to the table, lay a cushion upon it, set a basket at the side in which Goethe might lay his shawl. Goethe would then sit down, waiting to see whether a friend would visit him. His associates would have been informed in the meantime, and who would not gladly come when it was possible! Then he would sit with his small circle until nearly eleven, in familiar conversation, and have wine and cold dishes brought for them. For years he had himself taken nothing in the evening.

Now I was to see his deathbed. He did not die lying down; if not, as befits the Emperor, standing, at least sitting. To the left of the workroom is the bedroom. It, too, is quite small, without decoration, even shabbier than the workroom. Only in his last years did Goethe look to his health to the extent of hanging a woolen blanket on rings between the bed and the wall immediately next to it, as a shield against the coldness of the wall. Besides this arrangement, and a narrow rug before the bed, there is here no sign of softness or comfortable living. The bed itself is low, covered with an old blanket of red silk, so narrow that I cannot understand how his large body could find room in it.

In all these details one sees the image of a wise man, a great man, for whom decoration and fancywork had their place, but who wanted only absolute simplicity in his immediate environment, because he was his own finest ornament.

There at the head of the bed stands the chair in which this majestic life breathed its last. All are completely agreed that his death came without struggle, without pain, without outward sign of its approach, that no one even noted the actual moment of its coming . . .

Young people should be brought here, that they may gain an impression of a secure, honorable way of life. Here they should be required to take three oaths: that of diligence, of truthfulness, of consistency.

Part II   I   The Problem of Bourgeois Society

1   *Emile*, Chap. 1.
2   Cf. in the First Discourse, especially the speech of Fabricius in praise of Roman virtues; the Second Discourse sketches the problem of the *Contrat Social*, although it is a eulogy of prepolitical life. Rousseau dedicated it to the Councillors of Geneva, as the governors of a true *polis*. He acknowledged the consequences for himself by once more becoming Protestant for the sake of political allegiance.
3   On what follows, see the Marburg dissertation of K. D. Erdmann, *Das Verhältnis von Staat und Religion nach der Sozialphilosophie Rousseaus* (1955).
4   IV, 8. A summary of the *Contrat Social* is contained in the fifth book of *Emile* and the sixth letter of *Lettres de la Montagne*.
5   See *Napoleons Gespräche*, ed. Kircheisen, III (Stuttgart, 1913), 195 f., 256, 262.
6   G. Jellinek, *Die Erklärung der Menschen- und Bürgerrechte* (4th edition; Munich, 1927).
7   IX, 438 ff.; cf. XV, 534 f.; *Phänomenologie*, ed. Lasson, pp. 378 ff.
8   *Enc.*, Sect. 163, Zus. 1.
9   *Rechtsphilosophie*, Sect. 184.
10   *Ibid.*, Preface (2nd edition), p. 7, Sect. 268, Zus.
11   Cf. H. Freyer, *Einleitung in die Soziologie* (Leipzig, 1931), pp. 63 ff.
12   *Rechtsphilosophie*, Sects. 4 to 7; also the application of the analysis of the will to Rousseau and the French Revolution, Sect. 258.
13   *Ibid.*, Sect. 260, Zus.
14   *Ibid.*, Sect. 185; cf. Preface (2nd edition), p. 16; Sect. 46, Sect. 260, Zus. See also F. Rosenzweig, *Hegel und der Staat*, II (Munich, 1920), 77 ff.
15   *Rechtsphilosophie*, Sect. 185 and Zus.
16   *Enc.*, Sect. 482; cf. Sect. 163, Zus. 1; also XIV, 272 ff.
17   L. v. Stein, *Der Begriff der Gesellschaft*, ed. G. Salomon (Munich, 1921), pp. 52, 502 f.; see also S. Landshut, *Kritik der Soziologie* (Munich, 1929), pp. 82 ff.
18   Rousseau's ideal man was not the proletarian, but rather the plebeian, whom he ennobled. He distinguishes him from the upper classes, the rich and aristocratic. "Le peuple," that is, the middle class of craftsmen and peasants around Lake Geneva, the simple, common man who gains his living through the work of his own hands, to whom the father is the highest ideal. As the son of such a craftsman he was proudly aware of being nobly born. (Dedication of the Second Discourse, and letter to David Hume of August 4, 1766.) This was also the view of the Assembly. When Rousseau's remains were brought into the Pantheon, the Assembly had representatives of various trades march in procession carrying a tablet on which was written, "To the man who restored the honor of useful industry." It is precisely this "natural" and "good" man, in sociological terms the petit bourgeois, who is the perpetual object of attack by Marx. Marx sought to demonstrate to "bourgeois socialism" that this middle class is by no means the entire nation, nor even the best part of it, but rather

the reactionary mass of petit-bourgeois mediocrity. See E. Seillere, *Der demo-kratische Imperialismus* (2nd edition; Berlin, 1911), pp. 357 ff., 119, 163 f.

19 I/1, p. 593.

20 I/1, pp. 595 ff.; cf. V, 175 ff., 388 ff.; *Das kommunistische Manifest* (9th edition; Berlin, 1930), p. 28.

21 Cf. G. Sorel, *Reflexions sur la violence* (7th edition; Paris, 1930), p. 114; *Les illusions du progrès* (4th edition; Paris, 1927), p. 65.

22 *Das kommunistische Manifest, op. cit.,* pp. 33, 35, 47.

23 V, 389.

24 *Das eine was not tut, op. cit.,* p. 5; II, 224; cf. VI, 204, 208.

25 II, 225.

26 *Das eine was not tut,* p. 7; cf. *Kritik der Gegenwart,* p. 57; *Tagebücher,* 327; *Angriff auf die Christenheit,* p. 15.

27 Address on dictatorship, January 4, 1849, quoted in H. Barth's article on D. Cortes in *Schweizerische Rundschau* (August, 1935), p. 401.

28 *Der Staat Gottes,* ed. L. Fischer (Karlsruhe, 1935), Introduction, p. 58.

29 *Ibid.,* Chap. 4.

30 *De la création de l'ordre dans l'humanité, Oeuvres compl.* (nouvelle ed.; Paris, 1927), pp. 73 f.

31 Tome X, pp. 205 f., 187 f.

32 De Tocqueville, *Autorität und Freiheit,* ed. A. Salomon (Zürich, 1935), pp. 193 f., 15; cf. pp. 51, 207.

33 *Ibid.,* pp. 58 f., 130, 132; cf. pp. 44, 134, 213, 230, 232; *Das alte Staatswesen und die Revolution,* translated by A. Boscowitz (Leipzig, 1857), pp. 94, 318.

44 See G. Gurwitsch, "Kant und Fichte als Rousseau-Interpreten," *Kantstudien,* of freedom; it is a combination of a sense of freedom and success."

35 *Das alte Staatswesen . . . ,* p. xi.

36 *Autorität und Freiheit,* p. 154.

37 *Das alte Staatswesen . . . ,* p. 138; cf. Goethe's letter to Zelter of June 6, 1825.

38 *Autorität und Freiheit,* p. 197; cf. *M. Webers Politische Schriften* (Munich, 1921), p. 152.

39 Letter to B. Croce, *La Critica,* XXVIII (1930), p. 44.

40 *Reflexions sur la violence,* pp. 355 ff.

41 *Ibid.,* pp. 345 ff.; *Les illusions du progrès,* p. 285.

42 *Les illusions du progrès,* p. 336, note 2; pp. 378 ff.

43 The same problem is presented in Sorel's first work, *Le procès de Socrate* (1889), in which he takes the side of Aristophanes against Socrates and Plato. Socrates, he says, destroyed the old forms of society without laying the foundation for any new form; in the ideal State of his pupil, the state has become a church, since, as in the French Revolution, it represents a particular world view.

44 See G. Gurwitsch, "Kant und Fichte als. Rousseau-Interpreten," *Kantstudien,* XXVII (1929), pp. 138 ff.; E. Cassirer, "Das Problem J. J. Rousseau," *Archiv für Geschichte der Philosophie* (1932), pp. 177 ff., 479 ff.

45 X, 290.

46 XII, 417; cf. XIV, 411.

47 XVI, 336 f.

48 XV, 234.

49 XVI, 283; cf. XIV, 204; XV, 349 f.; XVI, 420.

II   The Problem of Work

1   Cf. M. Weber, *Wirtschaft und Gesellschaft* (Tübingen, 1925), p. 800: "It is simply a myth that new dignity was given to labor, e.g., in the New Testament."

2   *Pensées*, ed. L. Brunschvigg (Paris, 1909), pp. 390 ff.

3   See B. Groethuysen, *Die Entstehung der bürgerlichen Weltund Lebensanschauung in Frankreich*, II (Halle, 1930), 80 ff.

4   See the article on work in Voltaire's *Dictionnaire Philosophique*.

5   "In the older language, the dominant meaning of 'Arbeit' (work) was 'molestia,' 'labor'; the meaning 'opus' or 'opera' was secondary. In today's speech, however, the latter meaning is more common, the former less frequent. But both meanings were contained in the word itself. Man's activity has gradually become less and less servile, more free; it was natural to extend the concept of 'work' to the easier and more noble forms of business." Grimm, *Deutsches Wörterbuch*.

6   See H. Marcuse, "Über die philosophischen Grundlagen des wirtschaftswissenschaftlichen Arbeitsbegriff," *Archiv für Sozialwiss. und Sozialpol.*, No. 3 (1933).

7   *Jenenser Realphilosophie*, ed. J. Hoffmeister, I (Leipzig, 1932), 197 ff., 220 ff., 236 ff.; II, 197 ff., 213 ff.; cf. *Schr. zur Politik und Rechtsphilos.*, pp. 422 ff., 478.

8   Cf. XII, 218.

9   *Jenenser Realphilosophie*, I, 203 ff., 221.

10 In the *Phänomenologie*, in the analysis of the consciousness of "master and servant," Hegel makes a similar distinction between work and appetite. Work is a "restricted appetite," which prevents the vanishing of the object of appetite by creating it or giving it form. The worker gives recognition to the object on which he works by being in a negative relationship toward it. This formative activity is a "negative mean" because it mediates self-being with other-being through a positive act of negation. In it, the consciousness of the servant becomes "pure proseity," which achieves the element of permanence in the object on which he works for his master. "Thus the working consciousness achieves hereby a vision of independent being in the form of itself," that is, in working on something else, the servant objectifies his own self in something other, which remains permanent and gains more independence the more the worker puts of himself in the object on which he works. In forming an object, the proseity of a subject becomes object vis-à-vis itself. The master only enjoys the finished fruits of the work of others; in contrast, the servant furnishes the world with form. Through this rediscovery of the self in the object on which he works, he acquired individual, personal meaning, "self-will," and thus a kind of freedom within his servitude. The servile consciousness becomes "self-conscious," through this work in the service of others, it finally returns to itself, although it can never fully appropriate the object of its work, but must surrender it to the master to enjoy. On the other hand, the master has the "dispensation" of the object, but only imperfectly, because his enjoyment of it is bound up only with the aspects of it which are not independent. He must surrender the independent aspects of the object to the servant who works

on it. At the level of consciousness, work and enjoyment remain without complete mediation.

11 *Jenenser Realphilosophie*, II, 197 f.

12 *Ibid.*, I, 237; cf. *Enc.*, Sect. 526.

13 *Ibid.*, I, 239, with reference to Adam Smith's famous example of needle manufacture; cf. *Rechtsphilosophie*, Sect. 190, Zus.: "The need for clothing and shelter, the necessity for not leaving food in its unprepared state, but, rather, making it suitable for nourishment by destroying its natural state, in which it cannot be used—these result in man's having less ease than animals; since he is spirit, this ease is prohibited him. The mind, which comprehends the differences, multiplies and diversifies these needs. Taste and utility become criteria of judgment, to which the needs themselves become subject. Finally, it is no longer the need, but rather the opinion, which must be satisfied. Part of the task of education is to analyze the concrete into its particular aspects." Cf. Sect. 191, Zus.

14 Cf. *Rechtsphilosophie*, Sect. 192, Zus. Even so natural a need as that of nourishment cannot be satisfied at will in the "system" of needs, but only at definite, customary mealtimes, with provision made for hours of business. In this respect each man is made equal to his fellows; at the same time, each man begins to strive to distinguish himself in particular ways, with the result that work done for the satisfaction of needs is particularized once more, and becomes more abstract, that is, spiritual.

15 *Jenenser Realphilosophie*, I, 239 f.; cf. *Rechtsphilos.* Sect. 63, Zus. Besides Hegel and Marx, only G. Simmel produced a philosophical analysis of money; see *Philosophie des Geldes* (Leipzig, 1900).

16 *Jenenser Realphilosophie*, II, 254 ff.: In *Rechtsphilosophie*, Sects. 201 ff., Hegel includes the class of craftsmen, factory workers, and tradesmen in one class, the "business class." Its basis is the "substantial" class of peasants; at its head stands the "universal" class, dedicated to the universal interests of the state. This latter class must be freed from working for its needs either by independent wealth or compensation by the state.

17 See *Rechtsphilosophie*, Sects. 4, 5, Zus.; and also the "marginalia" (ed. Lasson; Leipzig, 1930), pp. 7 f.

18 *Rechtsphilosophie*, Sect. 196.

19 *Ibid.*, Sect. 197, Zus.; cf. *Enc.*, Sect. 525.

20 *Ibid.*, Sect. 198; cf. *Enc.*, Sect. 526.

21 *Ibid.*, Sect. 290, Zus.; Sects. 301 to 303.

22 *Ibid.*, Sects. 195 and 240 to 245.

23 *Ibid.*, Sects. 246 to 248.

24 See Rosenkranz, *Hegels Leben*, p. 86.

25 Constantin Roessler, *System der Staatslehre* (1857), pp. 155 ff.; also Rosenkranz' discussion in *Neue Studien*, IV, 353 ff. On the problem of work, cf. also L. von Stein, *Gesellschaftslehre* (1856), p. 99, and *Der Begriff der Gesellschaft*, ed. G. Salomon (Munich, 1921), pp. 17 ff. F. Lassalle, *Ges. Reden und Schriften*, ed. E. Bernstein (Berlin, 1919), Vol. V, pp. 31 ff.

26 Cf. L. von Stein, *Der Begriff der Gesellschaft*, pp. 88 ff., on the connection between education and the production of material goods.

27 *Aus früherer Zeit, op. cit.*, IV, 70 ff., 101 ff., 359 ff. See also Ruge's letter to Roessler: *Br.*, I, 426 ff., 440; II, 6, 12.

28 *Aus früherer Zeit*, IV, 84 f.
29 *Ibid.*, p. 101; cf. pp. 356 ff.
30 *Ibid.*, pp. 105 ff.
31 *Ibid.*, p. 360.
32 Marx, III, 33–172.
33 *Ibid.*, pp. 139 ff.
34 *Ibid.*, pp. 151 ff. Marx's entire discussion is determined by Feuerbach's theses and propositions, but the actual problem with which he deals is defined by his disagreement with Hegel.
35 *Ibid.*, pp. 116 f.
36 *Ibid.*, p. 97. *Kapital* is also a "system of work," the only one of its kind. This has been shown decisively by K. Dunkmann in his *Soziologie der Arbeit* (Halle, 1935), 71 ff. This is all the more reason why Dunkmann, in his criticism of the "abstract" concept of work should have taken note of the original meaning, in order to understand it properly.
37 *Vide supra*, Part I, Chap. II, Sect. 1. In the *Communist Manifesto*, Part II, we read: "In bourgeois society human labor is only a means of increasing accumulated labor. In a communistic society accumulated labor is only a means of extending, enriching, and promoting the life of the worker."
38 *Kapital*, III, 85.
39 *Ibid.*, pp. 129 f.; cf. M. Hess, *Sozialistische Aufsätze*, pp. 140 ff.
40 *Ibid.*, p. 118.
41 *Ibid.*, pp. 132 ff.
42 *Ibid.*, pp. 145 ff.; cf. *Kapital*, I⁶, pp. 59 ff.; II, 1 ff.; III¹, pp. 250 ff.; III², pp. 1–153.
43 *Ibid.*, p. 154.
44 *Ibid.*, p. 127.
45 *Ibid.*, p. 118.
46 *Ibid.*, p. 121.
47 *Ibid.*, pp. 155 f., 170 ff.
48 *Ibid.*, p. 168.
49 *Ibid.*, p. 154.
50 *Ibid.*, pp. 155, 157.
51 *Ibid.*, p. 155.
52 The absorption of the object of consciousness into the superior self-consciousness proceeds as follows: "1. The object as such presents itself to the consciousness as vanishing. 2. The alienation of self-consciousness produces reification. 3. This alienation has a positive meaning, as well as negative. 4. It has this meaning not only for us or in itself, but for its own self. 5. The negative aspect of the object, or its self-removal, has the positive meaning, or comes to know the worthlessness of the same, through its alienation of itself; for in this alienation it confronts itself as an object or as the object for the sake of the inseparable unity of proseity. 6. This also implies the converse aspect: it likewise abolishes and retracts this alienation and objectification, thus keeping its otherness as such" (*Ibid.*, pp. 158 f.).
53 *Ibid.*, pp. 155, 164.
54 See *Ibid.*, pp. 169 ff.: a criticism of the Hegelian transition from "idea" to "nature," and from "abstraction" to "observation."
55 *Ibid.*, pp. 159 f.

56 *Ibid.*, pp. 121 ff., 160 ff.
57 *Ibid.*, p. 161.
58 *Ibid.*, p. 156.
59 *Ibid.*, p. 156; cf. pp. 124 f., the resultant criticism of the theory of creation.
60 *Ibid.*, p. 157.
61 V, 531.
62 *Kapital*, III, 166. This reduction of dialectical negation to a one-sided concept of simple destruction is typical of the radicalism of all the left-wing Hegelians. The same simplification takes place in regard to Nietzsche when his "overcoming" of nihilism is taken as its elimination; for Nietzsche himself, nihilism, even when overcome, remains true.
63 Cf. the analysis of the process of work in *Kapital*, I⁶, pp. 139 ff.
64 Hegel, XV, 689.
65 *Kapital*, III, 26; cf. the second part of the *Communist Manifesto*, and also *Der Bürgerkrieg in Frankreich* (Berlin, 1931), p. 69, where the Paris Commune is said to have sought to make individual property a "truth" by means of expropriation, by transforming the means of production, the soil, and capital into mere tools of free and associated labor.
66 *Ibid.*, pp. 111 ff.; cf. M. Hess, *Sozialistische Aufsätze*, pp. 150 ff., 200 ff.
67 Cf. III, pp. 212 f., in opposition to Proudhon's idea of an abolition of unequal ownership "within the estrangement of the national economy," so that the reappropriation of the objective world would come about under the form of ownership, without any transformation of the manner of appropriation itself.
68 *Ibid.*, p. 114.
69 *Ibid.*, p. 119; on the deliberate renunciation of any possible solution to the problem as stated by Marx, cf. G. Simmel, "Der Begriff und die Tragödie der Kultur," in *Philosophische Kultur* (Potsdam, 1923), pp. 236 ff; also M. Weber, "Der Sozialismus," in *Ges. Aufsätze zur Soziologie und Sozialpol.* (Tübingen, 1924), pp. 492 ff.; also *Ges. politische Schriften* (Munich, 1921), pp. 139 ff. See also the author's "M. Weber und K. Marx," *Archiv für Sozialwiss. und Sozialpol.* (1932), Nos. 1 and 2.
70 *Lohn, Preis, und Profit*, ed. H. Duncker (Berlin, 1930).
71 Cf. F. Engels, *Anti-Dühring*, II, 6, on "simple and compound work," and III, 3, on the division of labor.
72 M. Scheler, *Schriften zur Soziologie und Weltanschauungslehre* (1923-24); *Versuche zu einer Soziologie des Wissens* (1924); *Die Wissensformen und die Gesellschaft* (1926); K. Mannheim, "Wissenssoziologie," in *Handwörterbuch der Soziologie*, ed. A. Vierkandt; K. Dunkmann, *Soziologie der Arbeit* (1933).
73 In Heidegger's *Sein und Zeit*, "care" is a kind of equivalent for the concept of work. It has the twofold meaning of "being anxious" and "taking care of one's needs." This existential-ontological "care," in accordance with its theological origin in Augustine's *cura*, has no creative overtones.
74 II, 236.
75 *Ibid.*, p. 241; cf. I, 255 ff. on the "cycle of alternation" between work and boredom.
76 *Ibid.*, p. 243.
77 Cf. *Drei fromme Reden*, ed. A. Bärthold (Halle), pp. 8 ff., and *Ausgewählte christliche Reden*, ed. Reineke (Giessen, 1909), pp. 19 ff.
78 Kierkegaard, II, 245 f.

79 *Ibid.*, pp. 255, 264.
80 *Ibid.*, p. 249; cf. *Buch des Richters*, loc. cit., p. 97.
81 *Tagebücher*, I, 248.
82 *Tagebücher*, I, 373; cf. *Buch des Richters*, p. 85.
83 For a sociological analysis of Kierkegaard's "inwardness," see Th. Wiesengrund, *Kierkegaard* (Tübingen, 1933), pp. 44 ff.
84 See *Tagebücher*, ed. Ulrich, pp. 23 f.
85 *Fröhliche Wiss.*, Aph. 329; cf. Aph. 42, 280; I, 229 f., 344 f.
86 *Jenseits von Gut und Böse*, Aph. 58.
87 *Fröhl. Wiss.*, Aph. 348, 349, 373.
88 *Morgenröte*, Aph. 173; cf. *Zur Genealogie der Moral*, III, Aph. 18.
89 See Tolstoy's reply to Zola in the Tolstoy Issue of *Neue Büchershau* (Sept., 1928); also *Was sollen wir denn tun*, Chap. 38.
90 XVI, 197, 196.

III   The Problem of Education

1   *Werke*, XVI, 133 ff.; cf. *Philosophische Propädeutik*, Sects. 41 ff.; *Rechtsphilosophie*, Sects. 187, 268. On Hegel's concept of education, see G. Thaulow, *Hegels Ansichten über die Erziehung und Unterricht* (Kiel, 1853 ff.); also K. Rosenkranz, *Die Pädagogik als System* (Königsberg, 1848).
2   XVI, 153 f.; for the application of this principle to philosophic instruction, see XVII, 342 f., 353.
3   *Ibid.*, pp. 134–139.
4   *Ibid.*, p. 142; cf. *Philos. Propädeutik*, Sect. 42.
5   *Ibid.*, p. 143.
6   *Ibid.*, pp. 143 f.; cf. the preface to the 2nd edition of the *Logik*.
7   Cf. Hegel's essay "Wer denkt abstrakt," XVII, 400 ff.
8   Hegel, *op. cit.*, XVI, 170.
9   *Ibid.*, pp. 151 f.
10 *Ibid.*, pp. 171 ff.
11 *Ibid.*, pp. 174 f.
12 *Ibid.*, p. 188.
13 *Ibid.*, pp. 188 f.
14 On the reformation of art according to the political principle of public community, see R. Wagner's *Die Kunst und die Revolution* (1849).
15 Echtermeyer and Ruge, "Der Protestantismus und die Romantik, Zur Verständigung über die Zeit und ihre Gegensätze," *Hallesche Jahrbücher*, II (1839), 1953 ff.; on criticism of Goethe, cf. pp. 65 ff., 153 ff., 2313 ff.
16 *Deutsche Jahrbücher*, V (1843): "Eine Selbstkritik des Liberalismus."
17 *Phänomenologie*, ed. Lasson, pp. 316 ff.
18 *Hallesche Jahrbücher*, I, 193 ff.; V, 61 ff.
19 "Das unwahre Prinzip unserer Erziehung oder der Humanismus und Realismus," *Kleinere Schriften*, pp. 237 ff.
20 Stirner, *op. cit.*, p. 249.
21 *Ibid.*, p. 253; cf. p. 369.
22 B. Bauer, *Vollständige Geschichte der Parteikämpfe.*

23 On the *Zeitschrift für Wissenschaft und Leben,* founded at this time, see *Vollständige Geschichte der Parteikämpfe,* III, 111 ff.
24 *Ibid.,* III, 13 ff., 88, 123.
25 *Ibid.,* III, 173.
26 *Ibid.,* III, 128.
27 *Ibid.,* III, 119.
28 *Ibid.,* III, 83.
29 *Ibid.,* III, 132 f.
30 *Ibid.,* III, 87.
31 *Ibid.,* II, 78 f.
32 *Ibid.,* III, 182 f.
33 *Briefe an G. und J. Kinkel* (Basel, 1921), pp. 81 f.
34 Letter to Schauenburg of February 28, 1846; cf. *Briefe an Kinkel,* pp. 137 f.
35 See the author's book on Burckhardt, pp. 233 ff.
36 *Ges. Ausg.,* V, 125.
37 The first publication was after Flaubert's death in 1881. *Oeuvres compl.* (Paris, 1923).
38 See the letter to L. Colet of December 1852 in *Correspondence,* II, 185. From the same period (1851), cf. Baudelaire's *Fusées* and his plan of composing a poetic "End of the World."
39 Guy de Maupassant, "G. Flaubert," contained in *In Memoriam G.F.* (Leipzig, 1913).
40 See Burckhardt, VII, 476, 478 f.
41 It is significant for the origin of the system of education of National Socialism that H. St. Chamberlain's *Grundlagen des 19. Jahrhunderts* was reprinted in a popular edition by A. Rosenberg. For a description of Chamberlain, see F. Overbeck, *Christentum und Kultur* (Basel, 1919), p. 198: he was a "rare specimen of the species of narrow-minded intellectual."
42 *Morgenröte,* Aph. 190.
43 *Jenseits von Gut und Böse,* Aph. 241; cf. XIII, 347 ff. From the same period comes a remark by K. Rosenkranz, to the effect that there is a general misconception that philosophy is an important element in the popular education of the Germans, a national study of general interest. In reality the epoch of German philosophy was of very short duration: down to the time of Leibniz and Wolff, we could surely not be considered a philosophic people, "but only warlike, diligent, and religious" (*Neue Studien,* II, 567 ff.).
44 VIII, 109; cf. IV, 163 f.; VII, 205 f.; XVI, 297 f.
45 See H. Fischer, *Nietzsche Apostata,* pp. 18 ff.; also A. Bäumler, *Nietzsche, der Philosoph und Politiker,* pp. 134 ff.
46 XV, 117; cf. I, 491 f.
47 X, 288 ff.
48 In its basic tendencies, Nietzsche's criticism of education goes back to Herder and Fichte. See Herder's *Briefe zur Beförderung der Humanität, 8. Sammlung, 7. Fragment* (1796), on "Schrift und Buchdrückerei"; Fichte, *Die Grundzüge des gegenwärtigen Zeitalters* (1804–05), *6. und 7. Vorlesung.* Cf. Goethe, *Gespräche,* III, 57 (1824), his letter to Zelter of June 6, 1825, and his conversation with Eckermann of March 12, 1828.
49 A criticism, both radical and concrete, of educational institutions (which Nietzsche mentions only in his title) is contained in two articles (1878 and

1881) by P. de Lagarde on the Education Law, contained in *Deutsche Schriften* (Göttingen, 1892), pp. 168 ff., 264 ff.
50 IX, 301 f.
51 On the original meaning of "Bildung," see P. de Lagarde, *op. cit.*, p. 171.

IV   The Problem of Man

1 *Enc.*, Sect. 384.
2 *Enc.*, Sect. 377.
3 I², p. 15; cf. pp. 31, 48, 75; XVI, 46, 205.
4 XI, 3.
5 See also *Theolog. Jugendschr.*, p. 57.
6 *Enc.*, Sect. 377, Zus.
7 *Enc.*, Sect. 163, Zus.; cf. Sect. 482.
8 VIII, Sect. 190.
9 VIII, Sect. 209, 270, note.
10 In his *Religionsphilosophie* (XII, 217), Hegel calls Christ the Son of Man the "second Adam"; by the "first man" he means "man as man," or "according to his proper notion," in contrast to one man who happens to be first among many others.
11 See N. Berdayev, *Das Schicksal des Menschen in unserer Zeit* (Luzern, 1935).
12 Foreword to the *Grundsätze der Philosophie der Zukunft*.
13 II, 413.
14 II, 267.
15 II, 266.
16 Grundsatz 54 and 63.
17 *Unser System, oder die Weltweisheit und Weltbewegung unserer Zeit* (1850).
18 *Aus früherer Zeit*, IV, 359 ff.; also *Unser System*, III, 1 ff.
19 *Unser System*, III, 85 f.
20 III, 151 f.; V, 535 ff.
21 I⁶, p. 11.
22 Cf. Ruge's letter to Marx (I¹, p. 558), where Ruge quotes Hölderlin's "Hyperion" as the "motto of his state of mind": "You see craftsmen, but not human beings; thinkers, but not human beings; masters and servants, but not human beings"; and also Marx's concurring reply.
23 On the concept of a "generic being," see particular III, 21, 116 f., 307 f.; *Zur Kritik der polit. Ökonomie*, p. xiv; *10. These über Feuerbach*.
24 I¹, p. 599; cf. pp. 591, 595; III, 112.
25 I¹, pp. 619 ff.; III, 206 f.
26 See G. Lukacs, *Geschichte und Klassenbewusstsein* (Berlin, 1923), pp. 188 ff.
27 V, 57 f.
28 For Marx, the "realm of freedom" begins on the far side of material production, the principle of which remains need and necessity, even under socialism. (*Kapital*, III², pp. 315 f.)
29 *Der Einzige und sein Eigentum*, pp. 196 ff., 217 ff., 420, 423, 428; also *Kleinere Schriften*, pp. 366 ff.
30 *Der Einzige und sein Eigentum*, p. 193.
31 VI, 204; cf. p. 208.

32 *Kritik der Gegenwart,* pp. 54, 56 f.
33 II, 224.
34 II, 285 ff.; III, 199 f.; *Tagebücher,* I, 334.
35 II, 220.
36 II, 288 f.
37 VII, 51.
38 *Vom Leben und Walten der Liebe* (Jena, 1924), pp. 19 ff., 48 ff.
39 XIV, 66.
40 VI, 14 f. (Preface to *Zarathustra*).
41 I, 423 f.
42 See Goethe, *Gespräche,* I, 456, 409.
43 R. Musil, *Der Mann ohne Eigenschaften* (Berlin, 1930).
44 *Maximen und Reflexionen,* Nos. 875 f.; cf. Nos. 216–219. See also Hegel's "Grundbegriff von der Anerkennung," *Jenenser Realphilosophie,* I, 226 ff.; 209 ff.; *Phänomenologie,* ed. Lasson, pp. 432 ff.; on the still unequal self-recognition-in-the-other, in the relationship between master and servant, see pp. 128 f.
45 *Maximen und Reflexionen,* No. 272; cf. Vol. XXV, p. 169.
46 Letter to Zelter of December 25, 1829.
47 Weimar edition, Section I, 41/2, p. 252.
48 Cf. Nietzsche, III, 62 ff.
49 *Maximen und Reflexionen,* Nos. 773 ff.
50 *Gespräche,* IV, 410; cf. letter to Carlyle of July 20, 1827; *Maximen und Reflexionen,* No. 214; on interpretation of Goethe's humanism, see Hegel, X/2, p. 235; G. Simmel, *Goethe* (5th edition; 1923), p. 263.

V   The Problem of Christianity

1 *Vide supra,* Part I, Chap. III, Sect. 4; cf. J. Wahl, *Études Kierkegaardiennes,* pp. 151 ff.
2 *Theolog. Jugendschr.,* pp. 378 ff. Even Spinoza had set up an antithesis between the "fleshly" attitude of fear and the "spiritual" attitude of love, the irreconcilability of the fear of God and the love of God. See also Leo Strauss, *Die Religionskritik Spinozas* (Berlin, 1930), pp. 199 ff.
3 *Theolog. Jugendschr.,* pp. 383 f.; cf. Novalis' fragment: "The logician takes the predicate as his point of departure, the mathematician the subject, the philosopher the copula."
4 I^2, p. 3.
5 *Die Vernunft in der Geschichte,* ed. Lasson, pp. 18 f.
6 XI, 5.
7 *Die Vernunft in der Geschichte,* ed. Lasson, pp. 20 f.
8 XI, 80.
9 I^2, p. 153; cf. XII, 235; *Phänomenologie,* ed. Lasson, p. 483.
10 See Michelet, *Geschichte der letzten Systeme der Philosophie,* II, 638 ff.
11 *Hegel als deutscher Nationalphilosoph,* p. 331.
12 On what follows, see Th. Ziegler, *D. F. Strauss,* I/II (Strassburg, 1908); E. Zeller, *Über das Wesen der Religion* (1845).
13 See *Streitschriften zur Verteidigung meiner Schrift über das Leben Jesu,* III

(Tübingen, 1938), 57 ff., 76 ff. For his dissolution of the "empirical certainty" of "theological phenomenology," Strauss appeals to the following passages from Hegel's works: XII, 246–250, 253–256; 260 f.; 263–266; XI, 82; XV, 249 f. Th. Ziegler remarks appositely that Hegel's *Theolog. Jugendschr.* are now an even better basis for Strauss's radical extension of Hegel's views on the historical reality of the Gospels (Th. Ziegler, *Strauss*, p. 249).

14 See E. Volhard, *Zwischen Hegel und Nietzsche. Der Ästhetiker F. Th. Vischer* (Frankfurt a. M., 1932).

15 See Feuerbach, VII[4], pp. 189 ff.; I, 1 ff.; Kierkegaard, IX, 82 ff., *Pap.* VIII[1], pp. 320 f. Cf. the discussion of the concept of "miracle" on the part of K. Daub, an Hegelian, whose lectures Feuerbach heard and whose work *Die Form der christlichen Dogmen- und Kirchenhistorie* (1836–37) Kierkegaard had studied (E. Hirsch, *Kierkegaard-Studien*, II, 97). On the problem of criticism of miracles, see Leo Strauss, *Die Religionskritik Spinozas*, pp. 204 ff.

16 Cf. S. Freud's *Unbehagen in der Kultur* (1930) and *Die Zukunft einer Illusion* (1927): man has become a kind of "prosthetic god."

17 Cf. Strauss, *Ges. Schriften*, ed. E. Zeller, V (1878), 181 f. Not only the Young Hegelians, but also J. E. Erdmann, R. Haym, K. Fischer, and F. Th. Fischer are under the influence of Feuerbach.

18 VII[4], p. 29; I, 248, referring to Bauer.

19 *Ibid.*, p. 47.

20 I, 249.

21 Feuerbach, VII[4], p. 50; Hegel, XIII, 88 f. Cf. Bauer's *Posaune*, Chap. XI, and J. Schaller, *op. cit.*, p. 165.

22 *Grundsätze der Philosophie der Zukunft*, p. 2.

23 VII[4], p. 31.

24 *Br.*, I, 408.

25 VII[4], p. 32.

26 "Furthermore, the conflict with the objections made by the natural sciences and the ensuing struggle has an analogy to that with the [Hegelian] system. In themselves, the objections are not particularly significant; but a powerful opinion, a secular education will be an embarrassment to the theologians. They will have to give an appearance of being themselves a bit scientific, etc.; they will be afraid of being behind the times, as was formerly true in respect to the system. . . . Thus the conflict between God and 'man' will probably conclude with 'man's' retreat behind the natural sciences. . . . Starting with the natural sciences, there will be an extension of that wretched distinction between the simple with their simple beliefs, and the scholars and semi-scholars, who have looked through the microscope. It is no longer possible, as in days gone by, to discuss at will the simple 'Supreme Being' with all men, regardless of whether they are black or green, whether they have large or small heads. It will be necessary to see first whether they have enough brains to believe in God. If Christ had known about the microscope, he would have subjected the Apostles to an examination" (Kierkegaard, *Buch des Richters*, pp. 123 ff.).

27 I, 253.

28 Cf. J. Ebbinghaus, "L. Feuerbach," *Deutsche Vierteljahrsschr. für Literatur-wiss. und Geistesgesch.*, Vol. VIII, No. 2, pp. 283 ff.

29 VII[4], p. 24.

30   *Br.*, I, 408.
31   VII⁴, p. 60.
32   I, 342 ff.; also Stirner's reply, in *Kleinere Schriften*, pp. 343 ff.; cf. Barnikol's edition of Bauer's *Entdecktes Christentum*, p. 74, note.
33   VII⁴, pp. 73 f. On the question of the connection between criticism of religion in general and the difference between Judaism and Christianity, see Leo Strauss, *op. cit.*, p. 199.
34   Cf. *Das Wesen der Religion*, lecture 20; also *Br.*, II, 236 ff., on Zinzendorf.
35   In Luther's sermon on Isa. 9:5, we read, "Make the two letters 'u s' as large as heaven and earth."
36   See K. Barth's criticism of Feuerbach in *Zwischen den Zeiten* (1927), Vol. 1; also the author's article in *Theol. Rundschau*, No. 5 (1930), pp. 341 ff.
37   IX, 437; XV, 253 ff. In a Catholic polemic by G. Müglich against "Die Hegelweisheit und ihre Früchte oder A. Ruge mit seinen Genossen" (Regensburg, 1849), we read: In Luther, God achieved consciousness, in Hegel self-consciousness—prior to 1517 no one had any idea of the "spirit"—only in the age of Protestantism has God appeared as the spirit of the age, to be present ever since Hegel.
38   *Aus früherer Zeit*, IV, 121 ff. For proof of this contradiction, Ruge refers to Hegel, XV, 114–117.
39   *Die Akademie*, pp. 1 ff., reprinted in the second volume of *Unser System*.
40   *Unser System*, II, 13.
41   *Neue Studien*, I (Leipzig, 1875), 317 ff. In his study of the "religious world-process" of the present, Rosenkranz explains the universal significance of Christianity for the modern world as the product of the education which it has acquired through science. The Christianity of today is the religion of self-conscious reason and humanism. There can be no doubt that in our epoch of technological civilization the religious process is everywhere also at work, changing the world in its very depths.
42   For a description of Bauer's personality, see K. Rosenkranz, *Aus einem Tagebuch* (Leipzig, 1854), p. 113; J. H. Mackacy, *M. Stirner* (2nd edition; Treptow bei Berlin, 1910), p. 221; Th. Fontane, *Briefe, 2. Sammlung*, II (Berlin, 1909), 392; P. Gast, *Briefe an Nietzsche*, II (Munich, 1924), 162; E. Barnikol, *Bauers Entdecktes Christentum*, pp. 67 f.
43   *Geschichte der Leben-Jesu-Forschung* (Tübingen, 1921), p. 161; cf. W. Nigg, *Geschichte des religiösen Liberalismus* (Zürich, 1937), pp. 166 ff.
44   The 2nd edition was prepared by Bauer; cf. *Posaune*, p. 149.
45   In *Entdecktes Christentum*, p. 156, Bauer defended just this thesis of "self-consciousness" which realises itself in history as the "only creative power in the universe," in opposition to Christianity. In *Die Heilige Familie*, Marx's criticism is directed against Bauer's Hegelian principle of "self-consciousness."
46   Cf. the discussion of Bauer's *Posaune* in *Hallesche Jahrbücher* (1841), Part II, p. 594.
47   *Die Posaune*, p. 148.
48   *Hegels Lehre von der Religion und Kunst*, p. 100.
49   *Ibid.*, p. 163.
50   *Ibid.*, p. 180.
51   *Ibid.*, p. 206.
52   Even before his conversion to the left wing of Hegelianism, Bauer had already

discarded Strauss's mythological view in principle, although for different reasons.

53 *Hegels Lehre von der Religion und Kunst*, pp. 190, 204.

54 *Ibid.*, p. 59.

55 Ruge, *Br.*, I, 243; cf. p. 239.

56 Feuerbach, *Br.*, I, 330, 364; cf. p. 337.

57 Ruge, *Br.*, I, 247; cf. pp. 255, 281, 290 f.

58 *Anekdota*, II (Zürich and Winterthur, 1843), 8.

59 Ruge, *Zwei Jahre in Paris, Studien und Erinnerungen* (Leipzig, 1846), pp. 59 ff.

60 Barnikol, *Das entdeckte Christentum im Vormärz.* In what follows, grateful use is made of Barnikol's well-documented material. For an explanation of the title of Bauer's work, see Barnikol's introduction, Sects. 78 ff. On Bauer's relationship to Edelmann, referred to in the subtitle, cf. his *Geschichte der Politik, Kultur und Aufklärung*, I, 204–236.

61 *Hegels Lehre von der Religion und Kunst*, p. 215.

62 E. Barnikol, *op. cit.*, p. 164.

63 Cf. the alternatives presented by Existentialism: Heidegger's "Selbstsein" and "Mansein" (personal being and impersonal being), Jaspers' "Selbstsein" and "Massendasein" (personal being and existence as part of a mass).

64 III, 251 f., 257 f.; cf. V, 75 ff.

65 V, 531 ff.

66 I/1, p. 607.

67 *Kapital* I[6], p. 336, note; cf. K. Korsch, *Marxismus und Philosophie* (Leipzig, 1930), p. 98.

68 V, 534 (*4. These über Feuerbach*).

69 I/1, p. 607; cf. Bauer's *Entdecktes Christentum*, Sect. 13.

70 I/1, pp. 607 f.; cf. Feuerbach, III[3], pp. 364 ff.

71 Cf. III, 125; cf. Lenin, *Über Religion* (Vienna, 1926), p. 24; as an extended example of Marxist criticism of religion, see Lenin and Plechanov, *Tolstoi im Spiegel des Marxismus* (Vienna, 1928).

72 Marx, letter to Kugelmann of July 27, 1871.

73 *Kleinere Schriften*, pp. 16, 23.

74 *Ibid.*, p. 19.

75 *Der Einzige und sein Eigentum*, pp. 147 ff.; *Kleinere Schriften*, pp. 343 ff.

76 *Der Einzige und sein Eigentum*, pp. 50 f.; cf. Bauer's criticism of the "religion of humanity" in *Vollständige Geschichte der Parteikämpfe*, II, 170 ff.

77 *Der Einzige und sein Eigentum*, p. 43.

78 I, 342 ff.

79 *Kleinere Schriften*, pp. 343 ff.; see also the author's *Das Individuum in der Rolle des Mitmenschen*, Sect. 45.

80 See also the author's "Kierkegaard und Nietzsche," *Deutsche Vierteljahrsschr. für Literaturwiss. und Geistesgeschichte*, No. 1 (1933), pp. 53 ff.

81 II, 224; cf. VI, 204, 208.

82 A detailed review of Kierkegaard's *Der Begriff der Ironie* can be found in Vol. V of the *Hallesche Jahrbücher* (1842–43), pp. 885 ff. Kierkegaard's familiarity with Bauer's writings may be assumed because the article by Daub which he studied (see note 15 *supra*) appeared in Bauer's *Zeitschrift für spekulative Theologie.* (See *Tagebücher*, ed. Ulrich, pp. 261, 270.) Further-

more, he was acquainted with Michelet's *Geschichte der letzten Systeme,* which contains many mentions of Bauer (see VI, 322, note).

83 VII, 259.

84 VII, 57.

85 IV, 418 f.; on Börne, cf. IV, 444. The significance of Börne for the philosophicopolitical movement of the forties is shown by Engels' statement that the job of the moment is to permeate Hegel with Börne (Marx-Engels, *Ges. Ausg.,* II, 102 f.).

86 IV, 426.

87 *Pap.* X², p. 129.

88 VII, 61 f.; see also Ruttenbeck, *Kierkegaard* (Berlin, 1929), pp. 236 ff.

89 *Tagebücher,* II, 285 ff.; 331 f., 388, 404.

90 The structure of the consciousness of this relationship is the theme of Hegel's analysis of "unhappy consciousness"; on what follows, see Ruttenbeck, *op. cit.,* pp. 230 ff., and J. Wahl, *op. cit.,* pp. 159 ff., 320.

91 *Tagebücher,* I, 284.

92 See the criticism by Th. Haecker, "Der Begriff der Wahrheit bei Kierkegaard," *Hochland,* No. 11 (1928–29); also: *Christentum und Kultur* (Munich, 1927), pp. 66 ff.

93 On Kierkegaard's destruction of the objective history of Christianity (in the *Philosophical Fragments*), cf. Feuerbach's *Wesen der Religion,* lecture 27: "What is historical is not religious, and what is religious is not historical" (VIII, 319).

94 On the basis of this existential concept of faith, Kierkegaard condemns both Schleiermacher's religion of feeling and Hegel's speculative concept of faith: "What Schleiermacher calls 'religion,' what the Hegelians call 'faith,' is ultimately nothing more than the primary, immediate prerequisite for everything —the 'vital fluid,'—the atmosphere we breathe when we think spiritually—and is therefore improperly called by these names" (*Tagebücher,* I, 54).

95 VI, 118.

96 VI, 275, note.

97 VI, 269.

98 VI, 272 ff.

99 VI, 274. The entire passage is underlined by Kierkegaard.

100 Cf. on the contrary the limitation of this thesis in *Begriff der Ironie,* p. 274.

101 VI, 279; see also Ruttenbeck, *op. cit.,* pp. 230 ff.

102 VI, 314; see also VII, 47 ff.; IX, 119 ff.; *Angriff auf die Christenheit,* pp. 5 ff., 11.

103 Cf. Jaspers, *Philosophie,* I (1932), 317; the reverse chain of reasoning in Th. Haecker, *op. cit.,* p. 477: "The answer to his major question, 'How am I to become a Christian?' does not, as he thought, lie solely in the 'how' of faith, nor solely in the world of faith, but also in the constitution of the world, which comes before faith. . . . Kierkegaard's enormous mistake is to take the 'how' as his point of departure, ultimately as everything; for man, the beginning is the 'what,' the dogmatic 'what' of faith that stands firm in the midst of a 'how' that is still frail and incipient. . . ." Cf. Jean Wahl, *Études Kierkegaardiennes,* pp. 440 ff.

104 *Tagebücher,* I, 407.

105 *Der Begriff des Auserwählten,* pp. 273 ff., 313 ff.

106 *Tagebücher,* I, 312.

107 *Angriff auf die Christenheit*, p. 149.
108 *Der Begriff des Auserwählten*, pp. 5 ff. Adler belonged originally to the right wing of Hegelianism. On the problems connected with Kierkegaard's *Angriff*, cf. *Tagebücher*, ed. Ulrich, pp. 130 ff.
109 *Der Begriff des Auserwählten*, pp. 102 f.; cf. *Angriff auf die Christenheit*, p. 401.
110 *Angriff auf die Christenheit*, p. 148.
111 *Tagebücher*, I, 300.
112 *Tagebücher*, I, 276 f., 333.
113 VI, 191.
114 *Buch des Richters*, pp. 94 f.; cf. pp. 85 f.
115 *Zur Genealogie der Moral*, Vol. II, Aph. 20.
116 E. Benz, "Nietzsches Ideen zur Geschichte des Christentums," *Zeitschr. für Kirchengeschichte*, No. 2–3 (1937), particularly pp. 194, 291. The thesis is that Nietzsche would continue a "genuinely German development of religious devotion," and, together with Strauss, B. Bauer, Lagarde, and Overbeck, assist the restoration of primitive Christianity! For a criticism of this interpretation of Nietzsche, see W. Nigg, *Overbeck* (Munich, 1931), p. 58.
117 See *Nietzsches Zusammenbruch* (Heidelberg, 1930); *Gestalten um Nietzsche* (Weimer, 1932); *Nietzsche und Lou Salome* (Zürich, 1938). On Nietzsche's "Christianity," cf. Bernoulli, *Overbeck und Nietzsche*, I, 217.
118 *Wille zur Macht*, Aph. 1021.
119 X, 289; cf. I, 341, where Nietzsche obviously makes use of one of Overbeck's ideas.
120 Musarion edition, I, 70 f.
121 *Antichrist*, p. 38.
122 *Fröhl. Wissenschaft*, Aph. 357; cf. I, 340.
123 XV, 70.
124 *Antichrist*, p. 10; cf. XIII, 14. Cf. also E. Dühring's differentiation between theology and philosophy as "priests of the first and second class," and his view that the task of pre-positivistic philosophy was to cover the retreat of theology (*Der Wert des Lebens*, Chap. 3).
125 *Wille zur Macht*, Aph. 87.
126 *Genealogie der Moral*, Vol. III, Aph. 24.
127 *Ibid.*, Aph. 27.
128 *Fröhl. Wissenschaft*, Aph. 377.
129 Letter to Rohde of May 23, 1887.
130 P. de Lagarde, *Deutsche Schriften* (Göttingen, 1892), p. 60.
131 *Ibid.*, p. 39.
132 *Ibid.*, p. 25.
133 *Ibid.*, p. 6.
134 *Ibid.*, p. 47.
135 *Ibid.*, pp. 11 f.
136 Lagarde distinguishes between Israel and Judaea; the former was a naïve people, unaffected by any kind of antipathy, and the latter an "artificial product," an "odium generis humani," comparable only to the Jesuits and the Germans of the Second Reich, who likewise (and justifiably) comprised the most hated nation in Europe (*Deutsche Schriften*, pp. 237 f.).
137 *Ibid.*, p. 62.

138 *Ibid.*, p. 64.
139 *Ibid.*, p. 233.
140 *Ibid.*, p. 234.
141 *Ibid.*, p. 240.
142 *Ibid.*, p. 247.
143 *Ibid.*, p. 68.
144 *Ibid.*, p. 76; cf. p. 97.
145 *Über die Christlichkeit unserer heutigen Theologie* (2nd edition; Leipzig, 1903), p. 25.
146 *Ibid.*, pp. 28 f.
147 *Ibid.*, p. 34.
148 *Ibid.*, p. 84; cf. Nietzsche, I, 340.
149 *Christentum und Kultur*, ed. C. A. Bernoulli (Basel, 1919), p. 291.
150 *Ibid.*, p. 279; cf. Overbeck's evaluation of Feuerbach in W. Nigg, *Overbeck*, p. 136.
151 *Theol. Lit. Zeitung* (1878), pp. 314 ff.
152 W. Nigg, *op. cit.*, p. 138.
153 *Studien zur Geschichte der alten Kirche*, I (1875), 159; cf. also the parallels in Nietzsche's *Wir Philologen* (X, 404 ff.) and also in Nigg, *op. cit.*, p. 44, note. For Nietzsche, the question of the "Hellenism" of classical philology had the same significance as did the question of the Christianity of theology for Overbeck.
154 *Hegels Lehre von der Religion und Kunst*, pp. 41 ff.; also *Entdecktes Christentum*, Sect. 16.
155 *Christlichkeit der Theologie*, p. 110.
156 *Ibid.*, p. 114. Nietzsche became acquainted with this work through Overbeck's *Exemplar des alten und neuen Glaubens*, and, as Overbeck noted, "used it for his execution."
157 *Ibid.*, p. 111.
158 *Ibid.*, p. 129; see also Overbeck's estimation of Lagarde as a person in Bernoulli, *Overbeck und Nietzsche*, I, 133.
159 *Christentum und Kultur*, p. 136; cf. pp. 286 f., and Bernoulli, *Overbeck und Nietzsche*, I, 273 ff.; II, 161.
160 *Christentum und Kultur*, p. 279.
161 *Ibid.*, pp. 268 f.
162 *Ibid.*, pp. 9 f.
163 *Ibid.*, pp. 64 f.
164 *Ibid.*, pp. 69 f.
165 Overbeck quotes from Treitschke's *Deutsche Geschichte* (3rd edition), III, 401, the statement that as early as the twenties the conversation at the table of the Prussian Minister Altenstein concerned whether Christianity would last a mere twenty years longer, or perhaps fifty—a story which throws interesting light upon Hegel and his pupils.
166 *Christentum und Kultur*, p. 7.
167 *Ibid.*, p. 10.
168 *Kritisch-historische Gesamtausgabe*, Vol. I, p. xlix.
169 *Christentum und Kultur*, p. 72.
170 *Christlichkeit und Theologie*, p. 87.
171 *Christentum und Kultur*, p. 289; cf. E. von Hartmann, *Die Selbstersetzung*

des Christentums und die Religion der Zukunft (1874), which contains many references to Lagarde and Overbeck.

172 *Ibid.*, p. 298.

173 Cf. Wellhausen's reservations: F. Boschwitz, *J. Wellhausen*, dissertation (Marburg, 1938), pp. 75 ff.

174 *Christentum und Kultur*, p. 270.

175 *Ibid.*, p. 77.

176 *Ibid.*, p. 69.

177 *Ibid.*, p. 64.

178 *Christlichkeit und Theologie*, p. 119.

179 *Christentum und Kultur*, pp. 101 ff.

180 W. Nigg, *op. cit.*, p. 153.

181 Cf. *Christentum und Kultur*, p. 247; cf. also Burckhardt's letters to Beyschlag of January 14 and 30, 1844 and his mature presentation of the relationship between Christianity and culture in VII, 111 f.

182 W. Nigg, *op. cit.*, pp. 165 f.

183 *Christentum und Kultur*, pp. 11, 147, 294 ff.; cf. Burckhardt, VII, 7.

184 *Ibid.*, Chap. 5.

Index

Index